# Comparative Development of India and China

*KUAN-I CHEN AND J. S. UPPAL*

Department of Economics
State University of New York at Albany



Fp THE FREE PRESS, NEW YORK
COLLIER-MACMILLAN LIMITED, LONDON

*Printed in the United States of America*



The Free Press
A Division of The Macmillan Company
866 Third Avenue, New York, New York 10022

COLLIER-MACMILLAN CANADA LTD., TORONTO, ONTARIO

Library of Congress Catalog Card Number: 71-142355

*Printing number*
1 2 3 4 5 6 7 8 9 10

# Comparative Development of India and China

# Preface

A STUDY OF the comparative development of India and China has strong fascination for students and scholars in various disciplines in the social sciences and also for general readers interested in international affairs. For economists the subject is important from the point of view of the effectiveness of planning and development strategies applied to solve the massive and difficult problems confronting these two most populous nations in the world.

It is interesting to note the many similarities between the two countries, especially the patterns of their physical and human resources. Both the countries are large in size and population. In size India is the seventh and China is the third largest in the world. In population China and India together have a total population of over one-third of the human race. At their present levels of development, both countries are overpopulated, and their rapidly growing populations present formidable barriers to economic progress. The utilization of huge manpower in these countries is a key factor in their development. Both India and China are predominantly agricultural economics with low productivity resulting from identical problems, such as inadequate irrigation facilities and flooding. The appalling poverty of the masses and the general economic backwardness of both countries is mostly a reflection of low yields in agriculture. In both countries industrial development, especially in large-scale industries, is not commensurate with the size of the countries, their huge population, and their varied and rich mineral resources. The present governments in both countries inherited economies torn by partition in the case of India and civil strife in China and exploited by foreign colonial interests. With more or less similar economic structures, the two countries embarked on the gigantic task of development and reconstruction at the same time—in the late 1940s and early 1950s—but under contrasting political systems. India's plans are formulated and implemented within a democratic structure, whereas China has adopted a centralized planning technique. The success and failure of planning in the two countries and the speed and effectiveness with which they can alleviate tragic poverty among their teeming millions and tackle other major social problems will be viewed by other nations in terms of the relative superiority of the two competing political systems. The future of democracy and socialism as political and economic systems for two-thirds of the world's population in underdeveloped countries may thus be influenced by the progress of the Indian and Chinese societies. This question is of great importance to students of political science and government. The ways in which the traditional societies of India and China are reshaped and the effectiveness with which the centuries-old cultural and religious values are changed or reinterpreted have great significance for sociologists and anthropologists. The educational philosophies and curriculum and instructional techniques used by democratic India and communist China are bound to shape the attitudes of youth toward our world of tomorrow.

Although numerous articles in many languages on various aspects of the Indian and Chinese societies are appearing in journals all over the world, there is no single source available that presents contrasting development in the two societies. Those interested in studying development contrasts in India and China have to dig deeply into numerous references for every single aspect. This volume attempts to fill the gap by presenting scholarly and up-to-date writings from specialists on India and China. In selecting the material from published sources all over the world, we have preferred readings that do not contain much technical detail. Introductions summarizing and synthesizing the readings have been added at the beginning of each section in order to present the problems and processes of development in the two societies from a comparative point of view. We have adopted the interdisciplinary approach to make the anthology useful to students and scholars in social sciences as well as to the general reader who is watching with interest and concern the development of more than half of our world living in the emerging nations of Asia.

STATE UNIVERSITY OF
NEW YORK AT ALBANY,
NEW YORK

Kuan-I Chen
J. S. Uppal

# Contents

## II. DEVELOPMENT POLICY AND PLANNING TECHNIQUES

### A. Planning Strategy and Industrial Policy



### B. Reorganization of Agrarian Structure and Land Reform



## III. DEMOGRAPHIC PATTERNS AND POPULATION POLICY



## IV. CAPITAL FORMATION AND DEVELOPMENT OF HUMAN RESOURCES

### A. Capital Formation

# Comparative Development of India and China

I

# Emerging Patterns in Economic Development

# A

# Patterns of Development in Agriculture

INDIA AND CHINA are still predominantly agricultural economies with agriculture continuing to be their economic backbone. The low economic standards of the great masses of people in the two countries are owing primarily to the backwardness of agriculture. Improvement of agriculture continues to be an integral part of the countries' development plans. The extent to which they are able to raise the standard of living of their people will depend largely on the effectiveness of their agricultural development plans.

On the eve of Indian independence and the downfall of the Nationalist regime on the Mainland China, the agricultural sectors of the two countries were characterized by similar and common problems: heavy population pressures on limited arable land; subsistence farming with semifeudal land tenure relationships; continuous subdivision and fragmentation of small holdings; widespread rural underemployment and unemployment; inadequate transportation and marketing facilities; and illiteracy among the rural population. The leadership in India and China correctly recognized the urgent necessity of tackling these difficult problems on a massive scale, but the methods adopted in the two countries were different. In his paper "Recent Development in Chinese and Indian Agriculture," Pranab Bardhan starts with a brief comparative survey of the major problems in the rural sectors of the two countries. After taking into account the statistical difficulties involved in comparing growth rates, Bardhan gives estimates of the per capita availability of food and rates of growth of food production during the period 1952–53 to 1967–68. The growth rates are quite close, 1.7 per cent for India and 1.9 per cent for China. Bardhan remarks that "on the whole it seems that the two countries had fairly similar and not very high rates of growth of food grains per capita over this period." The relative growth rates for total agricultural production also are not substantially different. Bardhan then considers the trends in the use of agricultural inputs and finds that Chinese land is more intensively cultivated than Indian land. Chinese farmers use comparatively larger quantities of organic manure. China has been able to utilize some part of her surplus manpower on construction of rural overhead capital, whereas India has largely failed in this respect. China's attempts to consolidate small fragmented and uneconomic holdings have been much more successful than India's. Despite comparatively favorable input use in China, the expected increase in productivity was severely counteracted by the disruptive impact of institutional reorganizations. Uncertainties resulting from constant experimentation, reorganization of rural institutions, and sporadic policy shifts had disruptive effects on productive efficiency in China. By the end of the 1950s China had attained a level of yield per hectare which seems about the maximum attainable within the framework of traditional agriculture. Much greater use of modern agricultural inputs will therefore be required to get further increases in yield. Because the policy of increasing modern inputs did not begin until 1962, the effects were not felt until the end of the 1960s.

The article "Indian Agriculture: An Analysis of Recent Performance" by Pranab Bardhan deals with the problems and process of development of Indian agriculture. The rate of growth of production during the period 1952–63 was 3.01 per cent for all crops and 2.5 per cent for food. The increase in population at the rate of 2.14 per cent during the same period rendered agricultural production inadequate. Apart from this inadequate increase in production, the proportion of total output marketed actually declined from 27.2 per cent in 1953–54 to 26.1 per cent in 1961–62, creating food shortages in the urban sector and increasingly inflationary pressures in the economy. Bardhan also looks into various factors affecting production and recommends measures to increase agricultural productivity.

Some of the measures recommended in Bardhan's second article, especially the use of improved varieties of seeds, have recently been adopted as a part of the new strategy in Indian agriculture. The Intensive Agricultural District Programme (IADP), originally tried as a pilot project in seven IADP districts in 1960–61, covered 6 million hectares by 1967–68. The new strategy aims at using high yield varieties (HYV) seeds of wheat and rice with recommended quantities of fertilizers in irrigated areas. The strategy has had spectacular success: by 1967–68 it led to an increase of 7.3 million tons in the production of food. Because of its spectacular success, the strategy is known as "The Green Revolution." Ruddar Datt and K. P. M. Sundharam have explained the present position and the future (at the end of Fourth Five Year Plan) prospects of the new strategy. If the expectations of the Indian government are realized, the production of food grain will touch 140 million tons by 1974–75 against the figure of 95.6 million in 1967–68. This target is characterized by many economists as overoptimism, because Indian economy is still vulnerable to the ravages of monsoons and other natural calamities.

The article "China's Agriculture Under Communism" by Marion Larsen is a comprehensive survey of the policies of the Communist regime for reorganization of the agriculture sector and use of improved inputs and modern technology since 1949. In their quest for establishing a socialist society, the Chinese government experimented with several forms of land reorganizations: peasant ownership; mutual team societies; cooperative and collective farms; and finally the communes. Many errors and much mismanagement that created a state of chaos in agriculture were observed. A period of adjustments to correct errors and maladjustments occurred in 1960–62. In 1962 new economic policy was outlined with the slogan: "Agriculture as the foundation and industry as the leading sector." Concrete proposals were made for improvements in the fields of culture, education, scientific research, and public health. In 1964 a "socialist education" drive was introduced to exhort peasants to place collective work ahead of individual desires. Emphasis was placed on the education of peasants, use of improved technology, and establishment of academies for research in agricultural sciences. Steps were also taken for the expansion of irrigation and flood control, development of better crop varieties, increase in livestock and rural electrification, and increase in the production of fertilizers. Agricultural production in China, however, has been sporadic. The greatest increase in production occurred during the decade of 1950. The best year for Chinese agriculture prior to 1966 was 1958. That year was followed by a serious decline in agricultural output caused mainly by disruptions from collectivization and the chaos resulting from the commune system. The regime and the peasants seemed to have lost contact with reality. There were reports of excessive destruction of livestock and crops. These chaotic conditions along with unfavorable weather conditions reduced agricultural production to a crisis level during 1959–61. Efforts to increase irrigation, fertilization, mechanization, seed selection, disease and pest control, and other measures were undertaken. Adjustments aiming at administrative reforms, increased peasant motivation, and modernization were made. By 1964 total agricultural output started increasing again and came close to the 1957–58 bumper crop output. A significant part of the increased output, especially of hogs, poultry, and vegetables, came from private plots. Latest estimates on the gains in food output in Mainland China show fairly good yields for 1967, 1968, and 1969.[1] Wider use of the strains of miracle rice (Los Banos seeds) and the improved varieties of wheat and corn are reported to have contributed to the higher yields, especially during 1969.

From the increased output in agriculture during recent years, it seems both India and China have been paying increasing attention to the use of modern agricultural inputs: irrigation, chemical fertilizers, improved seeds, and the like. Thus the prospects of further increase in output during the 1970s are quite promising. Although the yield of food gains per hectare is much higher in China than in India, the yield in China is close to the maximum attainable using traditional agricultural inputs. Thus the prospects for achieving a higher rate of growth in agricultural yield are more promising in India than in China.

**Note to this Part appears on page 391**

1

# Indian Agriculture: An Analysis of Recent Performance

*Pranab Bardhan*

*From* Current History, 54, no. 320 (*April 1968*): *212–18, 241 with omissions. Reprinted with permission.*

IN THE LAST few years, Indian agricultural problems have become a matter of international concern. The immediate occasion was, of course, the problem of acute food scarcity, caused mainly by two consecutive years of disastrous crop weather in 1965–66 and 1966–67, in a country of 500 million people. The acuteness of the crisis will certainly be relieved to some extent by the prospect of a bumper crop in the current year. But this should not divert attention from longer-run problems which afflict the Indian agrarian economy. We shall briefly discuss some of these problems in the context of the agricultural performance over the last decade and a half.

Describing the trends in production, 1952–53 can be regarded as the initial year in our calculations, since by 1952 the economy had substantially recovered from the disruptions and dislocations of the preceding decade like the war and partition, and the minimum technical and organizational foundations for long-range planning had been laid. It is also important to note that 1952–53 was a "good" agricultural year from the standpoint of crop weather compared to the two preceding years. In most of our calculations the end-year is 1964–65, which was another "good" agricultural year.[1] Although some data are available for 1965–66 and 1966–67, since they were exceptionally "bad" years, choosing either of them as an end-year would have biased our calculations, particularly since we are interested more in the long-run factors. Production of foodgrains is estimated to have been 61.68 million metric tons in 1952–53, 78.7 million metric tons in 1958–59 and about 89 million metric tons in 1964–65. In 1965–66 it was 72.3 million metric tons.

A more meaningful estimate would, of course, take foodgrains production per head of population. Per capita production of foodgrains was about 164 kilograms in 1952–53 and 182 kilograms in 1964–65. This, however, does not give the full picture of the net *availability* of foodgrains per head of Indian population, since part of the gross production goes to provide the seed and feed requirements and wastages which, taken together, are usually estimated at 12.5 per cent of gross production of foodgrains.

There is also the supplementary factor of imports. Imports of foodgrains increased, from an annual average of about 3 million metric tons during the 1950s to more than 6 million metric tons during the Third Plan period (1961–66). Even in the bumper crop year of 1964–65, imports of foodgrains amounted to about seven per cent of domestic output. Between 1952 and 1965, imports of cereals, however, never exceeded 10 per cent of total domestic cereals production. It has been calculated that the per capita net availability of foodgrains increased from 14.5 ounces per day in 1953 to 16.8 ounces per day in 1965. This implies that even in the good year of 1964–65, the "average" Indian could derive only about 2,145 calories per day from the foodgrains available to him. In this connection one may note that the *minimum* nutritional requirement for the Indian population on the basis of the scales prescribed by the Indian Nutrition Advisory Committee has been estimated to be 2,370 calories and 66.6 grams of protein per day per head.[2]

The rate of growth of production in this period has not been very low. Between 1952–53 and 1964–65, total crop production grew at an annual compound rate of 3.01 per cent, and total production of foodgrains at 2.5 per cent. One may compare this rate of growth with that in Japan after Meiji Restoration, a



**Notes to chapter 1 appear on page 391**

period in which Japan is generally regarded as having achieved an impressive rate of growth in agricultural production. Between 1880–84 and 1915–19, the Japanese rate of growth of agricultural output was 1.8 per cent.[3] But whereas Japan in this period had a rate of growth of population less than 1 per cent per year, the corresponding rate in India was 2.14 per cent in the period between 1952–53 and 1964–65. This largely explains why India has to run very fast to remain in the same place.

Apart from the fact that the high rate of population growth cancels much of the impact of agricultural growth, there is the added problem of mobilizing (either through the market or government procurement) from the villages enough food for the growing demand of the non-agricultural sector, in view of the rising tempo of industrialization and urbanization. Since farmers tend to retain a very large proportion of their rising grain output for their own consumption and for feeding livestock, the amount supplied to the industrial sector as a proportion of output does not rise fast enough to support the pace of industrialization. As a matter of fact, according to one rough estimate, marketed proportion of gross production of cereals in India went *down* slightly from 27.2 per cent in 1953–54 to 26.1 per cent in 1961–62.[4] This proportion may have declined further in more recent years. This tends to generate inflationary pressures in an economy where the major component of the cost-of-living index is the price of foodgrains.

## *Factors Affecting Production*

Once the urgent need for raising production and the actual performance in this respect has been noted, the next obvious step is to analyze the factors that affect production. The factor of production in agriculture that comes to mind is, of course, land. In India, gross sown acreage under all crops was 144.2 million hectares in 1954–55 and 153.8 million hectares in 1964–65. Although there was some addition to sown acreage in the early 1950s through land reclamation and so forth, on the whole it is true to say that the land "frontier" in India has been more or less exhausted. The possibilities of further expansion in acreage are not substantial, and the most promising means of increasing production is, and will increasingly be, more intensive and efficient cultivation of existing farmland.

This brings up the question of the land productivity situation in India. Yield per hectare of land was 0.81 metric tons in 1952–53 for rice and 1.07 metric tons in 1964–65; for wheat it was 0.78 metric tons in 1952–53 and 0.9 in 1964–65; for all foodgrains it was 0.59 metric tons in 1952–53 and 0.75 in 1964–65. These productivity figures are among the lowest in the world today. Even in China, the rice yield per hectare is about *three* times that in India; and the Japanese yield today is more than *four* times that in India. There is, therefore, a considerable scope for improving the productivity of Indian land provided the crucial agricultural inputs are available.

A major factor in improving and even maintaining soil fertility and increasing crop yields is the supply of soil nutrients in the form of organic manure and chemical fertilizers. Through centuries, farmers in India have been applying considerable amounts of organic manure and it is still the major source of crop nutrients. Information on the use of organic manure is very scant but, according to rough estimates, organic manure provided about 1 million metric tons of nitrogen (Indian soil is most deficient in nitrogen) in 1955–56.[5] Even substantial increases in the supply of organic fertilizers will, however, be grossly insufficient in view of the fertilizer requirements for the desired growth in agricultural production. The consequent need for a huge expansion of chemical fertilizer production and consumption is now recognized in all quarters. In India, the use of chemical fertilizers in agriculture is of comparatively recent date, and the amounts used per hectare of land are among the lowest in the world. Consumption of nitrogenous (N), phosphatic ($P_2O_5$) and potassic ($K_2O$) fertilizers per hectare of gross cropped area in India was 0.9 kilograms in terms of crop nutrients in 1955–56 and 4.9 kilograms in 1964–65. These figures are miserably low relative to those in countries like Japan; even in China use of chemical fertilizers per hectare is more than twice as large.

For effective application of chemical fertilizers, as for normal crop growth and more intensive cropping, an adequate supply and regulated use of water is necessary. In the last two decades, a great many flood-control and irrigation programs have been carried out. Gross irrigated area under all crops was 23.2 million hectares (16.9 per cent of gross cropped area) in 1952–53, and 30.6 million hectares (19.5 per cent) in 1963–64. These are not very high percentage figures, particularly in a country where vast areas do not have adequate and assured rainfall. In spite of much improvement, the agrarian economy is still considerably vulnerable to periodic floods and droughts, as evidenced by the extent of annual harvest fluctuations. Besides, the major emphasis so far has been on the protective harvest-stabilizing aspects of water projects; only in very recent years has irrigation started to play a more positive role of facilitating the use of improved farming techniques.

Apart from fertilizers and water, another—quite often complementary—crucial input in transforming traditional agriculture is improved seeds. In India, area sown under improved seeds increased from 1.3 per cent of total gross cropped area in 1955–56 to 29.5 per cent in 1964–65. Most of the improved varieties of seed developed in India were, until recently, designed for their drought-resisting quality. This was understandable under Indian conditions, where the major risk of cultivation was in the failure of monsoons. But the response of these varieties to high fertilizer doses was very limited. In very recent years there has been a major breakthrough in Indian agriculture which is expected to show up in production figures fairly soon. This is the introduction of high-yielding varieties of hybrid seeds which have a very high fertilizer response.

## *Remunerative Prices?*

It has sometimes been argued that Indian farmers are inhibited from using these productivity-raising inputs because they do not get remunerative prices for their crop or because the prices they have to pay for these inputs are extremely high.[6] Let us examine this question in some detail. Index numbers of wholesale prices of agricultural commodities went up from 100 in 1952–53 (it should be noted here that the 1952–53 level of wholesale prices of agricultural commodities was more than four times that of the immediate pre-World War II period) to 122.9 in 1961–62, after a short but sharp dip in the middle of the 1950s, and to 155.8 in 1964–65 (they shot up to 199 in the crisis year of 1966–67). So absolute prices of agricultural commodities have gone up considerably in this period. There is, still, some indication that the price of agricultural commodities relative to that of manufactured consumer goods which the farmers buy has declined to some extent over most of this period. Estimating the ratio of index numbers of wholesale prices of agricultural commodities to those of some of the major manufactured consumables like cotton manufactures, sugar, edible oils and "fuel, power light and lubricants" purchased by the agricultural sector, we find that it was *below* the 1952–53 level for the period between 1954–55 and 1963–64, and has been above the 1952–53 level only since 1964–65.[7]

It should, however, be pointed out here that in the Indian context of low inter-sectoral mobility of scarce resources, the adverse effect of low *relative* prices of agricultural commodities on *total* agricultural production is likely to be much weaker than in advanced countries. Production of individual crops is, of course, more sensitive to changes in relative prices of competing crops as they compete for acreage and other inputs like water and fertilizers. As an example, since 1952–53 the price of non-foodgrain crops like sugar, cotton jute and groundnut relative to that of foodgrains has steadily increased, which must have contributed to the fact that acreage under non-foodgrains has grown at a rate more than twice that under foodgrains.

In this connection one might also refer to

the price-dampening effect of imports of wheat from the United States under Public Law 480 agreements. Until 1964 the price of wheat remained below the 1952–53 level while that of other crops was much above, and this must have something to do with the fact that net import of wheat was between one-fourth and one-third of the net availability of wheat in India over most of the period. Imports of American wheat have been an important factor in relieving acute consumer distress in some years, but over the period as a whole they are likely to have had a depressing effect on incentives in domestic wheat production; the Indian government's policy of distributing imported wheat even in good crop years instead of building up an adequate buffer stock has accentuated this problem.

As for price of inputs purchased by farmers, the fertilizer-crop price ratio in India is one of the highest in the world. In 1957, the price of nitrogen relative to that of rice was 3.22 in India, 2.12 in Japan and 1.46 in the United States. But there is no evidence to suggest that this factor has inhibited the farmers' use of fertilizers. On all calculations, the net return of fertilizers is often so very large, particularly after the introduction of high-yielding varieties of seeds, at the present low rates of application in India that it is not surprising to find farmers' demand for fertilizers tending to outstrip available supply even at the existing extremely high fertilizer-crop price ratios. The major bottleneck in the extension of fertilizer use has been its scarcity. The old idea of the illiterate and superstitious Indian farmer not responding to the opportunity of using chemical fertilizers and other improved techniques on his farm is now terribly outdated.

## *Agricultural Investment*

There has been some complaint that India has not invested enough in her agricultural sector. Gross investment in agriculture and allied activities constituted about 20 per cent of total gross investment for the period 1951–52 to 1960–61.[8] This figure for investment allocation to agriculture is not very high, nor is it extremely low, particularly for a country with an urgent program of industrialization.[9] Certainly the share of investment used in building the industrial base of the economy was much higher, but then no country aiming at structural transformation of the economy can be expected to allocate investment in proportion to existing sector shares in national income. Besides, in Asian agriculture, investment in fixed capital may not always be the most important determinant of any significant productivity rise; much depends on *industrial* investment in producing fertilizers, pesticides and pumps.

## *Effective Investment?*

Even if complaints about neglect of agriculture in investment allocation are justified, there are probably stronger reasons to question the *effectiveness* of investment that has been made in the agricultural sector and the appropriateness of the investment priorities actually followed *within* the industrial sector itself. Let us take the second aspect first. In spite of planners' intentions to the contrary, while industries catering to luxury and semi-luxury consumption have often spawned an undue amount of investible resources including foreign exchange (this has been made possible largely due to the extremely unequal income distribution pattern and loose government control over investment) and have sometimes overfulfilled their production targets, investment and production performance have fallen grossly short of the desired pattern in respect of, say, chemical fertilizers. In the Third Five Year Plan period less than 30 per cent of the target was achieved in production of both nitrogenous and phosphatic fertilizers. In the Second Plan period also, actual production at the end-year was only 34 per cent of target in nitrogenous fertilizers and 45 per cent of target in phosphatic fertilizers.

As for effectiveness of investment, agricultural programs have suffered from serious technical deficiencies as well as poor management and coordination. As the different Program Evaluation Reports to the Planning Commission have amply testified, there have been serious shortcomings not only in the input distribution and extension service aspects of agricultural programs but also in the technical suitability or local adaptability of various items in those programs. Water, fertilizer or seed programs have been pushed without sufficient consideration of local soil, climate conditions, cropping patterns, cultivating practices and the crucial complementarities in the use of different factors of production. Farmers have sometimes refused to adopt new inputs and technology, not out of irrationality, ignorance or fatalism, but due to a better appreciation of their local unsuitability or technical complementarity than is to be found in the administrative officials pushing those programs (apart from the risk factors involved).

Talking about investment in the agricultural sector one might point to the fact that, given sufficient organization, there is considerable scope in India for mobilizing the vast masses of unemployed and seasonally underemployed rural labor on labor-intensive investment projects like minor irrigation, flood control, land reclamation, contour bunding, terracing, leveling and road building. The Indian plans and the Ford Foundation Agricultural Production Team in India in 1959 endorsed this policy, after pointing out that a vast number of such rural construction projects could be undertaken with very little extra equipment. In China, in recent years, staggering amounts of earthworks have been constructed by mass mobilization of labor in the countryside. In comparison, the Indian performance so far has been very poor.

Apart from organizational problems, one should take note of the important incentive problem in the distribution of benefits from such rural construction projects. In India a major problem in mobilizing labor on such projects is that those who work on them do not receive proportional benefits from them. As report after report of the Program Evaluation Committees has stressed, most of the benefits from Community Development Projects in India have accrued to richer farmers. No wonder that the mass of poor peasants and agricultural laborers do not feel excited by these projects. In irrigation projects also, the distribution of water is very inequitable and it is a major reason for the poor maintenance of field channels.[10] The rural institutional framework in India has severely constrained the effectiveness of much of the development program. This immediately raises the question of land organization and institutions in village India.

## *Land Legislation*

A great deal of land legislation has been undertaken in India in the last two decades. The major objectives of land policy were the abolition of intermediary tenures, reform of the tenancy system—including fixing of fair rent at one-fifth to one-fourth of the gross produce and security of tenure for the tenant —extension of owner-cultivation, ceilings on land holdings making possible a redistribution of surplus land among landless laborers, consolidation of agricultural holdings and increase in the size of the operational unit to an economic scale through cooperative methods. These programs have been enforced in part and have met varying degrees of success or failure.

The program for the abolition of intermediaries has been carried out practically all over the country; about 20 million tenants of former intermediaries have come into direct relationship with the state and became owners of their holdings. Far less effective has been the program of tenancy reform. A considerable proportion of the total area cultivated is still under tenancy. According to the 1961 census, of the total cultivated area in rural India, the proportion of holdings under "pure" and "mixed" tenancy is 22.4 per cent.[11] The actual importance of tenancy in rural India may, however, be more important than this figure suggests for two major reasons. First, since the prevalence of tenancy is significantly higher in the wet and therefore generally more productive areas (including irrigated land) than in the dry areas, loss from tenant cultivation is more than is suggested from the average all-India figure.[12]

Second, what may not have come out in official data is that land legislation in some areas has in fact driven underground some forms of tenancy; numerous cases of eviction of tenants have taken place under the guise of "voluntary surrenders" and informal arrangements have been made with share-croppers disguised as agricultural laborers. The high pressure of population on land as well as the balance of social and political forces in the countryside has made it possible for land owners to impose such arrangements on the landless and defenseless agricultural population.

This has tended to defeat the major aim of protective tenancy reforms. On the subject of the rights of tenants, it is worthwhile to quote from the Report of the Committee on Tenancy Reform for the Planning Commission:

> Even where the tenants are aware of their rights they are generally in too weak a position both economically and socially to insist on their rights. The landlord class includes money-lenders and tradesmen upon whom the tenants have frequently to depend for credit and other necessities of life. Socially the tenants often belong to the backward classes and are afraid of exercising their rights against the higher classes. If the tenancy laws are to be effective, it is necessary that they should be very simple and behind them there should be an administrative support to counteract the effects of the social and economic weaknesses of the tenants. On the contrary, in many States there is no administrative machinery within easy reach of tenants. In some States, there are no village records from which a tenant can establish his position . . . [even where there are], the landlord has so much influence in the village that frequently it is very difficult for the tenant to establish his position by oral evidence and, even if he tries to do so, the trouble and expense of taking his witness out of the village to a distant court frequently deters him from doing so. Finally, the attitude of the revenue officers may at times be unconsciously against him. . . . In the case of conflicting evidence, there is a greater tendency to believe the landlord rather than the tenant, the presumption being that a poor man is more likely to speak untruth with a view to obtaining some land than the rich landlord who, having already enough land, may not be under immediate pressure to do so.

The tenant cultivator with insecure tenure has little incentive to undertake long-run improvements in the land he cultivates. Besides, his capacity to invest is seriously limited by high rents and limited access to even cooperative credit. The rents as fixed by tenancy laws are still very high in several states and in others the rents charged are generally much higher than the legal maximum. As for credit, among all the occupational categories based on agriculture, the tenant cultivator figures the least in proportion to his importance among the beneficiaries of credit programs. This is mostly because even cooperative loans continue to be given generally against the mortgage of land, and there has not been any significant shift to the crop loan system in most states.

Among tenant farms a more acute incentive problem arises in the case of share-croppers. Little information on the extent of share-cropping is available from census publications, but from National Sample Survey data for the 8th Round (1954–55), it seems that at least 56.5 per cent of tenancy areas is under formal or informal share-cropping and that only 20.8 per cent of tenancy areas may be definitely free from share-cropping. Share-cropping may thus be regarded as still the predominant form of tenancy in rural India.

Crop-sharing tenancy without cost-sharing (as is generally the rule in India) obviously involves an added disincentive problem in application of new agricultural inputs like chemical fertilizers, compared to the case of tenancy with fixed cash rent. It is easily shown why the share-cropper paying a very high proportion of his gross produce as rent may be reluctant to adopt a new input even when he knows that this will bring some addition to output. One can cite from recent Farm Management Studies the case of Thanjavur district in Madras where with "moderate" response rates, the tenant receiving 40 per cent of the share of the crop has little incentive to apply the second one-third of the package of improved practices and none at all to apply the last third.

## Small Holdings

Leaving aside the problem of tenancy, a major affliction of Indian agriculture has been and still is the prevalence of small and fragmented holdings.[13] According to National Sample Survey 16th Round data on Land Holdings for 1959–60, 30.6 per cent of the total area operated is in holdings of less than 7.5 acres, 53.7 per cent is in holdings of less than 15 acres, 75.6 per cent is in holdings of less than 30 acres. A substantial proportion of cultivated area is thus being operated in holdings that are "uneconomic" by most standards.[14] Besides, compared to large farmers, small farmers suffer from extra disadvantages in getting enough supplies of credit, inputs and technical assistance. Although there has been some improvement in cooperative servicing in recent years, particularly in credit, marketing and provision of agricultural supplies,[15] many of the cooperatives tend to be dominated by the larger farmers and traders who take the lion's share of the facilities, thereby defeating one of the major aims of the cooperative movement.[16] As for cooperative farming, no significant progress has as yet been made in this direction.

Apart from being small, the holdings also consist of widely scattered fragments. According to National Sample Survey 16th Round data for 1959–60, the average number of parcels per operational holding in India is 5.82 and the average area of a parcel is 1.14 acres. Under the five year plans, up to 1964–65 a total of only about 55 million acres of area has been consolidated. Consolidation of holdings removes a lot of division strips, assists in soil conservation measures and irrigation projects, and economizes use of animal and human labor.

Thus it is generally true to say that in India, in spite of copious land legislation, some crucial land relations have remained basically unaltered. A substantial part of Indian agriculture still bears the burden of uneconomically small and fragmented holdings, tenurial insecurity and share-cropping. One can no doubt expect that with the significant improvement in supplies of agricultural inputs (particularly chemical fertilizers and high-yielding varieties of seeds) and investment, Indian agricultural performance may be much better in the next decade than it has been in the past. But a large part of her development effort will remain seriously constrained by her backward rural institutional framework.

2

# The Green Revolution

*Ruddar Datt*
*K. P. M. Sundharam*

*From Ruddar Datt and K. P. M. Sundharam,* Indian Economy, *(New Delhi: Niraj Prakashan, 1969), 465–76, with omissions. Reprinted with permission.*

## *New Strategy in Indian Agriculture*

THE INCREASE IN agricultural production that has taken place during 1967–68 and 1968–69 has revived new hopes and it is being felt that a break-through in Indian agriculture has been made. Some have gone so far as to proclaim that a green revolution is round the corner. Our purpose is to examine the true position as it stands in the light of the latest information gathered.

The new strategy in Indian agriculture was tried as a pilot project in 7 IADP districts in 1960–61. After the reports of initial success, the program was extended to other areas. By 1967–68, 6 million hectares (14.8 million acres) of land was brought under High Yielding Varieties and on the basis of official estimates, it has led to an increase of about 7.73 million tons in the production of foodgrains. By 1968–69, the coverage of HYV will extend to about 17 million acres. It is proposed to bring the entire irrigated area under high yielding varieties (HYV) during the Fourth Plan. In 1964–65, we had a total irrigated area of about 53 million acres. During the three Annual Plans, another 14 million acres have been extended irrigation facilities. Thus the total irrigated area by 1967–68 is of the order of about 67 million acres. It is hoped that during the new Fourth Plan irrigation facilities may be extended to another 20 million acres. Thus the program is to bring about 65–70 million acres under high yielding varieties. On the basis of the official yardsticks, the high yielding varieties are expected to yield 0.6 ton of additional produce per acre. Thus the arithmetic of HYV varieties is as under:

Irrigated area in 1964–65 = 53 million acres.
Irrigated area in 1968–69 = 53 + 14 = 67 million acres.
Irrigated area in 1974–75 = 67 + 20 = 87 million acres.
Area under HYV by 1968–69 = 17 million acres.
Additional area under HYV = 70 million acres.
Additional production expected = 70 × 0.6 = 42 million tons.
Production of foodgrains by 1967–68 = 95.6 million tons.
Expected target of production by 1974–75 = 137 million tons.
Percentage growth rate of foodgrain production = 7 per cent.

The average rate of growth of food production in the non-HYV area is estimated at the rate of 1.5 per cent per annum. Thus adding expected growth rate in HYV and non-HYV areas, the rate of growth of food production would be 8.5 per cent per annum. In other words, food production would touch 140 million tons by 1974–75. This would be a stupendous achievement. All this arithmetic is based on the assumption that there is no abnormal drought year during the Fourth Plan and that the yardstick of additional production of 0.6 ton per acre holds good. But the Planning Commission is targeting a growth rate of 5 per cent per annum. Why is it so? Obviously, it is legitimate to question the yardstick which seems to be an over-estimate. According to the official figures by 1967–68 (6.034 million hectares) or about 14.8 million acres of land was brought under HYV varieties and the contribution of High Yielding Varieties to food production is estimated at 7.73 million tons. Thus, the contribution of HYV per acre works out to be a little less than 0.5 ton per acre. Discounting the figure of additional production in

**Notes to chapter 2 appear on pages 391-392**

HYV areas by the achieved norm of 0.5 ton per acre and also making an allowance for bad weather conditions, it can be reasonably argued that the food production target may be kept at 6 per cent per annum. We can, therefore, argue that the Planning Commission target is an under-estimate. This may be the result of a cautious approach in fixing targets because of the experience of the Third Plan. Thus, it would be appropriate to fix a target of about 130 million tons of foodgrains by 1974–75.

To realize this target, the new agricultural strategy proposes to make a technological break-through in Indian agriculture which comprises of the introduction of new and high yielding varieties of improved seeds, increased application of the recommended doses of fertilizers and extension of the use of pesticides so that the crop produced can be saved from destruction by insects. For this purpose, research has to be directed to finding new high yielding varieties in each crop, stepping up the production of fertilizers and making the peasant familiar with the use of pesticides. In the initial stages, the program was restricted to areas which enjoyed better irrigation facilities and which were immune to natural hazards. But as the coverage of the program has to be extended further, irrigation facilities will have to be expanded. Need it be emphasized that water is a basic input in agriculture and better seeds and fertilizers can produce desired results only if adequate quantity of water is made available. Not only that, to enable the poor peasants to make use of better agricultural implements, install tubewells, apply heavy doses of fertilizers and use improved seeds, agricultural loans have to be provided. Steps are being taken in all these directions. It would be appropriate to examine the achievements of the strategy during the three year period (1965–66 to 1967–68) and also to know the future programs.

### ACHIEVEMENTS OF THE NEW STRATEGY

Table 1 below gives the area, production and yield of the principal crops during the last few years. A close look at the table will reveal that the production of wheat which stood at 12.3 million tons in 1964–65 rose to about 16.6 million tons in 1967–68, *i.e.*, an increase of 34.9 per cent in total wheat production. Part of this increase can be attributed to an extension of the area, but even the yield per acre rose from 913 Kgs. to 1,111 Kgs. per hectare, signifying an increase of 21.7 per cent. Increase in yield in maize during 1964–65 and 1967–68 is esti-

***Table 1—Area Production and Average Yield of Principal Crops***[a]

| | | *1960–61* | *1964–65* | *1965–66* | *1966–67* | *1967–68* |
|---|---|---|---|---|---|---|
| Rice | A | 34,128 | 36,364 | 35,273 | 35,251 | 36,722 |
| | P | 34,574 | 39,034 | 30,614 | 30,438 | 37,858 |
| | Y | 1,013 | 1,073 | 869 | 863 | 1,931 |
| Jowar | A | 18,412 | 17,938 | 17,504 | 18,504 | 18,630 |
| | P | 9,814 | 9,749 | 7,527 | 9,224 | 10,107 |
| | Y | 533 | 543 | 430 | 511 | 543 |
| Bajra | A | 11,469 | 11,726 | 11,563 | 12,239 | 12,539 |
| | P | 3,283 | 4,454 | 3,655 | 4,468 | 5,132 |
| | Y | 286 | 380 | 316 | 365 | 409 |
| Maize | A | 4,407 | 4,618 | 4,765 | 5,074 | 5,577 |
| | P | 4,080 | 4,658 | 4,760 | 4,894 | 6,275 |
| | Y | 926 | 1.009 | 999 | 964 | 1,125 |
| Wheat | A | 12,927 | 13,460 | 12,656 | 12,838 | 14,917 |
| | P | 10,997 | 12,290 | 10,424 | 11,393 | 16,568 |
| | Y | 851 | 913 | 824 | 887 | 1,111 |

[a] A: Area 000 hectares, P: Productivity 000 tons, Y: Yield per hectare in kgs.

mated at about 11.5 per cent, but increase in yield from jowar and bajra is insignificant. But the most disappointing feature of the prevailing situation is the decline in the total production of rice from 39.03 million tons in 1964–65 to 37.86 million tons in 1967–68. This only highlights the fact that whereas the new strategy has been able to make an impact on the wheat crop, the biggest crop of India, namely, rice has remained unaffected by it so far.

As a result of the new strategy, area under improved seeds has gone up from 112 million acres to 134.5 million acres in 1967–68. Besides this, the new varieties take a short-term duration and consequently, instead of growing one crop in several irrigated areas, two crops are being grown. In the case of wheat, unprecedented enthusiasm exists among farmers in the Punjab, Haryana, Delhi, Rajasthan and Western U.P. for the new Mexican varieties like Lerma Rojo, Sonara-64, Kalyan and P.V.-18 and a situation has developed in which the demand for seeds by the farmers has exceeded the supply. But in the case of rice, the new varieties like TN-1, IR-8, Tainen-3 and ADT-27 which were tried and found successful on a laboratory scale, have not been proved distinctively superior on the field. The peasants in rice areas which account for a big chunk of the total farming families have not accepted the new varieties with favor and enthusiasm. Rice varieties incorporating Dee-gee-woogen have proved capable of producing 8 to 10 tons per hectare, while the conventional varieties yield only 4 to 5 tons per hectare. Dr. M. S. Swaminathan,[1] Director of the Indian Agricultural Research Institute has adduced the following reasons for our failure in the case of new rice varieties:

1. The new "rice varieties which, due to their non-lodging habit, have the ability to respond well to good conditions of soil fertility, are unfortunately highly susceptible to virus and bacterial diseases. As a consequence, virus diseases are growing in importance for the first time in our long history of rice culture."

2. Several studies conducted about the HYV program reveal that cultural practices such as date of planting, depth of transplanting, age of seedlings at the time of transplanting, spacing, time and method of fertilizer application, type of water management adopted and time of harvesting, may all influence yield considerably."[2]

3. Bad water management is another cause of low productivity in rice areas. Mr. Swaminathan writes: "In many parts of India, rice yields are low more because of excess of water than due to a lack of it."[3]

4. Another factor responsible for low acceptance by the peasants of the new varieties is the wrong choice of a variety for propagation in the rural area. In this connection, Swaminathan mentions: "Kerala is reported to have shown the lowest degree of acceptance of high yielding varieties by farmers, while Punjab occupies the top position at the other end of the scale. Ironically, the highest percentage of literacy occurs in Kerala and literacy has often been cited as the first requisite for the adoption of new ideas. The reason for this enigma is the wrong choice of the rice variety used in the program, namely Tainen-3, the grains of which become sticky on cooking."[4]

### AREA UNDER HYV VARIETIES AND ITS CONTRIBUTION TO FOOD PRODUCTION

Figures regarding area under HYV are given in Table 2 which reveal that the achievement in all crops except wheat is below the target. It obviously shows that either the targets were set without adequate consideration of feasibility or the necessary extension effort and input supplies were not properly planned, or both were responsible for the gap between target and achievement. While assessing the role of Governmental agencies in the successful implementation of HYV program, P. N. Radhakrishnan writes: "Madras is the only example where the official plan was successfully implemented. In other states, whatever success was achieved has been attributed largely to the initiative and enthusiasm of the farmers themselves than to the efforts of the Governmental machinery. In Punjab, officials are reported to have stated that farmers in their area being well educated did not require any prodding from Government to adopt the HYVP."[5]

It has been estimated that during 1967–68, HYV program contributed 7.7 million tons to total food production. During 1968–69, 7.4 million tons is estimated to be the contribution to total kharif cereals. The contribution can be considered as significant though it may be stated that it is not the maximum achievable.

## Use of Fertilizers

The new agricultural strategy has recommended definite doses of fertilizer for each crop and consequently, it was imperative that efforts be made to expand the production of fertilizers. In the interim period of installation of fertilizer plants, the new strategy stepped up the imports of fertilizers. Table 4 reveals that during 1964–65 and 1968–69, the consumption of nitrogenous fertilizer (domestic plus imported) increased by 291 per cent, that of phosphate fertilizer by 339 per cent and of potassic fertilizer by 642 per cent. Need it be emphasized that the

### Table 2—Area under High Yielding Varieties of Seeds (thousand hectares)

| | 1966–67 | | 1967–68 | | 1968–69 |
|---|---|---|---|---|---|
| *Foodgrain* | *Target* | *Achievement* | *Target* | *Achievement* | *Target* |
| Rice | 1,315 | 887 | 2,428 | 1,784 | 3,440 |
| Jowar | 374 | 190 | 745 | 599 | 1,012 |
| Bajra | 151 | 59 | 741 | 420 | 1,012 |
| Maize | 376 | 207 | 741 | 289 | 1,012 |
| Total kharif cereals | 2,216 | 1,343 | 4,655 | 3,092 | 6,476 |
| Wheat | 644 | 540 | 1,416 | 2,942 | 2,023 |
| Total foodgrains | 2,860 | 1,883 | 6,071 | 6,034 | 8,499 |

### Table 3—Estimated Contribution of HYV to Food Production (thousand tons)

| *Foodgrain* | *1967–68[a] Estimated* | *1968–69[a] Target* |
|---|---|---|
| Rice | 2,013 | 3,880 |
| Jowar | 742 | 1,254 |
| Bajra | 306 | 738 |
| Maize | 435 | 1,528 |
| Total kharif cereals | 3,496 | 7,400 |
| Wheat | 4,231 | N.A. |
| Total foodgrains | 7,727 | N.A. |

[a] Official estimates. Production has been computed on the basis of statewise "yardsticks."
*Source: Eastern Economist,* Annual Number 1969.

### Table 4—Consumption of Fertilizers (thousand tons)

| | *Nitrogenous* | *Phosphate* | *Potassic* |
|---|---|---|---|
| 1950–51 | 56 | 7 | 6 |
| 1955–56 | 107 | 13 | 12 |
| 1960–61 | 210 | 70 | 26 |
| 1964–65 | 434 | 148 | 70 |
| 1965–66 | 600 | 132 | 90 |
| 1966–67 | 840 | 250 | 115 |
| 1967–68 (estimated) | 1,150 | 400 | 200 |
| 1968–69 (anticipated) | 1,700 | 650 | 450 |

achievement was spectacular if we compare it with the period of the 1950s when practically very little effort was made to step up fertilizer use in Indian agriculture.

MINOR IRRIGATION

During the First Plan, emphasis on irrigation was very pronounced and a large number of multi-purpose river valley projects were built. But in the subsequent plans, irrigation gave place to heavy industry as a priority item. Some progress in irrigation was, however, made but the progress was not sufficient. The drought of 1965–66 and 1966–67 which created famine conditions in Bihar and Eastern U.P. reinforced the need to develop minor irrigation as a priority item in agricultural planning. Consequently, development of minor irrigation was incorporated as an integral part of the new agricultural strategy. It is gratifying to note that an additional irrigation potential of about 10 million acres was created during the three-year period (1966–67 to 1968–69). The success of the new strategy will largely depend on the extension of irrigation facilities. In the first instance, the new strategy has decided to concentrate on areas of assured irrigation or rainfall, but for the agricultural revolution to become pervasive in the whole of rural India, extension of irrigation is a sine qua non.

## *Assessment of HYV Program under the New Strategy*

CASE FOR THE HIGH YIELDING VARIETIES PROGRAM

The apologists of the new strategy consider the intensive approach as the only means of making a break-through in Indian agriculture in the shortest possible time. To achieve self-sufficiency in foodgrains by the end of the Fourth Plan requires a production strategy which can promise an additional 25 to 30 million tons of food. The HYV program provides a short cut to reach this goal.

Secondly, it is admitted on all hands that agricultural inputs are scarce and it is not possible to meet the needs of the entire country in this respect. The choice is to have a thin layer of the inputs spread over the entire country or to apply concentrated doses in selected and promising areas. The latter choice, according to the apologists, is more rational as it ensures maximum production in the short period.

Thirdly, it is held that the application of high doses will be accompanied by increasing returns and, consequently, the application of high doses can be justified on economic grounds.

Fourthly, large-scale demonstration of better cultivation in actual field conditions will induce farmers in other areas to adopt improved techniques. Thus the intensive development program sets in motion a beneficient circle which will move on and on and thus gather momentum. In this way, the spread effect of the program will raise the over-all level of productivity in Indian agriculture.

Fifthly, increased agricultural production in a certain region will produce very healthy secondary and tertiary effects. For instance, the availability of more food in the country will decrease our dependence on food imports and thereby release scarce foreign exchange resources for other sectors of the

### *Table 5—Area under Minor Irrigation*

| *Period* | *Million acres (Gross)* |
|---|---|
| 1951–52 to 1955–56 | 9.5 |
| 1956–57 to 1960–61 | 9.0 |
| 1961–62 to 1965–66 (provisional) | 13.1 |
| Additional potential created during | |
| 1966–67 | 3.4 |
| 1967–68 | 3.0 |
| 1968–69 | 3.6 |

economy. Similarly, increased production of commercial crops will enable the expansion of agro-based industries.

Lastly, the program, by concentrating on areas of assured irrigation and rainfall, will lessen the fluctuations in agricultural output. Even in bad monsoon years, total output may not rise but shall not register a steep fall as it happened in 1965–66. In other words, the program is conceived as an insurance against the vagaries of monsoons. It shall, therefore, help to reduce wide fluctuations in agricultural output.

### CRITICISM OF HYV PROGRAM

Critics have seen in the agricultural revolution the signs of frustration and have therefore attacked the new strategy on several counts. Main points of criticism are:

1. Growth of black markets in agricultural inputs. It is really a healthy sign that the demand for agricultural inputs has broken the confidence bands of the forecasts made by the government. This is true in respect of seeds, fertilizers, insecticides which have shown an excess demand over supply. But the policy of the Indian government is, to say the least, muddleheaded. The agricultural revolution has become frustrated because of the existence of black markets in agricultural inputs. This has raised the cost of the application of the new inputs. To the extent peasants are forced to purchase these inputs at black market prices, there is a disincentive to the peasants—more especially, the small peasants. It is, therefore, necessary that measures be taken to make agricultural inputs available in adequate quantity at cheap rates.

2. Growth of capitalistic farming in Indian agriculture. The high yielding varieties necessitate heavy investment in fertilizers and water. These heavy investments are beyond the capacity of small and medium farmers. In India, there are about 60 million farms. Forty per cent of the farms are under one hectare (2.5 acres) and 35 per cent are between 1 and 3 hectares (*i.e.*, between 2.5 to 7.5 acres) and 12 per cent between 3 and 5 hectares (*i.e.*, 7.5 acres to 12.5 acres). It is only the remaining 13 per cent of the big farmers that account for 50 per cent of the land who are making heavy investments in the installation of tubewells, pumping sets, fertilizers and agricultural machinery required for the purpose. Consequently, the new agricultural strategy has helped the growth of capitalist farming in India. The agricultural revolution is lacking in spread effects and thus is fostering an enclave type development in Indian agriculture. The poor peasantry is not being benefited thereby, but it has led to concentration of wealth in the hands of the top 10 per cent of the rural population.

3. Side tracking the need for institutional reforms in Indian agriculture. The new strategy does not recognize the need for institutional reforms in agriculture. Among the institutional changes, the most important is the land-relations so that the technological changes sought to be achieved can be effected with maximum social benefit. It is a truism that in India agriculture is carried on by millions of cultivators and it is the absorption capacity of fertilizers by these millions of cultivators that will determine the total agricultural production. Needless to emphasize here that land reforms which were conceived to be a step in the right direction have failed in India. Not to speak of providing ownership rights to the bulk of the peasant population, we have failed to provide even fixity of tenure and large-scale evictions have already taken place. As a result, the tenants are being forced to accept the position of share-croppers. Minhas and Srinivasan have studied the effect of crop-sharing arrangements in fertilizer use. Their basic assumption is that the cost of fertilizers is met by the cultivator by borrowing, and interest charges amount to 10 per cent of the cost. Since the crop season is of about six months duration, the interest charges shall work out to be in the neighborhood of 20 per cent of the cost. Further assuming three crop-sharing arrangements, *i.e.*, full ownership (100 per cent) or 50 per cent ownership and 40 per cent ownership, they have worked out the net returns as percentages of fertilizer cost.

Their conclusions are summarized in table 6.

The logic of fertilizer use becomes crystal clear from the table. Basing our judgment on the capitalist principle of profit maximization, the owner-farmers reap a profit of 180 per cent on irrigated lands in the case of wheat and 183 per cent in the case of rice. Contrasting it with the tenant cultivation (50 per cent basis), this return is reduced to 65 per cent in wheat and 67 per cent in the case of rice. The return is further reduced to a level of 42 per cent in the case of share-cropping on a 40 per cent basis. The assumptions on the basis of which Minhas and Srinivasan have calculated the disparity in the rate of returns to owner-cultivators and share-croppers are questionable. They understate the disparity. For instance, the assumption that share-croppers can borrow at 10 per cent interest rate is of doubtful validity. Similarly, the assumption that all types of cultivators are able to grow two crops a year is also not true, and this is more so in the case of tenant-cultivators. Thus the conclusion is inescapable that tenancy cultivation poses itself as a big obstruction in the way of fertilizer use. Profit maximization criterion so very familiar to capitalist economics clearly indicates that larger dosages of fertilizers will be absorbed by owner-farmers than by tenants. Minhas and Srinivasan conclude their analysis in the following words: "It is probably needless to stress that the optimal levels of fertilizer use (and the profits per unit of investment) for tenants are lower than for owners. In the long run, share-cropping can obstruct the process of intensification of current input use far short of levels, which would be desirable from the point of view of extracting maximum output from the limited amount of available land."

### *Table 6—Net Returns as Percentage of Fertilizer Cost*[a]

| *Crop sharing basis* | *New variety of wheat* | *Existing variety of wheat* | | |
|---|---|---|---|---|
| | | *Irrigated* | *Unirrigated* | *Rice* |
| 100 per cent | 136 | 180 | 74 | 183 |
| 50 per cent | 89 | 65 | 12 | 67 |
| 40 per cent | 24 | 42 | — | 43 |

[a] Assumption: Variable cost is 20 per cent.

Some recent studies have shown that the landlords have started paying for the new inputs to the tenants. In other words, cost sharing of inputs is fast becoming a new norm in Indian agriculture, but this has also enhanced the bargaining position of the landlords and they are demanding a greater share of the produce. Sengupta and Ghosh, analyzing the conditions in West Bengal, comment: "Moreover, in the event of the owner bearing the additional cost (and ultimately realizing them from the output) the relative share of the share-cropper in the gross output will diminish sharply even though he may gain in terms of his absolute return. . . . Improved technology requiring large out of pocket investments puts the owner in a more favorable position and he can turn the terms of trade against the farmer. This has been happening in this area after the introduction of canal irrigation and the subsequent increase in profitability of land."

4. Socialist pattern of society and the new strategy. Dr. V. K. R. V. Rao has warned the Government against the pursuit of the new strategy to its "logical end." He opines: "The selective approach we are following certainly has its logic in production economics; but it is also going to increase interpersonal and regional inequalities among our farmers. Such a development is bound to lead to tensions and discontent in the 60 million families and threaten social stability in rural India. It will be out of tune with the socialist and egalitarian ideals that constitute the motivational base of Indian planning." The famine conditions in eastern U.P. and Bihar witnessed during recent years necessitate

urgent attention being given to such vulnerable areas in our economy but the new strategy tries to develop the more prosperous areas. The situation is just like making more investment on children in public schools so as to raise their levels and leave the large mass of poor children to the mercy of natural forces. While enunciating the concept of democratic socialism in our plans, we have always held maximum production as a goal of policy but in conjunction with equality of opportunity for all.

5. Absence of co-ordination among various agencies. The slow achievements under the new agricultural strategy as compared with the targets set by the government shows lack of comprehensive planning in the effort for agricultural development. It is the production of fertilizers which has been emphasized. It is quite possible that fertilizer supplies may not remain inadequate after a few years, but coordination in developing supporting measures like the timely availability of credit, fertilizers and seeds, extension of irrigation through minor irrigation works etc. has also to be ensured. Mr. V. S. Vyas is right when he asserts: "Many of the reasons for the unsatisfactory performance of the new strategy are the same as those for the lack of success in the IADP areas, namely, lack of coordination among the State Government's agriculture departments, panchayati raj institutions and cooperatives; failure of extension agencies to come up to the requirements of a sophisticated technology; and the failure of the cooperative movement in large parts of the country in timely distribution of inputs like fertilizers, and, more particularly, in toning up credit operations."

## *Is the Agricultural Revolution Round the Corner?*

On a balance of considerations, it would be too optimistic to assert that the agricultural revolution is round the corner. Much leeway has to be covered before an assertion of this type can be made. Our reasons for not being optimistic are as under:

Firstly, the agricultural revolution initiated by the new strategy is limited to wheat, maize, jowar and bajra only. The major crop of India, *i.e.*, rice, has not been affected by the high-yielding varieties. Besides this, progress in major commercial crops, oil seeds, cotton, jute and sugarcane is very slow. Agricultural research has not diverted attention to the development of new seeds in them. In addition to all this, pulses which account for about 10 to 12 per cent of the total food production have not registered any significant spurt in production. It would, therefore, be very premature to speak in terms of an agricultural revolution unless the projected upward trend in production in a few crops becomes pervasive in most of the major crops. If growth rate of food output is measured from the peak year 1964–65, in the year 1967–68, total foodgrain production was 96 million tons as compared to 89 million tons touched in 1964–65, signifying a growth rate of about 1.5 per cent per annum. During 1968–69, the total production of foodgrains is about the same as in the year 1967–68 which only shows that the target of reaching 100 million tons by 1968–69 could not be achieved. In the face of these facts, it is rather too optimistic to believe that the target of 130 million tons set for the Fourth Plan is achievable. Research has to be directed to other crops so that new high-yielding seeds can be developed in rice and pulses and other commercial crops. This shall enable the agricultural revolution which has been initiated in a few crops like wheat, maize, bajra and jowar to spread to other agricultural crops. There are possibilities of making a break-through if the experience of wheat and maize can be successfully transmitted to rice, oil seeds, jute, cotton, pulses, etc.

Secondly, the rise in food production has taken place in Punjab, Haryana, Western U.P. and in some selected districts of Andhra Pradesh, Maharashtra and Madras. But these areas cannot claim to cover the bulk of India. All that can be said is that they have shown the way to a big take-off in agricultural production. In other words, the already better-off areas have made their economic position still better. This has initiated a process of unbalanced growth in India. The regions which have lagged behind have to catch up with those that have marched ahead. Unless all the major states enter the take-off stage, it would not be fair to speak of an agricultural revolution.

Thirdly, the new strategy has created three kinds of conflicts, namely, between large and small farmers, between owners and tenant farmers and between employers and employees on agricultural farms. The holders of large farms are capable of making heavy investments in the form of fertilizers, pumping sets, tubewells and agricultural machinery. They are also able to procure credit from cooperatives, as also obtain fertilizers and better seeds. For all practical purposes, the large farmers enjoy the right of pre-emption of agricultural inputs and, thus, the small farmers are deprived of the much-needed inputs. This has, therefore, widened the inequalities of income and fostered the growth of capitalist agriculture in the country.

In India, quite a significant group of peasants have small size holdings and consequently, they hire land on tenancy from the large owners. Since the landlords pay for the new agricultural inputs, such farms are experiencing a dualism in agricultural production technique. The part of land hired by the tenants is provided with modern techniques and the small fragments of land owned by the tenants continue to be worked by traditional techniques. This conflict is the cause of social tension, more so when the landlords demand exploitative rents on the lands hired out by them.

The application of new technology in large farms has led to the substitution of human labor with mechanical processes. In other words, the back wash effects of new strategy in terms of displacement of human labor have also to be taken note of. The greatest sufferers in the process of agricultural revolution are landless laborers. Unless alternative opportunities of employment are provided to this most vulnerable section of the rural community, agricultural revolution will be meaningless to the millions of landless peasants in this country.

It is, therefore, essential that landless laborers and tenants are organized and a trade union mechanism is developed, so that non-exploitative forms of tenancy can be developed in rural India and the wages of landless laborers can be improved. The gains of high-yielding varieties are being pocketed by the rich land-owning classes and the new strategy has further tilted the scales of distribution in their favor. Organized peasant resistance alone can help the small peasant, the tenant, the share cropper and the landless laborer, *i.e.*, the agricultural proletariat in maintaining its relative share in agricultural income intact.

To sum up, the agricultural revolution is not round the corner. At best, it can be asserted that a technological break-through has been achieved in wheat, maize, bajra and jowar and that too in Punjab, Haryana, Western U.P. and parts of Andhra Pradesh, Maharashtra and Madras. The break-through has to be made pervasive by developing new high-yielding varieties in other crops and also by extending the geographical coverage of the new technology. But this production economics approach will not mean the end of poverty in rural India, unless the surplus agricultural population is drained off to alternative employments. Moreover, it is very necessary that the gains of the high-yielding varieties be shared by all sections of the rural population and not usurped by the top 10 per cent of the farming families. For this purpose, peasant organizations must endeavor to establish new norms in tenant-landlord relations so that non-exploitative forms of tenancy become the rule. Only then can the agricultural revolution be consummated.

3

# China's Agriculture Under Communism

*Marion R. Larsen*

*From* An Economic Profile of Mainland China, Vol. I, *Studies Prepared for the Joint Economic Committee, Congress of the United States, February 1967, U.S. Government Printing Office, 223–30, 235–52 and 257–61, with omissions. Reprinted by permission.*

## *Developments in Agriculture*

### BASIC POLICY THWARTED

THE COMMUNIST REGIME in China faced a formidable task of developing an isolated economy stagnated because of overpopulation, undeveloped industrial and resource base, primitive agriculture, low-level technology, extremely inadequate transportation and communication systems, and no reliable source for capital accumulation.

The regime accelerated its program of gaining control of the major sectors of the economy, and initiated its long-range development plan two years ahead of its formal acceptance. The following analyses attempt to evaluate these and subsequent developments in tracing the effect of the socialization program by the Communist regime on China's agriculture.

*Policy*—The Communist regime's plan was to establish a socialist society by socializing and industrializing all the sectors of the economy. Social welfare, while often mentioned, was relegated a secondary role. Agriculture was to enjoy the fruits of industrialization through mechanization, which was originally programed to take place over a period of 20 to 25 years, for the estimated 65 per cent of the cultivated area considered suitable for such developments. By the end of 1956, socialization had been completed for essentially all sectors of the economy. In agriculture, policy concentrated, for the most part, on the development of the socialist structure. Errors and mismanagement ended in a state of chaos in agriculture. Since 1960, there has been an embarrassingly long period of "readjustment" during which the Third Five-Year Plan was postponed three years.

Failure of the Second Five Year Plan resulted in drastic economic and political changes. Confronted with rapid decline in the agriculture sector and a heightening food crisis, the regime put together a patchwork of emergency measures to stave off national disaster. The withdrawal of Soviet technicians and technical aid made the problems more difficult. Capital construction was sharply reduced in 1961, and industrial output, particularly that of light industry, which is heavily dependent on agricultural raw materials, declined for the second straight year. Exports of agricultural commodities were drastically reduced and industrial produce imports were supplanted with imports of food. Rationing was intensified, the amounts were reduced and heavy penalties were imposed for speculation and black market activities in an attempt to stem inflation.

Implementation of agricultural plans failed partly because of a lack of funds in two critical areas. Short-term credit to individual farmers and collectives was inadequate, difficult to administer, and lacked flexibility. State investment funds for financing large projects on a long-term basis were spread too thinly among numerous improvement programs. Of the approximately 8 per cent of state investment funds which were allocated for agriculture during the First Five-Year Plan, about two-thirds went for water conservancy alone. Other measures such as mechanization, seed improvement, pest and disease control, land reclamation, multiple cropping, and chemical fertilizer were not applied in sufficient measure.

Although greater investment in agriculture was effected in 1961, much of the investment went to support industries such as chemical fertilizer and machine building. During 1965 there was a de-emphasis on sophisticated farm machines in favor of semimechanized equipment and tools.

NEW ECONOMIC POLICY

A new economic policy was outlined at the March-April session of the Second National People's Congress in 1962. A program announced by Premier Chou En-lai provided for an increase in agricultural production especially in grains, cotton and oil-bearing crops; gave agriculture first priority followed by light industry and heavy industry, with special emphasis on increasing the output of daily necessities; provided for a cutback on capital construction and set standards for inventorying materials and controlling the use of state funds and materials; provided for a reduction of urban population by returning workers to the country; strengthened state procurement and broadened the scope of foreign trade; provided for improvement in fields of culture, education, scientific research and public health; and set standards for reducing costs, increasing revenue, and for contributing to the improvement of the country through thrift and hard work.

The regime emphasized its new policy with the slogan "agriculture as the foundation and industry as the leading factor." Under the new policy no clear-cut guidelines were established nor concrete proposals formulated. Following the belated Second National Peoples' Congress in late 1963, the Lei Feng emulation campaign, which hit its peak in 1964, metamorphosed into a "class struggle" to convince the population that the overthrow of the capitalists and burgeoise was not complete and that "sprouts of capitalists" were emerging among young people who were not aware of the great struggle to establish and maintain the "people's republic" under the present regime.

Class struggle was enmeshed into the broader "Socialist education" drive of late 1964 in which the "collective spirit" was to be consolidated by convincing peasants to place collective work ahead on individual desires so that the individual's circumstances will improve as the collective economy becomes more affluent. This campaign was aimed at peasants who devoted their energies and inputs to their private plots at the expense of the production team effort. During 1965, the campaign was intensified under the banner of the Socialist education movement and was directed mainly at the supposedly "uncorrupted" poor, or former landless, peasants through a series of nationwide congresses. The intensity of the program during the year, the adoption of a new national Socialist hero, Wong Chieh, soundings by various officials about the potential of the economy to support a Great Leap Forward, which later were toned down to "new upsurge," indicate a continuing though modified belief by the regime that achievement of the goals of the Socialist education movement could be attained—hopefully in a comparatively short time.

During the latter part of 1965 a general "cleaning up" of the cadre resulted in closer cooperation between the working and administrative levels of supervision. Considerable streamlining in recordkeeping and statistical reporting was accomplished along with extending the system of political commissars to the agricultural sector.

Two major announcements were made during the latter part of 1965. The first was that state procurement in 1965 would not exceed that in 1964 in order to allow production teams to build up grain reserves. The second announcement reiterated the regime's support for private subsidiary production including that from private plots. The policy on private plots categorized them as "playing a very important supplementary role." Subsequent official statements, however, cast considerable doubt on the regime's sincerity in tolerating the private plots. Instead of announcing the Third Five-Year Plan at the National People's Congress, which was not held in December as originally announced, the regime closed out the year by stating "it is imperative to mobilize all the productive forces that can be mobilized and put them to work in order to make up for the deficiencies of the Socialist economy."

*Education and Technology in Agriculture*—The Communist regime recognized early in its tenure that in order to spread its Marxist gospel, as it unconditionally must, and to provide guidance in the development of the country, it must first elevate the 80 to 90 per cent of the population which was illiterate and which comprised most of the people engaged in agriculture to an acceptable level of literacy. Expediency became the guiding principle of educational development rather than quality. To launch its monolithic program of development, the regime drew heavily on the technical as well as the capital resources of other Communist countries, especially the U.S.S.R. It sent many of its more promising students abroad for training and began using as many of the indigenous trained and qualified personnel as their Marxist orientation would permit.

> To the Communists, education is far more than schooling. It is not distinguishable from indoctrination, propaganda, and agitation. Everything that produces an impact on the minds of men and brings about changes in behavior and thought must be considered a phase of education.

While admitting little or no progress in educational developments during the first three years when the economy was being stabilized, the regime accelerated the rate of expansion in the First Five-Year Plan. By 1957, 10 per cent of the national budget, a fourfold increase compared with 1951, was assigned to "social services, culture, education, and science." Under the expansive spirit of the Great Leap Forward upwards of 100 million persons reportedly were absorbed into the educational system and an even larger number into various types of spare time and on-the-job training and literacy programs including those for adults throughout the agricultural sector where about 50 million peasants were in illiteracy classes. As indicated in Hung-Chi (Red Flag) No. 3, February 1, 1960:

> We have put into effect a program with equal emphasis on schools operated by the state and those operated by factories, mines, enterprises, governmental organs, civic bodies, armed forces, peoples communes, cities and street organizations; on full-time, part-time, and spare-time education; on popular education; and on tuition-fee and tuition-paying education.

Although possibly overstated by Jen-min Jih-pao (*People's Daily*), December 31, 1965, that "everyone in China today—worker, peasant, soldier, intellectual, student, housewife—belongs to some kind of organized study group," the achievements in sheer numbers affected by the education program has been phenomenal.

The measure of literacy set by the government was the mastering of 1,500 Chinese characters by peasants and 2,000 for workers, less than half the number (4,000) required of primary-school graduates. Two linguistic reforms were introduced to speed the learning process. One was the development of simplified characters and the other was a romanized alphabet. The latter provided a unifying effect since the alphabet could be learned only by mastering the Peking dialect. Reportedly, the new system cut the time from two to three years to four to five months or about 120 hours of study to master 1,500 characters. This level of literacy is about sufficient to barely read the local newspaper. The most important accomplishment of the education program, however, is the fact that after seventeen years a large part of a new generation has grown up under the tutelage of the Communist system. The shorter life span thus is advantageous to the regime in its indoctrination program.

Western educators who have visited educational institutions in China observed that the work at agricultural colleges and universities is on the level appropriate to an apprentice or technician and that basic research is being neglected. In the newer formed institutions—since 1958—the level more nearly conforms to an even lower level in filling the country's need in terms of physical labor as well as technical training. Short-cut methods of training and part-work, part-study schools have reduced the number of courses and hours of study. Also, the newly adapted method of selecting students for admittance to institutions of higher learning most assuredly will lower standards even further.

By 1965, 75 to 90 per cent of the recipients of degrees from institutions of higher learning in the fields of engineering, science, agriculture scientists were 35 years of age and younger. Almost 60 per cent of the agricultural scientists were thirty years old and younger. Less than 6 per cent were fifty years of age and older. Thus, in a few years the younger, less experienced scientists—a very small percentage of whom have degrees beyond an equivalent four-year college degree in most Western countries—will replace the remnant of Western trained scientists who have played an important role in guiding the developments in agriculture under the Communist regime.

### TECHNOLOGY IN AGRICULTURE

Agriculture, along with industry and national defense, was singled out by the Chinese People's Political Consultative Conference before the Communist regime's formal assumption of power as one of the three major fields to be developed through the scientific approach. Rewards were to be given for scientific discoveries, developments, and inventions. The conference's emphasis on "love of science," however, had little consequence, since most of the Communist hierarchy had no knowledge of science or any concept of scientific methods and procedures. It was not until 1956 that the regime—with the assistance of Soviet experts—mapped out a general plan for the development of science and technology patterned after that of the Soviet system. The blueprint known as the twelve-year plan under the National Agricultural Development Program (1956–67), was hammered out over the issues of central control versus free development of science and technology, basic versus applied research, specialist research versus the "mass line," and gradual development versus the "leap forward" approach. Except for a brief period—during the "blooming and contending period" in 1957 when academic freedom was granted—the Party has maintained strict control over scientific and technological developments in agriculture.

The Academy of Agricultural Science was organized in 1957 as the national center for agricultural research and development. Its functions were:

> . . . to meet the requirements for national plans of development, for agricultural production practices, and for the development of agricultural sciences within and outside the country; thus it was to organize and lead the agro-scientists in basic as well as in applied research in agrotechnology.

The status of the Academy increased substantially in 1961 with the Party's decision to make agriculture the foundation of the national economy. One-third of the approximately eighty scientists at the Academy hold posts in the Chinese Academy of Sciences, and a large percentage are western trained. The Academy controls more than thirty institutes in different parts of the country together with numerous field research stations and seed development centers. The majority of these institutes are devoted to the study and analysis of single crops, while others concentrate on specific branches of agricultural science.

Over half of the existing agricultural colleges, including the Agricultural University at Peking (which has been moved to the countryside), are experimenting with the part-study, part-work schools, and over two-thirds of the 307 lower level secondary agricultural schools have adopted them. These schools, particularly those at the secondary level, serve the communes which supply the students and take them back at the end of the school term. By 1960, over a fourth of the students (3 million) in junior middle schools were enrolled in 30,000 agricultural middle schools. The curriculum was divided about equally between study and directed work. School schedules were coordinated with production plans and the type of agriculture, depending on the area. Formal courses include mathematics, physics, chemistry, biological and language studies taken during the slack season. Students in increasing numbers participate in all the varied activities of production during the cropping season. A recent national conference on education (August 1965) decided that apart from certain departments and classes for special purposes, all new agricultural colleges and lower level schools should conform to this system. The number of colleges and secondary schools is to be increased in the provinces, municipalities, and autonomous regions. The conference concluded on the note that:

> With the entire new generation equipped with Socialist consciousness and culture, scientific and technical knowledge, capable of both manual and mental labor, conditions for passing to Communism will have been created.

The various agricultural colleges and institutes are staffed by a large proportion of the roughly 135,000 graduates with agricultural degrees from institutions of higher learning in China since 1928 and an unknown number of graduates from colleges and universities in foreign countries. An additional large group which has received training in the middle and secondary agricultural schools assist as technicians. A very small percentage, only about 10 to 30 per cent, of those who pass entrance examinations have been admitted to the university. Major fields of research and development include general agriculture, forestry, sericulture, tea culture, plant protection, pomology, soil and agricultural chemistry, veterinary science, agricultural irrigation, agricultural economics, animal husbandry, agricultural mechanization and electrification, management of Socialist agricultural enterprises, landscape gardening, agricultural medicine, agricultural meteorology, pedology, forest and pasture management, and others.

Complementary to these specialists are a number of research academies under the direction of various ministries. They include the Research Academy of Water Conservation, the Academy of Machine Building and Manufacture, and the Research Institute of Food and Grains. These institutions concentrate mainly on practical problems rather than on basic research. Each agricultural college operates an experimental farm which must contribute somewhat to the upkeep of the school.

The central theme of agricultural development under the Communists has been the technical transformation of agriculture. Agricultural scientists were directed by Premier Chou En-lai at the 10th plenary session of the Eighth CCP Central Committee's Conference on developing agriculture in 1962 that:

> All the good achievements in agricultural science and technology gained by foreign countries, whether Socialist or capitalist, should warrant our study to see if these achievements are applicable to the actual conditions existing in our country.

General guidelines for modernizing agriculture included the expansion of irrigation and flood control, development of better crop varieties and increases in livestock, increased use of chemical fertilizers and pesticides, rural electrification, and farm mechanization. The role of the scientists was to develop through experimentation the best possible methods for developing and executing these programs. Despite the claimed rise in literacy, the regime holds to the traditional technique of the model to explain findings to the farmers. The model was the demonstration farm which has recently become a prominent part of China's rural scene. Technical and scientific personnel have been assigned to these farms. The major functions of the demonstration farms are to (1) consolidate peasants' experiences and techniques, (2) to set a consistent pattern for production, and (3) to conduct studies and experiments to assist nearby farmers. State farms also engage in essentially the same functions as do tractor stations.

The outgrowth of the demonstration farms is the "guaranteed high yield fields," the ultimate in farm production, whereby the factors of production are so accommodated that the success of a crop does not depend wholly on the weather. To gain this level requires intensive cultivation whose costs are considerably higher. The proportion of cultivated land in high yield fields is not large, but the movement is nationwide, is expanding, and is one of a number of projects which has governmental financial backing. The returns become less fruitful as the project reaches out beyond the areas which can readily and with little investment be brought into higher, more reliable production. There is little doubt that the program will be further delayed as the result of the Cultural Revolution now sweeping the country. At a conference of the Chinese Communist Party Committee of the Chinese Academy of Science in April 1966, the following guidelines were adopted for the "further" and "fast" development of science and technology:

> . . . take the thought of Mao Tse-tung as the guide; take class struggle as the key; let politics command work; adhere to the general line for Socialist construction; pursue the policy of self-reliance; make the intellectuals identify themselves with the workers and peasants, specialists with the masses, and scientific experiment with production practices; follow the mass line; continue to push the scientific and technical revolutions forward; and serve Socialist construction and proletarian politics.

Any scientist who still harbors thoughts about "red" versus "expert" need search no farther for an answer.

*Factors affecting production*—The 1956–67 National Agricultural Development Program (approved by the second session of the second National People's Congress, April 10, 1960) was formulated as the major guideline for the long-range development of agriculture. This program was to mesh with the three five-year plans extending through 1967. The general guidelines included in the plan draft were categorized and defined in terms of yearly goals under the five-year plans, but they were sidetracked by the overriding surge of the Great Leap Forward only to reappear as a submerged foundation for the yet undefined Third Five-Year Plan—to have been completed in 1967 had the original plans been successful.

The plan was designed—according to its preamble—to "increase productive capacity in agriculture rapidly, . . . to reinforce industrialization, . . . and raise the living standard of the peasants as well as all people . . ." The twelve-point program for agriculture included: (1) water conservation to develop irrigation and prevent floods; (2) increase the output of natural and chemical fertilizers; (3) improve traditional farm tools and develop mechanization; (4) develop and propagate new strains of seeds suitable to local environment; (5) expand the area of multiple cropping; (6) increase the area of high-yield crops; (7) improve cultural methods commensurate with local needs; (8) improve soil producing capacity and utilization; (9) promote water and soil conservation; (10) protect and increase production of draft animals; (11) exterminate insects and plant diseases; and (12) reclamation of wasteland to expand cultivated acreage.

Mismanagement in the agriculture section upset the balance of one of the most intricate farming enterprises the world has known. Yet the agricultural section was called upon to furnish beyond its capacity with only token response in the form of inputs in return. Allocations to agriculture under the Socialist economic plan have not been sufficient to lift agriculture to the level required for it to meet the contingencies imposed by the regime's industrialization program. Even the stepped-up emphasis for agriculture in post-Leap Forward programs and a de-emphasis on industry leaves China more agrarian than before communalization but less able to feed its population from domestic production, particularly the urban and industrial sectors. An increasing amount of light industry's output (consumer goods for home consumption) is exported and demands for national defense continue to increase.

The nearest agriculture came to fulfilling its role of supplying the economy with the essentials for economic expansion was during a comparatively few short years prior to 1959 when moderate economic expansion occurred. However, during this period large amounts of foreign aid and technical assistance were available. Radical policies, which spawned the Great Leap Forward, greatly altered the productive powers of agriculture and alienated foreign technical and economic aid. Three years of unfavorable weather heaped on top of this dealt a crippling blow to agriculture and the economy from which they have not fully recovered, upset the Communist regime's timetable for economic fulfillment, and forced the adoption of new economic policies.

The agricultural development program

was to be coordinated with the socialization program which also was to be completed by the end of 1967. The program became untracked, however, and numerous modifications—evidence of vacillation and disagreement within the Communist Party—have occurred. Estimates by officials at the beginning of the Third Five-Year Plan extended the period for modernizing agriculture up to twenty to thirty years and even beyond. An analysis of the progress of some of the more important developments in the long-range program enumerated above, as well as those related to the socialization program may shed some light on the lack of success in the development of agriculture.

### INVESTMENTS AND FINANCING

The effort to industrialize as rapidly as possible dealt a double blow to agriculture. In the first place, it denied the agricultural sector the initial volume of investment necessary to stimulate the high level of output required to meet the demands placed on agriculture to support industrial development. Secondly, it skimmed off such a large portion of the sector's production that self-generating funds, which otherwise would have been invested in development programs at lower administrative echelons, did not materialize in sufficient volume to compensate for low state investments. Peasants found it necessary to rely increasingly on credit for carry out farming operations with little or no means for capital improvement.

During the First Five-Year Plan (1953–57) the government allocated about 8 per cent of total state investment funds for agriculture, forestry, water conservancy, and meteorology compared with over four times that amount for industry. According to the draft of the First Five-Year Plan, 6.1 billion yuan were allocated to agriculture, water conservancy, and forestry departments of which 3.26 billion yuan were earmarked for capital construction within those departments. Funds to be used indirectly, in the agricultural sector in the form of relief funds, agricultural loans, and reclamation by units outside the agriculture sector increased the potential amount to 8.4 billion yuan. To this amount was added an expected 10 billion yuan representing investments by peasants, with 6 billion to be used to increase fixed assets and 4 billion for circulating capital.

Investment funds were categorized into (1) capital construction (building of houses, purchase of machinery, appliances and equipment, construction of dams and tunnels); (2) operating expenses (establishment of and maintenance of service organization, and operating expenses for projects aimed at increasing production, and subsidies for various projects utilizing peasant labor); (3) and working funds (working capital for various agricultural enterprises and undertakings including state farms, state livestock farms, state forests, machine tractor stations, and so on). Expenditures in the first two categories were almost equal: capital construction, 3,864 billion yuan and operating expenses, 3.82 billion yuan; working funds amounted to 213 million yuan. Not only did agriculture suffer a low priority for investment funds, the investments that materialized were confined mainly to the socialized area and particularly the development of state farms, state livestock farms, herb medicine enterprises, and other (Socialist) agricultural enterprises. Investment in reclamation of wasteland by state farms and livestock farms under the Ministry of Agricultural Reclamation was about 1.1 billion yuan during the First Five-Year Plan. A total of 93,000 hectares were reclaimed. The purchase of agricultural machinery for state farms and machine tractor stations (8.885 and 22,622 tractors, respectively, in 15 horsepower units) represented the major expenditure for agricultural machinery. Investments in water conservation constituted an estimated 2.34 billion yuan, 62 per cent of total state investments for capital construction in agriculture during the First Five-Year Plan. These were utilized for flood control (49.4 per cent), irrigation (20.2 per cent), drainage (19.9 per cent), and soil conservation (10.5 per cent).

Numerous limitations confront any effort to expand the area of cultivated land in China. Because of this, investments in agriculture have been of a yield-increasing type. The major effort has been toward reducing fluctuations in the harvests. These activities have been aimed at limiting flooding on the one hand and increasing the irrigated area on the other. The third element is the increased application of chemical fertilizer which combined with the other two was to insure the "guaranteed high-yield field". Irrigation and flood control projects have been of the labor-intensive types. The near exclusion of capital and basic materials has been a factor in limiting the effectiveness of the labor-intensive projects, and the mismanagement that has accompanied the making of plans and their implementation has resulted in many technically deficient projects.

The Second Five-Year Plan allocated about 10 per cent of total state investments to agriculture. The agricultural bank, which was in existence from 1955 to 1957 to finance the rapid collectivization drive, was re-established in the fall of 1963 to provide greater control over financial matters in rural areas by attempting to mobilize untapped rural savings which could be used to strengthen the available supply of rural credit at the so-called credit cooperatives. Available information does not indicate the scope nor the authority of the bank to handle the monetary affairs in the agricultural sector. However, much of the current investments in agriculture is not connected with the bank, since the major investments in agriculture are through the industries which support agriculture. The bank's main function so far (besides its control mechanism on local currency) is that of providing agricultural loans. Amounts of loans ranging up to 2 billion yuan per year have been claimed. This amount is questionable in light of other official statements that funds for loans would have to come primarily from repayments of previous loans.

Aside from the claim of 10 per cent of state investments earmarked for agriculture in the Second Five-Year Plan, which became defunct, information on the extent of investment in agriculture since the Great Leap Forward is extremely limited. Nevertheless, it is evident that increasing investments were poured into agriculture—much of it in the form of emergency programs during the depression years of 1959–61. After more than a year of reassessing the imbalance caused by the Great Leap Forward a new program for economic development—based on the slogan of "agriculture as the foundation and industry as the leading factor"—was announced at the National People's Congress in the spring of 1962. First priority was given to agriculture to help it catch up and second priority was given to light industry. The pattern of investment was drastically changed with a greater share allocated to agriculture and consumer goods industries. Farm incentive programs including lower taxes, price adjustments, reduction in crop collections and more autonomy at the production level were established. Emphasis was given to increasing the output of industries directly connected with agriculture, notably chemicals (especially chemical fertilizers), machinery, electricity, petroleum, and other related industries.

The new program has had a beneficial effect on agriculture and has resulted in substantial gains in certain sectors of the economy, although not all goals have been attained. Agricultural inputs have increased sharply. Had not unfavorable weather counteracted the beneficial effects of increased inputs in 1965 and 1966 there is little doubt that agricultural output would be at an all-time high. This was the goal the regime hoped to attain at the beginning of the Third Five-Year Plan, which began in 1966. Those industries supporting agriculture appeared to be continuing to increase output. The large imports of chemical fertilizer already contracted for delivery in 1967, the continued emphasis on expanding the production of chemical fertilizer, increases in the production of machinery for agricultural purposes and the continued high level of imports of goods to aid the agricultural sector indicate that the regime intends to continue a strong policy of supporting agriculture.

### IRRIGATION AND WATER CONSERVANCY

A major problem confronting China's agriculture is the unbalanced distribution of water. In the northern part (north of the Tsinling Mountain) the problem is scarcity, whereas in the southern part the problem is control of a generally overabundant supply.

In a wet year the north generally fares better, while flooding and water-logging may destroy crops in the south. A dry year brings great damage to crops in the north but often results in less crop loss in the south. Between these extremes local conditions of rainfall or lack of it presents the peasant with a continuing problem of attempting to make nature serve his purposes.

Efforts prior to 1949 to initiate country-wide water conservancy projects were meager and consisted mainly of simple irrigation of crops. Irrigation techniques were primitive and amounted to little more than drawing water directly from streams by gravity flow or by some simple mechanical (mainly human operated) means. Such systems were entirely dependent on streamflow. Limited utilization was made of wells in the northern areas of the country and reservoirs in the south, where water generally was abundant. Visiting western irrigation engineers had pointed out the impracticability of building reservoirs on the extensive loess areas of northern China because of erosion, a high rate of seepage, and silting problems. Silting of rivers over the years and the building up of river banks has resulted in river beds rising well above the level of the land through which the rivers flow in the northern flat country.

The water conservancy program was elevated to national scale by the Communist regime in 1949, and a considerable degree of success has been attained despite numerous failures. Officially, ". . . the main task of water conservancy are to alleviate the disasters of flood and drought to insure a steady increase in agricultural production, and to promote the development of industry and river navigation." The immediate goals of the new government were the prevention of floods, the drainage of waterlogged fields, and the construction of irrigation canals. In 1956 a program was outlined to eliminate ordinary floods and drought within seven to twelve years. It was claimed that of the approximately 58 million hectares of cultivated land in the plains area and about 47 million hectares in the hilly and mountain regions, only a small portion had an optimum supply of water. Roughly 20 million hectares of land were irrigated in Mainland China in 1932. The Communist regime claimed that by 1949 there were about 16 million hectares of irrigated land of which 76 per cent needed rebuilding.

Initially, irrigation programs assigned priority to flood control projects. This included the building and strengthening of river dikes along major rivers and their tributaries. This phase was essentially completed during the period 1949 to 1952. But haste in getting the projects under way and deficiencies in training and management resulted in numerous problems and failures. Programs were not coordinated between provinces; strengthening of the dikes along the Huai River in Honan Province contained waters from heavy rains, but downstream in Anhwei Province dikes were washed out. Other projects during the pre-1952 period included minor irrigation facilities, generally small-scale projects at the farm level. Large dams and multipurpose projects were to come later. Total hydroelectric power, for example, was only 180,000 kilowatts in 1952.

Major problems became apparent as the water conservancy program progressed. The most critical included an acute shortage of capable technical personnel, the inability or unwillingness of the regime to provide adequate funds, the absence of soil surveys to provide information of subsurface structure, and a lack of coordination between state and local officials on the scope and extent of projects to be undertaken. The state retained responsibility for harnessing large rivers and for constructing large irrigation projects. Medium-sized projects were to be built with state aid and small-scale projects by the masses. The state retained the better technicians including the Soviet experts and benefited from irrigation development plans inherited from the previous regime which had hired foreign technicians (mostly American) to construct them.

Beginning in 1952, a major spurt occurred in water conservancy. Large-scale projects were initiated by the government, and more emphasis was placed on the irrigation of farmland. Investment funds were allocated for a series of dams, reservoirs, and canals which were concentrated principally in provinces of east and central China along the Huai, Yungting, and Yangtze Rivers. When the Great Leap occurred in water conservancy, new projects also were started to the north and south of the initial thrust. The newer projects were located on the upper reaches of some of China's largest rivers and many of them dwarfed the earlier projects. While the largest reservoir of the earlier period had a capacity of about 2 billion cubic meters of water storage capacity, the Liukia Gorge project on the Yellow River near Lanchow had a storage capacity of about 5 billion cubic meters. The largest of all, the Sanmen Gorge project near Loyang, several hundred miles downstream in the same river, had a goal capacity of 65 billion cubic meters.

Projects based on Soviet design were begun during the First Five-Year Plan. The need for a more rapid increase in the irrigated area to increase agricultural production set off a new "upsurge" in irrigation in 1956. It was decided that further development of large projects was not possible, because of a lack of funds and material, and attention was shifted to the development of small projects. The water conservation program was considerably decentralized, and peasant labor was organized in a frenzied attempt to build a mass of small projects, primarily wells. Although the pace slackened in 1957—to allow time to rectify mistakes of previous years—it gathered momentum with the impetus of the Great Leap Forward in 1959. Small projects were stressed, and the emphasis was on storage of water.

Following the formation of communes, a more balanced approach toward water conservation was adopted, but greater reliance was placed on local resources. That is, local needs became the guiding factor and limited capital enforced labor intensive projects. This accounts, in part, for the shift in 1959 to the digging of canals and construction of fewer but larger reservoirs from natural material—to fight the drought in the north and to bring these types of projects up to the level of wells, ponds, and small reservoirs, which had received the major emphasis during the three previous years.

Beginning in 1959—with an apparent slowdown of new construction—peasants were directed to concentrate on "improving" the area under irrigation. During the ensuing period to 1963 the water conservancy program was confined mostly to consolidating existing projects by building auxiliary works and other improvements. Such direction was necessary following the reckless pace of construction during the Great Leap Forward when as many as 100 million persons were engaged at one time in conservancy projects. In 1964, efficiency of irrigation through good management of existing systems rather than starting, new, large-scale and capital-intensive projects was the guideline. There is little evidence of new construction in recent years. Increased emphasis has been given to improving the existing system. Drainage of fields subject to waterlogging in North China and the increased use of electric pumps in the hilly sections in the southern part of the country together with the drilling of deep wells in pasture areas have received major attention. Reports indicate that numerous problems are being encountered because of silting of waterways and reservoirs in the north. It has been known for some time that this problem was likely to be an eventual threat to the hydroelectric systems in the loess areas.

Tens of millions of people participated in the water conservancy projects including peasant farmers during the off season. Also members of the armed forces, students during vacation, large numbers of unemployed from cities, and prisoners are used in conservancy work. Work groups were organized and functioned in a quasi-military fashion. Although work on projects was continuous, the peak periods occurred during the seasons of least farm activity when about 80 per cent of the annual tasks were completed. From official reports, an estimated 50 billion man-days were expended in water conservancy between 1949 and the end of the peak labor period in early 1960.

Many laborers on the project were paid in goods. Others were paid wages of varying amounts and some "volunteer" groups donated their labor in addition to furnishing their own food and tools. A rough estimate of worker's compensation based on wages paid on the Haui River projects and projects in Kwangtung Province applied to estimated total work performed varies between 25 and 60 billion yuan (10 to 25 billion U.S. dollars). The Communist regime claimed that during the period 1949 to 1960 a total of 70 billion cubic meters of earthworks and masonry were completed, equivalent to excavating 960 Suez Canals.

An assessment of the water conservancy program can be made only in general terms, because of a lack of data on the one hand and the mass of conflicting reports of successes and failures on the other. Claimed increases in irrigated land (5.35 million hectates) during the period 1949–52 increased the total irrigated area to around the pre-World War II level of about 20 million hectares. The regime claimed 34.3 million hectares of land under irrigation by the end of 1957.

Plans for the Second Five-Year Plan (1958–62) varied from adding 13.4 million hectares announced in December 1957 to 33.3 million hectares announced in February 1958 for a total of 66.6 million hectares by the end of 1962. (The new plan figure implied a revision of the claimed 34.3 hectares in 1957.) But fantastic things happened in 1958 including a claim that the irrigated area increased more than 32 million hectares, compared to a goal of only 2.9 million hectares for the year. China's total claimed irrigated area thus amounted to 66.7 million hectares by the end of 1958. Mounting claims continued: 71.3 million hectares at the end of 1959. and a vague report intimating that an additional 9 million hectares would be added in 1960, for a total of 80 million hectares under irrigation.

Not even the success-minded officials were able to live with these claims. T'an Chen-lin, Deputy Premier, clarified the irrigation situation somewhat in the *People's Daily* of June 3, 1959, by stating that only 46.7 million of the claimed 71.3 million hectares under irrigation met requirements stipulated in the agricultural development program, that is, ability to withstand a drought ranging from 30 to 70 days. In other words, less than 40 per cent of the total claimed irrigated land had met the requirements of withstanding drought from 30 to 70 days. Thus, as much as 60 per cent of the irrigated land could not withstand drought extending beyond thirty days. Premier Chou En-lai substantiated this view before the standing committee of the Second National People's Congress, August 16, 1959, when he stated that only 500 million mow (33.3 million hectares) could be adequately irrigated, that over 300 million mow could be partly irrigated, and that 200 million mow needed leveling of fields and digging of ditches before they could be benefited. Hwang Hu-chen, president of the Water Conservation and Hydro-Electric Power College said that only 500 million mow were guaranteed three irrigations a year, while there was no irrigation facility for the remaining 1.1 billion mow (73.3 million hectares).

The accomplishments of the water conservancy program leaves many unanswered questions but there can be little doubt that much was accomplished. In years of near normal weather conditions the new water projects have proved beneficial in regulating water flow and in extending the irrigated acreage. Nevertheless, in retrospect, the effect expended in dam construction, reservoir excavation, dike repair, and others has not basically altered traditional vulnerability to the scourges of flood and drought.

The testing period of the effectiveness of the water conservancy program occurred during 1959–61 when severe widespread drought centered in the northern provinces which accounted for nearly one-half of the irrigated area claimed since 1952. Yet those areas suffered most from the elements the irrigation projects were designed to alleviate. Many projects that were undertaken during the Great Leap Forward have been allowed to deteriorate. Some can never be used. Even the problem of getting water to the projects appears to have been of secondary consideration, and many projects were completed without a source of water. T'an Chen-lin, quoted above, continued:

> In irrigation, the building of reservoirs itself does not mean that the irrigated acreage indicated in the construction figures has all actually received the benefits of irrigation.

These benefits can only be obtained when the reservoirs are filled, canals and ditches are dug, the land is leveled off, and lifting equipment is at hand.

This statement forces a second look at the water conservancy claims and provides some reason for T'an's remark that 60 million hectares would be "fully benefited" by 1967, although at the time of the statement (April 6, 1960) the regime was claiming that 71.3 million hectares were under irrigation.

If, as indicated by the regime, the main task of water conservancy was to alleviate the disasters of flood and drought and to insure a steady rise in agricultural production is taken at face value, it is evident that the Communist government over the past decade has been inadequate to the task. Although the amount of cropland which was taken out of production because of reservoirs, canals, ponds and other project-connected facilities is not known, it remains a debit factor in assessing the irrigation.

#### FERTILIZATION

The use of chemical fertilizers in Mainland China's agriculture is of comparatively recent date. Prior to 1949, the major use of chemical fertilizer on the mainland was by the Japanese who built a 200,000-ton (annual capacity) factory at Dairen. In 1951, American-trained Chinese technicians constructed a factory at Nanking with a 50,000-ton capacity. These factories did not produce at full capacity. Dismantling of the Darian factory after VJ Day and civil strife reduced production to a mere 27,000 tons in 1949. Imports were negligible.

The traditional methods of fertilizing utilized manure from farm animals, human excreta, oilseed cakes, plant residues and ashes from fibrous material, mud from streams and bottoms of ponds, fish and animal refuse, gypsum and lime, and green manure, particularly from legumes. The latter has increased materially in recent years. Compost piles have always been an integral part of the rural scene. Officials estimate it requires 30 to 40 per cent of farm labor to make, collect, and transport natural fertilizers.

The traditional fertilizers are still by far the most important source of plant nutrients. Despite efforts to increase these materials, however, it was immediately apparent to government officials that a huge expansion in the production of fertilizer was necessary if the needed increases in agricultural production were to be attained. Thus, development of the chemical fertilizer industry was one of four major measures included in the regime's National Program for Agricultural Development (1956–67). The development of the chemical fertilizer industry followed water conservancy according to government programing.

The general guidelines and goals for the production of natural and chemical fertilizers called for an average production of 1.5 to 2 hogs per rural family by 1962 and 2.5 to 3 head by 1967—for the production of manure to be combined with garbage and other plant materials, especially green manure crops—for making fertilizers. On the industrial side, 5 to 7 million tons of chemical fertilizers were to be produced by 1962 and 15 million tons by 1967. The production of chemical fertilizer made significant gains, but suffered numerous setbacks, particularly when the Soviet scientists were ordered home. According to available data, neither of the goals—hog production or chemical fertilizers—were attained in 1962, and the possibility of reaching the 1967 goals is even remote.

Soil deficiencies in Mainland China provided the guideline for production of chemical fertilizers. Nitrogen deficiency was by far the greatest with potash least. Despite the critical need for chemical fertilizers, China's chemical fertilizer industry developed slowly prior to 1953. The government claimed production of only 180,000 tons of ammonium sulfate, 7,486 tons of ammonium nitrate, and 6,000 tons of superphosphate by the end of 1952. Soviet technicians and Soviet aid provided the base for the chemical fertilizer industry in the First Five-Year Plan, which called for the construction of five large plants and expanding the capacity of the two existing ones. Construction was not started, however, until approval of the plan was given by the National People's Congress on July 30, 1955. Only one of the plants—in Kirin—began operation within the plan period. Through expansion of the older plants, however, and the construction of small ones, the industry reportedly was producing about 800,000 tons of chemical fertilizers in 1957.

With completion of the major plants started in the first plan, fertilizer producing capacity increased rapidly during the early part of the Second Five-Year Plan. A strenuous effort was made by the government during the Great Leap period to get local units to build small- and medium-sized plants to compliment the large state constructed one. Efforts to increase fertilizer production capacity is shown by budget allocations for fertilizer capacity expansion in the Second Five-Year Plan. It was four times the 375 million yuan allocated in the first plan period, and represented over 62 per cent of total investments for the chemical industry.

Neither synthetic urea nor chemically refined potassium fertilizers were produced in China prior to 1958, since their production required more complicated equipment and production techniques than were available. Experimental production of potassium began in 1958 at a small plant in Nanking. Fertilizers manufactured from other small plants included the more common ammonium chloride, ammonium cyanide, ammonium bicarbonate, and a few other ammonium solutions, most of which possessed a low nitrogen content.

The fertilizer industry suffered a temporary setback at the time of the departure of Soviet technicians, but a comparatively advanced degree of sophistication has developed since then with the import of plants from western countries and the hiring of western technicians to assemble and operate them. These activities have been accompanied by experimentations into the needs of fertilizers. According to American-trained Hou Tepang, Vice Minister of China's chemical industry, experiments now show that a combination of about equal parts of nitrogen and phosphate obtained about a 50 per cent higher response when applied to rice in south China.

One means of using phosphatic fertilizers to good advantage in the rice producing areas has been on green manure crops between rice crops. Not only does the green manure, especially legumes—milk vetch and cow vetch the most common in China—act as soil conditioners but also are nitrogen fixing plants. The use of green manure crops has expanded rapidly in the rice growing regions of the south in recent years. During the winter of 1965–66 the area reportedly was increased 50 per cent.

Deficiency of phosphorus in the southern soils as revealed and likely by recent surveys those in the likelihood of similar deficiencies in provide an answer at least in part, for the rapid increase in manufacturing capacity of this fertilizer. The lack of adequate capacity to produce the requisite increased volume of sulphuric acid the main ingredient in manufacturing phosphatic may be a limiting factor in increasing this fertilizer at a more rapid rate. If subsequent surveys show the same phosphorus deficiencies in the northern as in the southern part of the country, China's requirements for phosphate fertilizer could amount to 15 to 20 million tons. Assuming a ratio of 1.1 with nitrogen fertilizers, total fertilizer needs for the country could surpass 30 million tons annually. This amount likely would go a long way in satisfying the nutrient deficiencies. In studies prior to 1949 it was estimated that 80 to 96 per cent of the total cultivated land was deficient in nitrogen, 40 to 55 per cent was low in phosphate and 15 to 24 per cent lacked potash.

China's two-pronged attack to fill the demands for chemical fertilizers has resulted in a substantial increase in both production capacity and imports as shown in Table 1. Whole plants have been purchased from abroad in addition to domestic construction of large, medium, and small plants, with the smaller plants producing mostly phosphate fertilizers. This sharp increase in both domestic production and imports are expected to continue. Negotiations for imports in 1967 about equal to those in 1966 already have been completed and a large British ammonia plant which is to support the urea plan from the Netherlands located near Luchow in Szechwan Province recently began production. Provisions were made to double the output of these plans in the future.

Despite the rapid increase in the availability of chemical fertilizer, there has been little evidence of an increase in overall production of agricultural commodities. Major reasons are that not enough fertilizer is yet available to stimulate the necessary response plus problems of storage, distribution, and application by suspicious farmers who are slow to attempt new and progressive methods of crop cultivation. Low quality and types of fertilizer which deteriorates rapidly constitute a high proportion of the domestic production. Overriding these considerations has been an extended period of unfavorable weather which has cut heavily into production increases that could otherwise be attributed to increased application of fertilizer. The following tabulation (based on estimated available amounts for selected years in kilograms per acre, with nutrient values in parenthesis) indicates the small amount of chemical fertilizer available despite sharp increases in recent years:

| *Year* | *Arable land* | *Planted land* |
|---|---|---|
| 1952 | 1.6 (0.3) | 1.2 (0.2) |
| 1957 | 6.5 (1.3) | 4.6 (0.9) |
| 1962 | 11.7 (2.3) | 8.0 (1.6) |
| 1966 | 34.1 (6.8) | 22.8 (4.6) |

AGRICULTURAL MECHANIZATION

Mechanization of agriculture in China refers primarily to the mechanization of cultivation in north and northeast China, mechanized irrigation and drainage in the southern paddy regions with limited cultivation, and the construction of wells in the major pasture areas. Chinese officials have estimated that about 100 million hectares can be eventually mechanized. This includes approximately 80 million hectares of land currently adaptable to mechanical operation and a potential 20 million hectares which are expected to be added through reclamation.

### *Table 1—Production and Imports of Chemical Fertilizer, Mainland China[a] (thousands of metric tons)*

| *Year* | *Total Nitrogenous* | *Phosphatic and other* | *Total* | *Imports all types* | *Total Availability* |
|---|---|---|---|---|---|
| 1941 | 227 | | 227 | ([b]) | ([b]) |
| 1949 | 27 | | 27 | ([b]) | ([b]) |
| 1950 | 70 | | 70 | ([b]) | ([b]) |
| 1951 | 134 | | 134 | ([b]) | ([b]) |
| 1952 | 188 | 6 | 194 | 239 | 433 |
| 1953 | 249 | | 249 | 343 | 592 |
| 1954 | 321 | | 321 | 579 | 900 |
| 1955 | 324 | 21 | 345 | 875 | 1,220 |
| 1956 | 563 | 100 | 663 | 837 | 1,500 |
| 1957 | 683 | 120 | 803 | 997 | 1,800 |
| 1958 | 900 | 344 | 1,244 | 1,456 | 2,700 |
| 1959 | 1,390 | 375 | 1,765 | 1,190 | 2,955 |
| 1960 | 1,960 | 500 | 2,460 | 860 | 3,320 |
| 1961 | 1,080 | 320 | 1,400 | 883 | 2,283 |
| 1962 | 1,600 | 500 | 2,100 | 1,000 | 3,100 |
| 1963 | 2,200 | 700 | 2,900 | 1,700 | 4,600 |
| 1964 | 2,600 | 900 | 3,500 | 1,030 | 4,530 |
| 1965 | ([d]) | ([d]) | 4,500 | 2,500 | 7,000 |
| 1966[c] | ([d]) | ([d]) | 5,000 | 3,500 | 8,500 |

[a] These data, most of which are estimates, are based on sources in the U.S. Department of Agriculture.
[b] Not available.
[c] Preliminary
[d] Included in totals.

To accomplish mechanization officials estimated the utilization of 100 to 150 million horsepower divided among 1.2 million tractors (and complementary machinery), 300,000 to 350,000 combine harvesters and an equal number of trucks, and $3\frac{1}{2}$ to 4 million power pumps. This amount of equipment would provide each 100 hectares (247 acres) with one tractor, a combine and one truck for each 300 hectares (741 acres) and a 5-horsepower pump for each 13.3 hectares (33 acres).

This was an overwhelming goal in sight of the scarcity of even the simple farming tools, their inferior quality, poor design, and short life.

For centuries ploughs, picks, hoes, spades, sickles, rakes, flails, winnowing shovels, and so on, have constituted China's farming tools. These were made from cast iron, wrought iron, and wood which were the main ingredients in simple ploughs and harrows of the one-horse type. Motive power was (and still is) furnished by oxen, cows, horses, mules, donkeys, and water buffalo in the south. Made by artisan families, the design of these tools had changed only slightly. Although peasants were aware of tractors (the first one was imported by China in 1907), they were familiar only with foreign makes until 1958 when China successfully began producing its own tractors.

Significant progress has been made in mechanizing farming operations in certain areas of China, but for the country as a whole only a start has been made. Mechanization in the Western sense has been confined largely to state farms, which exist primarily for reclaiming land, and state tractor stations which serve the larger farming units. Throughout the First Five-Year Plan, of the slightly fewer than 25,000 tractors imported about half were used in agriculture. These units, distributed to 390 tractor stations provided motive power for about 4.5 million acres of land, or one tractor for 375 acres. A major problem which grew out of the imported machinery was that of unstandardized equipment and a serious shortage of spare parts. These drawbacks seriously interfered with the hoped for progress of the initial thrust of mechanization.

Mechanization did not become a serious program until the beginning of the Second Five-Year Plan when producing capacity expanded sufficiently within the country to enable commercial production of serial designs. The original plan (including mechanization of agricultural, forestry, animal husbandry, and sideline production) was to be completed in about ten years. A Ministry of Agricultural Machine Building Industry was established in 1959. This agency claimed in 1959 to have in operation 59,000 tractors. The Ministry also claimed to have in operation 4,900 combine-harvesters and 7,500 motor threshers and almost 3.4 million horsepower of mechanical equipment for irrigation and drainage work.

The Great Leap that occurred in both production and imports of tractors more than doubled the number by the end of 1962 (100,000) compared with 1958. The proportion of this increase produced domestically is not known, but it likely was comparatively small because of the lack of raw materials, particularly the various required types of steel. Even after China began producing its own tractors, it was necessary to import most of the 450 kinds of metal from which the roughly 10,000 parts of the "East In Red" tractor was made. As late as 1962, China was not producing all the metals necessary to manufacture its farm machinery. Of the metals domestically produced many were of inferior quality.

As the production capacity increased cutbacks occurred in the importation of tractors. The limited ability of native technicians to repair the large variety of foreign makes of tractors and other internal combustion engines was further reduced by a lack of spare parts. In six production brigades a visitor found eight models of engines consuming different fuels—gasoline, natural gas, and so on—and in one of the districts in Chekiang Province more than forty types of power-driven machines were used for irrigation and drainage. In 1961 as many as 20 per cent of the tractors and 20 to 30 per cent of the machines used in irrigation were idle because of a lack of repairs and spare parts.

Furthermore, despite much consolidation of farm plots following collectivization and communalization, it was difficult in many areas to join enough contiguous plots together into sufficiently large farming units to qualify for tractors under the prevailing regulations. Also, in many paddy rice areas, roads and bridges were too narrow and bridges were not strong enough to support the heavy tractors.

Mechanization of agriculture has been fraught with numerous problems including intra-Party differences as to the types of machines and the speed with which mechanization should be pushed. The most recent policy was outlined in the *People's Daily*, April 9, 1966. The announcement called for achievements of mechanization of agriculture on a national scale within fifteen years. More emphasis appeared to be on mechanization than on semimechanization, which received major emphasis in 1964 and 1965. The brigade and commune were cited as the units to implement mechanization. Amid the sober announcement was the flamboyant "revolutionary flying leap" which agricultural production would be enabled to achieve with mechanization. The announcement, however, followed the basic policy lines with heavy stress on gradualism, self-reliance, local investment, unsophisticated equipment, and a balance between mechanization and other inputs.

Farming implements currently produced besides include traditional handtools, animal-drawn implements such as the hand plow, single-row cotton planter, multitooth hoeing machine, seven-row wheat-sowing machine, manual- and power-operated corn thresher, and heavier machinery for use by tractors. Six standard tractors, products of domestic industry, were in use ranging from the (Worker Farmer) 7-horsepower hand tractor for use in rice paddies to the large 100 horsepower (Red Flag) caterpillar track tractor used by state farms in reclamation projects. The type of machines and tractors being produced are continually being modified to fulfill demands of local cultivation conditions. Factories are dispersed to cut transportation costs and to utilize local materials and labor.

The extent of mechanization at the present time, the prospect of attaining the goals and the success with which the regime is attaining these goals is difficult to assess. Some evidences of a successful speed-up in manufacturing farm implements and in organizing the industry to better serve the agricultural areas can be drawn from official reports. Local industries have been given the responsibility of producing all semimechanized and mechanized farm tools and all motor-driven machines generating 20 horsepower and less. New tractors designed for the rice growing areas have been modified for use in dry crop areas as well. Small motor driven sprayers, high-lift pumps, and small portable diesel and gasoline engines have grown in prominence in the last year or so. The increase in mechanization is uneven, however. Communes and brigades must purchase their own equipment, and reports indicate that some brigades have fully mechanized their agricultural operations, while others have barely begun. Reports from China's largest grain producing province, *Szechwan*, suggest that typical implements utilized in farm production are foot-pedaled threshers, hand-propelled corn shellers, and hand-operated potato slicing machines.

A series of emergency measures were taken in 1962 to find a solution to the problem of farm mechanization. The Ministry of Agricultural Machine Building Industry was aided by the Chinese Academy of Agricultural Mechanization, which was designated to provide guidance and develop farm machinery models and help advance the adaptation of mechanization in different regions at a uniform speed based on prevailing crops and other local conditions. In 1965 it was reported that there were 2,263 mechanical stations in over 1,300 hsien and municipalities with about 135,000 tractors (15 horsepower units) in 1965. If these figures are correct, they represent a net gain of about 35,000 tractors since 1962, a significant gain considering that most of this increase was the result of indigenous production and that the replacement of wornout imported tractors had to be replaced. On the other hand, it represents an extremely weak effort toward attaining the goal of 1.2 million tractors (15-horsepower units) not in twenty to twenty-five years, but in fifteen years according to Mao's newest estimate.

### OTHER AGRICULTURAL INPUTS

The First Five-Year Plan called for reclamation of 2.6 million hectares (6.4 million acres) of land. Much of the initial thrust of reclamation consisted in reactivating farms that had been abandoned during the civil strife prior to 1959. The plan for reclamation was expanded in 1956 to a goal of 6.7 million hectares (16.6 million acres) by 1967. The usual conflicting reports showed overwhelming success—5.3 million hectares (13.1 million acres) reclaimed during 1953–57. This figure was later reduced to 3.9 million hectares (9.6 million acres) in the State Statistical Bureau's report on the First Five-Year Plan. This addition boosted the total cultivated area from the claimed 107.9 million hectares (266.6 million acres) in 1952 to 111.8 million hectares (276.3 million acres) in 1957, according to official statistics, and increased the double cropping index to 141.

A high percentage of the land reclaimed during 1953–57 was in areas of marginal agricultural production, and some was in the mountainous areas adjacent to the southern boundary of Outer Mongolia in the Sunkiang-Liaoning Plain, extending east to west from Heluugkiang Province to western Singiang Province. In addition to land reclamation, a land consolidation program was carried out in connection with the collectivization of agriculture. How much cultivated land was added through the consolidation of small farms is not known; but likely it was not significant because field boundaries, banks, paths, and roads had already been reduced to a minimum prior to the collectivization drive. On the other hand, some of the farmland was taken for industrial and urban sites, farm building sites, extension of roads, and construction of irrigation facilities. Undisclosed amounts of cultivated land were lost to erosion and some was abandoned due to a loss of fertility. According to official reports, reclamation was very expensive compared with returns. In 1956, the regime reduced the original estimate of the potential for reclamation from 100 million hectares (247 million acres) to 43 million hectares (106 million acres). This was more in line with the Nationalist government's estimate prior to World War II. The preoccupation with communes in 1958 diverted much of Peking's attention from reclamation as a means of solving the productive land problem of China.

Sketchy reports indicate that reclamation in 1959–61 amounted primarily to an attempt to reclaim the land which was deserted during the Great Leap Forward. No indication of success is available. Official statistics indicate that since 1957 there has been a decline in the amount of cultivated land. As late as 1966 officials carried the area of cultivated land as 1.6 billion mow (106.67 million hectares) which is a reduction of 4.6 per cent from the peak of 111.8 million hectares (276.3 million acres) in 1957. The difference in the amount of land in official statistics, 5.13 million hectares (12.7 million acres) may be the amount of land which was allocated to private plots, or it may represent a total loss to irrigation projects, roads, industrial sites, and so on, or a combination of the two. Although the multiple cropping index has increased somewhat, it is unlikely that the total sown acreage per year has regained the level of 1957.

Although some progress is being made in crop breeding and in the control of insects and plant disease, not much information is available on the effectiveness of such programs. A major limitation is the relatively small number of trained agricultural scientists and technicians. Major programs in crop improvement have been confined mainly to seed selection and propagation. Developmental work has been carried out on hybrid corn and kaoliang and possibly other crops. From the limited yield and production data available, it is difficult to attach much significance to advancements in crop development. China's crops are afflicted with pests and diseases similar to those in other countries of the Far East. Control measures are being developed and modern equipment for applying insecticides and herbicides appear to be in serial production, but progress has been slow in light of the large amount of equipment needed by such a large country. Pest control has been carried out mainly through cooperative effort of the peasants using simple methods.

Losses from insects, diseases, destructive birds, and small animals probably are serious. Prewar estimates of damage from insects alone was estimated at 12 million tons of cereals each year. Nationwide networks have been set up to provide information and forecasts on insects, pests and crop diseases. Serious outbreaks of wheat rust in north China in the spring of 1964, damage by locusts in central China in 1965, and the outbreak of cutworms in north and northeast China and attacks by other pests in both north and south China in 1966 indicate weaknesses in the control mechanism. Reports indicate that in some areas peasants were forced to revert to more primitive methods of control after their supply of chemical insecticides had been exhausted.

Another important factor, the institutional nature of Communist control of the agricultural sector, has played a dominant role in shaping the character of the country's agriculture. The vacillation from centralized to decentralized control through the socialization process—previously discussed—to the present loosely defined socialist unit has destroyed the base for understanding between the peasant and the rulers. The various forms of control and their effects on agricultural production have been ably treated by Dwight H Perkins. Perkins points out that under the centralization of the communes the use of labor became more flexible but that the cadres were not sufficiently skilled or were too doctrinaire to utilize this added resource efficiently and that peasants' incentives (and consequently their output) declined as they became more removed from their connection with the land and that these problems increased with the size of the controlling unit. He concludes:

> ... there appears to be little that centralization accomplishes which cannot be done better through extension services, taxes, and market controls in the context of a free peasant economy. In Communist China, however, political and ideological considerations cannot be put aside. The political and ideological advantages to the regime of the collective form of organization in agriculture have been too great for this organization to be abandoned except under the most desperate circumstances. The real question for China, therefore, is not whether cooperatives (collectives) or communes work better than a free peasant alternative, but whether they can be made to work at all.

The radical economic convulsions that accompanied China's Great Leap Forward likely would reappear if another such Leap were attempted. To reinstate a new Leap Forward would require a return to greater centralization by the Communist Party, resulting in the denial of peasants' gains since 1960. The Chinese peasantry was not ready for the first Leap Forward episode, and, despite the socialist education movement, the cultural revolution, and other programs aimed at "uniting" the peasants into armies of workers for the state, they remained unmoved and passive to the drumbeat of the Communist Party. The Party's tampering with the peasant's soul has not wrested it from the soil nor its attachment to basic Chinese culture. The Communists will find this a difficult gap to bridge in their attempt to create the "new man" with the selfless oriented desire to place the collective, the party, the people, and the nation above self.

## AGRICULTURAL OUTPUT

The lack of official data since 1958 and the relatively unreliability of official data prior to that time prevent an accurate analysis of China's agricultural production. However, official reports of plan fulfillments, weather conditions, policy changes, the flow and balance of foreign trade and so on provides a basis for rough estimates of the current situation and trends. The following analysis is based on the accumulation of available data and on published and unpublished estimates by various agencies of the U.S. Department of Agriculture.

Agricultural production under Communist

leadership has been sporadic. The greatest advancement in production under the Communists occurred during the decade of the 1950s. Because of World War II action and that of the civil war which followed, agricultural production had reached a very low level. It is generally accepted that by the start of the First Five-Year Plan the production level of agriculture had about regained the prewar level. Then followed a few years of rapid expansion through 1955 for most crops and livestock according to official statistics. Official statistics show that the four major categories of cereal crops (wheat, rice, miscellaneous grain, and sweetpotatoes) and other food crops (vegetables, soybeans, fruits, peanuts, etc.) increased in the aggregate by almost 20 per cent from 1952 to 1957 and that population increased by about 11 per cent. This would represent about a 9 per cent increase in per capita production, or an annual rate of about 1.5 per cent a year.

Although these data place the results of the First Five-Year Plan in a favorable light, closer examination reveals that the real increase in crop production and also livestock production occurred between 1952 and the completion of the massive collectivization drive in 1955–56. By the time the collectivization drive culminated in 1957—with the consolidation of the higher level types of collectives—stagnation in agricultural production had already commenced. Had it not been for the exceptional good years 1956 and 1958 when favorable weather boosted crop production significantly, the decline, which became obvious in 1959, may have been worse. Although smaller increases in grains, cotton, tobacco, and tea were recorded up through 1957, production of soybeans, peanuts, rapeseed, and sesame declined between 1955 and 1957. Although a general decline had occurred in the number of cattle, horses, donkeys, and mules in 1957, numbers of all livestock increased between 1952 and 1957. Sheep and goats had the most consistent gains, whereas hog numbers varied greatly particularly in 1957 when unbelievable inventories were published.

Despite the low level of increase in production during this period, the export share of food crops and soybeans remained fairly stable and at a fairly high level, although mainland newspapers and periodicals complained of food shortages and tight rations, particularly in the cities. This condition may have arisen due to little or no change in government procurement, while, at the same time, there was a decided increase in urban population. The collectivization of agriculture which was to consolidate the regimes' control of both production and distribution of agricultural products, failed in both instances and likely was a major factor in the decline in the urban food supply.

There was no appreciable increase in the production of other major food crops during the 1952–57 period. Some increases occurred in the production of fruits and vegetables on private plots but vegetable oil-seeds, which provide a substantial source of fats in the diet, remained static; peanut production increased slightly but soybeans declined slightly. Cotton production was pushed under special programs in an attempt to make China self-sufficient and to accommodate the establishment of a huge light industrial complex with the textile industry as the base. Production of cotton increased substantially during the earlier years of the First Five-Year Plan but ran into competition with grain crops when it became necessary to expand the area of grains when increased yields failed to materialize. Thus, during the period of the First Five-Year Plan production in the agricultural sector responded favorably to the initial inputs, and the peasants took a keen interest in their status as new landowners. By the end of the plan period too little investment, too much central control, and too little personal incentive had taken their toll. Traditional patterns of farming were changed, the delicate balance of soil fertility had been impaired, traditional rotation and the complex interplanting systems had given way to a central plan, shortages of draft power and farm tools began to mount, and finally the peasant, the regime's greatest input became disillusioned and apathetic.

Despite these drawbacks the year 1958 provided agriculture with its best year ever.

However, disruptions of the farming system caused by collectivization were multiplied by the chaos which accompanied the emergence of the communal system during which time it appears that both the regime and the peasant lost contact with reality. Excessive destruction of livestock occurred, and considerable waste of foods, which unwittingly were in shorter supply than at first anticipated, occurred as centralized feeding became an integral part of communal living. The onslaught of three years of unfavorable weather on top of the administrative fiasco of the Great Leap Forward reduced agricultural production to a crisis level, forced the importation of grains to supplement dwindling stocks, brought about a new "agricultural first" policy and returned a certain amount of autonomy to local production units.

Agricultural production has not responded as hoped by the regime despite the efforts in irrigation, fertilization, mechanization, seed selection and development, and disease and insect control and other inputs. Adjustments are still being made but the combination of administration, peasant motivation, and modernization programs now under way have not solved China's food problem. Under the handicap of limited acreage expansion for crops, attention and capital have been concentrated on the more promising areas that respond to intensive cultivation.

Since the drastic reduction in food crop acreage in 1959, only the estimated acreage of miscellaneous grains presently exceeds the 1957–58 level; the acreage of wheat has remained significantly below that level; and the acreage of rice has not regained the 1957–58 level. Acreage of potatoes surpassed the 1957–58 level in the early 1960s but has declined during the past three years. Yields of rice are at their highest level and exceed those for 1957–58, whereas those for wheat, miscellaneous grains, and potatoes remain significantly less. This has been due primarily to the serious drought conditions in the major wheat and miscellaneous grain area of north China during the past two years and possibly to a shift of some potatoes to more marginal land. Total production of these crops, therefore, has not regained the 1957–58 level. Of the individual grains, only miscellaneous grains appear to have exceeded the 1957–58 level and only by a small margin. Production of potatoes continues to decline gradually.

Of the other major crops produced in China, the situation is similar to that for food crops except that recovery has not been so fast since the calamity years of 1959–61. A few exceptions are noteworthy, however. Great emphasis has been centered on reviving the cotton industry and this crop has been greatly expanded since 1961; but it has not regained its pre-Leap Forward prominence. One crop that has exceeded the pre-Leap Forward acreage and production is sugar, which has been a happy surprise to the regime. This was accomplished by devising a high incentive program with peasant farmers. The success of this program has enabled the regime to substantially reduce imports of sugar. Vegetable oilseed crops have not regained pre-Leap levels of acreage and production, although peanuts have made considerable progress in recent years. Tobacco, both the Flue-cured and native types, likely has exceeded former levels of production. Soybeans are still well below their former level of both acreage and production. Rapeseed's comeback has been slowed by the program to use this crop's area for the production of green manure crops as a measure to increase the fertility of riceland during the winter.

Essentially all of China's crops were affected similarly by the Great Leap policies and the bad weather, but their return to their former level of production has varied. Major emphasis was aimed at restoring the production of food crops. This involved not only the shifting of acreage of many nonfood crops but resulted in net losses of acreage of other crops when allocations were made to private plots. Intensive cultivation by peasants on their private plots resulted in a substantial increase in much needed foods high in nutritional value (vegetables, fruits, poultry, pork) and any other crop that would satisfy a food need. Because of these shifts and the lack of an effective reclamation program the multiple cropping index appears to have gained only slightly from the level of 141 in 1957. Even assuming it to be at 145 in 1966, there would still be a smaller sown area than in 1957. This analysis suggests that with all the shifting of crops during recent years a satisfactory combination of land utilization has not yet been established. It also points to the possibility that some of the former cropland may not be utilized for some time, particularly if the experimentation of the "guaranteed high yield field" project proves successful. Increasing imports of raw cotton and the gradual establishment of synthetic fibers industry point to a possibility of not utilizing all of the former cotton producing area.

The most significant development in land utilization following the Great Leap has been the intensified use of the private plots for both production of food and for sideline enterprises. Although a true measure of the value of production from the plots cannot be made, their contribution to the national economy is significant and their immediate benefit to the peasants has been important. Representing about 5 per cent of the total cultivated land, this private sector produces possibly as much as 80 per cent of the hogs and 95 per cent of the poultry in addition to a large proportion of the fruits and vegetables. Although data are not available, there is some evidence that private plots may supply up to 20 per cent of the daily food requirements. This is doubly significant since production from these plots supply a high percentage of the quality foods in the current Chinese diet. Furthermore, a very large share of the increase in farm exports (poultry, eggs, pork, bristles, other animal products, canned fruits and vegetables, etc.) during the last few years has come from the private plots.

## LIVESTOCK

The livestock industry is a significant factor in Mainland China's agricultural economy. While per capita consumption of meat is small, total production is relatively large. Pork accounts for the bulk of China's meat production, and in total output China ranks third in the world, after the United States and the U.S.S.R. The production of food grains has depended heavily on the livestock industry. Almost all the draft power is furnished by animals, and the maintenance of soil fertility is closely tied to the availability of animal manures. Many items of output from China's livestock are undervalued or not even recorded in national statistics. Yet the industry's total contribution to the total value of agriculture and subsidiary production probably equals about 20 per cent. Of vital importance in building up China's foreign exchange earnings is the export of livestock, meat, and animal products which have been increasing since the 1959–61 depression.

Under the Communist regime, livestock has continued to have a minor role but managed to increase under private ownership up to the time of collectivization. The Great Leap Forward dealt a serious blow to the industry. Peasants slaughtered animals rather than give them to the collectives and communes. Collective production proved costly and unproductive, and it was not until after the establishment of private plots and the inauguration of special programs in the pastoral areas of the country following the Great Leap Forward that progress again was made in building up the industry. Sheep and goats, which were least affected by the socialization drives, continued to increase after suffering an initial setback during the Great Leap Forward. The energetic program by the Government to entice farmers to raise hogs has been effective following the large losses during 1959–61. As a result of these programs, the number of hogs appears to have about regained or slightly exceeded preLeap Forward levels. The comeback of large animals (buffaloes, cattle, horses, mules, donkeys, and camels) has not been as rapid as for hogs, but substantial progress has been made. Shortages still exist for draft animals, but the increasing use of tractors in some areas is modifying this need.

The future of the livestock industry is not clear. No goals were mentioned in China's Third Five-Year Plan which commenced in 1966. Numerous problems confront the industry. Foremost of these is the limited supplies of feed, especially in the areas where hogs are produced. Numerous adjustments in the milling and other food industries in the countryside have been effected to provide a more even and a more direct supply of manufacturing wastes to bolster feed supplies. Despite Government help in supplying a certain amount of concentrates including grain, there is the continuous complaint of underfed and underweight hogs being sold to the state. The Government continues to encourage as rapid increase as possible of all categories of livestock. Despite the severe winter in the major livestock areas of northeast and northwest China plus continuous dry weather throughout a large portion of 1966 which adversely affected livestock, official reports indicated sizable gains. The sinking of new wells and the development of irrigation facilities in the Sinkiang and Inner Mongolian pastoral areas indicate the determination by the Communist regime to further expand livestock numbers. This effort, at least, will provide a much better base upon which to support larger numbers of livestock than before the Great Leap Forward provided proper management is maintained.

4

# Recent Development in Chinese and Indian Agriculture

*Pranab Bardhan*

AGRICULTURE IS THE key sector in both China and India and yet detailed comparisons of the two economies on the agricultural front are hard to come by.[1] Undoubtedly a major problem is that in both countries the state of availability and, in particular, reliability of economic information is worst with respect to agriculture. Even apart from problems of comparability of data across countries and problems of sheer non-availability of data at a national scale on many significant points, continuous changes in coverage and reporting systems, occasional cases of deliberate mis-reporting in official data (as, for example, is widely suspected of Chinese official production figures for 1958 and 1959) and frequent cases of one's being obliged to rely on sources that are not reputed for their impartiality (this is particularly serious because matters relating to Communist China tend to evoke very strong feelings in some quarters) are bound to frustrate the most heroic of research workers interested in a comparative study. Any such study is, therefore, grossly limited in its accuracy of appraisal, and the present paper is no exception. It is offered in the hope that despite the severe limitations on information, it may not be impossible to derive some rough generalizations, and in view of the importance of the subject, it may be worthwhile to draw attention to them. At the same time one has to bear in mind that whatever results this paper has should not lead anyone to jump to decisive ideological conclusions about the success or failure of a particular political system. Apart from the non-reliability of data, we have to take account of the numerous extraneous factors that complicate the actual operation of a system making it very difficult to have any straightforward judgement particularly in the relatively short period under consideration.

The agrarian economies that the Communists inherited in China after Liberation and that the Congress Government did in India after Independence were broadly similar in their essential structure and in the major problems afflicting them, with acute population pressure on limited arable land resources, with preponderance of subsistence farming and semi-feudal land relationships, with continuous sub-division and fragmentation of land holdings, widespread rural unemployment and underemployment, with peasants often having neither the ability nor the incentive to introduce improved methods of cultivation, with landlords, traders and village money-lenders channeling most of their investible funds into consumption credit (at exorbitantly high rates of interest), land purchases and speculation, with miserable transport and marketing conditions and, in general, with the prevalence of a self-perpetuating spiral of backwardness and poverty. For the first time in their recent history in both the countries, the new governments seriously committed themselves to long-run programs of agricultural transformation. By 1952, both the economies had substantially recovered from the disruptions and dislocations of the preceding decade and the minimum technical and organizational foundations for long-range planning had been laid. From this standpoint 1952 is a good starting point for a study of both the countries. Besides in terms of crop weather 1952 was a "good" year in both countries.

Table 1 gives the figures for (husked) foodgrains over the period for both countries. To Chinese output figures, which are normally in terms of unhusked grains, we have used a reduction factor of 0.81 for processing (this reduction factor has been used by Ishikawa [18] and is very close to the one used by Buck in [6]). Chinese grain statistics exclude soybeans but include, unlike in

 Notes to chapter 4 appear on pages 392-393

India, potatoes (in terms of 4–to–1 grain equivalents). Potatoes represent an inferior substitute for rice in South China like jowar and bajra for wheat in parts of India.

Let us now indicate the sources and also the reliability of the output figures in Table 1. The Chinese figures for 1952 to 1957 are from an officially published source [30]. The 1957 figure is widely regarded even among conservative Western observers as fairly reliable. But some of these observers regard the figures for the preceding few years as underestimates due to incomplete coverage and inadequacies of the crop reporting system. In spite of deficiencies of the crop reporting system, there are not, however, enough grounds to suspect underreporting on an organized scale in that period. Ishikawa [18] shows how the official figures of production for 1952 are quite consistent with estimates of consumption. On the basis of the nation-wide land survey of 1949–52 and other information Chi-Ming Hou [15] concludes that "it is highly doubtful that there was much, if any, understatements of cultivated acreage in the early years of 1952–57."

Hardly anybody,[2] however, believes in the inflated Chinese official figures for 1958 and 1959. For those two years we have taken the adjusted estimates of Dawson, the former Agricultural Attache of the USDA, as cited in Jones [21]. Since 1960 Peking has not published grain output estimates in the domestic press. So one has to depend on varieties of indirect estimates and sometimes nothing more than so-called "educated guessworks" of varying reliability for the post-1959 figures. For 1960–65 we have taken the reconstructed official figures (most of them based on Peking officials' claims at different points) cited in Jones [21]. The U.S. Consulate of Hong Kong provides some alternative estimates for these years which are, of course, much lower, particularly in the later years. But the Consulate data do not seem to be consistent with observations on foodgrains consumption and production potential from the estimates of use of fertilizers and other inputs; on this line Perkins [27] has given convincing reasons why Jones' reconstructed official figures seem to be a better approximation of actual output. Our 1966 figure for Chinese foodgrains output is cited by Han Suyin in her book *China in the Year 2001* (p. 54) and our 1967 figure is given by Anna Louise Strong in her January 15, 1968 "Letter from China," which reportedly gets official approval before being released. The difference between these 1966 and 1967 figures is consistent with Vice-Premier Hsieh Fu-chih's reported statement that 1967 grains (unhusked) production had increased over 1966 by about 10.5 million tons.[3]

***Table 1—Production of Foodgrains (Husked) (million tons)***

| China | | India | |
|---|---|---|---|
| 1952 | 125.0 | 1952–53 | 61.67 |
| 1953 | 127.1 | 1953–54 | 72.19 |
| 1954 | 130.0 | 1954–55 | 70.61 |
| 1955 | 141.6 | 1955–56 | 69.22 |
| 1956 | 147.8 | 1956–57 | 72.34 |
| 1957 | 149.9 | 1957–58 | 66.50 |
| 1958 | 165.2 | 1958–59 | 78.69 |
| 1959 | 137.7 | 1959–60 | 76.70 |
| 1960 | 121.5 | 1960–61 | 82.02 |
| 1961 | 131.2 | 1961–62 | 82.71 |
| 1962 | 140.9 | 1962–63 | 80.15 |
| 1963 | 148.2 | 1963–64 | 80.64 |
| 1964 | 162.0 | 1964–65 | 89.00 |
| 1965 | 162.0 | 1965–66 | 72.03 |
| 1966 | 178.2 | 1966–67 | 74.23 |
| 1967 | 186.3 | 1967–68 | 95.59 |

The Indian data are, of course, based on the officially revised index numbers of agricultural production (to take account of recent changes in coverage and methods of estimation) and the figures for the 1950s are derived by using these index numbers backwards from the official estimate of production in 1960–61.

Since China has a much larger population than India, the difference in foodgrains output between China and India is smaller in per capita terms than what appears from Table 1.[4] Assuming a Chinese population of 575 millions at the end of 1952 (as given by the State Statistical Bureau), and taking the official estimate of foodgrains for granted, per capita production of processed foodgrains in China was 237.2 kg. in 1952, whereas in India it was 164 kg. in 1952–53. Thus the Chinese per capita amount of processed foodgrains production was about 32 per cent higher than the Indian amount around 1952.

Assuming a population of 728 millions in China in 1965, from Table 1 we may say that the per capita production of processed foodgrains in China was about 222.3 kg. in 1965, whereas in India it was 182 kg. in 1964-65. Thus the Chinese per capita amount of foodgrains production was about 22 per cent higher than the Indian amount around 1965.

Even in the crisis year of 1960 in China, per capita production of processed foodgrains (assuming a Chinese population of 676 millions) did not go below the Indian amount for 1960–61 (which was a normal year in India).

India, of course, has been much more dependent on imports of foodgrains than China. Imports of foodgrains in India increased from an annual average of 3.8 million tons during the Second Plan to more than 6 million tons during the Third Plan. Even in the bumper crop year of 1964–65 imports of foodgrains amounted to about 7 per cent of output. In the beginning of the period studied China was a net *exporter* of foodgrains, although net exports were relatively insignificant (about 1 million tons each year over the most of the 1950s). In the 1960s China turned into a net importer of grains, but her imports of about 5 million tons of grains has not exceeded 3 per cent of output in any of the years.

Let us now have a look at the rates of growth in production. We fitted a semilog-linear equation, Log $Y = a + b$, to the data, with $b$ as the percentage rate of growth. When we take the data for sixteen years (1952–67 for China and 1952–53 to 1967–68 for India) as given in Table 1, we get the rate of growth $b = 1.9\%$ for China[5] (with standard error = .005), and $b = 1.7\%$ for India (with the standard error = .004). Since this series of data include the unusually disastrous years (which were the worst in several decades) of 1965–66 and 1966–67 for India and 1960 and 1961 for China, there is some point in calculating the rates of growth with these two years excluded from the set of data for the respective country. When we do this we get the rate of growth $b = 2.5\%$ for China (with standard error = .004), and $b = 2.5\%$ for India (with standard error = .003). On the whole it seems that the two countries had fairly similar, and not very high (relative to the rates of growth of population), rates of growth of foodgrains production over this period. Since the experience of Meiji Japan is often cited in discussion of agricultural growth, we may compare these rates of growth for China and India with the estimates by Yamada, according to whom the rate of growth of agricultural output in Japan between 1880–84 and 1915–19 was about 1.8 per cent.[6]

The rates of growth for India and China mentioned above are, of course, for foodgrains alone and not for total agricultural production. For India the compound rate of growth of total agricultural production between 1952–53 and 1964–65 was 3.01 per cent. The Chinese rate of growth of total agricultural production is likely to have been slightly lower than that of foodgrains.

The most important non-food crop in China is cotton. Its output went up from 1.3 million tons in 1952 to 1.64 million tons in 1957; then there was a substantial drop in production and it crept up to 1.4 million tons in 1965. Since 1959, shift of acreage from non-foodgrain crops to foodgrain crops has resulted in a relatively slow rate of growth of the former. In 1957 the area under foodgrain crops was 76.9 per cent of total cropped area, in 1965 it was 80.1 per cent.

In India, at least up to 1963, movements in relative prices of cash crops to food crops were favorable to the former, and some shift of acreage (as well as inputs like fertilizers and water) took place. Between 1952–53 and 1964–65 acreage under foodgrains grew at a rate of 1.1 per cent; the rate was 2.3 per cent for non-foodgrains. In 1964–65 the area under foodgrains was about 75 per cent of total cropped area.

Yields per acre in foodgrain production, particularly in rice, are much larger for China than in India, as can be seen from Table 2.

Let us now consider the trends in use of inputs.

Gross sown acreage under *all* crops was 151.1 million hectares in China in 1955 and 156 million hectares in 1965.[7] In India it was 144.1 million hectares in 1954–55 and 157.9 in 1964–65. The two countries, in spite of sizeable differences in geographical area and population, have a relatively similar amount of gross sown acreage under all crops. In both countries the possibilities of further expansion of acreage are very limited, and the most promising means of increasing production is, and will increasingly be, more intensive and efficient cultivation of existing farmland.

Chinese land is far more intensively cultivated than in India. The index of multiple cropping (i.e., the amount of gross sown acreage as a proportion of net sown acreage under all crops) was 137.2 in China in 1955 and 143.1 in 1965; in India it was 112.8 in 1954–55 and 115.3 in 1964–65.

**Table 2—Yields per Hectare in Processed Foodgrains (tons)**

| | *China* | | *India* | |
|---|---|---|---|---|
| | *1952* | *1965* | *1952–53* | *1964–65* |
| Rice | 1.78 | 2.19 | 0.81 | 1.07 |
| Wheat | 0.62 | 0.72 | 0.78 | 0.91 |
| All Foodgrains | 1.11 | 1.3 | 0.59 | 0.76 |

*Sources:* For India, calculations in Table 2 are made from the levels and indices of agricultural productivity given by the Ministry of Food and Agriculture. The Indian yield figures for total foodgrains are much lower than those for rice and wheat because of relatively low yields for pulses which are included in foodgrains. For China, the 1952 figures are calculated from State Statistical Bureau [30]; the 1965 figures are very rough estimates by Jones [21], p. 94 based on piecemeal official information and a lot of educated guesswork. We have used Buck's [5] reduction factors for processing 0.74 for rice, 0.85 for wheat and 0.81 for all foodgrains.

Through centuries farmers in both countries have been applying substantial amounts of organic manure and it is still the major source of crop nutrients. Information on the use of organic manure is very scanty, but it seems that the Chinese farmers use a much larger quantity of organic manure (in terms of plant nutrients) than their Indian counterparts. According to rough estimates, organic manure provided about 5.5 million tons of N (as is well known, both Chinese and Indian soils are most deficient in nitrogen) in China in 1957 and about 0.96 million tons of N in India in 1955–56.[8]

We did not have figures for *all* items of organic manure in India in recent years, but Table 3 provides information about the amount of N provided by the major items of organic manure in India and China. In

**Table 3—Estimates of Use of Organic Manure (thousand tons of N)**

| | *China (1965)* | *India (1964–65)* |
|---|---|---|
| Green manure | 259 | 951 |
| Farmyard manure | 2,930 | 659 |
| Compost (rural & urban) | 1,536 | 459 |
| | 4,725 | 2,069 |

preparing Table 3 we have taken the Chinese estimates from Ishikawa [18] and applied the fertilizer ingredient factors used in N.C.A.E.R. [25] to the Ministry of Food and Agriculture data on manures for 1964–65 (except that for rural compost we have used a factor of 0.4 per cent to get the amount of N).

In both countries the use of chemical fertilizers in agriculture is of comparatively recent date, and the amounts used per hectare are miserably low relative to countries like Japan today. Comparing India and China, it seems that the amount of nitrogenous, phosphatic and potassic fertilizers used per hectare is about thrice as large in China as in India around 1965. Organic (only the items in Table 3) and inorganic manure taken together, China used 38.5 kg. of N per hectare of cropped area in 1965 and India used 16.5 kg. of N per hectare of cropped area in 1964–65.

For effective application of fertilizers, as for normal crop growth and more intensive cropping, an adequate supply and regulated use of water is necessary. In the last two decades a great deal of water conservancy and irrigation programs have been carried out in both countries. According to Indian official data, gross irrigated area under all crops was 23.3 million hectares (16 per cent of gross cropped area) in 1952–53, 25.7 million hectares (17.2 per cent) in 1956–57 and 31.2 million hectares (19.7 per cent) in 1964–65.

For China, an assessment of the irrigation programs is more difficult because of a lack of data particularly for the later years and a variety of conflicting reports from official and semi-official sources, although there is no doubt that throughout the period irrigation projects on a massive scale had been undertaken and completed.[9] One of the most competent official sources of technical information places the 1952 total of irrigated area at 23.4 million hectares (this is an underestimate according to some Western observers) and the 1957 total at 38.3 million hectares (about 24 per cent of the gross cropped area).[10]

As in India, so in China, the increase in effective irrigation is much less than the potential created. Chinese engineers have stated that water from some of the projects never reached the farmer's land and that in other cases salinity and waterlogging developed because of high seepage from the large irrigation systems and inadequate drainage. In 1957 the Vice Minister of Water Conservancy stated that about 30 per cent of the area reported under irrigation was incapable of resisting drought. In August 1959, Premier Chou En-lai stated that only 33.3 million hectares (which was only half of the area claimed to be under irrigation at that time) could be adequately irrigated. Data on irrigation since that period are tenuous and it is very difficult to have a clear idea. Dawson [9] seems to think that the area irrigated by 1964 may have reached some 46 to 50 million hectares; i.e., about one-third of the total gross cropped area, which is much larger than the proportion in India.

It is well known in India that a substantial portion of the irrigation potential created is not utilized (because of, among other things, a lack of funds and incentives on the part of farmers to construct water courses and field channels, inappropriate phasing and coordination, etc.), although with recent measures of the Government in

***Table 4—Consumption of Chemical Fertilizers per Hectare of Gross Cropped Area (kilograms)***

| *China* | | *India* | |
|---|---|---|---|
| 1955 | 1.7 | 1955–56 | 0.9 |
| 1965 | 12.3 | 1964–65 | 4.1 |

*Sources:* For India, the fertilizer consumption data are from the *The Fourth Five-Year Plan, A Draft Outline* and gross cropped area data from the Ministry of Food and Agriculture publications. For China, the 1955 figure (which, incidentally, excludes ammonium nitrate in domestic production), is based on data in State Statistical Bureau [30]; the 1965 figure is calculated from estimates of fertilizer consumption in Ishikawa [18].

this direction, the utilization rate is improving. From official data it can be calculated that only about 48 per cent of the additional major and medium irrigation potential created since 1950–51 was utilized by 1955–56; the figure had gone up to 77 per cent by 1964–65.

Considering the extent of annual harvest fluctuations it is probably true to say that in spite of great improvements, the agrarian economies in both the countries are still considerably vulnerable to periodic floods and droughts. Besides, in both countries the major emphasis has been on the protective harvest-stabilizing aspects of water projects (the percentage of expenditure on water conservancy devoted to flood control is larger in China than in India because of difference in topographic, hydrologic and soil conditions); only in very recent years irrigation has started playing the more positive role of facilitating the use of improved farming techniques. It is also interesting to note that in both countries there has been a similar change in irrigation policy in recent years. In both countries attention has been remarkably shifted from constructing new large-scale grandiose projects to the development of numerous minor irrigation projects and to the consolidation of existing projects by building auxiliary works and other improvements.[11]

As for improved seeds, in India the area sown under improved seeds increased from 1.3 per cent of total gross cropped area in 1955–56 to 29.5 per cent in 1964–65. In China, according to official data, it went up from 4.7 per cent in 1952 to 77.5 per cent in 1958 for the area under foodgrains and from 50.2 per cent in 1952 to 97.0 per cent in 1958 for the area under cotton. But because of lack of information about the relative quality of improved seeds in the two countries it is difficult to compare the figures.

As for other agricultural inputs, both the countries are increasingly using mechanical and electric power in agricultural operations, irrigation and drainage and transportation, particularly in some advanced regions, although in aggregate terms this is still very small. The number of tractors in operation in China was 135,000 in 1956 (see *People's Daily*, April 13, 1966) compared to 2,719 in 1952. In India the number of tractors was 9,000 in 1951 and 31,000 in 1961. In 1965 nearly 6.6 million hectares of farm land in China were irrigated by mechanized pumps, doubling the area in 1961 (see *Far Eastern Economic Review Year Book*, 1966, p. 134). In India the number of electric pumps went up from 26,000 in 1951 to 400,000 in 1964–65. In China some of the increased use of agricultural machinery was, however, only in compensation for the drastic reduction[12] in the number of draft animals since the end of the 1950s. The number of total large animals (like cattle, buffaloes, horses) was 76.17 million in 1952, 85.38 million in 1957 and about 50.5 million in 1965 (see Ishikawa [19]). The ratio of total tracting power supplied by draft animals to that by tractors was 99:1 in 1957 in China, but it changed to 91:9 in 1965. From the livestock census data one finds that in India the total number of cattle and buffaloes used for work was 67.4 million in 1951 and 80.5 million in 1961.

In the application of new inputs like fertilizers, improved seeds, etc. there has been in recent years a remarkably similar shift in policy in both countries toward concentrating a large proportion of new inputs and administrative and technical personnel on a few selected districts. In India an Intensive Agricultural District Programme was undertaken in 1960–61 for some districts selected on the criterion of maximum irrigation facilities and a minimum of natural hazards where the cultivators were induced to adopt an integrated and intensive use of improved agricultural practices. The supply of high-yielding varieties of seeds, fertilizers, pesticides, etc., is pre-empted in favor of these selected areas which now constitute about 5 per cent of the total cultivated area in the country. However, as the Draft Fourth Five Year Plan observes, "evaluation done so far has shown that with the exception of some districts, progress has not matched expectation."

In China also certain areas—particularly in Yangtze and South China lake plains and deltas—have been selected for concentrated effort. These "modernizing" areas seem to constitute not more than 10 per cent of the farmland. According to Jones [21], marked results seem to have been achieved at relatively low total and State costs on these limited areas. Prosperous communes in these areas have sometimes provided the major part of the cost of investments, thus limiting State subsidies.

An important point to note here is that the mechanism for siphoning off some part of the agricultural surplus in these favored areas is more effective in China than in India, and this is a significant determinant of the efficacy of these package programs from the point of view of the economy as a whole.

On the general question of investment as well as price policy, there is a widespread impression that in both countries the agricultural sector has been relatively neglected. Let us first briefly take up price policy.[13] The major agricultural price policy in China has been the adjustment of Government purchase prices to stimulate or control agricultural production. The agricultural purchase price index went up sharply from 100 in 1950 and 121.6 in 1952 to 148.8 in 1957 and 188.3 in 1963; whereas the *rural* retail price index for industrial products went up from 100 in 1950 and 109.7 in 1952 to 112.1 in 1957 and 125.4 in 1963.[14] Thus the "terms of trade" have in general shifted in *favor* of the agricultural sector. For India data are not available on rural retail prices of industrial products for the country as a whole over a long enough period. On the basis of wholesale prices data and the value of the purchases of individual commodities by each sector from the other sector in 1960–61 as "weights," Thamarajakshi [33] has calculated the movement in intersectoral terms of trade in India. According to her calculation the index for prices received by the agricultural sector (for sales of goods of both intermediate and final use) went up from 82.5 in 1952–53 to 88.0 in 1957–85, 100.0 in 1960–61 and 126.8 in 1964–65, whereas the index for prices paid by the agricultural sector (for purchases of goods of both intermediate and final use) went up from 83.2 in 1952–53 to 89.4 in 1957–58, 100.0 in 1960–61 and 116.7 in 1964–65. The terms of trade seem to have improved over time for the Indian agricultural sector, although this improvement is marginal compared to that in China. One should, however, keep in mind that compared to the pre-war period the 1952 prices of agricultural relative to industrial products were in favor of the latter in China and the former in India.

Let us now take up the question of fixed investment in agriculture. According to estimates by Hollister [14] the agricultural sector in China accounted, on an average, for about 23 per cent of gross fixed investment in the economy in 1952–59. This includes, apart from state investment, investment by agricultural cooperatives and individual farmers. In India gross investment in agriculture and allied activities constituted about 20 per cent of total gross investment for the period 1951–52 to 1960–61.[15] These figures for investment allocation to agriculture are not very high, nor are they extremely low, particularly for a country with an urgent program of industrialization. Certainly the share of investment used in building the industrial base of the economy was much higher in both countries (higher in China than in India), but then no country aiming at structural transformation of the economy can be expected to allocate investment in proportion to existing sector shares in national income. Besides, in Asian agriculture investment in *fixed* capital may not always be the most important determinant of any significant productivity rise. One may also note here that in more recent years under pressures of agricultural crises the share of investment going to agriculture has appreciably increased in both countries.

Even if complaints about neglect of agriculture in investment allocation are justified, there are probably stronger reasons to question the *effectiveness* of investment that has been made in the agricultural sector and also (this is particularly true in India) the appropriateness of the investment priorities actually followed *within* the industrial sector itself. Let us take the second aspect first. In India, in spite of planners' intentions to the contrary, while industries catering to luxury and semi-luxury consumption have often spawned an undue amount of investible resources including foreign exchange (this has been made possible largely due to the extremely unequal income distribution pattern and loose government control over investment) and sometimes overfulfilled their production targets,[16] investment and production performance have fallen grossly short of the desired pattern in respect of, say, chemical fertilizers[17] (as in machinery-producing industries).

In China also up to the end of the First Five Year Plan too low a share of investment went into increasing chemical fertilizer production. In recent years, however, their rate of growth of production of chemical fertilizers has exceeded that of India.[18]

As for *effectiveness* of investment, agricultural programs in both countries have suffered from serious technical deficiencies as well as poor management and coordination. For the Chinese case let us quote from Eckstein's [10] general evaluation on this point. "Agricultural cadres often paid so little attention to the relationship between planting distance, depth of ploughing, soil moisture, crop strain, and soil fertility that applications of chemical fertilizer were at times not only wasted but even counterproductive. Similar difficulties plagued water conservation to an even greater extent.[19] Thus, it was officially admitted that 40 to 60 per cent of the water in the large irrigation systems was lost through leakage. This high seepage, coupled with inadequate drainage, caused water logging and sometimes serious alkalinization and salinization. The fact that local cadres were under tremendous pressure to fulfill and overfulfill the extremely ambitious targets for water conservation encouraged the withdrawal of land from cultivation in some areas. Technical deficiencies of these types characterized water conservation projects from the early 1950s on, but they became particularly pronounced during the Great Leap. The downgrading of the expert and the decentralization of economic management were felt perhaps more in this field than in any other. In the pursuit of the 'mass line', projects were designed locally by the peasants according to the availability of local construction materials," often causing considerable waste. Apart from fertilizer application or water conservation, even in other aspects of cultivation, programs have often been initiated by the Government and vigorously pushed through by party cadres without adequate consideration of the soil-climate complex and the varying economic and technical circumstances in different regions in the country (the resounding failure of the large-scale program of introducing the double-wheeled, double-bladed plough, as cited by Perkins [26] is only one example among many), and sometimes apparently sensible policies laid down by the central leadership have been carried to an absurd extreme by unskilled but overzealous cadres (for example, in following the principle of deep ploughing emphasized in Mao's "Eight Point Charter," in some areas ploughing was carried to a depth of six feet).

In India also, as the different Programme Evaluation Reports to the Planning Commission have amply testified, there have been serious shortcomings not only in the input distribution and extension service aspects of agricultural programs but also in the technical suitability or local adaptability of various items in those programs. Water, fertilizer or seed programs have been pushed without sufficient consideration of local soil-climate conditions, cropping patterns, cultivating practices and the crucial complementarities in the use of different factors of production. Farmers have often refused to adopt new inputs and technology, not out of irrationality, ignorance or fatalism, but due to a better appreciation of their local unsuitability or technical complementarity than is to be found in the administrative officials pushing those programs (apart from the risk factors involved). Programs have also suffered from a lack of coordination among different agencies engaged in research, administration, extension, and business and marketing in the field of agriculture.

In China, as we have noted, some of the technical deficiencies in agricultural programs became more pronounced in the Great Leap Forward period. But the failures and excesses of the Great Leap should not lead us to overlook the fact that the underlying strategy of the Leap involving mass mobilization of (especially seasonally) underemployed rural labor on labor-intensive investment projects like irrigation, flood control, land reclamation, contour bunding, terracing, leveling, and road building is in principle basically sound in overpopulated agrarian economies like China or India. The Indian Plans, and even the Ford Foundation Agricultural Production Team in India in 1959, have endorsed very similar policies after having pointed out that a vast amount of such rural construction projects could be undertaken with very little extra equipment. While we have duly noted how out of the staggering amounts of earthworks constructed by mass mobilization of labor in China in the Great Leap Forward period a significant proportion was ineffective in their intended purpose of coping with floods or droughts, it is worth mentioning at this point that no other country in recent history (not even the Soviet Union) has even attempted mobilization of rural labor on agricultural capital projects on such a massive scale, and the consequent organizational and economic stresses and strains should be judged in that context. In comparison the Indian performance with respect to the rural works programs has been very poor.

In connection with mobilization of labor on construction of rural "overhead" capital, it is important to point to the incentive effects of the different patterns in the distribution of benefits from these projects in the two countries. In India, as in pre-communist China,[20] a major problem in mobilizing labor on such projects is that those who work on them do not receive proportionate benefits from them.[21] As reports after reports of the Programme Evaluation Committees have stressed, most of the benefits from Community Development Projects in India have accrued to the richer farmers. No wonder that the mass of poor peasants and agricultural laborers do not feel excited by these projects. In irrigation projects also, the distribution of water is very much inequitable and is a major reason of the poor maintenance of field channels.[22] Through cooperative management of cultivation the Chinese have minimized this problem of conflicting self-interest between workers and beneficiaries of a rural capital project.

The emphasis in Indian Community Development Projects has been on coordinated administrative action by the Government agencies and not on any program deliberately planned to effect any change in the rural institutional framework. The village level workers and extension officers are not merely ill-paid and overworked; they have to operate within a severely constrained institutional set-up. This over-enthusiastic but technically incompetent Chinese party cadre in his visions of unprecedented socialist transformation attempts too much and quite often fails. The under-enthused Indian village-level worker does and can, under the given constraints, attempt too little.

The discussion of the institutional framework in which agriculture operates inevitably brings us to the question of land policy in the two countries and their important differences in this respect. Let us first take the case of India.

A great deal of land legislation has been undertaken in India in the last two decades. The major objectives of land policy were the abolition of intermediary tenures, reform of the tenancy system, including fixation of fair rent at one-fifth to one-fourth of the gross produce and security of tenure for the tenant, extension of owner-cultivation, ceilings on land holdings making possible a redistribution of surplus land among landless laborers, consolidation of agricultural holdings and increase in the size of the operational unit to an economic scale through cooperative methods. These programs have been enforced in part and have met varying degrees of success or failure.

The program for the abolition of intermediaries has been carried out practically all over the country; about 20 million tenants of former intermediaries came into direct relationship with the State and became owners of their holdings. Far less effective has been the program of tenancy reform. A considerable proportion of the total area cultivated is still under tenancy. From the 16th Round data of National Sample Survey

(1959–60) it is found that of the total cultivated area in rural India the proportion under tenancy is about 12.5 per cent.[23]

The tenant cultivator with insecure tenure has little incentive to undertake long-run improvements in the land he cultivates. Besides, his capacity to invest is seriously limited by high rents and limited access to even cooperative credit. The rents as fixed by tenancy laws are still very high in several States and in others the rents charged are generally much higher than the legal maximum. As for credit, among all the occupational categories based on agriculture the tenant cultivator figures the least in proportion to his importance among the beneficiaries of credit programs. This is mostly because even cooperative loans continue to be given generally against the mortgage of land, and there has not been any significant shift to the crop loan system in most States.

Among tenant farms a more acute incentive problem arises in the case of share-croppers. From National Sample Survey 15th Round data (1959–60) it seems that more than 43 per cent of total area under tenancy is under share-cropping. Except in South India share-cropping is still the predominant form of tenancy in rural India.

Crop-sharing tenancy without cost-sharing (as is generally the rule in India) obviously involves an added disincentive problem in application of new agricultural inputs like chemical fertilizers, compared to the case of tenancy with fixed cash rent. It is easily shown why the share-cropper paying a very high proportion of his gross produce as rent may be reluctant to adopt a new input even when he knows that this will bring some addition to output.

Of course, it is availability, and not tenurial disincentive, that is the major bottleneck for the expansion of the use of new inputs like fertilizers. But share-cropping gives rise to the problem of inefficient allocation of a given total amount of fertilizers among different farms. Under the existing tenurial conditions there will be "too much" fertilizers on owner-cultivator areas and too little on share-cropped areas. In principle, this particular problem of misallocation of a given total of fertilizers will, of course, disappear if all land were share-cropped with the same proportional shares. This point is relevant in a comparison between China and India, since in view of an agricultural tax fixed in proportion to output the Chinese cooperative farm may also be said to be operating under a kind of share-cropping system (with the share going to the Government).[24] The Chinese agricultural tax has a disincentive effect on the total amount of fertilizer demand, but because of its uniformity over cultivated areas the misallocation problem we have referred to is avoided.[25]

Leaving aside the problem of tenancy, a major affliction of Indian agriculture has been and still is the prevalence of small and fragmented holdings.[26] According to National Sample Survey 16th Round data on Land Holdings for 1959–60, 30.6 per cent of the total area operated is in holdings of less than 7.5 acres, 53.7 per cent is in holdings of less than 15 acres, 75.6 per cent is in holdings less than 30 acres. A substantial proportion of cultivated area is thus being operated in holdings that are "uneconomic" by most standards.[27] Besides, compared to large farmers small farmers suffer from extra disadvantages in getting enough supplies of credit, inputs, and technical assistance. Although there has been some improvement in cooperative servicing in recent years, particularly in credit, marketing, and provision of agricultural supplies, many of the cooperatives tend to be dominated by the larger farmers and traders who take the lion's share of the facilities, thereby defeating one of the major aims of the cooperative movement.[28]

Apart from being small, the holdings also consist of widely scattered fragments. According to National Sample Survey 16th Round data for 1959–60, the average number of parcels per operational holding in India is 5.82 and the average area of a parcel is 1.14 acres. Under the Five Year Plans, up to 1964–65 a total of only about 55 million acres of area had been consolidated.

Up to the middle of the 1950s, Chinese agriculture was also characterized by the prevalence of small, uneconomic, and widely fragmented holdings. In pre-Communist

China 60 per cent of the farms averaged less than three acres. According to J. L. Buck's survey [5] in twenty-two Chinese provinces the average farm in 1929–33 contained only 4.23 acres. Because of the inheritance practices and the extreme pressure of population on land, the situation must have worsened in the subsequent two decades. As for fragmentation, according to Buck's survey, the average number of fragments per farm was 5.6 and the average distance of the fragments from the farmstead was about half a mile. As for tenancy, according to Buck's survey, 28.7 per cent of cultivated land was rented and only 54.2 per cent of the farmers owned their land. The Land Reform of 1949–52 expropriated the holdings of the landlords (which constituted nearly 40 per cent of cultivated land) and redistributed a total of 116.7 million acres of land among 300 million poor and landless peasants. The resultant land situation was still marked by very small farms. An official survey in 1954 revealed that about 24 per cent of total cultivated area was being operated by households having, on an average, 2 acres of land (and one half of a draft animal and one third of a plough) and only 3.2 per cent of cultivated area was being operated by "rich" peasant households having on an average 5.8 acres of land (and two draft animals and one plough). This was a situation much worse (from the production efficiency point of view) than in India in the same period, so far as the size of holding is concerned.

Between 1953 and 1957 the small fragmented peasant farms in China were replaced in turn by mutual aid teams (with pooling of labor and other resources, labor reward fixed in work-day units, full private control over landholdings), agricultural producers' cooperatives "of the less advanced type" (pooling of both land and labor, peasants retaining their title and rights to the land, land share distributed according to size of owned land-holdings, labor reward in terms of work-day units, and a common accumulation fund), and then the collective farms or the agricultural producers' cooperatives "of the more advanced type" (nominal private ownership of land but no land share in income, joint management and cultivation, small garden plots permitted to private members for raising vegetables and livestock with rural free markets to sell the produce). A further stage in the socialization of agriculture was reached in 1958 with the introduction of communes. A number of collectives (on the average of thirty) was amalgamated into communes having an average membership of four to five thousand households. The basic unit in agriculture was enlarged to organize mass mobilization of rural labor on soil and water conservation projects and local industries and to coordinate economic and administrative functions at the local level. Private garden plots and rural free markets were abolished. Peasants were paid both in money and in kind, determined partly by work done (relative to the income of the whole commune) and partly by "free supply." Since 1960, after the agricultural crisis, there was a gradual movement back to smaller agricultural units. The production team, with an average membership of 60 to 80 households (which is much less than a half of the size of even the producers' cooperatives of 1955–56) has gradually become the basic unit for resource allocation and economic decision-making, although the commune has remained as a unit of local government. The private garden plots and the rural free market for subsidiary products have been restored. The partial "free supply" system in distribution has disappeared.

Let us briefly discuss the possible general impact of these institutional reorganizations on production efficiency in agriculture. First, the constant experimentations and reorganizations of rural institutions and the various policy shifts must have had disrupting effects on productive efficiency simply because of the uncertainties caused. This was probably inevitable in a period of transition in a country undertaking a fundamental rural transformation on an almost unparallelled scale, continuously groping for an optimum agrarian unit given the political and economic goals. Secondly, there must have been a considerable incentive problem from the point of view of individual peasants as they became more removed from their connection with the land and as their labor reward became more removed from the work they performed with each enlargement in the size of the basic unit of agricultural planning and income distribution. The disincentive problem may have been much less serious in recent years with the small production team now generally accepted as the basic unit. Besides, as Hoffman [13] points out, along with collectivization of agriculture the Chinese have rationalized their payment schemes and devised elaborate scaled work grades and piece-rate mechanisms to keep up material incentives. Except for a brief early phase of the communes when non-material incentives and distribution "according to need" were emphasized, agricultural wage payments have generally been geared to the quantity and quality of labor.

Against whatever losses there might have been due to disincentives in collectivization, one should weigh the undoubted gains from the pooling and consolidation of former uneconomic and fragmented holdings. Consolidation of holdings removes a lot of division strips, assists in soil conservation measures and irrigation projects, and economizes use of animal and human labor. As for joint farming, even if technological economies of scale of the usual type are not significant under traditional methods of cultivation there are some benefits apart from avoiding the serious problem of uneconomic holdings.[29] One example is the case where the family farm is frequently obliged to diversify in crop pattern even when specialization is more profitable on the small piece of land, whereas the joint unit can get the advantages of specialization without ceasing to meet the varied consumption needs of its member families. In addition to all this, cooperative management may facilitate introduction of new inputs and technology, improvement in the rates of saving and investment and mass organization of rural works meant to increase agricultural productivity'[30] Some of these advantages have not materialized in China since the rural party cadres who controlled the cooperatives were not sufficiently skilled in agricultural technology; in their zeal for reform they often carried out undue encroachments on private incentives and in their constant attempt to show spectacular results often went for ill-fated crash programs.

Contrary to usual expectations, the socialization of agriculture does not seem to have significantly improved the agricultural sector's sales proportion of foodgrains to the non-agricultural sector in China. From Table 5 based on Ishikawa's [6] estimate it seems that the marketed proportion (including the

### *Table 5—Marketed Ratio of Foodgrains Production in China*

| *Year* | *Percentage* |
|---|---|
| 1950 | 35.24 |
| 1953 | 37.74 |
| 1954 | 39.07 |
| 1955 | 34.22 |
| 1956 | 30.34 |
| 1957 | 30.69 |
| Average for 1953–57 | 34.18 |
| 1958 | 26.94 |
| 1959 | 30.00 |

*Sources:* Ishikawa [17], Table 8. Both the amounts produced and marketed were in terms of processed foodgrains. The marketed amount includes agricultural taxes, the amount sold to State and Cooperative commerce and also the amount (relatively small since 1954) sold in free markets. [The amount of return sale (as ration or relief measures) of the government to agricultural areas is, however, not included.] For extensive notes on the estimates, see Ishikawa [17]. Our estimates are slightly different from those in [17], since in order to make our figures comparable to those in Table 6 for India, we have deducted a wastage factor of 4 per cent for China (which seems to be the average wastage per cent for foodgrains for the economy as a whole as suggested in Shen [29], Appendix). In other words, as in Table 6, the figures here roughly refer to the ratio of the total amount of foodgrains available for consumption in the non-agricultural sector to the total gross output of processed foodgrains. One might comment here that Ishikawa has used official grain output data (which are greatly inflated) for 1958 and 1959 in deriving his percentages. But Ishikawa thinks that this has not led to any significant underestimation of the marketed *ratios* of production.

amount paid in agricultural taxes) of foodgrains production has (in spite of significant year-to-year variations) *in general* declined in China in the 1950s and although we do not have enough data for the subsequent period, on all indirect evidence the decline seems to have continued in the 1960s. Ishikawa thinks that the major factors responsible for this phenomenon are (1) very high income elasticity of demand for foodgrains on the part of the average farm household at the existing low levels of consumption, (2) more egalitarian income distribution pattern, and (3) the Government's general reluctance to impose an extractive policy at the risk of social unrest and loss of production incentives (peasant unrest in 1954 and 1959—years when the marketed ratio of foodgrains was relatively high—immediately led to a softening of Government procurement policy).

It is interesting to note that in India also the marketed proportion of foodgrains output has not significantly increased in recent years. On the basis of N.S.S. per capita cereals consumption data, Census population data and the Government production and distribution of cereals data we have estimated the time series of marketed proportion of output of cereals as in Table 6 (it is assumed that the non-agricultural rural population consumes cereals at a rate that is an average of that for rural and urban population).

From Table 6 it seems that over these thirteen years there has not been much of a trend in the marketed proportion of cereals output in India; if anything, there has been a mild declining trend, particularly since the middle of the 1950s. This is in spite of growth of cereals production at an annual compound rate of about 2.7 per cent over this period.

This general failure of the marketed proportion of foodgrains output to rise in India may be explained by: (1) a very high income-elasticity of demand for foodgrains on the part of farm households, as in China or any other poor peasant economy, (2) withholding of grains on the part of middle and big farmers in expectation of higher prices, particularly in very recent years (this is a short-run factor), and (3) increase in withholding capacity of these relatively better-off farmers on account of higher income and better credit and storage facilities.

On the whole it seems that agricultural production in the two countries has grown at fairly similar rates. In terms of absolute level Chinese yield per acre in most crops, of course, exceeds that of India by a significant margin, but this has been true for quite a long time in the past. (In fact, Ishikawa [5] notes that China had attained by the tenth century—with the establishment of the present-day rotation pattern—a level of per-hectare rice yield which was almost the same as its level in 1952). On the other hand, in provision of inputs, Chinese performance has been much better than that in India. Al-

### *Table 6—Marketed Proportion of Cereals Output*

| *Year* | *Percentage* |
|---|---|
| 1952–53 | 29.12 |
| 1953–54 | 29.65 |
| 1954–55 | 32.76 |
| 1955–56 | 35.13 |
| 1956–57 | 29.55 |
| 1957–58 | 32.99 |
| 1958–59 | 29.26 |
| 1959–60 | 29.65 |
| 1960–61 | 36.14 |
| 1961–62 | 29.47 |
| 1962–63 | 30.80 |
| 1963–64 | 28.55 |
| 1964–65 | 23.84 |

*Source:* See Bardhan and Bardhan [3].

though gross cropped area is very similar between the two countries (net sown area, of course, is smaller in China), the Chinese use much more manure and fertilizers, irrigation water, improved seeds, agricultural equipment and machinery, and labor per unit of cropped area than India. We have seen that their price policy also has been more favorable toward the agricultural sector. In trying to explain why the Chinese performance in terms of rate of growth has not been much higher than India in spite of more inputs and better prices, I think the two following points on the level of sweeping generalities are important.

1. In a large part of the period under study, certainly in most of the 1950s the Chinese tried to step up agricultural production mainly through a more intensive use of the traditional factors of production, more application of labor in production, shift to more labor-intensive crops (like paddy and potatoes), more farmyard manure and more minor irrigation of the traditional type (which heavily uses labor and local materials and was often of limited effectiveness from the long-run point of view).[31] An avowed purpose of agricultural collectivization was to accelerate this intensive use of traditional factors of production, to organize a fuller and more efficient use of labor in double cropping, collection and application of manure and construction of social overheads, like minor irrigation and flood-control projects. Although collectivization was amply successful in this respect, China by the end of the 1950s must have faced the serious problem of diminishing returns from more intensive application of traditional inputs to agriculture. In this period China had attained the level of land productivity which seems to be near the maximum attainable within the framework of traditional agriculture and since her initial base was much larger than the Indian, to grow at a significantly higher rate than India would have required a technological breakthrough on a larger scale than was attempted in China in the major part of the period under study. The Chinese leaders have now fully appreciated the limitations of traditional technology and inputs and since the beginning of the 1960s they have geared their agricultural policy to the so-called "four transformations," i.e., mechanization, electrification, increase of irrigation and the use of chemical fertilizers. Of course the weight of new inputs in total inputs is still very small (for example, although the proportion of total plant nutrients supplied by chemical fertilizers increased from 2.5 per cent in 1957 to 13.5 per cent in 1965 in China, it is still a relatively small percentage), but it is worth noting that China is now increasing the use of these new inputs in agriculture at a much faster rate than India.

2. A second major factor which must have adversely affected agricultural production in China was what might be called organizational instability and the trial-and-error land policy. Much of this period under consideration was taken up in China in bold experimentations—with the inevitable advances and retreats—in search of the optimum size of land management. The constant experimentations and reorganizations of rural institutions and the various policy shifts must have had disrupting effects on productivity simply because of the uncertainties caused. But as we have noted before, this was probably inevitable in a period of transition in a country undertaking a fundamental rural transformation on an almost unparallelled scale, and in that sense it is not quite fair to compare the performance of China and India in this period merely in terms of rates of growth of production.[32]

Since 1962, however, Chinese agriculture has had a period of relative organizational stability. By vesting planning, accounting and management authority in the small *production team*, the Chinese now seem to have reached a fairly good compromise; the production team which is less than half of the size of the producers' cooperatives of 1955–56, is large enough to make the unit of land management viable, but it is small enough not to stretch the connection of reward and individual work very much. The effectiveness of the production team as the basic unit and the organizational stability in agriculture along with increased use of modern inputs go a long way in explaining the steady growth of agricultural production in China since

1963. On all evidence the Cultural Revolution has not seriouly interrupted agricultural growth.

As regards marketed surplus of foodgrains, we have noted in this paper that in spite of collectivization of agriculture the marketed proportion of foodgrains output did not increase in China. This points to an important difference in the agricultural policy in China from that in the Soviet Union in the early decades of planning industrialization. Soviet policy toward agriculture had been primarily extractive rather than developmental. As Tang [32] notes, reduction in agricultural output in the Soviet Union were absorbed mainly by the agricultural population while the flow of agricultural surplus to the industrial sector was maintained (for example, while grain output declined from 82 million tons in 1913 to 63 million in 1932, in the Soviet Union total grain collected fell only from 21 million to 20 million tons), and because of this industrial growth could proceed unabated even with reduction in farm output (Tang finds that the correlation between rates of agricultural growth and rates of industrial growth in the Soviet Union for 1928–37 is low and statistically insignificant).

This correlation, however, is very high in China (and India). The pace of industrial advance in China (as in India) has been severely constrained by the vagaries of agricultural production. Tang [32] points out that the Soviet Union could afford to follow a more extractive policy toward agriculture because she had a larger extraction margin to start with (China's per capita food availability in grain terms in 1952 was less than half the Soviet Union's in 1928). Chinese agricultural population has been much closer to the subsistence margin and fluctuation in agricultural output could not be absorbed by the farm population; instead they were reflected in fluctuations in farm marketings, state procurements and total collections. But this also points to the difference in sensitivity of the Chinese leaders to peasant distress from that of their Soviet counterparts in the relevant period, and this is related to the substantial difference in the nature and origin of the Chinese and the Soviet Revolutions.

Before ending our discussion we may also point out that in this paper we have concentrated mainly on production performance in the Indian and Chinese agriculture, and have generally ignored the question of distribution of income and wealth in the rural sector. Even in discussing the institutional framework we have emphasized different aspects only insofar as they directly operate on production efficiency. No comparative study of two economies is complete without a consideration of the distribution patterns, but we have chosen not to discuss it here out of considerations of space as well as our belief that most people will hardly deny that the pattern of income and wealth is likely to be more egalitarian in China and in India. We may only note that the welfare effects of a more egalitarian distribution may be substantial in countries like India or China with millions of people at the near-subsistence level of consumption.

B

# Patterns of Development in Industry

TRANSFORMATION FROM THE present agricultural economy to an industrial economy is the major objective of the Indian and Chinese patterns of economic development. The slogan "agriculture as the foundation and industry as the leading sector" emphasized in the New Economic Policy of China (1962), and the Indian Planning Commission's ambitious plans for industrialization indicate this planning strategy. As Wilfred Malenbaum remarks, "Modern power plants, steel mills and machinery are indelible components of what the citizens and officials of a poor country 'need' in their quest for economic expansion." Heavy investments in the industrial sectors of both India and China are fulfilling this need in their quest for economic development.

The article by Malenbaum explains the background and strategy of industrial planning in India. The strategy is to expand the output of capital and intermediate goods in preference to consumer goods in order to reduce dependence on imports of machinery for future growth. About achievements in this direction, Malenbaum believes that though the actual output has been less than the planned target, "The Indian economic scene has literally been transformed through the vigor and diversity of the nation's industrial expansion." He analyses the progress of the steel and fertilizer industries and their future prospects. Output in the steel industry has been far below the target owing to delays in the scheduling of component parts and construction, especially in case of steel mills in the public sector. Expansion in fertilizer and machine tools industries has been quite impressive.

The article by Ruddar Datt and K. P. M. Sundharam explains the industrial pattern in India under the Five Year Plans. The overall index number of industrial production (1950–51 = 100) was 139 in 1955–56, 194 in 1960–61 and 329 in 1965–66. During the period 1951–67, the index of industrial production registered an increase of 177 per cent. Adding to this a 7 per cent increase in industrial production during 1968, the growth rate during the above period works out to be 6.6 per cent per annum. This figure is quite close (6.4 to 6.7 per cent) to that calculated by Barry Richman for the period 1950 to 1966.

The article by R. M. Field examines the growth rates of individual industries and total industrial production in China during the period 1949 to 1965. Field has not used the official published sources and has constructed his own indices of industrial production based on critical examination of various sources. The growth of industrial production is marked by great fluctuations over different periods. Field breaks the period 1949–65 into Economic Rehabilitation (1949–52); the Leap Forward (1958–60); and Recovery and Readjustment (1961–65).

During the period of Economic Rehabilitation, the growth rate was quite high: 27 per cent per annum. There was not much of an increase in productive capacity, but the economy was able to recover from the war damages (loss through the Soviet removal of equipment from Manchuria in 1945). Between 1953 and 1957, however, there was a substantial increase in the fixed productive capacity. The high growth rate continued through the first two years of the Leap Forward, followed by a serious decline in industrial production in 1960. The withdrawal of Soviet technicians in mid-1960 was one of the major causes for this decline. With more pragmatic policies, the industry gained recovery that continued until 1965. For the period of 1949–65, Field computes the average growth of industrial production at 11 per cent per annum. Interestingly enough, his estimate is close to Barry Richman's estimate of 11.5 to 12.0 per cent for the period of 1950–60. Discussing the high growth rate during 1963–65 and estimating future trends, Field remarks, "This growth, however, has been achieved by the gradual re-employment of capacity that had been installed during or prior to the leap forward rather than by the addition of new productive capacity. Because almost all idle capacity has now been put back into production and because few capital construction projects have been undertaken since 1960, further increases in output will be more difficult to achieve than those of the 3 years 1963–65."

Compared to India's growth rate of industrial production (6.4 to 6.7 per cent) during 1950–66, expansion of industrial production in China has been at a higher rate (11 per cent) during the same period.

By 1969 both countries had attained a much higher level of sophistication and diversification of their industrial products than that which had existed in the early 1950s. Diversification became a common feature of Indian industry during 1968–69, indigenously producing for the first time a wide range of hitherto imported products. This included cadmium, high density polyethylene, electrocardiographs, operation tables, needle roller bearings, malleable pipe fittings, industrial furnaces, and special electrodes. Another indicator of progress was the winning in global competition of large contracts for items such as railroad wagons, textile machinery, and power generators. India now exports technical know-how and capital on an increasing scale. It has joint industrial projects operating in a number of countries in Africa and southeast Asia. Indians are setting up manufacturing plants in Thailand, Afghanistan, Ghana, Yugoslavia, and Luxembourg, just to name a few. These firms produce a wide range of products—textiles, iron and steel, electrical goods, bicycles, paper pulp, trucks, tractors, asbestos cements, pharmaceuticals, pesticides, air conditioners, refrigerators, precision tools, plastics, chemicals, clocks, and others.[1]

A number of new engineering products have also been reported for China. Items built for the first time in 1969 include 125,000-kilowatt steam turbogenerators, 5,000-horsepower hydraulic drive locomotives, 15-ton heavy-duty tip trucks, trucks with 12-ton load capacity, and a 20-ton trailer. The machine-building industry also produces a wide range of industrial products including metallurgical and mining machinery, electric machinery and appliances, chemical and petroleum industry equipment, ships, instruments and meters, and others.[2]

Despite these gains in the industrial field, both nations still have a long way to go before they can attain the level of sophistication and diversification already achieved by the leading industrialized nations.

**Notes to this part appear on page 393**

5

# Industrial Progress in India Under Planning

*Wilfred Malenbaum*

*From* Current History *54, no. 320, (April 1968): p. 206–11, 246, with omissions. Reprinted with permission.*

In December 1967, India's National Development Council announced the termination of formal operations under the Fourth Five Year Plan, begun in April 1966. Continuation would have meant, in the official view, persistence in a program that was out of touch with the realities of the Indian economic situation: India was in recession. Demand for industrial goods had declined, on the part of farmers, because of two disastrous crop years; on the part of urban residents, because of limited purchasing power after meeting high food prices; on the part of government, because of reduced revenues and on the part of private business because of falling production. Industrial output was also restricted because of a shortage of raw materials. Overwhelming all was the upward surge of prices; the wholesale index for all commodities increased some 15 per cent a year after 1964. This combination of recession with inflation saw one-third of India's modern industries with declining product in 1966 and again in 1967. Such realities were certainly not in step with India's plans; hence the plan termination.

Other causes for the government's action were the high military expenditures arising from conflicts with China and Pakistan, and uncertainties about foreign aid. Apart from diminished enthusiasm in the United States about the role of massive foreign aid, active hostilities between India and Pakistan promoted a halt in commitments just as India's draft Fourth Plan was to be put in final form. It was never completed; development operations since early 1966 have proceeded on an interim, annual basis. There were also growing doubts about basic development strategy. Was industrailization being favored unduly over agricultural development? Within industry, was too much stress being put upon heavy capital goods? Was the government role in development, especially in industry, conducive to maximum growth, given the importance of private industry in India's economy? While the International Bank, with some $1.8 billion in loans authorized for India (and with its central position in the India Aid Consortium), has often raised such questions, there are important domestic critics also. Thus India's newly reconstituted Planning Commission has itself suggested the need for new plans and directions before the resumption of formal plan programs—perhaps in 1969.

A growing economy is an industrial, as distinct from an agricultural or extractive, economy. Economic progress is often measured by the rate of decline of primary activities, whether by share of national product, or share of total labor force. A growing nation has some sector which grows most rapidly. For a period this might be in agriculture, or extractive enterprises, or even services, but sooner or later this most-rapid growth area will best be characterized as "in industry." In industry, a nation can see continuous expansion; the modern factory offers ever-increasing productivity per man. The development task is the meshing of factory expansion with expansion in other parts of the economy so that total product will increase rapidly and continuously. Factories are thus tools of growth; they are also symbols. Modern power plants, steel mills and machinery that makes machinery are indelible components of what the citizens and officials of a poor country "need" in their quest for economic expansion.

One basic attribute of the potential diversity and efficiency of industry is the role it can

**Notes to chapter 5 appear on page 393**

play in providing the capital goods for expansion. Industry will produce the diverse consumer goods people want and the machinery that facilitates diversification. Moreover, industry offers a broader entry to the export market, to permit imports of goods and services better produced elsewhere. Industry has the potential to make a country more independent of foreign sources of supply for capital goods while it can enhance a country's ability to depend upon foreign sources of supply. It is the prime sector of "import substitution" and "export stimulation."

## *Planned Expansion*

The industrial emphasis of the plans indicates a hoped for twenty-fold expansion in industrial investment. From less than 20 per cent of all investment in the First Plan, industry was to receive 40 per cent in the Fourth and Fifth. Within industry, public investment was to grow even more rapidly. And the role of industrial product was to expand, more or less in line. Value added in modern industry was to show a fifteen-fold expansion from 1950–51 to 1975–76.

Within modern industry, planning became increasingly explicit with respect to the output of capital goods and of intermediate goods. Basic policy on this matter was formalized by 1955; with the Third Plan this policy was built scientifically into specific targets.[1] Intermediate goods and capital goods together were to be four times as important as consumer goods by the end of the Fifth Plan.

Such changes were essential to India's scheme for continued growth. Successive plans were expected to decrease the degree to which Indian investment needed to depend upon foreign assistance, from some 18 per cent during 1951–56 to essentially zero after fifteen to twenty-five years, as originally envisaged. Given the extent to which modernization itself depended upon machinery and intermediate goods from abroad, this objective called for a large (relative) expansion in India's exports or a large (relative) reduction in Indian imports. Since India would continue to require new industrial goods for many plan periods, and since export expansion was considered a difficult process, India's own intermediate goods and machinery were to supply the capital goods insofar as possible. These same products, plus diversified output from consumer goods industries, could also broaden the range of Indian exports.[2]

The import substitution process is readily illustrated in the case of machinery. India added approximately Rs. 850 crores of new machinery to its economy in 1960–61; it projected needs of roughly double that level for 1965–66. Machinery imports were 47 per cent of total supplies in 1960–61. If domestic production of machines had not expanded, India's imports would have had to be Rs. 1,250 crores to achieve its goal. If production had increased so that imports retained their relative importance (47 per cent) the import bill would be Rs. 800 crores. With a more rapid expansion projected in output imports would increase to Rs. 500 only. Eventually, by 1975–76 in recent projections, most machinery imports would be replaced by growth in domestic production. This illustration understates the import drain of machinery, since important intermediate products also originate abroad. There are foreign exchange costs in the Rs. 300 crores figure for 1960–61. But the very large expansion planned in this intermediate goods category suggests that there are possibilities for substitution there also.

Finally, where India exported a very small amount of machinery in 1960–61 (less than Rs. 15 crores), magnitudes twice as great were visualized in 1965–66, and ten to fifteen times as great during the Fifth Plan. In 1975–76, machinery exports alone could thus provide an eighth of the total of exports sufficient to pay for essentially all the imports of a nation which could then continue to grow without foreign assistance.

The very complexity of the industrial structure, with its high inter-industry and intersectoral relationships, imposes specific definition upon the plans. Planned industrial development demands technical knowledge. Expansion in one area, steel, must be coordinated with the supply of coking coal, coal-washing facilities, specialized transport, and other inputs on the output side, as well as on the demand side, with growth in industries which will need more steel. Without such knowledge, it remains difficult to decide where to start expansion or where action will induce other expansion. The needs of planning in industry demand the articulation of input-output tables and the calculation of dynamic capital coefficients. It is India's industrial programs that make the Planning Commission the home of India's promising statisticians and economists. An economy at once committed to freedom, to free markets and to planning discovers crisis problems in industry. The problems of Indian development are at least as much problems of making the plans work as they are the formulation of technically consistent and feasible plans.

## *Achievements*

The industrial achievement has been significant. Output in major industries is a multiple of production in the last pre-plan year: in 1967, finished steel output was 4.5 million tons, in 1951, just below one million; diesel engines were 75,000, as against 5,500; fertilizers (nitrogen content) 235,000 tons, against 9,000 tons; the value of machine tools increased 100 times. Many of the products that now flow from production lines were entirely imported in pre-plan years; tubes, transmitters, electric locomotives, hydrogenerators, heavy electric motors, tractors, mining machinery, and more. Industrial products are helping to reduce the imported percentage in India's new industrial installations, and in their current raw materials and intermediate inputs. They find their way throughout the world. The contribution of modern industry to India's total product has probably reached 15 per cent. The Indian economic scene has literally been transformed through the vigor and diversity of the nation's industrial expansion.

Yet the record is below what was planned. Some 85 per cent of the modern industrial growth projected in the first two plans was actually achieved. A more significant shortfall occurred in the Third Plan years: instead of about doubling, as planned, value added in 1965–66 rose by some 50 per cent above 1960–61. The ratios do not distinguish growth in capacity and in output. The 85 per cent figure for 1951–61 refers mostly to capacity; during the Third Plan the shortfalls were fairly even in capacity and in degree of use. In the past two (Fourth Plan) years, the important characteristic was the degree of underutilization of capacity. Through 1965–66 private enterprise seemed to be able more nearly to achieve officially announced goals (with such notable exceptions as fertilizer) than did public enterprise. The latter moved more slowly than resource availabilities would have permitted.

Increasingly, and especially during the Second Plan, costs began to rise and foreign exchange became more limited. Plans tended to commit completion dates and costs prematurely. There was thus a lag in new capacity, a need for arranging additional financing. Public and private sectors shared in this experience, although public industry had less prior experience on which to draw. Total expansion in industry to date, though significantly below target, seems to have involved total expenditures well above the level projected, even in real terms.

## *Steel and Fertilizer*

Some expansion in existing private steel mill output and some output from a new public mill were anticipated during the First Plan. Relatively little new production was in fact achieved, but plans were made for three one-million-ton public steel mills, as well as for private steel expansion, notably an essential doubling of the output of the Tata mill at Jamshedphur. These became core components of the Second Plan, which set a target of 4.3 million tons of finished steel by 1960–61, 2 million of which were to be in the three public mills. The actual figure in 1960–61 was 2.3 million tons, with 0.6 from the public sector. There were understandable delays in the scheduling of component parts and construction, complicated by the diverse foreign authorities (British, German, Russian) who were integrally part of the individual projects. Money costs turned out to be about double the original plan estimates.

The Third Plan target for finished steel was 6.8 million tons. The vast bulk of this was to come from expanded capacity of the three public mills (Bhilai, Durgapur and Rourkela) plus some very beginnings from the fourth mill in Bokaro. Total production in 1965–66 was actually about 4 million tons. Only the expansion in one mill (the "Russian" mill at Bhilai) was completed; the other two remain in process, delayed partly by problems of financing. After long international discussions on funding possibilities, construction at Bokaro was begun, with Russian cooperation, in 1967. Recent plans projected total steel capacity in India at nearly 15 million tons by 1970–71.

Growth of capacity in steel is primarily a record of public decision and implementation. Delays in plan fulfillment are inevitable aspects of a complicated engineering, financing and administrative task. Though steel has increasingly become a public sector product, about half of total mill output moves into the private sector: price and control policies for steel and for its products influence demand. The patterns of steel output and of steel imports have been senstive to quality and price differentials between Indian and foreign steel products. Changes in government policy on prices and controls since 1963–64 may have been as important as expansion of domestic capacity in reducing the import percentage. But even within the present year, licensing has had to be tightened; imports are authorized only with non-availability certificates from domestic steel producers. While India still anticipates annual imports of 1 to 2 million tons over the next five years, these are meant to be special steels. Exports should increase from their current very low levels to perhaps one million tons by the end of the Fifth Plan.

Production of fertilizer, and especially nitrogenous fertilizer, has been a major objective in India over the entire period of planning. In 1950–51, consumption of nitrogen was about 60,000 tons (N basis), with less than 10,000 tons produced domestically. Capacity of 300,000 tons was set for the First Plan, but less than one-third of this was achieved: actual output of 80,000 tons (N) is reported for 1955–56. Factory construction at Nangal, Neiveli, and Rourkela, scheduled to begin in the First Plan, was actually started during the Second. But some expansion did occur at the government plant at Sindri as well as at smaller private plants. The target for 1960–61 was again set at 300,000 tons, but of the new plants only Nangal was in production by that date. Total output did not quite reach 100,000 tons. Capacity in public plants was originally planned at 800,000 for 1965–66, with a national goal of one million tons. Private capacity was encouraged for expansion of existing and for new facilities. Discussions in the early 1960s were promising in this regard, so that the Third Plan scaled public plants down to some 650,000 tons. During the plan, however, total capacity reached less than 600,000 tons, and actual output in 1965–66 was but 225,000 tons. Very little of this was in private plants; two projects undertaken during the plan are still incomplete. Major public installations at Durgapur and Cochin are now scheduled for 1969. The draft Fourth Plan indicated production of 2 million tons by 1970–71, 4 million by 1975–76.

The record here reflects the indecision of national authorities on agricultural programs: public resources were committed here less enthusiastically than in steel, for example. Private interests were not attracted to an area so dominated by government. The complexity of the process and the extent to which inputs are shared with other industries have made capacity balance difficult for a central planning authority. Thus a major explanation of the gap between nitrogenous fertilizer capacity and output in 1965–66 was inadequate gas availability and power shortages, especially for the Rourkela plant.

India is proceeding with machine building plants as a central cog in her program for industry, overall growth and economic independence. In light machinery—machine tools, textile machinery, boilers, motors—

capacity is already large. But important investments are being made, mostly with foreign assistance, in major heavy industrial machinery complexes. Some of the largest are in machine building (Ranchi), electricals (Bhopal and Hardwar), mining (Durgapur), apart from machine construction intimately associated with the public steel centers. These vast industrial complexes are India's real thrust in the machine-building area. Conceived in the First Plan, and formally initiated in the Second, construction and assembly are now approaching production. Complex machines associated with an advanced stage of industrialization will become available—to replace imports and perhaps to provide new exports. Their ultimate pay-off in the economy cannot yet be appraised.

## *Prospects*

What significance does India's vigorous industrial expansion have for overall development and the prospect of a modern economy able to sustain continuous growth? It is true that performance has to date been below plan, but economic projections for a tradition-bound society "being modernized" are not straightforward tasks. Any answer must compare gains from alternative investment patterns, where projections might also differ from expectations. There is much that is appealing in the "assured" path of self-contained modernization presented by India's planners. The "gains from trade" of economic theory do not identify export possibilities. Traditional agricultural exports could have been expanded, but their relative economic merits over diverse goods from a flourishing industry are debatable. Uncertainties notwithstanding, some effects of India's industrial emphasis can be indicated.

It is possible that the government's concern with expanding industry has meant a relative neglect of agricultural output. While there is some tendency to attribute agricultural adversities to bad weather, official attention to agriculture was in fact stronger in words than in deeds. Nor need the two development efforts be competitive. Indian planners may have felt that industry deserved priority attention because success in industry would also stimulate agricultural output. Thus the greater employment elasticity of industrial expansion might attract labor from rural areas and increase agricultural productivity. Industry's agricultural products (fertilizer, pesticides, agricultural machinery) would enhance agricultural prospects, and an increasing diversity of new consumer goods would stimulate the desire of peasants to produce more.

Actually, industrial expansion turned out to be a reasonably straightforward process, once appropriate authorities decided to proceed. Agricultural expansion requires a decision by millions of entrepreneurs, very many of whom are not geared to commercial market activity. The record shows very diverse movements in output in the two sectors. High prices for food, limited supplies and high prices for raw materials and intermediate goods contributed to higher prices for all manufactures. Domestic terms of trade moved against industry in the Third Plan. High agricultural prices benefited middlemen and wealthy farmers; most farmers consumed their high-value grains and, like most urban consumers, were not buying industrial products. Even this very general presentation indicates the adverse influence of limited agricultural development upon industry. The sequence is in fact a still broader one. The very extensiveness of the labor commitment to agricultural and rural-based activities assures that poor crops mean limited growth in overall national product. There were thus disappointments in tax yields and in government borrowing from the private sector, which in turn had negative repercussions upon demand for industrial products, now on the part of government itself.[3]

While industry has increased its labor force (by 40–50 per cent over the fifteen years) and while industry has expanded investment, it is hard to identify significant derived employment from this expansion. Derived employment, so important to India's total plan of growth, has yet to become apparent. Similarly, the savings ratios in big business seem not to have grown more than savings in other private parts of the economy. As of the early

Fourth Plan, industrial expansion has not revealed itself as a propelling force on other sectors of the economy.

## *Imports*

With respect to industry's effect upon India's foreign economic independence, rapid industrialization initially means more imports—for machinery and parts, for many raw materials and intermediate products. Soon however some of these begin to be domestic; ". . . in machine tools we used to import 91.6 per cent of the total supply in 1950–51, the figure went down to 44.6 per cent in 1964–65";[4] "by the end of the Fourth Plan we would be meeting 75 per cent of a much larger demand."[5] "In sugar machinery the figure has gone down from 100 per cent to 4.1 per cent, textile machinery from 100 to 56.5 per cent" . . . "in petroleum products (other than kerosene) from 91.5 to 1.6 per cent and in aluminum from 74.8 to 29.7 per cent. However, in several cases the total demand has increased so much that in spite of a larger proportion being manufactured indigenously the total imports have tended to increase. In some cases there are substantial imports of components."

> . . . If the programme put forward in this Plan is implemented, the country would have by 1970–71 the capacity to build its own steel mills, fertilizer plants, equipment for power generation, transmission transport and a variety of other equipment.[6]

Still, total imports continue to grow relative to national income except where, as in recent years, the financing arrangements have not permitted the needed imports, with serious consequences for the economy as a whole. Whatever the inroads of domestic production into capital goods imports, the total position warranted a recent official judgment that "the impact [of import substitution] may be small considered in relation to total requirements." Nor has there yet been appreciable export stimulation from industrial output. India's dependence on net assistance has grown relative to total investment requirements. The record of foreign transactions to date does not support the prospect of a closing of the gap during the Fourth and Fifth Plans as revealed in perspective (official) drafts. While they have made allowances for the effects of rupee devaluation in June 1966, they obviously precede Fourth Plan termination in December 1967. In what direction are further changes apt to take place?

For the next decade or more of planning, the first order for success in Indian industry lies in success in Indian agriculture. More than 150 million persons in India's labor force are now more or less directly involved with agriculture's wellbeing. A significant percentage of these cannot be absorbed outside agriculture and rural-oriented work activities in any foreseeable plan period. Present agricultural emphasis on intensive development will need to reach small and poor farmers as well as large and wealthier ones. This is a major effort, still in its beginning stage in India. The key requirement for it lies with government policy, outside of industry; but there is an important complementary dimension that is industrial. Our fertilizer illustration is in point. Other chemicals, diesels, power pumps and electric motors are essential elements in balancing the progress in agricultural technology, seed improvement and irrigation: a better balance would have meant a very different Third Plan experience for the Indian economy. India's diverse industry suffers not only from high food prices and agricultural raw material shortage; of even greater importance is its need for continuous demand for its products. This requires that most of India's people be able to convert their needs into effective demands. This is the core problem in a populous, tradition-bound society. Until India succeeds in this transformation, modern industry will not play a lead sector role in the economy.

Export stimulation deserves higher priority in Indian development schemes. While import substitution for machinery and parts presents a reasonably clear prospect (in concept and in measurement) this is not true for so-called maintenance imports. Success in the former (substitution of machinery) brings new costs to the latter (maintenance imports), as is clearly indicated in the relative increase of the maintenance/project import ratio in recent years. The goal of substitution for maintenance imports may need to await a much more developed stage of industrialization. In the interim plans, the volume of exports must assure these imports. There needs to be a constant searching for new opportunities such as the recent "discovery" of markets for tea in Eastern Europe, new scope for ore shipments to Japan, cables, castings and engineering goods to African lands. The persistent need for export stimulation strengthens the case for maintenance imports when these seem to compete for foreign exchange with new project imports. Recent shifts in International Bank policy to permit financing of maintenance imports are to be commended. (Currently, in fact, new loans are not available for new projects.) Again the "maintenance vs. project" dichotomy illustrates the need for a higher priority for efficient resource use.

## *Prospects*

India's prospective emergence as a significant producer of heavy capital goods will yield benefits only as these products do in fact replace imports. In this regard the pro-foreign bias of Indian industry deserves attention. The record of steel expansion provides illustrations of the extent to which India's development relied upon foreign sources for plates and sheets. This is still the problem of emphasizing capacity use. Competition between use-of-existing vs. creation-of-new is apparent, not real. For efficient output today is the best assurance for continued growth of capacity.

India is making a major investment in industrial capacity. Its extent and scope are bold and imaginative. On the other hand, India is not an automatic recipient of more domestic output, even if it is modern output. Direct efforts are needed to assure that product meets needs, that quality and price will serve that purpose, in India and abroad. The intersectoral links of industry are technologically known, though the appropriate balance of capacity does not automatically assure the appropriate ratios of output. But the links between industry and the rest of the economy are economic. Only when they are joined can Indian industry best serve the nation's total economic expansion.

6

# Pattern of Industrial Development in India

*Ruddar Datt*
*K. P. M. Sundharam*

*From Ruddar Datt and K. P. M. Sundharam,* Indian Economy *(New Delhi: Niraj Prakashan, 1969), p. 483–93, with omissions. Reprinted with permission.*

WHAT HAS BEEN the pattern of industrial development in India? Has it been conducive to economic development? If not, what are the gaps and how can they be reduced? These are crucial questions. We shall consider below the historical evolution of India's industrial structure with a view to locate gaps in it.

Before the rise of the modern industrial system, Indian manufactures had a worldwide market. Indian muslin and calicoes were in great demand the world over. Indian industries not only supplied all local wants but also enabled India to export its finished products. Indian exports consisted chiefly of manufactures like cotton and silk fabrics, calicoes, artistic wares, silk and woollen cloth.

The impact of the British connection and industrial revolution led to the decay of Indian handicrafts. Instead, machine-made goods started pouring into India. The void created by decay of Indian handicrafts was not filled by the rise of modern industry in India because of the British policy of encouraging the import of manufactures and the export of raw materials from India. In the words of Dr. Vera Anstey, "In India there was a much more definite hiatus than in the West between the decay of handicrafts in the eighteenth century and the beginning of modern industry in the middle of the nineteenth century."

After the report of the Industrial Commission (1918), the British government in India provided discriminating protection to some selected industries. This protection was accompanied by the most-favored-nation clause for British goods. Despite this factor, some industries such as cotton textiles, sugar, paper, matches, and to some extent iron and steel did make progress. But one thing is quite obvious that during the British period no effort was made to foster the development of capital goods industries. Rather, the British Government put definite hindrances and cold-shouldered their development. The main features of the industrial pattern in India are as under:

(1) Lop-sided size pattern of industries. The Indian industrial structure till 1956 reflected a lop-sided size pattern. The total number of persons employed in manufacturing in mid-1956 was about 15 million. Out of this, only 3.9 million were employed in factories (as defined by the act as unit of production employing ten or more persons); 11.1 million were employed in household enterprises and workshops employing less than ten persons. The break-up of employment in different size groups of enterprises is given in Table 1.

***Table 1—Size Pattern of Industrial Employment***

| *Description* | *Definition (number employed)* | *Average daily employment in 1956 (million)* | *No. of establishments* |
|---|---|---|---|
| Household enterprises and small workshops | Less than 10 persons | 11.1 | 5,130,000 |
| Small factories | 10–49 persons | 1.2 | 61,000 |
| Medium factories | 50–499 persons | 1.0 | 8,050 |
| Large factories | 500 or more persons | 1.7 | 1,050 |
| Total | | 15.0 | 5,200,100 |



**Notes to chapter 6 appear on page 394**

From the data, it is obvious that out of a total factory employment of 3.9 million persons, 1.2 million or 30.8 per cent is in small factories, 1.0 million or 25.6 per cent is in medium factories and 1.7 million or 43.6 per cent is concentrated in large factories. The peculiarity of industrial pattern of India lies in the fact that there is a high concentration of employment either in small factories and household enterprises, *i.e.*, the lowest size-group or that there is a high concentration of employment in large factories, *i.e.*, highest size group. The medium-sized factories did not develop in India. The existence of this lop-sided industrial pattern is due to the colonial nature of our economy. The foreign firms and those owned by big business and industrial magnates were of a very large size coming at the top of the pyramid, and at the bottom were a very large number of indigenous small size firms. The lop-sidedness of the industrial pattern is reflected in the absence of the middle entrepreneur running medium-size firms.

Another point to be noted in this connection is that the total number of industrial establishments in 1956 was estimated at 52 lakhs. Out of these, 50 lakhs employed less than five persons each, while only 1,050 establishments employed over 500 persons each. Thus, there is a preponderance of small units engaged in manufacturing.

(2) Low capital intensity. Another feature of the Indian industrial pattern is the prevalence of low capital intensity. It is the result of two factors—first, the general level of wages in India is low, and second, the small size of the home market in view of the low capita increase and the limited use of mass production (or high capital intensity) techniques results in low capital per worker employed.

A comparison of the two sets of figures provided by the United Nations reveals that capital employed per worker is very low in India *vis-à-vis* America. Low capital intensity is reflected not only in consumer goods industries like bakery, cloth, sugar, etc., but also in capital goods industries like iron and steel.

(3) Composition of manufacturing output reflects the preponderance of consumer goods industries *vis-à-vis* producer goods industries. In 1953, the ratio of consumer goods to producer goods worked out to be 62:38. The composition of manufacturing output is given in Table 3.

According to the criteria suggested by Hoffman, India seems to have entered the second stage of industrial development. But

### *Table 2—Capital per Worker Employed in Some Industries*[a]

| | *U.S.A.* | *India* |
|---|---|---|
| Alcoholic beverages | 16.0 | 6.1 |
| Bread/bakery products | 5.0 | 3.5 |
| Cotton yarn and cloth | 8.7 | 1.8 |
| Flour and gristmill products | 39.1 | 5.6 |
| Iron and steel | 32.1 | 5.7 |
| Sugar refinery | 26.8 | 2.6 |
| Wood-pulp, paper and paper products | 10.2 | 0.6 |

[a] In thousands of dollars at 1950 prices.

*Source:* United Nations, *Industrialization and Productivity.* Bulletin No. 1, 1958.

### *Table 3—Composition of Manufacturing Output in India, 1953*

| *Commodity group* | *Percentage of total output in manufacturing* | *Index of domestic supplies to domestic output = 100* |
|---|---|---|
| Non-durable consumer goods | 62 | 112 |
| Producer goods (final and intermediate) | 38 | 80 |

even then, there is no doubt that the capital-goods sector is underdeveloped and there is a need for the expansion of this sector so as to ensure a rapid rate of growth, make the economy self-reliant and ultimately foster the pace of industrialization in the country. Only then can per capita income be pushed up at a fast rate.

The second column in Table 3 reveals a structural imbalance in the industrial pattern. In case of consumer goods, domestic supply is more than the demand. The index of domestic supplies of consumer goods is 112 as compared to domestic demand equal to 100. But in case of producer goods, the domestic supplies fall short of domestic demand. The index number of domestic supplies in relation to demand is 80. This increases our dependence on other countries in the capital goods sector. The conclusion is obvious: There is a great need for increasing the output of final and intermediate producer goods so as to correct the imbalance between their demand and supply. Industrial development "is not solely a process of expanding output to meet the rising demand created by growing per capita incomes; it is also a process in which existing demand for manufactures is met increasingly from domestic production instead of from foreign sources."

In short, the industrial pattern in India on the eve of planning was marked by low capital intensity, less development of medium size factory enterprises and imbalance between consumer goods and capital goods industries. It would be of interest to examine the extent to which the Five Year Plans have made an attempt to improve the industrial pattern, correct its lopsidedness and develop the capital goods sector.

## *Industrial Pattern and the Five Year Plans*

The era of planning started from the year 1951. Since then efforts have been made to evolve a suitable industrial pattern which should lead to industrialization of India. The efforts made in the various Five Year Plans to industrialize the economy are briefly discussed below.

### INDUSTRIES AND THE FIRST FIVE YEAR PLAN

During the First Five Year Plan, on account of the limitedness of the resources and because of the small size of the plan and the top priority assigned to agriculture, no big effort was contemplated to industrialize the economy. Rather the emphasis was to build basic services like power and irrigation so that the process of industrialization would be facilitated. In view of the limitation of resources, the First Plan laid down the following priorities:

1. Fuller utilization of existing capacity in producer goods industries like jute and plywood and consumer goods industries like cotton textiles, sugar, soap, vanaspati, paints and varnishes.
2. Expansion of capacity in capital and producer goods industries like iron and steel, aluminium, cement, fertilizers, heavy chemicals, machines, tools, etc.
3. Completion of industrial units on which a part of the capital expenditure had already been incurred.
4. Establishment of new plants which would lend strength to the industrial structure by rectifying as far as resources permited the existing lacunae and drawbacks, *e.g.*, manufacture of sulphur from gypsum, chemical pulp from rayon, etc.

The Industrial Policy Resolution, 1948, was to serve as the basis for the demarcation of public and private sector programs. A total investment of Rs. 707 crores was planned for industry, out of which investment in the public sector was to be of the order of Rs. 94 crores. The break-up of programs in the private sector showed an allocation of Rs. 463 crores on expansion, modernization, replacement and current depreciation and Rs. 150 crores as investment in working capital.

Out of the proposed public sector outlay of Rs. 94 crores, only about Rs. 57 crores were actually spent; and as against the proposed aggregate investment of Rs. 463 crores on new projects, replacements and modernization, only Rs. 340 crores were actually spent. Thus, there were shortfalls in the investment programs both in the public and the private sectors. Shortfalls in public sector outlays were due to the delay in the execution of iron and steel projects and conducting negotiations with foreign countries and firms for financial as well as technical assistance. Shortfall in private sector investment occurred in such industries which required heavy capital investment and offered a relatively small profit margin.

As a result of the efforts made in the First Plan, industrial production recorded a cumulative growth rate of about 7 per cent per annum.

Despite the fact that the First Plan only aimed to utilize the existing capacity to the full, the general index of industrial production recorded an increase of 39 per cent during the five-year period. This was no mean achievement. The progress in cotton textiles and iron and steel was 28 per cent and 22 per cent respectively.

During the First Plan, the Sindri Fertilizer Factory, Chittaranjan Locomotive Factory, Indian Telephone Industries, the Integral Coach Factory, the Cable Factory and the Penicillin Factory were established. Besides, this, Machine Tool Factory, U.P. Cement Factory, Nepa Factory and Bihar Superphosphate Factory were completed. In iron and steel industry, preparatory work for the establishment of three steel plants was completed and expansion of Mysore Iron and Steel Works was undertaken.

### *Table 4—Index Number of Industrial Production*[a]

| *Group* | *1955–56* |
|---|---|
| General index | 139 |
| Cotton textiles | 128 |
| Iron and steel | 122 |
| Machinery (all types) | 192 |
| Chemicals | 179 |

[a] 1950–51 × 100.

*Source: Third Five Year Plan,* p. 39.

The First Plan, therefore, was a modest effort on the industrial front. It did help to boost up industrial production but a big effort to develop the basic and heavy industries to lay the foundations for the industrial structure of the economy was still to be made. The development of village and small industries was also accorded a low priority, as only a sum of Rs. 43 crores (or 2 per cent of total plan expenditure) was devoted to their expansion. The limitation of resources was the principal factor in this regard as well.

## INDUSTRIES AND THE SECOND FIVE YEAR PLAN

The Second Five Year Plan program for industrialization was based on the Industrial

### *Table 5—Actual Outlay and Investment on Industries during the Second Plan*[a]

| | *Total Investment* | | |
|---|---|---|---|
| | *Public* | *Private* | *Total* |
| Organized industry and minerals | 870 | 675 | 1545 |
| Village and small industries | 90 | 175 | 265 |
| Total | 960 | 850 | 1,810 |

[a] In Rs. crores.

*Source: Third Five Year Plan,* p. 59.

Policy Resolution of 1956 which envisaged a big expansion of the public sector. Total outlay on industrial development in the public sector was proposed to be Rs. 890 crores, *i.e.*, 18.5 per cent of the total plan expenditure.

The actual outlay in the public sector on organized industry was about Rs. 900 crores, out of which Rs. 870 crores represented investment. Private sector investment was Rs. 675 crores during the Second Plan period —more than envisaged in the Plan. Similarly, investment in village and small industries was Rs. 265 crores (in both public and private sectors). Taken together, total investment in industries was Rs. 1,810 crores, *i.e.*, 27 per cent of the total investment during the Second Plan.

The industrial pattern sought to be developed during the Second Plan was conceived in terms of the following priorities:

1. Increased production of iron and steel and of heavy chemicals, including nitrogenous fertilizers, and development of the heavy engineering and machine building industries.
2. Expansion of capacity in respect of other developmental commodities and producer goods such as aluminium, cement, chemical pulp, dyestuffs and phosphatic fertilizers; and of essential drugs.
3. Modernization and re-equipment of important national industries which have already come into existence such as jute and cotton textiles and sugar.
4. Fuller utilization of existing installed capacity in industries where there are gaps between capacity and production.
5. Expansion of capacity of consumer goods keeping in view the requirements of common production programs and the production targets for the decentralized sector of industry.

During the Second Plan, a major task in industry was the building up of three steel plants of one million tons ingot capacity each in the public sector, and the production of 350,000 tons of foundry grade pig iron. The three steel plants are: Rourkela Steel Plant in Bihar estimated to cost Rs. 128 crores; Bhilai Steel Plant in Madhya Pradesh estimated to cost Rs. 110 crores and Durgapur Steel Plant in West Bengal estimated to cost Rs. 115 crores. Besides the three steel plants, the capacity of Mysore Iron and Steel Works was to be expanded.

The other programs of industrial development included the manufacture of electrical equipment, expansion of Hindustan Machine Tools, expansion of Sindri Fertilizer factory and the establishment of a fertilizer plant at Nangal, further expansion of Hindustan Shipyard and Chittaranjan Locomotives factory. Among light and medium industries in the public sector were D.D.T. and antibiotic factories, establishment of a second D.D.T. plant at Travancore-Cochin, the expansion of Hindustan Cables Ltd., the National Instruments Factory and Indian Telephone Industries.

A review of the progress during the Second Plan period revealed that the index of industrial production rose from 139 in 1955–56 to 194 in 1960–61.

Most of the investments in the Second Plan were in heavy and basic industries. Steel ingot production rose from 1.4 million tons in 1950–51 to 3.5 million tons in 1960–61. Besides this, there has been a rapid expansion of machine-building industries for use in

### *Table 6—Index Number of Industrial Production*[a]

| *Group* | *1955–56* | *1960–61* |
|---|---|---|
| General index | 139 | 194 |
| Cotton textiles | 128 | 133 |
| Iron | 122 | 238 |
| Machinery (all types) | 192 | 503 |
| Chemicals | 179 | 288 |

[a] 1950–51 = 100.

agriculture and transport and for such industries as chemicals, textiles, jute, cement, tea, sugar, flour and oil mills, paper, mining, etc. Good progress was also recorded in modernization and re-equipment of important industries such as jute, cotton textile and sugar. Quite a number of new industrial items, *e.g.*, industrial boilers, milling machines, tractors, motor cycles, scooters, etc., were also produced in large quantity. Consumer goods industries such as textiles and sugar recorded substantial progress. Rapid progress was achieved in durable consumer goods industries such as scooters, bicycles, electric fans, heaters, electric lamps, sewing machines, etc.

In the sphere of village and small industries, substantial progress was recorded. About 60 industrial estates comprising 1,000 small factories were set up. The period also witnessed the rise of a vigorous class of small entrepreneurs. In a number of items such as machine tools, sewing machines, electric motors, fans, bicycles, hand tools, etc., production increased from 25 to 50 per cent during the five-year period. Khadi, handloom and powerloom cloth production increased from 1,773 million yards in 1955–56 to 2,349 million yards in 1960–61.

### INDUSTRIES AND THE THIRD FIVE YEAR PLAN

The Second Five Year Plan by emphasizing the development of heavy and basic industries tried to strengthen the industrial base of the economy. The purpose of the Third Plan is to further the expansion of industries, especially capital and producers goods—with special emphasis on machine-building and development of managerial skill, technical know-how, etc. With this broad pattern, the Third Plan laid down the following priorities:

1. Completion of projects envisaged under the Second Five Year Plan which are under implementation or were deferred during 1957–58 owing to foreign exchange difficulties.
2. Expansion and diversification of capacity of the heavy engineering and machine-building industries, castings and forgings, alloy tools and special steels, iron and steel and ferro-alloys and stepping-up of output of fertilizers and petroleum products.
3. Increased production of major basic raw materials and producer goods like aluminum, mineral oils, dissolving pulp, basic organic and inorganic chemicals and intermediates inclusive of products of petro-chemical origin.
4. Increased production from domestic industries of commodities required to meet essential needs like essential drugs, paper, cloth, sugar, vegetable oils and housing material.

*Programs of Industrial Development*—The Third Plan proposed a total investment of Rs. 2,720 crores in the public and private sectors, out of which the public sector component of investment will be of the order of Rs. 1,520 crores and the private sector investment of the order of Rs. 1,050 crores. In addition to this, Rs. 150 crores will be forthcoming for replacement and modernization in certain pre-war industries.

The key role in industrial development programs belongs to the public sector. The aim is to make the economy self-sustaining in producer goods industries such as steel, machine-building, etc., so that the quantum of external assistance needed can be curtailed to a very low level. Expansion of production of consumer goods on a significant scale will be carried out in the private sector. An overall target of 70 per cent increase in industrial production is envisaged in the plan.

The targets as set out in the Third Plan are as given in Table 7.

A total investment of Rs. 425 crores has been allocated in the Third Plan for the development of village and small industries —Rs. 150 crores in the public sector and Rs. 275 crores in the private sector. The principal objective in this field is to provide more employment and increased production of consumer goods and some producer goods. It is proposed to set up 300 new industrial estates. Similarly, the production of Khadi, handloom and power-loom is expected to increase from 2,350 million yards to 3,500 million yards.

The overall financial outlay in organized industries and mining during the Third Plan period is now placed at Rs. 3,000 crores of which the outlay in the public sector is at about Rs. 1,700 crores and that in the private sector Rs. 1,300 crores. This is somewhat higher than the outlay of Rs. 2,720 crores—Rs. 1,520 crores in the public sector and Rs. 1,200 crores in the private sector—originally envisaged. The upward revision of costs was due to the availability of more reliable information, a general increase in construction costs and enlargement of the scope of some of the projects. However, the monetary outlay does not represent the full physical accomplishments.

But for 1965–66, industrial output increased steadily at the rate of 7.8 per cent per annum. The actual increase stood at 7 per cent in 1961–62, 7.7 per cent in 1962–63, 8.5 per cent in 1963–64, 7 per cent in 1964–65 and about 4 per cent in 1965–66. The achievement is lower than the average of 14 per cent per annum visualized in the plan. Although the increase in the output of producer and basic industries is higher than the actual growth in the general index of production yet it is much lower than the target set out in the Third Plan. But the growth of output in two major consumer goods industries—textiles and sugar—was barely 20 per cent and 13 per cent respectively during the entire plan period. Similarly, fertilizer production program has lagged behind the schedule. As against a target of 10.2 million tons the production of steel ingots rose to barely 6.2 million tons in 1965–66. Another disquieting feature has been the rise in the prices of essential consumer goods such as common varieties of textiles, sugar, kerosene, drugs, paper, etc. In short, there is an overall underachievement of targets in the industrial field in the Third Plan.

**Table 7—Targets of Industrial Production in Third Plan**[a]

| Group | 1960–61 | 1965–66 | Percentage increase in plan period |
|---|---|---|---|
| General Index | 194 | 329 | 70 |
| Cotton textiles | 133 | 157 | 18 |
| Iron and steel | 238 | 637 | 168 |
| Machinery (all types) | 503 | 1,224 | 143 |
| Chemicals | 288 | 720 | 150 |

[a] 1950–51 = 100.

*Source: Third Five Year Plan*, p. 64.

## *Industrial Development in India Since 1947—A Resume*

After a period of eighteen years of planning, it is relevant to have a stock-taking of the gains of the policies pursued so far, as

**Table 8—Structural Transformation of Indian Industries**

| INDUSTRIES | NET VALUE ADDED AT 1960–61 PRICES (RS. CRORES) | | Percentages | |
|---|---|---|---|---|
| | 1950–51 | 1965–66 | 1950–51 | 1965–66 |
| Consumer goods | 260.7 | 487.6 | 67.9 | 34.0 |
| Intermediate goods | 89.5 | 620.2 | 23.3 | 43.3 |
| Machinery | 30.9 | 315.9 | 8.0 | 22.0 |
| Others | 3.1 | 10.3 | 0.8 | 0.7 |
| Total | 384.2 | 1,434.0 | 100.0 | 100.0 |

*Source: Commerce Annual* 1968, p. 281.

also to note the deficiencies in planning policies aimed at the industrialization of the economy. The major gains of the industrial programs are as under:

Firstly, between 1951 and 1968, the index of industrial production registered an increase of 177 per cent. If we add to this 7 per cent increase in industrial production during 1968 we find that the growth rate of industrial production during the period 1951–68 works out to be 6.6 per cent per annum. During the First Plan, although the allocation to industry was very small, an increase of 41 per cent in industrial output was secured by better utilization of capacity. During the subsequent period, (1956–68) increases in industrial output were secured largely by creation of new capacity. During 1965–66 and 1966–67, the tempo of industrialization was slackened by the recession. Among the principal causes of recession were the cut-back in agricultural production as a consequence of drought, the reduction in government outlay and the erosion in the saving potential of the community as a result of inflation.

Secondly, during the period of planning, the structure of industries changed in favor of the machinery and capital goods sector. During 1950–51 and 1965–66, the share of machinery rose from 8 per cent to 22 per cent in value added by the manufacturing sector and that of intermediate goods from 23.3 per cent to 43.3 per cent. As against it, the share of consumer goods declined from 67.9 per cent to 34 per cent. In a nut-shell, a host of new industries hitherto unknown have come up. They include chemical fertilizers, locomotives, heavy and basic industries, machine tools, engineering goods, metallurgical industries, etc. However, rate of progress recorded in traditional industries—cotton textiles, jute, paper, sugar etc.—was relatively slow.

Thirdly, there is a widespread absorption of modern technology in the industrial sector. A measure of technological change consequent upon modernization is a change in the capital intensity. Since data on the stock of capital is defective, mainly because no time series at one set of prices is available, and also because the unscientific methods of measuring capital consumption through permissible rates of depreciation distort the analysis, capital-output ratios and capital-labor ratios are of little help. But the fact that electricity consumption per worker has increased from 1,477 Kw. in 1951 to 4,941 Kw. in 1966–67 is a good index of increase in capital intensity.

Fourthly, during the planning period, the country has been able to train a cadre of technical manpower which can handle cement factories, chemical fertilizer units (including plants), oil refineries, power houses, steel plants, locomotive factories, engineering industries, etc. About 1.6 lakh diploma holders are turned out by the technical institutions. Similarly, in-plant training and sending brilliant young men and women abroad for training in top skills has helped to generate skilled manpower and thus reduce dependence on foreign technicians and experts.

Lastly, there is the growth of the public sector on a big scale in the heavy and basic industries, the machine goods sector, engineering industries, etc. During the eighteen-year period of planning, Rs. 4,500 crores have been invested in the public sector on industry. The enlargement of the public sector is an index of the contribution of the government in the industrial growth of the economy. Besides this, the investment in the infrastructure—power, transport and communication, etc.—by the government is of the order of Rs. 8,000 crores during the same period.

### INADEQUACIES OF THE PROGRAMS OF INDUSTRIALIZATION

Without under-estimating the achievements of the process of industrial expansion initiated during the planning era, it may be emphasized that much of the industrial growth is only a myth. Our reasons for this are as under:

Firstly, it is unfair to consider that the index of industrial production is an adequate measure of industrial growth since it covers the factory sector alone. It is legitimate to add the production of the small scale sector. When a correct index of industrial production which is inclusive of the total real domestic product originating in mining and manufacturing sector is worked out, the growth of industrial production is reduced to 88 per cent during 1951 and 1968. This gives a growth rate of industrial production as 4 per cent per annum. Adjusting this to the growth rate of population which was 41 per cent during the period under reference, index of real per capita increase in industrial output just works out to be 33 per cent during the entire period, or barely 1.8 per cent per annum. Thus, industrialization has not resulted in a significant increase in per capita industrial output in the manufacturing sector as a whole.

Secondly, the share of industry in national income in 1948–49 was 17 per cent. As against it, in 1966–67, it has risen to 20 per cent. Even in terms of contribution to national product, the share of the manufacturing industry sector continues to be low. In most of the developed nations, this share is between 30 to 50 per cent.

Thirdly, the process of industrialization has not been able to make a dent on the problem of unemployment. During 1951–67, total labor force increased by 470 lakhs, but factory employment absorbed only 2 per cent of the increase in the labor force. Total labor force engaged in mining, manufacturing and construction in 1966–67 was 10.7 per cent. This includes 7.2 per cent of the labor force engaged in small scale industries. In the developed countries of the world, labor force engaged in manufacturing ranges between 30 to 50 per cent. Obviously, industrialization has not been able to make any serious impact on the problem of unemployment.

Professor Gunnar Myrdal studies the spread effects of industrialization on employment and also its back-wash effects in terms of unemployment on the traditional sector. Myrdal, after a careful examination of the situation, observes: "the employment effects of industrialization cannot be expected to be very large for several decades ahead, that is, until the region is much more industrialized. For a considerable time the net employment effects may even be negative. This dimension of the problem, as well as the wider consequences for labor utilization outside the modern sector, is overlooked in the vision that sees industrialization as the remedy for "unemployment" and "underemployment".[1] George Rosen, after studying the capital-labor coefficients in India's five major industries—cement, paper, iron and steel, sugar and textiles—reaches the same conclusion. To quote: "Even doubling the labor per unit of investment, as compared with the coefficients computed . . . would only increase the labor force in the five industries studied by about 100,000 more workers than projected in the Second Plan, assuming the same investment plans; the effect upon all organized manufacturing industry would increase employment in all factory manufacturing industries by less than one million workers in the Second Plan period (in contrast to a projected expansion in the labor force by ten million workers). Investment in this sector has today probably one of the lowest direct employment-expansion effects, compared with an equal investment within other sectors of the economy."[2]

Fourthly, the big business houses have been able to mold the licensing policies of the government in their favor and thus pre-empt licensing capacity. Although the 1956 industrial policy clearly underlined the need for prevention of monopoly and concentration of economic power, available evidence suggests that big business has gained enormously in the planning period. This has been brought out in the Monopolies Inquiry Commission Report by Mr. R. K. Hazari. The three big business houses which gained the most are: the Tatas, the Birlas and the Mafatlals. "In absolute terms the assets of Tata Group in 1966–67 were Rs. 551 crores, of the Birla Group Rs. 510 crores and of Mafatlal only Rs. 127 crores. The increase in assets recorded by the Mafatlal Group over the three year period (1963–64 to 1966–67) was Rs. 81 crores in absolute terms. The comparable figures for the Tata Group was about Rs. 133 crores and the Birla Group Rs. 217 crores."[3]

To sum up, the programs of industrialization have not generated sufficient growth potential either in terms of contribution of output or in terms of employment. The question of choice of techniques has, therefore, to be examined anew with reference to employment which should legitimately get a key position in any meaningful program of industrialization. Similarly, the implications of industrial programs and policies in terms of concentration of economic power and growth of monopolies have to be thoroughly examined so that our goals of establishing a socialist pattern of society are not mutilated.

7

# Chinese Communist Industrial Production

*Robert Michael Field*

*From* An Economic Profile of Mainland China, Vol. I, *Studies Prepared for the Joint Economic Committee, Congress of the United States, February 1967, U.S. Government Printing Office, pp. 271–77 and 283–85, with omissions. Reprinted by permission.*

## *Introduction*

TAKING TO HEART Lenin's admonition that only through industrialization could China become a socialist state, the Chinese Communists made the development of heavy industry the core of their First Five-Year Plan (1953–57). The rapid growth of heavy industry was to provide the material base for national defense, for the well-being of the people, and for still further increases in industrial capacity. The goal of industrialization soon became identified with overtaking Great Britain in the absolute level of industrial production. In 1958, with the optimism of the Great Leap Forward, the Chinese expected to achieve their goal in fifteen years. More recently they have said that it may take from thirty to fifty years, but the goal is the same: To convert China, step by step, from a backward, agricultural country into an advanced, socialist, industrial state.

This paper will present an independently constructed index of total industrial production in Communist China for 1949–65. Although data on the output of specific military items were not available, these items had to be included in the index by imputation, because the weights could not be adjusted satisfactorily to exclude military production. Because most military production is concentrated in the metal processing industry, the assumption implicit in the construction of the index is that the military component of the metal processing industry grew at the same rate as the civilian component. However, if the weight for the metal processing industry could have been adjusted, the rate of growth shown by the resulting index of civilian industrial production would have been lower than that of the index presented in this paper. On the other hand, if military production could have been included explicitly, the indexes for the metal processing industry and for total industrial production both would have been raised.

## *Summary of the Growth of Industrial Production*

Industrial production in Communist China, as measured by the index presented in this paper, grew rapidly during the years 1949–65, at an average annual rate of 11 per cent, but the differences from year to year and by branch of industry were extreme. My index and the official Chinese Communist index for total industrial production, industry, and handicrafts are shown in Table 1. The average annual rates of growth for individual branches of industry for the years 1950–52, 1953–57, and 1958–59 are presented in Table 2; and the structure of industrial production in 1949, 1952, 1957, and 1959 is presented in Table 3. It was not possible to calculate the rates of growth by branch of industry or the structure of industrial production for the years since 1959 because of the lack of data.

### ECONOMIC REHABILITATION, 1949–52

During the period of economic rehabilitation (1949–52), my index shows that industrial production more than doubled, growing at an average annual rate of 27 per cent. This rapid rate of growth was characterized by large increases in employment, but little or no growth in the net value of fixed capital assets. The capacity damaged by the war or lost through the Soviet removal of equipment from Manchuria in 1945 was repaired or replaced and put back into operation, and supplies of raw materials were improved. Industry grew at an average annual rate of 35 per cent and handicrafts at 8 per cent.

Within industry, the rates of growth ranged from 19 per cent in the electric power industry to 110 per cent in the ferrous metals industry. The branches of industry producing industrial materials, such as ferrous metals, chemical processing, and building materials,

### *Table 1—Indexes of Industrial Production in Communist China*[a]

| | *Field* | | | *Official*[b] | | |
|---|---|---|---|---|---|---|
| | *TOTAL* | *INDUSTRY* | *HANDI-CRAFTS* | *TOTAL* | *INDUSTRY* | *HANDI-CRAFTS* |
| 1949 | 27.2 | 21.8 | 56.9 | 19.9 | 18.4 | 27.7 |
| 1950 | 34.3 | 29.0 | 64.2 | 27.2 | 24.0 | 43.2 |
| 1951 | 45.6 | 41.2 | 70.2 | 37.5 | 34.5 | 52.5 |
| 1952 | 56.1 | 53.1 | 72.3 | 48.8 | 46.1 | 62.5 |
| 1953 | 70.2 | 65.2 | 97.9 | 63.5 | 60.6 | 77.9 |
| 1954 | 80.2 | 76.0 | 103.7 | 73.9 | 70.8 | 89.4 |
| 1955 | 80.7 | 78.8 | 91.2 | 78.0 | 76.3 | 86.5 |
| 1956 | 100.0 | 100.0 | 100.0 | 100.0 | 100.0 | 100.0 |
| 1957 | 109.4 | 111.0 | 100.2 | 111.4 | 110.8 | 114.3 |
| 1958 | 143.8 | 149.8 | 110.2 | 185.2 | | |
| 1959 | 181.6 | 192.4 | 121.3 | [c]257.9 | | |
| 1960 | 188.5 | | | [d]332.3 | | |
| 1961 | 124.5 | | | | | |
| 1962 | 109.6 | | | | | |
| 1963 | 120.7 | | | [e]184.0 | [f]198.7 | [g]110.7 |
| 1964 | 134.9 | | | [h]211.6 | | |
| 1965 | 147.6 | | | [i]234.9 | | |

[a] 1956 = 100.
[b] State Statistical Bureau, *Ten Great Years*, Peiping, 1960, pp. 87 and 94, except as noted.
[c] *Press Communique on the Growth of China's National Economy in 1959*, Peiping, 1960, p. 1.
[d] Planned. Li Fu-ch'un, "Report on the Draft Plan for 1959," *Jen-min jih-pao* (*People's Daily*), Mar. 31, 1960.
[e] Derived from the statement that the gross value of handicraft output was about 10 per cent of the gross value of total industrial production. See "Consolidate and Enhance Handicraft Cooperatives in Order to Actively Develop Handicraft Production," editorial, *Jen-min fih-pao* (*People's Daily*), Oct. 27, 1963. For the gross value of handicraft output, see footnote *g* below.
[f] Derived from the gross value of industrial output, which is the difference between the gross value of total industrial production and the gross value of handicraft output.
[g] Derived from the statement that the gross value of handicraft output was more than 4 times that of 1949. See T'ien P'ing, "Great Changes in the Handicraft Industry in the Past Fifteen Years," *Ta-kung pao* (*Impartial Daily*), Oct. 9, 1964. For the gross value of handicraft output in 1949, see footnote *b*, above.
[h] Derived from the 15 per cent increase reported in Chou En-lai's speech to the 1st session of the 3rd National People's Congress on Dec. 21–22, 1964. See American Consulate General, Hong Kong, *Survey of China Mainland Press* No. 3370, Jan. 5, 1965.
[i] Planned. Derived from the planned increase of 11 per cent. See *ibid.*

### *Table 2—Average Annual Rates of Growth of Industrial Production*

| | *1950–52* | *1953–57* | *1958–59* |
|---|---|---|---|
| Total industrial production | 27 | 14 | 29 |
| Industry | 35 | 16 | 32 |
| Electric power | 19 | 22 | 46 |
| Coal | 27 | 14 | 41 |
| Petroleum | 53 | 27 | 59 |
| Ferrous metals | 110 | 31 | 41 |
| Metal processing | 43 | 19 | 39 |
| Chemical processing | 60 | 26 | 40 |
| Building materials | 63 | 19 | 34 |
| Timber | 28 | 20 | 22 |
| Paper | 51 | 20 | 33 |
| Textiles | 36 | 9 | 26 |
| Food | 22 | 12 | 15 |
| Handicrafts | 8 | 7 | 10 |

had the highest rates of growth. These branches were followed by the metal processing industry and then less closely by the fuels and the light industries. Although the growth of the fuels and light industries was relatively slow, the rates achieved were quite high.

There are no reliable indexes of industrial production by branch of industry for the pre-Communist period with which my indexes for the period of economic recovery can be linked, but the production of key industrial commodities may be used as a rough measure. A comparison of the rates of growth shown by individual branches of industry for the years 1950–52 and the percentage decline in the production of key commodities from their peak to the level of output achieved in 1949 shows an inverse relationship. It is clear, therefore, that the rapid growth of total industrial production in this period represents a return to previously achieved levels of output rather than a growth in the productive capacity of industry and that the differences in the rates of growth shown by individual branches of industry are closely related to the extent to which production had fallen from the pre-Communist peak levels.

### THE FIRST FIVE-YEAR PLAN, 1953–57

During the First Five-Year Plan (1953–57), industrial production is estimated to have doubled again, reaching a level more than four times that of 1949, but the rate of growth was slower and less steady than it had been during the period of economic rehabilitation. Although averaging 14 per cent, the annual increases ranged from less than 1 per cent in 1955 to 25 per cent in 1953.

The large increase in output in 1953 resulted from a 9 per cent increase in the net value of fixed capital assets and an increase of 16 per cent in the average number of workers. The relatively slow growth in capital assets and the rapid growth in employment, however, are more typical of the period of economic rehabilitation than they are of the rest of the First Five-Year Plan, when capital assets increased at a rate in excess of 20 per cent annually, but employment increased at only 7 per cent. These data, together with fragmentary data on the

***Table 3—Structure of Industrial Production in Communist China***[a]

(Percent of value added)

| | *1949* | *1952* | *1957* | *1959* |
|---|---|---|---|---|
| Total industrial production | 100 | 100 | 100 | 100 |
| Industry | 68 | 80 | 86 | 90 |
| Electric power | 2 | 1 | 2 | 3 |
| Coal | 11 | 11 | 1 | 13 |
| Petroleum | ([b]) | 1 | 1 | 1 |
| Ferrous metals | 1 | 3 | 6 | 7 |
| Metal processing | 9 | 13 | 16 | 19 |
| Chemical processing | 1 | 2 | 3 | 3 |
| Building materials | 3 | 7 | 8 | 9 |
| Timber | 5 | 5 | 6 | 5 |
| Paper | 1 | 1 | 1 | 1 |
| Textiles | 16 | 20 | 15 | 15 |
| Food | 20 | 17 | 16 | 13 |
| Handicrafts | 32 | 20 | 14 | 10 |

[a] Because of rounding, components may not add to the totals shown.
[b] Negligible.

continued increase in the intensity with which existing capacity was used, indicate that the large increase in output achieved in 1953 was a continuation of the rapid growth achieved during the period of economic rehabilitation and tend to suggest that the pre-Communist peak level of production was not reached until 1953. Because 1953 was really part of the period of economic rehabilitation, the average annual rate of growth of 12 per cent achieved during the years 1954–57 is a better measure of industrial growth in China than the rate for the First Five-Year Plan as a whole.

During the five-year period, industry grew at an average annual rate of 16 per cent and handicrafts at a rate of 7 per cent. Within industry, the rates of growth for individual branches were lower and the range in the rates was narrower than it had been during the period of rehabilitation, varying from 9 per cent in the textile industry to 31 per cent in the ferrous metals industry. The general pattern of the rates of growth shown during the First Five-Year Plan was much the same as it had been during the period of recovery, the most marked change being the relative improvement in the rates of growth shown by the fuels industries.

Different factors determined the general pattern of growth in the two periods. Whereas the relative rates of growth during the period of rehabilitation had been determined largely by the extent to which the disruption of production has been repaired, the pattern of growth during the First Five-Year Plan was the result of investment-policy decisions made by the Chinese Communist regime. Since the regime decided to adopt the Soviet model of industrialization and concentrated investment in heavy industry, heavy industry, quite naturally, grew more rapidly than light.

### THE LEAP FORWARD, 1958–60

During the Leap Forward (1958–60), the average annual rate of growth in industrial production surged to 20 per cent. This growth was accompanied by a massive increase in industrial employment and by mass emulation campaigns requiring an intensity of work that could not be maintained. The rate of growth dropped from 31 per cent in 1958 to 26 per cent in 1959 and only 4 per cent in 1960.

Most of the growth in industrial production during the years 1958–60 would have occurred, even without a Leap Forward. The acceleration of the existing industrial construction program during 1958 and 1959 resulted in large additions to capacity and a rapid growth in the net value of fixed capital assets. For example, of the 921 major industrial construction projects started during the First Five-Year Plan, 428 were completed and in normal operation by the end of 1957, and 109 went into partial operation. But in 1958 alone, a large number of new construction projects were started and 500 were completed. Merely putting these new plants into operation would have been enough to guarantee China substantial gains in industrial production. The true accomplishments in industry during these 3 years, therefore, were achieved in spite of the excesses of the Leap Forward.

In 1958–59, industry grew at an average annual rate of 32 per cent and handicrafts at 10 per cent. Within industry, the rates of growth were nearly as high as those achieved during the period of economic rehabilitation, but the range was not as wide. The highest rate of growth was shown by the petroleum industry, which grew at 59 per cent, and the lowest was shown by the food industry, which grew at 15 per cent. The most striking change in the pattern of rates of growth shown by the individual branches of industry was the rise in the position of the fuels industries. Ranking the branches of industry by the rates of growth shown during the period of rehabilitation, the First Five-Year Plan, and the Leap Forward, it can be seen that the petroleum industry rose from fourth place in 1950–52 to become the fastest growing branch of industry during the Leap Forward. The electric power industry rose from eleventh place to second, and the coal industry from ninth to third. Thus, the fuels industries became the three fastest growing branches of industry.

### RECOVERY AND READJUSTMENT, 1961–65

Total industrial production fell sharply in 1961 and continued to fall, although less sharply, in 1962. Production in 1962 was slightly above the level of 1957 but only about 60 per cent of the peak reached in 1960. After the withdrawal of the Soviet technicians in mid-1960, the Chinese found they could not operate many of the key industrial plants that had been built as Soviet aid projects and were forced to close them down. In light industry, the levels of output achieved during the Leap Forward could not be maintained because of the failure of agriculture to supply needed raw materials. Even without these blows to the economy, however, the dislocation of industry, the exhaustion of the labor force, and the crisis in the food supply would probably have been severe enough to cause the collapse of the Leap Forward.

With the adoption of more pragmatic policies in 1962, industry began to recover. In each year since 1962, total industrial production has increased by about 10 per cent, reaching in 1965 a level slightly higher than that of 1958. This growth, however, has been achieved by the gradual reemployment of capacity that had been installed during or prior to the Leap Forward rather than by the addition of new productive capacity. Because almost all idle capacity has now been put back into production, and because few capital construction projects have been undertaken since 1960, further increases in output will be more difficult to achieve than those of the three years, 1963–65.

The number of output series available for the years since 1960 is not large enough to permit estimates for individual branches of industry, but the series do indicate the general pattern of growth. The output of primary energy is now about the level of 1958, but it is still far below the peak level of 1960. The relative importance of the various sources of energy has changed. Although coal still provides the bulk of the primary energy, it has declined in relative importance. In 1957 coal supplied 95 per cent of all primary energy, but in 1965 it supplied only 91 per cent. Petroleum has risen from 2 per cent in 1957 to 6 per cent in 1965, and water power has remained at about 3 per cent.

By far the most spectacular performance in the field of industrial materials has been shown by the chemical processing industry. The output of chemical fertilizer in 1965 was more than five times that of 1957 and nearly double the previous peak level of 1960, and the Chinese claim that by 1963 the chemical processing industry had become the fourth largest branch, having risen from seventh place in 1952. The output of most industrial materials, however, is not yet back to the peak levels of 1959 or 1960. The output of crude steel in 1965 was about equal to the volume of usable steel produced in 1959, and the output of cement and timber were at about the levels of 1958.

There are not sufficient data to make a precise estimate for the metal processing industry. Output is certainly well above the level of 1957, but has probably not yet reached the level of 1958. Output may be on the order of 30 to 40 per cent greater than that of 1957. On balance, the output of heavy industry as a whole in 1965 had not yet reached the level of 1959, although it probably exceeded the level of 1958.

The level of output in light industry has recovered more slowly than heavy industry, because of the failure of agriculture to provide an adequate supply of raw materials. The output of paper in 1965 was about 25 per cent above the level of 1957 but still nearly 10 per cent below that of 1958. The output of cotton cloth was less than 80 per cent of the output achieved in 1957. Although the output of woolen and silk cloth has recovered more rapidly than that of cotton cloth and may be approaching peak levels, the textile industry as a whole is probably still below the level of 1957, because of the importance of cotton cloth. The food industry has recovered more rapidly than the textile industry. The output of sugar has already exceeded the previous peak level achieved in 1959. Sugar, however, is not typical of the food industry as a whole.

The aggregate output of the food industry is certainly above the level of 1957 but has probably not yet reached the level of 1958. On balance, the output of light industry as a whole in 1965 was probably only slightly higher than the level of 1957.

## *The Prospects for Industry During the Third Five Year Plan, 1966–70*

The prospects for industry in Communist China during the Third Five-Year Plan (1966–70) are a matter of great concern, not only in China, but throughout the Western World. The current political turmoil in China, however, makes any attempt to forecast the growth of industrial production over the next five years unusually hazardous.

The current cultural revolution was not originally planned for economic reasons. Important documents such as the *Decision of the Central Committee of the Chinese Communist Party on the Great Proletarian Cultural Revolution* or the *Communique* of the Eleventh Plenary Session of the Central Committee (held on August 1–12, 1966) make only passing references to economic matters. But there are already rumors to the effect that production has declined, at least in some enterprises, because of the time and energy required of managers and workers alike for demonstrations, parades, and endless meetings to discuss the thought of Mao Tse-tung.

Since early September 1966, the regime has been concerned with the impact of the cultural revolution on production. The front-page editorial in *Jen-min jih-pao* on September 7 stated that production must not be interrupted. Workers were instructed to stay at their jobs, and the Red Guards were cautioned not to interfere. The frequency with which these themes have been repeated by national and provincial news media indicates that the concern is genuine. Production has been affected already, but it is not yet clear whether the cultural revolution will spill over directly into the field of economics. Statements such as the following have appeared frequently in the Chinese press:

> The unprecedented scale of the present great cultural revolution necessarily presages a flying leap in the development of our Socialist revolution and a new Great Leap Forward in Socialist construction.

The tone of these statements has led to the speculation that the Third Five-Year Plan may be superseded just as the Second Five-Year Plan was superseded by the Leap Forward.

If a new Leap were in the making, one would expect to see drastic increases in targets and production claims, and in fact, recent claims are strongly reminiscent of those made in 1958 and 1959. For example, the claims that industrial production in the first eight months of 1966 increased by 20 per cent over the corresponding period of last year and that the increase in the output of various industrial commodities ranged from 40 to 200 per cent appear to be unreasonably high. But there is, as yet, no evidence that targets have been raised.

On balance, it does not now appear likely that the Chinese Communists will attempt a new Leap, but given the current political instability, it is not impossible. If they did, however, it would be doomed to failure. Industrial production might spurt ahead briefly, but any new Leap would undoubtedly collapse. The collapse would be worse than that of 1961–62 because the Chinese do not have the cushion now that they had in 1958 and the population has increased by some 100 million persons.

Industrial production has increased at about 10 per cent annually during the last three years and has regained the level achieved in 1958, but even without a new Leap Forward or the disruptions of the cultural revolution, the Chinese would not be able to maintain such a high rate of growth. The increases in production during this period of readjustment have been based on the reemployment of existing capacity. Very little new capacity has been installed since the collapse of the Leap Forward in 1960, and the margin for investment is small.

The chief determinants of the growth in industrial production over the next few years will be the manner in which the limited resources available for investment and defense are allocated and the performance of agriculture. If the limited resources available, the scarce materials and skilled manpower, continue to be concentrated in the weapons program, the output of heavy industry will expand only slowly.

Most of the capacity not now in production is concentrated in light industry, especially in textiles, but the failure of agricultural production to keep up with the increase in population means that agriculture will not be able to supply the raw materials necessary for light industry. The output of industrial crops will continue to be sacrificed in favor of food crops. Continued weak performance of agriculture will mean that light industry will not grow rapidly and that the output of many light industrial products probably will not reach their previous peak levels during the Third Five-Year Plan.

In summary, the drain of the weapons program on heavy industry and the dependence of light industry on agricultural raw materials would seem to preclude a rapid rate of growth during the Third Five-Year Plan. Simply to regain the level of production achieved in 1960 by the end of the Third Five-Year Plan, industrial production will have to grow at a rate in excess of 5 per cent annually. If the Chinese do not attempt a new Leap, they probably can maintain a rate of growth of 5 per cent and may well regain the previous peak level of industrial production by 1970, but the misguided economic policies of the Leap Forward will have cost China a full decade's industrial growth.

8

# Quantitative Dimension of Communist China's Aggregate Economic and Industrial Performance

*Barry M. Richman*

*Specified excerpts from pages 595–605 and 607–08 from* Industrial Society in Communist China, *by Barry M. Richman, Copyright © 1969 by Barry M. Richman. Reprinted by permission of Random House, Inc.*

WE SHALL BRIEFLY examine peak levels of industrial and economic performance in pre-1949 China, before the Communists came to power, and see when these peaks were surpassed under the Communists. We shall also examine key trends for the entire 1949–67 period as well as for different segments of this period. And we shall compare critical aspects of China's performance with that of India, in particular, but also, to some extent, with those of the Soviet Union, Japan, and the United States. Finally, a suggestive quantitative rating of the environmental constraints under study in this book will be undertaken in terms of their impact on managerial effectiveness and industrial progress in Red China and the other four countries.

As can be seen on several of the tables to be presented, I have used ranges—some of them relatively large—in estimating various aspects of China's performance. This is necessary because the available data to work with are quite speculative and sparse in many instances, and there are frequently significant variations in the estimates made by experts and secondary sources which I must draw on for my own analysis. However, I strongly believe that suggestive estimates and comparisons based on a careful analysis of available information, sound reasoning, interpretation, and plausible assumptions are better than bypassing the entire problem—particularly for as large, important, and unique a country as Red China. Moreover, in spite of differences in the precise magnitudes of the estimates available in various reputable sources, there is almost universal consensus with regard to broad performance trends during the 1949–66 period.

In general, statistics and estimates involving Communist China's performance tend to be most reliable for the 1952–58 period, particularly the 1953–57 portion. For the other periods the reader will see that the estimates of performance tend to be in even broader ranges. In my opinion, the low points of most ranges understate China's performance, but I have presented them anyway since they have some basis in information, reasoning, and assumptions. The low-point estimates are in large part from the same studies written by experts who, in my opinion, tend to significantly underestimate China's industrial progress and economic growth. At the same time, some of the upper limits of the estimate ranges in the following tables are, in my opinion, too high, but here again, I present them anyway for the same reasons that I include those that I personally feel are too low. However, I have ignored available estimates involving China's performance which seem to be unrealistically high or low, and are inadequately supported.

## *Aggregate Growth Trends: 1949–66*

If we look at key quantitative indicators of Communist China's aggregate performance for the 1949–66 period as a whole (see Tables 1 and 2). it is evident that China has achieved substantial economic growth, industrial progress and, by implication, sizable gains in managerial effectiveness. As we shall see shortly, Red China's growth and development record appears to be substantially better than India's to date, better than the

## Table 1—Some Key Growth Rate Estimates for Communist China's Economy and Industrial Sector[a]

| *Period* | *Gross National Product*[b] | *Per Capita GNP*[b] | *Industrial Production (Including manufacturing and mining and public utilities)* | *Industrial Employment* | *Industrial Labor Productivity*[c] *(Output per man-year, all industrial employees)* |
|---|---|---|---|---|---|
| 1950–66 | 5.5–7.2 | 3.4–5.2 | 11.5–12.0 | 9.7–10.0 | 1.7–2.0 |
| 1950–65 | 5.3–7.0 | 3.2–5.0 | 11.0–11.6 | 9.5–9.8 | 1.4–1.7 |
| 1950–52 | 21.0–26.0 | 19.2–24.0 | 25.0–29.0 | 19.0–21.0 | 6.0–8.0 |
| 1953–66 | 3.5–4.7 | 1.4–2.6 | 9.7–10.7 | 6.4–6.8 | 1.1–1.5 |
| 1953–65 | 3.3–4.5 | 1.2–2.4 | 8.8–9.4 | 7.0–8.0 | 1.2–1.4 |
| 1953–57 | 6.2–8.8 | 3.9–6.6 | 15.0–16.0 | 8.4–8.6 | 6.0–6.2 |
| 1958 to mid-1960[d] | 7.0–15.0 | 4.5–12.6 | 20.0–30.0 | 80.0–90.0 (nearly tripled in 1958) | – 33.0 to – 40.0 |
| 1960–62[e] (low point from 1958–60 peak) | – 20.0 to – 35.0 | – 22.0 to – 37.0 | – 40.0 to – 45.0 | – 45.0 to – 50.0 | 1.0 to 2.0 (for period) |
| 1957–65 | 1.6–2.6 | (– 0.5) to 0.6 | 4.6–5.3 | 7.1–7.2 | – 2.0 to – 2.5 |
| 1957–66 | 1.8–2.9 | (– .02) to 1.0 | 5.5–6.5 | 7.3–7.4 | – 1.5 to 0 |
| 1963–65 | 5.7–8.0 | 3.3–5.7 | 10.0–11.3 | 5.1–5.6 | 4.7–5.7 |
| 1963–66 | 6.0–8.3 | 3.6–6.0 | 10.5–12.0 | 5.5–6.0 | 5.0–6.0 |

[a] Estimates are annual average compounded growth rates in per cent. The estimates are based on a careful study of many available studies and sources, the most important of which are cited below. I have used ranges for all of my estimates, eliminating figures and estimates from other sources which seem to be unrealistically high or low. The most reliable estimates in this table are for the 1952–57 period. The least reliable are probably for the 1958–60 and 1961–62 periods.

[b] My GNP estimates are based on a variety of national-income-type data including figures for gross and net national product, gross and net national income per se, gross and net domestic product, net material product, etc. For definitions of these terms with particular reference to the case of Communist China, see T. C. Liu and K. C. Yeh, *The Economy of the Chinese Mainland* (Princeton: Princeton University Press, 1965), especially p. 119 and pp. 214 ff.

[c] I have computed labor-productivity growth rates from a labor-productivity index which I have constructed from industrial production and employment data.

[d] Peak-level GNP during 1958–60 was probably reached in 1959, although some experts place it in 1960, and one (T. C. Liu) at the end of 1958. The different estimates regarding the GNP peak level and the subsequently low point account in part for the sizable ranges in GNP and per capita growth rates after 1957. Industrial production probably roughly doubled during the 1958–60 period, although some official Red Chinese pronouncements claimed that it tripled. The highest rate of industrial growth probably came in 1958, with somewhat lower growth in 1959, and a rate of probably well under 10 per cent in 1960. It is likely that industrial production actually declined in the second half of 1960. Industrial employment nearly tripled in 1958 and may have begun to decline somewhat by the end of 1959.

[e] For the 1960–62 period the figures indicate total percentage declines from the peak levels reached during 1958–60, except for labor productivity which is an average-growth-rate estimate.

*Sources:* For data on total GNP and per capita GNP: Liu and Yeh, *op. cit.;* T. C. Liu, "The Tempo of Economic Development of the Chinese Mainland," *An Economic Profile of Mainland China,* Vol. I (Washington: U.S. Government Printing Office, 1967), pp. 45–75; E. Jones, "The Emerging Pattern of China's Economic Revolution," *Economic Profile,* Vol. I, pp. 77–95. Statements, comments, and papers by A. Eckstein, J. Gurley, K. Chao, T. C. Liu, E. Jones, and W. Proxmire, *Mainland China in the World Economy* (Washington: U.S. Government Printing Office, 1967), pp. 108, 159; W. Hollister, *China's Gross National Product and Social Accounts, 1950–57* (Glencoe, Ill.: Free Press, 1958); Y. L. Wu, F. Hoeber, M. Rockwell, *The Economic Potential of Communist China* (Menlo Park, Calif.: Stanford Research Institute, 1964); Y. L. Wu, *The Economy of Communist China* (New York: Praeger, 1965); A. Eckstein, *The National Income of Communist China* (Glencoe, Ill.: Free Press, 1961); A. Eckstein, *Communist China's Economic Growth and Foreign Trade* (New York: McGraw-Hill, 1966); C. M. Li, *Economic Development of Communist China* (Berkeley and Los Angeles: University of California Press, 1959); *Ten Great Years* (Peking: Foreign Languages Press, 1960); *Current Scene,* Vol. IV, No. 3 (February 1, 1966); *World Bank Atlas of Per Capita Product and Population* (published by the International Bank for Reconstruction and Development, 1966); "Economic Indicators for the Soviet Bloc," *Annual Economic Indicators for the USSR* (Washington: U.S. Government Printing Office, 1964); D. Perkins, "Economic Growth in China and the Cultural Revolution," *The China Quarterly,* No. 30 (1967). See also my comments in Note 53 in Chapter 6 of this book. An important new book published in 1968 (a few parts of which I have seen in manuscript) is W. Galenson, A. Eckstein, and T. C. Liu, eds., *Economic Trends in Communist China* (Chicago: Aldine Publishing Co. 1968).

For population estimates used in estimating per capita GNP: J. Aird, "Population Growth and Distribution in Mainland China," *An Economic Profile of Mainland China,* Vol. II (Washington: U.S. Government Printing Office, 1967), pp. 341–400; and E. Jones in *Economic Profile,* Vol. I, pp. 80–82, 93, Table II.

For data on industrial production: R. Field, "Chinese Communist Industrial Production," *Economic Profile,* Vol. I, pp. 269–95; Jones, *Economic Profile,* Vol. I, pp. 85–88, p. 95, Table V; K. Chao, *The Rate and Pattern of Industrial Growth in Communist China* (Ann Arbor: University of Michigan Press, 1965), especially pp. 88 and 96; Liu and Yeh, *op. cit.,* especially pp. 66, 146, 573, and 585; Perkins, *op. cit.; Far Eastern Economic Review,* September 29, 1966; *Peking Review,* Nos. 1, 2 (1967). *New China News Agency, International Broadcast,* September 30, 1966; Ta Kung Po (Peking), September 10, 1965; *Peking People's Daily* (in Chinese), January 1, 1967.

For data on industrial employment: J. Emerson, "Employment in Mainland China," *Economic Profile,* Vol. II, pp. 403–69; L. Orleans, *Professional Manpower and Education in Communist China* (Washington: National Science Foundation, 1961), Chap. VIII.

Soviet Union's from 1918–35, and roughly as good as Soviet performance during the 1928–40 period, after Russia embarked on a vigorous development campaign through her five-year plans beginning in 1927–28. But Red China's performance is not nearly as impressive as Japan's "economic miracle" since the late 1940s.

China's impressive growth record, so far, has been achieved in spite of erratic industrial performance and extreme periods of economic instability, most notably during the superficial and short-lived boom of the Great Leap and the severe economic depression which followed. The Great Leap and subsequent depression cost Red China at least several years, and perhaps as many as six or seven, in overall economic growth and industrial production.

Had it not been for the Leap and the depression, Red China's GNP, per capita income, and industrial production would have probably been at least 40 or 50 per cent greater than what they were as of 1966–67 and, conceivably, even double that.

Poor weather caused poor agricultural performance, and the Soviet pullout of mid-1960 contributed greatly to China's general economic and industrial crisis, but I am strongly convinced that ideological extremism was, by far, the most important basic cause of the crisis. Ideological extremism did great direct damage not only to managerial effectiveness, productive efficiency, and general progress in the overall industrial sector, but it also contributed greatly to the agricultural crisis, and probably to the Soviet pullout as well.

## GROWTH IN GNP AND PER CAPITA INCOME

Table 1 indicates that gross national product in Communist China grew at an average annual rate of 5.5 to 7.2 per cent during the 1950–66 period, and per capita GNP at 3.4 to 5.2 per cent, and only slightly less if one wishes to ignore 1966 because of the uncertainty caused by the Cultural Revolution. In my opinion, GNP probably grew at a rate of 6 per cent or slightly more, and per capita GNP at about 4 per cent. Even if we take the low point of these ranges, China's GNP and per capita growth are significantly higher than India's for this period. Table 3 indicates that India's GNP grew at a maximum average annual rate of 3.7 per cent, and per capita GNP at a maximum rate of 1.4 per cent. Some experts may claim that I am making an unfair comparison between China and India for the 1950–66 period, and there is some justification for the criticism. It is true that China achieved abnormally high growth rates during the 1949–52 period of economic rehabilitation in large part by putting a vast amount of existing, but idle, productive capacity and skilled human resources back into operation; while India, which was not so seriously torn by war or civil strife, had to rely much more on the creation of new capacity and critical resources for growth during this period. But the point still remains that when the Chinese Communists came to power they did bring about, create, and put into effect an overall environment much more conducive to managerial effectiveness, industrial progress, and economic growth than had ever previously existed in China.

If we compare Red China's economic growth for only the 1953–66 period—after economic rehabilitation—with the 1950–66 period in India, China would still probably come out ahead. China's GNP growth averaged 3.5 to 4.7 per cent annually, and, in my opinion, it was probably at least 4 per cent, while India's was in the range of 3.5 to 3.7 per cent. (See Tables 1 and 3.) Even if we take the low point of the range for China—which I feel would be a mistake—China did about as well as India. China's per capita GNP grew at an average annual rate of 1.4 to 2.6 per cent (I would place it around 2 per cent), during the 1953–66 period—while India's rate was 1.2 to 1.4 per cent during 1950–66. Here again, China's low-point estimate is as good as India's maximum rate estimate.

Red China has done roughly as well in GNP growth as the Soviet Union during its first two five-year plan periods, 1928–38, when its growth rate was about 6 per cent, and during the 1950–66 period in Russia when GNP growth averaged 6 per cent to 7

### Table 2—Estimates for China of Some Key Aspects of Performance: Pre-1949 and under Communist Rule

| *Period* | *Gross National Product*[a] | *Per Capita GNP*[a] | *Index of Industrial Production* | *Industrial Employment* |
|---|---|---|---|---|
| (Year-end estimates) | (Figures through 1952 are in 1952 yuan; after 1952, they are in current U.S. dollars.) | (Figures through 1952 are in 1952 yuan; after 1952 they are in current U.S. dollars.) | (1952 = 100) | (Millions of people) |
| Pre-1949 peak level | 58–62 billion yuan | 117–121 yuan (under $60) | 66–69[b] | Probably well under 3 million |
| Year of pre-1949 peak | (1933) | (1933) | (1933)[b] | (Possibly 1936 or 1942–44; in 1933 about 2 million) |
| 1949 | 40–45 billion yuan | 70–80 yuan (under $50) | 48–50 | 3.059 (at year's end) |
| Year pre-1949 peak was surpassed | (1951) | (1952) | (1951) | (1949) |
| 1952 | 68–73 billion yuan | 121–126 yuan | 100 | 5.26 |
| 1957 | (a) $40–$50 billion (official exchange rate)<br>(b) $60–$70 billion (internal purchasing power rate) | (a) $63–$80<br>(b) $95–$108 | 195–205 | 7.9 |
| 1958–60 peak year | (a) $50–$65 billion (official exchange rate)<br>(b) $70–$88 billion (internal purchasing power rate) | (a) $73–100<br>(b) $110–$132 | 390–400 | 23–24 |
| 1961–62 low year | (a) $35–$45 billion (official exchange rate)<br>(b) $50–$65 billion (internal purchasing power rate) | (a) $50–$67<br>(b) $75–$90 | 200–240 | 11.5–12.0 |
| 1965 | (a) $47–$72 billion (official exchange rate)<br>(b) $70–$95 billion (internal purchasing power rate) | (a) $65–$93[c]<br>(b) $95–$125 | 265–300 | 13.7–14.0 |
| 1966 | (a) $50–$75 billion (official exchange rate)<br>(b) $75–$100 billion (internal purchasing power rate) | (a) $69–$105[c]<br>(b) $100–$137 | 292–360 | 14.6–15.0[d] |

[a] I have not attempted to convert yuan to U.S. dollars for 1952 or previous years since I do not consider myself an expert on yuan-dollar conversion rates. For the conversions for 1957 and later years I have estimated GNP and GNP per capita in current U.S. dollars at both the official exchange rate prevailing in 1965 (roughly 2.5 yuan to the dollar) and the internal purchasing power rate estimated by people more knowledgeable in this area than myself. It is possible that the official exchange rate undervalues China's output of the producer-goods industries and undervalues agricultural output and various other types of goods and services.

At the hearings on Communist China's economy conducted by the Joint Economic Committee of the U.S. Congress in April 1967, there seemed to be general agreement—with only a few minority dissenters, on the high and low side, among experts that Red China's GNP in the 1965–66 period was in the range of \$70 to \$100 billion in terms of internal purchasing power or in comparison to the United States' GNP; the majority opinion placed it around \$90 billion.

These hearings were based, in large part, on an analysis of the two-volume study prepared for the Joint Economic Committee in early 1967 and published under the title *An Economic Profile of Mainland China* by the U.S. Government Printing Office. The hearings themselves were published under the title *Mainland China in the World Economy.* See pages 108 and 159 of this volume for the majority position among the participants regarding the dollar value of China's GNP.

For other estimates of China's GNP and per capita GNP in U.S. dollar values, see E. Jones, in *Economic Profile of Mainland China*, Vol. I, p. 96, Table 6; "Economic Indicators for the Soviet Bloc," *Annual Economic Indicators for the U.S.S.R.* (Washington: U.S. Government Printing Office, 1964), p. 131; especially Table xl–1; *Current Scene*, Vol. IV, No. 3 (February 1, 1966), p. 1; *World Bank Atlas of Per Capita Product and Population;* H. Kahn, "Uncertain Road to the 21st Century," *Think*, Vol. 33, No. 1 (January–February 1967), p. 5; Eckstein, *op. cit.*, p. 249, Table 7–1; *Indicators of Economic Strength of Western Europe, Canada, United States, and Soviet Bloc, 1959–62* (Washington: Department of State Intelligence Reports, 1963).

[b] It is possible that industrial production was somewhat higher during 1936 and/or sometimes during the 1942–44 period under Japanese occupation.

[c] I was told by a Chinese Communist central-planning official in Peking in May 1966 that he thought that per capita income in Communist China "might currently be around 225 to 250 yuan." He made it clear that this was a personal opinion rather than an official estimate—although he no doubt has access to key economics statistics. He would not elaborate as to what definition of national income or GNP he was referring to or whether the yuan were in 1966 or earlier prices. He would not say whether all services were included in his figures. He also would not say whether his figures were for 1965 or expected 1966 performance. In any event, his per capita income range, when worked out, approximates the upper limits of my GNP and per capita income estimates for 1965 and 1966 in U.S. dollars at the official exchange rate.

[d] I was told by a Chinese Ministry of Labor official in Peking in May 1966 that the industrial labor force was expected to grow by roughly 5 per cent to 7 per cent in 1966 over 1965. He would not give me an absolute employment figure, however. Industrial employment was around 14 million in 1965 (as estimated by Emerson, *op. cit.*, p. 445), and an increase of 5 per cent to 7 per cent in 1966 would place it around 14.6 to 15 million in 1966.

*Sources:* The estimates in this table are based on a careful study of the sources cited in Table 1 of this chapter. The 1933 and 1949 figures are from Liu and Yeh, *op. cit.*, pp. 69 and 181; Chao, *op. cit.*, Table C–1; Field, *op. cit.*, appendix D, p. 295, Table 10; Eckstein, *op. cit.*, pp. 20 ff. and Table 2–1, and A. Eckstein, *The Economic Heritage* (mimeographed), prepared for the Conference on Economic Trends in Communist China sponsored by the Social Science Research Council's Committee on the Economy of China held in Chicago, October 21–24, 1965.

### *Table 3—Statistics of Some Key Aspects of India's Economic and Industrial Performance*

#### *Part I: Critical Growth Rates*[a]

| | *GNP* | *GNP Per Capita* | *Industrial Production (Including manufacturing, mining and public utilities)* | *Industrial Employment*[b] | *Industrial Labor Production*[b] *(Output per man-year)* |
|---|---|---|---|---|---|
| 1950–66 period | 3.5–3.7% | 1.2–1.4% | 6.4–6.7% | 2.2–2.4% | 3.6–4.3% |

#### *Part II: Absolute Levels of Performance*[a]

| | *1950* | *1966* |
|---|---|---|
| *Gross national product* | | |
| In current U.S. dollars at 1965 official exchange rate of 4.75 rupees = \$1 (U.S.) | \$20–\$22 billion | \$34–\$38 billion |
| In current U.S. dollars at internal purchasing power rate estimated by expert sources | \$25–\$27 billion | \$47–\$51 billion |
| *Per capita GNP* | | |
| In current U.S. dollars at official exchange rate | \$55–\$60 | \$68–\$75 |
| In current U.S. dollars at internal purchasing power rate | \$75–\$80 | \$75–\$104 |
| *Industrial employment (in millions)*[b] (Includes manufacturing, mining, utilities) | 5.9–6.2 | 9.5–9.8 |

[a] Average annual compounded rates of growth in percentage. Ranges are used—although much smaller than those for China—since there is some disagreement among basic sources as to India's precise level of economic and industrial performance during various periods. This is due to several factors. Different concepts and measurements of GNP, national income, etc., as well as industrial production and employment indexes, are used. Some sources report results for calendar years, others for fiscal years (April 1–March 31 in India), and some do not indicate which of the two they are reporting for. Similarly, some sources do not indicate whether constant prices for a base period or current prices are used in computing national-income figures. There are also deviations in the internal purchasing power rates used in converting rupees to U.S. dollars.

[b] Industrial employment does not include the roughly 8 to 10 million persons engaged in "household industry," which is essentially like handicrafts where a portion of the output is consumed by the producers and their families. However, much of the output of this sector goes through regular marketing channels and is probably included in industrial-output statistics. Whereas the large majority of handicraftsmen making factory-type consumer or producer goods have been absorbed in the "modern" or factory industrial sector in China, this is not true for India. Moreover, there is apparently much more seasonal and contract labor in Indian industry than in Chinese industry which is not reported in official employment statistics. This also means that industrial-labor productivity tends to be overstated in India in relation to China.

*Sources: India's Draft Fourth Plan* (New Delhi: National Planning Commission, Government of India, 1966). *Gross National Product, Growth Rates and Trend Data by Region and Country* (Washington: Agency for International Development, Statistics and Reports Division, March 31, 1967). *World Bank Atlas on Per Capita Product and Population* (International Bank for Reconstruction and Development, 1966). *Eastern Economist*, 1965 and 1966 (New Delhi). *United Nations Statistical Yearbook* (various years during 1950–65 period). *Monthly Commentary on Indian Economic Conditions*, September, October, and December 1966, January and February 1967 (New Delhi Indian Institute of Public Opinion). *India: Pocket Book of Economic Information*, 1964 and 1965 (New Delhi Ministry of Finance, Government of India). *Statistical Outline of India*, 1964 and 1965 (Bombay: Prepared by Tata Industries Private Limited, published by Popular Prakashan).

per cent. However, the Soviet Union may have had a somewhat higher per capita income-growth rate—about 4.5 per cent—because of her lower rate of population growth. Since the early 1960s the Soviet Union's GNP average growth rate has fallen slightly below 5.5 per cent, and in per capita terms to about 3.5 per cent.

The United States has had a long-term historical GNP growth rate of only about 4 per cent, and in per capita terms about 2.5 per cent, although in the 1960s it has averaged about 5.5 per cent and 4.0 per cent, respectively.

But China has not done as well as Japan since 1950. Japan's GNP has grown at an average annual rate of 7 per cent to 8 per cent, and in per capita terms at 6 to 7 since 1950, with rates exceeding 10 per cent during some periods and in the 1960s.

#### GROWTH IN INDUSTRIAL PRODUCTION

Table 1 indicates that industrial production grew at an average annual rate of 11.5 to 12 per cent during the 1950–66 period, and only slightly less if we ignore 1966. This is substantially higher than India's rate of about 6.5 per cent noted on Table 3. Even for the 1953–66 period China's industrial production grew at an annual average rate of around 10 per cent. China's rate of industrial growth is roughly equal to the Soviet Union's during the 1928–38 period, when it was 10 per cent to 14 per cent (depending on whose production index is used), and a bit higher than the 1950–55 Soviet rate of about 9.5 per cent. In the United States, industrial production has grown at a somewhat lower rate than in Russia since 1960. Red China has not done as well as Japan, which has had a fantastic average annual rate of growth in industrial production of more than 14 per cent since 1950.

### *Aggregate Performance in Real Terms: 1933–66*

#### ABSOLUTE LEVELS OF GNP AND PER CAPITA INCOME

Table 2 indicates that in absolute terms, Red China's GNP as of 1966 (year-end) was probably in the range of $75 to $100 billion if we convert yuan into U.S. dollars at an internal purchasing power (IPP) rate, and $50 to $75 billion at the official exchange (OE) rate. The latter rate probably leads to a significant understatement of China's GNP in terms of living standards—which are still very low with either rate—and economic and industrial strength, not to mention military power. Using the IPP rate, China's per capita GNP was probably in the range of $100 to $137 as of 1966, and at the OE rate $69 to $105. The majority of experts place Red China's 1966 population at around 750 million and her real GNP in 1966 at about $90 billion. (See the sources and notes in Tables 1 and 2. It should be pointed out that Note *c* in Table 2 comments on a per capita income estimate given to me by a central Chinese Communist official in May 1966). At this population level, and with a GNP of $90 billion, per capita income would be $120. This seems to be a pretty realistic figure to me. I do not feel that China's per capita GNP at the IPP rate was significantly lower than $120 in 1966, and it could conceivably have been higher.

In pre-1949 China, before the Communists came to power, the peak GNP for a single year was probably around $36 billion (in present U.S. dollars) at the IPP rate, and $24 billion at the OE rate. (See Table 2.) Peak per capita income was probably never higher than $60 at the IPP rate in pre-1949 China. In 1949, when the Communists took over, GNP at the IPP rate was only about $27 billion, and at the OE rate $18 billion, while per capita income at the former, and higher, rate was probably significantly less than $50. Hence, during China's Communist era until 1966, GNP and per capita GNP probably more than doubled. The pre-1949 peak levels of GNP and per capita income were surpassed in 1951 and 1952, respectively.

I am sure that in 1966 the average citizen in China was living substantially better—and could expect to live twelve to sixteen years longer—than the average citizen did at any time before the Communist takeover. I know that some veteran Sinologists will disagree with this statement, but I am convinced they are wrong.

Table 3 indicates that India's GNP as of 1966 was approximately $48 or $49 billion at the IPP rate of conversion, and about $36 billion at the OE rate, or substantially less, perhaps as much as 50 per cent, than in Red China—at either rate. Per capita income in India in 1966 was in the range of $90 to $104 at the IPP rate, and $68 to $75 at the OE rate. The high points of the ranges for India's 1966 per capita GNP are approximately equal to the low points of China's ranges. It is quite likely that China's real per capita GNP was at least 20 per cent higher than India's as of 1966. Moreover, India's GNP increased by no more than 70 to 80 per cent during the 1950–66 period, while China's probably increased by more than 100 per cent. Similarly, India's per capita income —which was about $58 (current U.S. dollars) at the OE rate and $78 at the IPP rate in 1950 —increased by roughly 20 per cent during the 1950–66 period, while China's increased by approximately 75 to 100 per cent. Even if we compare the 1952 or 1953–66 period for Red China with the 1950–66 period for India, China comes out ahead. In general, very few poor or developing countries have done as well as China in terms of growth and development since 1950.

II

# Development Policy and Planning Techniques

A

# Planning Strategy and Industrial Policy

THE PAPERS IN this section deal with the strategies and techniques adopted by India and China for the planning and development of their economies. The major economic policies in both countries relate to their respective plans, which contain statements on objectives, past achievements, and targets in the different sectors. Both societies are very much plan-conscious, and their major prides and disappointments emanate from the extent of the plans' fulfillment. The planning techniques in the two countries reflect differences in their political ideologies and economic systems. These differences are explained in the papers in this section.

The Chinese National Plan governs all Chinese economic activities in general. It seeks to achieve balance between the supply and demand of the nation's resources, labor, and finances on both the national and regional levels. The national plan also covers aggregates for industrial and agricultural production, transportation, labor, and employment, allocation of materials, commodity flows, capital construction, social, cultural, and welfare undertakings, foreign trade, technological development, and the like. The financial plan is also included in the national plan, and it covers the consolidated state budget, the credit and cash plans of the banking system, the financial plans of the ministries, the enterprises and communes, and the estimated receipts and expenditures of government agencies and enterprises. These national aggregates are the sum total of the plans of various provinces, autonomous regions, and enterprises. The process of plan preparation starts with the State Economic Commission's formulating "control figures" (or general guidelines) which take into consideration the major economic and political factors. The control figures, which consist of a set of production targets, input and cost coefficients, and indicators of performance described for the enterprises, are then sent to the central government ministries and to the provincial governments for transmission to the enterprises and agencies under their respective jurisdictions. On the basis of these control figures, the individual enterprises formulate their operational plans and submit them to the higher provincial, regional, and national levels. The operational plans are integrated at the provincial or regional levels and transmitted to the State Economic Commission, where they are reviewed and integrated into a plan of material and labor balances. The revised figures are reissued as targets to the individual operating agencies and enterprises. Thus, theoretically, the economic plan in China covers every aspect of the national economy. It encompasses production plans of all the industrial, agricultural, and other enterprises.

From a survey of literature one observes a great amount of divergence between theory and practice or plan and reality. In theory the Chinese planning system is well planned in every detail with reasonable intersectoral balance within an input-output matrix, perfect regional cooperation, correspondence between the plan in real terms and its counterpart in terms of monetary flows and the steady growth of the entire system at predetermined rates. In practice, however, there are intersectoral and interregional imbalances. In many sectors, especially agriculture, communes do not always follow a planned course. In the non-agricultural sector, it has not been possible to follow the control figures of the national plan. There has been a lack of cooperation between the different levels of government leading to defiance of the directives from the central government by the provincial governments and autonomous regions. In practice the Chinese planning system is not so centralized as it appears in theory. Several factors can cause the difference between theory and practice: The national economic plan may be based on inaccurate information leading to overfulfillment and underfulfillment of the initial plan; frequent changes in the plan to take care of the underfulfillment or overfulfillment; or nonfulfillment of the plan because of exogenous "shocks" and unexpected "windfalls." Thus the Chinese planning system is different from what it appears to be from the official pronouncements of the Chinese government or the Communist party. In theory the Chinese planning system seems centralized, but in her paper "Central Economic Control," Audrey Donnithorne cautions against the view that Chinese economic planning is under tight control by the central government. She delineates the process of decentralization, showing the increasing part being played by the provincial governments, autonomous regions, and even by individual enterprises. According to Donnithorne, even the role of the Communist party, as an instrument of the center's control over the country, has not been able to stop the decentralization process. In "Incentives and Profits in Chinese Industry" Dwight H. Perkins explains the extent of decentralization arising out of the existence of a large number of small-scale industrial enterprises using primitive technology and out of the economy's being agricultural and exposed to vagaries of nature. Centralized planning of hundreds and thousands of small enterprises and farms is an insurmountable task. Perkins also notes the increasing role of profit and bonus incentives in Chinese industry.

One may conclude that Communist China does not really have a truly comprehensive national plan. The formulation of the First Five Year Plan, 1953–57, was not formally completed until half of that period had elapsed. The Second and Third Plans were largely overshadowed by the crises stemming from the Great Leap Forward and the Cultural Revolution. Thus during most of the past two decades China's economic development has been guided by a partial plan on a year-to-year basis and largely on a regional level. Further decentralization of industry was reported to have occurred during 1969. It seems this trend may continue in the immediate future.

The structure of the Indian Planning Commission and the planning strategies adopted by it are different from those of China in several respects. The Indian Planning Commission is an advisory body created by an executive order of the union government. Its function is to "make an assessment of the material, capital and human resources of the country," recommend a plan for "the most effective and balanced utilization of the country's resources," and "determine the nature of the machinery which will be necessary for securing the successful implementation of each stage of the plan in all its aspects." The Commission recommends Five Year Plans on an all-India basis, for execution by the union and state governments in their respective constitutional spheres. The central and state governments share equal jurisdiction over economic and social planning, but vital areas of development such as public health, education, agriculture, irrigation and electricity, and a wide range of industrial and transportation activities are dealt with only by the state. Thus constitutionally the states are under no compulsion to accept the plan recommended by the Central Planning Commission on any subject in the state list. But for various reasons the states generally have so far cooperated with the central government in implementing the plan. First, the Planning Commission prepares the plan with initial consultation and close cooperation of the state governments. Also the states have been accepting guidance from the Planning Commission because of factors such as the political authority of the union government's leadership (which is also represented on the Planning Commission), the general acceptance in the country of the necessity of national economic planning, the greater competence of the union authorities; and various kinds of financial inducements that the Planning Commission and the central government can offer if the schemes and programs suggested by them are agreed to by the States.

India's Five Year Plans are not comprehensive in the sense that every sector of the economy is planned in detail. According to the paper, "The Role of Planning in the Indian Economy," the "greater part of the plan refers to programs of development undertaken by the central and state governments and by local authorities." These programs constitute a minor part of the national economy. A large proportion of the economy—agriculture, small scale industries, and large scale industries (except the ones in the public sector as outlined in the paper "Industrial Policy in India")—is in private ownership and is guided through the indirect mechanism of the market. In several areas there are controls and regulations, but this does not change the general conclusion. The plans of the private sector are the estimates and forecasts undertaken in consultation with private industry; such plans serve as target guides. In India's plans private and public sectors are viewed as being complementary.

The major political and administrative problems of implementing the Indian plans are discussed by M. Abel in his paper, "Administrative Problems of Economic Development." The major problems arise from the autonomy of the states, interstate rivalries and parochialism, incompetent administrative machinery, lack of horizontal coordination between different departments, lack of vertical coordination between various levels within the same department, and lack of competent and imaginative personnel.

9

# The Role of Planning in the Indian Economy

*Government of India*

*From Government of India, Planning Commission* The Planning Process *(Delhi: Manager of Publications, 1963), p. 1–4, 8, 11–18, with omissions. Reprinted with permission.*

## *India's Five Year Plans*

INDIA HAS COMPLETED twelve years of planned development. These include five years of the First Plan (April 1951–March 1956), five years of the Second Plan (April 1956–March 1961) and the first two years of the Third Plan (April 1961–March 1966). These Plans form a continuing series, both in terms of investments and in benefits. They also present a picture of continuity and evolution in basic economic and social policies. Inevitably, there are important adaptations from one phase to another, reflecting both changing conditions and problems and the results of fresh experience and evaluation.

Each Five Year Plan is conceived against a longer perspective. The First Plan was set against a simple projection of economic growth over a period of thirty years from 1951 to 1981. The Second Plan was worked out in relation to a perspective up to 1976. The Third Plan has been drawn up and is being implemented explicitly as the first phase of a fifteen-year plan for the period 1961–76. Preliminary work on the formulation of a long-term plan for this period is in hand. This should greatly facilitate the task of filling in the details of the Fourth Plan (April 1966–March 1971).

## *Historical Background*

During the long period of India's struggle for freedom, there was deep and growing concern with the problems of mass poverty, protection of the farmer and the artisan, the need for industrialization and, generally, with the reconstruction of the entire fabric of social and economic life. A long line of national leaders looked upon political freedom primarily as the means to solve these fundamental problems. As the national movement grew and spread among the people, its social content became deeper. To Mahatma Gandhi, freedom was not merely a political objective but the very condition for raising of the masses of the people from poverty and stagnation. The social and economic aims of the struggle for freedom came to be more precisely defined during the thirties. The setting up by the Indian National Congress of a National Planning Committee toward the end of 1938—nine years before Independence—indicated both the important place held by social and economic objectives and the influence which the Soviet Five Year Plans had begun to exert in other lands.

The objectives of India's planning and its social premises derive from "the Directive Principles of State Policy" set forth in the Constitution. Among these "Directive Principles" were that:

> The State shall strive to promote the welfare of the people securing and protecting, as effectively as it may, a social order in which justice, social, economic and political, shall inform all the institutions of national life.

Further that:

> The State shall, in particular, direct its policy towards securing—
> (a) that the citizens, men and women equally, have the right to an adequate means of livelihood;
> (b) that the ownership and control of the

material resources of the community are so distributed as best to subserve the common good;

(c) that the operation of the economic system does not result in the concentration of wealth and means of production to the common detriment.

Against the background of these Directive Principles, the functions assigned to the Planning Commission were to:

(1) make an assessment of the material, capital and human resources of the country, including technical personnel, and investigate the possibilities of augmenting such of these resources as are found to be deficient in relation to the nation's requirements;
(2) formulate a Plan for the most effective and balanced utilization of the country's resources;
(3) on a determination of priorities, define the stages in which the Plan should be carried out and propose the allocation of resources for the due completion of each stage;
(4) indicate the factors which are tending to retard economic development, and determine the conditions which, in view of the current social and political situation, should be established for the successful execution of the Plan;
(5) determine the nature of the machinery which will be necessary for securing the successful implementation of each stage of the Plan in all its aspects;
(6) appraise from time to time the progress achieved in the execution of each stage of the Plan and recommend the adjustments of policy and measures that such appraisal may show to be necessary; and
(7) make such interim or ancillary recommendations as appear to it to be appropriate either for facilitating the discharge of the duties assigned to it; or, on a consideration of the prevailing economic conditions, current policies, measures and development programmes; or on an examination of such specific problems as may be referred to it for advice by Central or State Governments.

Since 1950, each Plan has marked an important phase in India's economic history. The beginning and the end of a Five Year Plan are regarded as vital dates in the national life, each Plan being at once an appraisal of the past, a guide map for action in the future and a reformulation of basic national policies in the light of experience and the new problems facing the country. Events now move faster than a few years ago, and adjustments over shorter periods have gained in importance.

### CENTRALIZATION AND DECENTRALIZATION OF PLANNING

The question of centralization and decentralization of planning has three main facets. The first concerns the political and administrative structure which is served through planning. India has a federal structure in which the powers and functions of the Central and the State Governments are defined by the Constitution. "Economic and social planning" is in the "concurrent" list, but vital areas of development, such as public health, education, land, agriculture, irrigation, electricity, local government and a wide range of activities under industries and transport fall within the State list. In practice, the Five Year Plans, comprehend the entire range of development activities and cross over the lines set by the Constitution. In other words, planning in India has made possible a degree of inter-penetration of interest and concern between the Central and State Governments. In such a structure, the Center assumes a large role in the formulation of policy and overall plans, while the States take on steadily expanding administrative and development functions. Since important development programs have to be undertaken at the local level in towns and villages, as a consequence of planned development, the Center's interest also extends to the institutions closest to the people, through which local resources are mobilized and local plans implemented.

The second aspect of the question of centralization and decentralization bears on the techniques employed in the management of the economy. As explained later, while there is a large and growing sector in which direct planning is undertaken, a large proportion of economic activity is undertaken privately and guided through the indirect mechanisms of the market. In several areas there is of course a measure of control or regulation, but this does not detract from the general conclusion.

In the third place, from the aspect of the management of enterprises undertaken by the Government, it is significant that the vast majority of public enterprises are functioning as corporations and companies with their own autonomous Boards and management, and are expected to operate on a commercial basis, paying taxes to the State, building up their own resources for development and with an increasing degree of freedom in internal management, if not yet in determination of pricing and investment policies.

### PUBLIC AND PRIVATE SECTORS

In the scheme of planned development the public and private sectors are viewed as being complementary. The private sector includes not only organized industry, but also agriculture, small industry, trade and a great deal of activity in housing and construction and other fields. Over the greater part of activities comprised in the private sector, individual effort and private initiative are regarded as necessary and desirable, the aim of policy being to assist development on the basis of voluntary cooperation to the utmost extent feasible. Much of the activity undertaken by Government by way of provision of transport and power and education and social services and the establishment of basic industries supports and makes possible the spread of economic activity on the part of individuals and groups.

### PUBLIC PARTICIPATION AND COOPERATION

The enlistment of voluntary effort and public participation has been one of the keystones of India's planning. As was stated in the First Plan:

> Public cooperation and public opinion constitute the principal force and sanction behind planning. A democracy working for social ends has to base itself on the willing assent of the people and not the coercive powers of the State. . . . In the way any programme is conceived, offered and carried out, action by the agencies of the government must be inspired by an understanding of the role of the people and supported by practical steps to enlist their enthusiastic participation.

With each Plan an attempt is made to assess the elements of strength and weakness in the prevailing system of public cooperation and national development and from time to time new ways of enlarging public cooperation are tried out. Considerable encouragement is given to voluntary organizations and an attempt is made to coordinate their efforts through the National Advisory Committee for Public Cooperation. In the formulation of each Plan and in its subsequent implementation, at the local, state and national level efforts are made to enlist public cooperation and comment and criticism and constructive suggestions are sought from all quarters. As a Five Year Plan takes shape, having passed through a prolonged process of consultation and public debate, it emerges as a national consensus largely passing beyond party lines.

### INSTITUTIONAL CHANGES

An important pre-condition for development in each sector of the economy concerns policies and measures for creating an adequate institutional framework. This is a task of extreme difficulty and one calling for continuous adaptation, for which no ready-made solutions are available and there is need for considerable experimentation and evaluation of experience.

In agriculture there are three essential institutional steps: (a) creation of a network of extension services, (b) reform of land tenures and (c) development of cooperation in credit, marketing and other activities including, so far as may be possible, production. Important measures in these directions were initiated in the First Five Year Plan and have been further developed in the Second and the Third Plan.

### BALANCED DEVELOPMENT

The question of balanced development in relation to different sectors is essentially one of priorities during a given phase of development as expressed in allocations of real and financial resources. In each Plan this issue has to be determined after taking into account urgent objectives and the stage of development reached in different fields. On the whole, planning in India has been based on the premise that balanced development in different sectors is a desirable goal, even though it may for a period lead to comparatively less progress in some selected fields. The overall cumulative effect of balanced development is expected to be not only greater but also better calculated to lead to even progress and social stability.

Considerations governing balanced regional development have been set out at length in India's Third Plan. The Plan points out that the balanced development of different parts of the country, extension of the benefits of economic progress to the less developed regions and widespread diffusion of industry are among the major aims of planned development. Considerations of the growth of the economy as a whole, however, cannot be neglected. Means have to be found for the transfer of resources from the more rapidly developing and advanced areas to those which have for some reason remained backward. The measure in which such transfers of resources may take place and the capacity of the economy to achieve a better balance between consumption and savings increase when economic growth is both rapid and sustained. It has been emphasised that the development of particular regions should not be achieved at the cost of the economy as a whole. The aim is to develop the growth potential of each region, having regard to its special problems and possibilities and its stage of development without, however, coming in the way of the growth of the economy as a whole.

Each Five Year Plan provides for a scheme of investment and for basic policies and institutional changes which are designed to achieve certain major aims. In drawing up the Third Plan in India, the principal aims have been as follows:

1. To secure an increase in national income of over five per cent per annum, the pattern of investment being designed also to sustain this rate of growth during subsequent Plan periods.

2. To achieve self-sufficiency in foodgrains and increase agricultural production to meet the requirements of industry and exports.

3. To expand basic industries like steel, chemical industries, fuel and power and establish machine-building capacity, so that the requirements of further industrialization can be met within a period of ten years or so mainly from the country's own resources.

4. To utilize to the fullest possible extent the manpower resources of the country and to secure a substantial expansion in employment opportunities.

5. To establish progressively greater equality of opportunity and to bring about reduction in disparities in income and wealth and a more even distribution of economic power.

In proposing these aims an attempt was made to take account equally of the progress of the economy over the previous decade and the objectives to be realized in the course of the next ten or fifteen years.

The Five Year Plans in India do not have the force of legal enactment. Legislation is undertaken in the context of the specific objects to be achieved in any field of development. A reference has been made to legislation for industries. There has been similar legislation in other fields, for instance, for establishing State Electricity Boards or for conservation of coal or for public health and town planning. In all sectors, the Plan provides important guidelines to policy, but these are not intended to be rigid. Conditions vary widely in different parts of India and there must also be much adaptation and innovation as new problems emerge and greater experience is gained. The scale of investment and allocations between different sectors are necessarily matters of judgement and decision rather than legislation. Within limits the scale of investment must also vary from year to year, but a steadily growing volume of investment is necessarily implicit in the scheme of development.

The Indian Plan is not comprehensive in the sense that every sector of development is planned in detail. In the main the greater part of the Plan refers to programs of development undertaken by the Central and State Governments and by local authorities. These include a variety of measures, some involving direct enterprise and management, some in the nature of extension and promotion and others providing for training, research and other methods of raising productivity. Plans in the private sector are in the nature of estimates and forecasts undertaken in consultation with the representatives of industry, but sufficient provision is made for financial resources, including foreign exchange, and the requisite material resources to facilitate the execution of these plans. The levels of production aimed at are also in the nature of estimates, although they serve as target guides.

Annual plans are drawn up in the context of Five Year Plans. Work on the annual plan precedes the preparation of the annual budget. Each annual plan seeks to provide not only for the following year but also includes investments and other preliminary action whose benefits are intended to accrue in later years.

Broad projections for a long-term plan for the period up to 1975–76 have been set out in India's Third Plan. A more detailed long-term plan has yet to be drawn up. However, in several fields studies have been undertaken and further studies are being initiated, specially in industry, power and transport and for obtaining fuller data on natural resources.

## *Strategy for Long-term Economic Development*

As has been explained in the Third Five Year Plan, India's plans are based on a broad strategy of economic development which will ensure that the economy expands rapidly and becomes self-reliant and self-generating within the shortest possible period. In this strategy there is emphasis on interdependence between agriculture and industry, between economic and social development and between national and regional development and on the mobilization of domestic and external resources. Considerable stress is also placed on measures for scientific and technological advance and for raising the general levels of productivity as well as on policies relating to population, employment and social change.

It is considered that the development of agriculture holds the key to the rapid development of the country. In agriculture the maximum increase in production physically possible has to be secured. There is considerable scope for the intensive utilization of manpower resources. The present crop yields are so low that with adequate irrigation, supplies of fertilizers, improved seeds and implements, education and extension, reform of land tenures and development of the rural economy along cooperative lines, large increases in levels of production can be attained. In the present stage of development, production of sufficient foodgrains as well as of cotton, oilseeds and other commercial crops is regarded as being equally urgent.

While agriculture and industry are regarded as closely linked parts of the same process of development, industry is assigned a leading role in securing rapid economic advance. India has large industrial resources and, therefore, a considerable potential for industrial growth. In particular, she has the potential for producing steel and other basic materials relatively cheaply. Her large and growing domestic market places her in a favorable position to produce machinery and a wide range of engineering and chemical and electric goods needed for development. In turn, these are essential for stimulating the growth of medium and small industries and for expanding both urban and rural employment. Over a period, therefore, it should be possible to build up an integrated industrial structure and expand industrial production efficiently along the lines of real comparative advantages. This implies that for a period special emphasis must be placed on industries such as steel, coal, oil, electric power, machine-building and chemicals. With these developing rapidly, the requirements of further industrialization can be met increasingly from the country's own resources.

At the base of the effort to build up industry and agriculture and expand transport and power are the vital programs for the development of human resources, specially education and health, and measures for raising levels of skill and technical know-how and scientific and technological research.

An adequate level of domestic capital formation, the maximum effort possible in developing exports and availability of external assistance during the critical period of transition are among the pre-conditions for building up a self-reliant economy which can sustain a high rate of growth. Mobilization of domestic savings and development of exports will involve considerable burdens for the community but, in the interest of development, for many years only a limited rise in consumption standards will be possible, specially in commodities or services which may be less essential for the bulk of the population. A basic objective is to create the conditions in which dependence on external assistance will disappear as early as possible. A very large expansion of exports is essential for this purpose. In the transitional period, however, the development effort entails a large increase in import requirements, both for specialized capital equipment and for raw materials and components, for which it will be difficult to pay from export earnings. In this situation, external assistance has an important contribution to make to the economic development of the country.

Against the background of the strategy outlined above, development over the next fifteen years or so is postulated in terms of a cumulative rate of growth as close as possible to 6 per cent per annum. With population increasing at over 2 per cent per annum and the labor force expected to increased by about 70 million over the period 1961–76, a rate of growth such as this is to be regarded as the very minimum for achieving a significant rise in levels of living, adequate expansion of opportunities for productive employment outside agriculture and solution of deep-rooted social problems. In the coming years, on account of the increasing and inescapable burdens of defense, the tasks of economic development, complex as they are, will become even more difficult. Inevitably, larger claims will be made on the community. Moreover, in seeking closer integration between defense and development, while there will be opportunity for stimulating growth in some directions, in others the present scheme of priorities may have to be modified, specially for the immediate future.

## *Possibilities and Limitations of Planning*

For an underdeveloped economy planning has a manifold significance. Since resources, whether natural, material, capital or human, are severely limited, planning provides a method of rational and considered choice for securing the optimum combination of inputs. Secondly, planning helps to identify those deficiencies in the economy and the social structure which demand the largest attention from the standpoint of economic growth. Thirdly, a plan for mobilizing resources is a necessary counterpart of the scheme of investment. By posing various critical problems in development and attempting to give them a quantitative dimension, planning is calculated to lead to a higher degree of capital formation than might be otherwise attainable. By drawing attention to the social prerequisites of growth, planning also paves the way for the acceptance of large institutional changes. The very processes associated with planning and the implementation of plans enlarge the scope for public participation and cooperation. Finally, as planning techniques improve and more precise statistical data become available, the interrelationships within the national economy can be seen more clearly and to that extent the effects of different policies and measures can be traced more systematically.

Experience over the past decade or more

suggests that practical success in planning is often limited by a variety of factors, more specially inadequate statistical, economic and technical data, weaknesses in the social structure, lack of trained personnel, and inadequacies of management, in particular in large enterprises, both in the public and the private sector.

# 10

# Administrative Problems of Economic Development

M. Abel

*Reprinted from* Religion and Society *12, no. 3 (1965): 36–50, with permission.*

ECONOMIC DEVELOPMENT IS not a simple matter of inputs and outputs. It is shot through and through with many an intricate political and administrative problem pertaining mainly to human behavior. Bad administration can destroy even a good idea or a sound plan of economic development. Poor administration can lead to waste and general inefficiency in the use of resources. It might mean bad planning and execution of projects, resulting in excessive cost of schemes and projects. Therefore the critical importance of a suitable organization and sound administrative structure and procedures for successful economic planning can hardly be exaggerated. A sound and adequate public administration is, indeed, an essential prerequisite for economic growth.

Indian experience in the process of economic development through planning has tended to reveal that the existing governmental organization is rather insufficient to carry out the greatly expanded public investment and development programs. The reports of the economic survey commissions sent out by the United Nations and the International Bank for Reconstruction and Development are replete with references to the handicaps to Indian economic growth imposed by poorly developed public administration and the shortage of competent officials. The late Prime Minister Jawaharlal Nehru testified to this when he said: "In many cases implementation of (these) projects was delayed, giving rise to increase in cost. To some extent the fault was with the administration."[1] The Planning Commission also has admitted that "the administrative machinery has been strained and, at many points in the structure, the available personnel are not adequate in quality and number."[2]

Thus it cannot be denied that the planning and implementation of the Five-Year Plans in India are hampered to a certain extent, apart from other factors, by the limitations of the Indian political and administrative system. These limitations, according to a statement of the Planning Commission, include: "the slow pace of execution in many fields, problems involved in the planning, construction and operation of large projects, especially increase in costs and non-adherence to time schedules, difficulties in training men on a large enough scale and securing personnel with the requisite calibre and experience, achieving co-ordination in detail in related sectors of the economy and, above all, enlisting the widespread support and co-operation from the community as a whole."[3]

The following analysis is an attempt to show how the limitations of the Indian political and administrative system—mainly the administrative shortcomings of the system—raise certain road-blocks in the way of Indian economic growth. It also emphasizes the need for removing these road-blocks in order to enable Indian economy to reach the goal of self-sustained growth within the time limit stipulated in the Five-Year Plans.

## *Autonomy of States and Planning*

The political system of India accords an autonomous status to the states and empowers them to exercise legislative and administrative jurisdiction over certain defined areas of governmental action. The

**Notes to chapter 10 appear on page 394**

Constitution of India makes provision for the division of power between the Center and states according to which 47 items, including economic and social planning, are placed under the concurrent jurisdiction of the states and the Center, 97 items within the exclusive control of the Center and 66 items within the exclusive control of the states. Among the items included in the State List are Public Health, Education, Roads, Agriculture, Animal Husbandry, Irrigation, Land Policy, Forests, Fisheries and other items of fundamental importance in any plan of general economic and social development like the Five-Year Plans of India.[4] The fact that these are under the exclusive jurisdiction of the states carries with it the implication that many of the developmental projects fall within the jurisdiction of the states and that planning and authorization of projects must be done by the state governments and legislatures. This introduces several obstacles in the way of rational and objective planning.

The political and legislative autonomy of the states hinders proper planning of projects to some extent. Each state is interested in getting as much aid as possible from the Center to put through as many of its own projects as possible. Further, the states are aware of the pruning effect of the Planning Commission on the number of projects they propose. Therefore, they are tempted to propose a large number of projects with the hope of getting at least some of them approved by the Center. Such a state of affairs encourages the states to put forward projects which are hastily conceived and ill-planned for consideration at the Center. In the absence of sound projects, the Center may be forced to select some uneconomical projects. Sometimes political expediency may dictate to the Government of India the exclusion of some sound and economical projects. Pork-barrel politics may result in the inclusion of uneconomical projects with Plans. This may be proved by the fact that many irrigation and power projects were included in the first two Five-Year Plans without fully or adequately exploring the technical and financial soundness of the projects concerned. The Technical Advisory Committees which examined the technical and financial soundness of the projects put forward by the state governments for inclusion in the Second Five-Year Plan drew "pointed attention to the unsatisfactory condition regarding the investigation and finalization of the projects."[5] It pointed out that the investigations were not complete and the project reports lacked details essential for technical and financial scrutiny. The Planning Commission also has admitted that "for many irrigation and power projects sponsored by various State Governments for inclusion in the Second Five-Year Plan, supporting data were either incomplete or inadequate."[6] There is no evidence to believe that matters during the Third Five-Year Plan had improved.

The adverse effects of the autonomy of the states are nowhere more acutely felt than in the schemes of river valley development. Where two or more states are involved in planning and implementing projects like river valley development, hydro-electric power schemes, water supply schemes, etc., states' autonomy, coupled with parochialism, has engendered interstate rivalries and conflicts of interests that draw out negotiations and bargaining, and delay action. The dispute that is now going on among Andhra Pradesh, Mysore and Maharashtra for the allocation of the waters of the Krishna and the Godavari is a case in point. Sometimes projects included in the plans could not be undertaken immediately for implementation for want of workable solutions to interstate disputes. For example, the Upper Sileru hydroelectric project of Andhra Pradesh, which was included in the Second Five-Year Plan, remains still unexecuted because of the difference of opinion between the Governments of Andhra Pradesh and Orissa in regard to the site of the project. The project is again included in the Third Five-Year Plan but has not yet been allotted the needed foreign exchange. Explaining the reason for this, the Central Minister for Irrigation and Power stated in the Parliament that "in regard to the Upper Sileru Stage II, foreign exchange would be arranged only after the difference of opinion between the Governments of Andhra Pradesh and Orissa in regard to the site has been resolved."[7] Even if workable solutions are ultimately found to these interstate disputes, they may not be the best or the most economical solutions.

The remedy for such interstate disputes that hamper sound and proper planning lies in evolving a suitable organization whose jurisdictional boundaries go beyond those of the states as defined in the Constitution. In order to reap optimum benefits from the development of water resources, different states have to cooperate and their schemes of development should be coordinated. As the Planning Commission has put it:

> Water stored in reservoirs in one state may be used with advantage for irrigation in adjoining states. Similarly, power available in one state may be distributed in other states. In certain cases, it may be useful to divert waters from one basin to another for the benefit of the region as a whole. Co-operation between states is, therefore, essential for investigations, allocation of waters and sharing of costs.[8]

That the existing unit of political organization, namely the state, is not conducive to promote interstate cooperation for the integrated and economic development of the large river basins is quite evident from the number of interstate disputes going on for the allocation of the resources of the various interstate rivers. Therefore, the unit of political organization for such items of development as river valley development should be larger than the state. Such a larger unit of political organization cannot be the Union of India for it would be too large and too remote to deal effectively with the public and the political community involved in water disputes. The inability of the Union Government to solve interstate water disputes is proved by the fact that it has not been able to implement effectively the River Boards Act of 1955 and the Interstate Water Dispute Act of 1955. On the other hand, it could not be the state, which is too small and too much preoccupied with its own development to take cognizance of the legitimate interests of other states and bring an objective approach to the planning of the management and development of water resources. Neither centralization nor decentralization affords an equitable and workable solution to such problems as involved in interstate water disputes. Therefore, in order to facilitate rational planning of river valley development schemes, an organization with a scale of jurisdiction smaller than the Union government but larger than the state government has to be evolved.

This does not mean that the present set-up should be scrapped, states abolished and new political units established. The state provides a suitable scale of organization for such items as education, agriculture, cooperation, community development, etc., and so it cannot be abolished. Moreover, the sentimental force that lies behind the present state set-up makes it rather difficult to envisage the possibility of abolishing the states and establishing a unitary state in India. Therefore, the need of the hour is to evolve an organization with jurisdictional boundaries large enough to include such items that are difficult to be dealt with by individual states in isolation. Such an organization should consist of the representatives of two or three states of a particular region to bring a regional approach to planning. The Zonal Councils which came into existence in the wake of the reorganization of the boundaries of the states in 1956 can offer a solution to this problem. Though they were primarily established to deal with interstate boundary disputes, they are capable of being developed into full-fledged units of political organization with certain defined functions and powers relating to such subjects as development of interstate river basins. These Zonal Councils, supported by the technical expertise of advisory bodies such as the River Boards (which are yet to be constituted) might offer an adequate scale of organization to deal with problems of planning arising out of inter-state disputes.

## *Administrative Structure and Procedure*

In the execution of the projects included in the Plans the administrative departments concerned assume major responsibility. In some projects, more than one department is involved. Further, different projects are implemented at different levels in the administrative set-up, namely, national, state, district, block and village. The successful implementation of projects, therefore, requires horizontal coordination between different departments as well as vertical coordination between the various levels within the same department at different levels of administration. The maintenance of such coordination largely depends upon the nature of the prevailing administrative structures and procedures, and also on the calibre of personnel. Therefore, the chief problem when trying to assess the efficiency with which projects are implemented, is to know how far Indian administrative structures and procedures, facilitate interdepartmental cooperation and coordination on the one hand and cooperation and coordination among different hierarchical levels within the same department, and between central and local levels of administration, on the other. This section endeavors to indicate that weaknesses inherent in the administrative structures and procedures and personnel practices affect unfavorably the efficient execution of the Plan projects.

### PROBLEMS OF ADMINISTRATIVE STRUCTURE

The organizational structure of the administrative departments at the Center as well as in the states is not very conducive to sound planning and efficient execution of projects. As Paul H. Appleby has observed: "Hierarchies are not set up with a sufficient number of levels of a relatively slight differentiation in responsibility; the levels are too far apart for good communication, underpinning, effective delegation, and more constant development of personnel capacities."[9] Such hierarchical structures which are not well filled in and which do not have much pyramidal form cannot facilitate free and continued flow of information and commands up and down the administrative line. This makes it difficult for those in command to secure an adequate informational basis to understand the problem in all its varied aspects and formulate sound judgments and decisions. The existing structure of administrative departments does not facilitate a vertical discussion of matters within the departmental hierarchy which is very essential for sound and effective decision-making. Further, it does not make room for delegation of authority and responsibility to the lower echelon. So much so, the top officials in the department who are expected to be responsible for making important decisions and inventing ideas to execute projects are preoccupied with routine, trivial matters of departmental housekeeping. Consequently the projects may fail to be properly conceived or efficiently executed.

Even interdepartmental coordination suffers under the present structure because sometimes departments are set up with undifferentiated but overlapping functions. For example, two agencies, namely, the Community Development Department and the Central Social Welfare Board, are functioning within the same jurisdictional area and with similar functions. The latter was brought into existence to coordinate women's and children's welfare programs and especially assist voluntary agencies. It was not originally intended to start its own welfare extension programs on a uniform pattern with centralized direction. The Government resolution adjured it "to promote the setting up of social welfare organizatiosn on a voluntary basis in places where no such organizations exist."[10] But in course of time, the Central Social Welfare Board began to organize welfare extension projects, one in each district in the country, each serving a group of about 25 villages. Very often these villages would have already been included in a community development block. One often sees the gram sevikas of the Community Development Department and the workers of the Social Welfare Department invading the same village for the same purposes. The result is confusion, waste and overlapping. To rectify this, the Central Government ordered an integrated pattern of activities in December 1956. The Programme Evaluation Organization made a study of this problem and recommended that what was needed was a coordinated pattern of work. But so far nothing has happened. The vested interests which have grown up in the past six or seven years are too strong to be eliminated easily. But in the interests of economy and efficiency it is better to reduce the multiplicity of overlapping agencies than to talk about coordination between two agencies which are performing similar functions in the same areas.

The implementation of plan projects is further impeded by lack of adequate cooperation between the Central and State Governments. The division of powers between the Center and the States as set forth in the Constitution refers not only to legislative but also to administrative powers, for the Constitution provides that "the executive power of the state shall extend to the matters with respect to which the legislature has the power to make laws."[11] This implies that the primary responsibility for developing those areas of governmental activity that are assigned to the state by the Constitution lies with the state and that the administrative machinery needed for that purpose should, on the whole, be the state administrative machinery. As a result, sometimes the Government of India does not have much say in the issuing of construction contracts, personnel recruitment, supervision and other details pertaining to the execution of the projects concerned, and its hopes for success are dependent on its capacity for "influencing and coordinating administration actually in the states' systems and not directing or controlling the States or holding them strictly and specifically accountable."[12]

No doubt the Central Government does have control over its own grants-in-aid, and it is as much concerned as the states in the proper administration of even those projects within the exclusive control of the latter if such concern is demanded by the principles and policies underlying the development plans. There are ministries at the Center with functional fields akin to those of the state, charged with the "overall responsibility for helping, coordinating and guiding the work of the states so that national policies can be evolved and satisfactorily worked."[13] However, too much of administrative responsibility is left to the states with the result that there is a danger of the policies and programs not being effectively implemented."[14] The Central ministries, being restricted in function to only "diluted and incomplete coordination" with only "staff functions" and no administrative line, "do not exercise any real, formal and continuing power of control" but only promote "an excess of cross-reference and conference antecedent to action, and a delaying of action."[15] The difficulty of the Central government to control and coordinate the activities of the State governments makes it rather difficult to ensure the proper use of the funds, and expeditious and efficient execution of projects.

### PROBLEM OF ADMINISTRATIVE PROCEDURE

Indian administrative procedures often hinder bold and imaginative planning and execution of projects. The whole administrative procedure is dominated by the process of review which discourages initiative and enterprise on the part of the officials and dissuades them from assuming responsibility to take sound decisions.

A project may be included in the Five-Year Plan and may have been allotted the required foreign exchange, the required amount of steel, and necessary funds. But the ministry designated to execute the project cannot go ahead with the project unless it secures the prior approval of the Finance Ministry for funds, the Home Ministry for personnel, and the Ministry of Industry and Commerce to obtain steel. It must also secure the approval for the use of foreign exchange, and of any other ministry which might have some remote connection with the project. All this involves re-reviewing, by different ministries at different hierarchical levels, of the project which has already been reviewed and recommended for inclusion in the Plan. For example, Paul H. Appleby, who has studied closely the Indian administrative system, has observed: "Granted prior agreement in principle on kind and dimension of program to be undertaken and the amount of money to be made available for the purpose, specific decisions incident to effectuation of purpose in India are reviewed by too many persons in too many organs of the government in too detailed, too repetitive and too negative terms."[16] The result, as Mr. U. Ananda Rau, the Chairman of the Central Board of Irrigation and Power, has observed, is that it takes years of correspondence to get through the clearance of the ministries concerned for getting the exchange allotted (for procurement of machinery and other implements from abroad) and it thus involves considerable loss of time and slowing down of progress."[17]

This process of review is rendered futile by the fact that it is conducted at different hierarchial levels in the states and at the Center without much differentiation along the same lines, and is directed toward discovering whether the purpose "is fully in accord with the precedent."[18] Further, the entire process seems to be irrational in view of the fact that a project of a designated ministry which has been recommended by experts in the ministry concerned, when sent for approval by another ministry, is reviewed by some subordinate staff "who have no experience or knowledge of the kind of project being dealt with," and yet do not hesitate to challenge the technical findings of the experts.[19]

The net result of this "unbelievably petty and frustrating" process of "precedent-oriented", negative and repetitive review is that it necessitates "too many references of too many matters . . . to get agreement on everything by everybody before anybody risks doing anything."[20] Consequently, besides much loss of valuable time and effort, the designated ministry, denied of discretion in the selection of its own personnel and lacking authority to draw on funds and supplies without the prior approval of other ministries, feels less accountable for its performance than it ought to, and tends to evade responsibility for making decisions. Thus the present procedure of preliminary process of consultation and conference between departments and ministries serves only to undermine the sense of individual responsibility. Any review of past actions by too many persons in too detailed, repetitive and negative terms makes officials chary of taking much on themselves. Such a state of affairs is not conducive to sound planning and effective execution of projects. The remedy for this lies, as the Planning Commission has pointed out, in making "a concentrated attempt to make the administration much more action-oriented than at present", and by giving to the agency and particular individuals within it "full responsibility and, with it, the necessary measure of support and trust" within defined limits.[21] Consultations, which are at present too frequent and too concerned with detail and, therefore, impede effective action, should be reduced to the minimum and be confined to broader matters. Therefore, the real issue is whether "programming ministries," as Dr. Appleby calls them, may safely be given the necessary autonomy to draw upon funds and recruit personnel without having to wait for the Finance Ministry to sanction their estimates or the Public Service Commission to select their personnel. The Finance and Home Ministries, which have special powers of supervision and coordination of the work of others, must therefore reconsider and relax their rules with a view to increasing the responsibility and initiative of officials in charge of projects.

The existing budget procedures also contribute somewhat to the inefficient planning and administration of projects. In present practice projects are submitted to the Finance Ministry all the year round even after the budget has been approved by Parliament or a State Legislature. Allotment of funds is made to some projects immediately while others are kept on file for re-reference and activation later on. The result is that the ministries, knowing full well that the Finance Ministry will reduce their requests, submit many loosely estimated projects for inclusion in the budget. Commenting on the evils of such a practice of re-reference of development schemes for final administrative and financial sanction, the Foodgrains Enquiry Committee has stated that the final sanction of schemes after the budget is passed, means that "money for the schemes does not in many cases start flowing until towards the end of the financial year. The result is, quite often, confusion, injudicious expenditure and either a sacrifice of quality for quantity, or a partial or total lapse of the sums allotted. What is needed is synchronizing the procedure for executive approval and financial sanction of schemes to suit the development needs."[22] If projects are to be properly planned and executed, the Ministry of Finance must encourage and stimulate good budgeting practices in the various departments by giving immediate and maximum approval to projects that are proposed on the basis of rational and firm cost estimates.

## *Personnel Problems*

Successful execution of the Plan Projects, with necessary funds and supplies of materials given, depends largely on the adequacy and competence of the personnel employed to carry out the projects under the programs. The main problem of India in the personnel field is to find adequate numbers of competent personnel to administer and carry out the projects. It is generally agreed that Indian Government agency staffs are shorthanded and overloaded with work at top levels. In its report on the Second Five-Year Plan, the Planning Commission has stated that "in several fields the average state is not able to recruit personnel of high quality, organize adequate training and provide reserves of personnel to cope with continually expanding needs."[23] This shortage of technical and administrative personnel, as the Planning Commission has admitted, "has been the most important single cause for shortfalls in the expenditure and consequent failure to fulfil targets set by the (First) Five-Year Plan."

The execution of development projects also requires proper approach and attitude on the part of the administrative personnel to the problems of economic and social development. The role of the administrative personnel in a dynamic and revolutionary situation such as social and economic development is different from that of just maintaining law and order, and collecting revenue and taxes. The task of development requires the administrator to transform himself into what Dr. R. G. Karve, the Director of Programme Evaluation Organization, has called the "Executive-*cum*-Development Officer." The administrator should become more "action-oriented," more receptive to the technical advice of the experts in matters of planning development, and identify himself more and more with the people and their welfare. But in actual practice, as the Programme Evaluation Organization has reported, "while instances of personalities transcending the limitations of administrative relationship and forms might be treated as exceptional, the normal working of the executive-*cum*-developmental officer at the project or block level has yielded disappointing, but by no means unexpected results."[24] In order to understand why this has happened one must find out whether the Indian administrative personnel, under existing conditions of training and incentives, are capable at all to adapt themselves to new conditions and economic and social development. This problem may be conveniently tackled through an analysis of the personnel problems encountered in the execution of community development projects.

The community projects which are intended to change the outlook of the people and infuse the spirit of self-reliance need a new type of officer to convey the message of these projects to the villagers. The district collector and his revenue staff are neither suited for the job nor capable of adapting themselves to the new requirements. The training of the personnel of the Indian Administrative Services is still modeled on that of the old Indian Civil Service. It is based on the same old generalist tradition and does not make provision for the candidates to gain practical understanding and experience of the problems of development in the district. Further, the collectors and revenue staff are too conscious of their rank and dignity of office to cooperate with technical experts of lower ranks when such cooperation is essential for conducting successfully the operations of a development program. For example, the Programme Evaluation Organization has reported that one-fifth of the "agricultural specialists feel that they do not share in decision-making regarding their program. . . . In the field of cooperation the block specialists and the Block Development Officers meet often enough, but more than 50 per cent of the specialists feel that they do not participate in planning and decision-making."[25] Moreover, the image of the revenue officials as tax gatherers and revenue collectors is not congenial to evoke public enthusiasm for and participation in projects. Thus the generalist type of intellectual orientation of the administrative personnel, their status-consciousness and dependence on authority and power to obtain public cooperation, and their reluctance to cooperate with specialists in the various fields of community development make it rather difficult for the collector and his revenue staff to adapt what Paul H. Appleby has called the "human relations orientation" which is essential for the success of the community development projects. Therefore, instead of trying to bring about a reorientation in the outlook of the revenue officials, it is better to disassociate them from developmental projects and recruit a new type of people who by temperament, upbringing and training are well qualified and suited to implement projects of economic and social development. As long as revenue staff is charged with developmental and social welfare functions "the result in terms of a real change in the outlook and habits of the people are found to be disappointing."

## *Organizing People for Action*

The process of development in India has so far been conducted mainly in terms of achieving production targets, financial outlays and other physical assets. The emphasis has been on completing projects within the target dates, establishing the specified number of development blocks, distributing a given quantity of improved seeds and fertilizers, etc. The disadvantage of this kind of target-oriented approach is that it neglects the development of social assets such as labor, and the full utilization of the potential created by the newly executed projects. There is a tremendous responsibility on the administration to organize people to make effective use of existing social and economic assets as well as exploit to the maximum extent the potential of the new projects. That the administrators have failed to discharge this responsibility may be illustrated by the unsatisfactory exploitation of the potential of many major irrigation schemes.

During the last decade India has executed many river valley development schemes. These have created a large potential of irrigation but not all of this potential is being used. According to the Foodgrains Enquiry Committee report, "at the end of the First Plan the potential created was 5.59 lakh (559,000) acres in Bihar and 4.65 lakh (465,000) acres in West Bengal, of which only 2.65 and 2.23 lakh acres were actually irrigated.[26] Thus about 50 per cent of the potential benefits from major irrigation has been left unharnessed. In Mysore State, as against the irrigation potential of 10.6 million acres, the actual irrigated area was only 1.2 million acres. The respective figures for the Tungabhadra Project are 580,000 and 33,000 acres.

Several factors, most of them administrative, are responsible for this non-utilization of the new irrigation potential to the fullest extent. It requires the administration to take effective steps for organizing and educating people to make use of the available irrigation facilities. In some states cultivators are not accustomed to using irrigation facilities and are reluctant to switch over from dry to irrigated farming, either for want of necessary capital or out of conservative habits. In such cases the Community Development and National Extension Service Blocks should intensify their campaign to teach the cultivators the use and benefits of irrigation projects and other developmental schemes.

Further, the Government constructs only the head-works and in some cases the main distributary canals, and leaves the construction of branch channels and field channels to farmers. It is estimated that "for every million acres of irrigated area, the Government has to provide approximately on an average, 2,500 miles of canals and the village has to provide four times that length, *viz.*, 10,000 miles of field channels."[27] Therefore, the solution to the problem of utilizing the irrigation potential ultimately hinges on how enthusiastic the people are to construct the field channels. Here is a tremendous responsibility on the administrators to organize people for effective and enthusiastic action. Unless the democratic processes of India evolve some ways and means of organizing and mobilizing all available labor for developmental purposes, maximum utilization of the full potential of the new projects cannot be achieved.

India has tried to organize the human resources of the country through organizations like the Bharat Sevak Samaj. But the predominance of the leadership of the Congress Party has hindered the participation of others of different political faiths in the activities of the Samaj. Therefore it is very essential that such popular organizations be actively led by non-partisan social workers instead of political leaders to ensure enthusiastic cooperation and participation of all people irrespective of political prejudices. Further, representative institutions like the Panchayats and Panchayat Samitis must be strengthened and endowed with adequate resources to organize and mobilize people for effective action.

## *Evaluation*

The need for evaluation exists in all purposive, planned and organized action in any field—social, private or governmental. Parliamentary Committees like the Public Accounts Committee and the Estimates Committee do conduct periodical evaluation of the performance of the Plans. The Committee for Plan Projects constituted by the Planning Commission also makes mid-term appraisals of the Plan performances. Further review of activities and appraisal of results are normally undertaken by the Central Coordinating Committee through a system of regular checks, inspections and stocktaking. Besides such routine administrative assessment of quality and quantity of the end-product and targets, there is another type of evaluation which is of much fundamental importance from the point of view of collecting information to serve as a basis for future policy changes. No administrative policy can claim final validity. As it is pointed out by Dewey "every measure of policy put into operation is logically, and actually, of the nature of an experiment."[28] In this sense, every scheme of economic development is an experiment and its results should be carefully and objectively evaluated in order to facilitate the planning of the future course of action in the light of the past experience and the attitudes and reactions of people to changing economic and social conditions. For example, evaluation may be conducted with a view to discovering the groups that function as agents and carriers of change in villages so as to find the proper channel to introduce changes successfully. In all the fields of development effort, in which the objectives are not merely the accomplishment of stated administrative tasks but are related to consciously inducing social and economic changes, evaluation can be a valuable aid to administrative action. By furnishing an objective appraisal of progress, by indicating which methods have proved effective and successful and by furnishing more detailed quantitative data through specially carried out surveys, it can provide valuable material for the guidance of field workers.

The Planning Commission emphasized the need for program evaluation in its report on the Second Five-Year Plan:

> In all planned development many unknown factors have to be reckoned with. Understanding of the interaction of different elements that enter into the programs which bear closely on the life of the people can be of material help in enhancing their contribution to the welfare of the community. Evaluation has, therefore, to be increasingly oriented towards studies of a selective and intensive type, motivated by and leading to purposive action.[29]

To perform this task, the Programme Evaluation Organization was established with the help of the Ford Foundation as an independent organization but attached to the Planning Commission. This organization has been doing valuable work in the field of community development projects and national extension service blocks and has so far published *Evaluation Reports on the Com-*

*munity Projects* and has also conducted several sociological surveys and studies of health and levels of living.[30] There is much need for enlarging the activities of the Programme Evaluation Organization to include other projects and further intensifying its studies and surveys in the existing areas. The universities and other autonomous institutions of higher learning and research should be encouraged to participate in the evaluation of the various development programs and projects.

# Industrial Policy in India

*Government of India*

*From Government of India, Department of Industries,* Industrial Development in India *(Delhi: Manager of Publications 1965), p. 11–16 with omissions. Reprinted with permission.*

## *Industrial Policy Resolution, 1948*

AFTER INDEPENDENCE THE Government decided to encourage the existing industries to step up their production, and to promote the establishment of new industries. The main aim was to strengthen the economy and to initiate institutional changes which would facilitate more rapid advance in the future. In order to achieve these objectives, a comprehensive statement of policy was necessary. Accordingly, the Government adopted the Industrial Policy Resolution in April 1948.

The Resolution emphasized clearly the responsibilities of Government in promoting, assisting and regulating the development of industry in the national interest. It laid down a certain demarcation of fields for the public and private sectors. For example, the Resolution reserved some industries exclusively for the Central Government. These were the manufacture of arms and ammunition, the production and control of atomic energy and the ownership and management of railway transport. In some other industries, such as coal, iron and steel, aircraft manufacture, ship-building, manufacture of telegraph, telephone and wireless apparatus and mineral oils, both Central and State Governments as well as other public authorities were to be responsible for further development. However, cooperation of private enterprise was to be enlisted where necessary.

The rest of the industrial field was left open to private and cooperative enterprise. But the state could intervene whenever the progress of any industry, under private enterprise, was unsatisfactory. Central regulation and control was envisaged for eighteen specified industries, such as automobiles and tractors, machine tools, cement and air and sea transport, which were of special importance from the viewpoints of investment and technical skill involved.

### INDUSTRIES (DEVELOPMENT AND REGULATION) ACT, 1951

To implement the industrial policy, the Government decided to acquire powers to regulate and develop industries along the prescribed lines. To this end, the Constitution was amended and the Industries (Development and Regulation) Act of 1951 was enacted.

Initially, the Act applied to 37 industries listed in the first schedule. These included fuel, machinery, electrical goods, electric energy, automobiles, telephones and telegraphs, arms and ammunition, agricultural implements and various other consumer, producer and capital goods industries. The Act was amended in 1953 to provide, among other things, for the addition of a few industries like silk, artificial silk, dyestuffs, soap, plywood and ferromanganese to the list. It was again amended in 1956 to bring 34 more industries under the control of the Union Government. At present, 162 industries come within the scope of the Act.

Under the Act, all existing undertakings were required to be registered with the Government. Substantial extensions to the existing units, or the setting up of new units, could not be undertaken without license from the Government. The Act authorized the Government to examine the working of any scheduled industry or undertaking in cases where there was a fall in the quantity or quality of its products or when there was an unjustified rise in their prices. If the undertaking continued to be mismanaged, and did not carry out the directions issued after an investigation, the Government was empowered to take over the management.

The Act also provided for the establishment of a Central Advisory Council of Industries, consisting of representatives of industry, labor, consumers and primary producers, to advise the Government on all matters concerning the development and regulation of industries. The Council was established in May 1952.

One of the main provisions of the Act was the setting up of development councils for individual industries. The councils would draw up plans for development, determine targets of production, promote improvement in efficiency and formulate measures for the maximum utilization of the existing industrial capacity.

At present, fourteen councils are functioning covering the following industries:

(1) Art silk, (2) woollen, (3) paper, pulp and allied industries, (4) food processing, (5) oils, detergents and paints, (6) sugar, (7) organic chemicals, (8) inorganic chemicals, (9) machine tools, (10) non-ferrous metals and alloys, (11) automobiles, automobile ancillary industries, transport vehicle industries, tractors and earthmoving equipment, (12) drugs and pharmaceuticals, (13) heavy electricals, and (14) textile machinery.

Five councils, set up earlier, have since been abolished. These covered:

(1) glass and ceramics, (2) leather and leather goods, (3) instruments, bicycles and sewing machines, (4) internal combustion engines, power driven pumps, etc., and (5) light electrical industries.

Besides, a number of panels and expert committees have been appointed to examine the policies and problems facing some industries which are not sufficiently developed or advanced to need a development council.

By exercising the powers under the Act, the Government aim at securing (1) a proper utilization of the country's resources; (2) a balanced development of large and small-scale industries; and (3) a proper regional distribution of the various industries.

## *Industrial Policy Resolution, 1956*

The 1948 Industrial Policy Resolution guided India's industrial development for eight years. These years witnessed many important changes and developments in the country. The Constitution of free India was adopted, guaranteeing certain fundamental rights and enunciating the Directive Principles of State Policy. Parliament adopted the socialist pattern of society as the objective of social and economic policy. The First Five Year Plan was completed, laying a new foundation for future growth and the Second Plan was formulated, with emphasis on industry. These developments necessitated a fresh statement of industrial policy, based on the principles laid down in the Constitution, the socialist pattern and the experience gained during these eight years.

In April 1956, the Government adopted the new Industrial Policy Resolution. It envisaged the enlargement of the public sector so as to include in it all industries of basic and strategic importance or in the nature of public utility services. Other industries, which were essential and required investment on a scale which the state alone could provide, had also to be in the public sector.

### THREE CATEGORIES

The new Resolution classified industries into three categories and defined the part the state was to play in each of them. In the first category were included seventeen heavy, basic or strategic industries, such as arms and ammunition, aircraft and railway transport, the future development of which was to be the exclusive responsibility of the state. The second category consisted of twelve industries such as machine tools, fertilizers and antibiotics which were to be progressively owned by the state. In order to accelerate their future development, the state was to establish new undertakings in those industries. At the same time, private enterprise was also expected to supplement the efforts of the state either on its own or with state participation. The third category included all the remaining industries. The future development of these was left to the initiative and enterprise of the private sector, although it was open to the state to enter any field, if necessary. It is necessary to emphasize that the three categories were not meant to be water-tight compartments. The public and private sectors were to work as complementary to each other. A good deal of flexibility was permitted in practice. For instance, major expansions in steel were allowed in the private sector although steel was in Schedule A, reserved for the public sector.

### ENCOURAGEMENT TO PRIVATE SECTOR

The development of industries in the private sector was to be in accordance with the programs formulated in successive Five Year Plans by ensuring the development of transport, power and other services and by appropriate fiscal and other measures. The state was to continue promoting institutions to provide financial aid to these industries.

Special assistance was to be given to enterprises organized on cooperative lines for industrial and agricultural purposes. But industrial undertakings in the private sector had necessarily to fit into the framework of the social and economic policy of the state. They were subject to control and regulation in terms of the Industries (Development and Regulation) Act and other relevant legislation.

### SMALL-SCALE AND COTTAGE INDUSTRIES

The Resolution also stressed the role of cottage and village and small-scale industries in the development of the country's national economy. These industries offer some distinct advantages. For example, they provide immediate employment to a large number of people. At the same time, such industries generally ensure a more equitable distribution of the national income. They facilitate an effective mobilization of resources of capital and skill which might otherwise remain unutilized. The aim of the state policy was to ensure that the decentralized sector acquired sufficient vitality to be self-supporting and its development was integrated with that of large-scale industry.

### REGIONAL DISPARITIES

In order that industrialization might benefit the economy of the country as a whole, the Resolution stressed that disparities in levels of development between different regions should be progressively reduced. One of the aims of national planning, therefore, was to ensure that the various facilities, such as raw materials, power, water supply and transport, were steadily made available to areas that lagged behind industrially or where there was greater need for providing employment opportunities. Only by securing a balanced and coordinated development of industrial and agricultural economy in each region could the entire country attain higher standards of living.

### TECHNICAL AND MANAGERIAL PERSONNEL

The Resolution recognized that such a program of industrial development would require large numbers of technical and managerial personnel. Accordingly, managerial and technical cadres were to be established in the public services. Steps had also to be taken to meet shortages at supervisory levels, to organize apprenticeship schemes for training on a large scale, both in public and private enterprises, and to extend training facilities in business management in universities and other institutions.

### LABOR ASSOCIATION IN MANAGEMENT

The new policy laid stress on the provision of proper amenities and incentives for all those engaged in industry. The living and working conditions of workers needed to be improved and their standard of efficiency raised. It was laid down that there should be joint consultation and workers and technicians should be associated progressively with management. Enterprises in the public sector had to set an example in this respect.

DECENTRALIZATION OF AUTHORITY

Finally, the new policy emphasized that, with the growing participation of the state in industry and trade, the manner in which these activities should be conducted and managed assumed considerable importance. Speedy decisions and a willingness to assume responsibility were essential if these enterprises were to succeed. To achieve this objective, there was to be decentralization of authority and management was to be along business lines.

12

# Central Economic Control

*Audrey Donnithorne*

*From* Bulletin of the Atomic Scientists, Science and Public Affairs *22, no. 6, (June 1966): 11–20, with omissions. Reprinted by permission. The subject of central economic control in China is treated at greater length in Audrey Donnithorne's book,* China's Economic System *(New York: Frederick A. Praeger, 1967).*

WESTERNERS COMMONLY ASSUME present-day China to be a monolith under tight control by the central government in Peking. This article questions that assumption and discusses the degree and manner of central control, particularly in economic matters, although these cannot be dissociated from political factors.

We will first detail those categories of economic undertakings still remaining under the direct management of the central government, and those economic targets which the center still lays down. Most of our information about these dates from the decentralization measures of 1957–58. (On the decentralization movement in general, see Donnithorne, "Background to the People's Communes: Changes in China's Economic Organization in 1958," *Pacific Affairs, XXXII*, 4, December 1959.) Since then information has, of course, been scantier, but had there been a radical change of direction it is unlikely to have been completely concealed. We will then discuss the extent to which central authorities have been able to maintain control of the economy, despite administrative decentralization, through the instrumentality of the Party and the army. Finally we shall consider features of the Chinese scene which render close control difficult by any level of government, central or local.

The decree of November 1957 on the reform of the industrial management system was implemented faster than originally anticipated. By June 1958 no textile factories remained under the direct control of the central Ministry of Textile Industry, and all but five of the factories under the Ministry of Light Industry had similarly been handed over to the management of local authorities (*People's Daily*, June 25, 1958, p. 1), primarily to those on the provincial level. (By the "provincial level authorities" is meant the administrations of the twenty-one provinces, five autonomous regions, and the cities of Peking and Shanghai, all of which come directly under the central government. In this article these will often be referred to as "the provinces.") By the middle of 1958, therefore, the central government directly controlled virtually no manufacture of consumer goods. In producer goods industries, most undertakings of importance were, by terms of the decree, to remain under direct control of the central ministries. These undertakings included large metallurgical and chemical enterprises; important coal fields; large power stations and electricity grids; oil refineries (no size qualification specified for these last); factories making large and precision machines, electric motors and instruments; the whole of the military equipment industry; and other technically complex branches of industry, together with experimental plants and other special cases. (*Collected Laws and Regulations of the Chinese People's Republic* [in Chinese], *VI*, p. 392; Hsiao Liu, "The Problem of Building Industrial Bases and of the Balanced Development of Local Economies," *Planned Economy, VII*, July 1958, p. 8.) The decentralization of heavy industry was reported to have covered a wider range than indicated by the original decree. (*People's Daily*, June 25, 1958, p. 1; *Collected Laws and Regulations, VII*, p. 331.)

The group of state farms, factories, mines, and other undertakings operated by the People's Liberation Army Production and Construction Corps in Sinkiang is under the immediate control of the Ministry of State Farms and Land Reclamation, as is the important group of state farms (also founded by ex-servicemen) in Heilungkiang, and another group of farms in a frontier district of Inner Mongolia. This gives the central government a close hold over certain strategic areas, as well as sources of grain supplies under its immediate control.

In transport, the main railway system, other than small local railways and lines built to serve individual coalfields, factories, or lumber areas, is under direct central control, together with the major civil aviation services. Road transport is mainly under local control, but the central government has been responsible for building—and presumably maintaining—certain major highways, notably some of strategic importance. The main coastal shipping services are directly under the central government (although there may be some difference in this respect between shipping services along the north China and the south China coasts), while a central governmental organ—the Yangtze Navigation Administrative Bureau—exercises general supervision of shipping on the Yangtze. In addition to the Bureau's own vessels, local authorities and joint state-private companies also run ships on the river. Transoceanic shipping under the Chinese flag, whether Chinese-owned or chartered, may be presumed to come directly under the central government, as would the China Ocean Steamship Agency, which handles the clearing of foreign ships and agency work at all ports at which foreign ships are accustomed to call.

The main national level organs of radio, telecommunications, and the press come directly under the central authorities.

The central government has direct control of the river conservancy commissions, of which the chief are the Yellow River Water Conservancy Commission, the Huai River Water Conservancy Commission, and the Yangtze River Planning Office. These commissions span several provinces and are charged with the multi-purpose development of the respective rivers. Similarly, the Grand Canal Committee, established to improve the Grand Canal for purposes of both navigation and water conservancy, was placed under the chairmanship of the Minister of Communications.

The banking system, coming directly under the central government, and especially the ubiquitous People's Bank, is an all-important instrument of supervision and control over the entire economy. The main foreign trade corporations also fall under direct control, although local foreign trade corporations appear to have some independence in their dealings.

The chief institutions of higher learning and of scientific research have been maintained as national, rather than provincial, organs and their subordination to the central government has furthered its control over both the economy and the armed forces.

## *Targets for Control*

After considering those economic undertakings which remained directly under the central government after the 1957–58 administrative decentralization, our attention must now turn to the economic indices which the center announced its intention of still controlling. After 1959 their number was reduced to the following seven:

1. Output and transfer balances to and from provinces of certain major industrial products.
2. Output and transfer balances to and from provinces of major agricultural products.
3. Total exports and imports and the volume of important export and import commodities.
4. Volume of freight of railways and of transport undertakings directly under the Ministry of Communications.
5. Total investment, new productive capacity, major projects, and scale of capital investment. (The phrase "scale of capital investment" is vague in Chinese. It may mean the investment ratio in the national income.)
6. Total wages and average number of staff and workers.
7. Enrollment in higher educational institutions and allocation of graduates.

Other targets which now ceased to be fixed by the central authorities included total value of industrial output, irrigated acreage, arbale acreage, total circulation of commodities, total retail sales, local transport, rate and total of cost reduction, and volume of building and installation work. These targets were in future to be settled by the local authorities and the ministries among themselves. In order to provide flexibility, even the centrally-controlled targets might be adjusted by local authorities so long as state plans were fulfilled and more especially those plans concerning construction projects, productive capacity, level of production, transfer balances, and revenue. (Wang Kuei-wu, "An Important Change in the Method of Drawing up Annual Plans," *Planned Economy*, IX, September 1958, p. 14.)

With respect to material allocation, the central government since 1959 appears to have concentrated on trying to control interprovincial transfers of certain major commodities, both agricultural and industrial (notably grain, cotton, vegetable oil, pigs, steel, iron, coal, lathes, and cotton yarn). It is true that the list of centrally-controlled indices includes the output as well as the transfer balances of such commodities. However, in agriculture from 1965 onward the intention had been to change from unrealistic production planning to procurement planning, at least as far as central government plans were concerned. (*Collected Laws and Regulations, IV*, p. 376.) And in grain procurement, the main concern of the central authorities is not with what happens within any province so long as that province meets its external obligations, *i.e.*, so long as it delivers its required quota for interprovincial transfer or for export or, in the case of a grain-deficient province, so long as it does not demand more than its stipulated inward transfer. (*Ibid., VII*, pp. 281–82.) While the circumstances of agriculture make production planning particularly hazardous, this is also very difficult with that substantial proportion of China's industrial output which comes from small enterprises. As far as coal is concerned, the central government does not attempt to allocate, much less to enforce, a close output plan on that considerable part of the country's total production which comes from the smaller and less accessible mines.

Provincial control over allocations of raw materials was extended when it was laid down that from 1959 on, even central government enterprises were to apply to the planning organs of provincial level authorities for supplies. Exceptions to this were made in special cases, such as materials for the armed forces, armament industries, and the railways; fuel for civil aviation; and goods for export, for which requisition would continue to be made to the central ministries concerned. (*Ibid., VIII*, p. 101; She Yi-san, "A Discussion on the System for Distributing Commodities," *Planned Economy, X*, October 1958, p. 34.)

Overall control of the rate and direction of investment is, as we have seen, one of the targets retained in the hands of the central government, as it must be if any claim is made to have a planned economy. Central control of enrollment in institutions of higher education and of the allocation of graduates can be seen to be a special instance, and a vitally important one, of the control of investment. Closely connected with central control of investment is another centrally controlled target—that of total wages, which, if inflation is to be avoided, must be kept in step with the supply of consumer goods. Joined with the target for total wages is that of the average number of employees: together they constitute control of wage levels and, given the system of urban residence permits, of immigration into towns. Control over the disposition of the country's foreign exchange reserves strengthens the central government's control over investment, and also over allocation of certain key commodities, notably (in the past few years) grain and machinery. Central control of the volume of freight carried by railways and the major modern transport enterprises helps to reinforce central controls over other targets.

In addition to those targets specifically listed as continuing under central control from 1959 are the figures for revenue transfers between the central government and the provincial level authorities. From 1959 onward the centrally approved figure for a provincial level authority's budgetary expenditure was to be compared with the figure for the total revenue the authority was responsible for raising (*i.e.*, all the revenue from its area, except for customs duties and the profits of enterprises under direct central control). Approved deficits were to be made up by the central government, to which also a proportion of estimated excess revenue had to be transferred. Figures for these balances were the only financial targets at provincial level still to be directly controlled by the central government. (Hsu Fei-ch'ing, "Unified Leadership and Delegated Management is the Correct Policy for Budgetary Control," *Finance*, *XIX*, October 9, 1959, p. 13.) Separate from these block transfers of revenue, the central government makes budgetary grants for major investment projects and also *ad hoc* grants for emergency and other special purposes.

## *Price Controls*

Decentralization was also applied to price fixing. According to regulations of October 1958, the appropriate ministries of the central government were to continue to control the procurement prices of major agricultural products: grain, raw cotton, vegetable oils, jute, ramie, tea, tobacco, timber, and live pigs. They were also still to control the selling prices (presumably both wholesale and retail), at important commercial centers, of grain, edible oil, pork, timber, cotton yarn and cloth, woolen cloth, edible salt, sugar, coal, petroleum, chemical fertilizers, and wrist watches. The centrally fixed prices of both kinds—procurement and selling prices —were to apply to standard types of the goods in question while prices of other types, and of standard types at places other than the main commercial centers, were to be determined by the local authorities, with reference to the prices of standard types. The prices of all other goods, both agricultural and manufactured, were also to be under local control. (*Collected Laws and Regulations*, *VIII*, pp. 168–69.) This list of centrally controlled prices excludes those industrial goods subject to central allocation, the allocation prices of which would also be centrally fixed.

Another important item supposedly determined by the central authorities has been the annual budgetary allotment of additional credit funds to the banks. However, it was found difficult to keep the total of bank loans down to the figure in the budget, and in 1957–59, the last years for which figures have been published, budgetary funds actually expended for this purpose greatly exceeded estimates. (*People's Handbook*, 1958, p. 214; 1959, pp. 226–27; 1960, pp. 182 and 184; also *Collected Laws and Regulations*, *IX*, pp. 63–64.) The estimated loanable funds of the Agricultural Bank in 1965 were at the beginning of the year allocated between various provincial level authorities. ("The Agricultural Bank of China: Review of the Work in 1964 and Arrangements for the Work in 1965," Minutes of the Third National Conference of Branch Managers, *Rural Finance*, *IV* and *V*, February 28, 1965 [SCMM 468].) It is likely that a similar division of loanable funds was also made by the People's Bank.

This account of targets under the control of the central government dates largely from the decentralization measures of 1957–58. Since then the ban on the export (and possibly on the open circulation within China) of journals on economic planning, and the paucity of other sources, make it difficult to speak with assurance about the regulations in force at later dates. In 1961–62 reports were current of a move back toward greater financial centralization. (Fan Yeh-chun, Li Te-sheng, and Chang Chih-tao, "The Problem of Centralization and Unification in Financial Work," *Ta Kung Daily* [*Dagong Bao*], Peking, June 25, 1962, p. 3.) This however, as far as can be seen, consisted mainly of improvements in accounting procedures. If such improvement were successful, it would do more than any organizational change in actually increasing the financial powers of the center, for one of the chief limits on central control or control by lower levels of the government lies in administrative and accounting weaknesses.

In general, instead of greater centralization, such evidence as we have suggests that in the 1960s relaxation (whether *de jure* or just *de facto*) of central control occurred in the case even of some items, such as procurement prices of grain, (*Kweichow Daily*, August 30, 1959 [SCMP 2142]), which earlier had been reserved to the central authorities. This, too, is what might be expected after the decentralization of 1957–58 gave great powers to the provinces, powers which it would be difficult for the center to circumscribe within the limits it had propounded.

The vital economic matters between the provinces and the central government are, therefore, net transfers of revenue (including *ad hoc* central grants for investment and other purposes); net transfers of grain and other major commodities, agricultural and industrial; and the allocation between provinces of banks' loanable funds. Another item of transfer between provinces and the center is manpower for the armed services. Provinces are responsible for carrying out conscription. (See Jung Tze-ho, Vice Minister of Finance, "Some Problems in the Reform of the System of Financial Management," where expenditure on organizing conscription is included in the "regular annual expenditure" of provinces, *Finance*, January 1958, p. 1.) The fact that a large part of the central government's revenues is collected by provincial organs and forwarded by the provinces to the central Ministry of Finance is likely to strengthen the provinces' position in negotiations with the central government, at least in those provinces which have a net outward transfer of revenue. Those authorities, such as Sinkiang, which are subsidized by the central government are, of course, in a weaker position in this respect.

The only revenues directly collected by the central government are import duties, profits accruing from foreign trade, and profits of those enterprises under direct central management. In the 1958 budget local authorities were responsible for collecting 77 per cent of the budgetary revenue, but for spending only 44 per cent of total expenditure. These figures are for the *ex ante* budget of 1958, and not for the realized budget of that year, for which a similar analysis is not available. (Yang Chao-chi'ao, "Financial Work Must Serve the Party's General Line," *Finance*, October 1958, p. 1.) The Chinese state budget, like that of the Soviet Union, is an aggregate of the revenues and expenditures of all levels of the government. As the 1958 budget was balanced, it can be seen that in that year the central government's estimated direct revenues sufficed for only 41 per cent of its budgeted expenditure. The center's dependence on the provinces is therefore very marked.

The economic relations between center and provinces are concerned only with marginal transfers. The great bulk of production, consumption, and exchange is intraprovincial, if not intra-*hsien*. What goes on within a province is of little direct concern to the central government, so long as the province meets its external obligations. The Party, of course, demands more. It demands from its provincial and other local branches, and thus indirectly from the local administrations they control, obedience to policies, programs, and campaigns. The degree of verbal obedience it receives is overwhelming. A slogan launched one day in the capital will be repeated on the morrow throughout the country. It was intended that after administrative decentralization, control by the Party should insure enforcement of central policy throughout the country. This did in fact occur in 1958. However, it is by no means so certain whether the local branches of the Party still remain dependable agents for carrying out central policies which may conflict with local interests. To this question we will now direct our attention.

## *The Party Role*

The role of the Communist Party, as the instrument of the center's control over the country, demands that its branches should be omnipresent, extending into all administrative and economic units of the country, and yet that it should maintain its own separate identity; that it should be amenable to central commands, and yet be on good terms with the masses. These requirements have often proved incompatible.

The two hierarchies, that of the Party and of the government administration, are supposed to run parallel to each other through the political and economic systems right down to the lowest units of local authority and to individual enterprises and institutions. The Party hierarchy ranks the higher of the two. The system of dual hierarchies is, of course, copied from the Soviet Union, where the Party committee at each level has usually been more influential than the corresponding government organ. The tendency toward direct Party control in economic matters has been stronger in China because that country has had proportionately fewer educated people than the Soviet Union, even than the Soviet Union in its early days; hence the maintenance in China of fully-staffed dual hierarchies is difficult, if impossible. Another reason for the tendency, no doubt, is the more recent date of the Chinese revolution and the necessity of continuing to employ as managers and professional personnel many members of the old bourgeoisie who cannot be considered politically reliable. The Party therefore keeps a tight rein on their activities.

Direct executive control of political and economic life by the Party was especially evident during the Great Leap. This period saw an increase in provincial autarky. Despite the good harvest of 1958, in that year interprovincial transfers of grain declined. (Kao Yu-huang, "The Need for Vigorous Organization of Rational Transport in the Economic Activities of the Nation," *Economic Research*, *VII*, July 1959, p. 5.) Chaotic conditions in the allocation system and in transport made it more necessary than ever for each administrative unit to reach for the highest possible degree of self-sufficiency. The desire for self-sufficiency, whether industrial (by each industrial ministry), by enterprises, or by localities is endemic in the type of economic planning practiced by China, where the complexities of allocating raw materials and the uncertainties involved encourage individual units to become self-sufficient. The decentralization measures of 1957–58 provided the framework for greater autonomy of the provincial level authorities. In the circumstances of the time this meant increased authority for the provincial Party secretaries, who were supposed to be agents for maintaining the Party's centralized hold on the provinces. However, once a provincial Party secretary becomes *de facto* responsible for the government of a province, he necessarily becomes identified with the provincial administration, with its particular interests and problems. He also finds himself making his province's case, in negotiations with the central government, on the size of the all-important transfers of revenue and commodities, of which we have spoken above. (See, for example, the case of P'an Fu-sheng from 1953 to 1958, First Secretary of the Honan CCP Provincial Committee, *Honan Daily*, July 4, 1958 [CB 515, pp. 7 and 10]; Wu Chih-p'u, First Secretary, Honan CCP Provincial Committee, "Rightist Opportunism is the Principal Danger in the Party Now," *Honan Daily*, July 4, 1958 [CB 515, pp. 20–21]; Editorial, *Honan Daily*, July 15, 1958 [CB 515, p. 41]. This example of a First Secretary's opposition to central policy on grain procurement and grain transfers dates from the period of centralization, when his powers were less than in subsequent years.)

These considerations seriously weakened the usefulness of provincial Party committees as agents of the central authorities. It is thought that the chief reason for the reestablishment of the six regional bureaus of the Party, reported in 1961, was to restrain the growing independence of the provincial Party committees. In 1965 the role of the first secretaries of the Party regional bureaus as agents of the center was emphasized by the appointment of four of the six to concurrent high offices in the central government. At one time there were several cases of the first secretaryship of regional bureaus of the Party being held concurrently with the first secretaryship of the Party committee of the most important provincial level unit within the region. From 1965 the tendency was for the two positions to be separated, perhaps to prevent the Party regional bureaus from being absorbed into the general administration as the Party provincial committees had been. The fact that there is no governmental administrative unit corresponding to the region should lessen the danger of this fate befalling the Party regional bureaus.

At lower levels of the political and economic administration the same difficulty has been apparent of preserving the separate identity of the Party. At the time of the Great Leap the tendency to direct Party control intensified. In some places Party organs merged with organs of *hsien* and communes, while in factories Party committees usurped managerial functions. After the Leap it was attempted to disentangle the Party from too close identification with the administrations of geographic units and of enterprises. However, in 1961 it was still necessary for *Red Flag* to oppose "tendencies that do not distinguish between the Party and the government and between the Party and the commune (Huang Chih-kang, "Strengthen Leadership over Basic Level Rural Cadres' Study," *Red Flag*, *XIX*, October 10, 1961, p. 28); and for it to be urged that a Party committee in an enterprise should avoid involvement in routine matters, lest it be "demoted to the status of an ordinary operational department and its leadership role weakened." (*Liberation*, June 5, 1961 [SCMM 312].)

In 1957 Party cadres in enterprises were assessed for bonuses within the enterprises in which they worked, often by enterprise staff. This, and the fact that the bonuses were probably dependent, at least in part, on the fortunes of the enterprise, must have been an important factor in causing political cadres to identify themselves with enterprise management. (Yu Shu-fang, "Political and Mass Organization Cadres in Enterprises Who Are Not Engaged in Production Should Not Receive Bonuses," *Labor*, November 11, 1957, p. 17.) Yu argues the case against these cadres receiving bonuses, but assumes it is still an open question. He writes, "At present bonuses for Party and mass organization cadres not engaged in production are decided by the director of the enterprise, or even by the wages department or some are not even assessed by anyone. Thus the work of such cadres is not judged by higher levels of the Party, Youth League or trade union." During the Great Leap, bonuses for all staff and workers were widely discontinued, but soon appear to have been resumed. No information is available about assessment of bonuses for Party cadres in enterprises after the Leap.

The attempt to prevent Party committees of enterprises from being absorbed into the ordinary administration was apparently not successful. In any case, from 1964 on, it was thought necessary to provide additional political leadership in economic life through establishing special political departments, first only at the national level, but before long at provincial and *hsien* levels as well, inside the ordinary administrative departments of finance, commerce, industry, and communications. New political departments were also formed inside some corporations presumably alongside their Party committees. (Sometimes a number of enterprises [*ch'i yeh*] are grouped under the control of a corporation [*kungsze*]. *Kungsze* is also on occasion appended to the name of and used to denote a single enterprise.) In some places special "guides" or "instructors" were assigned to individual enterprises by political departments of *hsien* or higher levels. (*Ta Kung Daily* [*Dagong Bao*], Peking, June 16, 1965, p. 1, editorial and news item. See also *China News Analysis*, No. 581.) Clearly it was felt that the strictly political tasks had been neglected and that a stiffening of the political element was needed throughout the economy.

Doubt may be permitted on whether these political departments, in their turn, may not go the same way as the Party committees. As long as the main task of Party organs in economic sectors is to produce certain economic results—and even if their tasks are expressed in political terms, success in these may be measured by the degree of subsequent economic success, *i.e.*, the attainment of targets is the most easily ascertainable proof of ideological zeal—so long must the leading elements in these Party organs concentrate their energies on economic matters. "Whether or not an enterprise is able to fulfill the whole of the plan laid down by the State is the chief way of determining if theoretical political work in the enterprise has been done well or badly." (Chang Feng-lin, "The Appropriate Distribution of Enterprises'

Bonus Funds," *Labor*, August 8, 1964, p. 27.) This inevitably involves taking sides on economic issues, such as, for example, which method of production to prefer in a given instance. Before long these problems engross the group which has to decide and mold them, rather than the group molding the economic matters with which it deals. That the group in question continues to repeat the approved political slogans may disguise rather than demonstrate its chief preoccupations. This trend may be hastened if, as often seems the case, new industrial recruits to the Party are chosen in great measure for competence in their jobs, so that their interests are likely to be more professional than political.

In any case, the new political departments can only be as effective as the quality of their staff permits. Figures available for one province, Heilungkiang, show that the majority (54 per cent) of the new political instructors assigned to the particularly sensitive sector of finance and trade were secretaries of Party branches, *i.e.*, from the category whose defects presumably made the new departments necessary; 10 per cent were chosen from administrative staff; and 32 per cent were ex-servicemen. (*Ta Kung Daily* [*Dagong Bao*], Peking, June 16, 1965, p. 1.) It is on the last category that the most sanguine hopes have been placed, yet the ex-servicemen's ignorance of economic affairs is likely to weaken their ability to enforce political control over economic life.

Altogether then, we must conclude that the Party will continue to become assimilated to administration and management at all levels. In this way the Party, especially in urban areas, is in process of being transformed from a revolutionary controlling group to a managerial elite, a club for meritocrats. The Party cannot, therefore, necessarily be depended on to be an effective instrument for enforcing central policies against the interests of provinces and lower local authorities, and of enterprises. It might be thought that the army could fulfill this role, or at least ensure that local Party branches accede to central wishes in these matters. While the army may be presumed to be under firm central control it is a blunt instrument for carrying out central policies in economic matters. (I am indebted to John Gittings for the information that provincial first secretaries are concurrently political commissars of their provincial military districts, except for Szechuan and Shantung, which are military regions.) As we have just seen, the military men given economic appointments in the new political departments are seldom likely to have sufficient understanding of economic matters to be able to exert the desired influence.

## *Control over Appointments*

There remains another channel of possible central influence and control. Within the Party, yet in some way additional to it, the public security system provides a potential centralizing agency. Its vertical lines of responsibility are thought to be especially strong, at least up to the level of the province; it is uncertain how strong they are above this level. (I am indebted to Professor A. Doak Barnett for allowing me here to draw on the findings of his research.)

The control of appointments is probably one of the chief means available to the central authorities for controlling affairs within provinces, although it is by no means clear what degree of control over appointments is still exercised by the center. In 1954 the State Council was made responsible *inter alia* for the appointment and dismissal of directors and deputy directors of departments and bureaus of provincial level authorities, *i.e.*, the local counterparts of central ministries; below these and the other officials under State Council jurisdiction came grades whose occupants fell under the jurisdiction of individual central ministries. The duties of the State Council in this sphere have been discharged by the Ministry of Internal Affairs since 1959, when it took over the responsibilities of the defunct Personnel Bureau of the State Council, which had dealt with appointments of officials of the rank of *hsien* magistrate and above, employed by ministries. (*Collected Laws and Regulations, I*, pp. 103, 109, and 122.) Presumably, the administrative staff of state enterprises were included, subject to the provisions of the decentralization decrees. In enterprises handed down to them by the decentralization directive of November 1957 provinces were to have the same authority over personnel as they had in the enterprises they already controlled. Even in the case of enterprises that remained in the control of central ministries, local authorities were permitted "to adjust the cadres appropriately" so long as they did not weaken the staff of major factories and mines. When transferring cadres of grades controlled by the State Council, approval was to be obtained from the State Council; similarly, consultation with the central ministries was required before transferring cadres of those categories falling under the jurisdiction of ministries. (*Ibid.*, *VI*, p. 394.)

Behind the state apparatus for the assignment of officials lies that of the Party. In the Soviet Union the Party controls the distribution of cadres through the *nomenklatura* system, by which given Party committees are responsible for making particular appointments in the state administration, in enterprises, trade unions, and other bodies; the word can also be used to signify the list of persons qualified to hold these posts. Little information is available on this topic in respect to China, but it is probable that a similar system is in operation. A provincial report in 1958 mentions that "the appointment or dismissal of cadres must first of all be decided by the Party committees." (Report by Chang Chung-liang, First Secretary of the Kansu Provincial CCP Committee, *Kansu Daily*, August 16, 1958 [CB 528].) The context makes it clear that cadres in all sectors of national life are included. This must imply an apportioning out of the responsibility among Party committees at different levels, according to the importance and type of the appointment to be made.

Thus, the degree of central control over appointments would depend on the degree of central control over the Party committee making them, and this depends in part on the degree of control of central appointees to Party committees once they had been appointed—that is, the extent to which the center could afford to dismiss them if they championed local interests, or whether such dismissal would generate ill will between center and provinces which the center would be unwilling to risk. We cannot speak with any certainty on this topic until more study has been done on the turnover rate and mobility between provinces of members of provincial Party secretariats. Even with this knowledge, assessment of its significance would be difficult. We know, for example, of certain cases where the central authorities have dismissed such officials. We do not know how often the center may have wished to order dismissals but refrained because of reasons cited above. (Michael Oksenberg, who is studying career patterns and channels of upward mobility in China, and to whom I am grateful for a discussion of the topics, would give greater weight to central power than I have done here.)

In any case the extent of decentralization must not be exaggerated. The centripetal factors mentioned earlier make possible a greater degree of unification and of control by the central government than has ever existed in China before. In any large country or organization, centripetal and centrifugal trends are liable to alternate. This is natural and need cause no surprise. However, the "norm" around which these oscillations take place must vary with the size, nature, and traditions of the units in question. All these factors point to a greater degree of decentralization from the national government to the next lower level in China than in most other countries. Thus we may judge the degree of centralization attempted in the first Five-Year Plan period to have been abnormal. The corollary is that the decentralization that subsequently occurred in China is less likely to be reversed than the decentralization in the Soviet Union, to which it bore many resemblances and by which the Chinese decrees were no doubt influenced.

The provincial level authorities were the primary beneficiaries of the devolution of authority from the center. (In the northeast, formerly known as Manchuria, historic and economic ties lessen the force of provincialism and make the whole region more of a unit in itself.) The overwhelming advantage possessed by these authorities as against the national government in the task of economic control and development is that of size. Averaging 20 to 30 million population each (30 to 40 million if only the provinces of China proper are taken into account) their administrations are better placed than the ministries at Peking for making decisions on policies and priorities for most types of industrial growth and agricultural improvement. The province has become the main unit for the promotion of agricultural mechanization. Powered irrigation and electrically motivated processing industries have been based on transmission lines radiating mainly from provincial capitals. These power systems rarely span provincial boundaries, unlike the regional electric grids. For many agricultural functions even the province is too large a unit; this explains the leadership of the *hsien* in such activities as demonstration farms. But for the promotion of industry, except on the very largest and the very smallest scales, the provincial level is now the most significant.

## The Province and Local Authorities

When we consider relations between the province and its subordinate units—the special administrative districts, the *hsien*, and the municipalities—we know much less than we do with regard to central-provincial dealings. The latter are the subject of national directives, many of which are accessible in the volumes of *Collected Laws and Regulations.* These directives also have something to say about the provincial level's relations with lower units as, for example, when maximum permitted rates of agricultural tax are specified. However, a large degree of latitude is given by the directives to the major local authorities in the manner and extent of their control of the affairs of subordinate authorities. This presumably means that in different provinces and autonomous regions the amount of power exercised by these subordinate authorities may differ considerably. However, we hazard the opinion that political and economic factors combine to make the province and its equivalents the key units for economic development in China today.

These provincial level authorities vary in resources (even after making allowance for the greater levies made by the center on the wealthier ones) and in efficiency. For example, in 1958 certain coal mines in Yunnan, Kweichow, and Ninghsia were to remain for the time being under the management of the central Ministry of Coal on the grounds that these authorities were not administratively capable of managing them. (*People's Daily*, June 25, 1958.) Differences in policy are manifest in matters such as interprovincial variations in size of communes not always accounted for by differing circumstances; as in the formation of communes among the Yi national minority in Yunnan but not among the Yi in neighboring Szechuan, among whom the unit or organization is reported still to be the agricultural producers' cooperative (NCNA Kunming, July 26, 1965; NCNA Chengtu, July 19, 1965; whether this difference is merely verbal or more substantial is admittedly uncertain); and in the pioneering of linear programming, especially in transport, by Shantung, and the use of special features, notably the multi-branched Labor University, which in Kiangsi characterizes the movement for "sending down" youths to remote mountainous areas of the province.

The position of the provinces might be thought to be threatened by the campaign waged from 1962 onward to restore commerce to its former channels and directions according to economic regions instead of according to administrative units, as had tended to be the case since the growth of local self-sufficiency in 1958. However, the deliberate restoration by administrative means of old trading patterns, as by the resituating of state commercial organs, has been slow and cumbersome, especially compared with the apparently spontaneous revival of two other instruments of the traditional channels of trade: rural markets and trade warehouses. The trade warehouse is a traditional wholesaling unit where, in the old days, traders not only stored goods, but also did business and were boarded. The managers would also provide them with commercial contacts. (The fluctuations in the fortunes of the trade warehouses in recent years will be treated in the author's forthcoming book.) In 1965 the change was still far from complete (*Ta Kung Daily*, Peking, August 9, 1965, p. 1); perhaps local Party committees were far from enthusiastic. It may be wondered how far the reaction can go against the organization of trade according to administrative units without causing wide repercussions, not only in the economy but also in the political structure.

Since 1957–58 almost all activities occurring within a province, with the limited exception of the army and the most important economic enterprises, have come under the surveillance of the provincial Party committee and more especially of its first secretary. Beneath the provincial level, the Party committees and secretaries of lower local authorities have enjoyed a similar sway. If commerce is no longer to be based on the administrative units of province, district, and *hsien*, transport and production are likely to follow suit. The planning and fiscal jurisdictions of the units of local government will then be difficult to maintain in their present form. The real professionals in the commercial systems probably hope that by basing their activities on nonpolitical units, they may lessen the hold of the political men on them. Whether the local politicians, especially the provincial first secretaries, will accept this situation remains to be seen. Awareness of the political implications involved may perhaps be shown by the leading role taken in encouraging the change by the regional bureaus of the Party, which each control several provinces (*Ta Kung Daily*, Peking, August 9, 1965, p. 1), and which may see in the movement a way of limiting the power of provincial and other local Party secretaries. If political and economic administration were disjoined at the provincial level, it might assuage the anxiety of the center about waxing provincial autonomy, but it would leave in its place the problem which decentralization was designed to solve —the administrative impossibility of far-reaching direct control throughout the country from Peking. The choice before the central government, if it has one, may therefore be between seeing provinces develop on increasingly autonomous lines, or permitting a considerable relaxation of political control over the economy. Perhaps a measure of each will be unavoidable.

## *Provincial Autonomy*

In any case the strengthening of autonomy at the provincial level is unlikely to be quickly reversed. In the short and medium term, we may conclude, the future of China lies in great measure with the provinces. Our present ignorance of what is happening at the provincial level, in both political and economic matters, is profound. Presumably in some provinces strong administrations are being built up. Negotiations between provinces and the central government are likely to be tough on the matter of transfer balances—the net transfers of revenue, grain, and other major commodities; the allocation among provinces of raw materials, central budgetary investment, and banks' loanable funds. The permitted total wage payments within a province may also be the subject of hard bargaining and even harder struggle in enforcement. The onus for enforcing this must fall largely on the provincial branches of the People's Bank, for it is their duty to refuse to release cash for unauthorized wage payments. A number of press references indicate that overspending the wage fund has been difficult to prevent. However, it has not occurred on a scale to undermine the value of the currency, and for this the People's Bank must have been kept under firm central control on all vital matters and be able to stand up to pressure from organs of the provincial authorities. Indeed, it may be that the Bank has succeeded in this respect where the Party has failed, in that it has kept its identity as an organ of central control while local Party branches have tended to be assimilated with their corresponding local authorities. In the past, weakness in organizing the large impersonal undertakings of modern economic life has characterized the

Chinese scene. Without an opportunity for close study on the spot at the present time, we must speak with caution, but it seems at least probable that the People's Bank has, to a large extent, overcome this weakness. This is relevant to the question of central control of the army, for the Bank presumably is the channel for paying the army. It will be remembered that during the period of warlord rule in China, control of local military units was determined by who paid them.

When linked with the question of provincial-central relations, China's imports of grain take on an additional significance. While five to six million tons a year (the approximate rate at which these imports were running in the early 1960s) represents only some three per cent of China's total grain output, it is the equivalent of around 20 per cent of total grain procurement, and probably a good deal more of total interprovincial transfers. Hence the imports of grain serve to ease relations between the center and the provinces, as otherwise Peking would be forced to try to squeeze larger grain transfers out of grain-surplus provinces. Thus this supply of imported grain, which is under its direct control, strengthens the central government by making it to that extent less dependent on provincial compliance with its levies. Foreign trade in this way fulfills the same role as the "key economic areas" which in days past gave the imperial government of China much of the grain supplies for its own needs. (Chi Ch'ao-ting, *Key Economic Areas of Chinese History*, New York, 1963.) As well as importing grain, the present government of China is also fostering "key economic areas" for the same purpose in the form of "areas of high and stable yield." These areas receive priority for central government investment funds for agriculture, which presumably gives the center a greater hold on their surpluses of grain and cotton.

## Cellular Society

China is not a monolithic society or economy, but a cellular one. This is the burden of the evidence. Repeatedly, economic discussions in the Chinese press refer to the "responsibility (or guarantee) system" (*pao-kan chihtu*). According to this traditional and deeply rooted concept, a unit guarantees performance in a certain sphere to the authorities of the level immediately above it, in return for which it is allowed a very wide latitude in the conduct of its internal affairs, including its relations with its lower units, without interference from superior authority. Thus, so long as a province, localized lineage, village, or other group fulfilled its obligations to the outside world, it would be left alone in peace to deal with its members or subordinates. This satisfied the Chinese attachment to the notion of harmonious self-sufficient groups. At the same time, it was an eminently practical arrangement in a society where direct administration down to the grassroots was impossible. This "responsibility system" is so taken for granted in China that it is seldom explicitly set forth, but is something that the observer must always bear in mind. The concentration of center-provincial relations on marginal transfers, and not on total production, revenue, or expenditure within provinces is fully consonant with the "responsibility system." Practical considerations contributed in 1958, and the subsequent years of disaster, to the trend toward autonomous self-sufficiency implied in this concept. At a deeper level, the process may have been hastened by the instinctive return in times of crisis to familiar patterns of doing things.

We must indicate certain consequences which flow from this organizational pattern of the Chinese economy. Any direct revenue or expenditure by the central government—for example, on the nuclear program, other military expenditure, foreign aid, etc.—should, to determine its relative internal significance, be calculated as a percentage of *direct central government* revenue or expenditure and not only as a percentage of total budgetary revenue or expenditure; similarly with the quantities of grain and other commodities at the disposal of the central authorities. In other words, the central government cannot draw directly on the total taxable capacity of the country. The center can always, of course, call on the major local authorities to increase their contributions of cash or commodities. Even when a definite period of years is stipulated before changes can be made in any regulations, there are always loopholes, and in any case plenty of examples can be quoted of the free way in which law is interpreted, or ignored. The real limit on the expansion of central revenues lies in the relations between the center and the major local authorities. The center depends on the cooperation of these authorities, and only in an extreme situation could it afford openly to use crude force—*i.e.*, its control over the armed forces—to secure increased levies of revenue or commodities. The tension between center and provinces with respect to transfers in cash and kind must be seen in the context of their mutual dependence.

While stressing the cellular nature of the present-day Chinese economy, a word of warning is necessary. As the economy becomes modernized, the tendency will be for its cellular nature to evolve into more complex systems of relationships. Even now the economy is less cellular than in the past, as exemplified in particular by the countrywide operations of the People's Bank and also in the changes taking place in the more modernized parts of the country. (The latter is brought out in the study of Tangshan, Hopeh, being undertaken by Professor John W. Lewis, to whom I am indebted for a discussion of this point.)

Another point must be emphasized. Given the size and circumstances of China, the surprising thing is not the amount of provincial autonomy, but the extent of central control; not any fissiparous strains we may have noted, but the degree of underlying and persisting unity which binds this quarter of the human family, and which must claim our tribute of admiration.

Apart from the growth of local autonomy, other basic causes weaken the control both of the center and also of local authorities over the economy. Deficiencies in statistical work and accountancy figure prominently in this list. These weaknesses set very severe limits to the possibility of any kind of control. The same result follows from the shortage of competent administrators and managers. In discussing the difference between developed and underdeveloped economies, too much prominence is usually given to technological matters and not enough to management and to financial and statistical know-how. Administrative failures may have been one reason for the frequent choppings and changings of policy which have marked the economic scene in Communist China.

The concentration of central control on marginal transfer balances is due in good measure to the virtual impossibility, given the deficiencies just mentioned, of trying to ascertain—much less to control—output and revenue totals; transfers are easier to check. A similar importance has come to devolve on profits as a success indicator for enterprises. (This topic will be developed in the author's forthcoming book. See also F. Schurmann, "Economic Policy and Political Power in Communist China," *Annals of the American Academy of Political and Social Science, 349*, September 1963, p. 63.) Whether a given amount of profit has or has not been remitted to the state by an enterprise is less liable to uncertainty or abuse than is the use of output, quality, cost of production or labor productivity as success indicators. This is apart from the economic superiority of the profit index over the alternatives.

To return to the limitations placed on economic control by administrative and accountancy weaknesses in China, a major example is the inability to prevent the illicit use of extra-budgetary funds. These were originally those items of revenue at the disposal of local authorities of different grades, or of economic enterprises and of institutions of various kinds and their controlling ministries, which were not entered in the budget and which might be used without higher authorization. Large sums from this source have been diverted to unplanned investment, thus making nonsense of state investment plans. Also this unplanned investment has often led to the diversion of state-allocated raw materials from their planned use. Apparently the People's Bank was not able to prevent all this, possibly because the transactions involved were settled in cash, contrary to regulations.

## Public Face and Private Face

The Chinese have a sophisticated attitude to outward expression of opinion, which renders government control simultaneously easier and more difficult. Words are regarded as symbolic counters, to be moved about the chessboard of life in order to produce the desired effect. This results in reservations and subtleties of expression and action which need to be interpreted within the framework of the Chinese environment and which a stranger might not understand. The effect is that outward compliance is easily obtained; but an individual's or a group's "public face" must not be taken as an indication of their "private face." Thus conformity, although easily won, is apt to remain superficial. Alongside this, however, is an implicit understanding by both government and people of the limits to which both can go, an understanding which was ruptured during the Great Leap but which may now have been restored. It is relatively simple in these circumstances for a government to see that stipulated formulas are repeated throughout the country or that demonstrations are held when ordered, but quite another thing for it to insure that its writ should run in enforcing policies against local interests. In this case there may be little in the way of outward protest (although occasionally, as in the Hundred Flowers period, submerged feelings may well out), but sabotage need be none the less effective for being done in silence. Indeed, the more contrary to central orders that local cadres may be acting, the more loudly they may give verbal support to those orders.

Connected with this trait is another, the strong tradition in China of not discussing family difficulties and dissensions with outsiders. This holds not only for families but also for larger groups and for the nation itself. Thus the Chinese are apt to present a seemingly monolithic front to foreigners. Added to this, foreigners at present are restricted mainly to those places and sectors of Chinese life which are directly controlled by the central government: the capital and other large cities and their environs, diplomacy, international trade, and institutions of higher education. In consequence, the picture given to the outside world is of a gigantic slab of humanity under tight centralized control, whose actions are based on certain highly simplified slogans. An impression so untrue, so dull, and so terrifying may be thought to serve the purposes of prestige: certainly it ill serves the cause of international understanding, of world peace, or even of China's national safety.

13

# Incentives and Profits in Chinese Industry

*Dwight H. Perkins*

*From* Current Scene, Developments In Mainland China *4, no. 10, (May 15, 1966): pp. 1–10, with omissions. Reprinted by permission.*

IN THE YEARS since the "Great Leap" and the rupture in Sino-Soviet relations, the Chinese Communist leadership has been deeply engaged in a struggle against "revisionism" both at home and abroad. Within China the campaigns for "socialist education" and to "learn from the army" have been vigorously pushed. Abroad the primary effort has been directed against Soviet foreign policies, particularly "peaceful co-existence" with the West. But "revisionist" domestic policies have not been spared. In the eyes of Peking:

> Khrushchev's "communism" takes the United States for its model. Imitation of the methods of management of U.S. capitalism and the bourgeois way of life has been raised by Khrushchev to the level of state policy. . . . He wants to copy the United States in the sphere of industry . . . and, in particular, to imitate the profit motive of U.S. capitalist enterprises.[1]

To the outside observer perhaps the most interesting question is whether these polemics deal with real differences between the Soviet and Chinese economies or are merely a smokescreen for other sources of conflict. Does the regime in China, for example, treat enterprise profits differently from the Soviet Union? If it does, is the divergence in practice due to ideology or is there an economic explanation?

Peking's reliance on private incentives in varying forms in the countryside is well known and need not detain us here. The reintroduction of private plots, rural trade fairs, and the transfer of most management functions to the production team since 1959 were all undertaken with the realization that the attempt to do away with many forms of private incentive was, at best, premature.

Chinese policies with respect to the use of private incentives—whether profits or other devices—in industry are less well known. Before attempting to describe these policies and to analyse their origin, a brief summary of Soviet efforts in this area is in order.

## *Soviet Reforms*

Emphasis on private incentives in industry did not begin with Khrushchev or his successors. It was Stalin who insisted on significant differences in wages for Soviet workers depending on their skills and performance. It was also under Stalin that the system of large bonuses for managers who overfulfilled their plans was developed and refined.

By the mid-1950s and particularly in the 1960s, the problem of centrally planning Soviet production was becoming increasingly complex. The number of commodities produced was multiplying rapidly and, more important, problems of quality and style, particularly in the consumers' goods sector, were becoming acute. For example, the Soviet plant manager did not lack incentive to produce hats, but he did lack the incentive to produce hats that the average Soviet citizen was willing to wear. As a result, retail stocks of apparel in the retail trade network nearly tripled between January 1, 1959 and January 1, 1964.[2]

The issues were, if anything, more acute in East Europe where industries had not only to satisfy domestic consumers, but also had to produce for export to much more demanding markets in West Europe. As a result, first in such countries as Poland and Hungary, and increasingly in the Soviet Union itself, alternatives began to be discussed. The best publicized parts of these discussions were the proposals by Liberman and others to substitute profits for gross value of output as the principal basis for appraising enterprise performance. Profits, it should be pointed out, had always been an indicator of success or the lack of it, but not the primary indicator.

## *Marx Mute*

Khrushchev and then Kosygin allowed this discussion to continue relatively free from counterattacks based on ideology (although not from those based on pragmatic considerations). Nevertheless, only very modest attempts have been made to implement the economists' suggestions. Most of the reforms put into effect by both Krhushchev and Kosygin have been concerned primarily with administrative reorganization, *i.e.*, the shift in authority to the various Soviet republics and now back to the ministries in Moscow. Where the more radical reforms were given a trial, as in the case of two clothing manufacturers, the results fell well short of expectations. This was partly due to inadequacies of the Soviet price structure and partly because old administrative habits were difficult to break and constantly interfered with the efficient operation of the new techniques.

The principal point of this brief summary is to emphasize that changes in Soviet economic organization have been in response to pragmatic economic considerations. They have not involved the extension of the role of private property nor of much else that can be clearly labelled as un-Marxist. In fact Marx, as has often been pointed out, had little if anything to say about how socialist enterprises should be organized or run.[3] Although the erosion of Marxist-Leninist ideology within the Soviet Union is real, and industrial reform may have become politically feasible as a result of that erosion, there is little ideological content in most of the specific reforms tested.

## *Dissimilar Economies*

It is not surprising, therefore, that when one turns to the case of China one finds discussion and often actual adoption of many of the same measures. Where there have been significant differences between the economic policies of China and the Soviet Union, the explanation can often be found in the dissimilar natures of the two economies.

China today is still basically an underdeveloped economy. The number of commodities produced by her industrial sector is significantly smaller than is the case in the Soviet Union, and the problems of planning or coordinating their production and output are correspondingly fewer. It will be a long time before Chinese consumers can be much concerned with questions of quality and style. The problem today is more one of insuring that enough cloth, shoes, and the like are produced to take care of basic needs.

Nor is China a major exporter of goods whose markets are dependent on maintenance of high quality or style. The mainland's principal exports are agricultural products and industrial raw materials, together with cheap textiles for the markets of Asia and other developing nations.[4]

China's dependence on agriculture does complicate centralized planning in other ways, however. Farm output, subject to influences of weather and organizational changes, is and will remain unstable. Textile mills, food processing plants, and other factories using agricultural raw materials cannot know more than a few months ahead of time whether they will be producing at capacity or whether their equipment will be left standing idle. As a result, annual plans drawn up for these plants are little more than hopeful guesses about what is really going to happen. The difficulties that such uncertainty causes planners, however, should not be exaggerated. If they guess wrong it simply means that a few workers will have to be laid off and rations of consumers reduced. In contrast, a decline in steel output would significantly affect dozens of other industries using steel. But most such industries, *i.e.*, those whose output is a major input in many other products, are in the heavy industrial sector and do not depend on agricultural raw materials.

## *Small-Scale Firms*

The greatest single factor militating against highly centralized planning in China is the existence of large numbers of small-scale industrial enterprises using widely varying, often primitive, techniques. There were over 100,000 such firms in the mid-1950s and their number must have been greatly expanded during the "Great Leap Forward" of 1958–59.[5] Even when these enterprises possessed adequately trained accountants and statistical workers, the obstacles to getting accurate data to Peking in time to be of any use to the planners were virtually insurmountable.

The Chinese Communists have struggled with the problem of controlling these small-scale firms almost from the beginning of their attainment of power in 1949. At the Eighth Party Congress meetings in September 1956, the regime decided to allow many of these firms to buy their raw materials directly from the market and sell their produce to the market rather than having to work through wholesale companies whose allocations were determined by centralized plans. Over-centralization of the inputs and outputs of these firms was sharply criticized.[6]

These measures were not simply a product of the brief liberalization of late 1956 and early 1957, made famous by the slogan "let a hundred flowers bloom." Nor did they result from the well known preferences of Party economist Ch'en Yün for a "rational" economic policy. During the "Great Leap" there was a shift in emphasis towards administrative decentralization rather than reliance on the market. New and old, small and medium scale firms were turned over to provincial and lower level authorities, particularly to commune level organizations. This transfer of control was not unlike the shift in authority to the Soviet Republics. But in China, major heavy industries never were removed from Peking's direction.

## *Outside the Rules*

Decentralization of administrative control, however, probably did not eliminate direct contacts between firms for the purchase and supply of materials. In fact, given the disruption of planning procedures in 1958–59 and the lack of reliable statistics upon which to base allocation decisions, it is likely that firms had constantly to resort to sources of supply outside the formal state commercial network, whether or not such actions were sanctioned by regulations.

By 1964 production outside the state plan and commercial network was again given public approval by the authorities, at least after the state plan had been fulfilled by the particular enterprise concerned.[7] Such measures may seem modest by the standards of a free enterprise economy, but direct production for the market, or rather for retail outlets, has commonly been considered one of the most "radical" elements in the Soviet experiments with reform.

## *Role of Profits*

The Chinese Communists have also attempted to enhance the role of profits in industry. Here the changes seem not to have been motivated solely or even primarily by the existence of large numbers of small-scale firms. Rather, it has been the realization that control over all firms, both large and small, could benefit from some relaxation and from increased attention to lowering costs. Profit under such circumstances is an ideal indicator, since it encourages a firm to pay attention both to increasing output and decreasing cost, but allows the firm to determine the relative emphasis given to each.

In 1954 the Ministry of Finance issued a directive stating that enterprises could keep 40 per cent of profits that were in excess of the plan's profit target, and that these funds could be used to meet shortages in the firm's circulating capital and several other items.[8] Regulations controlling the use of these funds were liberalized slightly in 1956 and bonuses were given for exceeding planned profits. In 1958 the rules for determining the level and use of retained profits were thoroughly overhauled, the net effect being to increase significantly the portion retained by the enterprise.[9]

Another measure initiated in 1957 was to reduce the number of compulsory plan targets from twelve to four. In effect this enhanced the importance of the remaining four, one of which was profits. The net influence of these measures should not be exaggerated, however. At all times output targets were given first priority by both central planners and enterprise managers. These priorities prevailed even when Peking's economic policies were most "conservative," as in 1957. During more "radical" periods, such as the "Great Leap Forward" in 1958–59, the role of profits was almost completely obscured.

## *Theory and Practice*

The real importance of enterprise profits to the plant manager, in contrast to the role assigned them in the formal regulations, depended on the enforcement of a whole panoply of financial controls. For example, the incentive to surpass the profits target in order to obtain additional funds for working capital existed only so long as funds could not be readily obtained from other sources. A reading of the formal regulations would lead one to believe that tight financial control was the normal state of affairs. Firms were allowed enough cash on hand for only three days' operations. Even the use of their own deposits in the bank, let alone obtaining short term credit, depended on the bank's approval. This would be given only after the bank was assured the funds were being properly spent.

In actual practice it was often easy to obtain large sums for working capital. The rules were not changed; they were simply ignored, particularly when pressure was on all economic personnel to perform near miracles in increasing physical output. Such pressure was especially severe in 1956 and 1958–59, but was always present in one form or another. Thus the reforms in the profit regulations in 1958 were at least temporarily accompanied by, but did not cause, a decline in the real significance of the profits target.

The explanation for this lack of concern with financial regulations was partly ideological. Party personnel tended to equate finance in general and profits in particular with capitalism. Moreover, many individuals were given positions of trust because of their participation in the revolution and not because of their educational or technical background. A lack of economic sophistication thus was at least as important an explanation of the financial rule-breaking. In addition, centralized planning of the type practised in Moscow and Peking virtually necessitates emphasis on physical output as against financial considerations.[10]

## *Finance and Control*

With the exception of the year 1956, however, the general trend through 1957 was toward gradual tightening of financial control and an enhancement of the role of profits. This trend was sharply reversed in 1958–59, and control did not begin to be re-tightened until perhaps 1961. In the first half of 1962 there was even talk in the economic journals of giving first priority to the profits target over the output target. As far as one can tell, these recommendations were never implemented. The 1958 profits regulation appears to have remained in force with little major alteration, except that an effort was made to reduce the size of the retained portion.[11]

The problem from 1961 through 1965 was not so much one of improving or tinkering with the basic system of centralized planning and control as it was one of restoring that system or any other system of control, so that the regime could re-attain some direction over the course of the economy. As a result, articles on finance, prices and profits tended to reiterate, with minor variations, themes common in the 1950s, such as what is the proper sphere of finance and how should the relative prices of items of different quality be determined.[12] The general purpose of such articles would appear to be a desire to get economic personnel to pay more attention to the proper handling of financial matters and not to set the stage for revisions in the system itself.

Emphasis on financial considerations will continue to be of particular importance in China as long as the need for giving special attention to problems of quality and cost is recognized, as it has been during the past few years. It is unlikely, on the other hand, that this need will of itself dictate any major change in the control system.

### *The Bonus Incentive*

One of the few areas in Communist China's control apparatus over enterprises where there is a major difference from the procedures followed in the Soviet Union is in the treatment of bonuses. And here the contrasting methods can, in a significant way, be traced to ideological differences. In the Soviet Union factory managers in the 1930s could double and triple their base salaries by fulfilling and overfulfilling their plan targets. In 1947 the average premium for managerial personnel in the Soviet iron and steel industry was 51.4 per cent of base salaries. In the food industry, which had much more difficulty in meeting and surpassing its plan targets, the average was 21 per cent.[13]

In sharp contrast, bonuses in Chinese enterprises are meant primarily for the workers, not the managers. Furthermore, the funds available for this purpose have seldom been large. They have generally not been paid directly to the workers at all, but have been used to finance projects designed to promote collective, not individual, welfare.[14] The Chinese have also made somewhat less use of piece-rate wages, a key method of encouraging maximum effort from workers in the Soviet Union. It is possible to argue with respect to workers that in China there was less need to encourage maximum performance. In China, with its large surplus of unskilled and semi-skilled labor, the threat of being laid off was a real and effective stimulus. But in the Soviet Union the labor shortage insured that one could usually find work elsewhere.

Soviet managerial bonuses were not designed simply to make people work harder. They were also a powerful tool for enforcing state-set priorities and other directives. Peking, however, appears to prefer to rely on tight Party supervision to make certain that managers follow the spirit as well as the letter of Party directives. The regime has always shied away from excessive use of material incentives for Party personnel, both high and low, and most factory managers are long standing Party members. Party personnel who hold high posts do get salaries roughly commensurate with their rank. But their salaries may be topped by those of subordinate engineering executives, although evidence on this point is limited.

The principal explanation for Peking's lack of reliance on bonuses and other similar incentive mechanisms would appear to be the leadership's underlying belief that one cannot maintain communist discipline and elan by following what they consider to be capitalist incentive systems. Such features are all right for workers and technicians who have not overcome their bourgeois past, but if introduced into the Party itself they quickly change the character of the Party. Party members' incentives, it is believed, can only be properly sustained by a genuine commitment to communist ideals and by constant re-education to make sure those ideals are properly understood.

### *Wage Incentives*

Whatever the case with managerial motivation, it is wages and wage differentials that provide the principal source of incentives for most other enterprise personnel. Briefly, during 1958–59, the Chinese Communists reduced the use of piece-work wages and generally pushed some egalitarianism in the wage system. As with so many other aspects of the economy, however, the "Great Leap Forward" in wage policy was more of a temporary aberration than a continuing and characteristic policy line.

If wage differentials in China are less pronounced than in the Soviet Union—and it is not at all clear that they are—further research will undoubtedly uncover economic, not ideological, explanations. For example, China's reluctance to push the use of piece-rates more vigorously has, except during the "Great Leap," resulted from difficulties in properly setting norms for calculating the piece rates.[15] These difficulties in turn were caused by the underdeveloped nature of China's economy and the rapid changes that were taking place in that economy's structure.

In effect, it was difficult to pay wages on the basis of how much a worker produced on any given day because increases in his productivity were frequent. Often they were unconnected with any effort exerted by the worker himself, but instead resulted from the introduction of machinery, or reflected routine increases in skill and dexterity common during the first few years of operation of any new plant.

## *Buying Power*

Of even greater significance to worker and peasant incentives than wage differentials was what those wages would buy. In China and in the Soviet Union of the 1930s and 1940s, widespread rationing of consumers' goods reduced the meaning of these differentials. Additional income could not readily be used to buy more of the items most important to the worker. The amount of grain or edible oil that an individual could buy in China was generally fixed without regard to his income. Only on the black market was it possible to obtain more of these items, and then only at exorbitant prices.

The need for rationing in both China and the Soviet Union resulted essentially from the fact that money incomes outstripped the availability of consumers' goods on the market and prices were not allowed to rise fast enough to fill the gap. The situation was particularly severe when preceded by a sharp decline in farm output as happened in China in 1959–61 and in the Soviet Union following collectivization.

## *Heavy Industry*

The emphasis on heavy industry was the principal reason for the disparity between incomes and the availability of goods and, to a significant degree, for the organizational changes in agriculture that caused a sharp drop in farm output. In both China and the Soviet Union investment funds were directed toward industries producing machines and steel and away from agriculture and factories making consumers' goods.

The original reasons for adopting such an investment policy had little to do with ideology, although Marx did tend to equate economic development with heavy industrial growth. Of more importance was the fact that heavy industry was the basis for military strength and for maximum independence of foreign trade. As time has passed, however, concentration on heavy industry has tended to become part of the dogma. In fact, except for state ownership of enterprises and some form of central planning, centering investment in heavy industry has become the key economic dogma. There is every reason to believe that when China was drawing up its first five-year plan the basic thrust of the plan —its emphasis on heavy industry—was the subject of little if any debate.

## *The Food Factor*

In recent years in the Soviet Union a number of economists have criticized what they believe has been an overemphasis on machinery and steel. Discussion, however, has produced little action and the Stalinist investment pattern continues with minor alterations. Not so in China. Unlike the Soviet Union, the Chinese economy was too near the subsistence level for the regime to ignore the drop in farm output which occurred in 1959–61. Although the regime might have been able to avoid outright starvation and still have maintained the investment pattern of the 1950s, incentives and hence productivity would have remained at a low level. Even if Peking cared about nothing other than heavy industry, which was far from the case, agricultural difficulties would still have dictated a shift of investment to consumers' goods and to farm support industries (*e.g.*, chemical fertilizer and farm machinery).

There is evidence that this shift, which began in a major way in 1961–62 and has continued to the present, was not greeted enthusiastically by many Party cadres who looked on the Stalinist pattern as dogma. A number of cadres apparently particularly disliked the decision to lower the rate of investment and hence to raise the portion of national income devoted to consumption.[16] Nevertheless, the decision was made.

## *Pragmatism vs. Dogma*

The evidence presented, therefore, suggests that Chinese Communist control of industry and the methods of maintaining worker incentives have been determined for the most part by pragmatic considerations, just as in the Soviet Union. Dogma has played a role, but has seldom been sustained for long in opposition to clear indications that the dogmatic solution was not working. The period of the "Great Leap Forward" was the one time in which Chinese economic policy seems to have been governed for a substantial period of time by heavily ideological considerations. But even this period was not really an exception to the rule that the Chinese have been governed by what works because in 1958–59 they believed that the policies of the "Great Leap" did work. That it took so long to discover that the contrary was true must be attributed to the fact that one of the "Great Leap" policies was to rid the system of most means of checking on success or failure. Principally this meant the dismantling of the statistical apparatus.

It does not follow from this analysis, however, that because the Chinese follow a pragmatic economic policy their criticisms of the Soviet Union are insincere. What they are really against is not Soviet tinkering with the relative importance of the profits target or some other device, but what they consider to be the basic thrust of Soviet domestic (and foreign) policy. Whereas all Chinese policies are ultimately directed toward the building of a socialist society—or at least that is their intent—the same cannot, in Chinese eyes, be said for the Soviet Union. Where compromises are made in China for the sake of economic growth, they generally are looked on as compromises, not transformed into ultimate goals.

It is far from certain, however, that the Chinese Communist leadership can continue compromising with its revolutionary ideology and still maintain the vitality of that ideology as a determining force in Chinese society. It is just this problem that forms a central part of Chairman Mao Tse-tung's worries about the younger generation in China.

B

# Reorganization of Agrarian Structure and Land Reform

AS NOTED IN the section on Development of Agriculture, on the eve of Indian Independence and the Communist take-over of mainland China, the Indian and Chinese economies were characterized by backward and subsistence agriculture with semi-feudal land tenure relationships, continuous subdivision and fragmentation of small land holdings, and widespread rural unemployment and underemployment. In this chaotic state of affairs, the peasants were illiterate, poor, and exploited by the landlords and the money-lenders. The land tenure system prevailing in the two countries did not leave any incentive for the peasants to increase output, for a large share of the output accrued to the absentee landlords with little or no stake in the land. This agrarian system thus acted as a strong obstacle to economic development, and it reduced the actual tillers of land to a semistarvation level and being a virtual slave of the exploitative landlords. During the period of struggle for India's independence and before the Communist takeover of China, people vying for leadership in the two countries vowed to end this sad state of affairs. Accordingly in both countries bold programs for reorganization of agrarian structures have been undertaken. The objectives of this reorganization, according to the Indian Planning Commission are ". . . to remove such motivational and other impediments to increase agricultural production as arise from the agrarian structure inherited from the past, to create conditions for evolving an agricultural economy with a high level of efficiency and productivity and to eliminate [redacted] of exploitation and social injustice within the agrarian system." The steps taken to achieve these objectives have, however, been different in the two countries.

India's land reform measures aimed at "transferring ownership of the land to the tillers and security of tenure to the tenants." Land reform legislation enacted in different states between 1950–60 was built around the following measures: (1) abolition of intermediaries and big absentee landlords and transferring ownership rights to the actual tillers; (2) security of tenure to the tenants and fixing fair rents; and (3) fixing an upper ceiling on landholdings by one family and distribution of surplus land to the cultivators holding less than the upper ceiling. The pattern of land reforms in different states is more or less similar.

Uppal's paper on implementation of land reform legislation summarizes the legal provisions and findings of various studies undertaken in different states. Uppal explains the implementation of legislation in two villages in Punjab, showing how provisions in the legislation have been defied against the interests of tenants and landless laborers. On the whole, good progress has been made in the abolition of large estates of absentee landlords, and, as the excerpts from the Fourth Five Year Plan suggest, "The program for the abolition of intermediaries has been carried out practically all over the country. About 20 million tenants of former intermediaries came into direct relationship with the State and became owners of their holdings." On other land reform measures, the progress has been less than satisfactory. For some years, especially during the 1950s, the Indian government encouraged cooperative farming mainly as a measure to consolidate small and fragmented holdings and to enable the farmers to pool their resources. Not much progress was made in this respect, and at present the country is divided on the question of the feasibility of cooperative farming from political and economic points of view. The Indian government is, however, encouraging formation of agricultural cooperative societies to provide credit to farmers and cooperative societies for marketing agricultural produce and providing fertilizers, insecticides, and improved seeds. The cooperative societies are, however, still not within the reach of the majority of Indian peasants.

For improving rural conditions, India launched, with assistance from the United States, a comprehensive program called the Community Development Project scheme. Datt and Sundharam have outlined the working of the scheme and the progress achieved in improvement of agriculture, irrigation, communications, education, and public health. The program, started in October 1952 on an experimental basis, now covers entire rural India. The program draws material and human resources from the people and channels them for improving rural conditions under guidance from the government. To draw more voluntary cooperation from the people, participation of the elected village councils in the Community Development Program is being encouraged.

China's land policy and methods of reorganization of agrarian structure have been markedly different from India. China's main objective was to transform agriculture from a system of private ownership into a system of public ownership without alienating the peasants. This objective was achieved in five successive stages during the decade 1950–60. It started with simple land reforms (more or less like Indian land reforms) involving reduction of rents and transferring ownership to the actual tillers. This was followed by forming Mutual Aid Teams comprising five to ten or more households pooling their agricultural tools and farm animals for common use for farm production and subsidiary occupations. The next step was setting up Agricultural Producers Cooperatives consisting of thirty to forty households pooling their land and other agricultural resources and drawing compensation based on members' contributions of labor, land, and other inputs. These cooperative farms were transformed into collective farms, each containing about 100 households and their members organized into production brigades and production teams. From August 1958 on communes came into existence, engulfing collective farms and other enterprises in a designated area. Excerpts from the Burki book on Chinese communes explain the organization and working of the communes. Burki also explains the administrative machinery, the financial structure, and the techniques of manpower utilization in the communes. The striking feature of the communes is that they enable the planners to obtain planned funds for capital investment. The payment of wages to workers according to work points and organization of communes into production brigades and work teams assure utilization of available manpower. The success of China in increasing capital accumulation from agriculture and utilizing its huge manpower resources is likely to accelerate her growth rate. India's record on these two counts has been less than satisfactory. India's attempts to utilize rural manpower through the Community Development Project Scheme have not met with much success. However, when the promise of Green Revolution is fully materialized, India may be able to increase capital accumulation through an increase in agricultural productivity achieved largely in the medium and large farm units. Prior to World War II, the increase in productivity in the Japanese agricultural sector, achieved largely through improved agricultural techniques, did contribute to capital accumulation for her economic development. This was accomplished without a comprehensive land reform such as that introduced later during the Allied occupation period after World War II. It is quite possible that India may well already be on the threshold of repeating the Japanese experience.

14

# Land Reforms in India

## *Government of India*

*From Government of India, Planning Commission,* Fourth Five Year Plan—A Draft Outline *(Delhi: Manager of Publications, 1966), p. 125–31, with omissions. Reprinted with permission.*

### *Progress*

FIFTEEN YEARS AGO when the First Plan was being formulated, intermediary tenures like *zamindaris*, *jagirs* and *inams* covered more than 40 per cent of the area. There were large disparities in the ownership of land held under ryotwari tenure which covered the other 60 per cent area; and a substantial portion of the land was cultivated through tenants-at-will and share-croppers who paid about one-half the produce as rent. Most holdings were small and fragmented. Besides, there was a large population of landless agricultural laborers. In these conditions, the principal measures recommended for securing the objectives of the land policy were the abolition of intermediary tenures, reform of the tenancy system, including fixation of fair rent at one-fifth to one-fourth of the gross produce, security of tenure for the tenant, bringing tenants into direct relationship with the State and investing in them ownership of land. A ceiling on land holding was also recommended so that some surplus land may be made available for redistribution to the landless agricultural workers. Another important part of the program was consolidation of agricultural holdings and increase in the size of the operational unit to an economic scale through cooperative methods.

#### ABOLITION OF INTERMEDIARIES

During the past fifteen years, progress has been made in several directions. The program for the abolition of intermediaries has been carried out practically all over the country. About 20 million tenants of former intermediaries came into direct relationship with the State and became owners of their holdings. State Governments are now engaged in the assessment and payment of compensation. There were some initial delays but considerable progress has been made in this direction in recent years and it is hoped that the issue of compensatory bonds will be completed in another two years.

#### TENANCY REFORM

To deal with the problem of tenants-at-will in the ryotwari areas and of sub-tenants in the zamindari areas, a good deal of legislation has been enacted. Provisions for security of tenure, for bringing them into direct relation with the State and converting them into owners have been made in several States. As a result, about 3 million tenants and share-croppers have acquired ownership of more than 7 million acres, as shown in Table 1.

***Table 1***

| *State* | *Number of Tenants*[a] | *Area*[b] |
|---|---|---|
| Gujarat | 462 | 1,408 |
| Madhya Pradesh | 358 | — |
| Maharashtra | 618 | 1,674 |
| Punjab | 22 | 147[c] |
| Uttar Pradesh | 1,500 | 2,000 |
| West Bengal | — | 800 |
| Telangana region of Andhra Pradesh | 33 | 202 |
| Delhi | 29 | 39 |
| Himachal Pradesh | 24 | 28 |
| Tripura | 10 | 12 |

[a] In thousands.
[b] In respect of which ownership conferred (in thousand acres).
[c] Area in standard acres.

Provisions for regulation of rent have been adopted in all States. In Assam, Bihar, Gujarat, Kerala, Maharashtra, Mysore, Orissa, Rajasthan and the Union Territories, the maximum rent has been fixed at a quarter or less of the produce. In Andhra area, Jammu and Kashmir, Madras, Punjab and West Bengal, the fair rent or the share of the produce as fixed by law is still a third to one-half of the gross produce.

### CEILING ON HOLDINGS

Laws imposing ceiling on agricultural holdings have been enacted in all the States. In the former Punjab area, however, the State Government has the power to settle tenants on land in excess of the permissible limit of the landowners although it has not set a ceiling on ownership. According to available reports over 2 million acres of surplus lands in excess of the ceiling limits have been declared or taken possession of by Government in the States shown in Table 2.

**Table 2**

| State | Surplus Area[a] |
|---|---|
| Assam | 34.0 |
| Gujarat | 38.8 |
| Jammu and Kashmir | 450.0 |
| Maharashtra | 162.5 |
| Madhya Pradesh | 67.1 |
| Madras | 20.2 |
| Punjab | 368.5[b] |
| West Bengal | 776.5 |
| Uttar Pradesh | 222.7 |

[a] In thousand acres.
[b] Area in standard acres.

More lands will become available as implementation proceeds. The surplus lands are being distributed to tenants, uneconomic holders and landless agriculturists.

### EXTENSION OF OWNER-CULTIVATION

The "land to the tiller" policy followed during the last fifteen years has helped to establish owner-cultivation on a large scale. This is borne out by the data collected in the Census of 1961. Out of every 100 cultivators 76 were owner-cultivators, 16 were owner-cum-tenant cultivators and only 8 were pure tenant-cultivators.

There were, however, shortcomings in several directions. Substantial areas in some regions of the country are still cultivated through informal crop-sharing arrangements; there were ejectments of tenants through the device of voluntary surrenders; the fair rent provisions were not enforced effectively in all cases; and the ceiling had been evaded through the well-known device of transfers and partitions and not much land was made available for distribution to the landless.

### REVIEW BY N.D.C. COMMITTEE

In November 1963, following the Mid-term Appraisal of the Third Plan, the National Development Council reviewed the progress made in the implementation of land reforms in different States. It noted that on account of legal and other factors in some States the laws had not been fully enforced. The Council emphasized that speedy execution of land reforms was vital for increasing agricultural production and strengthening the rural economy, and called upon all State Governments to complete the implementation of land reform programs before the end of the Third Plan. The Council constituted a Committee with the Minister of Home Affairs as Chairman and the five Chief Ministers who are Vice-Chairmen of Zonal Councils, the Minister of Food and Agriculture and the Member in charge of land reforms in the Planning Commission as members to review the progress of land reform in different States and propose measures for securing the implementation of the land reform legislation. Officers were deputed to visit the States to review the progress of implementation and examine the difficulties encountered in giving effect to the program. Most of the States have since been visited by the officers. Their reports and the resulting recommendations in respect of the States of Andhra Pradesh, Bihar, Gujarat, Madras, Maharashtra, Orissa, Rajasthan, Uttar Pradesh and Himachal Pradesh have been examined in the Committee in consultation with the States concerned and their attention has been drawn to the problems faced. As a result several States have taken steps to strengthen implementation.

## *Program for the Fourth Plan*

The land policy to be pursued in the States has been outlined in the first three Plans. The emphasis in the Fourth Plan should necessarily be on finding solutions to the problems which have been observed in the States in which implementation has lagged behind. The main points which call for immediate attention are set out in the following paragraphs:

(1) Administrative arrangements for enforcement and supervision are often inadequate and public opinion has not been sufficiently built up to quicken the pace of reforms. These arrangements need to be strengthened to ensure better implementation by following a phased program to be drawn up by the State Governments. It would be necessary to supplement administrative action by enlisting support and assistance of public workers. A high-level committee comprising Ministers and representatives of public opinion may be set up in each State, which should keep the progress of implementation of the policy under constant review, district by district, so that timely action is taken to fill the gaps in the law and expedite implementation.

(2) Records of tenants do not exist in several States and are often incomplete and out of date even where they do. For effective enforcement of tenancy reform, it is imperative that records of tenancies should be prepared and kept up to date whatever the difficulties in the way. It should assist in the preparation and revision of records if tripartite committees representing landlords and tenants and presided over by an independent person or a revenue official are constituted for groups of villages. Entries in the records so prepared should have presumptive evidence value. Each tenant, so recorded, should be issued a certificate indicating his rights in the land and the rent payable by him. Such a step will facilitate enforcement of the legal provisions. To help the States to bring the records of tenancies up-to-date, a Centrally sponsored scheme has been included in the Fourth Plan.

(3) The economic condition of tenants, even where they have been conferred permanent rights, still continues to be weak. It is important to confer on them the right to make permanent improvements to the land and to ensure adequate compensation in the event of eviction. Adequate and timely agricultural credit should be available to them. For this purpose, they should enjoy the right to mortgage their interest and title with the Government agency, cooperative society and other lending institutions for raising loans for effecting various improvements on their land. It will help expeditious disposal of loan applications if the cooperative societies are supplied with a copy of the tenants' record of rights.

(4) In some States, such as Andhra Pradesh, Assam, Bihar, Madras and West Bengal (in respect of *bargadars*), the existing provisions for security of tenure are of an interim nature. Comprehensive measures for converting tenants and share-croppers into owners have not yet been adopted. Delay in enacting comprehensive legislation creates a great deal of uncertainty which is inimical to efforts for increasing agricultural production. Speedy action is called for to rectify this situation.

(5) Even the apparently restricted right of resumption for personal cultivation has, in practice, widened the scope of ejectments. Besides, such resumption upsets the economy of small owner-*cum*-tenant farmers who had leased in small areas to make up viable units of cultivation. The right of resumption was originally intended for exercise only during a limited period of five years. This period having elapsed the right of resumption should now be terminated, and permanent and heritable rights conferred on all tenants.

(6) Numerous ejectments of tenants have occurred under the guise of "voluntary surrenders." This has tended to defeat one of the major aims of land reform, namely, providing security of tenure for the tiller of the soil. The Third Plan document drew the attention of State Governments to this distressing phenomenon and made two recommendations: (*a*) surrenders should not be regarded as valid unless they were duly registered with the revenue authorities; and (*b*) even where the surrender was held to be

valid, the landowner should be entitled to take possession only up to his right of resumption permitted by law.

This has been acted upon by only a few States, namely, Kerala, Madhya Pradesh, Mysore, Manipur and Tripura and partially by Bihar, Gujarat, Jammu & Kashmir, Maharashtra and Rajasthan. As the *bona fides* of most surrenders are open to doubt, it is important that early steps are taken to remove legal and administrative loop-holes. As no more resumption is visualized, all surrenders should here after be made to Government only, without any right for the landowner to take possession of the land so surrendered.

(7) The rents as fixed by law are still high in Andhra area, Jammu and Kashmir, Madras, Punjab and West Bengal and should be brought down to the level recommended in the Plans—to one-fourth or one-fifth of the gross produce. Besides, produce rents which are difficult to enforce should be abolished and replaced by fixed cash rents so that uncertainties arising out of annual fluctuations in rents may be eliminated and the tiller assured of the full benefits of his investment. As suggested in the Third Plan, it would facilitate enforcement if fair rent is fixed as a multiple of land revenue. The difficulty arising out of variations in the land revenue rates for lands of equal productivity owing to different dates of settlement and other factors might be met by adopting a range of multiples so that different multiples can be adopted in different areas according to local conditions and the date of settlement. In areas where regular settlement has not taken place, it might be convenient to work out and notify cash equivalents of one-fourth or one-fifth of the gross produce on the basis of data available with the State Governments about yields of different classes of lands.

Security of tenure for the tiller is crucial to the whole scheme of tenancy reform. It enables him to obtain various aids and inputs and to participate fully in the production programs. Experience has shown that it is difficult to ensure security of tenure and effective enforcement of rentals so long as the landlord-tenant bond remains unbroken. Besides, ownership provides the psychological stimulus for maximizing agricultural production. The objective should therefore be to put a complete end to the landlord-tenant nexus and convert the tenants into full owners. To this end, the State might step in, acquire ownership of leased land and transfer it to the tenants. In States where legislation has been enacted for converting tenants into owners, gaps in the law, if any, should be filled immediately and the legislation implemented with speed. In States where such legislation has not been enacted, steps should be taken to pass the necessary law. As a first minimum step, there should be immediate legislation to break the direct landlord-tenant relationship, the State interposing between landlords and tenants to collect fair rents from tenants and pay them to landlords after deducting land revenue and a collection charge. As State Governments are already equipped to collect land revenue from millions of small holders, such a step is not likely to throw any excessive additional burden on them. This should apply to all tenants who held land on a given date, say, April 1, 1966. Provision should also be made for the restoration on application of those who may have been illegally dispossessed, say, during the past three years. The tenants who thus came into direct relationship with the State should have, besides permanent and heritable rights, an optional right to purchase ownership on payment of reasonable compensation to be prescribed in the law.

The program of ceilings set out in the Plan has been diluted in implementation. There were deficiencies in the law and delays in its enactment and implementation resulting in large scale evasions. Several States had made provisions for disregarding transfers made after a specified date, but often these provisions proved to be ineffective and not much surplus land has been available for redistribution. The main object of ceilings which is to re-distribute land to the landless at a reasonable price on a planned basis has thus been largely defeated. In the absence of any reliable data it would also be difficult to say that as a result of transfers much land has passed into the hands of agricultural laborers or small farmers. However, as stated in the Third Plan, once legislation has been enacted, amendments should aim primarily at eliminating deficiencies and facilitating implementation rather that at introducing fundamental changes in the principles underlying the legislation. As transfers take place generally between the members of a family, the States might consider the suggestion earlier made by the Panel on Land Reform (and this has already been provided in some laws), namely, to apply ceilings to the aggregate area held by all the members of a family rather than to individual holdings, the family being defined to include husband and wife, their dependent children and grandchildren.

Land reform has been too often regarded as something extraneous to the scheme of agricultural development and implemented in isolation. It needs to be re-emphasized that it is an integral part of the program of agricultural development as it helps to establish owner-cultivation and removes an important impediment arising out of defects in the agrarian structure. At the same time it should be recognized that land ownership is just one of the components, though an important one, of the package required for higher production. Unless the beneficiaries of land reform, namely, the tenants and the new owners created as a result of tenancy reform and settlements on lands, are provided with adequate agricultural credit, physical inputs and other essential services and facilities, it could not yield the expected results. This aspect needs special attention.

15

# Implementation of Land Reform Legislation in India—A Study of Two Villages in Punjab

*J. S. Uppal*

*From* Asian Survey *9, no. 5 (May 1969): 359–72, with omissions. Reprinted with permission.*

According to a United Nations Report,[1] the agrarian system generally prevailing in underdeveloped countries acts as a strong obstacle to economic development in a number of ways. First, the tenants have little incentive to increase output, for a large share of the output accrues to absentee landlords with little or no stake in the land. Second, a very small margin is left with the actual tiller, and this amount is quite insufficient to provide for capital investment in land. In order to remove these impediments to economic advancement and to promote social justice, each of India's Five Year Plans has laid great emphasis on land reforms. Accordingly, the objectives of the Fourth Five Year Plan are:

> . . . to remove such motivational and other impediments to increase agricultural production as arise from the agrarian structure inherited from the past, to create conditions for evolving an agricultural economy with high level of efficiency and productivity, and to eliminate elements of exploitation and social injustice within the agrarian system.[2]

Despite the great importance attached to land reform by India's central government, the direct powers to enact and implement land reform legislation are vested in the states. Land rights and agriculture are constitutionally under the domain of the states. In accordance with the broad objectives laid down by the Planning Commission and the central government, the states have been enacting legislation on different aspects of land reform since 1949. Though the underlying principles of land reform in different states incorporate common basic features, the pattern of land tenure that has emerged varies from state to state. This is due, first, to the multiplicity of tenures that existed in the states before 1947. Second, the diverse cultures, socioeconomic conditions, history, and geography of India have left different states with markedly different land reform programs. A major part of the land reform legislation was enacted by the states between 1950 and 1960 and the related programs have been built around the following measures: (1) abolition of intermediaries; (2) tenancy reforms, *e.g.*, security of tenure to the tenants, fixing of fair rents, and provision of the tenant's right to purchase land; and (3) ceiling on land holdings and distribution of surplus lands.

The passing of a law is one thing and its implementation another. Recognizing the importance of the implementation of land reform laws, several studies have been made to determine the extent to which the legislation has been enforced and also to recommend measures for rendering legislation more effective. The Research Program Committee of the Planning Commission sponsored a phased program of such studies, and their findings throw light on many aspects of the land reform measures. In a study in Bombay, Dandekar and Khudanpur remarked:

> The main facts brought out by this investigation are: firstly, the extensive resumption and changes of tenants that took place even after the enforcing of the Act showing that the protection given to the tenants could not be effective in practice; secondly, a more or less normal market in land showing that the provisions for promoting the transfer of lands into the hands of the tillers were not quite effective; and thirdly, an almost complete absence of any sign of lowering the share and cash rents or of any changes in the tenancy practices.[3]

**Notes to chapter 15 appear on page 395**

The studies sponsored by the Planning Commission in Andhra, Hyderabad, West Bengal, Saurashtra, and Gujarat reached similar conclusions and pointed out the basic failure in implementing the tenancy legislation effectively.[4] On the basis of results of these studies, the Planning Commission has recognized the slow progress in the implementation of land reform legislation and the frustration of some of the objectives:

> . . . the total impact of land reform has been less than hoped for. . . . there has been insufficient attention to the administrative aspects of land reform. Frequently, at the lower levels of administration, collusion and evasion have gone unchecked.[5]

In addition to the Planning Commission's studies, several investigations were conducted in the different states in India.[6] Professors Nanavati and Anjaria have summarized the results of these investigations as follows:

> Inquiries into the working of the tenancy legislation have revealed that the implementation of the law has been far from satisfactory. Rents higher than the legally prescribed minimum continue to be paid; there were also several cases of unlawful evictions, sometimes with the acquiescence of the tenant himself through the so-called voluntary surrenders. . . . In a number of cases the protection given to the tenant has not benefited him in practice because of the right of resumption given to landlord, the exercise of which has converted the tenant into an agricultural laborer and the landlord into the so-called "personal cultivator."[7]

According to C. B. Mamoria, land reform legislation

> has failed to solve the problem of uneconomic holdings or to correct the structural imbalance between land and labour. . . . The legislated intention of the land reform was lost through faulty, ineffective and sometimes even unsympathetic implementation.[8]

An analysis of the studies and investigations shows that in most cases provisions in land reform legislation have been rendered ineffective for the following reasons:

1. The legislation has gone far enough and has fallen short of fulfilling the objectives.

2. The legislation was formulated in an unsystematic and uncoordinated manner, and contains technical defects and contradictions. For example, in many states, such as Rajasthan, Punjab and Madhya Pradesh, no legal sanctions were provided against the landowner in case of a tenant being ejected unlawfully or the landowner realizing more than the statutory rent.

3. The legislation has not been properly implemented because of administrative difficulties and inadequacies. The failure of the government to maintain correct and up-to-date land records has created a great lacuna. The record does not provide information in respect of holdings of the tenants and crop sharer. For example, in some cases holdings are shown to be cultivated by proprietors who do not even live in that village.

4. The spirit of the legislation is not consistent with the prevailing social and economic forces. In fixing maximum rent payable or providing security of tenure for the tenants, scarcity of land and overcrowding in agriculture without alternative means of subsistence for tenants are often forgotten. In the circumstances, provisions in the legislation are not enforced because tenants may be willing to cultivate land without taking advantage of any of the tenancy provisions.

Most of the studies indicating failure of land reform legislation have emphasized the legal and administrative aspects of the situation. Sufficient attention has not been given to the attitudes and opinions of the rural population in framing land legislation. No legislation, however perfect it may be, can achieve the desired results if the parties involved are indifferent or hostile to it. Moreover, little attention has been paid to the Northwestern region in India in general, and to the state of Punjab in particular, in studying the implementation and impact of land reform legislation.

This study examines the implementation of land reform legislation in Punjab and the opinions held about that legislation by rural households in different tenure situations.

## THE VILLAGES

During the summer of 1966 data were collected from two villages, Chanalon and

Santa Majra, in Kharar *tehsil* in the Ambala district (Rupar district after reorganization of the state of Punjab) in the Punjab. The village of Chanalon has a total area of 619 acres, with a population of 892 (480 males, 412 females) living in 143 households. Eighty per cent of the population derive their livelihood from agriculture. Out of the village's total area, 448 acres are under cultivation and distributed among various land tenures as follows: 282 acres (62 per cent of the cultivated area) are self-cultivated by owners; 166 acres (37 per cent) are cultivated by tenants. Only 11.4 per cent of the cultivated area is under irrigation through wells.

Santa Majra has a total area of 737 acres, with a population of 702 (374 males, 328 females) living in 146 households. Eighty-three per cent of the population derive their livelihood from agriculture. Out of the total area, 656 acres are under cultivation and distributed as follows: 538 acres (82 per cent of the cultivated area) are self-cultivated by owners; 118 acres (18 per cent) are cultivated by tenants. Only 12 per cent of the cultivated area is under well irrigation.

These villages were not much affected by the refugee movement caused by the partition of the province in 1947. There are only two refugee families from Pakistan in Chanalon, and only one in Santa Majra—all three having originally belonged to these villages and having gone to Lyallpur and Montgomery districts (now in West Pakistan) during the 'twenties to settle in the canal colonies. Undisturbed by partition, these villages thus provided a good opportunity to study the effect of the legislation from an historical perspective.

Information was collected from all the households in the villages on major aspects of land reform legislation in the Punjab contained in the Punjab Tenancy Act of 1887, the Punjab Occupancy Tenants (Vesting of Proprietory Rights) Act of 1952, and the Punjab Security of Land Tenure Act of 1953 with later amendments. For eliciting the opinions on the legislation, however, a stratified random sample of 100 households (50 from each village) was selected from the households in different categories of land tenure, and these were interviewed in depth.

Of the data collected, background information included household composition, occupation of the household members, landholdings under different tenures with changes in ownership and management pattern (with details of transactions) since 1950, details of the holdings rented in or rented out, and occupancy rights. Supplementing the information and opinions collected from the households was information obtained through interviews with the revenue officials.

## *Salient Features of the Legislation*

1. *Regulation of Rent:*

   Maximum rent payable by a tenant is not to exceed one-third of the crop or value thereof. Where the customary rent is less than such one-third, it is to be deemed the maximum rent.

2. *Security of Tenure:*

   (a) Ceiling on existing holdings: 30 standard acres[9] not exceeding 60 ordinary acres; in the case of displaced persons from Pakistan, 50 standard acres not exceeding 100 ordinary acres. Any surplus area will be utilized for the purpose of settlement of tenants. Any transfer or disposition of land (except by way of inheritance) made after April 1953 will be disregarded. Orchard or tea estates, cooperative garden colonies (existing before April 1953), lands granted to members of the armed forces, and well-run farms[10] are exempt from the ceiling.

   (b) Ceiling on future acquisitions for personal cultivation: Permissible area is the same as in (a) above and subject to the conditions that each tenant is entitled to retain (i) the entire area, where he holds land from a person who owns land exceeding the above limits, and (ii) up to 5 standard acres in other cases until alternative land is provided by the state government.

   Self-cultivation means cultivation by a landowner either personally or through his wife or children, or through his brothers or collaterals in the first degree, or through his real uncles and nephews, whether maternal or paternal, under his supervision.

   (c) There are two categories of tenants: (i) *Occupancy tenants*—tenants who have held land for two generations or have occupied lands for a continuous period of some time on payment of rent or services to the proprietor. From 1953, there will be no new occupancy tenants and the existing ones will have the right to purchase the land. (ii) *Other tenants*—tenants who have full security of tenure. The minimum period of tenancy is 10 years; if allowed to hold over thereafter, it is deemed as renewed for a further period of 10 years, subject, however, to resumption rights granted to landowners for self-cultivation as outlined above.

(d) Ejection: A tenant can be ejected on the following grounds—failure to pay rent or its arrears, failure to cultivate land, use of land in such a way as to render it unfit for cultivation, subletting of land, holding of an area in excess of the permissible amount.

3. *Tenant's Right to Purchase Land:*

(a) Occupancy tenants: Effective from June 15, 1952, property rights will be vested in the occupancy tenants in respect of the land under their cultivation on payment of compensation to the landowner at the rate of (i) 20 times the annual rent of occupancy right if acquired under the Punjab Tenancy Act of 1885, or (ii) an amount equal to 25 times the annual rent in other cases.

(b) Other tenants: Other tenants have an optional right of purchase in respect of non-resumable lands provided that such tenants have been in possession of the land for a continuous period of 6 years.

## *Impact of the Land Reform Legislation*

The data were drawn from two sources—(1) the households and (2) the revenue records. The households were asked two sets of questions:

1. Pattern of cultivation of the owned land:
   (a) was it under self-cultivation?
   (b) was it cultivated through hired labor or through relatives?
   (c) was it rented out to others?
2. Sources of obtaining land for cultivation:
   (a) was it their own land?
   (b) was it rented?

The information was collected for two periods, 1950–51 and 1965–66, to study the changes before and after the land reform legislation.

### PATTERN OF OWNERSHIP AND MANAGEMENT

The land reform legislation altered the pattern of ownership and the management of land and also the economic status and occupation of the households. Table 1 shows changes in the occupation of the families under study.

On the whole, there was a sharp increase in the number of agricultural laborer families—from 9.3 per cent of the total families in 1950 to 29.4 per cent in 1966. The number of non-owning cultivator families (*i.e.*, tenants) decreased from 9.7 per cent in 1950 to 2.4 per cent in 1966, while the number of cultivating owners increased from 35.8 per cent in 1950 to 40.1 per cent in 1966. From these changes in status of the families, the following trends emerge:

1. The number of cultivating owner families has increased. More and more owners are cultivating their land themselves or through hired labor.
2. The number of non-owning cultivator families (tenants) has decreased. The tenants are being removed from the land.
3. The number of landless laborer families has increased. The ex-tenants have been removed from their land and have joined the ranks of landless laborers.

Table 2 shows changes in the pattern of cultivation in the two villages. During the period of 1950–66, the area under cultivation increased from 66.2 per cent to 74.2 per cent of the total area under cultivation. In the same period the area under tenancy (both under cash rent and *batai*)[11] declined from 33.8 per cent to 25.8 per cent of the total area under cultivation. These and other changes in the land tenure situation will be discussed under the headings *Cultivation by Owners* and *Cultivation by Tenants.*

### CULTIVATION BY OWNERS

As already mentioned, the data show a definite trend toward an increasing proportion of total land under owner cultivation. In both the villages, the total area under owner cultivation increased from 66.2 per cent in 1950 to 74.2 per cent in 1966. As shown in Table 1, the number of cultivating owner families in the two villages also registered an increase, from 35.8 per cent to 40.2 per cent of the total number of families. In order to analyze this trend we investigated the changes in pattern of cultivation by the owners (see Table 3).

The reason for the decrease in the proportion of area cultivated by owners themselves is that the male members of many families either have found jobs in the nearby urban centers (*e.g.*, Kharar and Chandigarh) or

***Table 1—Changes in Agricultural Status and Occupation of Families***

| AGRICULTURAL STATUS AND OCCUPATION | 1950 NO. OF FAMILIES | | | | | | 1966 NO. OF FAMILIES | | | | | |
|---|---|---|---|---|---|---|---|---|---|---|---|---|
| | Chanalon | | Santa Majra | | Total | | Chanalon | | Santa Majra | | Tota | |
| | No. | % | No. | % | No. | % | No. | % | No. | % | No. | % |
| I. Cultivating Owners: | 53 | 37.6 | 47 | 34.0 | 100 | 35.8 | 57 | 39.9 | 59 | 40.4 | 116 | 40.1 |
| Cultivating one's land only | 27 | 50.9 | 21 | 44.7 | 48 | 48.0 | 29 | 50.8 | 33 | 55.9 | 62 | 53.4 |
| Cultivating one's own land and also renting | 22 | 41.4 | 19 | 40.4 | 41 | 41.0 | 25 | 43.9 | 22 | 37.2 | 47 | 40.5 |
| Cultivating one's own land partly and leasing out the rest | 4 | 7.7 | 7 | 14.9 | 11 | 11.0 | 3 | 5.3 | 4 | 6.9 | 7 | 6.1 |
| II. Non-Cultivating Owners: | | | | | | | | | | | | |
| Owning but not cultivating | 66 | 46.8 | 60 | 43.5 | 126 | 45.2 | 41 | 28.8 | 40 | 27.5 | 81 | 28.1 |
| III. Non-Owning Cultivators | 12 | 8.6 | 15 | 10.9 | 27 | 9.7 | 6 | 4.0 | 1 | 0.6 | 7 | 2.4 |
| IV. Agricultural Laborers | 10 | 7.0 | 16 | 11.6 | 26 | 9.3 | 39 | 27.3 | 46 | 31.5 | 85 | 29.4 |
| Total | 141 | 100.0 | 138 | 100.0 | 279 | 100.0 | 143 | 100.0 | 146 | 100.0 | 289 | 100.0 |

***Table 2—Changes in the Pattern of Land Cultivation***

| PATTERN | 1950 CHANALON | | 1950 SANTA MAJRA | | 1950 TOTAL | | 1966 CHANALON | | 1966 SANTA MAJRA | | 1966 TOTAL | |
|---|---|---|---|---|---|---|---|---|---|---|---|---|
| | Area (acres) | % of Total | Area (acres) | % of Total | Area (acres) | % of Total | Area (acres) | % of Total | Area (acres) | % of Total | Area (acres) | % of Total |
| I. Under Owner Cultivation | 235 | 53 | 481 | 75 | 716 | 66 | 282 | 63 | 538 | 82 | 820 | 74 |
| II. Under Tenancy Cultivation | 206 | 47 | 161 | 25 | 367 | 34 | 166 | 37 | 118 | 18 | 284 | 26 |
| (a) *Batai* System | 195 | 95 | 129 | 80 | 324 | 88 | 143 | 86 | 76 | 64 | 219 | 77 |
| (b) Cash Rent System | 11 | 5 | 32 | 20 | 43 | 12 | 26 | 14 | 42 | 36 | 65 | 23 |
| Total Area | 441 | 100 | 642 | 100 | 1083 | 100 | 448 | 100 | 656 | 100 | 1,104 | 100 |

have joined the armed services. Some owners have declared themselves to be self-cultivators in the official record, though in fact they are getting land cultivated by tenants (cases of concealed tenancy) or by hired laborers under the supervision of their family members.

## *Table 3—Pattern of Cultivation by Owners*

| PATTERN OF CULTIVATION | 1950 AREA IN ACRES | 1950 PER CENT OF TOTAL | 1966 AREA IN ACRES | 1966 PER CENT OF TOTAL |
|---|---|---|---|---|
| Cultivated by self | 548.62 | 76.6 | 519.11 | 63.3 |
| Cultivated by relatives | 132.00 | 18.4 | 123.00 | 15.1 |
| Cultivated by hired labor | 35.50 | 5.0 | 177.75 | 21.6 |
| Total land | 716.12 | 100.0 | 819.86 | 100.0 |

The area cultivated with the assistance of relatives has remained more or less constant. There has been a large increase in the area cultivated by the owners through hired labor —from 5 per cent of the total area cultivated in 1950 to 216 per cent in 1966.

It is interesting to note that the increasing trend toward getting land cultivated by hired labor has given rise to a new type of land tenure arrangement known in the area as *sanjhee*. The landowners, who in many cases work outside the village, or engage in other occupations such as shopkeeping and carpentry in the same village, get the land tilled and seeded by hired labor and then contract with a *sanjhee* (one of the hired laborers) to look after the land, perform day-to-day operations such as weeding, and harvesting the crop. A *sanjhee* receives one-sixth to one-eighth of the gross produce, as against one-half of the gross produce as rent in the case of regular tenants. In the revenue records the land is registered under owner cultivation, since this new arrangement of *sanjhee* is not recognized by law.

### CULTIVATION BY TENANTS

Table 2 indicates a decline in the proportion of area under tenancy cultivation—from 34 per cent of the total land under cultivation in 1950 to 26 per cent in 1966. Tenancy as a legal land tenure arrangement is on the decline as the landowners are resuming personal cultivation through hired laborers or the *sanjhee* system. The landowners indicate that they are not prepared to take the risk of losing their land to tenants by renting it on a regular basis. The prevailing opinion among the landowners is that if one lets the land remain with a tenant for two to three years, the tenant is likely to become owner of the land.

To avoid this risk, the landowners in these villages are either renting their land for one year only, or making the rental arrangement on a verbal basis, or in some cases concealing the tenancies.

Out of the total area of 284.50 acres under tenancy, 215.7 acres (75.8 per cent) were rented on yearly basis. In most cases, the tenants were changed every year, *not* because there was anything wrong with them but because of the prevailing fear that if a tenant occupies land for more than a year he establishes some sort of ownership claim to the land. It is surprising how the tenants have been surrendering land voluntarily after a year. When questioned about voluntary surrenders most of the tenants remarked that in order to live in the village and get any land for cultivation, they have to establish a good reputation for being "cooperative" and "honest" tenants. During the last fifteen years there have been two cases where the tenants, at the suggestion of some outside influence, refused to surrender land to the landowners after one year and threatened to go to court to retain the land. Many villagers still remember how these two families got the reputation of being "troublemakers" and were looked down upon even by their own social and caste groups since they were creating hardship for other tenants by setting bad examples. Eventually they had to surrender the land voluntarily (though under social pressure). One tenant left the village to settle elsewhere, and the other apologized to the landowner. The voluntary surrender of land after one year is evident from Table 4.

While in 1950 only 24 per cent of the land under tenancy was rented for less than two years, the figure rose to 80 per cent in 1965–66.

We could not understand the logic behind changing tenants *every* year. Under the legislation, a tenant cannot be ejected from the land (except in case of failure to pay rent, subletting, etc.) irrespective of the period of his occupying the land. Technically, a tenant cannot be asked to surrender the land even after a year. However, he becomes eligible to buy the rented land after six years of continuous occupation. From discussion with the revenue officials we found that the landowners somehow have the erroneous impression based on long-standing practice in the villages, that after one year a tenant cannot be ejected.

We also noticed some cases of concealed tenancy in both villages—(one in Chanalon, and two in Santa Majra) where the land was in fact cultivated by tenants, but in the revenue records it was reported to be under "owner's personal cultivation." It is difficult to determine the exact number of such cases, since, obviously, neither the landowners nor the tenants are willing to divulge the information. Our source of information was village gossip, later confirmed by our confidential probe of the parties concerned. When questioned, the tenants observed that the choice before them was between having the land in a concealed manner or not having it at all. The landowners indulged in this concealed practice to safeguard themselves from the alleged complications of legal tenancy under the land reform legislation. The local land revenue official (*patwari*) expressed his ignorance about the concealed tenancy cases. As one of the landowners aptly remarked, "If the parties concerned—landowner and tenant—wish to keep a land transaction confidential, what can the *patwari* do?"

**Table 4—Land Cultivated by Tenants — Percentage of Rented Land and Duration of Renting Arrangements**

| | Land Rented | | | |
|---|---|---|---|---|
| | 1950–51 | | 1966 | |
| No. of Years | Acres | % of Rented Land | Acres | % of Rented Land |
| 5–10 | 40.3 | 11.0 | 16.8 | 6.0 |
| 4– 5 | 87.7 | 24.0 | 15.0 | 5.0 |
| 3– 4 | 91.2 | 25.0 | 12.3 | 4.0 |
| 2– 3 | 59.2 | 16.0 | 14.2 | 5.0 |
| 1– 2 | 44.2 | 12.0 | 71.1 | 25.0 |
| 0– 1 | 44.2 | 12.0 | 155.1 | 55.0 |
| Total | 366.8 | 100.0 | 284.5 | 100.0 |

PAYMENT OF RENT

Under the provisions of land reform legislation, the maximum rent payable by a tenant is not to exceed one-third of the crop or value thereof. Where the customary rent is less than such one-third, it is to be deemed the maximum rent.

Our data show the following trends on the payment of rent: (1) All the tenants renting land on *batai* rent basis were paying rent at the rate of one-half of the gross produce of the land. This is a clear defiance of the maximum legal limit on the rent payable. (2) There is a shift from *batai* rent to cash rent arrangement. (3) Some new rental arrangements are being evolved to defy the legislation. The patterns and practices of payment of rent are given in Table 5.

Tables 2 and 5 show a changing pattern of rent payment in the villages. There is a sharp decline in both the area and number of families under *batai* rent, and an increase in the area under own cultivation and the number of tenant families paying cash rent. The *sanjhee* system, which did not even exist in 1950, has come to occupy an important place in tenancy arrangements. As already explained, there is no legal limitation on the rent paid under the *sanjhee* arrangement. The increasing tendency toward renting land under cash rent is due to the prevalent view among landowners that there is no maximum per acre is explained by the scarcity of land. It also shows how the legal provision of the upper limit on rent has been defied. As regards the *batai* rental arrangement, all the tenants in both the villages are paying at the rate of one-half of the total gross produce per acre. It is a matter of common knowledge that the maximum rent payable is a third of the gross produce per acre, but nobody seems perturbed over the excessive rent being charged. As already pointed out, a tenant simply cannot rent land at the rate of less than half of the produce, and if he complains against the excessive rent he will find himself in trouble. It is a situation where the spirit of legislation regarding the maximum rent payable is inconsistent with the underlying economic situation: a scarcity of land arising

**Table 5—Pattern of Rent Payments by Tenants**

| Pattern of Rent Payments | 1950 NO. OF FAMILIES | | | | | | 1966 NO. OF FAMILIES | | | | | |
|---|---|---|---|---|---|---|---|---|---|---|---|---|
| | Chanalon | | Santa Majra | | Total | | Chanalon | | Santa Majra | | Total | |
| | No. | % | No. | % | No. | % | No. | % | No. | % | No. | % |
| *Batai* Rent | 30 | 88.2 | 28 | 82.3 | 58 | 85.3 | 13 | 41.9 | 14 | 60.8 | 27 | 50.0 |
| Cash Rent | 4 | 11.8 | 6 | 17.7 | 10 | 14.7 | 15 | 48.3 | 5 | 21.7 | 20 | 37.0 |
| *Sanjhee* Arrangement | — | 0.0 | — | — | — | — | 3 | 9.8 | 4 | 17.5 | 7 | 13.0 |
| Total | 34 | 100.0 | 34 | 100.0 | 68 | 100.0 | 31 | 100.0 | 23 | 100.0 | 54 | 100.0 |

**Table 6—Average Cash Rent Per Acre[a]**

| TYPE OF LAND | 1950 CHANALON | | 1950 SANTA MAJRA | | 1966 CHANALON | | 1966 SANTA MAJRA | |
|---|---|---|---|---|---|---|---|---|
| | Amount Rs | % of Gross Produce | Amount Rs | % of Gross Produce | Amount Rs | % of Gross Produce | Amount Rs | % of Gross Produce |
| Unirrigated | 72 | 46 | 70 | 45 | 115 | 52 | 112 | 51 |
| Irrigated | 105 | 49 | 103 | 51 | 159 | 56 | 156 | 57 |

[a] At 1950 prices.

limit on the cash rent under the land reform legislation. The common practice for fixing cash rent is to rent the land to the tenant offering the highest cash rent, taking into account, however, his reputation. During the last sixteen years the average amount of cash rent per acre has increased considerably, as shown in Table 6.

The increase in the amount of cash rent from overcrowding in agriculture without alternative employment opportunities.

## *Information and Opinion on the Land Reform Legislation*

There is great variation in the extent of information landowners and tenants have about different provisions in the legislation. The provision on regulation of rent is the most widely known among both groups; the provision least known is the ceiling on future acquisition of land for personal cultivation. The tenants are better informed than the landowners about the security of tenure, but less informed on their rights to purchase land. It is our impression that on the whole the respondents—both landowners and tenants—are generally well informed on the land reform legislation, and that the ineffective implementation of the legislation is due mainly to economic and social factors, rather than to lack of information.

There is a general feeling among the tenants that they have not benefited from the legislation. They are more insecure in the terms of their tenure, continue to pay more than the maximum legal rent, feel that their relations with the landowners are no longer cordial, etc. This feeling of being worse off than before has led to frustration among them. Results from the legislation have fallen far short of expectations, and the tenants generally have developed a cynical attitude towards the government's efforts to reform tenancy conditions. Most tenants demand stern government action against the landowners charging rents in excess of the legally prescribed limit and using concealed tenancy practices. They feel that any half-hearted measures create more problems for them.

The landowners also express disappointment over the legislation. They feel that the government has given too many rights to the tenants to the utter neglect of the landowners' interests. Their defiance of the land reform legislation is a desperate attempt to preserve the ownership of their land, which they fear is in danger under the provision regarding the tenant's right to purchase land. They know that charging rent at a rate greater than a third of gross produce is illegal, but they justify it on the following grounds: Rent equivalent to one-half is traditional and has been in existence for many, many years. There is an acute shortage of land available for rent. Tenants are willing to pay rent greater than one-half of the produce. With increasing taxes and rising prices in general, it is difficult to live on rent less than one-half of the gross produce. The landowners assert that the government should not reduce the rent from the present rate of one-half the gross produce, since that would be inconsistent with the economic reality of a growing scarcity of land because of overcrowding in agriculture.

The landowners have suggested that to alleviate their fear and concern, the limit of 5 acres regarding acquisition for personal cultivation should be abolished. They suggest that a landowner should be able to get his land for personal cultivation whenever he needs it to support his family members. Until the 5-acre limit is removed, the illegal practices of concealed tenancies, changing tenants every year, and using hired labor rather than renting to regular tenants will continue.

Our findings suggest that in formulating any further policies on land reform, social and economic factors in the villages should be taken into account. The government should then take strict measures in implementing whatever legislation and policies are formulated. As we have observed, half-hearted measures do more harm than good to the tenants. It is very important that an up-to-date record of tenancies be kept, and it would be of further help if the record were verified constantly by independent committees consisting of revenue officials and representatives of landowners and tenants. Each tenant so recorded should be issued a certificate indicating his rights regarding the land and the rent payable by him. Since there is a big shift under way from *batai* rent to a cash rent arrangement, it is important that the provision regarding the limit on rent be extended also to cash rent. As we have observed, the tenants are at a great disadvantage in dealing with landowners over security of tenure and limit on rent because of social and economic factors. A recent recommendation of the Indian Planning Commission for "immediate legislation to break the direct landlord-tenant relationship, the state interposing between landlords and tenants to collect fair rents from tenants and pay them to landlords after deducting land revenue and collection charges," is worthy of consideration.[12]

Those who have suffered most from the ineffective implementation of the land reform legislation, worsening tenant-landowner relationships, and increasing overcrowding in agriculture have been the former tenants (now landless agricultural laborers) and the very small owners. The landless laborers are not afforded much protection by the land reform legislation, and they face uncertainties of employment and income. The period of transition from tenants to laborers has been very painful for them. The small landowners must rent additional lands in order to subsist.

High priority should be given to providing employment opportunities to the landless laborers and small landowners on the village work projects and cottage industries being organized under the community development schemes. Encouragement should also be given to landless agricultural laborers to move to other areas in the country in order to settle on newly reclaimed lands or to find employment in the industrial sector.

## *Conclusions*

Our study has pointed up the ineffective implementation of the main provisions in the land reform legislation. Tenants continue to pay rent at the rate of one-half of the gross produce, in violation of the legal upper limit of one-third. There has been an extensive voluntary surrender of land by tenants. There has been a sharp increase in the area under personal cultivation, giving rise to concealed tenancy practices as well as new tenure arrangements such as the *sanjhee* system. Many former tenants have become landless laborers. The landowners generally do not rent land for more than a year, and they have become very careful and strict in renting land. The tenants are dismayed and frustrated, many of them feeling that they have lost several advantages formerly enjoyed *vis-à-vis* the landowners, and they seem to be of general opinion that the government should either take strong measures (*e.g.*, take over the land and distribute it among peasants, or declare the charging of excessive rent to be a cognizable offense) or not interfere with the landlord-tenant relationship. The landowners, on the other hand, feel that the tenants have been given too many benefits and that the provisions regarding the upper limit on rent payable are not consistent with economic reality, *i.e.*, with the acute and growing scarcity of land arising from increasing population pressures and the lack of alternative avenues of employment. The tenants are in a weak position in dealing with the landowners. The closed social system and the unity among landowners prevent tenants from demanding the rights allowed them under the land legislation. There have been cases of social ostracism against those families threatening to go to court to get the legislation implemented.

To sum up our suggestions, socioeconomic factors should be kept in mind when formulating any further policies; the government should take strict measures to implement whatever legislation and policies are formulated; an up-to-date record of tenancies should be maintained, with each tenant issued a certificate indicating his right regarding the land and the rent payable by him; and steps should be taken to provide employment opportunities to the landless laborers and the small landowners.

*Community Development Projects*

16

# Community Development and Panchayati Raj

*Ruddar Datt*
*K. P. M. Sundharam*

*From Ruddar Datt and K. P. M. Sundharam,* Indian Economy *(New Delhi: Niraj Prakasham), pp. 418–29, with omissions. Reprinted with permission.*

THE GROW MORE Food Enquiry Committee, after a study of the experience of the late forties, came to the conclusion that agricultural production could not be stepped up merely as a result of the government effort. The technical departments of the government can at best carry the message of new technology to the countryside, but unless the whole village community accepts the technological change, substantial results in agricultural upliftment cannot be achieved. A group of economists felt that improved technology should first be introduced by a few progressive farmers and then others would follow the queue and take to methods of modern agriculture. This trickle-down concept of rural uplift might appear to be quite appealing, but the result expected of it would be so slow that the hopes of building a prosperous village India might not be realized within a lifetime and thus, the slow pace of the movement might bring an end to the whole process of rural revitalization. Consequently, it was felt that a movement should be launched to further the cause of rural upliftment and this explains the birth of the Community Development approach on the basis of the recommendations of the Grow More Food Enquiry Committee.

*Need for Community Projects*—The basic idea behind the scheme of community projects is to exterminate the triple enemies—Poverty, Disease and Ignorance—from rural India. Any amount of effort on the part of the Government to revitalize the Indian economy is bound to end in failure if it is not supported by people's enthusiasm. The task of the State is to define clearly the goals of the community and also to clear the hurdles on the road to progress and furnish the necessary leadership and provide the requisite finance. But the success of the scheme will depend upon the extent to which people's effort can be harnessed in the task of rural reconstruction. This is implied in the term "Community Development."

According to the report of the United Nations "the term 'Community Development' has come to connote . . . the process by which the efforts of the people themselves are united with those of government authorities to improve the economic, social and cultural conditions of communities, to integrate these communities into the life of the nation and to enable them to contribute fully to national progress." Obviously, the community development program is directed to the task of rural upliftment. For this the government and the people have to work together—the government for instance, can provide technical assistance in the form of better seeds, manures, expert knowledge, better agricultural implements, etc., and the people can contribute labor, management, locally available materials, etc.

Though it is quite important to provide education and better health facilities to the rural people, yet the principle problem is that of rural poverty. Rural poverty is the result of low productivity and the prevalence of under-employment in Indian agriculture. In order to transform "subsistence agriculture" into "progressive agriculture," we have to improve the technique of production. Consequently, the Indian farmers are to be persuaded to use better scientific methods and superior inputs in agriculture. Besides, they have to be provided credit facilities and irrigation so that optimum results can be achieved by the application of better seeds, manures, etc. In order to reduce the burden of persons dependent on agriculture, wider opportunities for subsidiary and cottage industries have to be provided. In a nutshell, community development projects aim at eliminating underproduction and underemployment in agriculture. The community development program, therefore, endeavors to bring within its scope all rural families, especially those who are "underprivileged" and enable them to take their place in the cooperative movement and other spheres in their own right.

To achieve these twin objectives of more production and fuller employment, a comprehensive program should be launched. The scheme of community projects provides an integrated approach to revive village India.

*Main lines of activity*—The main lines of activity undertaken in the C.D. schemes are as follows:

Agricultural and related matters include reclamation of waste land, provision of fertilizers and improved seeds, the promotion of improved agricultural techniques and land utilization, supply of technical information, improved agricultural implements, improved marketing and credit facilities, prevention of soil erosion, encouragement of the use of natural and compost manure, improvement of cattle, etc. All this is to be achieved by fostering the growth of a healthy cooperative movement.

Irrigation program entails provision of water for agriculture through minor irrigation works, *e.g.*, tanks, canals, surface wells, tube wells, etc. It is proposed that at least half of the agricultural land be served with such irrigation facilities.

Communications program emphasizes the construction of roads linking different villages as also to improve roads within a village. Road building should be encouraged through voluntary labor. The state or public agencies should take the responsibility of providing main roads.

Education has to be extended in two ways. First, in order to remove illiteracy, expansion and improvement of primary and secondary education should be emphasized. Secondly, in order to encourage small rural industries, training facilities should be developed for artisans and technicians in modern techniques.

Health program includes the provision of dispensaries and hospitals. Not only should dispensaries and hospitals be provided for men, women and children, but veterinary hospitals be provided to take care of cattle diseases. Besides, control of epidemic diseases, such as malaria, cholera, tuberculosis, etc., is an essential part of the program in addition to improvement in general sanitation.

Supplementary employment be provided for the underemployed persons by the development of cottage and small industries using local materials.

Housing, training and social welfare programs include provision of audio-visual aids for instruction and recreation, organization of community entertainment, sports and fairs, opening of training centers for village level workers, development of parks and playgrounds and assistance in the supply of building materials.

### ORGANIZATION AND ADMINISTRATION

For each community project planned, a region of approximately 300 villages with a total area of 450 to 500 square miles, a cultivated area of about 1,50,000 acres and a population of about 2 lakhs is taken for intensive work. The project area is divided into three development blocks, each consisting of about 100 villages and a population of about 60,000 to 70,000. The development block is in turn divided into groups of five villages each, each group being the field of operation of a village level worker.

The organization and administration of the scheme at various levels is carried out as under:—

*At the Center*—The Ministry of Community Development, Panchayati Raj and Cooperation frames overall broad policy outlines.

*In the States*—The execution of the program is the responsibility of the State Governments. Each State has a State Development Committee consisting of the Chief Minister (Chairman), the ministers of the development departments and the Development Commissioner as Secretary. The Development Commissioner is the executive head of the Scheme at the State level.

*At the district level*—The Zila Parishads organized under the Panchayati Raj are responsible for the implementation of the program.

*At the block level*—The Block Panchayat Samiti is the overall in-charge of the program at the Block level. This is an elected body of Sarpanches (Presidents of Village Panchayats) and a few coopted persons.

On the administrative side, the executive head is the Block Development Officer who is assisted by eight extension officers who are experts in agriculture, rural engineering, cooperation, village industries, animal husbandry, public health, social education, etc. These persons act as guides on the technical aspects of the program.

*At the village level*—Panchayat possesses overall control of the village program. All the schemes of the improvement of the village are to be approved by the panchayats.

From the administrative side, the Gramsevak (village level) worker acts as a multipurpose extension agent. A group of four to five villages is allotted to him for intensive work. He seeks the cooperation of the village panchayat and other voluntary organizations in drawing up schemes concerning the improvement of the village. In other words, the Gramsevak is the pivot round which the whole C.D. program hinges.

PROGRAMS AND PROGRESS

The Community Project program was started in October, 1952 with 55 pilot projects on an experimental basis. It was, however, felt that the scheme should be extended to all the villages as early as possible. But, the Community Development program which required a budget allotment of Rs. 15 lakhs for each block could not be extended to the entire countryside for want of resources. To meet the demand of the villages for the extension of benefits under the program as also to keep in view the limitation of resources, a less intensive scheme called National Extension Service was created. Thus were added to the C.D. Blocks, the N.E.S. Blocks. The aims and objects of National Extension Organization and Community Projects "are based on the same ideas. Their methods and aims are identical. The only differences are, firstly, that a higher standard of development is attempted in the Community Project areas by allotting them large funds; and, secondly, the Community Projects are temporary for three years, while the National Extension Organization is permanent." Thus community development is the method and rural extension is the agency through which the process of transformation of the social and economic life of villages is initiated.

Up to 1958, the program of community development followed a pattern under which every new development block was first taken up under the N.E.S. scheme with a budget allotment of Rs. 4.5 lakhs. After a period varying from one to two years, a proportion of the N.E.S. projects were included in the community development program with a budget allotment of Rs. 15 lakhs for a development block. According to the revised pattern, adopted in April, 1958, on completion of the first stage of intensive development for five years the block enters the second stage during which development is continued with a relatively reduced budget allotment under the C.D. program for another five years but with increased provision from the respective subject-matter departments. When the block completes stage II, it becomes the permanent unit of planning and development and an established channel for development expenditure. Where this is not achieved to any substantial extent, the State Governments provide post-stage II blocks with a minimum outlay of Rs. 1 lakh a year. Before entering stage I, every block has to undergo a pre-extension phase of one year with the program exclusively confined to agricultural development.

At the end of First Five Year Plan (*i.e.*, by 1955–56), the total number of blocks undertaken were 1,200—300 blocks were under the community development scheme and 900 blocks were under the national extension scheme, covering about 1.23 lakh villages and a population of about 80 million.

The study team headed by Mr. Balwantrai Mehta in 1957 recommended the adoption of a single scheme of community development to be carried out in two stages, each of five years. The first stage envisaged a budget allotment of Rs. 12 lakhs and the second of Rs. 5 lakhs. Before entering the first stage, every block enters a "pre-extension phase" of one year during which exclusive emphasis is given to agricultural development. By the end of the Second Plan the C.D. program served 3,100 development blocks comprising about 3.7 lakh villages. The total outlay incurred on the C.D. program in the first two plans was of the order of Rs. 233 crores.

The C.D. program now covers the entire rural India. As on 1st January, 1968 there were 1,717 blocks in stage I, 2,207 in stage II and 1,337 in post-stage II, while four blocks were in pre-extension stage. During the Third Plan, the actual expenditure in Third Plan is estimated at Rs. 269 crores.

### RESOURCES AND PEOPLE'S CONTRIBUTION

The community development program draws resources from the people and the Government. Several schemes such as the construction of roads, street lanes, hospitals, schools, etc., are financed by the government on the basis of matching contribution from the people. The people's voluntary contribution may be in cash or kind or voluntary labor. In case of recurring items pertaining to approved schemes, the expenses to be shared between the Center and State governments are in the ratio of 1:1 and in case of non-recurring items in the ratio of 3:1. Besides this, the Central government also advances loans to State governments for productive works like irrigation, reclamation of land, etc.

The total government expenditure till March 31, 1966 amounted to Rs. 502 crores. As against it, people's contribution amounted to Rs. 151 crores, *i.e.*, 32 per cent of government expenditure.

### A CRITICAL APPRAISAL OF THE COMMUNITY DEVELOPMENT PROGRAM

The scheme of Community Development was described as a "pilgrimage" by Shri S. K. Dey. He also emphasized: "pilgrimage is a process. It is not a consummation." The pilgrimage of village India through the agency of community development projects was started on the 2nd of October, 1952 and fifteen years have passed by now. It is, therefore, necessary to pause and review whether the process of change initiated was in the right direction and whether we have been able to accomplish what we planned for.

Commenting on the Community Development Program Professor Toynbee described it as "one of the most beneficient revolutions in the peasantry's life that have been known, so far, to history." Similarly, Mr. Nehru stressing their importance said: "The Community Projects are the bright, vital and the dynamic sparks all over India from which radiate rays of energy, hope and enthusiasm. With this spark we have to light a few lamps, which will in turn light newer and newer lamps and thus proceeding in a geometric progression, we have to light all the lamps in the hearths and homes of five and half lakh villages of India."

While nobody can deny the positive aspect of the program of community development and national extension, the program was the subject of a good deal of criticism. Many of the criticisms are justified. It would be worthwhile to examine them.

(1) More emphasis on welfare activities than on economic development. In the community projects, the project officers and staff have been giving undue importance to welfare activities such as building a school, a hospital, a link road, street pavements,

street lights, etc. The villagers have donated plots of land, contributed money, materials or voluntary labor to create these tangible welfare projects. The project officers were purposively emphasizing this aspect because they could show to the visiting dignitaries some tangible results of their efforts. But the creation of these welfare activities only kindled the dissatisfaction with the present economic condition of the rural people. Neglect of activities connected with economic development—for instance, the failure to increase yield per acre, or to provide non-agricultural rural employment—did not create the capacity to make use of welfare activities. Consequently, the facilities created at schools, hospitals, recreation centers, etc., have remained beyond the reach of the poor and weak sections of our rural population. In this connection Myrdal writes: "When the government suddenly opened new vistas for improvement, but limited its initial offer of assistance to the short span of three years, it was natural for both villagers and civil servants to put other things aside in order to seize this unprecedented opportunity. Those who took an active part in the program became absorbed in planning and carrying out programs for schools, wells, roads, paved village streets, and so on." The Study Team on Community Development, therefore, recommended a shift of emphasis in favor of economic development if community development is to win the confidence of the people.

(2) Distribution of benefits of the program in favor of the privileged classes. An important disquieting feature of the program has been the uneven distribution of benefits in the community. Various study teams and groups have highlighted this weakness of the program. Govind Sahay Committee for U.P. after an analysis of the benefits reached the conclusion: "The whole programme has suffered from a lack of vitality and is tending to degenerate only into a number of material benefits for a limited few." In another study pertaining to U.P. it was pointed out: "A closer analysis of the agricultural extension work itself reveals that nearly 70 per cent of its benefits went to the elite group or to the more influential and affluent agriculturists." It is now an admitted fact that only those persons in the village who have an access to the Block Officials are able to obtain government assistance. The artisans, the landless laborers and the small agriculturists, for whom the program was launched, hardly receive any of the grants or loans, or superior agricultural inputs or help provided by the State. In other words, the program has not been able to earn the much-coveted title of "Community development programme." Shri S. K. Dey has admitted this fact in the following words, "One of the disabilities under which the Community Development Programme has suffered till now is that the Programme has functioned more as one for the development of individuals. The catalyst for community-making has not been easily obtaining." Thus the bulk of our rural population continues to live in poverty, ill-health and conditions of starvation, while we may boast of an extension service extending over the entire country. Myrdal categorically states: "The agricultural extension service, which from the beginning was a part of the community development program, was most valuable to the substantial landholders; it had little to offer the landless. . . . As things worked out, there was a tendency to favor not only the wealthier residents within a village but also the wealthier villages and regions."

(3) Pace of extension of the program faster than justified by economic and social factors. A very meaningful criticism of the program is that the rate at which development blocks were opened was unjustified. The principal reasons for this criticism are: firstly, the scarcity of resources was a big limiting factor. We tried to overcome this by having N.E.S. blocks where less intensive work was undertaken. Actually we have only created an illusion of coverage of the entire village India by this program. The actual achievements in terms of economic and social development are much too small. Secondly, we have not been able to train the requisite number of technical personnel to meet the fast growing needs of more and more development blocks. Consequently, the quantum and quality of work done by extension

staff have suffered. Incompetent and half-trained persons were recruited to fill the large number of vacancies. In many blocks, shortage of adequate staff has meant more burden of work on the village level workers. Gramsevak—the pivot of the scheme—is at best a half-literate, half-trained and technically ill-equipped person. Under the circumstances, it would have been far better to concentrate on a fewer projects and after consolidating the work on them to proceed to open new projects. But this suggestion has gone unheeded because of the political reason of satisfying every region that extension facilities have been provided to it. Mr. Rajeshwar Dayal condemning this tendency opines: "The demands for opening more and more blocks were made and now almost the whole of the country stands covered under this programme. In this way, we have taxed the future for certain achievements for the present, we have taxed the abstract and real achievements for material and unreal achievements. This has been suicidal, because these blocks have not been working as satisfactorily as could be wished and the nation has not been getting good dividend for its money from this programme."

(4) Agricultural Extension effort has been inadequate. Various studies pertaining to the use of better seeds, fertilizers, compost and green manure, plant protection and breeding have pointed out that the targets have not been achieved in the various fields. At the end of the Second Plan, the consumption of nitrogenous fertilizers reached only 52 per cent of the target and of phosphatic fertilizers only 58 per cent. Similarly, during the Third Plan the targets in respect of improved seed, fertilizers and plant protection had been achieved to the extent of 31 per cent or less. The target for minor irrigation was fulfilled to the extent of 54 per cent. Agricultural production in a given agrarian set-up is dependent upon the growth of better production methods. In other words, there is a shortfall in making available the targeted inputs.

(5) Absence of clearly defined priorities in community development program. The scope of the community development program is too wide so as to encompass all aspects of human life. In this sense, the program has been adjudged as too ambitious. The range of activities comprises fostering agricultural development, setting up rural industries, improving health, education, youth welfare, women welfare, adult literacy, organization of recreation centers, fairs, exhibitions, etc. All these things cannot be accomplished simultaneously. The result is that it has not been able to do anything satisfactorily. There are no clearly defined priorities. It is far better to concentrate on programs of stepping up agricultural production and employment first of all. Other low priority activities like provision of youth welfare activities, recreation centers, welfare activities, can wait for some time. Topmost priority should be given to raising the level of production and employment. Once a dent is made on poverty and unemployment, other ancillary activities can be developed later on. Only recently, the government has realized the necessity of assigning priorities.

(6) The Community Development Program, by-passing land reform, encouraged the growth of capitalistic agriculture. The C.D. program was launched before the completion of land reform. The rich peasants treated it as an opportunity to grab the liberal grants offered by the State for the modernization of agriculture. Consequently, resistance to land reform measures increased. In a very strong comment, Myrdal writes: "At least some of the members of this (peasant landlord) politically influential group—mainly those who cultivated the land themselves—learned that money can be earned by the modernization of agriculture and that liberal aid can be obtained from the government for this purpose. Having absorbed that lesson peasant landlords are less disposed than ever to agree that their holdings should be broken up for the benefit of less fortunate villagers. Because it preceded rather than followed the completion of land reforms, the extension program has impeded ceiling legislation, tenancy reform, and attempts to foster cooperative farming. Although Indian leaders profess to want to see agriculture assume a more 'socialist

pattern,' their own community development program has the effect of making agricultural practice more capitalistic."

The fact of the matter is that the Community Development Program has degenerated into a "routine affair." This is a dangerous situation. Mr. S. S. Iyer in a frank though sharp comment on the working of the program mentions: "The fate of the community development program is another instance of the distortion of the original objective in the course of its actual implementation. While this program was aimed at, and had the potentialities of, creating a nation-wide movement of resurgent self-reliant activity, it has, ultimately, turned out to be another machinery for the distribution of grants and loans to the richer classes in the rural areas and has made the people more dependent on the government. Neither the purely economic objective of increased agricultural production, nor the broader objective of creating a mass movement of self-help has been achieved. It is a case of the proverbial fall between two stools. Today this program is in a state of comfortable and convenient confusion and is no more than a skeleton."

From time to time, demands have been made in the Parliament for the abolition of the Ministry of Community Development. As a result of constant pressure, the Ministry of Community Development and Cooperation ceased to exist as a separate ministry, and thus the community development program has now become an appendage of the Ministry of Food and Agriculture. Mr. V. T. Krishnamachari, the father of the Community Development Program said to Mr. Sudhir Ghosh after a conference on community development in 1964, "You remember, Sudhir, you and I had a fight over Community Projects back in 1953! Well, the whole thing has become damned bureaucratic."

## *Panchayati Raj (Democratic Decentralization)*

We have already emphasized that the success of community development depended upon the participation of the people in the programs of village uplift. Merely asking people for participation was not enough; they had to be genuinely associated with the work of rural development. For this purpose, it was of vital necessity that power be shared with the people in the villages of India. The government officers could lead the movement in community development, but it was not possible to enlist people's participation through fear. Consequently, attention was directed to the search for a new set-up where democracy could function in a more real manner in the task of nation-building. Development was impossible through bureaucratic officers. Mr. S. K. Dey rightly puts it: "Fear and democracy do not mix together. Democracy administered with a galaxy of government servants through long-distance control may offer a pastime for some. A backward economy cannot afford such a luxury."

Balwantrai Mehta's study team to examine the community development program realized the necessity of democratic decentralization of administration so as to create institutions of democratic administration at the village block and the district level. The term "democratic decentralization" was replaced by an indigenous coinage 'Panchayati Raj' which now embodies all the institutions of local self-government. Balwantrai Mehta team recommended a three-tier system of decentralization. At the grass roots in the villages were to be formed village-panchayats, in the middle come Panchayat Samitis at the block level and at the top, Zila Parishads were to be at the district level. The village panchayats are elected bodies of village people. All adults (men and women) vote to elect the panchayats. The village panchayats send their elected representatives to block Panchayat Samiti. Besides, the elected representatives, a few coopted members representing women, depressed and scheduled classes are also included. The Samiti elects its president and vice-president. The Zila Parishad is constituted by the president of Panchayat Samitis along with the

MPs and MLAs in the district. The Zila Parishad functions in collaboration with the Collector, and, the technical departments of the government offer guidance and assistance to the Block Panchayat Samitis. The Samitis are autonomous because they are not controlled by the departments. In short, people's representatives, at all levels—center, states, district, block and village—are associated with the Panchayati Raj. In this way, the goal of Panchayat Raj "Destination Man" is sought to be realized. The principal objectives of Panchayati Raj as given in the Third Plan are as under:

1. Increasing agricultural production. 2. Development of rural industries. 3. Fostering cooperative institutions. 4. Full utilization of local manpower and other resources and the resources, physical and financial, available to Panchayati Raj institutions. 5. Assisting the economically weaker sections of the village community. 6. Progressive dispersal of authority and initiative, with special emphasis on the role of voluntary organizations, and 7. Fostering cohesion and encouraging the spirit of self-help within the community.

On January 12, 1958, the National Development Council approved the scheme of the Balwantrai Mehta Committee regarding the establishment of Panchayati Raj. Rajasthan accepted the scheme in October, 1959 and formulated the necessary legislation in this regard. In November, 1959 Andhra adopted the scheme. With some variation depending upon local conditions, Panchayati Raj is under implementation besides Rajasthan and Andhra—the pioneers—in other states such as Assam, Bihar, Gujarat, Madras, Maharashtra, Mysore, Orissa, Punjab and Uttar Pradesh. A provision of about Rs. 28 crores was made for the implementation of Panchayati Raj in the Third Plan.

### PANCHAYATI RAJ AND PLAN IMPLEMENTATION

Out of the Village Panchayat, Block Panchayat Samiti and Zila Parishad, the Block Panchayat Samiti holds the key position in the context of planning. The State government indicates to the Panchayat Samitis the funds that are likely to become available for development and aid them to prepare plans on the basis of local needs. The Panchayat Samitis allot funds to village panchayats and after consolidating the block development plan on the basis of the recommendations of the Panchayats, forward it to the Zila Parishad to be included in the District Plan. Thus, an important function of the Panchayat Samitis is to prepare a production plan and then take steps to implement the plan. Besides the resources placed at the disposal of the Panchayati Raj institutions by the State government, the Panchayats are authorized to impose taxes, namely, on profession, fairs, education, cess on land revenue, etc., to supplement the resources for development.

The Village Production Plan includes, according to the Third Plan, two main groups of programs, namely: (a) supply of credit, fertilizers, improved seed, assistance for plant protection, minor irrigation, etc., for which a measure of assistance has to come from outside the village, and (b) programs such as the digging of field channels for utilizing irrigation from large projects, maintenance of bunds and field channels, contour bunding, digging and maintenance of village tanks, development and utilization of local manurial resources, village fuel plantations, etc., which call for effort on the part of the village community or beneficiaries.

Thus, the Panchayati Raj scheme accepts in principle the system of democratic decentralization. The responsibility of implementing the block development plan belongs to the Panchayat Samiti which enlists the cooperation of the Panchayats operating within its fold.

### A CRITICAL APPRAISAL OF PANCHAYATI RAJ IN ACTION

Panchayati Raj institutions are yet in an infant stage of development. In various states, their age varies from four to nine years—a period too short for making any judgment. For instance, there are about half a million presidents and a similar number of vice-presidents of village panchayats. Besides these, the representatives in other local bodies are estimated to be nearly ten times. Thus the total number of representatives works out to be nearly ten million. Most of these persons do not have the education and training in working these institutions or shouldering the executive, judicial or social responsibility they are called upon to bear. Mr. S. K. Dey rightly points out, "Mere manpower is no asset to a nation. We know it to our cost. Mere institutions of people—representative or associate—can be no asset either. For, these may grow easily into a dead weight adding to the tax burden on the people. A programme for education and training has, therefore, to be organized en masse all along the line." Consequently, while critically assessing the working of Panchayati Raj we must keep the limitations of transforming a society steeped in ignorance, superstition and conservatism.

Some of the weaknesses of the Panchayati Raj which have been noticed in recent years are as follows:

(1) Reluctance to impose taxes. There has been a reluctance on the part of Panchayat Samitis to impose taxes to raise local resources for development. This is either the result of a fear that the Panchayat may become unpopular or that there is a general resistance to pay taxes. Panchayati Raj has not so far been able to overcome the resistance to taxes. People are prepared to pay taxes only if there is a direct link between the taxes imposed and the benefits that accrue from them. Obviously, Panchayar Samitis should impose taxes for specific projects like a school, a village road or an irrigation tank or canal, etc. Permanent taxes of a general nature should be imposed by bodies farther removed from the people than the Panchayat Samitis.

(2) Ready use of loans, grants, etc., but no enthusiasm for raising local resources. Mr. P. K. Chaudhuri in his study of Panchayati Raj in action in Rajasthan observed: "Panchayat Samitis and village panchayats are prompt to take up and execute programmes for which funds are provided by the Government in the form of loans, subsidies, grants, etc., so as to utilize the assistance provided. But programmes which are to be carried out with local resources and initiative lag behind." It is, therefore, alleged that Panchayati Raj institutions are bodies which limit their functions to receive government grants, loans and subsidies, and make use of them for the benefit of the select few in the villages. The government may boast of distributing impressive quantities of seeds, fertilizers, implements, etc., through these institutions, but the results in higher productivity are hardly noticeable. There is a fear that if misdirection of resources continues, the mass of the people may lose faith in this democratic institution, considered to be a panacea for village India.

(3) Dual control of extension staff promotes indiscipline and groupism. Under the Panchayati Raj set-up, the extension officers for agriculture, animal husbandry, cooperation, etc., work on deputation with the Panchayat Samitis. Since these persons are on deputation, the Block Development Officer cannot take any administrative action against them for any of their faults. Similarly, since substantively, they are linked to administrative departments, the Panchayat Samitis cannot initiate any disciplinary action. In this dual control, indiscipline and inefficiency thrive and the controlling bodies feel helpless about the whole situation. Moreover, dual control sometimes leads to a clash between the Block Development Officer and the President of Panchayat Samitis. In case of conflict, the extension staff indulges in groupism. Some align themselves with the Block Development Officer, while others associate themselves with the Samiti president. Dual control, therefore, is a serious weakness which undermines the utility of Panchayati Raj.

(4) Village production plans are paper plans. An important function of Panchayat Samitis is to prepare village production plans. "Panchayati Raj institutions were expected to give the lead in this matter but this they have failed to do so far. The so-called village production plans that we have today are nothing but paper plans casually prepared by the Village Level Workers in

consultation with a couple of village elders and the sarpanch of the village panchayat. No serious attempt has yet been made to prepare an authentic village production plan incorporating production targets for each crop and for every family in the village."

(5) No specific role of Zila Parishads. The Zila Parishads are just advisory bodies and their suggestions or instructions are not mandatory. It would have been a healthy practice had Panchayat Samitis developed a tradition of accepting the suggestions of Zila Parishads or give cogent reasons for not accepting them. In the absence of this tradition, Zila Parishads appear to be redundant institutions. It would be worthwhile to assign a more specific role to Zila Parishads in the Panchayati Raj.

(6) Control of Panchayats by undesirable elements. Panchayats and Panchayat Samitis are seats of power. They are, therefore, the seats of patronage, in the economic as well as the non-economic sphere. Consequently, the upper castes, the privileges classes in the rural areas, use all sorts of methods to capture these seats of power. For this purpose, the doling out of money to buy votes is a very common practice. Kidnapping and forceful confinement of sarpanches have occurred on an alarming scale. Thus indirect elections to Panchayat Samitis have let loose a chain of evils. Suitable amendments in Panchayati Raj legislation are called for to avoid the evils associated with indirect election.

## CONCLUSION

Panchayati Raj institutions are a step in the right direction. The weaknesses listed above are those of organization and implementation. It is imperative that if planning and democracy are to survive in this country, the institution of Panchayati Raj will have to be strengthened further.

# A Study of Chinese Communes

*Shahid Javed Burki*

*Reprinted by permission of the publishers from Shahid Javed Burki,* A Study of Chinese Communes, *1965, Cambridge, Mass.: Harvard University Press, copyright, 1969, by the President and Fellows of Harvard College, pp. 8–32, with omissions.*

CHINA'S COMMUNE SYSTEM has "three levels of management and ownership." A commune is usually broken up into ten to twelve production brigades; a production brigade is further subdivided into ten to fifteen production teams. Production assets are owned at all three levels and, as such, all these production units (communes, production brigades, and production teams) can generate income from their own sources. However, in theory as well as in practice, the management at the commune level exercises considerable influence on the management at the levels of production brigades and teams; the leadership at the level of the production brigade, on the other hand, exercises control over that of the production team more in theory than in practice. The system as it has evolved over the years has, therefore, tended to play down the importance of production brigades. In some latter-day communes, for instance, this tier was altogether done away with. For example, the Leap Forward Commune of Inner Mongolia, formed in 1960, has 48 production teams but no brigades. Table 1 below provides similar details about other communes visited by the delegation from Pakistan. All these communes (not counting Leap Forward) have 135 production brigades, or 11.25 production brigades per commune. These production brigades are further subdivided into 1,212 production teams, or very nearly 9 production teams per brigade.

### THE COMMUNE CONGRESS

There is "democratically centralized leadership" at all three levels of management and ownership. The body with most authority, at least in theory, is the Commune Congress with a membership of between 100 and 150. It is an elected body with a term of two years. The electoral college for the congress is formed by production brigade

***Table 1—Organization of the Communes***

| *Commune* | *No. of Production Brigades* | *No. of Production Teams* | *Land per Production Team (hectares)* | *Workers per Production Team* |
|---|---|---|---|---|
| Evergreen | 12 | 125 | 22.4 | 112.2 |
| Red Star | 9 | 157 | 71.7 | 153.3 |
| Leap Forward | — | 48 | — | 7.2 |
| Kawkang | 11 | 59 | 37.0 | 67.8 |
| August First | 14 | 73 | 46.6 | 60.3 |
| Tsin Yah | 7 | 59 | 49.9 | 55.2 |
| Hsin Lung San | 20 | 200 | 67.4 | 64.0 |
| Peng Pu | 9 | 101 | 9.5 | 84.7 |
| Hsu Hang | 11 | 127 | 13.1 | 72.0 |
| West Lake | 14 | 54 | 6.2 | 88.9 |
| Tung Chun | 10 | 81 | 7.3 | 63.1 |
| People's Suburban | 5 | 26 | — | 52.5 |
| Stonewell | 13 | 150 | 20.0 | 147.8 |

congresses. The electoral system gives proportional representation to groups like peasants, craftsmen, women, youth, minorities, ex-service men and overseas Chinese. Most of the power which rests with the congress is delegated by it to the Commune Management Committee. The members of the committee as well as its director were elected for a two-year term by the congress. The committee has a membership of between ten and fifteen.

A quasi-democratic procedure is followed for electing the chief executive of the commune. All those interested in holding the office submit their names to the local county council. The county officials examine the biographical data and antecedents of all the would-be candidates. An approved list of candidates is then sent back to the Commune Congress for final selection. The slate of candidates seldom has a non-cadre represented on it. After approving the names of the candidates, the county council does not put any pressure on the members of the Commune Congress; they are left to vote much as they please.

We were provided with one particularly interesting example of a change in directorship that had been brought about by this democratic process.

In this case the incumbent, who was defeated by a newcomer, stayed on in the Management Committee as the deputy director (we shall cite below another example of the working of this process). It is possible for a non-cadre to be elected to the directorship of the commune; if that happens, the person so elected automatically becomes a government cadre. This is why it is not possible to come across a non-cadre functioning as director of a commune. For instance, all the thirteen commune directors that we met with were government cadres.

The commune director supervises, with the help of the members of the Management Committee, the working of the commune secretariat. The secretariat is organized into a number of departments. The secretariat of Kawkang Commune, for instance, includes the departments of general administration, finance and accounting, civil affairs (resolution of disputes), education, culture and public health, people's militia, agricultural production, women's activities, youth clubs, and workshop management. In this, as in all other communes, the heads of the administrative departments are taken from the Management Committee.

The Commune Congress meets once a year primarily to review the work done by the Management Committee. Sometimes very important decisions are taken in these meetings. For instance, in 1960, the Congress of Hsu Hang Commune in the suburb of Shanghai decided to hand over the management of a vegetable-producing brigade to the Commune Committee. This was done against the wishes of the director who was then dropped from the Management Committee.

Every two years, the Commune Congress also elects a Supervisory Committee which draws its entire membership of between twenty to twenty-five from the Communist Party. The main function of this committee is to insure that the policies laid down by the Communist Party are faithfully and dutifully carried out by the Commune Management Committee. No duplication is allowed in the membership of the two committees.

The Congress-Supervisory Committee-Management Committee apparatus exists at the level of the production brigades as well. The Production Brigade Congress has a membership of about fifty and is elected once every year by the production team congresses. The Brigade Congress elects every year a Management Committee and its director who is usually not a cadre. (Only very large production brigades have cadres as their directors. For instance, six of the thirteen production brigades of Stonewell Commune have cadre-directors.) The Supervisory Committee, also elected by the Brigade Congress, has a term of one year. As for the communes, all members of the Supervisory Committee belong to the Communist Party.

All the able-bodied workers of a production team automatically become the members of the Production Team Congress. Every year the congress elects a Management Committee (seven to ten members) and a Production Team Leader. There is, however, no Supervisory Committee at the level of the production teams. Since 1961, the production team congresses have been electing one supervisor to oversee the work of the Management Committee.

All the land, cultivated or not cultivated, is owned by the commune. It may not, however, be directly managed by its management committee. For management purposes, it may be leased out either to production brigades or to production teams. This division of responsibility between ownership and management gives the Commune Management Committee the power of overseeing the work of other production units. The commune management, therefore, can and sometimes does order production units to make important changes in the way the leased-out land is being used.

### SOURCES OF INCOME

The production units do not make any payments to the commune for using land leased out to them. The Commune Management Committee has, therefore, to look for other sources of income. Ownership of machinery and equipment provides it with one important source. Tractors, threshers, trucks, and pumping stations are more often than not owned by the commune. These are rented out to production units. Maintenance of the rented machinery is the responsibility of the production units. However, repair workshops are owned by the communes and the production units have to pay for getting their equipment repaired in them.

In 1964, the Peng Pu Commune Tractor and Agriculture Implement Repair Station contributed 7,531 yuan to the income of the commune. Small industrial enterprises are another source of income for the communes. The share of industry in the total income of the communes declined considerably after 1961. Some important industrial units have remained even after the reorganization of communal economy in the period 1959–61. These contribute substantial additional income to the communes. Red Star Commune of Peking is still operating a wrapping-paper plant. The plant employs 520 workers and yields an income of about 250,000 yuan every year. Brick-making, straw mat-weaving, rice-husking, and grain-milling are some of the favorite forms of industrial activity at the commune level. The third important source of commune income is the ownership of specialized production brigades. Many communes have production brigades engaged in such specialized activities as producing vegetables in hothouses, growing fruits, honey bee-keeping, etc. These brigades are usually directly managed by the commune directorate. A fourth source of income for the commune is the share that they receive from the reserve and welfare funds managed by the lower production units. Amounts thus received from the production units can be used only for specific purposes.

Very few production brigades have independent sources of income. The production brigade was an important level of ownership and management in the earlier communes. These communes were very big; many had more than 150 production teams in their control In their case, it was essential to have an intermediate tier between the commune and production team levels. With the breakup of the bigger communes in the period 1959–61, production brigades automatically ceased to function as effective units of production and management. Production brigades continue to retain their importance in the areas where the communes, for one reason or another, were not reorganized. Production brigades in Hsin Lung San Commune, which has 200 teams, and in Stonewell Commune, which has 150 teams, continue to perform important management and production functions. Stonewell Commune is the only example we saw of a commune being enlarged in size as a result of the 1959–61 reorganization program. This was done in order to operate more effectively the water drainage and irrigation system that was being installed in this area. Here the Commune Management Committee had delegated most of its powers to the brigade management committees. It is no wonder, therefore, that six of the thirteen brigades have government cadres as directors of their management committees.

The bulk of the communes' agricultural income accrues to the production teams. The teams are entitled to manage themselves the returns they receive from the lands they cultivate. That is why they are called "basic units of accounting in the commune system." By management of returns is meant the distribution among the workers who produce it, the government, the reserve fund, the welfare fund, and a fund established for meeting future (next year's) production costs. The teams, however, have to manage their resources according to the principles laid down by the state and in conformity to the wishes of the commune leaders. The latter can and often do exercise considerable influence on the decisions of the production team leaders. The communes can exert pressure on the production teams for two reasons. We have already seen that the commune management is made up almost totally of cadres who, because of their official status and close connection with government bureaucracy and party leadership, wield tremendous power. The production team draws its leadership from the peasants who are easily awed by the position and status of the cadres. Also, as we saw above, communes have large financial resources at their disposal which are given to the production teams for capital investment purposes. It would naturally be very difficult for truant teams to claim these resources. In matters of distribution of funds for development purposes, the commune cadres seem to have the final say and the production team cannot hope for any intervention from above (county or province). While the management of production resources within the commune hierarchy was considerably decentralized in the period 1959–61, it does not seem right to read into this development a process of a total disintegration of the system.

### STATE CONTROL

The Communist state exercises direct as well as indirect control of the communes. An elaborate government machinery exists to supervise the working of the communes, to render advice to the commune level cadres, to coordinate the development plans of the communes, and to provide financial and technical assistance to relatively backward production units. The Department of People's Communes' Affairs in the Ministry of Agriculture in Peking is one of the fourteen departments into which the Ministry is divided. (The other thirteen are: General Administration, Agricultural Science and Technology, Agricultural Education and Propaganda, Agricultural Finance and Capital Construction, Animal Husbandry and Fisheries, Land Improvement and Soil Amelioration, Plant Protection, Disease Control and Insecticides, Fertilizer Production, Distribution and Procurement, Industrial Crops, Oil-bearing Crops, Food-Grains, Foreign Trade and Foreign Relations, and Political Work.) All provincial agricultural departments also have "commune affairs offices". The county governments have "commune management sections" as well. A parallel exists under the Bureau of Commune Management located at Peking. There are bureaus in all the provinces and counties. However, there is no duplication between the working of the department-office-section under the Ministry of Agriculture and that under the Bureau of Commune Management. The former is concerned only with insuring that the development plans drawn up by the communes are in keeping with its own overall agricultural development program. On the other hand, the latter organization is concerned with supervising the day-to-day working of the communes. The bureau, therefore, works as the field-arm of the Ministry. The plans drawn up by the Ministry are based on the data supplied by the bureau; once the plans have been forwarded, it is the business of the bureau to break them down according to provinces, counties and communes. The plan that is eventually handed down to the communes is in the form of production targets. The communes are left to devise the programs for achieving these targets themselves. The programs so drawn up are submitted by the communes to the county governments for purposes of scrutiny and approval.

The commune management, therefore, comes in touch, for the most part, with the administrations at the county level. All the counties have an elaborate organization to maintain close liaison with the communes in their areas. For instance, Tsin Yah Commune of Changchun is controlled by a county council whose department of agriculture is divided into several sections. The section responsible for commune affairs has twenty-three personnel, thirteen of whom are agro-technicians, and ten administrators. The section looks after 11 communes, 100 production brigades, and 1,000 production teams. It receives annual development programs from all the communes at least three months before they are launched. It is also provided with a monthly statement of accounts from every commune. The commune cadres are encouraged to keep themselves in close touch with the section officials; the officials themselves visit all the communes at least once every six months.

The cadres exercise indirect control on the working of the communes. The number of cadres working in a particular commune depends upon its size and income. Peng Pu Commune of Shanghai, with a gross income of 3.862 million yuan has thirteen cadres working in various capacities. People's Suburban Commune of Kiangsu Province has been given only six cadres, but then it has a gross income of only 1.1 million yuan. Cadres are appointed by the county councils but usually belong to the communes in which they work. They are, therefore, seldom transferred from one commune to another. Nine of the thirteen communes that we visited had cadre-directors who had been appointed immediately after the formation of the communes.

#### CADRES IN THE COMMUNES

Cadres are paid by the state but have to spend at least sixty working days in the field along with the ordinary members of the commune. The average salary of a commune level cadre is 60.6 yuan per month which is, as we shall see below, slightly less than twice the amount earned by an average able-bodied worker in the Chinese agricultural sector. The director of production brigades and leaders of production teams do not receive their salaries from the government. They have to work on the land like ordinary peasants. Most brigades and teams, however, subsidize the incomes of their leaders to bring them to the level of the income of an average worker. The leader of Mei Chi Hwu Production Brigade of West Lake Commune of Chekiang Province was able to put in enough work in the field in 1964 to receive 26.0 yuan from income distributed among the workers by his management committee. However, the leader had spent several days out of the village trying to secure funds from the local branch of the Agricultural Bank for the construction of a pumping station. The management committee, accordingly, allowed a subsidy of 11.0 yuan to be paid out to him every month. The subsidy is given to the leaders out of the production team's "production costs" in recognition of the fact that these officials cannot spend enough time in the field to earn the same number of "work points" as other able-bodied workers.

It is, therefore, in a rigid framework of direct and indirect control that the "decentralized democratic system of leadership and management" works in the communes. However, this does not mean that decentralization of operation has been achieved only on paper. For, despite the controls described above, the commune managements and leaders of the production units are able to make important decisions on their own.

### *Generation of Income and its Distribution*

The analysis presented in this chapter is based mostly on the data collected from the thirteen communes visited by the delegation. This data has to be handled with caution for at least three important reasons. First, a sample of thirteen communes can hardly be used with confidence in drawing general conclusions. Four of the thirteen communes would, most probably, not figure in a randomly drawn sample; two of them (Evergreen and Red Star Communes of Peking municipality) are obviously showpieces, shown to most foreigners; one of them (Leap

Forward Commune in Inner Mongolia) belongs to a relatively underdeveloped region of the country, has organizational aspects not shared by other communes in China, and is concerned almost totally with animal husbandry; and the fourth (People's Suburban Commune of Kiangsu province) is a highly specialized commune, deriving one hundred per cent of its income from fishing. For this reason, in most of this section of the study, we shall not be using data obtained from the Inner Mongolia and Kiangsu communes. At times we shall drop Evergreen and Red Star communes from our analysis in order to obtain more meaningful conclusions for Chinese agriculture. Second, time series data for a commune may not refer to the same geographical units. We have already seen that many changes were made in the boundaries of the communes in the period 1959–61. This fact may have been ignored by the commune management at the time of the presentation of data to the delegation. Third, our sample narrows even further when we discuss important matters like the rate of increase in the use of chemical fertilizer or the pattern of distribution of production costs. This happens because the commune cadres did not present data according to any unified pattern. Some cadres were able to provide more information than others.

Our caution about the smallness of the sample is highlighted by the tremendous differences in size, composition, etc. (see Table 2) among the communes.

### THE SYSTEM OF ACCOUNTING

All production units (communes, brigades, teams) follow the same system of accounting. Uniformity is further insured by the use of the same or very similar account books all over the country. The income of the production unit is entered in the account book in gross terms; various items of expenditure are grouped together under five main headings. The first charge on the gross income of a production unit is agricultural tax. In addition to this, there are two more obligatory charges on gross income: contributions made by the production units into the reserve and welfare funds. A production unit is also expected to set aside a portion of its current income for meeting future (usually only the subsequent year's) production costs. What remains after all these deductions have been made is distributed among all the able-bodied workers listed in the production units employment ledger. "Distributed income" or "net income," as this last item is called, is, therefore, a residual item.

Deductions from the gross income, under the five items listed above, are made by the production unit managers according to a very broad formula laid down by the government in 1961. The production units, apart from meeting fully the obligation of the state, are obliged to contribute at least 10 per cent of their incomes into the reserve fund and

**Table 2—Area Cultivated and Population of Communes Visited**

| Commune | Province | Cultivated land (hectares) | Number of Families | Number of Workers | Workers per Hectare |
|---|---|---|---|---|---|
| Evergreen | Peking | 2,805 | 8,100 | 14,000 | 4.99 |
| Red Star | Peking | 11,251 | 11,000 | 24,000 | 2.13 |
| Leap Forward | Inner Mongolia | — | 252 | 350 | — |
| Kawkang | Liaoning | 2,183 | 2,988 | 4,000 | 1.83 |
| August First | Liaoning | 3,401 | 2,800 | 4,400 | 1.29 |
| Tsin Yah | Kirin | 4,329 | 3,000 | 4,800 | 1.11 |
| Hsin Lung San | Kirin | 13,528 | 10,130 | 12,790 | 0.95 |
| Peng Pu | Shanghai | 958 | 3,721 | 8,552 | 8.93 |
| Hsu Hang | Shanghai | 1,664 | 4,629 | 9,149 | 5.50 |
| West Lake | Chekiang | 333 | 1,800 | 4,800 | 14.41 |
| Tung Chun | Chekiang | 588 | 2,014 | 5,112 | 8.69 |
| Peoples Suburban | Kiangsu | — | 553 | 1,365 | — |
| Stonewell | Kwangtung | 3,000 | 11,900 | 22,000 | 7.33 |

2 per cent into the welfare fund. It is also mandatory for them to distribute at least 50 per cent among their able-bodied members.

The production team leaders may, on the receipt of permission from the country administration, deviate from the state's prescribed formula. The following can be advanced as legitimate reasons. First, exceptionally poor production units may contribute less than 10 per cent to the reserve fund in order to distribute a greater proportion of income among their workers. In their case the state undertakes to provide funds for development schemes. Second, relatively more prosperous production units may distribute less than 50 per cent among their workers. In their case the state insists that payments of savings so made be put into the reserve or welfare funds. Third, during emergencies, the production units may not set aside any amount for meeting anticipated production costs during the following year. In such contingencies, the Agricultural Bank of China advances short term, low interest loans to cover the outlay on production costs. County administrators all over China seem to have been fairly liberal in granting production units permission to deviate from the distribution formula. This is indicated by the statistics furnished by the Bureau of Commune Management in Peking. (See Table 3 below.) According to this, the agricultural workers in China in 1964 received 5 per cent more income than had been actually stipulated by the state. The total contributions to the welfare funds were also a percentage point higher.

***Table 3—Distribution of Gross Agricultural Income in China, 1964***

| *Item* | *Percentage of Gross Income* |
|---|---|
| Agriculture Tax | 7.0 |
| Reserve Fund | 10.0 |
| Welfare Fund | 3.0 |
| Production Cost | 25.0 |
| Distributed Income | 55.0 |
| Total | 100.0 |

Table 4 gives an income distributional breakdown for all the thirteen communes visited by the delegation. As was perhaps to be expected, there are considerable differences in the proportions of gross incomes set aside by different communes for different purposes.

### AGRICULTURAL TAX

The collection of tax from the agricultural sector was first systematized by the state in 1953. A simple formula was adopted. Almost all the cooperatives (those exempted or charged at lower rates were the very poor ones) were ordered to pay 10 per cent of their gross income to the state as a tax on agriculture. Tax assessment was to be made at

***Table 4—Distribution of Gross Income in the Thirteen Communes, 1964***

| *Commune* | *Gross Income (G.I.)* | *AGRICULTURE TAX* | | *RESERVE FUND* | | *WELFARE FUND* | | *PRODUCTION COST* | | *DISTRIBUTED INCOME* | |
|---|---|---|---|---|---|---|---|---|---|---|---|
| | | *Amount* | *% of G.I.* | *Amount* | *% of G.I.* | *Amount* | *% of G.I.* | *Amount* | *% of G.I.* | *Amount* | *% of G.I.* |
| Evergreen | 13.300 | 0.399 | 3.0 | 1.590 | 12.0 | 0.133 | 1.1 | 4.520 | 34.0 | 6.650 | 50.0 |
| Red Star | 27.000 | 1.700 | 6.3 | 4.100 | 15.2 | 1.400 | 5.2 | 6.200 | 23.0 | 13.600 | 50.4 |
| Leap Forward | 0.250 | 0.010 | 4.0 | 0.025 | 10.0 | 0.008 | 3.0 | 0.033 | 13.0 | 0.175 | 70.0 |
| Kawkang | 2.202 | 0.111 | 5.1 | 0.178 | 8.0 | 0.051 | 2.3 | 0.660 | 30.1 | 1.211 | 54.5 |
| August First | 3.900 | 0.200 | 5.1 | 0.660 | 16.9 | 0.200 | 5.1 | 0.780 | 20.0 | 2.060 | 52.8 |
| Tsin Yah | 2.250 | 0.100 | 4.4 | 0.180 | 8.0 | 0.050 | 2.2 | 0.673 | 29.9 | 1.247 | 55.4 |
| Hsin Lung San | 6.600 | 0.530 | 8.0 | 0.330 | 5.0 | 0.130 | 2.0 | 1.650 | 25.0 | 3.960 | 60.6 |
| Peng Pu | 3.862 | 0.250 | 6.5 | 0.480 | 12.4 | 0.070 | 1.8 | 0.859 | 22.2 | 2.203 | 57.0 |
| Hsu Hang | 4.250 | 0.220 | 5.2 | 0.390 | 9.2 | 0.153 | 3.6 | 1.150 | 27.0 | 2.340 | 55.1 |
| West Lake | 1.760 | 0.170 | 6.1 | 0.112 | 6.4 | 0.018 | 1.0 | 0.333 | 18.9 | 1.190 | 67.6 |
| Tung Chun | 1.320 | 0.066 | 5.0 | 0.092 | 7.0 | 0.026 | 2.0 | 0.286 | 21.7 | 0.850 | 64.4 |
| People's Suburban | 1.100 | 0 006 | 0.5 | 0.110 | 10.0 | 0.028 | 2.5 | 0.187 | 17.0 | 0.770 | 70.0 |
| Stonewell | 9.000 | 0.360 | 4.0 | 0.450 | 5.0 | 0.090 | 1.0 | 2.700 | 30.0 | 5.400 | 60.0 |
| Total | 76.794 | 4.122 | 5.4 | 8.697 | 11.3 | 2.357 | 3.1 | 20.031 | 26.0 | 41.656 | 54.2 |

the beginning of every year; in this way the state reserved for itself the right to claim subsequently any proportion of the gross agricultural income. In 1954, however, the government took the important decision to fix the level of agricultural tax in perpetuity. In the future the cooperatives were to pay the same amount in money terms as they had actually paid in 1953. Some adjustments were made; those cooperatives which had had exceptionally good output in 1953 had their assessments scaled down by a little. By adopting this form of assessment, the government provided the cooperatives with a positive incentive to develop their resources and increase their incomes. As the government claimed nothing out of the increases in incomes registered in the period 1953–58, variations in the incidence of taxation in 1958 ranged between 7.4 per cent to 10.3 per cent of the gross incomes of the cooperatives.

In 1958, at the time of communization of agriculture, the government did not adopt a new formula of assessing agricultural tax. The government specified that the communes, over the years, would pay to the state the sum of the amounts the federating cooperatives would have paid had they continued to exist independently. Some adjustments were made following the reorganization of the communes in 1959–61.

That the proportion of the gross income paid to the government in 1964 as agricultural tax can serve as an indicator of the rate of growth of agricultural incomes is borne out by the data presented in Table 5 above. In 1964, Hsin Lung San Commune of Kirin province was paying more tax in absolute terms as compared with Evergreen Commune of Peking, although the former had a gross income almost exactly half that of the latter. In 1958, at the time of their formation, the two communes had almost the same incomes. Even then, Hsin Lung San paid a larger proportion of agricultural tax than Evergreen. (These figures indicate that the growth patterns in the two communes were established even before their formation.) By 1964, this difference had widened even further.

### RESERVE FUND

The contribution to the reserve fund is the second charge on the income of the production units. These funds are operated separately by the communes and production teams. The accumulation of resources at the commune level is usually employed for financing the development projects of those production teams that cannot afford to execute them without outside assistance. Some communes also use their reserves for creating facilities like repair shops, cold storages, hothouses, etc. In this way the commune is able to add to its income-generating capacity.

The main purpose for making production units contribute at least a tenth of their gross incomes to the reserve funds is to make it possible for them to execute development schemes financed largely from their own resources. Earlier, we got a general idea of the type of development activity that has been undertaken by the communes in their areas.

**Table 5—Growth in Incomes and Agricultural Tax as Percentage of Gross Incomes of Evergreen and Hsin Lung San Communes, 1958-1964**

| | *Evergreen* | | | | *Hsin Lung San* | | | |
|---|---|---|---|---|---|---|---|---|
| *Year* | *Gross Income (millions)* | *Rate of Increase, %* | *Ag. Tax* | *Ag. Tax as % of Income* | *Gross Income (millions)* | *Rate of Increase, %* | *Ag. Tax* | *Ag. Tax as % of Income* |
| 1958 | 5.32 | — | 0.399 | 7.5 | 5.29 | — | 0.53 | 10.0 |
| 1959 | 6.07 | 14.0 | 0.399 | 6.6 | 5.32 | 0.6 | 0.53 | 9.9 |
| 1960 | 6.94 | 14.3 | 0.399 | 6.2 | 5.01 | -5.8 | 0.53 | 10.6 |
| 1961 | 7.74 | 11.5 | 0.399 | 5.2 | 4.92 | -1.8 | 0.53 | 10.8 |
| 1962 | 9.32 | 22.1 | 0.399 | 4.3 | 5.24 | 6.5 | 0.53 | 10.1 |
| 1963 | 12.01 | 28.8 | 0.399 | 3.3 | 6.21 | 18.5 | 0.53 | 8.5 |
| 1964 | 13.30 | 10.8 | 0.399 | 3.0 | 6.60 | 6.3 | 0.53 | 8.0 |

The data of Table 4 are in aggregative terms; they provide figures for total contributions made by all the production units within the communes. Data in Table 6 give some idea of the breakdown of contributions to the reserve fund between the commune itself and its production teams. In the period 1959–64, all the production units in Hsu Hang made a total contribution of 1.94 million yuan to the reserve fund. Out of this, 1.375 million yuan, or 70.9 per cent of the total was contributed by the commune from the income earned from its own enterprises. The main source of income for the commune is a production brigade that specializes in producing vegetables. The production teams also pay the commune management to have their implements repaired in the central workshop. By 1964, the commune had spent only 530,000 yuan, or 27.3 per cent of the total accumulated reserves for development purposes. If this pattern is repeated in all the other Chinese communes, it is easy to see why the commune management exercises so much control over the leadership of the production teams.

While the commune managements discourage production teams from saving less than 10 per cent of their incomes for development purposes, the teams are allowed to save more if they can afford to do so. For instance, in 1964 all the production units of Tsin Yah Commune together saved 8 per cent of their total income for this purpose, but Chao Tien Production Team was able to set aside as much as 15 per cent. In 1964 this team exhausted all its reserves by purchasing a grain milling machine. Over the years, the same team has been able to buy six low-lift pumps, three hand carts, and two hand-power tillers.

### *Table 6—Breakdown of Contributions to the Reserve Fund in Hsu Hang Commune*

| | *Gross Income (millions)* | | | | | *Contribution to Reserve Fund (millions)* | | | | | *Expenditure (millions)* | |
|---|---|---|---|---|---|---|---|---|---|---|---|---|
| *Year* | *Total for the Commune* | *Prod. Teams* | *Comm. Enterprises* | *2 as % of 1* | *3 as % of 1* | *Total* | *By Comm. Enterprises* | *By Prod. Teams* | *7 as % of 6* | *8 as % of 6* | *Cumulative* | *11 as % of 1* |
| | *1* | *2* | *3* | *4* | *5* | *6* | *7* | *8* | *9* | *10* | *11* | *12* |
| 1959 | 3.100 | 1.600 | 1.500 | 51.6 | 48.4 | 0.300 | 0.210 | 0.090 | 70.0 | 30.0 | 0.280 | 90.3 |
| 1960 | 2.570 | 1.090 | 1.480 | 42.4 | 57.6 | 0.250 | 0.175 | 0.075 | 70.0 | 30.0 | 0.400 | 72.6 |
| 1961 | 2.804 | 1.304 | 1.500 | 46.4 | 53.4 | 0.300 | 0.220 | 0.080 | 73.3 | 26.7 | 0.405 | 52.9 |
| 1962 | 3.300 | 1.650 | 1.650 | 50.0 | 50.0 | 0.325 | 0.225 | 0.100 | 69.2 | 31.8 | 0.419 | 35.6 |
| 1963 | 3.810 | 2.040 | 1.770 | 53.5 | 46.5 | 0.375 | 0.275 | 0.100 | 73.3 | 26.7 | 0.442 | 27.9 |
| 1964 | 4.250 | 2.280 | 1.970 | 53.6 | 46.4 | 0.390 | 0.270 | 0.120 | 69.2 | 30.8 | 0.530 | 27.3 |
| 1959–64 | 19.834 | 9.964 | 9.870 | 50.3 | 49.7 | 1.940 | 1.375 | 0.565 | 70.9 | 29.1 | 0.530 | 27.3 |

#### WELFARE FUND

Welfare funds are also operated separately by all the production units within a commune. Accumulations in the funds are used for a variety of purposes. Expenditures are made on meeting the current and not the capital costs of welfare projects undertaken by the production units. The production units of Peng Pu Commune of Shanghai and Stonewell Commune of Kwangtung contributed a total amount of 160,000 yuan to the welfare funds. Out of this 158,000 yuan were spent by the two communes on various welfare activities, as detailed in Table 7 below. In Stonewell Commune the expenditure exceeded the total contributions made to the fund by 11,000 yuan. This difference was made up by borrowing 6,000 yuan from the savings made in the past and 5,000 yuan from the Credit Cooperative Society. The latter has lent 22,000 yuan to the commune for welfare activities in the period 1958–64.

As we see from the table, the bulk of the expenditure is in the form of relief payments made to poor families. A family qualifies as "poor" for two reasons: first it may have a very low worker to non-worker ratio; second, its able-bodied workers may not be able to accumulate enough work points to afford a decent living to the members. In Peng Pu Commune, the non-worker to worker ratio is 2.3 (see Table 2), which means that an able-bodied worker here supports, apart from himself, on the average, 1.3 non-workers. In this commune, a family with a ratio of 3.5 qualifies for support from the welfare fund. A typical family supported by the fund would be made up of two workers (husband and wife), six children, and an old person. Peng Pu production units were providing this type of relief to 213 families. In 1964 a poor family received, on the average, 244 yuan per year.

### *Table 7—Expenditure on Welfare Activities in Peng Pu and Stonewell Communes, 1964*

| | *Peng Pu* | | *Stonewell* | |
|---|---|---|---|---|
| *Item of Expenditure* | *EXPENDITURE (YUAN)* | *% OF TOTAL* | *EXPENDITURE (YUAN)* | *% OF TOTAL* |
| Relief to poor families | 52,000 | 74.3 | 74,000 | 73.3 |
| School feeding | 9,000 | 12.9 | 13,000 | 12.9 |
| Food for patients | 7,000 | 10.0 | 3,000 | 2.8 |
| Reading room supplies | 1,000 | 1.4 | — | — |
| Sports | 1,000 | 1.4 | — | — |
| Community dining rooms | — | — | 1,000 | 0.1 |
| Poor people's home | — | — | 10,000 | 10.0 |
| Total | 70,000 | 100.0 | 101,000 | 100.0 |

PRODUCTION COSTS

Included in production costs are all those agricultural inputs which a production unit has to purchase from the outside. Thus, if a production team itself grows all the fodder needed for its animals, then expenditure on fodder would not figure under production costs. Figures of Table 4, therefore, do not give the real cost of inputs used by the various communes. There is no way of gauging the extent of underestimation involved. Items that tend to get excluded include animal fodder, seeds, and farm manure.

Table 8 provides a breakdown of production costs for all communes in China. These data were supplied by the Bureau of Commune Management. Table 9 supplies the same breakdown for those communes visited by the delegation.

Seed, fuel, power, chemical fertilizer and insecticides are obtained by the commune management from various state trading corporations and distributed to the production teams. For these inputs the state charges the same price for most of China. For instance the price charged for a ton of ammonium sulphate all over China in 1965 was 340.0 yuan and electric power for electric pumps was being sold at 7 cents per kwh. Animal feed is either grown by the production teams themselves or purchased from neighboring teams that happen to have a surplus. We saw considerable evidence of this type of trading between the production teams within the

### *Table 8—Breakdown of Production Costs for all Chinese Communes, 1964*

| *Item* | *Expenditure as percentage of total production cost* |
|---|---|
| Seed | 18.0 |
| Animal Feed | 35.0 |
| Chemical Fertilizer and Insecticides | 10.4 |
| Tractor Ploughing Charges | 2.8 |
| Electricity Charges | 0.8 |
| Fuel for Transportation | 2.0 |
| Maintenance of Trucks and Carts | 11.0 |
| Maintenance of Implements | 13.0 |
| Miscellaneous | 7.0 |
| Total | 100.0 |

same commune. Trucks, tractors, threshers, etc., are generally owned by the commune and hired out to the production teams at the rentals fixed by the Commune Management Committee. Workshops for repairing farm implements are also owned by the communes. For instance, the Evergreen Commune workshop had ten lathes and employed 110 workers. The net income from this workshop was more than 80,000 yuan.

***Table 9—Breakdown of Production Costs in Peng Pu, Tsin Yah, and West Lake Communes, 1964***

| | *Peng Pu* | | *Tsin Yah* | | *West Lake* | |
|---|---|---|---|---|---|---|
| *Item of Expenditure* | *COST (YUAN)* | *% OF TOTAL* | *COST (YUAN)* | *% OF TOTAL* | *COST (YUAN)* | *% OF TOTAL* |
| Seed | 194,700 | 22.7 | 150,000 | 22.3 | 74,000 | 22.2 |
| Animal Feed | 320,000 | 37.3 | 290,000 | 43.1 | 1,200 | 0.4 |
| Fertilizer | 151,000 | 17.6 | 85,000 | 12.6 | 119,880 | 36.0 |
| Tractor Ploughing | 9,250 | 1.1 | 30,000) | 4.5) | — | — |
| Electricity | 2,400 | 0.3 | ) | ) | 680 | 0.2 |
| Fuel | 4,500 | 0.5 | ) | ) | 1,400 | 0.4 |
| Workshop Charges | 14,490 | 1.7 | 17,200 | 2.6 | 8,900 | 2.7 |
| Miscellaneous | 162,110 | 18.9 | 100,800 | 15.0 | 126,940 | 38.1 |
| Total | 859,000 | 100.0 | 673,000 | 100.0 | 330,000 | 100.0 |

In Peng Pu and Tsin Yah Communes, expenditure on animal feed was even higher than the national average of 35 per cent; in West Lake Commune it was considerably smaller. An outstanding item of expenditure in West Lake Commune was fertilizer. In China according to the official view, the use of fertilizer for specialized production (vegetables, fruits, tea, etc.) has been encouraged even when this was at the expense of food grain production.

### PERSONAL INCOMES

What is left from the gross income after making all these deductions is distributed among the able-bodied workers of a production unit. On the average, 50 per cent of peasant wages are paid in grain and 50 per cent in cash. Wages are paid on the basis of "work points" allotted to a worker by the production team and the number of work days he puts in in a year. Work points are allotted on the basis of a worker's ability to do work in the field and his general attitude toward manual labor. Thus eight hours of work may entitle one worker to ten points while another, for the same number of hours in the field, may get only six points. If a worker puts in less than eight hours of work on a particular day, his work points for that day are correspondingly reduced. Points are allotted at the beginning of every month in an open meeting in which all the peasants participate enthusiastically. We attended one such meeting in which the final formula was accepted by all the members of the production team after what appeared to be at times a fairly heated debate. At the end of the agricultural year, the net income of the production unit is calculated by making all the deductions mentioned above; the residual is then divided by the total number of points obtained by all the members. This calculation determines the money value of a work point. The yearly wage of the workers is determined by multiplying the value of the work point with the number of points obtained by each one of them over the year.

In 1964, the average wage received by the workers in the thirteen communes was 388.5 yuan. This is reduced to only 272 yuan if we exclude the not very typical communes of Evergreen, Red Star, Leap Forward and People's Suburban. The Bureau of Communes' figure for the average agricultural wage in China in 1964 was 408 yuan. Able-bodied workers in our typical communes seem to have earned one-third less than typical workers in Chinese agriculture. The following factors may be responsible for this difference: first, our figures do not include incomes earned from private plots. The bureau's figures may not only include these but may also incorporate incomes from subsidiary occupations like handicrafts, etc. Second, only 50 per cent of the wages are paid in cash, the rest is received by the workers in kind. The money value of the agricultural wage, therefore, depends on the prices at which distributed food grains, etc., are valued. There is a difference in the price that the state pays to the production units for their agricultural produce and what it charges itself from the communes. Valuation of wages in kind at these two different prices would naturally lead to an overestimation by the state. Third, we have calculated average wages by simply dividing the total distributed income by the number of able-bodied workers. No transfer payments (payments to poor families out of the welfare fund) have been included. The government figure may also incorporate these.

Of the thirteen communes visited by us, only five (Evergreen, Red Star, August First, Leap Forward and People's Suburban) had paid out higher than average national wages to their able-bodied workers. In this group of five, we can identify two different communes: the very rich ones (Evergreen, Red Star and August First) and the very poor ones (Leap Forward and People's Suburban). The latter group had achieved higher wages for its workers by distributing to them 70 per cent of their gross income (Table 4). The former group had achieved a higher standard of living for its workers in spite of the fact that only half of the gross income was given out as wages. In fact, the percentage of gross income distributed to the able-bodied workers of Evergreen, Red Star and August First Communes was less than that for any other commune visited by us. This result appears to have been deliberately achieved; the most likely and probable aim being to reduce the gap between the distributed income per worker in rich and poor communes. The average distributed income per able-bodied worker in Evergreen, Red Star and August First Commune was 526.2 yuan in 1964. The average for the remaining communes, not counting Leap Forward and People's Suburban Communes, was only 264.2 yuan. This gap appeared despite different rates of distributing incomes adopted by the rich and poor communes. Thus the three richer communes distributed to their workers 50.5 per cent of their gross income while the remaining communes distributed as

### *Table 10—Family Income and Agricultural Wages in the Thirteen Communes, 1964*

| Communes | NET INCOME DISTRIBUTED (YUAN MILLION) | Families: NUMBER | Families: RECEIVED INCOME PER FAMILY (YUAN) | Workers: NUMBER | Workers: RECEIVED INCOME PER WORKER (YUAN) |
|---|---|---|---|---|---|
| Evergreen | 6.650 | 8,100 | 821.0 | 14,000 | 475.0 |
| Red Star | 13.600 | 11,000 | 1,236.4 | 24,000 | 567.6 |
| Leap Forward | 0.175 | 252 | 694.4 | 350 | 500.0 |
| Kawkang | 1.211 | 2,988 | 405.3 | 4,000 | 302.8 |
| August First | 2.060 | 2,800 | 735.7 | 4,400 | 468.2 |
| Tsin Yah | 1.247 | 3,000 | 415.6 | 4,800 | 259.8 |
| Hsin Lung San | 3.960 | 10,130 | 390.9 | 12,790 | 309.6 |
| Peng Pu | 2.203 | 3,721 | 592.0 | 8,552 | 257.6 |
| Hsu Hang | 2.340 | 4,649 | 503.3 | 9,149 | 255.8 |
| West Lake | 1.190 | 1,800 | 661.1 | 4,800 | 247.9 |
| Tung Chun | 0.850 | 2,014 | 422.1 | 5,112 | 166.3 |
| People's Suburban | 0.770 | 553 | 1,392.4 | 1,365 | 564.1 |
| Stonewell | 5.400 | 11,900 | 453.8 | 22,000 | 245.5 |
| Total | 41.656 | 62,907 | 662.2 | 115,318 | 361.2 |

much as 58.5 per cent. Had the comparatively richer communes also distributed their gross incomes in the same proportion as the others, the received income per worker for them would have been 609.4 yuan. This would have increased the income gap to 354.2 yuan. Or, conversely, had the poorer communes adopted the same distribution pattern as the richer ones, income per worker in their case would have been reduced to 228.2 yuan, making the income gap equal to 298.0 yuan.

Despite the effort to equalize wages, a wide income differential exists in Chinese agriculture. For instance, the workers of the Red Star Commune of Peking received wages almost two-and-a-half times those received by workers of Chekiang's Tung Chun Commune. The agricultural wage of Red Star Commune workers was 39.2 per cent higher than the national average; that of an average worker in Tung Chun Commune was less than two-fifths. This disparity is somewhat reduced if we remove the non-typical communes from this part of the analysis. Even then, the wages of workers in the August First Commune were 187 per cent higher than those in Tung Chun Commune.

Some idea of regional disparities can be had from Table 11. As is to be expected, high population areas have lower incomes per able-bodied worker. Thus as we move down from the northeastern provinces of Kirin and Liaoning toward the southeastern province of Kwangtung, there is a steady decline in the income of agricultural workers. Kiangsu province appears to present an exception. In this province, however, the delegation visited only one commune and that too was engaged in fishing. In order to pull its population out of desperate poverty, the Commune Management Committee was distributing 70 per cent of its gross earnings as wages. The figure of 47.00 yuan as monthly wage is, therefore, not representative of the area.

### *Table 11—Agricultural Wages Received per Month by Able-Bodied Workers in Eight Chinese Provinces, 1964*

| | (*yuan*) |
|---|---|
| Peking | 44.41 |
| Inner Mongolia | 47.22 |
| Liaoning | 32.45 |
| Kirin | 24.66 |
| Shanghai | 21.39 |
| Chekiang | 17.15 |
| Kiangsu | 47.00 |
| Kwangtung | 18.75 |

*Note:* Wages per worker have been calculated by taking weighted averages of the communes visited in the areas.

The Chinese communes have declared that their policy is to remove this difference as rapidly as possible. The government expects to achieve equality in the following ways. First, by providing state assistance to the relatively less developed regions of the country. Second, by identifying really poor production units, scientifically determining the reasons for their poverty, and trying to solve their peculiar problems by giving them massive financial and technical assistance. "Identification and separation" of poor production units has been done at two different levels. Every county has a few backward areas; if geographically contiguous and large enough (in population or area), they have been formed into communes, earmarked for special treatment. Similarly, poorer production teams within the communes have also been set aside for special attention. In fact at the time of the reorganization of the communes, the poverty factor was constantly kept in view by the county officials.

Third, by diversifying the economies of the poorer production brigades. By "diversification," the Chinese no longer mean the adoption of a mixed agricultural-industrial economy by the communes. Having tried this in 1958 and failed, the Chinese have turned to another form of diversification—"production spread to be achieved within the agricultural sector." The purely grain-growing areas are being encouraged to grow fruits, vegetables, medicinal herbs, etc. In order to encourage this type of "production-spread," the Chinese press gives prominence to success stories in which the turning point came when the production units partially switched from traditional to non-traditional crops. Under the pricing policy followed at present by the government, there is no doubt that the communes going in for "special crops" stand to earn a good deal more than those that only produce food grains. In Chekiang province, for instance, the West Lake Commune, which derives 80 per cent of its gross income from tea, is able to distribute 50 per cent more wages to its workers than Tung Chun Commune which grows mostly food grains.

Fourth, to adopt a labor policy which makes the industrial sector depend largely on hands recruited from the poorer regions. Such a policy, it is hoped, would reduce the pressure of population in the relatively less developed regions of the country. The officials are, however, aware that this policy can remove from these areas their only economically important asset, able-bodied workers. A lowered man-to-land ratio in which the composition of population has changed in favor of the very old and the very young cannot be regarded as an improvement. It is to prevent this sort of thing from happening that the leadership within a production unit has a strict control on labor migration.

III

# Demographic Patterns and Population Policy

# Demographic Patterns and Population Policy

PAPERS IN THIS section describe the demographic patterns in India and China. Both countries suffer from serious overpopulation problems. The runaway population growth is reflected in tragically low economic standards and serious unemployment, both overt and disguised. A dramatic decline in the death rate from improved public health facilities and a slower reduction in the fertility rate explain the population explosion. As the eminent demographer, S. Chandrasekhar, says about India, "Demographically, India is running so fast that economically, despite all the progress made, she is almost standing still." Both India and China have adopted family planning as a national goal, and serious efforts have been made to check the fast growing numbers. In India, to date, efforts have not been able to bring about a significant decline in the birth rate. Obviously the prospects for economic development in the two countries are inextricably bound up with population growth.

The papers by Thomas Dow, Jr. and Sripati Chandrasekhar and excerpts from India's Fourth Five Year Plan explain the present level of India's population, the main factors behind its growth, efforts to check the runaway population growth, and the progress achieved up to date. An encouraging indication pointed out by Chandrasekhar are the results of attitude surveys showing that "more than 70 per cent of mothers and fathers of all castes, religions and income groups are in favor of learning and practicing family planning." An all-out effort to make use of this hopeful attitude is suggested. As Chandrasekhar warns, if the problem is not tackled with a sense of urgency and spirit of dedication, the outlook is gloomy indeed. The prospect of a billion Indians by 2,000 A.D. is alarming indeed.

Leo A. Orleans suggests the difficulties of dealing with China's population problems. He points out that we are still ignorant about the composition and pattern of China's population, and calls attention to problems in interpreting census data issued by the government on the mainland. In his most recent work Orleans attempted to estimate the population of China during the past twenty years without using complicated demographic projection techniques.[1] His estimates took into account the impact of several relevant social, political, and

**Note to this Part appears on page 395**

economic factors, including the birth control campaign. He estimated a population of 746 million in 1969 with a growth rate of 14 to 15 per 1,000 in the recent few years. Some other sinologists have estimated the growth rate of China's population at less than 20 per 1,000 for the recent years. In his comprehensive paper on "Population Growth and Distribution in Mainland China," John S. Aird presents estimates of the present population and projections for the future under different assumptions about fertility and mortality rates. According to Aird, under all but the most pessimistic expectations, the population of China will surpass 1 billion by 1985. Due to the drastic decline in the mortality rates for both the urban and rural areas, the official birth control campaigns have not been successful. The seriousness of the growing numbers in China is, as Aird points out, that "Meeting the minimal needs of a growing population in all sectors at once is a formidable task requiring planned national investment on a scale well beyond the capacity of the economy or of the administrative system at the present time."

18

# The Population of India

Thomas E. Dow, Jr.

*From* Current History *54, no. 320, (April 1968): 219–24, 241–42, with omissions. Reprinted with permission.*

ONE OUT OF every seven people on the earth today inhabits the Indian subcontinent. Indians occupy less than 2.5 per cent of the world's land area while accounting for more than 14 per cent of the world's population. Numbering more than 500 million, they make India the earth's second most populous nation. The significance of this figure is apparent when one considers that the combined population of either the U.S.S.R. and the United States, or the combined population of sub-Saharan Africa and Latin America, is *less* than the population of India.

One consequence of such great numbers is high density of population. Estimates vary, but there appear to be over 370 persons per square mile in India. This represents a density approximately fifteen times greater than that of Africa, Latin America, North America, and the U.S.S.R. Yet it is a density which Europe is beginning to approach, and which Japan and the Netherlands—with 685 and 935 people per square mile, respectively—have already exceeded.

Such figures suggest that average density measures alone have little discriminative power; they are, for example, poor indicators of a country's prosperity, "have" and "have-not" nations being randomly mixed in high and low density groupings. Under these circumstances, it is useful to consider actual rather than average distribution.

In India, despite some urbanization and industrialization, the bulk of the population remains on the land. Roughly 400 million people are classified as rural residents, and the great majority of these are directly engaged in agriculture. This creates an extremely high rural density and this, more than anything else, distinguishes the Indian pattern of distribution from that of the developed world; that is, *vis-à-vis* Europe, India has proportionately more of its population living outside of cities and working directly in agriculture. In this sense, India is still a rural agrarian society, but a society nevertheless dedicated to its own modernization, and to the maintenance and control of its huge population. All this is to be accomplished under conditions of tremendous cultural diversity.

Indian society is a mosaic of immensely varied political, social, ethnic, linguistic and religious groups. There are, for example, seventeen separate states—with populations ranging from under 4 million to over 70 million—and almost as many major languages. This provides the opportunity for a rich cultural pluralism, but it also holds the threat of dissension and separatism. At the moment, India continues to seek an elusive unity within this diversity. The search for this unity, and the corresponding quest for modernity, are closely related to the question of India's population—its size and rate of growth.

Kingsley Davis estimates that the population of the subcontinent was 125 million in 300 B.C., and that almost 2,000 years later it was very much the same.[1] This stability was the product of a high constant birth rate and a high variable death rate, which—over the course of time—tended to balance each other out. The result, measured in centuries, was a roughly equal incidence of life and death, which permitted neither population growth nor population decline.

This pattern was gradually modified in the colonial period, to the extent that a limited control of death permitted some population gains. In spite of this, years of advance continued to alternate with years of decline, so that the resulting growth rate was still very moderate up until 1921.

After 1921, this alternating pattern ceased and the rate of population growth increased.

**Notes to chapter 18 appear on page 395**

Fundamental to this change was an extensive curtailment of mortality without a corresponding reduction in fertility. The death rate fell from perhaps 47 per thousand in 1911–21 to 17 per thousand in 1967, while the birth rate declined from 48 per thousand to 42 per thousand in the same period; that is, the death rate fell by *more* than 50 per cent, while the birth rate fell by *less* than 20 per cent. The resulting imbalance was and is responsible for the accelerating growth of Indian population.

At the moment this differential—of a birth rate in excess of forty per thousand and a death rate of less than twenty per thousand—results in a growth rate of 2.5 per cent per year which, if sustained, would double the Indian population in 28 years. It is doubtful that India could support such an increase in this short period of time; it is certain that she could not support subsequent increases of the same size. Barring an increase in mortality, only a curtailment of fertility will bring this cycle of growth to a close. In this connection, it is instructive to consider some of the reasons for the high birth rate in India.

Fertility is high in India because:

1. The age of marriage for most women is still very low (less than sixteen years on the average) and the proportion marrying is very high.
2. The needs and demands of traditional rural society tend to eliminate childlessness and to require generous reproduction, particularly to ensure the presence of one or more sons (male offspring being considered necessary for economic and religious reasons).
3. The early consequences of modernization, by reducing infant and maternal mortality, tend to increase rather than decrease the birth rate.
4. The practice of birth control, in spite of a growing interest in family planning, is still very limited.

These factors, as part of a larger social structure, tend to sustain the birth rate at a traditionally high level while—at the same time—allowing and encouraging rapid reductions in mortality. The result of this disjunction between the frequencies of births and deaths is a rate of increase that will bring the Indian population to 775 million by 1985 and to more than billion before the end of the century.

In the face of such rapid population growth, it will be difficult, if not impossible, for India to meet her development goals. In fact, no modernizing effort, no matter how vigorous, will be sufficient to offset the retarding effect of a rapid increase in numbers. This relationship is seen most clearly in the areas of economic and agricultural development.

## *Economic Development*

Since gaining independence in 1947, India can claim some major economic and agricultural achievements. Foremost among these are a 150 per cent increase in industrial productivity, a 400 per cent increase in steel production and in electrical power capacity, and a 62 per cent increase in agricultural production.

Unfortunately, most of these aggregate advances have not resulted in comparable per capita gains. In spite of a substantial national performance, the average citizen is not much better off today than he was a generation ago, and in some areas—particularly food consumption—his situation is actually worse.

This apparent paradox is resolved when one recognizes that this increase in national productivity was offset by a comparable increase in population; there was more to share, but there were more people to share it. The breaking of this cycle will require that the economy grow much more rapidly than the population. This and only this will permit sustained improvement at the individual level. Unfortunately, it is difficult to increase the economic growth rate when the population is increasing rapidly.

Under rapid growth conditions, a nation must set aside a disproportionate amount of its product for the support of its new members. To take a simple illustration, if a nation is increasing its product by four per cent a year, and if its population is growing at two per cent per year, this will leave only two per cent for the improvement of the standard of living, the remaining surplus being consumed by the demands of the increased population. Thus the necessity of providing for additional population tends to impoverish both the government and the family, leaving very little for saving, investment and economic growth.

India's rate of population growth has virtually nullified almost all the economic progress of the last twenty years. One dramatic example of this is the attempt to provide adequate employment for her increasing population. In 1961, there were 8 million unemployed; in 1966, approximately 12 million; and in 1971, there will probably be 15 million unemployed—all this in spite of the fact that the Indian government created 13 million new jobs between 1961 and 1966, and expects to create 20 million more jobs between 1966 and 1971. The government's effort is not at fault here, but rather the impossibility of creating jobs as rapidly as applicants at the present rate of population growth.

This same problem is evident in the recent setback of India's total development program. The Third Five-Year Plan, ending in 1966, fell short of its targets in almost all categories, while the present Five-Year-Plan —1966–71—has already been characterized as unrealistic in the face of India's immediate subsistence needs. It is clear that both these disappointments are the result of the sacrifice of long-range development goals to the immediate needs of a rapidly increasing population. This is most apparent in the slow increase of personal income in India. Over the entire period of independence, per capita annual income has probably increased by less than $25, being not less than $50 in 1950, and not more than $75 in 1967.[2] It remains to be seen how much more rapid this income growth would be if it did not have to compete with expansive population growth.

In approaching this problem, demographer Ansley Coale works with two different assumptions: (a), that fertility will remain unchanged; (b), that it will be reduced by 50 per cent in 25 years. Income per consumer is then calculated for each model. Significantly, after thirty years, income per consumer in the low fertility population would be 40 per cent higher than income per consumer in the high fertility population. After sixty years, the difference would be 100 per cent, and "after 150 years the low fertility population would have an income per consumer six times as high as the faster growing population with unchanged fertility."[3]

Clearly, India's developmental prospects are inextricably bound up with its population growth. If this growth rate can be markedly reduced, the chances for an economic breakthrough will be greatly enhanced; if not, one is hard pressed to imagine how the standard of living is to be sustained, much less improved.

## *A Population Control Program*

Prior to 1947, there was a long history of elite interest in family planning. Within the nationalist leadership, for example, the need for population control was apparently accepted by both Mahatma Gandhi and Jawaharlal Nehru.[4] Unfortunately, this interest was not shared by the British government and no action was taken.

Under these circumstances, one would have anticipated the inauguration of a major program immediately after independence, but this was not the case. Actually—once in power—the new leadership preferred to interpret India's problems in terms of colonialism, or the consequences of colonialism, rather than population growth. Under this assumption, India was suddenly regarded as an underpopulated country. The resulting confusion of indigenous population pressure with British economic exploitation tended to prevent an objective study of the population question, and thus any meaningful action in this area was delayed.

By 1951, however, with the inauguration of the First Five-Year Plan, there was at last an official recognition of the need for population control: "The objective of stabilizing the growth of population . . . must be at the very center of planned development."[5] Accordingly, a budget of $1.5 million was provided for this purpose.

As its first subsequent official act, India asked the World Health Organization for aid in promoting family planning. This assistance took the form of an experimental program designed to test the effectiveness of the rhythm method. The resulting field tests demonstrated the unsuitability of this method under existing conditions. The net effect was a loss of valuable time.

In the Second Five-Year Plan, 1956–61, the family planning appropriation was increased to over $10 million, but there was still no sense of urgency and certainly nothing resembling an effective national program. In fact, a major portion of this budget was not even spent. This indifference is partially explained by the fact that India believed its rate of population growth to be much lower than it actually was. As a result, the government underestimated population growth during the 1950s by roughly 30 million people. The magnitude of this error, and hence the enormity of actual population growth, acted as a stimulant to the family planning program.

For the period 1961–66, the budget was increased ten-fold, to over $100 million. There were also corresponding increases in medical facilities and relevant personnel, and yet the results were still meager. In part, the problem seemed to be one of finding a suitable contraceptive technique that would be both acceptable and effective in India. In spite of extensive and continuing experiments in this area, there was no major breakthrough until 1965, and even then, the results were mixed.

In 1965, the Indian Government decided to commit itself to a mass program of intrauterine device (I.U.D.) insertions. This method clearly avoided most of the difficulties and limitations of conventional contraception, and had apparently been reasonably effective in both Indian clinical experiments and large-scale field programs in Korea and Taiwan. The following goals were set:

1 million I.U.D. insertions in the first year;

6 million U.I.D. insertions in the second year;

50 million I.U.D. insertions over a ten year period.

Used in connection with other methods, it was hoped that this program would bring the birth rate down to 25 per thousand within a decade. Progress to date suggests that this goal may be difficult to achieve. In the first year of the program, 80 per cent of the desired insertions were accomplished; in the second year, this proportion fell to less than 15 per cent. Against a goal of 6 million, there were only 900,000 insertions.

There are numerous reasons for this lag. In part, it reflects a shortage of medical personnel. In general, there are not enough physicians; in particular, there are not enough female physicians. In a culture where many women will not allow a man to perform the I.U.D. insertion procedure, this deficiency in female personnel is very serious.

Equally serious are the problems involving the actual or potential recipient of the I.U.D. In a small percentage of cases (perhaps 5 per cent) the device will be involuntarily expelled; in a larger percentage of cases (perhaps 15 per cent) there will be side effects, which may or may not require removal. These side effects, if untreated and unexplained, can cause anxiety in the woman and apprehension among her neighbors. The result is two-fold: first, a large proportion of present users (perhaps as high as 50 per cent) will have the device removed within 24 months; second, their negative experience will tend to inhibit other potential users. In both instances, more extensive medical care, particularly after insertion, would greatly reduce the problem. Unfortunately, such care is not presently available. As a result, the I.U.D. program has so far reached only a small proportion of the more than 90 million women between fifteen and forty-five years of age who are potential recipients.

In the face of this delay, the government decided to make more extensive use of male sterilization. This, it believes, may be the answer to India's problem. Past efforts in this direction resulted in 500,000 sterilizations in 1965, and 650,000 in 1966. Prior to that, *i.e.*, from 1947 to 1965, a total of 1.1 million vasectomies were performed.

In an attempt to accelerate these rates, a compulsory sterilization bill is being considered which would apply to all men who have three or more children. The bill is sponsored by Dr. Sripati Chandrasekhar, Minister of State for Health and Family Planning, who claims to have considerable support for its passage.[6] At this point, the intent of the bill is not to introduce severe penalties—light fines are envisioned for those who fail to comply—but to establish an official sanction against large families. This would add the weight of legislative pressure to the present financial rewards being offered for voluntary sterilization.

It may be true that sterilization can do for India what abortion did for Japan, but that is yet to be fully demonstrated.[7] In spite of the gains made in 1967—800,000 vasectomies performed in the 6 months from May through October—the program will still have to overcome considerable resistance on the part of the male population. And, if it can do this, it will then have to provide the medical facilities necessary to capitalize upon this new motivation. In both areas, there is a long way to go.

### *Prospects*

Thus, all India's efforts to date have failed to bring about a significant decline in the national birth rate. Surprisingly, high fertility exists in spite of a general interest in family planning and a desire, on the part of most couples, to limit the size of their families.[8] This suggests that the basic problem of the future will be to bring acceptable contraceptive services to these people, to effect a decline in fertility. Unfortunately, there is some disagreement as to precisely how much the birth rate would be reduced even under these optimum conditions.

Kingsley Davis argues, for example, that neither an interest in birth control, nor a desire to control family size, is inconsistent with high fertility.[9] Indeed, those interested in family planning in India still want comparatively large families—of perhaps four children—and do not tend to seek contraceptive assistance until they have achieved their desired family size. Under these circumstances, the level of wanted and planned fertility would still be high, and a further decline in the birth rate would be necessary.

Davis feels that this subsequent reduction may be impossible without far-reaching changes in the society. He suggests that the problem at this point may not be one of merely getting people to accept family planning, or developing more effective contraceptives, but of providing the basic social and economic conditions under which such techniques will be used to achieve small family size.[10]

Granting the validity of much of this argument, it still does not follow that the success of present programs, *i.e.*, the distribution of effective contraceptive methods to presently motivated people, will be inconsenquential. The effective use of birth control by older couples will not go unnoticed by their younger peers. Hopefully, the resulting diffusion of contraceptive control would eliminate all unwanted births. Demographically, this might mean the difference between six births and fourth births for the average Indian woman. The result would be a major decline in the rate of population growth. Such a decline, in turn, would make it easier to achieve still further reductions in desired family size, and it would also help to bring about those broader conditions of modernization on which demographic stabilization ultimately depends. That is, even if present efforts do not immediately end the increase in human numbers, they will prepare the way for greater progress in this direction.

Thus if one assumes the eventual success of the current family planning program, it is not hard to anticipate the control of population growth in India. There are reasons for believing that this assumption is not unwarranted. An increasing literature now exists on the likelihood of a favorable outcome in the emerging world. The following elements are usually cited in support of such optimistic predictions: (1) "the development of national policies favoring family planning; (2) the demonstrated public interest in limiting childbearing; [and] (3) the improvement of contraceptive technology. . . ."[11]

When applied to India, however, each of these points must be appropriately qualified: the commitment of the government in this area is very recent and—at different levels—may still involve a certain ambivalence toward population control;[12] the problems of translating family planning approval into effective use are far from solved; and the search for an entirely suitable contraceptive methodology is still going on.

Such reservations are meant to suggest nothing more than the need to maximize all efforts toward the elimination of these difficulties. It is apparent that nothing short of this will be adequate. The United Nation's 1966 summary of India's situation makes this point quite clearly:

> Without . . . a true priority to family planning, which inevitably means the diversion of effort and resources from other desirable objectives, the program will not succeed. With it, there is great hope that it will.[13]

The problem is clear. That India can fully mobilize her almost infinite diversity to meet this challenge is problematic. Regional, linguistic, religious and cultural differences will have to be superseded by a sense of national urgency and purpose. Assuming such cooperation, the control of fertility will require further changes in law and custom, an increase in the number of social, medical and paramedical personnel,[14] and the continuation of present contraceptive research and development programs—all this necessarily taking place while the government strives to maintain acceptable levels of health, nutrition, literacy, income, employment and political stability.

Obviously, this burden will become first intolerable and then impossible in the face of population growth. Conversely, were fertility to be significantly controlled, one could expect a more rapid rate of modernization. Unfortunately, it seems unlikely that this control can be accomplished with domestic resources alone. Indeed, even with the fullest possible effort at home, India will be unable to ensure either a marked decline in fertility, or the maintenance of acceptable social and economic standards. External assistance will be required.

For the first time in its history, the United Nations may be prepared to provide such assistance. After twenty years in the demographic wilderness, the United Nations has finally agreed to take a more active role in cooperating with nations desiring to develop family planning programs. So far, however, the change has been more verbal than monetary. Appropriations in this area have been very limited, and—in view of the U.N.s overall financial situation—are not likely to increase markedly in the near future.

That leaves the Western world, which has shown a remarkable indifference to the developmental problems of India. Our own record in this area is mixed. On the one hand, much of the $15 billion Food for Peace program has gone to India, and there is every evidence that we will continue to meet her food deficits; on the other hand, our general aid to India over the entire twenty years of her independence has cost us less than has four months of the Vietnamese war, and has been much less than our per capita aid to other smaller Asian nations. Worse still, our most recent foreign aid bill was the lowest in history, and suggests further disengagement from these obligations. In the area of population control, the situation is hardly better. The United States is now spending some $25 million overall for this purpose, with India as a "major" recipient.

Clearly, India needs more assistance if she is to control her population growth while maintaining some degree of internal coherence. If she receives such increased aid, while *maintaining* and *expanding* her domestic effort, we should reasonably anticipate a decline in fertility and a marked acceleration in the process of development. But if there is any failure of total resolve, any flagging of effort—either in India or the West—we should recognize the certainty of a much less desirable outcome.

19

# A Billion Indians by 2000 A.D.?

*Sripati Chandrasekhar*

*From Sripati Chandrasekhar,* A Billion Indians by 2000 A.D.?, *The New York Times Magazine, April 4, 1965, pp. 32, 33, 110, 112, 114, and 117, with omissions. Reprinted with permission.*

THE RECENT ANNOUNCEMENT of the despatch of a United Nations team to study India's population problems and possibly advise the Government of India on ways to accelerate the current family planning efforts highlights India's pressing population problem and her desperate need to curb the birth rate. India's alarming increase of some ten million people each year tragically nullifies almost all the considerable progress the country has made in agricultural and industrial production during the last seventeen years of her freedom.

The dimensions and magnitude of India's population problem can be briefly summarized. She ranks second in population (Red China tops the list) and seventh in land area in the world. Today she claims about 15 per cent of the world's population, on about 2.4 per cent of the world's area. Although India is only about two-fifths the size of the continental United States of America she shelters about two and a half times the U.S. population.

## *India's 470 Million*

In 1891 India's population (adjusted to the present area) was 236 millions. In 1921, three decades later, the population increased to 248 millions—only a 12 million increase in thirty years thanks to epidemics and famines. And during the next thirty years, 1921–51, the population increased by not another 12 millions but by 110 millions! And during the last single decade, 1951–61, the population increased by 77.26 millions to reach a total of 438 millions. Today India's population is about 470 millions.

It must be remembered that last decade's increase of 77 millions is more than the entire population of any country in Europe with the exception of the Soviet Union or any country in Latin America. India's total population today (though only second largest in the world) equals that of 55 states of Africa and Latin America put together.

An explanation of India's population growth must be sought in the nation's birth and death rates, for emigration from and immigration into the country are practically nil. India's birth rate is around 40 per 1,000 but is not increasing. One reason for this high birth rate is that millions of girls still marry early—often below the age of consent, which is fourteen—and go on bearing children. Another is the universality of the married state (in India) which ensured that practically every adult male and female in the country participate in reproduction.

However, the decisive factor behind India's explosive population growth is the definitive decline in the nation's death rate, particularly the infant mortality rate. The estimated death rate has declined from 42.6 per thousand in 1901 to an estimated 19 in 1964. Even more revealing is the decline in the infant mortality rate (the number of infants under the age of one year who die per 1,000 live births in the course of a year) which dropped from 232 in 1901 to 92 in 1962.

This significant decline in the death rate has been brought about by the government's efforts in various directions: an increase in trained medical and para-medical personnel, D.D.T. spraying, B.C.G. vaccination, the services of trained midwives, the spread of a modicum of health education. American technical aid, particularly in malaria eradication, and the overall assistance of WHO and the Colombo Plan. In response to all this the expectation of life at birth has increased from 23 years in 1931 to 46 in 1961.

And with the population increasing today by about ten millions a year—that is, at the current rate of increase of 2.2 per cent—India's population can reach a billion by 2000 A.D., only thirty-five years away.

A statement of India's population problem can be summarized as follows: how can India raise the standard of living of her people (and this means more food, goods and services for everybody) and cut down the still relatively high death rate (and this means keeping alive more people and taking care of them) when it is so difficult to support the existing population even at a low standard of living, *if the population continues to increase by about ten million every year?* In other words, demographically India is running so fast that economically, despite all the progress being made, she is almost standing still.

The prospect of a billion Indians by 2000 A.D. is an alarming one. Theoretically this may never come to pass, for if food production (or supply) does not keep pace with this increase in numbers famine conditions would come to prevail all over the country, with their aftermath of an increase in disease and the death rate. The resulting poverty and miserable level of living can hardly be imagined. A government that could control India's millions in a state of such misery would clearly have to be some form of totalitarianism, embracing every aspect of the citizen's life with the tentacles of an octopus. Individual freedom as we understand it would be extinct, for teeming millions with almost literally no elbow room would imply choking government and social organization and control, utterly incompatible with individual human liberty, freedom or dignity. However, let us not dwell on this possible future Indian hell; sufficient unto the day is the evil thereof.

## *The Planning Commission*

Fortunately, the Government of India, dedicated to the task of promoting a welfare state, has been aware of this problem of population increase almost ever since the country attained independence in 1947. The first tangible recognition of the problem came with the publication of the First Five Year Plan which pointed out that "the objective of stabilizing the growth of population over a reasonable period must be at the very centre of planned development . . . in the circumstances of the country family planning has to be undertaken not merely as a major development program, but as a nation-wide movement which embodies a basic attitude towards a better life for the individual, the family and the community . . . (therefore) the reduction in the rate of growth of the population must be regarded as a major desideratum." To achieve this end the Five Year Plan recommended certain measures for the inculcation of the need and technique of family planning.

The Government of India approached the United Nations and asked the WHO for technical aid to promote its family planning program in 1950. As certain Catholic member nations of WHO objected to the world body offering scientific contraceptive advice even to non-Catholic countries, and as India's then Health Minister was "Gandhian" on the birth control question (Mahatma Gandhi opposed contraception and favored moral restraint for India), WHO's response was to send the late Dr. Abraham Stone, America's planned parenthood expert, to India to set up a series of pilot projects to try out the rhythm or safe period method of family planning. The WHO assignment specifically stated that family planning was to be confined to the rhythm method "on the assumption that if this method were to prove successful on a large population basis it would represent a simple method for dealing with family planning in India." The Health Minister felt that this method would not go against the traditions, culture and mores of the Indian people, and in addition it would have the advantage of not requiring any expenditure for supplies.

## *The Rhythm Method*

As a result, five centers were set up in New Delhi, Mysore and West Bengal States where the rhythm method was taught to selected couples. But teaching the safe period to illiterate wives in backward rural conditions raised its own problems. Reliance on the rhythm method implies accurate records and careful calculations of the menstrual cycle and of fertile and infertile days. Some simple techniques therefore had to be developed. Dr. Stone and some Indian physicians hit upon the idea of constructing a special necklace of 28 beads, one bead for each day of the menstrual cycle. There were orange beads for the days of menstruation, green beads for the safe non-conception days, and red beads for the fertile or "baby" days. The beads were strung for the individual woman on the basis of her menstrual cycle and she was instructed to move one bead daily from one side of the string of the necklace to the other, beginning with the first day of menstruation. During the time that the green beads appeared she was in the safe period and when the red beads came around sexual relations were to be avoided.

When the necklaces of colored beads were distributed to the women willing to practice family planning no one anticipated how many snags there were going to be in translating this apparently simple device into effective action. After a week the women came to the clinic with the complaints that they could not distinguish the colour of the beads in the middle of the night! An improvement was effected in retaining the color but changing the shape of the beads into round and square ones: round red beads were unsafe, square green beads were safe. The wife could feel their shape in the night and say "yes" or "no" to her husband accordingly. (The question of fluorescent beads was even considered.)

Then some women complained that the beads went both clockwise and anti-clockwise. This was a minor problem, however. Since the beads had to be pushed every day, a necklace with a safety catch permitting the movement of the beads in only one direction was devised.

Some orthodox Hindu women would not even wear the beads during their monthly periods as they consider themselves ritually unclean during this time. Some one else had to push the beads for them during those days.

Some women simply forgot to push the beads. Some decided not to wear the necklaces because they didn't want the whole village to know that they were practicing family planning. And some mistook the beads for charmed amulets distributed through the courtesy of the Government of India. They thought it was enough to simply push the beads to space or limit their families. Needless to say, the rhythm method failed to bring down the birth rate.

Besides these more bizarre difficulties, there are the well known biological difficulties inherent in the rhythm method itself. Not only has each individual women a different cycle, the cycle itself may vary from time to time. When nature deviates from the statistical norm, who can complain?

## *Diaphragm and Jelly*

The setting up of these rhythm method experiments by WHO were not India's first attempts at birth control. In fact, as early as 1928 two distinguished citizens of Madras, one a Justice of the High Court who was the father of ten children and the other a Member of the Governor's Executive Council who was childless, opened a birth control clinic in the city. In 1930 the Government of Mysore opened a birth control clinic in Bangalore and a few years later the Poona Birth Control League was founded. During the thirties both the All-India Women's Conference at their regular annual session and the National Planning Committee appointed by the Congress Party, under the chairmanship of Jawaharlal Nehru, strongly endorsed family planning. So even during those early years scientific contraception was not unknown in India, though it was probably confined to about one per cent of the high-income, educated population.

When the rhythm method failed to show any favorable results the Ministry of Health approved the supply of such modern methods of birth control as sheaths and diaphragms and jellies, which the early clinics had been using all along, for distribution in government hospitals and clinics to needy mothers free of cost.

The difficulties in the use of such conventional Western contraceptives as diaphragms in the backward rural conditions of India can easily be imagined. To begin with a strong motivation is necessary to get the rural mother to a clinic where she can be fitted with a diaphragm. Village dwellings are plagued by unhygienic conditions, insufficient running water and often no readily available water at all, lack of lighting and bathrooms. And predominant illiteracy means that even basic directions on a tube of jelly cannot be read. Backward living conditions apart, the diaphragm and jelly method implies some knowledge on the part of the woman of the structure and function of her reproductive organs.

Once after a detailed talk to a large group of rural women, made with the aid of charts and diagrams, a diaphragm was shown and one young woman promptly asked "Isn't it too *large* to swallow?" The village mind expects contraception in the form of a medicine—a pill or a mixture—to be swallowed once or twice a day to cure fertility. Knowledge of human physiology and reproduction seems to be rare even in towns and cities. Mothers who have been taught the diaphragm and jelly methods and given free supplies to last for a few months have returned to the clinics within a few weeks complaining that their periods have stopped and the birth control materials didn't work. "Did you use the diaphragm and jelly as instructed?" "Yes." "Regularly?" "Yes." But on further questioning it was discovered that they forgot sometimes and didn't think it would really matter! The fact that the contraceptives have to be used every time is apparently a problem demanding too much perseverance. And many Indian women have complained after a few attempts at contraception that it is messy and meddlesome, awkward and unaesthetic. Some confess that contraception is just too revolting even for such a desirable purpose as preventing conception.

## *Foam Tablets*

A family planning experiment under government auspices was undertaken in the Punjab where foam tablets were distributed free of cost to all mothers anxious to space or limit the size of their families. The Health Ministry believed that this method was relatively inexpensive and simple to use and the fact that no apparatus was needed was an added advantage. Trained women social workers visited willing mothers at regular intervals with foam tablets. The mothers were asked to insert a tablet up into the vagina prior to intercourse and wait for a few minutes for the tablet to disintegrate, creating a dense foam which would act both as a mechanical and chemical barrier. This experiment also failed in effecting a reduction in the birth rate. Some of the women who failed pointed out on questioning that they had simply forgotten to use the tablets and a few stated, "I didn't like the taste of the tablets."! It was not ascertained whether the women did not understand what they were to do with the tablets or whether they found it repugnant to use them as instructed.

A decade ago everyone was pleading for a simple oral contraceptiive. The magic pill. But now that the pill is here India has not taken to it, for swallowing twenty pills a month for months on end is expensive. And, expense apart, there will always be women who will forget to take their daily doses. Also the Government feels that the pill has not been tried long enough to make certain that there will be no adverse side effects after its prolonged use.

Another contraceptive, the intrauterine coil, a small plastic device worn by women, has recently come into vogue in Europe and the United States. The advantage of this apparatus for a country like India is that it is cheap (it can be produced for less than 2 cents) and can be put in place easily by a doctor without the use of anesthetics.

However, in clinical tests in India the coil has been effective in only 75 per cent of the cases. In some instances, it proved too uncomfortable; in others it was spontaneously expelled from the body, a fact the woman didn't discover until she found she was pregnant. But in the view of many experts, the real difficulty is that this is only a temporary measure.

### *Sterilization*

An ideal method of family planning should be cheap, harmless, reliable and effective in preventing conception, and acceptable to the people who use it. Under Indian conditions an additional important qualification must be added—the method must be good for numerous exposures, or must be a method of permanent conception control. This means surgical sterilization: vasectomy for fathers or salpingectomy for mothers. In view of the current Indian socio-economic-cultural conditions, certainly the most effective method is sterilization. The present writer has been pleading for this for nearly two decades.

Madras State embarked upon a policy of voluntary subsidized sterilization (a free operation plus a bonus of $7.50, and a three to six day holiday with pay for government employees) and Maharashtra and Kerala states have followed suit. They have done fairly well—the program began in 1957 and took time to get underway—in the sense that of all the methods tried so far only sterilization has yielded significant results, and a small dent has been made in the high birth rates of these states. So far nearly a million sterilizations have been performed, mostly on fathers, and the government hopes to step up the program in India's Fourth Five Year Plan (1966–71). About 700,000 operations have been performed in government hospitals, the rest by private surgeons. But India will have to perform three operations per 100 of population annually for ten years if the nation's birth rate is to be reduced from 40 to 20. The government might be wise to try much harder to motivate women to undergo sterilization when they are in the hospital delivering their third or fourth baby. However, the difficulty is that the majority of women deliver their babies in homes, largely unattended by medical personnel. And no wife would agree to sterilization, however much she might want it, unless the husband was prepared to endorse it. The men definitely wear the pants in India.

The advantage of sterilization is that it solves the problem once and for all for those couples who have had from two to four children and are certain that they do not want any more for health, economic or other reasons. So far the Indian experience shows that after sterilization of the mother or father (preferably the father for a variety of reasons, not least of which is that the operation is much simpler for the male) the couple can enjoy sexual relations with the great psychological satisfaction that pregnancy can never occur again. In India a written declaration from both the husband and wife that the couple do not want any more children is obtained and the irreversible nature of the operation (under normal conditions) is emphasized.

At first the Federal Government of India was skeptical and the then Minister of Health was opposed to it. But a few of the State governments went ahead with sterilization. Later the federal government came out in its favor and today almost all the sixteen states of the Indian Union have programs of sterilization as a method of family planning, although in many of the states the program has hardly gotten off the ground. Had India embarked on this policy fifteen years ago with fervor the country by now could have cut its birth rate by half.

### *The Future—Motivation*

It is late, but not yet too late, to do something concrete about India's runaway population growth. But unfortunately although today everybody talks about family planning, the country is still waiting for a crash program. Despite all the debate and discussion, the money and effort, the foreign aid and advice, the family planning program in India has been a failure so far. No significant decline in the nation's birth rate has been achieved, and only in those areas where the summary method of sterilization has been adopted has even a slight dent in the birth rate been made. While the Government of India as a whole under the leadership of Nehru took a refreshingly courageous attitude on the population question, actual efforts throughout these years of freedom have been half-hearted at best. A variety of problems have been responsible for this failure. There are problems of motivation, methods, money and men.

All the attitude surveys conducted so far show that more than 70 per cent of mothers and fathers of all castes, religions and income groups are in favor of learning and practicing family planning. But this desire is not sufficient motivation to go to a clinic, learn about a method of family planning, and rationally use it. The average Hindu wants sons. This attitude is understandable in a country where there is neither social security nor old age pensions, sickness benefits nor unemployment insurance for an overwhelming majority of the population. Parents have to depend on gainfully employed adult sons for their support in old age. Daughters are "married off" as soon as possible and it is bad Hindu manners to expect any financial aid from daughters or sons-in-law. It is much easier to motivate a couple who have three sons in favor of family planning than a couple with four daughters who want to keep on trying for sons. If only we could fix the sex of India's babies!

It is true that everyone wants the good things of life. Nobody loves poverty. But it is one thing to aspire and hope for a higher level of living and entirely another thing to persistently seek ways and means to achieve this. The motive is weak and dormant. Research is needed in this area of motivation in the context of Indian conditions.

As for methods, as already observed India needs a simple method which cannot go wrong. It must be foolproof. Since people marry early, once they have had two or three children the government must make every effort to persuade fathers or mothers to undergo sterilization. (It is also desirable to raise the age at marriage, but in the absence of prolonged education and training postponing the age at marriage becomes a formidable problem.)

As for money, many a desirable program has floundered on the rock of financial stringency. The Government of India must spend considerably larger sums of money than have been spent so far, for with a relatively small population it will eventually save money on its national food, education and medical bills. One solution would be for the Indian Government to ask the United States Government to allow them to use United States counterpart funds (rupees accumulated in India) for promoting sterilization. A cash bonus of Rs. 100 per vasectomy might do the trick. I have suggested this in Parliament but both the governments are extremely sensitive in this area. But in a problem this crucial perhaps we need more action and less sensitivity.

Another problem has been that the subject of population control has been saddled on the Ministry of Health, which has a hundred other pressing problems to tackle. The prevention and control of disease and the eradication of India's unenviable filth and the improvement of sanitation and hygiene alone could keep the ministry busy night and day for the next half a century. As Sir Julian Huxley pleaded some time ago, India should create a separate ministry of population control.

A population ministry, with sufficient funds at its disposal, could train a large band of dedicated men and women to go into the countryside and convert their underprivileged fellow citizens to the philosophy of small families. Given dynamic leadership—civil servants in a vast bureaucracy usually adjust their attitudes and pace to the minister in charge—this can be accomplished. Resistance to change is universal but methods must and can be found to overcome it.

Given the four "m's" that I have talked about, it should be possible to spread the family planning habit in India within the next crucial decade. As India's Planning Commission puts it, "Given a sense of urgency and a spirit of dedicated endeavour it is fully within the capacity of the nation to achieve the goals it has set itself." If this sense of urgency and spirit of dedication can be created soon, the population problem can be solved. If not, the outlook is gloomy indeed.

20

# Family Planning in India

Government of India

*From Government of India Planning Commission,* Fourth Five Year Plan—A Draft Outline, *(Delhi: Manager of Publications, 1966), pp. 346–49, with omissions. Reprinted with permission.*

INDIA'S POPULATION ACCORDING to the 1961 Census was 439.2 million. The estimated mid-year population of 1966 is 498.9 million. Improvement in public health has caused a sharp fall in the death rate without any significant change in the fertility rate. As a result, there has been a steady rise in the annual growth of population. It rose from 1.26 per cent per annum during the decade 1941–51 to 1.97 per cent per annum during 1951–61. The growth rate was estimated to be 2.4 per cent per annum during the period 1961–65. This rate of growth is expected to rise still further to 2.5 per cent per annum during the period 1966–70. Expectation of life at birth which used to be only twenty-seven in 1920s and nearly thirty-two in 1945 is now reckoned at fifty years. With the all round improvement in health conditions, the death rate will fall still further and the expectation of life will increase. The rate of growth of population is bound to rise unless action is taken on a national scale to bring it down.

India's objective of attaining socio-economic betterment of the people can only be fulfilled if the rate of growth of population is controlled and human skill and resources are developed to the desired extent. The Government of India have recognized family planning as a key program for the success of the country's Five Year Plans of development and have adopted a nation-wide program with the objective of reducing the birth rate from 40 per thousand at present to 25 per thousand as expeditiously as possible. The operational goal for achieving this objective is to create facilities for 90 per cent of the married population of India, for the adoption of family planning by:

1. Group acceptance of a small sized family.
2. Personal knowledge about family planning methods.
3. Ready availability of supplies and services.

India is one of the few countries which has taken up family planning as a national program. In the First Plan, a modest beginning was made. During the Second Plan, an action-*cum*-research program was initiated. The program was intensified toward the middle of the Third Plan when the emphasis was shifted from the clinical approach to a more vigorous extension education approach for motivating the people to accept the norm of a small family. The program involves various aspects of community life and social behavior of the people. Its successful implementation requires: (1) large numbers of trained staff such as doctors, nurses, midwives, health educators and other experts as well as non-technical administrative and executive personnel, (2) training facilities on a very wide scale for training of all categories of staff, (3) supplies of contraceptives, intra-uterine device (IUCD), equipment, transport, etc.

There were only 147 Family Planning centers at the end of the First Plan period. This number increased to 11,474 by the end of the Third Plan. In addition to these centers, nearly 9,329 centers for distribution of contraceptives have been located particularly in the rural areas. These centers provide supplies, services and advice on family planning. The program has all along been integrated with the maternity and child health program. All known methods of contraception are being followed with particular emphasis on the IUCD, which was introduced in the last year of the Third Plan. The response of the people has been encouraging both in urban and rural areas, particularly the response of women to the IUCD. Over 0.8 million IUCD were inserted and more than 1.5 million sterilization operations were performed by the end of the Third Plan.

Certain organizational changes have been introduced in order to facilitate speedy implementation of the program. The Ministry of Health has been redesignated as the Ministry of Health and Family Planning. A Department of Family Planning has been created with a separate Secretary. A Commissioner of Family Planning has been appointed with Regional Directors for better liaison with the State Governments and State organizations for Family Planning. For technical support, a Central Family Planning Institute has been established as an autonomous organization. For giving advice on demography and communication research, two committees have been formed, viz. the Demographic Advisory Committee and the Communication Action Research Committee. For medical and biological research, an Advisory Committee has been formed under the auspices of the Indian Council of Medical Research. A Cabinet Committee has been constituted with the Minister for Planning as Chairman and the Ministers of Finance, Information and Broadcasting, Food and Agriculture and Health as Members. This Committee will facilitate the taking of quick decisions and speeding up the implementation of the program.

## *Program for the Fourth Plan*

In keeping with the basic objective of reducing the birth rate from 40 to 25 per thousand as expeditiously as possible, the outlay of Family Planning has been stepped up from Rs. 27 crores in the Third Plan to Rs. 95 crores in the Fourth Plan. The programs include the recruitment and training of doctors and other workers at various levels to implement the campaign and the provision of supplies and services that go with it. It is intended to cover all the 5,200 Community Development blocks as well as the urban areas where there are large concentrations of population. Provision is being made for audio-visual equipment, technical equipment, mobile units, etc. The Department of Family Planning has, since the preparation of this Chapter proposed an additional outlay of Rs. 144 crores in the Fourth Plan for further intensification of the program. These proposals will be considered and any additional amount that this program can usefully spend will be provided through the Annual Plans.

Although it is intended to promote all methods of contraception, emphasis is being laid on the IUCD because of its efficacy, reversibility and acceptability. Stress is also being laid on all other conventional methods. The successful implementation of this program requires large number of women doctors and steps are being taken to ensure their availability for the purpose. A Central "task force" of doctors has been created and special stipends are being given to women medical students who agree to serve in the family planning program after their graduation. It is also intended to involve private medical practitioners in the program.

The mass education and motivation program will be intensified during the Fourth Plan. Steps have already been taken to make fuller use of various media like films, radio, press, etc., for promoting the acceptance of the family planning program as a way of life. These include mobile audio-visual vans, transistorized radio sets for villages not having electricity and the production of a large number of feature films and short films on family planning.

As already mentioned, the program will be implemented on a coordinated basis involving several Ministries. The most important is the professional work of doctors and other medical personnel under the Ministry of Health and Family Planning. Steps have already been taken to start the manufacture of loops for the IUCD program and the manufacture of condoms, both in private and public sectors. The Ministry of Information and Broadcasting will play a major role in the mass education field. The Block staff of the Department of Community Development and the staff of the Ministries of Education, Local Self Government and Social Security and various industrial organizations will be utilized for the propagation of family planning programs. The overall coordination will be done through the Committee of the Cabinet.

The active participation of Voluntary Agencies, Local Leaders, Local Bodies, Labor Organizations and other associations in various fields of national life is essential to the successful implementation of the program. Since it involves mass contact with the people it is vital that representatives of the people themselves are fully associated with the program. With this end in view, enhanced provision has been made for voluntary organizations and steps are being taken to associate local leadership both in the rural and urban areas.

21

# Population Growth and Distribution in Mainland China

*John S. Aird*

*From* An Economic Profile of Mainland China, Vol. II, *Studies Prepared for the Joint Economic Committee, Congress of the United States, February 1967 U.S. Government Printing Office pp. 357–68 with omissions. Reprinted by permission.*

## *Estimates for the Period 1953–65*

ESTIMATING THE POPULATION by age and sex for the years from 1953 to the present requires certain assumptions about general trends in fertility, mortality, and natural increase, assignment of levels at key points along the trend lines, and interpolation of values for intermediate years. Net migration is a negligible factor and may be ignored. During the First Five-Year Plan period, age specific fertility levels probably did not change much. There may have been some increase in marriage rates during the first years of the regime as a result of the increasing general security of life after many years of war and civil disturbance. Higher marriage rates would have meant an increase in the fertility rates for younger women. There may also have been some general increase in the fertility of women in the child-bearing ages due to improvements in general health and nutrition brought about by the public health programs and the system of food distribution set up by the new regime. On the other hand, the increasing separation of husbands and wives due to the Korean war, the large-scale migration of males from rural areas into the cities, the compulsory labor transfers, frontier settlement movements, and projects involving large numbers of laborers away from their home communities may have caused some reductions in fertility for the groups most directly affected.

The birth control campaign of the 1954–58 period did not receive strong official endorsement until late in 1956 and seems to have encountered much popular resistance and only limited cooperation from local cadres and health workers by the time it lost its priority about June 1958. Though some effects may have been achieved among women cadres and among female workers in the few factories where demonstration campaigns were pursued with vigor, it is doubtful whether the drive to popularize birth control could have affected perceptibly the birth rate for all China.

During the years of acute food shortage and general economic crisis, 1959–62, some of the factors sustaining a high marriage rate and high marital fertility rates were reversed. Not only was there general concern about whether the regime would be able to maintain order, but there were also signs of demoralization among Party, Government, and military personnel. Malnutrition reached such extremes that in some areas the list of symptoms included loss of libido and amenorrhea. It is hard to know how widespread these phenomena actually were or what effect they may have had on the birth rate. The accounts of the most severe distress came, of course, from refugees fleeing the mainland, who for a short period in the spring of 1962 were allowed to enter Hong Kong without restraint by the Chinese Communist border guards. But the refugees undoubtedly came from areas in which conditions were most depressed or anxieties most heightened; their representations, even if accurate, would not have been typical of the entire country. Furthermore, it is doubtful whether fertility could be extremely susceptible to the effects of undernutrition in a species which must have evolved under circumstances in which hunger was a common experience. Though definitive research is lacking, there is reason to believe that the effects of food crises on fertility are slight and of short duration. By the end of 1962, a general economic recovery was evidently under way. More recently this has leveled off somewhat, but economic distress is probably not a factor in determining fertility levels for the time being.

Even though fertility may have shown little reflection of the crisis years, the response of mortality must have been immediate and marked. The symptoms of undernutrition reported from some areas were such as to suggest not only deficiencies in particular food elements but also generally low caloric intake. Though the distress was by no means uniform, varying degrees of undernutrition must have been extremely widespread, and it is to be expected that resistance to disease and capacity to recover would both have been affected. Though there may have been few deaths directly attributable to starvation, there must have been a general increase in mortality from other causes during the worst years of the crisis.

These assumptions lead to the conclusion that age-specific fertility rates were fairly stable from 1953 through 1965, but that age-specific mortality rates followed a decelerating downward trend between 1953 and 1958, took a sharp rise from 1958 through the winter of 1961–62, and dropped back again rather quickly during 1963 and 1964, remaining constant thereafter. The trend of natural increase during the entire period would have been affected primarily by the trends in mortality, though influenced slightly by a downward trend in the crude birth rate caused by changing age composition. However, since the appropriate levels of mortality for the several critical years cannot be determined directly from the information available, they have been derived as a residuals of the assumed levels of fertility and natural increase.

Two fertility assumptions were made for the 1953–65 period, consistent with the two assumptions employed in the reconstruction of the 1953 age-sex structure—one equivalent to a crude birth rate of 40 per thousand and the other equivalent to a crude birth rate of 45 per thousand in 1953. Four assumptions about natural increase in 1953 are associated, two each, with the two assumptions about fertility, making a total of four series of estimates for the period. Increase rates of 22.5 to 20.0 per thousand are combined with the higher birth rate and 20.0 and 17.5 per thousand with the lower. (See Table 2.) The increase rates for all four models are permitted to rise about 2.5 points through falling mortality levels by the end of the First Five-Year Plan period. During the crisis years, natural increase declines in the various models until it is as low as 15.0 per thousand in the highest model and below 10.0 per thousand in the lowest. By 1965, natural increase is almost back to the 1953 levels, though mortality is as low as it was in 1958; the reason is that the crude birth rate had been depressed by a decline in the proportion of the population who are females in the childbearing ages. This decline results largely from the relative increase in the portion of children under fifteen years of age.

## *Projections for the Period 1966–85*

Positing assumptions about the determinants of future demographic trends in Mainland China is even more problematical than making assumptions about those of the recent past. In the latter case there is at least descriptive information to be interpreted and represented in quantitative terms which, however uncertain, presumably bear at least some resemblance to reality. Projections for the future require alternate assessments of prospective economic, social, and political conditions specific to China. The past experience of other countries may be totally irrelevant. Assumptions for China must make adequate allowance for what cannot presently be known, and are necessarily widely divergent.

The immediate prospects for the population of China are in large measure contingent on the outcome of the struggle to make the rate of increase in food production exceed the rate of increase in population. During the First Five-Year Plan period, when official figures were being compiled on food and population, the per capita grain figures declined in two years out of the five, and some doubts were expressed in the press as to whether the five-year average gains indicated by the figures could be trusted or whether, in fact, the food situation was worse than before 1949. After 1957, there were no figures comparable with those for earlier years, but the food crisis of 1959–62 indicates more clearly than official data could that the subsistence margin in China remains very narrow. Extrapolations of economic takeoff based on the easing of food problems during the past four years may therefore be premature. The possibility that China might presently begin to escape from the pressures of population on food supply and proceed at an accelerating pace along a stable course of general economic development cannot be excluded categorially. But it is at least equally possible that China will continue for an indefinite period, as in the immediate past, to labor through cycles of alternating crisis and recovery without much forward motion. It is not impossible that a coincidence of unfavorable circumstances in agriculture, perhaps exacerbated by problems in the economic, political, social, or military spheres, may precipitate a major catastrophe resulting in a net decrement in the population.

Turning to the demographic implications of these alternative prospects, the outlook for fertility ranges from continued high age-specific fertility levels to the beginning within the next few years of a gradual downward trend. High levels will probably persist as long as neither deliberate policies nor domestic economic and social changes are able to alter the basic social institutions which have maintained high birth rates in centuries past. Falling birth rates could be achieved through changes in the customs affecting average age at marriage, the proportion of women marrying, the stability of marital relationships, and the acceptance of contraception, sterilization, and abortion. Official policies may influence the direction and speed of these changes if properly conceived, but policy cannot be expected to bring about a revolution in values and social institutions unless reinforced by other major social changes. In most parts of the world, changes in fertility patterns seem to have been associated with changes in the basis of economic security and in general living levels. Only when the enhancement of both is clearly dependent upon restricting the number of children born will there be sufficient motivation to overcome whatever traditional barriers stand in the way of widespread adoption of methods of family limitation. In Mainland China, the relative scarcity of consumer goods, the relative uniformity of wages, and the relative security of employment and of health and welfare services do not uniformly point to the advantages of having fewer children in the effort to improve the family's economic status.

For the present, it is doubtful whether the changes in political and economic institutions attempted by the Chinese Communists have sufficiently penetrated the institutional infrastructure which is most directly responsible for fertility behavior to reverse customs and motivations toward high fertility. The discussions in Chinese newspapers and journals of the "socialist transformation" of the countryside contrast sharply with some reports of visitors and refugees which describe the persistence of traditional practices and relationships in villages. Despite some sanguine views expressed in the press in 1957 and 1958, it is doubtful whether the conspicuous mass propaganda that climaxed the first birth control campaign, which began in 1954 and ended in 1958, had achieved a significant degree of success in either urban or rural areas before its termination. In a population as large as China's, in which fertility control is virtually unknown, what may be significant for the pharmaceutical and rubber industries may not be significant for the crude birth rate.

Moreover, it is not completely clear what the official position now is on the question of fertility control. Since 1962, encouragement has again been given to contraception, sterilization, and the postponement of marriage. The three-child family has been declared ideal, and abortion is once more available under the liberal provisions which had been attacked by the China Medical Association in 1957. However, the implication in some official statements that the matter is not regarded as very urgent is at least consistent with the moderate tone and scale of the current propaganda campaign. Though there have been some reports that food and cloth rations and maternity leave are not granted after the fourth child, these potentially repressive measures are apparently not universally or strictly applied. Falling birth rates would no doubt be welcome, but China's leaders do not seem to have attached high priority to this objective during recent years.

The prospects for mortality range from a resumption of the downward trend of the early 1950s at a somewhat more gradual pace to a continuation of present average levels with periodic sharp increases during intervals of domestic crisis. If a moderate economic development gets underway in the near future, a part of the investment capital created by the growing economy will probably be set aside for general health improvement. Health services are popular with the people, whose cooperation must be cultivated even in an authoritarian system, and may also increase the productivity of labor by cutting worktime losses due to illness and by extending the average working life and thus recouping more on the investment in labor force training and experience. The Chinese Communist commitment to general health improvement has been one of the more stable elements of domestic policy, though, like most other elements, it has not been served with unvarying funds and efforts. However, beyond a certain point, which may already have been reached, the per capita costs of further health improvements rise very sharply and the effects of these improvements on the death rate becomes less and less apparent. Moreover, it is one thing to provide the latest medical and surgical advances for Party leaders and important technical personnel in the major cities and quite another thing to make the same services generally available throughout the countryside. The dissemination of high cost services is not likely to be rapid under the most favorable circumstances. Hence, in Mainland China there is little possibility of an immediate marked decline in mortality levels.

Radical fluctuations in mortality levels during periodic food crises would probably mean no appreciable reduction of general mortality during successive periods of recovery, since a long-term downward trend in mortality would probably be possible only under conditions which would preclude food crises. In fact, the overall mortality trend implicit in a situation of recurrent crisis would probably be upward unless the severity of the crises was diminishing. If the crises were to become more severe, the general trend of mortality might be sharply upward. If one such crisis reached sufficient severity and extent, perhaps in conjunction with other kinds of civil disturbance, to disorganize the system of emergency food distribution over a large and populous part of the country, mortality could attain a level not seen in China since the major famines of the nineteenth century. The scale of the catastrophe could well be far greater and the recovery less rapid than in former famines since the Chinese population today is probably more dependent than ever before in its history on the centrally planned and controlled storage, movement, and distribution of food in times of local distress. The return to a condition of local self-sufficiency would probably mean a lowering of the maximum population which the affected areas would be able to sustain even in normal times, and the combination of factors could result in a considerable ecological readjustment. Once the readjustment was completed, the relationship of human numbers to food resources and the general economic situation could be quite different from those which have prevailed during the past century.

The possibilities for future trends in fertility and mortality in China are derivative of alternate assumptions about future economic, political, and social developments, hence not all combinations and permutations can be incorporated into rational models. Generally speaking, models which anticipate successful national development imply falling birth and death rates, and ultimately, if the results of that development are not risked in a world conflagration, declining population increase rates associated with rising living levels. Anticipations of faltering or unsuccessful national development have more ambiguous implications for demographic model construction. If the degree of failure is enough to produce recurrent or chronic undernutrition, fertility may be somewhat depressed; if it is simply enough to cause a return to higher infant mortality rates and thus to remove some of the incentive for family planning, birth rates may remain relatively high or even increase. If China's economy continues as in the recent past to flounder periodically without making any significant per capita gains, the rate of increase in the population will probably be higher over a more prolonged period than if the economy gains or fails more rapidly hereafter.

Demographic models which embody assumptions of periodic crisis or a major catastrophe cannot be constructed by means of the simple extrapolation of trends in vital rates which serve reasonably well for countries in which more stable demographic development is expected. Some stylization of the demographic particularities of a given configuration of socioeconomic events is possible, but even so the models tend to have a specificity beyond what is customary in population projections. A recurrent crisis model must show fluctuating birth and death rates, but before their cycles can be laid out it is necessary to decide on the time of occurrence, degree of severity, and duration of each crisis, and also to make certain assumptions about the extent to which fertility and mortality are to be affected in each instance. Since there is no basic research along these lines to serve as a guide in making assumptions, all such decisions are extremely arbitrary. Hence, it is obvious that no meaning can be attached to the demographic values projected for any particular year; it is only the overall pattern that is significant, and even that is only one representation of the general conception of recurrent crisis which might have been represented in a variety of other ways.

Four projection models for the 1966–85 period are presented here, each a continuation of one of the four models for the preceeding period. Model III embodies the most optimistic prospects for economic development, with falling fertility and mortality levels. In model IV, development proceeds slowly for the next ten years, followed by a period of deterioration during which fertility ceases to fall and mortality reverses its previous trend and begins to rise once more. Model I assumes that two crises similar in nature to that of the 1959–62 period occur within the next twenty years, each more severe and prolonged than its predecessor; fertility and mortality show corresponding variation, but the long-term trend in mortality is upward and that for fertility is unchanged. Model II traces the demographic effects of a catastrophic famine resulting in a net decrement of 100 million in the population of China over a four-year period, 1970–73, followed by a recovery which restored fertility and mortality by 1985 to the levels assumed for 1965.

The estimated and projected populations for selected years from 1953 through 1985 generated by the four models just described are given in Table 1. Crude birth, death, and natural increase rates for the same years are given in Table 2. Age-sex structures for each model as of midyear 1953, yearend 1965, and yearend 1985, are given in Tables 3 and 4.

It can be seen from Table 1 that under all but the most pessimistic expectations the population of China surpasses 1 billion by 1985, but the demographic circumstances accompanying this growth are quite different from one model to another, as Table 2 shows. For model III, both birth and death rates fall at about the same rate through most of the period of the projections, with the result that natural increase is relatively constant at around 2 per cent per year until almost the end of the period. For model IV, birth and death rates are higher and almost constant for most of the period, with the result that natural increase is also relatively constant though not as high as for model III.

Model I has even higher fertility levels and high and irregular mortality levels. During the pit of each crisis there is some net decrease in population. The effects of the catastrophe in the early 1970s assumed in model II is apparent in the high death rates during the worst years and in the very high birth rates in subsequent years as a result of the concentration of surviving population in

## *Table 1—Estimates and Projections of the Population of Mainland China*[a]

| *Model and series* | *1953* | *1955* | *1960* | *1965* | *1970* | *1975* | *1980* | *1985* |
|---|---|---|---|---|---|---|---|---|
| Model I: | | | | | | | | |
| Census-based series | 576 | 603 | 682 | 743 | 817 | 868 | 926 | 960 |
| 5 per cent undercount series | 606 | 635 | 718 | 783 | 860 | 914 | 975 | 1,011 |
| 10 per cent undercount series | 640 | 671 | 758 | 826 | 908 | 964 | 1,029 | 1,067 |
| 15 per cent undercount series | 678 | 710 | 802 | 875 | 962 | 1,021 | 1,090 | 1,130 |
| Model II: | | | | | | | | |
| Census-based series | 577 | 601 | 671 | 718 | 788 | 696 | 765 | 859 |
| 5 per cent undercount series | 607 | 633 | 707 | 755 | 830 | 733 | 805 | 904 |
| 10 per cent undercount series | 641 | 668 | 746 | 797 | 876 | 774 | 850 | 955 |
| 15 per cent undercount series | 679 | 707 | 790 | 844 | 927 | 819 | 900 | 1,011 |
| Model III: | | | | | | | | |
| Census-based series | 577 | 601 | 672 | 734 | 814 | 904 | 1,003 | 1,104 |
| 5 per cent undercount series | 607 | 633 | 708 | 772 | 857 | 951 | 1,056 | 1,162 |
| 10 per cent undercount series | 641 | 668 | 747 | 815 | 904 | 1,004 | 1,114 | 1,226 |
| 15 per cent under count series | 679 | 707 | 791 | 863 | 957 | 1,063 | 1,180 | 1,298 |
| Model IV: | | | | | | | | |
| Census-based series | 578 | 599 | 662 | 715 | 779 | 853 | 938 | 1,026 |
| 5 per cent undercount series | 608 | 631 | 697 | 752 | 821 | 897 | 987 | 1,080 |
| 10 per cent undercount series | 642 | 666 | 736 | 794 | 866 | 947 | 1,042 | 1,140 |
| 15 per cent undercount series | 679 | 705 | 779 | 841 | 917 | 1,003 | 1,104 | 1,207 |

[a] January 1st figures in millions.

## *Table 2—Estimated and Projected Crude Birth, Death, and Natural Increase Rates for Mainland China*[a]

| *Year* | *Model I* | *Model II* | *Model III* | *Model IV* |
|---|---|---|---|---|
| Crude birth rates: | | | | |
| 1953 | 45.0 | 45.0 | 40.0 | 40.0 |
| 1955 | 44.3 | 44.4 | 39.6 | 39.7 |
| 1960 | 42.3 | 42.6 | 38.1 | 38.4 |
| 1965 | 40.8 | 41.5 | 36.8 | 37.3 |
| 1970 | 38.2 | 36.0 | 35.5 | 36.7 |
| 1975 | 41.1 | 45.9 | 34.2 | 37.0 |
| 1980 | 39.1 | 48.8 | 31.8 | 37.6 |
| 1985 | 41.5 | 47.7 | 26.5 | 37.9 |
| Crude death rates: | | | | |
| 1953 | 22.5 | 25.0 | 20.0 | 22.5 |
| 1955 | 19.5 | 22.2 | 17.3 | 19.6 |
| 1960 | 22.5 | 26.1 | 19.3 | 21.8 |
| 1965 | 18.4 | 20.9 | 16.1 | 18.6 |
| 1970 | 39.7 | 55.2 | 14.6 | 19.4 |
| 1975 | 21.1 | 31.7 | 13.2 | 17.8 |
| 1980 | 48.1 | 26.2 | 11.6 | 19.6 |
| 1985 | 27.5 | 24.6 | 9.8 | 21.5 |
| Natural increase rates: | | | | |
| 1953 | 22.5 | 20.0 | 20.0 | 17.5 |
| 1955 | 24.8 | 22.2 | 22.3 | 20.1 |
| 1960 | 19.7 | 16.4 | 18.8 | 16.7 |
| 1965 | 22.4 | 20.6 | 20.8 | 18.7 |
| 1970 | −1.4 | −19.2 | 20.9 | 17.2 |
| 1975 | 20.1 | 14.3 | 21.0 | 19.2 |
| 1980 | −9.0 | 22.6 | 20.2 | 18.0 |
| 1985 | 14.0 | 23.1 | 16.7 | 16.5 |

[a] Per thousand population per year.

## *Table 3—Reported and Estimated Distributions of the Population of Mainland China, 1953[a]*

| Age | Official data[a] BOTH SEXES | Official data MALE | Official data FEMALE | Models I and II BOTH SEXES | Models I and II MALE | Models I and II FEMALE | Models III and IV BOTH SEXES | Models III and IV MALE | Models III and IV FEMALE |
|---|---|---|---|---|---|---|---|---|---|
| All ages | 100.0 | 51.8 | 48.2 | 100.0 | 50.6 | 49.4 | 100.0 | 50.2 | 49.8 |
| 0 to 4 years | 15.6 | 8.0 | 7.6 | 16.3 | 8.3 | 8.0 | 15.1 | 7.7 | 7.4 |
| 5 to 14 years | 20.3 | 10.9 | 9.4 | 22.4 | 11.5 | 10.9 | 21.4 | 10.9 | 10.5 |
| 15 to 24 years | 17.3 | 9.1 | 8.2 | 19.2 | 9.8 | 9.4 | 19.1 | 9.8 | 9.3 |
| 25 to 34 years | 14.6 | 7.8 | 6.8 | 14.7 | 7.3 | 7.4 | 14.2 | 7.0 | 7.2 |
| 35 to 44 years | 12.0 | 6.2 | 5.8 | 11.1 | 5.6 | 5.5 | 11.1 | 5.4 | 5.7 |
| 45 to 54 years | 9.3 | 4.7 | 4.6 | 8.2 | 4.2 | 4.0 | 9.0 | 4.5 | 4.5 |
| 55 to 64 years | 6.5 | 3.3 | 3.2 | 5.1 | 2.5 | 2.6 | 6.1 | 3.0 | 3.1 |
| 65 to 74 years | 3.4 | 1.5 | 1.9 | 2.4 | 1.1 | 1.3 | 3.1 | 1.5 | 1.6 |
| 75 years and over | 1.0 | .3 | .7 | .6 | .3 | .3 | .9 | .4 | .5 |
| 0 to 14 years | 35.9 | 18.9 | 17.0 | 38.7 | 19.7 | 19.0 | 36.5 | 18.6 | 17.9 |
| 15 to 59 years | 56.8 | 29.6 | 27.2 | 56.1 | 28.4 | 27.7 | 56.8 | 28.4 | 28.4 |
| 60 years and over | 7.3 | 3.3 | 4.0 | 5.2 | 2.5 | 2.7 | 6.7 | 3.2 | 3.5 |

[a] Midyear figures in percentage of the total population.
[b] According to data provided by Ch'en Ta and T'ien Feng-t'iao.

## *Table 4—Estimated and Projected Distributions of the Population of Mainland China, Both Sexes*

[Year end figures in per cent]

| Age | Model I | Model II | Model III | Model IV |
|---|---|---|---|---|
| *1965* | | | | |
| All ages | 100.0 | 100.0 | 100.0 | 100.0 |
| 0 to 4 years | 15.6 | 15.3 | 14.7 | 14.5 |
| 5 to 14 years | 26.2 | 25.8 | 24.9 | 24.7 |
| 15 to 24 years | 17.5 | 18.0 | 17.2 | 17.5 |
| 25 to 34 years | 13.7 | 14.0 | 14.1 | 14.3 |
| 35 to 44 years | 10.7 | 10.8 | 10.9 | 11.0 |
| 45 to 54 years | 7.6 | 7.7 | 7.9 | 7.9 |
| 55 to 64 years | 5.2 | 5.1 | 5.9 | 5.8 |
| 65 to 74 years | 2.7 | 2.6 | 3.3 | 3.2 |
| 75 years and over | .8 | .7 | 1.1 | 1.1 |
| 0 to 14 years | 41.8 | 41.1 | 39.7 | 39.2 |
| 15 to 59 years | 52.5 | 53.4 | 53.3 | 53.9 |
| 60 years and over | 5.7 | 5.5 | 7.0 | 6.9 |
| *1985* | | | | |
| All ages | 100.0 | 100.0 | 100.0 | 100.0 |
| 0 to 4 years | 14.7 | 17.9 | 12.5 | 14.7 |
| 5 to 14 years | 23.0 | 21.6 | 23.6 | 23.7 |
| 15 to 24 years | 19.9 | 16.6 | 19.2 | 18.6 |
| 25 to 34 years | 16.7 | 17.2 | 15.5 | 15.2 |
| 35 to 44 years | 10.4 | 11.1 | 10.4 | 10.3 |
| 45 to 54 years | 7.4 | 7.8 | 8.2 | 8.0 |
| 55 to 64 years | 4.8 | 4.9 | 5.8 | 5.5 |
| 65 to 74 years | 2.4 | 2.3 | 3.3 | 2.9 |
| 75 years and over | .7 | .6 | 1.5 | 1.1 |
| 0 to 14 years | 37.7 | 39.5 | 36.1 | 38.3 |
| 15 to 59 years | 57.1 | 55.5 | 56.6 | 55.3 |
| 60 years and over | 5.2 | 5.0 | 7.3 | 6.4 |

the childbearing ages. Other comments on age composition will be reserved until the discussion of characteristics of the population in section III.

What is most important for users of these population estimates and projections is to take notice of the range of population figures that is possible within particular models and between one model and another. For 1953, the range within any given model produced by the varying base totals is 100 million; by 1985 this has widened to almost 200 million in some cases. The varying assumptions for different models, though they result in no appreciable difference in the totals in 1953, yield a range of almost 300 million by 1985. The total range of the figures by 1985 is from 859 to 1,298 million, or just under half a billion persons. Moreover, the varying magnitudes apply proportionately to the numbers of persons in various age groups by sex and the numbers of birth and deaths implied by the different models. If these ranges convey nothing else, they should serve to underline one important fact about the present and prospective population of Mainland China: the wide margin of uncertainty about its size and rate of growth.

## *Characteristics and Distribution of the Population*

Whatever the exact total, the magnitude of China's population is its most conspicuous characteristic, and certainly an impressive one. But once the observation has been made that the Chinese mainland has the largest concentration of human beings under a single political authority anywhere in the world, very few of the essential questions that this observation prompts can be answered without going further into the characteristics of that population. From the standpoint of economic, political, and military power it is by no means a certainty that a large population is an unqualified advantage in proportion to its size, or that China's position and influence in world affairs should be accorded gratuitously on the basis of proportional representation. What matters most about a large population with a high rate of increase is whether its productive members have achieved a high and rising level of skill and productivity or whether numbers and increase rate alike constitute an impediment to development. Answers to these questions must be found by analysis of the characteristics of the population and of the economy as a whole and their changes over time.

However, there is very little that can be said with assurance about the characteristics of the population on the basis of available data. The 1953 census did not collect infortion on literacy, educational attainment, occupation, employment, or income, and though there were subsequent censuses and surveys of specific segments of the nonagricultural labor force which did collect some of these kinds of information, the coverage of the urban population in general is incomplete and there is virtually no coverage of the rural population. Although the census was supposed to provide data needed for national economic planning, economic characteristics of the population were not included on the grounds that this would have made the task of census taking impossible. General inferences may be drawn as to how the population is distributed with respect to these characteristics, but definitive official data are lacking. Only the strictly demographic characteristics of age and sex may be estimated for the whole population with any degree of assurance.

### DISTRIBUTION BY AGE AND SEX

Regardless of the model used, the population of China has a relatively heavy concentration of persons in the younger ages in 1953. Between 35 and 40 per cent of the population is under fifteen years of age, whereas persons aged sixty and over account for only 5 to 7 per cent of the total population. The 1953 age-sex structure is much influenced by the fact that mortality rates, including infant mortality, had fallen sharply from traditionally high levels after the pacification of the Chinese mainland in 1949; lower infant mortality rates combined with continuing high birth rates resulted in much larger cohorts of children in the ages zero through four than had previously been found in those ages.

As the new larger cohorts grow older and are replaced by other enlarged cohorts, the proportion of the total population at ages under fifteen actually increases for a time, until by 1965 it is either just below or a little above 40 per cent in all models. The population aged sixty and over increases only slightly during the period 1953–65, but as a result of the increasing percentages of old and young, the proportion of the population in the adult years declines about 3 percentage points. By 1985, the proportion of adults rises in all models, but the population remains comparatively youthful, with 35 to 40 per cent younger than fifteen years of age. There are fairly marked differences between models in the proportion at ages zero to four in 1985 as a result of the differences in the birth rates in the preceding five years. For example, model III has only 12.5 per cent of the population in the ages under five, whereas model II has nearly 18.0 per cent in these ages.

The 1953 census gave an overall sex ratio for Mainland China of 107.6 males per 100 females, which would mean that males exceeded females by over 20 million. The model age-sex distributions used in constructing the estimates and projections presented here include varying allowances for high mortality among males in wars, civil disturbances, and political executions during the century prior to 1953. They show sex ratios well below that of the 1953 census: 102.3 under one set of assumptions and 100.6 under the other. Even taking into account the range of totals for the base population as of 1953, these sex ratios imply a surplus of males of only from 1 to 7 million. Between 1953 and 1965, the models show very little change in the overall sex ratios; in models I and II they fall somewhat, whereas in models III and IV they rise somewhat, the difference due mainly to the differences in age-sex structure between the four models at the outset. Between 1966 and 1985, a long-term trend toward higher sex ratios is evident as the male-deficient cohorts from earlier years become a less and less significant part of the total population. By 1985, sex ratios for all four models exceed 101, and that for model II has almost reached 104 as a result of the especially high mortality levels for females in the childbearing ages and among older age groups in the course of the catastrophe assumed in that model in the early 1970s.

The variability of estimates of China's age-sex structure can best be illustrated by citing the ranges in absolute figures for certain key age groups. Applying the maximum range in base totals to the various models, the total number of births in China is between 23 and 31 million in 1953, between 27 and 36 million in 1965, and between 30 and 50 million in 1985. The annual population increment is between 10 and 15 million in 1953, between 14 and 20 million in 1965, and between 14 and 24 million in 1985. The population in the primary school ages, seven through twelve years, is roughly 75 to 90 million in 1953, 110 to 140 million in 1965, and 125 to 190 million in 1985. If both primary and secondarly school-age children are considered, the total number is roughly 145 to 175 million in 1953, 200 to 250 million in 1965, and 180 to 350 million in 1985. In the labor force ages, eighteen through sixty years for men and eighteen through fifty-five years for women, the range is roughly 290 to 340 million in 1953, 330 to 400 million in 1965, and 450 to 650 million in 1985.

These figures also indicate how the magnitude of China's population affects the scale of whatever economic, social, and political arrangements must be made to provide the food, clothing, housing, health care, employment, education, welfare services, and other essential goods and services needed by particular age and sex groupings of a growing population. For example, around 1953 there is an annual increment of 1.0 to 2.0 million in the population of primary school ages; by 1965 this age group is increasing at the rate of 1.6 to 3.0 million a year; by 1985 the increase reaches 3.5 million a year under the most optimistic projections for economic development and fertility control. To have universal education through the secondary level by 1985, the schools in China would have to accommodate over 6 million new students annually under the same optimistic assumptions.

The number of new people entering the

labor force ages each year is between 11 and 13 million in 1953 but rises to between 15 and 26 million by 1985; the annual net increase in the labor force ages rises from around 4 to 6 million in 1953 to a maximum of 15 million in 1985. The population seventy-five years and older, which amounts to only 3 to 6 million persons in 1953, reaches a maximum of nearly 19 million by 1985, according to the model with the lowest mortality levels (model III). If current policies tending to separate aged persons from their families and accommodate them in old people's homes, euphemistically called "happiness houses" in China, are still in force by 1985, the national budget for this kind of "happiness" will have to be greatly expanded. Needless to say, meeting the minimal needs of a growing population in all sectors at once is a formidable task requiring planned national investment on a scale well beyond the capacity of the economy or of the administrative system at the present time. Given the scale of this problem, foreign aid is not likely to be a significant factor even if China's relations with other countries were such that it could be invited and received.

22

# Dealing with Population Problems

*Leo A. Orleans*

*From* Bulletin of the Atomic Scientists, Science and Public Affairs *22, no. 6, (June 1966): 22–26 with omissions. Reprinted by permission.*

It is, of course, well known that the study of Communist China is seriously hampered by the paucity and questionable validity of the published data. Nevertheless, an economist, although lacking the detailed statistics, can pick up enough bits and pieces from the mainland newspapers and other publications to assume certain activities and developments and to support his estimates. A specialist in foreign affairs can screen the daily flow of propaganda from Peking, follow China's exchanges with the Soviet Union, and observe her activities in the developing countries of Asia, Africa, and Latin America.

A demographer, however, is at a particular disadvantage, not only because during the past half-dozen or more years there has been virtually no mention of the subject of population, but also because most of the population data published during the early and middle 1950s were insufficient in quantity and inadequate in quality. Furthermore, there is no pre-1950 base for population analysis—no reliable benchmark that would permit meaningful projections and analogies. The few published population statistics have been thoroughly and repeatedly analyzed, digested, and debated.

## *Estimates of Size*

This article will not attempt to come up with yet another estimate of the size and rate of growth of China's population, but rather will examine three major premises:

1. The government in Peking knows neither the size nor the rate of growth of China's population.
2. The size and rate of growth of the population have been of continuous concern to the regime, despite vacillating population policies.
3. Given the desire to reduce fertility and a willingness to expend the necessary resources and effort, there is reason to believe that the communists may now be able to achieve a measurable drop in the birthrate.

Virtually all population estimates for China move forward and backward from the mid-1953 figure of 582.6 million—a product of a year-long intensive effort to count and register the country's population. Although frequently maligned, the figure is nevertheless generally accepted as the best available and the most usable approximation of China's population. The enumerators and registrars received training courses, while the general population was informed about the importance of cooperation and accuracy. There is no reason to believe that the 1953 effort was not genuine or that there was politically motivated tampering with the figures once they reached Peking.

Theoretically, the registers established after 1953 should have provided the regime both with a total population count and with the necessary data to calculate the nation's birth and death rates. Current population registers were to contain basic information on the number of permanent residents, as well as on births and deaths.

It was, presumably, on the basis of these registers that in 1957 Peking published the official year-end estimates for the country's population for 1954, 1955, and 1956 and followed them up with a series of population totals by province as of the end of 1957. The question, of course, is whether the registers and special surveys conducted during these years were capable of providing the government with accurate and acceptable population statistics.

Although population registers for China go back hundreds of years, neither the *pao chia* records of the Ch'ing dynasty, nor the various population counts of the Republic of China, were established for the purpose of deriving demographic data. In all cases the major intention was political control as much as the need for taxation, military draft, or labor conscription. The motivation for population registers of the present regime, since 1956 under the Ministry of Public Security, continues to be political control, as explicitly stated in the 1958 regulations governing population registers: "These regulations are enacted to maintain social order, to protect the rights and interests of the citizens, and to serve Socialist construction." This alone would be a major handicap to the collection of data for population analysis.

Other factors responsible for the inadequacy of statistical reporting in China are the poorly organized and directed statistical system, the shortage of trained statistical personnel, and the absence of motivation and integrity on the part of many of the people handling statistics. Finally, the post-1953 population figures may be questioned on the basis of demographic considerations, since the reported high rates of population growth imply death rates that are inconsistent with the medical, social, political, and economic conditions of the country. Whatever their defects, however, the figures are accepted and used, and for all practical purposes constitute the most recent population data of any consequence.

Since 1957 there have been virtually no population statistics emanating from Communist China. The reason for this may well be the fact that the already weak statistical system received two grave setbacks. First, as part of the Great Leap, much of the statistical responsibility was taken away from the experienced personnel and given to party leaders, who were instructed to produce only figures that would be politically acceptable. Many of the standard statistical principles were termed capitalistic and were discredited and discarded, while literally millions of people with no formal training were reported to be participating in "statistical work," with predictable results. The second setback to statistics resulted from the economic crisis that came on the heels of the Great Leap, when survival, rather than accurate statistical reporting, was uppermost in the minds of the Chinese leaders. Since 1961, along with the gradual improvement in China's economy, there has been an apparent return of some of the statistical responsibilities to the statisticians. Much of their effort, however, has been devoted to reconstituting the demolished system; there has been no evidence of sufficient progress to produce current population statistics.

A good example of the flagrant and unsophisticated use and abuse of population figures was provided by a series of recently published figures for Tibet. The report stated that between 1960 and 1965 the population of Tibet Autonomous Region increased at a rate of two per cent each year, and grew from 1,197,000 to 1,321,500. Is this reasonable? Not entirely. In the first place, considering the years of complete absence of population data, remote and sparsely settled Tibet would seem to be the most unlikely region to produce any precise population figures. In the second place, considering the economic and medical backwardness of the area, the lasting consequences of the 1959 uprising, and the still unstable political situation, the reported two per cent rate of growth between 1960 and 1965 seems excessive. Finally, if the 2 per cent growth rate is applied to the reported 1960 base population for five consecutive years, the exact 1965 figure is obtained. Unfortunately, real populations, particularly those undergoing the type of change implied by the reports, simply do not grow in this orderly fashion. It would have been much more realistic to show an ascending trend.

Why then would the Chinese report a 2 per cent rate of growth for Tibet's population? Because this rate has come to represent an acceptable minimum for a developing country. A lower rate would imply that perhaps the regime has not been able to introduce the necessary reforms, improve the standard of living, and thus reduce mortality.

The figures were obviously designed to make a point and to impress.

Is it possible that the Chinese actually do have population figures for the country, but do not publish them because of security considerations? This is a most unlikely premise. They published national totals for some ten years, and there is no reason to believe they would cease publication if the data were available for the following years. Provincial population distributions were released for 1953, 1954, and 1957 and individual *hsien* populations were reported in various dispatches. The fact that so few data have been published on population charactierstics such as age and sex composition, for example, may well be an admission that the system has been unable to produce such information.

On the other hand, because in the past the basic population figures were reported when available does not necessarily insure publication of any future figures, should the registration system again begin to function. It is quite possible that the regime would have difficulty in rationalizing the past with the present and in explaining any contradictions and implications inherent in the new figures. The new total population for the mainland may reveal the full intensity of the food crisis of the early sixties, for example. It may also be difficult to make the new total fit the reported growth rates of the middle fifties, if the latter were as unrealistically high as suspected. Another deterrent to the publication of the new figures may arise if the actual or implied death rate turned out to be higher than the incredibly low death rates of 13 and 11, reported for 1952 and 1957 by the Ministry of Health. Since statistics in Communist China must always show progress, it would be most surprising if Peking reported any figures that would imply a higher mortality.

The above discussion should not suggest that there is complete ignorance of the composition of the country's population. Certainly, there is a fairly accurate count of individuals with higher education and special skills; there should be adequate figures on the number and occupational distribution of workers and employees in the state sector of the economy; the population registers within individual cities probably provide usable estimates of the number of people living in these centers; even in the rural areas, the individual team leader undoubtedly knows the number of families under his control and the number of hands that are available for work. What is suggested, however, is that the system breaks down as statistics move up through the various rural and urban administrative levels, and that Peking is, in fact, ignorant of the size of the country's population.

## *The Absorption of Labour*

Although the Chinese Communists do not know the size and rate of growth of the country's population, they do know that the enormous obstacles facing the country would be easier to tackle if the annual population increment were five or eight million, rather than 10 or 15 million. Ignorance of whether there are 500 or 600 million peasants in the country may not basically affect China's overall plans and policies, but the absence of precise information has not clouded the leadership's recognition of the problems associated with a large population. For example, according to Edgar Snow, "China's leaders are clearly aware that a substantial gain in living standards can only come about through a reduction in birthrates."

Thus China's leaders were never oblivious to the immediate and potential consequences of the 15 million or more births that occur annually. Their minds did not fluctuate along with the vacillations of the prescribed population policies; the problem of numbers was too great and too pervasive.

It is to the credit of the regime that, despite the limitations of resources, China has been able to give almost all children at least a four-year primary education, to provide them at least with the minimum medical facilities, and, of course, to feed and clothe this unproductive multitude.

But after a child is reared and educated, he must be put to work in such a way as to assure the maximum benefit to the state from his activities, be he peasant, worker, or professor. How well has China been able to utilize her manpower in the past and what are these policies at present?

The ability of China to utilize effectively the hundreds of millions of persons in the working ages depends directly on the well-being of the country's economy and on a balanced growth of both its industrial and agricultural sectors.

To examine the problems of labor absorption, let us consider separately the urban and rural sectors of the economy.

## *In the Urban Sector*

The 1953 urban population of China was reported at 77 million, or just over 13 per cent of the total population. A few years later, when the State Statistical Bureau published China's total population, it also included an urban population series covering the years 1949 through 1956. These figures, ranging from 57.6 to 89.2 million, indicate an average annual growth of 4.5 million, but with significant fluctuations from year to year. The rapid growth of the urban population was the result of two major forces: (1) the push applied by the ruthlessly enforced collectivization of agriculture, and (2) the pull exerted by rapid industrial development. The migration of some 20 million peasants into the cities between 1949 and 1957 resulted in serious problems of housing, feeding, and employment of rural migrants. Throughout this period, efforts were made to return peasants to their villages and to restrict the continuous flow of the "non-productive elements" into the cities. Yet despite new and stringent regulations, the unplanned rural-to-urban flow of migrants was never entirely halted and, in fact, received new impetus with the introduction of the Leap Forward in 1958.

Past experience and reason make it obvious that the cities of China could not possibly absorb a reported 20 million persons in less than a year. Apparently the figure was related to the almost overnight increase in the reported number of workers and employees in the productive sector of the economy, which, in turn, was actually the result of a reclassification of millions of persons, both urban and rural, to the category of the labor force that receives wages and salaries from the state.

Because the definition of "urban" is partly based on the occupational composition of the labor force in a particular locality, such a reclassification could have shifted many communities into the "urban" category, without any major shifts of population. There was also, however, an actual acceleration of migration into the cities during this period.

In 1959 the Minister of Building stated that the urban population had grown to "about 100 million", probably a fairly reasonable estimate. At any rate, within the context of the present discussion, the important factor is that even during this period of most rapid industrialization, China's cities have not been able to accommodate the surplus rural manpower.

The serious internal crisis that developed on the heels of the Leap, and the ensuing natural calamities, forced a complete re-evaluation of China's economic policies.

The accent on agriculture instead of industry went hand in hand with renewed efforts to control and reduce the urban population. Many of the industrial enterprises in urban areas were forced out of operation by the shortage of raw materials, particularly food processing and textile industries. Other enterprises that were designated as uneconomic were closed down and the excess labor thus created was sent back to the rural areas. Every extra person in the city was considered to be a burden on agriculture.

Although the authorities probably were unable to transfer all the surplus urban manpower to the rural areas, "the urban population was appropriately reduced." Despite reports that the 1963 grain output in Communist China had returned to approximately the 1957 level and has continued to increase gradually, urban growth is still restricted. This is not only the result of the continued emphasis on agriculture and a shortage of industrial crops effected by the diversion of acreage to food production, but also because many thousands of young urban "intellectuals" are still being evacuated to the countryside.

There are indications that, at least for the time being, the communists may be willing to limit urban growth to little more than its own natural increase, which would amount annually to perhaps two million persons.

The purpose of this discussion is not to arrive at a specific estimate of the urban population, but simply to indicate that during the foreseeable future, the expansion of the industrial sector of the economy cannot be relied on to accommodate even the annual increment into the labor force. Rural China has had to find a place for them in the past, and will have to do so in the future.

## *In the Rural Sector*

The communists made no secret of their awareness of the problems posed by disguised underemployment and seasonal unemployment in rural China. As with everything else, the drastic change came in 1958 with the introduction of the people's communes and the Great Leap: Peking abandoned its propaganda for birth control, "liberated" the women from domestic chores to work in the field and factory, and proclaimed a severe manpower shortage throughout China.

The manpower shortage was real, but artificially created. A nationwide campaign was initiated to mobilize every available pair of hands for some form of productive labor.

Most significant was the diversion of millions of male peasants from farming to irrigation projects, manure collection, and various other water and soil conservation activities, as well as to the much-publicized production of steel in backyard furnaces. Whereas it was reported that in 1957 about 90 per cent of the peasant's time was devoted to agricultural and subsidiary production, by 1960 it was stated that "only a little over 50 per cent of the manpower is actually engaged in agricultural production." The natural calamities, held to be solely responsible for the crisis, were actually superimposed on already critical rural conditions resulting from the inefficient utilization of available manpower, attempts to do too much in too short a time, and general mismanagement. The consequences were disastrous and, according to some, brought China to the brink of collapse.

It is important to note here that, despite the economic crisis, the communist approach to labor utilization during the late 1950s was economically sound. There was a reasonable effort to reallocate individuals who were not fully active economically into alternative employment, where they could make a positive contribution, no matter how slight. The problem was that reclamation projects—irrigation, drainage, desalinization, and other mass programs—became the primary purpose, rather than a bonus, and millions of people spent their time in marginal labor at the expense of agriculture. Similarly, the idea of introducing some basic, handicraft-type industries into rural areas was a sensible attempt at utilizing excess manpower; it was the unreasonable emphasis on industrial production, suitable neither to manpower nor resources, that was so harmful to the effort. There are indications, however, that China is now following a much more reasonable approach toward effective utilization of excess labor forces.

During the last few years many of the Leap Forward schemes for utilizing surplus manpower have been reintroduced in a different wrapping and with a more rational approach. The emphasis is on developing "multiple operations" and striving for general improvement and expansion of "subsidiary occupations" by "fully developing the human potential, fully utilizing the natural resources, and opening up ways for multiple operations." Translated, this means, that when people can be spared from basic agricultural production, they should be utilized in reclamation projects, in expanding arable land, in developing mountain lands, in planting subsidiary crops, and in providing special care for domestic animals.

It is quite apparent to China's leaders that high population growth tends to perpetuate the labor surplus characteristic of the economy, that the growth of rural population increases agriculture's own consumption requirements, and that the implementation of the prescribed measures would be facilitated by reducing numbers. They are also aware that as the increasing numbers of women reaching childbearing age themselves bear children, there will be secondary waves of an even larger birthrate to cope with.

## *The Future of Population Control*

There were three main reasons why efforts to control fertility in the middle fifties did not meet with the success of some of the other mass campaigns: (1) there was no receptiveness or motivation on the part of the millions of largely illiterate or poorly educated peasants; (2) the government was not able to provide the population with effective, acceptable, and inexpensive means of control; and (3) given the absence of both means and motivation, the pervasive channels of communist control dissipated at the threshold of the commune bedrooms. Now there are reasons to believe that the government may be able to overcome these obstacles. If China assigns the program the necessary priorities, there is a possibility that some progress can be made in reducing the country's birthrate.

First, the question of receptivity. In 1965 people under thirty constituted approximately two-thirds of China's total population. They have few memories that predate 1950. If the current campaign can reach just this group, its success is assured. They comprise the most thoroughly indoctrinated and, coincidentally, the most fertile group. They have been saturated with government policies against the family, against cultural traditions, and against domesticity; but for socialist conformity, for service and sacrifice to the motherland. They are also better educated—most of them with at least a four-year primary school education. It is quite conceivable that they would be willing both to postpone marriage and within the marriage relationship to practice birth control, provided the means were readily available.

This introduces the second requirement. Although in China there are no cultural obstacles to the use of contraceptives nor, for that matter, to induced abortions or sterilization, in the earlier campaign contraceptive devices were apparently inadequate and too expensive. The supply and distribution of all contraceptives have now probably increased, but the most promising aspect of the current effort lies in the availability in China of the intrauterine contraceptive device (IUCD), so widely publicized in the West in recent years.

The IUCD has all the characteristics necessary for a successful contraceptive under the conditions prevailing in China: (1) Consisting of a small plastic coil, it is easy to produce at a very small cost. IUCDs are known to be manufactured in China, and presumably also are imported from Hong Kong. (2) Although some women cannot use the IUCD, the device is well over 90 per cent effective for those who can. The level is more than adequate for China, especially because of the increasing availability of induced abortion. (3) Whereas in the United States the insertion of the IUCD requires the services of a medical doctor, this is not the case in China. The process is relatively simple and, after a short course of instruction, may be performed by a rural medical assistant, by a midwife, or by other specially trained personnel. (4) The man, who is usually less receptive to troublesome precautionary measures, is not involved in any way. (5) Finally, one of the most important advantages of the intrauterine device is that effective limitation to impregnation can be achieved by a single decision and action on the part of the woman. She does not have to remember to take a pill, she does not have to count days, and she does not have to go through any pre-intercourse or post-intercourse procedures.

## *The Public Health System*

In addition to the requirements of receptivity and means, there is the problem of organization and implementation of any full-scale, centrally directed endeavor aimed at birth control. The natural channel for any such effort is the expanded public health service, the organization of which parallels the general administrative structure of the country, reaching down from Peking and the provincial capitals to the lowest level of the communes—the production team. Reportedly all cities and *hsien* centers have medical bureaus, which, in turn, control all the hospitals, clinics, and other medical facilities under their jurisdiction. All production brigades are supposed to have at least one health center while health services in the production units are provided by part-time workers, midwives, and nurses working under the direction of brigade health centers.

Adequate sources confirm that the health system permeates down to the lowest rural administrative unit. But what are the quality and quantity of the medical personnel? As in the case of other statistics from China, quantitative information on public health is inadequate and lacking uniform definitions. In 1958, the last year for which integrated health statistics are available, there were 75,000 doctors trained in Western medicine, 131,000 medical assistants, 138,000 nurses, 35,000 midwives, and 1,781,000 others. For the most part the "others" were practitioners of traditional medicine, midwives, and paramedical personnel with little formal training, who were responsible for peasant's care.

Based on scattered data, it may be estimated that by 1965 there were perhaps 135,000 persons with higher medical education and some 350,000 graduates of secondary medical education on the mainland. These staff most of the urban health facilities and probably represent the leadership in the *hsien* medical bureaus and some of the rural facilities. The number of health workers in the rural areas is, of course, even more difficult to obtain, but based on descriptions of health organizations in specific communes, they may now number in the vicinity of eight million—most of them engaged in public health work on a part-time basis.

Only the graduates of the formal medical schools, both higher and middle level, can be said to have adequate medical training. Most of the part-time rural health workers have only a rudimentary knowledge of human anatomy. But for the present discussion the number of people with some medical responsibilities is more important than their overall competence. Presumably, their number has reached significant proportions, they are widely dispersed, they operate within a chain of control, and they are accessible and trainable. A large proportion of the health personnel are women. Not only have many medical personnel been transferred to rural health centers, but the much publicized mobile medical teams apparently reach the most isolated areas of the country. The lines of control go down through government agencies and Party channels, as well as through the public health system.

It is important to remember that to a certain extent this discussion is speculative. There is some evidence in the Chinese press and elsewhere that the birth control campaign now in progress has considerable impetus and is, in fact, operating through the public health system, but there is no indication that the regime has assigned to it the high priority necessary for effective fertility control. It is impossible to determine whether the intrauterine devices have become an integral part of the program and there is no sign that a training program—essential if intrauterine devices are made available in rural China on a mass scale—is in progress. And yet, despite the absence of direct evidence, it is quite conceivable that the investment in financial and human resources necessary for an all-out effort to reduce the birthrate is contemplated in the near future. The ingredients for success appear to be present.

# Capital Formation and Development of Human Resources

# A

# Capital Formation

CAPITAL FORMATION REFERS to the increase in the production facilities in an economy. Because the process of capital formation will increase the productive capacity of an economy, it becomes a crucial factor in the economic development and growth of any country. Both India and China are still in the early stages of industrialization; the process of capital formation in both countries during the past two decades has been especially important in laying the foundation for their further economic growth. Thus the trends of capital formation in both countries not only will influence the growth of their aggregate economies but also the directions of growth in their various sectors.

The paper on the "Various Estimates of Physical Capital Formation for the Indian Economy" presents the estimates of capital formation made by three separate agencies: the National Council of Applied Economic Research, the Central Statistical Organization, and the Reserve Bank of India. The estimates of these agencies were based on different assumptions and are thus not comparable in a strict sense. Nevertheless taking these estimates together, some trends in capital formation become discernible.

The saving-income ratio of the Indian economy must have increased from 6 per cent around 1949–50 to about 9 to 10 per cent in the early 1960s. During the First Plan period the saving-income ratio of the government sector (government saving as a percentage of national income) was about 1.0 per cent increasing to about 2.3 per cent during the period 1961–62 to 1962–63. Although the ratio of the household sector increased from some 5 per cent during the First Plan to over 6 per cent during the period 1961–62 to 1962–63, the ratio of the corporate sector registered a minor change from 0.5 per cent to 0.7 per cent. The relative shares of sectorial savings to the national saving also showed some changes. The share of the household sector declined from 74 per cent during the First Plan to 66 per cent during the period 1961–62 to 1962–63, whereas the share from the government sector increased from 18 per cent to 26 per cent. The share from the corporate sector remained around 7 to 8 per cent during these different periods.

The rate of net capital formation was found to increase from 6 to 8 per cent during the First Plan to 11 to 14 per cent around 1957–58 or as late as 1960–61. The capital-output ratio was estimated at 3.86:1 during the First Plan and 3.58:1 during the period 1961–62 to 1962–63.

The article, "Estimates of Saving and Investment in the Indian Economy: 1950–51 to 1962–63", presents the revised estimates made by the Reserve Bank of India. A number of trends can be observed from this study. Total saving as a percentage of national income decreased from 5.7 per cent in 1950–51 to 4.2 per cent in 1952–53 and rose to 9.7 per cent in 1955–56; it again declined to 7.0 per cent in 1957–58 and thereafter steadily climbed up to 9.7 per cent in 1962–63. Thus the long-term trend is an upward one with major fluctuations. The government sector saving (as a percentage of national income) shows an upward trend with relatively minor fluctuations, increasing from 1.0 per cent in 1950–51 to 2.6 per cent in 1962–63. Corporate saving shows an upward trend with considerable fluctuations, from 0.4 per cent in 1950–51 to 0.7 per cent in 1962–63. Rural household saving shows a minor drop from 1.7 per cent in 1950–51 to 1.5 per cent in 1962–63. Urban household saving also fluctuated between 1.1 per cent and 6.4 per cent, with a rate of 2.6 per cent in 1950–51 and 4.9 per cent in 1962–63.

The value of saving in all sectors, except the rural household sector, increased at a rate faster than the value of national saving. As a result, the shares of rural household saving in the total national saving declined from 29.3 per cent in 1950–51 to 15.2 per cent in 1962–63. The shares of other sectors in these two years respectively are: government sector: 17.7 per cent and 27.4 per cent; corporate sector: 6.4 per cent and 7.0 per cent; and urban household sector: 46.6 per cent and 50.4 per cent. Because the saving of the urban household sector increased very rapidly during this period, its share of total (rural and urban) household saving increased from 61.3 per cent in 1950–51 to 76.9 per cent in 1962–63.

The composition of household savings also shows significant changes during the period 1950–51 to 1962–63. The value of financial assets (at 1948–49 prices) increased more than twenty-two times, whereas the value of physical assets (at 1948–49 prices) increased by only 17 per cent. As a result, the share of financial assets in total household savings increased from 4.7 per cent in 1950–51 to 50.0 per cent in 1962–63. Among various categories of financial assets, the value of currency and corporate, cooperative shares and securities accounted for a declining share of total household saving during this period whereas net bank deposits, insurance policies, and provident funds increased their shares.

The aggregate investment as a percentage of national income (at 1948–49 prices) increased with fluctuation from 4 to 7 per cent during the early 1950s to 11 to 13 per cent in the early 1960s. During the period 1950–51 to 1962–63, net capital inflow occurred in ten of these thirteen years, while there was small net capital outflow in the three earlier years: 1950–51, 1952–53, and 1953–54. For the first four years of this thirteen-year period, the total net capital inflow accounted for 8.5 per cent of the aggregate investments while for the last four years of this period, the total net capital inflow made up 22.9 per cent of the aggregate investment. The revised estimate gives a capital-output ratio of 3.86:1 for the Second Plan period and 3.53:1 for the period 1961–62 to 1962–63. A finer breakdown of this long period shows that the ratio first increased from 2.22:1 during the period 1953–54 to 1955–56, to 4.21:1 during the period 1956–57 to 1958–59, and it then dropped to 3.91:1 during the period 1959–60 to 1962–63.

Hollister's paper on China finds that gross investment as a percentage of GNP increased from 13 per cent in 1950 to 23 per cent in 1957, with a dramatic jump to 33 per cent in 1959. It dropped greatly during the following few years and has probably climbed back to the level of around 20 per cent since 1965. This rate of saving and investment is rather high for a low-income country, but it is relatively low when compared to the rate of 30 per cent in Sweden, USSR, and Japan.

When inventory is deducted from the gross investment figure, the difference becomes gross fixed investment. The latter includes mainly new installations and equipment and thus reflects the new physical facilities for production. The gross fixed investment as a percentage of GNP increased from 7 per cent in 1950 to 17 per cent in 1957. The rates in recent years are probably close to that in 1957.

The allocation of the gross fixed investment into various sectors of the economy reflects mainly the policy of the Chinese planners. The economic policy in the 1950s pursued the strategy of "heavy industry first," thus the share of gross fixed investment in heavy industry jumped rapidly from less than 15 per cent in early 1950s to 41 per cent in 1959. The shares in light industry, residential construction, and services and trade registered a decline during the 1950s. The policy of "agriculture first" since 1961 reduced the share in heavy industry and thus allowed greater shares for the other sectors, especially light industry.

The share of gross fixed investment that went into the agricultural sector remained around 21 to 24 per cent during the 1950s. This rate of investment in agriculture should not be considered low for a country undergoing industrialization. The reason the agriculture sector did not grow as fast as one would anticipate from such an investment share can be partly explained by the heavy industry bias that stressed the building and import of machinery and equipment for the machine-building industry, steel industry, and other basic industries during the 1950s. Since 1961 the policy has been shifted to the one of importing fertilizer plants and other plants supplying inputs for agriculture. Thus heavy industry is now oriented toward supporting agriculture and light industry and not toward supporting more basic heavy industry.

The relatively low share of investment in residential construction indicated that the rise of urban housing has, if not deteriorated, barely kept up with the rapid rise of urban population. The same situation existed in the transportation sector. The relatively small share of investment funds for the trade and non-agricultural services has been compensated to a large extent by the state-sponsored programs for education, health, recreation, and other communal services.

The trends of capital formation in China described above indicate why heavy industry grew more rapidly than other sectors and created an imbalance in growth among the sectors of the economy by the end of the 1950s. The new trends of capital formation since 1964, as estimated by Hollister, reflect a more balanced allocation of investment funds among the sectors. Heavy industry has been oriented toward the support of agriculture and light industry. In the sector of light industry emphasis has been placed on producing synthetic fibers to release more acreage from cotton production to foodgrain production. Finally the Chinese planners have freed themselves from the tendency to identify success or failure of economic development largely in terms of more or less steel mills and other key commodities of heavy industry.

23

# Various Estimates of Physical Capital Formation for the Indian Economy

*Ruddar Datt*
*K. P. M. Sundharam*

*From Ruddar Datt and K. P. M. Sundharam,* Indian Economy *(New Delhi: Niraj Prakashan, 1969), pp. 137–41, with omissions. Reprinted with permission.*

IN THE POST-INDEPENDENCE period, three estimates of physical capital formation have been made. The Reserve Bank of India made an estimate of capital formation for the Indian Economy. Similarly, in 1961 the Central Statistical Organisation (C.S.O.) prepared estimates of Gross Capital Formation in India for 1948–49 to 1960–61. Similarly, the National Council of Applied Economic Research in its monograph "Saving in India" published in April 1961, has prepared the estimates of national savings for the period 1948–49 to 1957–58.

While preparing an estimate, it is customary to divide the economy into three sectors—the household sector which comprises of productive economic units either run on an individual basis, or partnership or unincorporated business; the corporate sector which includes the joint stock companies and the government sector which includes the capital assets of the government as also the assets of the enterprises run under government control. If we sum up the net change in the value of the assets in a given period in these sectors, we arrive at a total of net domestic capital formation. To this if we add the net inflow of foreign capital, we arrive at an estimate of net capital formation for the economy.

## *NCAER Estimates of Net Investment and Saving*

The estimates of the National Council of Applied Economic Research pertain to 1948–49 to 1957–58. On the basis of the NCAER estimates, the following conclusions about the savings of the Indian economy can be drawn:

1. National average saving-income ratio of the Indian economy increased from 6 per cent in the period 1948–49 to 1950–51 to about 9 to 10 per cent in 1956–57 and 1957–58, the first two years of the Second Plan.
2. Marginal savings-income ratio was estimated to be in the neighborhood of 20 per cent.
3. The personal or individual saving-income ratio (including farm and non-farm unincorporated business) increased from 5 per cent in 1948–49 to 1950–51 to 8 or 9 per cent in 1956–57 and 1957–58.
4. The corporate saving-income ratio varied around an average of 30 per cent.
5. The government saving-income ratio rose from 7 per cent in 1948–49 to 1950–51 to 10 per cent in 1956–57 to 1957–58.
6. Corporations have never played a substantial role in the Indian economy or in the saving total as they have in other countries, accounting for only 2 to 3 per cent of national saving in 1948–49 to 1957–58 period, while the share of the individuals and the government works out roughly to be 81 to 82 per cent and 16 per cent respectively.

## *C.S.O.'s Estimate of Gross Capital Formation*

The Central Statistical Organization of the Government of India in 1963 prepared estimates of gross capital formation for the Indian economy pertaining to 1948–49 to 1960–61. Following conclusions can be drawn from the C.S.O. estimates of capital formation:

(1) During the twelve-year period (1948–49 to 1960–61) gross fixed capital formation and gross capital formation have shown an upward trend. The index of gross capital formation which stood at 100 with 1948–49 as the base jumped to 283.4 in 1960–61. As compared to this, the index of net capital formation rose to 417.8 in 1960–61 (this was mainly due to the fact that index of depreciation moved rather slowly from 100 in 1948–49 to 149.2 in 1960–61). These figures very clearly reveal that the share of depreciation in gross capital formation continued to decline. The share of depreciation in gross capital formation declined from 56.6 per cent in 1948–49 to 31.8 per cent in 1960–61. Consequently the share of net capital formation which was 43.4 per cent in 1948–49 improved to 58.2 per cent in 1960–61. This is an index of a developing economy.

(2) From Table 1, it can be observed that gross capital formation in the private and public sectors was in the ratio of 83:17 in 1948–49 and it changed to 66:34 in 1960–61. This shows that during the First and the Second Plan period, the expansion of the public sector has taken place at a faster rate than the expansion of the private sector.

(3) Net capital formation which was about 5.3 per cent during 1948–49 to 1950–51 (pre-Plan period) improved to about 7.5 per cent during the First Plan period and to nearly 14 per cent during the Second Plan period. As compared to this gross capital formation as percentage of gross national produce was 11.7, 17.3 and 19.3 per cent in 1950–51, 1955–56 and 1960–61 respectively.

***Table 1—Percentage Contribution of Private and Public Sectors to Gross Capital Formation***[a]

| | *Gross Capital Formation* | | |
|---|---|---|---|
| | *PUBLIC* | *PRIVATE* | *TOTAL* |
| 1948–49 | 82.7 | 17.3 | 100 |
| 1950–51 | 80.2 | 19.8 | 100 |
| 1955–56 | 72.4 | 27.6 | 100 |
| 1960–61 | 66.4 | 33.6 | 100 |

[a] At current prices.

## *Reserve Bank of India's Estimate of Saving and Investment*

The Reserve Bank of India's estimate of saving in the Indian economy was first published in March 1960 for the period 1950–51 to 1958–59. The revised series of the estimate

***Table 2—Relative Share of Different Sectors***

| *Sector* | *Saving as per cent of national income* | | *Percentage share in total saving* | |
|---|---|---|---|---|
| | *1960–61* | *1967–68* | *1960–61* | *1967–68* |
| Government | 1.7 | 0.8 | 17.4 | 10.4 |
| Corporate | 0.8 | 1.1 | 7.8 | 13.6 |
| Household | 7.2 | 6.1 | 74.8 | 76.4 |
| (a) Urban | 5.7 | — | 58.6 | — |
| (b) Rural | 1.5 | — | 16.2 | — |
| Total | 9.7 | 8.0 | 100.0 | 100.0 |

*Source: RBI Bulletin,* March 1965 *and Fourth Five Year Plan—Draft.*

were published in August 1961 and March 1965. These estimates present the sector-wise breakdown of the saving in the Indian Union. By adding to the total saving, the capital inflow during the period, the estimates arrive at the totals of investment. From the estimates of saving, the following conclusions emerge:

(a) The Reserve Bank estimate reveals that the household sector which consists of individuals, non-corporate business, educational institutions and charitable foundations contributes about 75 per cent of the total savings. As against it the share of the corporate sector is barely 8 per cent. This shows the high degree of importance of the household sector. Government sector savings are a little more than one-sixth of the total savings.

(b) During the first two Plan periods, the saving-income ratio has improved from 6.5 to 8.4 per cent of national income. Bulk of the increase in total savings is accounted for by urban household sector whose share in the total saving moved up from 48 per cent to 58 per cent. The rural household sector, however, showed a decline. Two reasons can be ascribed for this change. One reason could be increase in the size of the urban areas and secondly, it can be asserted that institutional efforts to raise savings have made a great impact in the urban areas.

The Third Plan figures pertain to the first two years and are hence not strictly comparable. The Planning Commission, in its preliminary Draft of the Fourth Plan, expected the value of saving-income ratio to be of the order of 13.1 per cent for 1965–66.

(c) In Table 4 aggregate investment is defined as the increase in the aggregate reproducible capital stock of an economy. This is derived by adding the estimated saving and estimated capital-flow from abroad. The table reveals how saving and investment were increasing quite rapidly during this period. From 5.6 per cent in 1950–51, the ratio of investment to national income has gone up to 12.7 per cent in 1962–63. (In 1960–61, it was actually higher at 13.2 per cent.)

(d) The capital-output ratio defined as the ratio of investment to increase in national income during a given period, declined from 3.86:1 during the Second period to 3.53:1

## *Table 3—Saving-Income Ratios*

| | *Plan I 1951–52 to 1955–56* | | *Plan II 1956–57 to 1960–61* | | *Plan III 1961–62 to 1962–63* | |
|---|---|---|---|---|---|---|
| | *% of N. I.* | *% of Total* | *% of N. I.* | *% of Total* | *% of N. I.* | *% of Total* |
| Government | 1.2 | 18 | 1.5 | 18 | 2.5 | 26.3 |
| Corporate | 0.5 | 8 | 0.4 | 5 | 0.7 | 7.4 |
| Household | 4.9 | 74 | 6.5 | 77 | 6.3 | 66.3 |
| Total | 6.5 | 100 | 8.4 | 100 | 9.5 | 100.0 |

*Source: Reserve Bank of India Bulletin,* March 1965.

## *Table 4—Estimates of Aggregate Investment*[a]

| | *Saving* | *Net capital inflow from abroad* | *Investment (1 + 2)* | *Investment as proportion (per cent) of National Income* |
|---|---|---|---|---|
| | *1* | *2* | *3* | *4* |
| 1950–51 | 503.2 | −7.3 | 495.9 | 5.6 |
| 1955–56 | 1,019.2 | +66.4 | 1,085.6 | 10.4 |
| 1960–61 | 1,235.2 | +447.7 | 1,682.9 | 13.2 |
| 1961–62 | 1,212.2 | +336.5 | 1,548.7 | 11.9 |
| 1962–63 | 1,300.7 | +393.7 | 1,694.4 | 12.7 |

[a] Rs. crores, at 1948–49 prices.

during the first two years of the Third Plan. A decline in the capital-output ratio, states the study, in the later phases of planning process is to be ordinarily expected due to greater utilization of the capacity created through the past investment and reduction of the gestation lags of the various types of investment.

There is no doubt that these estimates are not very accurate. The Reserve Bank realizing this mentions: "On the basis of such fragmentary information as is available, and taking a qualitative view, it appears that the aggregate saving-income ratio may be about two percentage points higher than that estimated in the study."

**Table 5—Investment, Investment-Income Ratios and Capital-Output Ratios[a]**

| | Investment (Annual Average) | Investment-income Ratio (per cent) | Capital-output Ratio |
|---|---|---|---|
| First Plan Period | 711.0 | 7.2 | . . |
| Second Plan Period | 1,360.8 | 11.7 | 3.86 : 1 |
| Third Plan Period (1961–62 and 1962–63) | 1,621.6 | 12.3 | 3.53 : 1 |

[a] Rs. crores, at 1948–49 prices.

## *Comparative Study of the Various Estimates of Capital Formation*

The estimates of capital formation by the Reserve Bank of India, the National Council of Applied Economic Research and the Central Statistical Organization are based on different assumptions. It is, therefore, not possible to compare them in the strict sense of the term. Moreover, the estimates of capital formation by the C.S.O. are based on the product method, whereas the estimate of the NCAER and RBI make use of the investment method approach. Besides the estimates are based on different price levels. The Reserve Bank estimates are computed at 1948–49 prices, the National Council estimates at 1952–53 prices and C.S.O. estimates at current prices.

A comparative study of these estimates reveals that the Reserve Bank estimate is the lowest. For the period of the First Plan (1951–52 to 1955–56), the Reserve Bank estimated the average net capital formation at 6.5. per cent, the NCAER as 8.2 per cent and the CSO at 7.5 per cent. By 1955–56, the last year of the First Plan, the economy had attained a rate of 10.4 per cent according to RBI estimate, 11.5 per cent according to NCAER estimate and 10.0 per cent according to CSO estimate. Similarly in 1957–58, net capital formation according to RBI, NCAER and CSO estimates is 11.3 per cent, 14.4 per cent and 11.1 per cent respectively.

From the RBI data (Table 2), it is clear that urban household savings account for approximately three and a half times the rural household savings. But the NCAER survey of savings estimated the rural savings to be of the order of Rs. 479 crores against the RBI estimate of Rs. 237 crores. The NCAER report asserts: "The survey clearly shows that the savings of the rural households are not as low as they are generally thought to be." There is no doubt that the NCAER estimate is based on a sample survey and that the RBI estimate is based on the net worth approach, but the magnitude of the difference is very large and cannot be explained away by the difference in methodology.

The estimates of net capital formation are tentative in nature because they are based on such statistics which are not very reliable. The statistics of the agricultural sector, the statistics about prices, imports, value added, etc., are all not dependable. In various fields, due to inadequacy of data, the estimator has to make some sweeping assumptions. But, there is no doubt that the computation of such estimates is a step in the right direction, viz., of constructing national accounts. As we are able to improve the quality of our basic statistics, such estimates will help us greatly to analyze the working of the Indian economy.

# Estimates of Saving and Investment in the Indian Economy: 1950-51 to 1962-63

*Reserve Bank of India*

*From* Reserve Bank of India Bulletin, *March 1965, "Estimates of Saving and Investment in the Indian Economy, 1950–51 to 1962–63" by D. R. Khatkhate and K. L. Deshpande, pp. 314–33, with omissions. Reprinted with permission.*

ESTIMATES OF SAVING in the Indian economy for the period 1950–51 to 1957–58 were published in the March 1960 issue of this Bulletin; in another article on the subject in the August 1961 issue, the estimates were extended to 1958–59 and certain refinements in methodology were introduced. In the present study, saving estimates are made for four more years, viz., 1959–60 to 1962–63, while those for the earlier years have been further revised, partly as a result of the refinement in methodology and partly due to the inclusion, for the first time, of estimates relating to inventories in (non-corporate) trade and agriculture. Thus, the saving estimates are now more complete than before. Basically, however, the method of estimation remains unaltered. As in the earlier studies, the estimates are exclusive of non-monetised investment and consumers' durables as the data necessary for estimating these are not available. The difficulties in estimating replacement of assets, whether in the corporate sector, or in the household sector, or in the Government sector, render the figures of *net* saving and investment rather imprecise; in the absence of any reliable guide to actual replacement expenditure, recourse has had to be taken to the analysis of the respective accounts for deriving figures of depreciation of assets. While, generally, the same sources of data as for the earlier studies have been continued, the results of new surveys, such as the preliminary results of the All-India Rural Debt and Investment Survey, and other sources such as reports of the Department of Company Law Administration have been used, wherever possible. Necessary information is still not available for all the individual years, and the deficiency has been made good by applying certain relevant proportions in the years for which data are available to other years for which no such data can be obtained. This renders year-to-year variations in saving less reliable.

The following section presents the aggregate and sector-wise saving estimates for the entire period, viz., 1950–51 to 1962–63, and seeks to explain the divergence between the revised estimates for the period 1950–51 to 1958–59 and the earlier estimates for the same period. The next section deals with the aggregate and sectoral saving-income ratios and the last section estimates total investment and discusses the trends in saving and investment.

## *Saving Estimates: 1950–51 to 1962–63*

The estimates of aggregate saving at current prices as also its sector-wise distribution for the period 1950–51 to 1962–63 are presented in Table 1 and the same estimates at constant prices are given in Table 2. Tables 3 and 4 embody the pattern of household sector's saving at current and constant prices, respectively.

### COMPARISON WITH THE EARLIER ESTIMATES

A revised series of the estimates of saving is given below, as also the earlier series. The revised estimates of aggregate saving are higher than the old ones for four years, viz., 1951–52 and 1954–55 to 1956–57. A marked difference is observed for four years, 1950–51, 1952–53, 1954–55 and 1956–57. The annual

## Table 1—Volume and Pattern of Saving[a]

| | 1950–51 | 1951–52 | 1952–53 | 1953–54 | 1954–55 | 1955–56 | 1956–57 | 1957–58 | 1958–59 | 1959–60 | 1960–61 | 1961–62 | 1962–63 |
|---|---|---|---|---|---|---|---|---|---|---|---|---|---|
| 1. Government Sector | 95.9 | 187.0 | 102.1 | 92.6 | 93.4 | 111.4 | 176.7 | 156.7 | 138.0 | 202.8 | 239.4 | 353.8 | 410.1 |
| 2. Domestic Corporate Sector | 35.0 | 63.6 | 1.1 | 25.9 | 50.3 | 60.0 | 58.5 | 18.0 | 32.4 | 57.6 | 106.7 | 97.8 | 104.7 |
| 3. Household Sector | 411.0 | 278.8 | 305.1 | 446.5 | 620.5 | 799.1 | 841.2 | 623.1 | 761.0 | 841.6 | 1,025.8 | 922.2 | 983.6 |
| Of which | | | | | | | | | | | | | |
| (a) Rural Householder Sector | 166.3 | 170.7 | 163.5 | 180.5 | 147.9 | 153.7 | 187.7 | 179.5 | 212.2 | 212.5 | 234.3 | 236.6 | 237.0 |
| (b) Urban Household Sector | 244.7 | 108.1 | 141.6 | 266.0 | 472.6 | 645.4 | 653.5 | 443.6 | 548.8 | 629.1 | 791.5 | 685.6 | 746.6 |
| 4. Total Saving (1 + 2 + 3) | 541.9 | 529.4 | 408.3 | 565.0 | 764.2 | 970.5 | 1,076.4 | 797.8 | 931.4 | 1,102.0 | 1,371.9 | 1,373.8 | 1,438.4 |

[a] In Rs. crores, at current prices.

## Table 2—Volume and Pattern of Saving

| | 1950–51 | 1951–52 | 1952–53 | 1953–54 | 1954–55 | 1955–56 | 1956–57 | 1957–58 | 1958–59 | 1959–60 | 1960–61 | 1961–62 | 1962–63 |
|---|---|---|---|---|---|---|---|---|---|---|---|---|---|
| 1. Government Sector | 89.1 | 170.7 | 98.4 | 88.6 | 99.9 | 117.0 | 172.0 | 149.8 | 127.6 | 185.7 | 215.5 | 312.1 | 356.0 |
| (a) | 17.7 | 35.3 | 25.0 | 16.4 | 12.2 | 11.5 | 16.4 | 19.6 | 14.8 | 18.4 | 17.4 | 25.7 | 27.4 |
| (b) | 1.0 | 1.9 | 1.1 | 0.9 | 1.0 | 1.1 | 1.6 | 1.4 | 1.1 | 1.1 | 1.7 | 2.4 | 2.6 |
| 2. Domestic Corporate Sector | 32.4 | 58.1 | 1.0 | 24.8 | 53.8 | 63.1 | 56.9 | 17.1 | 29.9 | 52.8 | 96.1 | 86.3 | 90.8 |
| (a) | 6.4 | 12.0 | 0.3 | 4.6 | 6.6 | 6.2 | 5.4 | 2.2 | 3.5 | 5.2 | 7.8 | 7.1 | 7.0 |
| (b) | 0.4 | 0.6 | — | 0.2 | 0.5 | 0.6 | 0.5 | 0.1 | 0.3 | 0.4 | 0.7 | 0.7 | 0.7 |
| 3. Household Sector (i + ii) | 381.7 | 254.4 | 293.9 | 427.5 | 663.7 | 839.1 | 818.3 | 595.8 | 703.6 | 770.7 | 923.6 | 813.8 | 853.9 |
| (a) | 75.9 | 52.7 | 74.7 | 79.0 | 81.2 | 82.3 | 78.2 | 78.2 | 81.7 | 76.4 | 74.8 | 67.2 | 65.6 |
| (b) | 4.3 | 2.8 | 3.1 | 4.3 | 6.5 | 8.0 | 7.4 | 5.5 | 6.0 | 6.5 | 7.3 | 6.2 | 6.4 |
| (i) Rural Household Sector | 147.6 | 151.0 | 156.4 | 169.3 | 171.0 | 170.7 | 178.5 | 170.3 | 189.0 | 187.3 | 200.6 | 200.0 | 197.2 |
| (a) | 29.3 | 31.3 | 39.8 | 31.3 | 20.9 | 16.7 | 17.0 | 22.3 | 21.9 | 18.6 | 16.2 | 16.6 | 15.2 |
| (b) | 1.7 | 1.7 | 1.7 | 1.7 | 1.7 | 1.6 | 1.6 | 1.6 | 1.6 | 1.6 | 1.6 | 1.5 | 1.5 |
| (c) | 38.7 | 59.4 | 53.2 | 39.6 | 25.8 | 20.3 | 21.8 | 28.6 | 26.9 | 24.3 | 21.7 | 24.7 | 23.1 |
| (ii) Urban Household Sector | 234.1 | 103.4 | 137.5 | 258.2 | 492.7 | 668.4 | 639.8 | 425.5 | 514.6 | 583.4 | 723.0 | 612.9 | 656.7 |
| (a) | 46.6 | 21.4 | 34.9 | 47.7 | 60.3 | 65.6 | 61.2 | 55.9 | 59.8 | 57.8 | 58.6 | 50.6 | 50.4 |
| (b) | 2.6 | 1.1 | 1.4 | 2.6 | 4.8 | 6.4 | 5.8 | 3.9 | 4.4 | 4.9 | 5.7 | 4.7 | 4.9 |
| (c) | 61.3 | 40.6 | 46.8 | 60.4 | 74.2 | 79.7 | 78.2 | 71.4 | 73.1 | 75.7 | 78.3 | 75.3 | 76.9 |
| 4. Total Saving (1 + 2 + 3) | 503.2 | 483.2 | 393.3 | 540.9 | 817.4 | 1,019.2 | 1,047.2 | 7,62.7 | 861.1 | 1,009.2 | 1,235.2 | 1,212.2 | 1,300.7 |
| (b) | 5.7 | 5.3 | 4.2 | 5.4 | 8.0 | 9.7 | 9.5 | 7.0 | 7.4 | 8.5 | 9.7 | 9.3 | 9.7 |

(a) Proportion (per cent) of Total Savings.
(b) Proportion (per cent) of National Income.
(c) Proportion (per cent) of Savings of the Household Sector.
*Note:* Saving in current prices is converted to 1948–49 prices by using the National Income deflator. All in Rs. crores, at 1948–49 prices.

## *Table 3—Volume and Pattern of Saving of the Household Sector*[a]

| | *1950–51* | *1951–52* | *1952–53* | *1953–54* | *1954–55* | *1955–56* | *1956–57* | *1957–58* | *1958–59* | *1959–60* | *1960–61* | *1961–62* | *1962–63* |
|---|---|---|---|---|---|---|---|---|---|---|---|---|---|
| A. Financial Assets (1 to 6) | 19.3 | −21.6 | 42.6 | 83.0 | 307.8 | 385.6 | 320.0 | 323.6 | 341.4 | 388.1 | 436.0 | 476.6 | 492.3 |
| 1. Currency | 79.6 | −114.6 | −22.4 | 24.5 | 85.4 | 190.3 | 51.9 | 45.3 | 112.4 | 130.2 | 160.3 | 95.2 | 173.1 |
| 2. Net Bank Deposits | −37.7 | −44.8 | 28.1 | −8.4 | 32.2 | 0.2 | 5.0 | 55.3 | 28.0 | 62.8 | − 6.0 | 111.1 | 49.2 |
| 3. Insurance Policies | 17.8 | 11.4 | 17.6 | 21.1 | 23.6 | 27.3 | 21.7 | 25.1 | 34.3 | 43.3 | 50.3 | 63.1 | 66.0 |
| 4. Provident Funds | 31.8 | 34.1 | 42.9 | 78.0 | 87.2 | 86.2 | 93.0 | 102.8 | 107.3 | 112.6 | 150 6 | 150.9 | 166.7 |
| 5. Net Claims on the Government Sector | −105.1 | 69.5 | −36.7 | −56.6 | 41.0 | 30.7 | 63.9 | 41.4 | 20.1 | −13.3 | 21.5 | −21.3 | −27.6 |
| 6. Corporate and Co-operative Shares and Securities | 32.9 | 22.8 | 13.1 | 24.4 | 38.4 | 50.9 | 84.5 | 53.7 | 39.3 | 52.5 | 59.3 | 77.6 | 64.9 |
| B. Physical Assets | 391.7 | 300.4 | 262.5 | 363.5 | 312.7 | 413.5 | 521.2 | 299.5 | 419.6 | 453.5 | 589.8 | 445.6 | 491.3 |
| C. Saving of the Household Sector (A + B) | 411.0 | 278.8 | 305.1 | 446.5 | 620.5 | 799.1 | 841.2 | 623.1 | 761.0 | 841.6 | 1,025.8 | 922.2 | 983.6 |

[a] In RS. crores, at current prices.

## Table 4—Volume and Pattern of Saving of the Household Sector

| | 1950–51 | 1951–52 | 1952–53 | 1953–54 | 1954–55 | 1955–56 | 1956–57 | 1957–58 | 1958–59 | 1959–60 | 1960–61 | 1961–62 | 1962–63 |
|---|---|---|---|---|---|---|---|---|---|---|---|---|---|
| A. Financial Assets (1 to 6) | 17.9 | −19.8 | 41.0 | 79.6 | 329.3 | 404.9 | 311.4 | 309.4 | 315.6 | 355.4 | 392.6 | 420.6 | 427.4 |
| (a) | 4.7 | −7.8 | 14.0 | 18.6 | 49.6 | 48.3 | 38.1 | 51.9 | 44.9 | 46.1 | 42.5 | 51.7 | 50.0 |
| (b) | 0.2 | −0.2 | 0.4 | 0.8 | 3.2 | 3.9 | 2.8 | 2.8 | 2.7 | 3.0 | 3.1 | 3.2 | 3.2 |
| 1. Currency | 73.9 | −104.6 | −21.6 | 23.5 | 91.4 | 199.8 | 50.5 | 43.3 | 103.9 | 119.2 | 144.3 | 84.0 | 150.3 |
| (a) | 19.4 | −41.1 | − 7.4 | 5.5 | 13.8 | 23.8 | 6.2 | 7.3 | 14.8 | 15.5 | 15.6 | 10.3 | 17.6 |
| (b) | 0.8 | − 1.1 | − 0.2 | 0.2 | 0.9 | 1.9 | 0.5 | 0.4 | 0.9 | 1.0 | 1.1 | 0.6 | 1 1 |
| 2. Net Bank Deposits | −35.0 | −40.9 | 27.1 | − 8.0 | 34.4 | 0.2 | 4.9 | 52.9 | 25.9 | 57.5 | − 5.4 | 98.0 | 42.7 |
| (a) | − 9.1 | −16.1 | 9.2 | − 1.9 | 5.2 | — | 0.6 | 8.9 | 3.7 | 7.5 | − 0.6 | 12.0 | 5.0 |
| (b) | 0.4 | 0.4 | 0.3 | − 0.1 | 0.3 | — | — | 0.5 | 0.2 | 0.5 | — | 0.8 | 0.3 |
| 3. Insurance Policies | 16.5 | 10.4 | 17.0 | 20.2 | 25.2 | 28.7 | 21.1 | 24.0 | 31.7 | 39.7 | 45.3 | 55.7 | 57.3 |
| (a) | 4.3 | 4.1 | 5.8 | 4.7 | 3.8 | 3.4 | 2.6 | 4.0 | 4.5 | 5.1 | 4.9 | 6.9 | 6.7 |
| (b) | 0.2 | 0.1 | 0.2 | 0.2 | 0.3 | 0.3 | 0.2 | 0.2 | 0.3 | 0.3 | 0.4 | 0.4 | 0.4 |
| 4. Provident Funds | 29.5 | 31.1 | 41.3 | 74.7 | 93.3 | 90.5 | 90.5 | 98.3 | 99.2 | 103.1 | 135.6 | 133.2 | 144.7 |
| (a) | 7.7 | 12.2 | 14.1 | 17.5 | 14.0 | 10.8 | 11.1 | 16.5 | 14.1 | 13.4 | 14.7 | 16.4 | 16.9 |
| (b) | 0.3 | 0.3 | 0.4 | 0.8 | 0.9 | 0.9 | 0.8 | 0.9 | 0.8 | 0.9 | 1.1 | 1.0 | 1.1 |
| 5. Net Claims on the Government Sector | −97.6 | 63.4 | −35.4 | −54.2 | 43.9 | 32.2 | 62.2 | 39.6 | 18.6 | −12.2 | 19.4 | −18.8 | −24.0 |
| (a) | −25.6 | 24.9 | −12.0 | −12.7 | 6.6 | 3.9 | 7.6 | 6.6 | 2.6 | − 1.6 | 2.1 | − 2.3 | − 2.8 |
| (b) | − 1.1 | 0.7 | − 0.4 | − 0.5 | 0.4 | 0.3 | 0.6 | 0.3 | 0.2 | − 0.1 | 0.1 | − 0.1 | − 0.2 |
| 6. Corporate and Cooperative Shares and Securities | 30.6 | 20.8 | 12.6 | 23.4 | 41.1 | 53.5 | 82.2 | 51.3 | 36.3 | 48.1 | 53.4 | 68.5 | 56.4 |
| (a) | 8.0 | 8.2 | 4.3 | 5.5 | 6.2 | 6.4 | 10.0 | 8.6 | 5.2 | 6.2 | 5.8 | 8.4 | 6.6 |
| (b) | 6.4 | 0.2 | 0.1 | 0.2 | 0.4 | 0.5 | 0.7 | 0.5 | 0.3 | 0.4 | 0.4 | 0.5 | 0.5 |
| B. Physical Assets | 363.8 | 274.2 | 252.9 | 347.9 | 334.4 | 434.2 | 506.9 | 286.4 | 388.0 | 415.3 | 531.0 | 393.2 | 426.5 |
| (a) | 95.3 | 107.8 | 86.0 | 81.4 | 50.4 | 51.7 | 61.9 | 48.1 | 55.1 | 58.9 | 57.5 | 48.3 | 50.0 |
| (b) | 4.1 | 3.0 | 2.7 | 3.5 | 3.3 | 4.1 | 4.6 | 2.7 | 3.3 | 3.5 | 4.2 | 3.0 | 3.2 |
| C. Saving of the Household Sector (A + B) | 381.7 | 254.4 | 293.9 | 427.5 | 663.7 | 839.1 | 818.3 | 595.8 | 703.6 | 770.7 | 923.6 | 813.8 | 853.9 |
| (b) | 4.3 | 2.8 | 3.1 | 4.3 | 6.5 | 8.0 | 7.4 | 5.5 | 6.0 | 6.5 | 7.3 | 6.2 | 6.4 |

(a) Proportion (percentage) of Household Sector's Saving, in Rs. crores, at 1948–49 prices.
(b) Proportion (percentage) of National Income, in Rs. crores, at 1948–49 prices.

average of saving-income ratios during the entire period of 1950–51 to 1958–59 is slightly lower at 7.0 per cent as against 7.1 per cent in the earlier study. The figure for 1952–53 in particular shows two changes: (*a*) sizeable fall in the total saving as compared to 1951–52—this was mainly under corporate sector which showed virtually no saving in 1952–53, and (*b*) a large decline in revised estimates for the year as compared to earlier estimates—this is under household sector. This was partly due to a sharp fall in inventories in trade (non-corporate) as there was a downward pressure on prices, and the fall in revised estimates relating to urban investment which was due to an estimated smaller rise in income originating from urban house property than in the earlier estimates. The fall in saving in 1957–58, as compared to previous two years, was largely in respect of urban household sector, and in physical assets. A running down of inventories in agriculture and trade and a sharp drop in investment in urban housing were partly responsible for the decline in saving.

### Table 5—Comparison of Earlier Estimates of Saving with the Revised Estimates[a]

| | *Earlier Estimates (August 1961 article)* | *Revised Estimates* |
|---|---|---|
| 1950–51 | 591 (6.7) | 503 (5.7) |
| 1951–52 | 460 (5.1) | 483 (5.3) |
| 1952–53 | 564 (6.0) | 393 (4.2) |
| 1953–54 | 573 (5.7) | 541 (5.4) |
| 1954–55 | 731 (7.1) | 817 (8 0) |
| 1955–56 | 955 (9.1) | 1,019 (9.7) |
| 1956–57 | 966 (8.8) | 1,047 (9.5) |
| 1957–58 | 782 (7.2) | 763 (7.0) |
| 1958–59 | 902 (7.7) | 861 (7.4) |
| 1950–51 to 1958–59 Annual Average | 725 (7.1) | 714 (7.0) |

[a] Rs. crores, at 1948–49 prices. Figures within parentheses represent percentage to national income.

Under the revised series of estimates, the saving of the Government sector and the corporate sector are higher than before, except for a year or two, while that of the household sector shows variations both ways as would be seen from Table 6.



The year to year deviations in the new estimates of aggregate saving from the old ones are to be explained, apart from the inclusion of estimates of inventories in agriculture and non-corporate enterprises, by the procedural changes indicated at the beginning of this article. These changes have affected the saving estimates, particularly changes in the assets, both physical and financial, of the household sector. Within the physical assets, investment in agriculture as well as urban housing has been now estimated throughout at a lower level. Aside from this, the saving in gold is now excluded as it is treated as a consumer durable rather than a capital asset.

## *Saving-Income Ratios—Aggregate and Sector-wise*

This section describes the trends in aggregate and sector-wise saving-income ratios during the period 1950–51 to 1962–63. For this purpose, the entire span of thirteen years is broken down into four periods, of which period IV comprises four years, while others cover three years each. The recourse to period analysis is because the fluctuations in year-to-year saving-income ratios are rather wide, partly due to the method adopted for estimating saving in this study. Apart from this, the trends in the saving-income ratios, Plan-wise, have been discussed to the extent possible.

The marginal saving-income ratio is calculated for the later three periods, *viz.*, period II to period IV; and the base with reference to which each of these ratios is calculated is the preceding period. Besides, the marginal saving-income ratios, Plan-wise, are also calculated.

In this study, marginal saving-income ratio is estimated by fitting a trend line because the number of observations has now increased to enable this. However, too much reliance should not be placed on this for the reason that year-to-year estimates of saving are not quite firm as explained earlier, and as the

### *Table 6—Comparison with Previous[a] Estimates of Saving: Sector-Wise[b]*

| | *TOTAL* | | | *GOVERNMENT SECTOR* | | | *DOMESTIC CORPORATE SECTOR* | | | *HOUSEHOLD SECTOR* | | |
|---|---|---|---|---|---|---|---|---|---|---|---|---|
| | *Previous* | *Present* | *Difference* | *Previous* | *Present* | *Difference* | *Previous* | *Present* | *Difference* | *Previous* | *Present* | *Difference* |
| 1950–51 | 635.9 | 541.9 | − 94.0 | 93.8 | 95.9 | + 2.1 | 32.2 | 35.0 | + 2.8 | 509.9 | 411.0 | − 98.9 |
| 1951–52 | 503.6 | 529.4 | + 25.8 | 192.3 | 187.0 | − 5.3 | 56.5 | 63.6 | + 7.1 | 254.8 | 278.8 | + 24.0 |
| 1952–53 | 585.3 | 408.3 | −177.0 | 88.4 | 102.1 | +13.7 | 4.3 | 1.1 | − 3.2 | 492.6 | 305.1 | −187.5 |
| 1953–54 | 598.7 | 565.0 | − 33.7 | 71.0 | 92.6 | +21.6 | 22.8 | 25.9 | + 3.1 | 504.9 | 446.5 | − 58.4 |
| 1954–55 | 682.7 | 764.2 | + 81.5 | 82.2 | 93.4 | +11.2 | 38.9 | 50.3 | +11.4 | 561.6 | 620.5 | + 58.9 |
| 1955–56 | 910.2 | 970.5 | + 60.3 | 69.9 | 111 4 | +41.5 | 54.3 | 60.0 | + 5.7 | 786.0 | 799.1 | + 13.1 |
| 1956–57 | 993.0 | 1,076.4 | + 83.4 | 128.9 | 176.7 | +47.8 | 53.7 | 58.5 | + 4.8 | 810.4 | 841.2 | + 30.8 |
| 1957–58 | 818.2 | 797.8 | − 20.4 | 114.4 | 156.7 | +42.3 | 17.2 | 18.0 | + 0.8 | 686.6 | 623.1 | − 63.5 |
| 1958–59 | 974.8 | 931.4 | − 43.4 | 103.0 | 138.0 | +35.0 | 34.3 | 32.4 | − 1.9 | 837.5 | 761.0 | − 76.5 |

*Note:* All differences are worked out with reference to present estimates.
[a] August 1961 article.
[b] Rs. crores, at current prices.

number of observations is still not fully adequate.

The method used to estimate income of the corporate, government and household sectors as also the income of the rural and urban households remains the same as in the earlier study.

The procedure adopted to estimate the saving of the rural and urban household sectors is changed to some extent. In the earlier studies the saving of the rural household sector was arrived at on the basis of the relationship revealed in 1951–52 and 1956–57 (in the All-India Rural Credit Survey 1951–52, and the Follow-up Survey for 1956–57) between rural saving and agricultural income. This ratio was 4 per cent. By applying this ratio to the agricultural income in other years, rural saving for these years was estimated. By deducting rural household sector's saving from the total household sector's saving, saving of the urban household sector was arrived at.

Some data are now available for 1962 through the Rural Household Saving Survey (RHSS) of the National Council of Applied Economic Research. The rural saving is estimated for 1961–62 by using partly the figures from the RHSS and partly the figures of saving in the form of physical assets, *e.g.*, the agriculture, rural housing and non-farm business, the estimation procedure of which is described earlier. This is done by adding the estimates of financial investments of the rural sector based on the RHSS data to the saving in physical assets of the rural sector, and then the net borrowings from the urban sector are deducted from that figure to obtain net saving of the rural household sector. This formed 3.3 per cent of the agricultural income in 1961–62. Thus, the ratios of rural saving to agricultural income have become available for three years, 1951–52, 1956–57 and 1961–62; these ratios are 3.3 per cent, 3.7 per cent and 3.3 per cent, respectively, for these years. In view of these differences in the ratio of rural saving to agricultural income in these years an average of these ratios (3.4 per cent) is applied to agricultural income to derive rural saving in each of the years of the study. The rural household sector's saving so estimated is deducted from the total household sector's saving to get the saving of the urban household sector.

The estimated saving-income ratios, both average and marginal, are presented in Table 7.

The average aggregate saving-income ratio steadily increased from period to period from 5.0 per cent during period I (*i.e.*, 1950–51 to

### *Table 7—Average Saving-Income Ratios: Aggregate and Sector-Wise*[a]

| | *Period I (1950–51 to 1952–53)* | *Period II (1953–54 to 1955–56)* | *Period III (1956–57 to 1958–59)* | *Period IV (1959–60 to 1962–63)* | *I Plan period* | *II Plan period* | *1961–62 and 1962–63* | *1950–51 to 1962–63* |
|---|---|---|---|---|---|---|---|---|
| Government Sector | 14.1 | 9.9 | 11.0 | 13.8 | 11.9 | 11.2 | 15.6 | 12.5 |
| Domestic Corporate Sector | 39.6 | 44.1 | 32.0 | 40.7 | 42.8 | 35.8 | 12.5 | 39.6 |
| Household Sector | 3.5 | 6.4 | 6.4 | 6.7 | 5.1 | 6.7 | 6.4 | 6.0 |
| (*i*) Rural Household Sector | 2.2 | 2.4 | 2.3 | 2.3 | 2.3 | 2.3 | 2.2 | 2.3 |
| (*ii*) Urban Household Sector | 7.3 | 16.3 | 16.5 | 17.0 | 12.7 | 17.1 | 10.1 | 15.1 |
| Aggregate Saving-Income Ratio | 5.0 | 7.7 | 7.9 | 9.3 | 6.6 | 8.5 | 9.5 | 7.8 |
| Aggregate Marginal Saving-Income Ratio | . . | 29.5 | 10.7 | 19.0 | . . | 18.9 | 14.6 | . . |

[a] The marginal saving-income ratios are in relation to the previous period. For the period 1961–62 and 1962–63, it is in relation to the last two years of the Second Plan (i.e. 1959–60 and 1960–61). In percentages.

1952–53) to 7.7 per cent during period II (*i.e.*, 1953–54 to 1955–56) and further to 7.9 per cent and 9.3 per cent in the subsequent periods (1956–57 to 1958–59 and 1959–60 to 1962–63). The saving-income ratio of the household sector rose from 3.5 per cent during period I to 6.4 per cent during periods II and III and further to 6.7 per cent in the following period. The saving-income ratio of the domestic corporate sector rose from 39.6 per cent during period I to 44.1 per cent in period II, declined sharply to 32.0 per cent in period III before increasing again to 40.7 per cent in period IV. The average saving-income ratio of the Government sector, on the other hand, declined from 14.1 per cent in period I to 9.9 per cent in period II but increased thereafter to 11.0 per cent and 13.8 per cent in periods III and IV, respectively.

Within the household sector, in most years covered by this study, the share of rural saving is much less than that of urban, considered in relation to total saving, or in proportion to national income or income of the respective sectors; *among other factors*, is the existence of non-monetary part of the rural economy though this part is likely to have declined somewhat during the later years as a result of the impact of planned economic development. The saving-income ratio of the urban household sector sharply increased from 7.3 per cent in period I to 16.3 per cent in period II and further to 16.5 per cent in period III and to 17.0 per cent in period IV. On the other hand, the saving-income ratio of the rural household sector remained virtually unchanged around 2.3 per cent in all the periods.

Plan-wise, the average saving-income ratio showed a steady growth. Thus, the average saving-income ratio increased from 6.6 per cent during the First Plan period to 8.5 per cent during the Second Plan period; this ratio worked out to 9.5 per cent during the first two years of the Third Plan period.

The aggregate marginal saving-income ratio calculated in each period with reference to the preceding period was 29.5 per cent in period II, 10.7 per cent in period III and 19.0 per cent in period IV. The wide swings in the marginal saving-income ratio are partly statistical and partly due to the fluctuations in the inventories particularly in agriculture and non-corporate business. The base with reference to which the marginal saving-income ratio in period II is calculated is unduly influenced by the saving in one year, *viz.*, 1952–53 when it reached the lowest level in the last thirteen years. This tended to make the marginal saving-income ratio in period II look unduly high. Furthermore, during period II, when bank credit to trade showed marked expansion, increase in stocks was large in relation to period I, while the stocks showed only a moderate rise in period III, with the slowing down in the rate of rise in bank credit to trade. The fluctuations in stocks as estimated here are also due to the method of estimation itself, which relies on changes in bank credit for deriving changes in stocks. It follows thus that when bank credit expands or contracts markedly, the corresponding estimate of variations in stocks in non-corporate business would also be sharp. The annual average rise in inventories at constant prices fluctuated from over Rs. 35 crores in period I to over Rs. 90 crores in period II and to Rs. 60 crores and Rs. 75 crores, respectively, in the subsequent periods. This limitation should be borne in mind in interpreting the marginal saving-income ratios period-wise.

But Plan-wise trends in the marginal saving-income ratio give a better picture as within each Plan period sharp rises and falls in stocks are averaged out. Thus during the Second Plan period, the aggregate marginal saving-income ratio is estimated at 18.9 per cent with reference to the First Plan period; the corresponding ratio during the first two years of the Third Plan with reference to the last two years of the Second Plan is estimated at 14.6 per cent. That the marginal rate of saving is around 15 to 19 per cent is also supported broadly by the estimate of marginal saving-income ratio, as derived by fitting a trend line to the saving-income ratios during 1950–51 to 1962–63. The ratio so estimated is 17.7.

## *Investment Estimates: 1950–51 to 1962–63, and Trends in Saving and Investment*

This section gives estimates of aggregate investment in the Indian economy and trends in saving and investment during the period 1950–51 to 1962–63. Investment is arrived at by adding the estimated inflow of capital to the total domestic saving estimated earlier. The method adopted to estimate capital inflow remains the same as in the earlier study. Thus, the current account deficit in the Indian balance of payments, excluding official donations and including 50 per cent of "Errors and Omissions," retained earnings of subsidiaries and branches of foreign concerns and their imports in kind are taken to represent inflow of capital. Since gold holding of the household sector is treated as a consumer durable rather than a capital asset, no adjustment is made in current account deficit for estimating capital inflow. The estimates of investment at current and constant prices are given in Tables 8 and 9,

**Table 8—Estimates of Aggregate Investment[a]**

| | *Saving* 1 | *Net Capital Inflow* 2 | *Investment (1 + 2)* 3 |
|---|---|---|---|
| 1950–51 | 541.9 | − 7.9 | 584.0 |
| 1951–52 | 529.4 | +224.4 | 753.8 |
| 1952–53 | 408.3 | − 17.0 | 391.3 |
| 1953–54 | 565.0 | − 3.5 | 561.5 |
| 1954–55 | 764.2 | + 46.5 | 810.7 |
| 1955–56 | 970.5 | + 63.2 | 1,063.7 |
| 1956–57 | 1,076.4 | +377.9 | 1,454.3 |
| 1957–58 | 797.8 | +489.1 | 1,286.9 |
| 1958–59 | 931.4 | +399.3 | 1,330.7 |
| 1959–60 | 1,102.0 | +258.3 | 1,360.3 |
| 1960–61 | 1,371.9 | +497.3 | 1,869.2 |
| 1961–62 | 1,373.8 | +381.3 | 1,755.1 |
| 1962–63 | 1,498.4 | +453.5 | 1,951.9 |

[a] Rs. crores, at current prices.

**Table 9—Estimates of Aggregate Investment[a]**

| | *Saving* 1 | *Net Capital - Inflow* 2 | *Investment (1 + 2)* 3 | *Investment as proportion (percentage) of National Income* 4 |
|---|---|---|---|---|
| 1950–51 | 503.2 | − 7.3 | 495.9 | 5.6 |
| 1951–52 | 483.2 | +204.8 | 688.0 | 7.6 |
| 1952–53 | 393.3 | − 16.4 | 376.9 | 4.0 |
| 1953–54 | 540.9 | − 3.3 | 537.6 | 5.4 |
| 1954–55 | 817.4 | + 49.7 | 867.1 | 8.4 |
| 1955–56 | 1,019.2 | + 66.4 | 1,085.6 | 10.4 |
| 1956–57 | 1,047.2 | +367.5 | 1,414.7 | 12.9 |
| 1957–58 | 762.7 | +467.6 | 1,230.3 | 11.3 |
| 1958–59 | 861.1 | +369.2 | 1,230.3 | 10.6 |
| 1959–60 | 1,009.2 | +236.6 | 1,215.8 | 10.5 |
| 1960–61 | 1,235.2 | +447.7 | 1,682.9 | 13.2 |
| 1961–62 | 1,212.2 | +336.5 | 1,548.7 | 11.9 |
| 1962–63 | 1,300.7 | +393.7 | 1,694.4 | 12.7 |

[a] Rs. crores, at 1948–49 prices.

respectively; the estimates of inflow of capital at current prices are presented in Table 10.

The inflow of capital in 1959–60 was much less than in the previous three years, and this kept down the aggregate investment level despite the marked rise in domestic saving. Similarly, capital inflow in 1961–62 was considerably less than in 1960–61 (when it was the highest for any year during the thirteen year period covered in this study) which in turn accounted for a reduced level of investment in that year as compared to 1960–61. *On the whole*, aggregate investment in 1960–61 was the highest during the entire period; at constant prices, total amount was slightly larger in 1962–63, but as a proportion to national income, investment was 13.2 per cent in 1960–61 and 12.7 per cent in 1962–63.

The trends in saving and investment which are presented in Tables 11 and 12, respectively, are discussed period-wise, and plan-wise, only at constant prices.

It would be seen from both these tables that aggregate investment as well as domestic saving in absolute terms, and as a proportion of national income, increased uninterruptedly in all the periods. The aggregate investment increased from an annual average of Rs. 520 crores during period I to Rs. 1,543 crores during period IV, and the annual average aggregate saving from Rs. 460 crores in period I to Rs. 1,189 crores in period IV. As a proportion of national income also, the saving has increased from 5 per cent in period I to 7.7 per cent in period II, 7.9 per cent in period III and to 9.3 per cent in period IV. The investment-income ratio has risen from 5.7 per cent in period I to 8.1 per cent in period II, 11.5 per cent in period III and to 12.1 per cent in period IV.

Plan-wise, the average investment-income ratio, which was 7.2 per cent during the First Plan, increased to 11.7 per cent during the Second Plan period and reached 12.3 per cent in the first two years of the Third Plan. Corresponding to this, the average aggregate saving-income ratio was 6.6 per cent, 8.5 per cent and 9.5 per cent, respectively.

The capital-output ratio which may be taken to describe a relationship between investment and an increase in income in a given period was 2.22:1 in period II and it increased to 4.21:1 in period III. However, this ratio somewhat declined to 3.91:1 in period IV. The trends in this ratio, Plan-wise, were similar. Thus, capital-output ratio which was 3.86:1 during the Second Plan, declined to 3.53:1 during the first two years of the Third

**Table 10—Inflow of Capital**[a]

| | *Current account deficit (excluding official donations and including half of errors and omissions) (Deficit +)* | *Non-cash Inflow* | *Retained earnings of branches and subsidiaries of foreign companies* | *Capital Inflow (1 + 2 + 3)* |
|---|---|---|---|---|
| | *1* | *2* | *3* | *4* |
| 1950–51 | − 33.4 | +15.5 | +10.0 | − 7.9 |
| 1951–52 | +190.4 | +15.5 | +18.5 | +224.4 |
| 1952–53 | − 36.5 | +15.5 | + 4.0 | − 17.0 |
| 1953–54 | − 29.6 | +15.5 | +10.6 | − 3.5 |
| 1954–55 | + 21.8 | + 6.4 | +18.3 | + 46.5 |
| 1955–56 | + 54.0 | + 6.4 | + 2.8 | + 63.2 |
| 1956–57 | +349.9 | + 8.5 | +19.5 | +377.9 |
| 1957–58 | +468.2[b] | +11.4 | + 9.5 | +489.1 |
| 1958–59 | +377.2 | +12.3 | + 9.8 | +399.3 |
| 1959–60 | +235.8 | + 7.2 | +15.3 | +258.3 |
| 1960–61 | +441.0 | +41.8 | +14.5 | +497.3 |
| 1961–62 | +348.4 | +17.6 | +15.3 | +381.3 |
| 1962–63 | +424.3 | +13.4 | +15.8 | +453.5 |

[a] Rs. crores, at current prices.
[b] Includes silver despatches to the U.S.A. in fulfilment of Lend—lease obligations.

Plan. A decline in the capital-output ratio in the later phases of the planning process is to be ordinarily expected due to greater utilization of the capacity created through past investment and reduction of the gestation lags of the various types of investment etc.

During the period 1950–51 to 1962–63, average share of the household sector's saving in the total saving was the largest at 74.6 per cent, as against 19.5 per cent of the Government sector and 5.9 per cent of the

### *Table 11—Volume and Pattern of Saving (Annual Average)*

| | *Period I (1950–51 to 1952–53)* | *Period II (1953–54 to 1955–56)* | *Period III (1956–57 to 1958–59)* | *Period IV (1959–60 to 1962–63)* | *1st Plan (1951–52 to 1955–56)* | *IInd Plan (1956–57 to 1960–61)* | *(1961–62 and 1962–63)* | *(1950–51 to 1962–63)* |
|---|---|---|---|---|---|---|---|---|
| Government Sector | 119.4 | 101.8 | 149.8 | 267.3 | 114.9 | 170.1 | 334.0 | 167.9 |
| (a) | 26.0 | 12.8 | 16.8 | 22.5 | 17.6 | 17.3 | 26.6 | 19.5 |
| (b) | 1.3 | 1.0 | 1.3 | 2.1 | 1.2 | 1.5 | 2.5 | 1.5 |
| Domestic Corporate Sector | 30.5 | 47.2 | 34.6 | 81.5 | 40.2 | 50.6 | 88.6 | 51.0 |
| (a) | 6.6 | 6.0 | 3.9 | 6.8 | 6.2 | 5.1 | 7.0 | 5.9 |
| (b) | 0.3 | 0.5 | 0.3 | 0.6 | 0.4 | 0.4 | 0.7 | 0.5 |
| Household Sector | 310.0 | 643.5 | 705.9 | 840.5 | 495.7 | 762.4 | 833.9 | 641.5 |
| (a) | 67.4 | 81.2 | 79.3 | 70.7 | 76.2 | 77.6 | 66.4 | 74.6 |
| (b) | 3.4 | 6.2 | 6.3 | 6.6 | 5.0 | 6.6 | 6.3 | 5.8 |
| (*i*) Rural Household Sector | 151.7 | 170.4 | 179.3 | 196.5 | 163.7 | 185.2 | 199.1 | 176.1 |
| (a) | 33.0 | 21.6 | 20.1 | 16.5 | 25.1 | 18.8 | 15.8 | 20.5 |
| (b) | 1.7 | 1.7 | 1.6 | 1.5 | 1.6 | 1.6 | 1.5 | 1.6 |
| (c) | 48.9 | 26.5 | 25.4 | 23.4 | 33.0 | 24.3 | 23.9 | 27.4 |
| (*ii*) Urban Household Sector | 158.3 | 473.1 | 526.6 | 644.0 | 332.0 | 577.2 | 634.8 | 465.4 |
| (a) | 34.4 | 59.6 | 59.2 | 54.2 | 51.1 | 58.8 | 50.6 | 54.1 |
| (b) | 1.7 | 4.5 | 4.7 | 5.1 | 3.4 | 5.0 | 4.8 | 4.2 |
| (c) | 51.1 | 73.5 | 74.6 | 76.6 | 67.0 | 75.7 | 76.1 | 72.6 |
| Total Saving | 459.9 | 792.5 | 890.3 | 1,189.3 | 650.8 | 933.1 | 1,256.5 | 860.4 |
| (b) | 5.0 | 7.7 | 7.9 | 9.3 | 6.6 | 8.5 | 9.5 | 7.8 |

(a) Proportion (percentage) of Total Saving.
(b) Proportion (percentage) of National Income,
(c) Proportion (percentage) of the Household Sector's Saving, in Rs. crores, at 1948–49 prices.

### *Table 12—Investment, Investment-Income Ratios and Capital-Ouput Ratios*[a]

| | *Investment (Annual Average)* | *Investment/ Income Ratio (Per cent)* | *Capital/ Output Ratio* |
|---|---|---|---|
| Period I (1950–51 to 1952–53) | 520.3 | 5.7 | — |
| Period II (1953–54 to 1955–56) | 830.1 | 8.1 | 2.22 :1 |
| Period III (1956–57 to 1958–59) | 1,291.8 | 11.5 | 4.21 :1 |
| Period IV (1959–60 to 1962–63) | 1,542.9 | 12.1 | 3.91 :1 |
| First Plan Period | 711.0 | 7.2 | — |
| Second Plan Period | 1,360.8 | 11.7 | 3.86 :1 |
| Third Plan Period (1961–62 and 1962–63) | 1,621.6 | 12.3 | 3.53 :1 |

[a] Rs. crores, at 1948–49 prices. Marginal Capital-output ratios are in relation with the previous period. The ratio in respect of the period 1961–62 and 1962–63 is in relation with the last two years of the Second Plan (1959–60 and 1960–61).

domestic corporate sector. Within the household sector, the average share of the urban household sector was 54.1 per cent during the period.

The proportion of Government saving to total saving sharply declined from 26.0 per cent in period I to 12.8 per cent in the next period; in subsequent periods it steadily increased to 16.8 per cent and 22.5 per cent, respectively. On the other hand, saving of the household sector, which was 67 per cent in period I, spurted up to 81 per cent and 79 per cent in periods II and III, respectively, before dipping again to 71 per cent in period IV. The share of domestic corporate sector which was 6.6 per cent in period I fell to 3.9 per cent in period III but increased to 6.8 per cent in period IV. Within the household sector, the share of the urban household sector in total saving rose sharply during period II and was generally maintained in the subsequent periods. Only in two years, 1951–52 and 1952–53, was the share of rural household sector larger than that of urban in the total savings of the household sector. These were the years when total saving of this sector was depressed, and especially so in financial assets.

The volume and pattern of the household sector's saving at constant prices are given in Table 13.

The largest share of the household sector's saving is accounted for by saving in physical assets. The average saving of the household sector in the form of physical assets was 59.4 per cent during the entire period 1950–51 to

## *Table 13—Volume and Pattern of Saving of the Household Sector (Annual Average)*

| | *Period I (1950–51 to 1952–53)* | *Period II (1953–54 to 1955–56)* | *Period III (1956–57 to 1958–59)* | *Period IV (1959–60 to 1962–63)* | *Ist Plan (1951–52 to 1955–56)* | *IInd Plan (1956–57 to 1960–61)* | *(1961–62 and 1962–63)* | *(1950–51 to 1962–63)* |
|---|---|---|---|---|---|---|---|---|
| A. Financial Assets (1 to 6) | 13.0 | 271.3 | 312.1 | 399.0 | 167.0 | 336.9 | 424.0 | 260.4 |
| (a) | 4.2 | 42.2 | 44.2 | 47.5 | 33.7 | 44.2 | 50.8 | 40.6 |
| (b) | 0.2 | 2.7 | 2.8 | 3.1 | 1.7 | 2.9 | 3.2 | 2.4 |
| 1. Currency | −17.4 | 104.9 | 65.9 | 124.5 | 37.7 | 92.2 | 117.2 | 73.7 |
| (a) | − 5.6 | 16.3 | 9.3 | 14.8 | 7.6 | 12.1 | 14.0 | 11.5 |
| (b) | − 0.2 | 1.0 | 0.6 | 1.0 | 0.4 | 0.8 | 0.9 | 0.7 |
| 2. Net Bank Deposits | −16.3 | 8.9 | 27.9 | 48.2 | 2.5 | 27.2 | 70.4 | 19.6 |
| (a) | − 5.3 | 1.4 | 4.0 | 5.7 | 0.5 | 3.6 | 8.4 | 3.1 |
| (b) | − 0.2 | 0.1 | 0.2 | 0.4 | — | 0.2 | 0.5 | 0.2 |
| 3. Insurance Policies | 14.6 | 24.7 | 25.6 | 49.5 | 20.3 | 32.4 | 56.5 | 30.2 |
| (a) | 4.7 | 3.9 | 3.6 | 5.9 | 4.1 | 4.2 | 6.8 | 4.7 |
| (b) | 0.2 | 0.2 | 0.2 | 0.4 | 0.2 | 0.3 | 0.4 | 0.3 |
| 4. Provident Funds | 34.0 | 86.2 | 96.0 | 129.1 | 66.2 | 105.3 | 138.9 | 89.6 |
| (a) | 11.0 | 13.4 | 13.6 | 15.4 | 13.4 | 13.8 | 16.7 | 14.0 |
| (b) | 0.4 | 0.9 | 0.9 | 1.0 | 0.7 | 0.9 | 1.1 | 0.8 |
| 5. Net Claims on the Government Sector | −23.2 | 7.3 | 40.1 | −8.9 | 10.0 | 25.5 | −21.4 | 2.8 |
| (a) | − 7.5 | 1.1 | 5.7 | −1.0 | 2.0 | 3.4 | − 2.6 | 0.4 |
| (b) | − 0.3 | 0.1 | 0.4 | −0.1 | 0.1 | 0.2 | − 0.2 | — |
| 6. Corporate and Cooperative Shares and Securities | 21.3 | 39.3 | 56.6 | 56.6 | 30.3 | 54.3 | 62.4 | 44.5 |
| (a) | 6.9 | 6.1 | 8.0 | 6.7 | 6.1 | 7.1 | 7.5 | 6.9 |
| (b) | 0.3 | 0.4 | 0.5 | 0.4 | 0.3 | 0.5 | 0.5 | 0.4 |
| B. Physical Assets | 297.0 | 372.2 | 393.8 | 441.5 | 328.7 | 425.5 | 409.9 | 381.1 |
| (a) | 95.8 | 57.8 | 55.8 | 52.5 | 66.3 | 55.8 | 49.2 | 59.4 |
| (b) | 3.2 | 3.5 | 3.5 | 3.5 | 3.3 | 3.7 | 3.1 | 3.4 |
| C. Saving of the Household Sector (A + B) | 310.0 | 643.5 | 705.9 | 840.5 | 495.7 | 762.4 | 833.9 | 641.5 |
| (b) | 3.4 | 6.2 | 6.3 | 6.6 | 5.0 | 6.6 | 6.3 | 5.8 |

(a) Proportion (percentage) of Saving of the Household Sector, in Rs. crores, at 1948–49 prices.
(b) Proportion (percentage) of National Income, in Rs. crores, at 1948–49 prices.

1962–63. It accounted for 95–8 per cent in period I but declined sharply to 57.8 per cent in period II and steadily declined in the subsequent periods.

Within the category of household sector's saving in the form of financial assets, prominent were saving through provident funds, whose average share in household sector's saving during 1950–51 to 1962–63 was 14.0 per cent, and currency whose corresponding share was 11.5 per cent. Next in importance were the shares of saving in corporate and cooperative shares and securities (6.9 per cent), insurance policies (4.7 per cent) and bank deposits (3.1 per cent).

Period-wise, the share of saving in the form of corporate and cooperative shares and securities in the total saving of the household sector remained, by and large, steady. Those which showed marked variations, period-wise, were saving in the form of currency, net claims on Government sector and insurance policies. Thus, the share of saving in currency in total household sector's saving rose from −5.6 per cent during period I to 16.3 per cent in period II and after declining in period III to 9.3 per cent again increased to 14.8 per cent in period IV. Net claims on the Government sector as a proportion of household saving increased from −7.5 per cent in period I to 5.7 per cent in period III and dropped to −1.0 per cent in the next period. The share of insurance policies declined from 4.7 per cent in period I to 3.6 per cent in period III but increased in the subsequent period to 5.9 per cent. The shares of provident funds and net bank deposits showed a steady rise from period to period. Thus, bank deposits increased from —5.3 per cent in period I to 5.7 per cent in period IV, and provident funds rose from 11.0 per cent to 15.4 per cent over the period.

25

# Trends in Capital Formation in Communist China

*William W. Hollister*

*From* An Economic Profile of Mainland China, Vol. I, *Studies Prepared for the Joint Economic Committee, Congress of the United States, February 1967, U.S. Government Printing Office, pp. 123–32 and 145–50, with omissions. Reprinted by permission.*

## *Introduction*

THIS PAPER IS concerned with the process of capital formation and its relation to the trends that have occurred in Mainland China since 1950. Capital formation refers to the increases that have taken place in the productive facilities of the Chinese economy in inventories, installations, and equipment for production of goods and services. This study will concentrate on *gross fixed investment* excluding that portion of gross investment that involves increases in inventories. The broadest definition of fixed investment would include all net acquisitions of goods or facilities for production or use in future time periods. On this basis the acquisition of consumer durables by households and the procurement of military equipment would be included under investment. Neither of these categories is included in investment as defined in this study. In Communist China household purchases of consumer durables other than housing are small; furniture and bicycles are typical items excluded. Expenditures for military equipment represent nonconsumption expenditures that must be financed in the same way as state investment, and such equipment represents capital available to the military establishment that is cumulative over time. Unfortunately, there is no data sufficiently reliable to justify the inclusion of such expenditures in fixed investment.

Measurement of capital formation is difficult because of the usual problems in the use of official Communist data. The limitations in such data with the inevitable distortions and deficiencies are compounded in the case of China by the kaleidoscopic shifts in economic policies that have taken place in the comparatively short period of time since 1950. Officially the period 1950–52 was a period of recovery when production was rising to levels already attained in the 1930s for China proper and in the early 1940s for Manchuria. Actually this process of recovery continued in the years 1953–55. The period 1950–55, therefore, represents a period of substantial recovery in all sectors from the disruptions of the Sino-Japanese war and the civil war that followed. The period of the First Five-Year Plan—1953–57—represents a planning framework for rapid industrialization made familiar by the Soviet program for economic development. This Chinese program was only taking hold in the years 1953–55 and did not become a dominant feature until the years 1956–57. The Leap Forward program for the years 1958–60 represents a drastically new policy framework introducing many changes in economic organization and production. This Leap Forward framework was superimposed on the First Five-Year Plan program for rapid industrialization that was gaining momentum in heavy industry in the years 1958–59. Since 1960 with the drastic setbacks in the Chinese economy following the Leap Forward there has been a prolong period of retrenchment, officially termed the "period of consolidation and readjustment." This readjustment period is now considered to have ended in 1965, and 1966 is termed the first year of a Third Five-Year Plan scheduled for 1966–70. With most of 1966 behind us, however, it is clear that this Third Five-Year Plan bears little resemblance to the planning pattern established for the Soviet economy. Annual production targets that are to be fulfilled or overfulfilled seem to be scorned by the Chinese Communist leaders as a "revisionist" approach to economic development. Political campaigns and *ad hoc* planning have taken the place of planning on the Soviet model.

The data permits estimates for fixed investment with any degree of reliability only for the years 1950–59. Even in this period the data for 1950–53 and for 1958–59 are less reliable than the far from satisfactory data for 1954–57. For the seven-year period 1960–66, only the skimpiest of data is available and there are no aggregate figures permitting direct estimates of fixed investment in these years. This paper will concentrate on the main conclusions to be drawn from the author's estimates of fixed investment, and not on the methods and procedures used in securing these estimates. Important differences between our conclusions and those of other scholars will be noted for the reader's benefit. In general, differences in the underlying estimates of capital formation are overshadowed by differences in interpretation and judgment as to the important trends in the Chinese economy.

## *The Rate of Investment and Growth*

Analysis of the growth potential of an underdeveloped economy like China's has usually proceeded in terms of two key aggregates. First, a definite ratio exists between savings and national income and this rate is considered to be a function of per capita incomes. China, with a very low level of per capita income, is expected to have a low rate of saving. Second, the rates of saving determines the proportion of output going to increments in the capital stock and a specific relation exists between increments to capital and increments to national income. The rate of saving and the incremental capital-output ratio (ICOR) together determine the rate of growth in national income. The problem of economic development in this approach is to raise the rate of saving and thereby permit an important increase in the rate of growth of total output.

Using this framework of analysis and given the low level of per capita incomes in China, it is clear that the Chinese Communist system has been successful in raising the rate of investment to levels that should permit important and sustained increases in per capita income. Table 1 presents the key estimates for the rate of investment in current market prices for the years 1950–59.

Table 1 gives estimates for depreciation for those readers interested in calculating net investment rates. Depreciation allowances represent provisions for financing replacements of the capital stock and vary widely as between various economies and various types of economic institutions. Depreciation is not a measure of the amount of capital that has been scrapped or has worn out. This

### *Table 1—Gross Investment in Communist China*[a]

| | 1950 | 1951 | 1952 | 1953 | 1954 | 1955 | 1956 | 1957 | 1958 | 1959 |
|---|---|---|---|---|---|---|---|---|---|---|
| | | | | | *Billion yuan* | | | | | |
| Gross domestic investment | 6.09 | 11.47 | 14.57 | 18.45 | 19.40 | 19.14 | 19.69 | 25.31 | 44.27 | 49.14 |
| Net balance of foreign claims | .15 | —.96 | —.92 | —1.01 | —.31 | —1.08 | .32 | .51 | —.07 | —.50 |
| Gross fixed investment | 3.24 | 5.77 | 8.42 | 12.59 | 14.12 | 13.92 | 19.87 | 18.77 | 33.47 | 38.73 |
| Gross national product | 46.98 | 63.94 | 70.12 | 85.28 | 90.47 | 92.55 | 104.66 | 112.21 | 136.1 | 147.8 |
| Depreciation | 2.62 | 2.98 | 3.31 | 3.75 | 4.15 | 4.50 | 4.97 | 6.29 | 7.03 | 8.08 |
| | | | | | *Percentages* | | | | | |
| Gross investment | 13.0 | 17.9 | 20.8 | 21.6 | 21.4 | 20.7 | 18.8 | 22.6 | 32.3 | 33.2 |
| Change in inventories | (6.1) | (8.9) | (8.8) | (6.9) | (5.8) | (5.6) | (—0.2) | (5.8) | (7.9) | (7.0) |
| Gross fixed investment | (6.9) | (9.0) | (12.0) | (14.8) | (15.3) | (15.0) | (19.0) | (16.7) | (24.6) | (26.2) |

[a] Current market prices.

analysis follows the United Nations study of European economics—in concentrating on gross fixed investment as the key aggregate for analysis. Rates of saving involve not only fixed investment but changes in inventories, and so figures for gross domestic investment are also given in Table 1. The data on inventories are far less reliable than for fixed investment. The importance of foreign investment in the form of grants or loans is also of interest, and rough magnitudes are given for net foreign investment showing that in the case of China most savings have been achieved internally.

The figures in Table 1 show that by 1952 the rate of gross investment was raised to one-fifth of total output and maintained at that level through the period of the First Five-Year Plan (1953–57). The Leap Forward push raised the rate of investment dramatically to about one-third of output in 1958–59. These rates include substantial percentages of output for increases in inventories in all years except 1956, but gross fixed investment is estimated at 12 per cent of GNP in 1952 and increased to about 15 to 17 per cent in the years 1953–57. The Leap Forward rates for gross fixed investment are one-quarter of total output and more than double the 1952 rate. These rates of capital formation are very much higher than the rate in 1933. According to estimates made by Liu and Yeh, gross fixed investment in 1933 in current prices was about 5 per cent of gross domestic product.

The rates for fixed investment shown in Table 1 can be compared to the estimates made for Japan—a country that is almost a perfect model for a successful long-term rate of economic development. Rosovsky's figures for Japan are as in Table 2.

A comparison of these estimates with the China figures for 1953–57 and allowing for small amounts of military construction in the China estimates indicates about the same rate of investment as in Japan in the 1931–40 decade and only a slightly higher rate than in the period after World War I. The China figures for 1958–59 were achieved in Japan only in the 1950s.

For the period since World War I, Rosovsky's figures for gross fixed investment excluding military investment average 14.8 per cent and the average annual rate of growth is about 4.8 per cent—giving an implied long-term incremental capital-output ratio (ICOR) of about 3.0. For the earlier period, 1887 to 1912, the implied ICOR is lower than this—closer to 2.0 than to 3.0. The ICOR for China has shown no stability over the period 1950–59. Allowing a year lag, for the whole period 1950–59, the ICOR was 1.65. For the recovery period 1950–53 the ICOR was quite low—0.8; for the 1953–57 period the ICOR was 2.0; and for the Leap Forward years about 1.3

***Table 2—Fixed Investment Excluding Military Investment as Percentage of GNP for Japan***

| | *(Overlapping decade averages)* | | *(Overlapping decade averages)* |
|---|---|---|---|
| 1887–96 | 9.1 | 1912–21 | 12.8 |
| 1892–1901 | 8.4 | 1917–26 | 14.4 |
| 1897–1906 | 8.4 | 1922–31 | 14.7 |
| 1902–11 | 10.1 | 1927–36 | 14.3 |
| 1907–16 | 10.6 | 1931–40 | 15.8 |

Figures for Asian countries in the 1950–59 period for gross fixed investment, growth rates, and ICOR's are shown in Table 3.

In Table 3, figures for China for 1958–59 are omitted because of problems in the data and because subsequent years clearly show that their inclusion would distort the comparisons. The 1950–53 years in China are recovery years, but they are also recovery years for most other Asian countries. No clear conclusions emerge from the comparisons in Table 3. The rate of gross fixed capital formation in China does not show that a Communist system is the only way to get high rates of fixed capital formation, because most of the Asian countries also achieved rates close to China's in the 1950–57 period. South Korea and Taiwan, however, financed a large portion of investment with foreign aid. The ICOR for China is in the expected range but why it is much lower than India's; pretty much the same as the ICOR for Japan, Ceylon, and Thailand; and higher than the ICOR for Taiwan and the Philippines is far from clear. The differences might lie in the estimates themselves, but the most likely hypothesis is that there is no simple and direct relationship between the three variables: the rate of investment, the rate of growth, and the incremental capital-output ratio.

In a paper of this scope it is not possible to go into all the considerations that are involved in the assumption that incremental capital-output ratios constitute a valid basis for analyzing trends in underdeveloped economies. It is our conviction that incremental capital-output ratios are only surface reflections of the underlying factors operating in the course of economic development. In themselves incremental capital-output ratios tells us nothing that we need to know about economic trends. In the rest of this paper we will attempt to analyze the alternatives faced by the Communist planners in formulating their investment policies and the implications of the kaleidoscopic shifts in investment policies that have occurred.

## *Sector Allocations of Fixed Investment*

Our estimates of fixed investment use a methodology that permits allocations of investment to the various sectors. Table 4 presents percentage shares in each year for fixed investment in the major sectors of the economy. The share for agriculture has remained stable over the period 1954–59 in spite of large increases in the absolute amounts of fixed investment. Transport has also commanded a fairly stable share of total fixed investment. The main feature of trends in sector allocations has been a steady rise in investment allocations for industry, construction, and utilities. The share for heavy industry alone reflects the very high priority given to this sector by the Communist planners with rising percentages throughout the period. There has been some decline in the share for residential construction, but the rising share for industry, construction, and utilities has been mainly counterbalanced by a decline in the share for services and trade.

The percentage shares for some European market economies are given in Table 5. The allocations for China for agriculture are roughly twice those for Western economies

### *Table 3—Gross Fixed Investment as a Percentage of GNP[a] Rates of Growth, and Incremental Capital-Output Ratios[b]*

| *Country* | *Average rate of gross fixed capital formation (percentage)* | *Average rate of growth in product (percentage)* | *ICOR* |
|---|---|---|---|
| Japan, 1950 to 1959 | 21.6 | 9.1 | 2.4 |
| Burma, 1951 to 1959 | 17.1 | 5.1 | 3.4 |
| India, 1950 to 1959 | 14.9 | 3.1 | 4.8 |
| Thailand, 1952 to 1959 | 14.4 | 5.5 | 2.6 |
| Taiwan, 1950 to 1959 | 13.1 | 7.9 | 1.7 |
| South Korea, 1953 to 1959 | 12.3 | 5.1 | 2.2 |
| Ceylon, 1950 to 1959 | 11.3 | 3.9 | 2.9 |
| Pakistan, 1950 to 1959 | 7.8 | 2.6 | 3.0 |
| Philippines, 1950 to 1959 | 7.0 | 6.0 | 1.2 |
| Indonesia, 1951 to 1959 | 6.2 | 3.6 | 1.7 |
| China (estimates): | | | |
| 1950 to 1957 | 15.9 | 8.9 | 1.8 |
| 1952 to 1957 | (17.5) | (7.6) | (2.3) |

[a] In constant market prices.
[b] Figures for Asian economies given in the *Economic Survey for Asia and the Far East, 1961*.

with the exception of Turkey, where agricultural investment is nearly as high a percentage as for China. The percentages for industry, construction, and public utilities in China are not much higher than for Western economies except for the years 1958–59 when one-half of total investment go to these sectors. Only Yugoslavia has as high an allocation for these sectors as that shown for China in 1958–59. No data are available on the breakdown between heavy industry and light industry in the Communist classification, but it is not likely that the European market economies allocated so preponderant a share of industrial investment to heavy industry as the allocations shown for China. Transport and residential housing command much smaller shares in China than in these countries.

### INVESTMENT IN AGRICULTURE

The most familiar charge against the investment policies followed by Communist planners during the period 1953–57 is that the priority for heavy industry starved agriculture of the investment funds that could have yielded larger increases in agricultural

## *Table 4—Sector Shares of Gross Fixed Investment*[a]

| *Sector* | *1950* | *1951* | *1952* | *1953* | *1954* | *1955* | *1956* | *1957* | *1958* | *1959* |
|---|---|---|---|---|---|---|---|---|---|---|
| Agriculture[b] | 31.5 | 25.5 | 24.9 | 20.7 | 22.4 | 24.5 | 22.8 | 23.0 | 24.0 | 23.2 |
| Industry, construction, and public utilities | 21.0 | 27.7 | 28.7 | 33.0 | 34.4 | 34.3 | 37.8 | 41.3 | 50.9 | 49.8 |
| Heavy industry | ([c]) | ([c]) | (15.0) | (17.1) | (20.2) | (24.6) | (26.2) | (29.2) | (41.0) | (40.6) |
| Light industry | ([c]) | ([c]) | (10.0) | (10.2) | (8.2) | (4.0) | (4.6) | (5.7) | (5.9) | (5.9) |
| Transportation and communications | 12.3 | 11.8 | 10.3 | 9.4 | 11.0 | 13.8 | 13.8 | 12.6 | 10.0 | 12.2 |
| Residential construction[b] | 12.4 | 12.8 | 14.6 | 10.2 | 9.5 | 10.5 | 8.4 | 9.7 | 6.6 | 6.6 |
| Service and trade | 22.8 | 22.2 | 21.6 | 26.5 | 22.8 | 16.8 | 17.0 | 13.4 | 8.4 | 8.3 |
| Total fixed investment[d] | 100.0 | 100.0 | 100.0 | 100.0 | 100.0 | 100.0 | 100.0 | 100.0 | 100.0 | 100.0 |

[a] Sector investment are based on estimates of investment for nonproductive purposes that are subtracted from the sector allocations for State investment. All private investment other than industrial investment, handicrafts, and native transportation have been included under investment in trade although small amounts of this investment may properly have fallen under other sectors.

[b] One-third of self-financed agricultural investment is estimated to be construction and half of this is assumed to be for housing.

[c] Not available.

[d] Subtotals do not necessarily add to the total because of rounding.

## *Table 5—Sector Shares of Gross Fixed Investment; Average 1949-58*

| *Country* | *Agriculture* | *Mining, manufacturing, construction, public utilities* | *Transport* | *Dwellings* | *Services* | *Total* |
|---|---|---|---|---|---|---|
| Southern European countries | | | | | | |
| Greece | 10.5 | 26.1 | 14.2 | 34.6 | 14.1 | 100.0 |
| Italy | 13.0 | 33.2 | 19.9 | 21.9 | 12.0 | 100.0 |
| Turkey (1950–58) | 21.6 | 29.5 | 21.3 | 18.6 | 9.0 | 100.0 |
| Yugoslavia | 8.8 | 49.7 | 15.6 | 14.8 | 11.1 | 100.0 |
| Spain | 10.4 | 32.7 | | 15.9 | | 100.0 |
| Portugal (1952–58) | 12.5 | 34.4 | 16.9 | 20.2 | 16.1 | 100.0 |
| Selected developed economies: | | | | | | |
| Western Germany | 8.8 | 37.1 | 14.8 | 22.7 | 16.6 | 100.0 |
| France | 11.2 | 38.2 | 14.5 | 24.5 | 11.7 | 100.0 |
| United States | 6.6 | 31.9[a] | 14.3 | 28.6 | | 100.0 |
| United Kingdom | 4.4 | 41.0 | 13.4 | 21.2 | 20.0 | 100.0 |

[a] Excludes construction.

*Source:* United Nations Publication, *op. cit.*, ch. II, p. 51.

output. In the discussion that follows, it must be remembered that the actual estimates for agricultural investment are higher than estimates made by others. The year-to-year changes in agriculture investment, however, are not greatly different in these alternative estimates.

The percentage shares for agriculture shown in Table 4 do not show that this sector has received insufficient investment. Agriculture in China contributes perhaps twice as much to national income as the percentages shown—about 22 per cent of fixed investment—but no country undergoing economic development can be expected to have investment allocated in proportion to existing sector shares of GNP. In the five-year period (1953–57) fixed investment for agriculture approximately doubled in magnitude. In the 1958–59 Leap Forward effort, agricultural investment again doubled in absolute magnitude. The Soviet analogy has often been cited in this context, but even in the Soviet case the problem probably lies more with the ineffectiveness of the agricultural investment undertaken than with the magnitude of the agricultural investment effort itself. In the case of China the strategy for agriculture outlined in the First Five-Year Plan seems quite sensible in concentrating on labor-intensive investment such as irrigation rather than pushing mechanization of agriculture. With China's large population, any very large release of manpower from agriculture was not indicated. The major problem is in increasing yields per acre, and for this objective the major emphasis needs to be on greater supplies of chemical fertilizer and other key inputs.

The heavy industry bias in China stressed imports of machinery and equipment for heavy industry when imports would much more wisely have been in the form of chemical fertilizer and other supporting inputs for agriculture. In the 1953–55 period too low a priority was given to increasing chemical fertilizer production; and this is a defect that applies not to the allocations of investment to agriculture, but to the allocations of heavy industry investment within heavy industry itself. The chemicals industries were relatively weak in China, and the greater priority needed for chemical fertilizer would have meant a somewhat slower increase in heavy industry output. The problem of increasing agricultural production in China is a problem of modernization—of improving farm technology. Given the traditional system of production and the usual deficiencies in Communist methods of socializing agriculture, definite limits are set on potential increases in output as a result of agricultural investment. The problems being faced by the Communist planners at the present time would be very much simplified if additional allocations of investment to agriculture would be all that is needed to increase production.

RESIDENTIAL CONSTRUCTION

Table 4 shows the percentage of fixed investment for residential construction at less than 10 per cent in the 1953–57 period. The percentages are far below those shown in Table 5 for European market economies. Most European countries show a pattern of sector allocation for dwellings between 20 and 30 per cent, with Turkey, Yugoslavia, and Spain in the 15 to 20 per cent range. A comparison for Asian economies with the estimates made in this paper would not show such differences. The estimates for Taiwan show the average percentage of fixed investment for 1957–63 for dwellings as 12 per cent. Rosovsky's figures for Japan show residential housing as percentages of total fixed investment excluding military construction as follows:

| | | | |
|---|---|---|---|
| 1887–96 | 27.7 | 1912–21 | 12.9 |
| 1892–1901 | 23.4 | 1916–26 | 11.4 |
| 1897–1906 | 17.3 | 1922–31 | 9.1 |
| 1902–11 | 10.3 | 1927–36 | 7.5 |
| 1907–16 | 11.8 | 1931–40 | 5.4 |

Since 1954 residential construction in Japan has run between 9 and 7 per cent of total fixed investment.

The estimates for China have taken as the starting point investment by all socialist enterprises furnished in the official data. But it has been estimated that in the 1950–55 period substantial amounts of residental construction were undertaken in the private sector. As late as 1954, half of the urban labor force was in the private sector. The estimates for private investment in urban housing for the years 1950–55 is about 70 per cent of the official figures for investment by socialist enterprises. There is no question that official policy by the planners was concerned with holding housing construction to a minimum, but even for State investment, the planners' efforts were not completely successful. State investment in urban housing for 1953–57 was much higher than the First Five-Year Plan targets, and so-called nonproductive investment exceeded the quotas in the plan by much more than investment in productive fixed assets. Less important in the estimates for investment are estimates for major repairs equal to 1 per cent of the value of the housing stock. Such major repairs are estimated to have been sufficient to keep the existing stock of urban housing habitable and inhabited in the 1950–59 period. The picture shown by the estimates is a rise in urban housing barely sufficient to maintain a low living standard in urban areas for housing in view of the rapid rise of the urban population.

Kang Chao's study of urban housing reaches a very different conclusion—that there has been a drastic deterioration in urban housing in the period 1949–60. By 1957 per capita housing is found to have declined by one-third from the 1949 level and by 1960 the urban housing situation is estimated to be one-half of the 1949 level. Actually such a trend would involve massive efforts in rationing housing space in urban areas and tensions that do not seem to have occurred in the period under consideration. The article was received too late for a detailed analysis of the sources cited. The data, however, would have to be quite reliable to substantiate the conclusions in our view, because the general assumptions are most implausible. Much urban residential construction uses dirt to be packed into walls and other materials not subject to the system of state controls for cement and other key commodities. Most of the labor involved can be furnished by the residents themselves in many cases and by handicrafts labor available locally outside the state apparatus.

Even if private investment in housing was not undertaken because of the prevailing situation, it is most unlikely that the major repairs necessary to maintain the urban housing stock that existed in 1949 were not undertaken. Kang Chao estimates that 2 per cent of the urban housing stock disappeared each year and by 1960 one-fifth of all housing that existed in 1949 had simply disappeared. For every square meter built under state investment, two-thirds of a square meter of housing had collapsed or was razed. The estimates in this study involve increments of living space per person of 3.24 square meters—well below the average urban living space as estimated by Kang Chao for all years through 1957. The main difference is that the housing standards in 1949 are estimated to be much lower than for Kang Chao's estimates. Many conclusions about trends in Communist China are not verifiable when all the research has been undertaken that is necessary. But the difference between these estimates of residential construction and Kang Chao's estimates does not fall in this category. Pending this research, the reader will have to make his own judgment.

### INVESTMENT IN TRANSPORTATION

Table 4 shows the percentage allocations for transportation in a range between 10 and 14 per cent. As with residential construction, transportation was clearly a grudging recipient of investment funds in the Communist planning framework. The percentage share for transport in most years is somewhat lower than the percentages shown in Table 5 for the European market economics. Etienne considers the Communist policy with respect to investment in the transportation system as plainly inadequate. In terms of per capita meters of highways or railway track or any other yardstick that might be used, the transportation system in China is at a very low level in relation to the economy.

Over the long run the level of investment for transportation will probably rise above the levels for the 1950–59 period. The trends in 1950–57 are accounted for in part by the large Japanese investment in Manchuria and in north China prior to and during the Sino-Japanese war. In north China the rail system was built up for military reasons on a scale not justified in terms of the pre-Communist production levels. Judged by the population and by total GNP the transportation system may be considered inadequate. Judged by the capabilities of the transportation system to support the existing heavy industrial base, however, the situation was relatively favorable.

#### INVESTMENT IN LIGHT INDUSTRY

The allocations of investment for light industry represent an attempt to hold the allotments for such industries as textiles and food processing to a minimum, but at the same time furnish sufficient investment to process the flow of raw materials from agriculture. A source of much potential additional investment in light industry consists of equipment to process the existing supply of agricultural raw materials more efficiently and reduce costs of production. Such a program would have displaced handicrafts production more rapidly and reduced the labor requirements for light industry production. Light industry investment undertaken, particularly for textiles, was concentrated in larger scale production facilities and tended to be labor displacing. Except for canneries and certain food industries, however, extensive labor-displacing investment in light industry does not seem to have occurred in the 1953–57 period. Considering the situation in China, this investment policy was reasonable. The central defect in the allocation of investment for light industry was the failure of the Communist planners to increase the potential for production of raw materials that could substitute for raw materials dependent on agriculture and on the land. Communist North Korea in this period, for example, was attempting to develop synthetic fibers for its textile industry, but the textile industry in China remained overwhelmingly concentrated in cotton textiles. Such a change in investment policy for light industry, however, would depend on heavy industry to produce the necessary raw materials, and involves the allocations of investment within heavy industry even more than the direct investment in light industry itself. As with chemical fertilizer production, production of synthetic fibers would require development of the chemicals industry. In the 1960s, there was a shift in investment policies in this direction. This effort should have started a decade sooner.

#### INVESTMENT IN TRADE AND NONAGRICULTURAL SERVICES

Allocations for trade and nonagricultural services declined in the years 1955–57 compared with earlier years. This investment includes military construction in substantial amounts up through 1954. Trends in income originating in government reflect a large military and administrative apparatus already established by 1952 and only small increases in the 1953–57 period. The percentage share for these sectors even in 1955–57 is about the same as those for the European economies shown in Table 5. The Communist bias against nonproductive investment is compensated for to a large extent by the political and ideological advantages of a state-sponsored program for education and communal services.

## *Capital Formation and the Actual Trends Since 1957*

In the last section we discussed the alternative policy frameworks that could have been adopted in 1957. We now turn to the actual course of events in the years since

1957. The Leap Forward strategy adopted in the 1958–60 years in our frame of reference is simply the heavy industry push strategy carried far beyond the framework established during the 1953–57 period. We have argued that the 1953–57 framework if followed in the 1958–62 period would imply a rate of urbanization that would put serious new strains on wage and price relationships. The Leap Forward strategy was based on the confident expectation that mass mobilization of rural labor for irrigation and a sharp increase in the flow of producer goods to agriculture would create an agricultural breakthrough, sharply increasing agricultural production beyond the rate of growth achieved for 1953–57. The agricultural surplus would, therefore, increase so much that even a Leap Forward rate of industrialization could be achieved. Furthermore, the Leap Forward strategy by stressing both large-scale and small-scale production methods and by glorifying the solidarity of all laborers blurred the distinction between workers in the modern sectors and workers in the traditional sectors.

The new strategy was striking at the whole trend involved in the First Five-Year Plan strategy—oriented as it was toward building up a skilled and disciplined labor force in the modern sectors as rapidly as possible while workers in the traditional sectors were to find some supporting role in the pattern of development. In fact, the Leap Forward strategy with the establishment of the communes and the campaigns to send students and urban workers to rural areas was aimed not only at abolishing the distinction between nonagricultural workers in the modern and the handicrafts sectors, but at the whole distinction between peasants and urban workers. In this context the Leap Forward strategy was aimed at all-out industrialization without any corresponding increase in the urban population simply because there would no longer be any distinction between workers in any occupation and output would expand as a result of a general upsurge in labor productivity in all sectors simultaneously. Wage differentials would be sharply reduced in the new psychology of peasant-worker solidarity. The investment in social overhead capital for workers developing skills in modern and more technical lines of production could be minimized in favor of investment in support of productive facilities.

In the aftermath of the Leap Forward when sharp declines in agricultural output in 1959–61 below 1957 levels showed that the agricultural surplus was going to fall below the 1953–57 levels, the leadership certainly could not press for all-out industrialization and had every reason to continue its political drive to abolish as many of the distinctions between peasant and worker as possible. The general consequence of continuing this part of the Leap Forward strategy would be to hold the rate of urbanization down as much as possible and lessen the pressure for increasing real wages for workers in the modern sectors as an incentive for increases in skills and disciplined effort.

The second main problem for the heavy industry push strategy was the tendency for heavy industry output to become an end in itself as an increasing portion of output was plowed back into further expansion of heavy industry irrespective of trends in the flow of heavy industry output to the other sectors. This limitation only operates if planners retain in some measure the idea that the objective of building up heavy industry is an increase in the capability of heavy industry to support the modernizing of the rest of the economy. The Leap Forward strategy took the heavy industry push approach far beyond the limits discussed because production targets for steel and other items were glorified as true indicators of industrial progress. In other words, the Leap Forward effort for heavy industry became progressively less rational as it proceeded.

We can easily adapt our heavy industry push projection for a Leap Forward projection based on the actual trends in 1958–59, some scattered indications for 1960, and a hypothetical 1961–62 period if the Leap Forward had run its course. Our first modification is in the level of imports for investment goods to be plowed back into the capital goods sectors. The Leap Forward effort pushed these imports far above our projected trend. Our first adjustment is to use the actual figures for 1958–60 for these imports, but we will assume that the 1961 and 1962 levels would have had to return to our projected levels because of limits in securing the necessary foreign exchange even if the agricultural difficulties and the Sino-Soviet dispute had not occurred. Second, the heavy industry push projection shows sales in support of consumption sectors increasing at an average annual rate of 16.7 per cent. The 1958–59 experience shows an average annual rate for the two years of 19.8 per cent. There is no question that this rate of increase was not viable, but our wish is to trace the Leap Forward to a successful completion by 1962, and so the 19.8 per cent rate will be used. Third, the heavy industry push projection was based on the judgment that investment in modern transportation in particular would be such that heavy industry investment as a percentage of total investment in the capital goods sectors would remain at the 1957 level of 65 per cent. The Leap Forward strategy pushed this percentage far above 65 per cent in the 1958–59 years and for 1960 as outlined in the 1960 plan. All the evidence shows that this investment policy was a mistake because the transportation network was under increasingly severe strains during the 1958–60 years, but we will also use the 1960 percentage for 1961 and 1962. Our fourth and final modification represents a single Leap Forward injection of effort in 1958 in which tremendous pressure was put on workers in large-scale heavy industries for overtime and extra effort, and large numbers of handicrafts people were pressed into the production of producer goods.

This Leap Forward injection decreased the capital-output ratio well below that of 1957 representing a level of sales well above the normal use of capacity. By 1959, however, the policymakers were trying to bring the Leap Forward effort in heavy industry into some semblance of order and the record shows that by 1959 the problem was to bring up production to a full utilization of the rapidly expanding capacity of heavy industry. For the years 1959 through 1962, therefore, we can simply maintain the capital-output ratio at the 1957 level.

With these five assumptions our projection for the Leap Forward strategy can be made. Table 6 presents the growth path for heavy industry involved.

The projected level of output in 1962 in the Leap Forward projection is 399.2 per cent of the 1957 level for an average annual rate of

## *Table 6—The Leap Forward, Heavy Industry Projection, Final Sales of Heavy Industry Plus Imports of Investment Goods*[a]

| | *1957* | *1958* | *1959* | *1960* | *1961* | *1962* |
|---|---|---|---|---|---|---|
| To other sectors except construction[b] | 7.20 | 7.70 | 10.22 | | | |
| To construction for investment in consumption sectors[b] | 4.90 | 6.60 | 7.65 | 21.41 | 25.65 | 30.73 |
| To construction for investment in capital goods sectors[c] | 5.70 | 11.80 | 13.98 | 18.55 | 23.73 | 33.11 |
| Heavy industry | (3.60) | (8.78) | (10.43) | (12.99) | (16.61) | (23.18) |
| Total sales: | | | | | | |
| Imports[d] | 2.90 | 4.94 | 6.20 | 5.63 | 4.01 | 4.35 |
| Domestic sales | 14.90 | 21.06 | 25.65 | 34.33 | 45.37 | 59.59 |
| Sales desired by domestic producers[e] | 14.90 | 18.00 | 25.46 | 34.33 | 45.37 | 59.49 |
| Leap Forward effort | 0 | 3.06 | .19 | 0 | 0 | 0 |

[a] In billion 1957 yuan.

[b] For 1957–59 based on index for total heavy industry output from Liu and Yeh (Liu and Yeh, *op. cit.*), less sales for investment from estimates in this study. For 1960–62 based on the 19.8 per cent a year increase for 1958–59.

[c] Total investment in capital goods sectors based on our estimates for 1957–59. For 1960–62, such investment is the residual. The proportion of total investment in these sectors for heavy industry is based on the actual record for 1957–59. The 1960 plan scheduled investment indicates that heavy industry would be 70 per cent of planned investment in the capital goods sectors, and this percentage is used for 1960–62.

[d] Based on the 1957 estimate against trends in these imports as shown in Eckstein's data for foreign trade; Alexander Eckstein, *Communist China's Economic Growth and Foreign Trade,* (New York; McGraw-Hill Book Co., 1966).

[e] Sales desired by producers to be always in the ratio of $\frac{1}{1.26}$ of fixed assets. Fixed assets added taken to be $\frac{1.5}{1.4}$ of final sales for investment in heavy industry. Therefore for every level of sales by heavy industry or imports plowed back into heavy industry, the increase in the desired level of sales will be 0.85 of plowback sales.

increase for the five-year period of 31.9 per cent. Of course, the projected trend could not possibly have occurred. Even without the difficulties in agriculture and the termination of Soviet aid, the projected trend involved severe imbalances in heavy industry because steel output was in excess of possible uses and other input-output imbalances were developing. The labor requirements would also have been clearly excessive. But supposing these limitations had not operated and the projection had gone through in 1960–62 as shown in Table 6. The proportion of domestic output plus imports plowed back into the capital goods sectors would have increased from 32 per cent in 1957 to 52 per cent in 1962. Of the total increase in domestic sales, 63 per cent would be for plowback sales into the capital goods sectors. The Leap Forward plowback propensity in 1962 is double the proportion estimated for the demand-oriented strategy.

The Leap Forward set as its goal overtaking the United Kingdom in the value of industrial output by 1967, and the whole logic was to expand heavy industry output so as to overtake the most advanced industrialized countries. If the industrialization goal is conceived as production in the form of chemical fertilizer, airplanes, and all other items flowing to the rest of the economy, that might be justified. But if the goal is to expand heavy industry as rapidly as possible without any reference to the modernizing potential involved, this could best be achieved by holding down the flow of goods to the rest of the economy to the level of imports, plowing back 100 per cent of domestic sales into the capital goods sectors. Given the capital-output ratio and the 70 per cent figure for heavy industry investment as a proportion of capital goods investment, total heavy industry output could then grow at the rate of 60 per cent a year, almost twice the Leap Forward rate. Such an effort would clearly be absurd, but the Leap Forward effort was well on the way toward such an absurdity.

The experience of the Leap Forward seems to have acted as a kind of catharsis removing from the leadership any tendency to look at heavy industry as an end in itself. Both from necessity and from bitter experience, the policymakers are now following what we have called a demand-oriented policy toward heavy industry. This is the policy that has been operating throughout the 1961–66 period, and our next problem is to sketch out the implications. Such a shift in policy in itself would have led to enormous changes in 1961. Instead of the Leap Forward projection for 1961 in Table 5, a shift to the demand-oriented policy framework would have meant that sales of investment goods for plowback investment in the capital goods sectors would have been cut in half. Instead of sales of heavy industry increasing by about 32 per cent as in Table 6, sales in 1961 would have declined. But we must also take into account the fact that the demand-oriented policy was forced upon the planners because agricultural failures and the termination of Soviet aid affected the feasible level of final sales by heavy industry to the other sectors. Some of the Soviet aid projects were going into production to support the final sales for military purposes and other flows to the consumer sectors. It is safe to say that the heavy industry push projection for these sales would be the maximum feasible level for increases rather than the Leap Forward levels. With the declines in agricultural production investment in light industry and trade would fall drastically on the order of 80 per cent of the 1960 level. With the overall decline indicated both for light industry and heavy industry the problem would be to reduce the labor force in the modern sectors rather than adding to them. The process of reversing the Leap Forward flow of workers into the nonagricultural labor force and moving large numbers back to the rural areas could not be pursued without freezing the social overhead capital of more established workers at 1960 levels. It is safe to say that investment in the nonagricultural consumption sectors in the 1961 situation would be reduced by something like 75 per cent from the 1960 level. Agricultural investment was troubled by poor quality and inefficiency in production and would have to stay at the 1960 level.

With the events of the 1961–65 period we have huge amounts of excess capacity in heavy industry but in spite of this excess capacity it is probable that new investment would have to be undertaken to support increases in final sales. Our assumption is that only half of the increase in sales can be met by greater use of excess capacity, and the other half must require new investment. Table 7 presents a sketch of the trends in heavy industry in the 1961–64 period.

The sketch of trends as shown in Table 7 is conjectural but the main conclusions are probably correct. Heavy industry output even by 1964 is still below the 1959 level and 70 per cent higher than in 1957. The under-utilization of capacity shown is such that final sales by heavy industry would have to be 90 per cent higher in 1964 to get back to the sort of pressure on producers to maximize output that existed during the First Five-Year Plan and during the Leap Forward. It is clear that there is absolutely no incentive on the part of the leadership to return to the heavy industry push model followed in the 1953–59 period. The whole system of production targets geared as they are to maximum use of industrial capital simply is not relevant for the 1960s. There is no likelihood that a heavy industry push policy framework will be resumed. If such a program were resumed it would only represent stupidity on the part of the Communist policymakers and not any indication of a successful solution to the economic problems of this decade.

The estimates for 1964 show total fixed investment in 1964 except for self-financed agricultural investment well below the 1957 level. This estimate is a little low but fixed investment was probably no higher than in 1957. This situation is possible first because the planners are investing in heavy industry only as needed to support final sales. This should have been the objective of the planners from the very beginning, and this paper has tried to show that the heavy industry bias simply absorbed economic resources beyond any possible justification. The level of investment shown for 1964 also can occur only because the planners have sharply reduced the rate of urbanization from early periods. The present peasant-worker alliance approach and the onslaught against intellectuals makes economic progress more difficult but it sharply reduces the amount of investment that is needed to build up the necessary social overhead capital in the cities to support rapid urbanization. This second investment policy is much more dubious than the demand-oriented approach to heavy industry. The first step releases economic resources for modernizing the economy. The second step puts the burden of modernization on a program for the whole population rather than specific training programs for selected groups of workers in the modern sectors.

Because the heavy industry push program has been terminated and the level of fixed

***Table 7—Aftermath of the Leap Forward, Heavy Industry Sales Plus Imports of Investment Goods***

| | *1960* | *1961* | *1962* | *1963* | *1964* | *1965* |
|---|---|---|---|---|---|---|
| To other sectors except construction[a] | 12.24 | 12.51 | 14.40 | 16.55 | 19.00 | 21.85 |
| To construction for Investment in the consumption sectors[b] | 9.17 | 4.20 | 4.20 | 4.40 | 4.50 | 4.60 |
| Total sales | 21.41 | 16.71 | 18.60 | 20.95 | 23.50 | 26.45 |
| To construction for investment in the capital goods sectors[c] | 18.55 | 1.70 | 2.12 | 2.30 | 2.66 | |
| Imports | 5.63 | 1.45 | .72 | .88 | .88 | |
| Domestic sales | 34.33 | 16.96 | 20.00 | 22.37 | 25.28 | |
| Domestic sales desired by producers[d] | 34.33 | 45.37 | 46.32 | 47.50 | 48.78 | |

[a] Final sales to other sectors for 1961–64 based on the trend projected for the heavy industry push projection.
[b] Gross investment in the consumption sectors estimated at 4,000,000,000 for agriculture and 1,900,000,000 for nonagricultural consumer service sectors for the years 1961–65. Light industry and trade at 1/5 the 1960 level for 1961–62 rising gradually in 1963–65 with a shift toward synthetic fibers and other investment. Sales by heavy industry 2/3 of investment sales.
[c] Normal desired investment for increases in sales in next year would be 1.8 times these increases but half of this attained by use of existing excess capacity. Indirect investment also unnecessary because of very large amounts of excess capacity.
[d] Desired level of sales based on maintaining the 1957 capital-output ratio for maximum utilization of industrial capital.

investment sharply reduced, there is a tendency to arrive at wrong conclusions about the general state of heavy industry. Table 7 projects a very satisfactory rate of increase in the sales of heavy industry to the other sectors (exclusive of sales for investment). These increases in production have been in the form of heavy industry output substituting for petroleum and other commodities previously imported, in the flow of military equipment, and in the flow of chemical fertilizer and many other items that constitute substantial progress in economic development. The Communist leaders seem to have freed themselves of the tendency to identify increases in production of steel and other key commodities of heavy industry with success or failure in economic development. The central thesis of this paper is that observers of the China scene must also find new criteria for success and failure to replace those used in the 1950–59 period.

B

# Improvement of Human Resources

THE IMPORTANCE OF education in accelerating the economic development of underdeveloped countries is increasingly recognized. One of the most difficult problems in planning for educational development is that of designing educational policies appropriate to the specific economic conditions and requirements of a particular country. There is no ready-made solution. The experiences of India and China can illustrate some of the difficulties involved in the problem.

The article, "Indian Education: Search for Economic and Political Independence," stresses the need for new educational policies to meet India's current socioeconomic problems. These problems include providing food for a fast-growing population, inequalities in land ownership and income distribution, lack of national unity, language diversity, social immobility, and opposition to cultural change. The article then discusses the administration of education in India. Education is under the states' control with the important exception of higher and advanced technical education, which is under the central government. The educational influence of the central government on the states is accomplished through three devices: making financial grants to the states, acting as collector and clearinghouse for statistical information, and the domination of both state and national politics by the same political party. The relationship and functions of the National Ministry of Education and the state ministries of Education are also discussed in the paper.

The goals and achievements in the field of education are analyzed. In the field of primary education a new pattern of basic education emphasizing the study of crafts has been introduced to aid rural reconstruction. In the field of secondary education a three- or four-year multipurpose secondary school curriculum, following eight years of basic education, has been adopted. Efforts have been made to meet the needs for vocational training, including crafts and agriculture. Emphasis has been placed on regional and national languages, teacher training, and the provision of scholarships for able but poor students.

In the field of higher education attempts have been made to adjust enrollment to the manpower need, to modernize the curriculum, especially in the natural and social sciences, to increase opportunities for women in education, and to synthesize India's cultural tradition and values with the newer knowledge from the West. Other innovations have been made in education to support community development programs. In order to establish closer ties between higher education and rural life, two experiments have been made. One experiment involves the development of the people's college inspired by the famous Danish folk schools. The other involves the creation of a number of rural higher institutes whose purpose is to carry out extension education and research on rural problems.

During the period of the first three Five Year Plans (1951–66), India has made impressive progress in the field of education. The targets of enrollments at all levels of education were fulfilled or overfulfilled, especially during the period of the Second and Third Plans. According to the Fourth Five Year Plan, the enrollment in the primary schools, (Classes I to V) increased about 170 per cent. In 1950–51 only 42.6 per cent of children in the age group 6 to 11 attended primary schools; by 1965–66 this proportion reached 78.5 per cent. The enrollment in middle schools (Classes VI to VIII) increased about 253 per cent; the proportion of children in the age group 11 to 14 attending middle schools increased from 12.7 per cent to 32.2 per cent. The number of students enrolled in secondary schools (Classes IX to XI) showed an increase of 330 per cent. The proportion of those in the age group 14 to 17 attending secondary schools thus increased from 5.8 per cent in 1950–51 to 17.8 per cent in 1965–66. University enrollment increased by 267 per cent and the proportion of those in the age group 17 to 23 attending universities rose from 0.7 per cent to 1.9 per cent. In the field of technical education the enrollment capacity of the diploma program increased from 5,900 in 1950–51 to 49,000 in 1965–66 and that for the degree program, from 4,120 to 24,700.

Because the proportion of girls in the age group 6 to 14 attending schools was substantially lower than that of boys, several steps were taken to increase facilities for female education. These steps included the provision of quarters for women teachers, special allowances to women teachers working in rural areas, and stipends for women teacher trainees. Educational facilities in backward areas were expanded. Attempts were made to meet the problem of parents taking children out of school as soon as they became able to work by implementing the provisions of compulsory education, providing more qualified teachers, better methods of teaching, and planning school holidays to coincide with harvesting and sowing seasons. In addition the system of basic schools was further extended, and communities were encouraged to increase school attendance, expand female enrollment, and add to school facilities.

Secondary schools were reorganized to provide diversified services to students according to their needs. The measures taken in this connection were the conversion of high schools into higher secondary schools and the development of multipurpose schools with facilities for the teaching of science and vocational preparation. The training of teachers for both the elementary and secondary schools was expanded, and teacher education was adjusted to meet the changes taking place. The programs adopted for university education include evening colleges, correspondence courses, the expansion of science education and women's education, rural institutes, and three-year degree courses as well as post-graduate studies and research.

Orleans' article starts with an analysis of the goal of education in China. China's goal is to create conditions for the gradual elimination of differences between industry and agriculture, between town and country, and between manual and mental labor. To pursue this goal a system of education would have to be established that would raise the overall literacy and the educational level of the masses, thus enabling them to be both "expert" (trained) and "red" (ideologically correct). During the past two decades the vacillations of China's educational policies have reflected the shifts in emphasis between "expert" and "red."

During the Great Leap period, 1958–59, a significant change was made in the field of education. The existing schools incorporated a variety of labor programs, including political education, into their basic curriculums—some of them actually operated limited production facilities. The aim was to create the "all-around man" by integrating manual work and intellectual pursuits. By 1961–62 the emphasis was again placed on diligent study, *i.e.*, "expertness." Ideological education and physical labor for students were increased somewhat in 1963, with greater emphasis being placed on the "work-study" and "farm-study" schools. The Cultural Revolution, 1967–68, further intensified this trend. The demands of the Red Guard for changes in educational emphasis included more political education, more integration of study with production and reality, remolding of all teaching staffs, and abolition of college entrance examinations in order to increase the proportion of workers, poor former peasants, and veterans among the student body. The latter demand resembles the advocacy of the "open admission" policy and "educational opportunity programs" for culturally disadvantaged groups in other countries. However in 1965 at least 50 to 55 per cent of the total student body in higher education already came from worker and peasant backgrounds.

Although the basic goals and policies of Chinese education are the same throughout the country, the educational system is extremely diversified and decentralized, utilizing various forms, methods, and practices. A variety of schools and colleges exists in China: government-managed schools; schools run by factories, mines, communes and other enterprises; general and technical schools; schools for adults and for children; full-time, part-time, spare-time, and correspondence schools; free schools and schools that require tuition. Within each category there are great variations in the length, content, and course of the program.

The enrollment in nursery schools and kindergartens was approximately 30 million in the later 1950s; primary schools (six-year) enrollment was somewhat below 100 million. The lowest school attendance rate was usually found in rural areas. One of the ways to combat this tendency was found to be to establish farm-study primary schools in the rural areas. The enrollment in general secondary schools (six-year) was between 8 and 9 million in the late 1950s. In addition to the programs offered by the general schools, numerous specialized secondary schools offer training in the fields of industrial vocation, agriculture and forestry, public health, and finance and economics, as well as teacher training. Prior to 1959 all full-time general secondary schools and the greater proportion of specialized secondary schools were located in urban areas. Since 1958–59 more middle schools have been established in the rural areas.

In 1969 a new pattern for the school system emerged. Schools were opened not as part of the state education system but as enterprises run by communes, neighborhoods, and factories. Within a commune primary schools were to be run by the production brigades and secondary schools by the commune itself. Total primary and secondary school education was to be compressed from twelve years to nine years. Emphasis was to be on vocational training combined with the work-study program. The current economic policy of moving industries from the cities to the countryside and emphasizing the development of small-scale industries in the commune should hasten the development of such vocational schools and work-study programs in the rural areas.[1]

The full-time enrollment in regular institutions of higher education reached 700,000 to 800,000 around 1960, and there were 430,000 students in spare-time and correspondence programs in 1965. To support economic development the system of higher education has been reorganized with emphasis on technical education. In 1948–49 23 per cent of the college graduates were in the fields of engineering, and this proportion rose to 35 per cent in 1965–66. Consequently the number of new college graduates in engineering increased from less than 5,000 in 1948–49 to 60,000 in 1965–66. The proportion of graduates in natural sciences, medicine, and agriculture increased from 22 per cent in 1948–49 to 26 per cent in 1965–66. Because of the great need for teachers, the proportion of graduates in education also increased from 9 per cent to 28 per cent. As a result the proportion in the remaining fields declined from 46 per cent to 11 per cent. The training of post-graduate students was provided by the Academy of Science, other academies, and universities.

Thus during the past twenty years China has continued to redesign and reorganize its system of education hoping to raise the overall literacy and educational level of the masses and at the same time provide the necessary trained personnel for industrial and agricultural development. In Orleans' view, education in China will truly be on the right track of "expertness" and will take precedence over "redness."

Note to this Part appears on page 396

26

# Indian Education: Search for Economic and Political Independence

*I. N. Thut and Don Adams*



SINCE 1947, WHEN the Indian subcontinent emerged from British colonial rule, Indians have optimistically referred to their nation as the New India (Bharat). And the republic of India is new in the sense that for the first time in its history India has become a politically unified nation. India is new also in its increasing influence in world affairs and in the democratic political pattern on which its government is structured. Moreover, the introduction, on a larger scale, of modern techniques and institutions designed to promote social and economic changes portend a permanency for such "newness." Yet dramatic changes notwithstanding, the progressive label, New India, should not be understood to mean that India has sloughed off her past and is an entirely new cultural creation. Modern India is deeply marked by her past, both ancient and recent.

## *A New Nation and New Educational Policies*

The Union of India was designed as a republic dedicated to the concept of progress through democracy. While free from the shackles of foreign rule, India still had many chains to loosen before the goals envisioned by such leaders as Tagore and Gandhi would be achieved. The new India emerged with a doctrine of universal suffrage extended to a population nearly 90 per cent illiterate. There was little industry, and agricultural efficiency was low. There were conflicts and distrusts between urbanites and villagers, educated and noneducated. Poverty, disease, and a passive view of life loomed as monstrous obstacles to the Gandhian vision of self-initiated change; yet there was some room for optimism. Great physical resources remained untapped, and educated, honest, and experienced leaders were available in numbers unknown in most developing areas.

### ECONOMIC PROBLEMS

The most serious economic problem facing independent India and one with which the nation has traditionally been plagued was the inability of the agricultural sector to provide sufficient food for the population. The low fertility of the soil, irregular monsoon rains, marketing defects, and antiquated farming methods resulted in one of the lowest agricultural yields per acre in the world. With the assistance of exceptionally favorable weather conditions, India has succeeded during the last few years in raising rice production nearly to the level of need. However, large quantities of other basic foodstuffs still have to be imported. The drain on foreign reserves, brought about by such importations, restricts India's efforts to purchase the tools and equipment necessary to develop its industrial sector. Because of the Hindu principle of *ahimsa*, or nonviolence, which prevents the slaughter or eating of cattle, efforts to improve the diet of the Indian population have not been widely successful. The vast number of cattle and other nonproductive animals that are kept consume large quantities of food yearly. The cattle may be used in plowing the land and transporting the produce, but their puniness makes for low efficiency even in such functions. Moreover, owing to poor breeding and improper feeding, the cows give little milk; the cow dung, which is burned for fuel, is perhaps the most useful contribution these animals make to the economy.

The problem of producing sufficient foodstuffs is compounded by India's rapidly growing population, which by 1961 had reached approximately 400 million. Medical improvements and humanitarian reforms have reduced famine and disease, but these factors combined with a high birth rate have resulted in a population growth rate of 2 per cent per annum. To counteract the perpetuation of starvation conditions brought on by population pressures a national program of planned parenthood has been initiated. Fortunately neither the Hindus nor the Moslems have religious strictures regarding birth control; but the tradition of large families and the importance of male lineage have proved to be formidable obstacles. Because of increasing concern over the population problem and the necessity for dramatic action, Nehru had suggested that Indian women consider voluntary sterilization after having borne three children.

Landownership and distribution form an Indian problem of both economic and social dimensions. Land in India has traditionally been a main source of wealth and status; and in recognition of this fact, the states in India after 1947 began a land-reform movement. As outlined in the third Five-Year Plan the overall land-reform objectives are to "reduce disparities in the ownership of land," create a condition where "the vast majority of cultivators . . . would consist of peasant-proprietors" who would be encouraged and interested in organizing themselves in voluntary cooperative bodies for credit, marketing, processing, and distribution and, with their consent, progressively also for production. Even with the unofficial assistance of the Gandhian disciple, Vinoba Brave, who traveled about the countryside urging landlords to voluntarily give up portions of their land, the Indian government admits only partial success. The land problem is more than one of maldistribution, for simple arithmetic shows that there is less than one tillable acre per capita. Indian leaders of the reform movement fully realize that overfragmentation of the larger estates may result in landholdings of uneconomic size. The goals, therefore, have a more moderate ring about them than might be expected in the case of such an explosive issue.

The combination of private responsibility within the framework of group planning, backstopped when necessary by direct government action, typifies India's approach to improvement of its agricultural sector and to economic development in general. Perpetual indebtedness to moneylenders and landlords has sapped the spirit of the Indian farmer, for as a popular Indian saying goes, "the bania (moneylender) goes in like a needle and comes out like a sword." Direct government action to help states and local communities make credit available at reasonable rates of interest has been a helpful stopgap measure, while community-development projects and cottage industries may be a long-term solution for making the underemployed farmer more self-sufficient. (It is estimated that the average farmer is productively employed only 150 days of the year.) One of the greatest boons to reducing the indebtedness of rural and city folk alike, however, has been the enactment of the so-called "dowry law," prohibiting the traditional lavish gifts of money and land by the bride's family.

Economic development in a nation the size of India also demands a rapid program of industrialization, balanced with light, medium, and heavy industries and designed to meet immediate consumer needs while not neglecting capital goods industries. Finding and training the skilled manpower needed for such an undertaking requires enlargement of Indian educational facilities and extensive utilization of foreign institutions. Financing large-scale industrial operations requires close cooperation between government and private enterprise and since the government is the biggest holder of capital, it has become responsible for the establishment of most of the major industries, as well as the infrastructures of power and transportation that make their operation possible. Yet in spite of its socialist philosophy, the government by 1961 had allowed private ownership of 90 per cent of industry.

During India's first and second Five-Year Plans, covering the period 1951–61, progress could be recorded in agricultural and industrial production, including the production of consumer goods. Per capita income increased 11.1 per cent during the first five-year plan and by approximately the same percentage during the second five-year plan. Aggregate real income was increasing at the yearly rate of nearly 4 per cent. India's productive efforts are receiving well-deserved plaudits throughout the world, with industrial production in particular causing surprise among the mature countries and envy in the underdeveloped ones.

Yet all is far from well with India's economic-development plan. Certain rural groups, particularly in the mountainous and desert sections of the country, have been little affected. India's industries are producing far below their capacities, owing in no small part, according to foreign observers, to inefficient management. Moreover, when the growth of national income is adjusted by the increase in population, the rate of real growth becomes nearly 1.5 per cent. Substantial as the progress under the first two Five-Year Plans has been, it is still not dramatic enough to produce the level of development expressed in India's goals.

#### SOCIAL AND POLITICAL PROBLEMS

At least five social major and political problems face India in its struggle for development. The first of these concerns the very existence of a unified India. Independence has not merely meant substitution of Indian rule over the territories formerly ruled by the British, but has also meant the establishment of a federation which includes 561 of the 562 princely states. These states had not been subject to British control, but rather had been ruled in an authoritarian manner by hereditary princes. The amalgamation of all these states but one (Kashmir) was a masterpiece of statesmanship on the part of the new central government.

But the process of unification had other more formidable obstacles. The Moslem minority, long uneasy about the prospect of Hindu majority rule, took steps through its own political party, the Moslem League, to form a separate nation; "the Indian Moslems felt themselves to be Moslems before they were Indians."

A second problem which thwarted rapid unity was the lack of a national language. English was well known to the educated elite who occupied high governmental, professional, and commercial positions, but it was practically unknown among the masses where the regional vernaculars remained strong. Acknowledging the need for a national language for political as well as economic and social reasons, the national government considered its alternatives. Since English was unacceptable for cultural as well as nationalistic reasons, the most popular vernacular, Hindi, became the logical choice, and 1965 was set by the government as a target date for making it the national language.

The language problem, however, is far from being solved, for Hindi was the language of only half of the Indian population. Nine other major languages are each spoken by at least 1 million Indians. Opposition to Hindi has been particularly strong in the southern part of the nation where fears were voiced that language would be used as a weapon to assist the northern region in perpetuating its traditional dominance in Indian affairs. The specific educational implications of the language problem are analyzed in a later section.

Social cleavages in the new nation resulting from traditions of caste posed a third problem which had economic and social dimensions. Caste hindered mobility of labor, for traditionally children were expected to take up the occupation of the parent. This situation had unfortunate implications for both the dying skills, for which there tended to be an oversupply of labor, and the expanding of new occupations, for which there tended to be labor shortages. Financial and other rewards assisted in removing the economic defects of the caste society but the inherent social evils remain.

Social mobility while on the increase was still limited in the highly divisive Indian society. The untouchables, the caste outside the caste system, were given official recognition; but since custom often transcended law, they still moved only on the fringe of civilized society in many regions. Although the national Constitution promises no discrimination on the basis of color, race, caste, or sex, the age-old prejudices are dying slowly. Repugnant and irrational though discrimination is to most Indian leaders, they feel its disappearance will necessarily be slow. It is their hope that the closer contact of people required in a modern industrial and urban society will be more effective than official proclamations.

A fourth condition affecting social and political development, one which does not lend itself to easy or brief description, has been the attitude of the Indian people toward the process of change. While some students of India have been favorably impressed with the ability of the Indian villagers to adopt new methods of crop cultivation, sanitation, and health care, other observers have emphasized the resistance to new ideas and methods. As in countries all over the world, the villages and rural areas in India are much less susceptible to change than are the urban centers. Recognizing that the villager often lives a precarious existence would lead one to hypothesize that a mixture of hope and apprehension may be rather widespread among the poverty-stricken masses. Villagers often suspect the government of ulterior motives when officials offer help; moreover, the traditional paternalistic role of the government militates against a cooperative approach by government and governed to the solution of problems. And living as they often do on the borderline of starvation, the Indian villagers well understand that any change in living or working habits literally becomes a gamble with life and death.

But attitudes implicit in Indian culture, not conducive to economic and social development, can be traced to other than rural influences. The extended family which has afforded security has discouraged initiative, enterprise, and risk taking on the part of the individual. A traditional hierarchical society, with power closely correlated with position, has made vertical cooperation difficult with all organizations. The multiplication of new occupational caste groups has hindered communication and promoted new separateness. The traditionally subordinate role of women has frustrated the optimum use of this part of the population in carrying out development plans. Moslem groups in particular have been slow to accept public education, especially coeducation, for their girls. And acting as a cloak sheltering the Indian youth from new ideas is the illiterate adult population.

A final problem, related to the foregoing, is concerned with defining the political character of the new nation and giving leadership to it. During the turbulent struggle for independence and in the uneasy years of nation building, India has been guided by persons of unusual intellectual and moral strength. Mahatma Gandhi and Jawaharlal Nehru provided charismatic but responsible leadership in their efforts to bring unity out of diversity and stimulate greater national effort. These men, so unlike in many respects, were in agreement that the New India should be both socialistic and democratic. Gandhi and Nehru, however, gave special qualifications to these terms, for each had found grave limitations in the practice of the political philosophies in other nations bearing such names. Gandhi distrusted concentration of wealth and power in the state as much as he did their concentration in the hands of a few individuals. Nehru did not share Gandhi's fear of industrialization or his great preoccupation with the spiritual aspects of development. While Nehru had shown a certain approval of the theoretical concepts of Marxism and admiration for the material progress in the Soviet Union, his actions and his words made it clear that his goal was a mixed economy, involving both government and private participation.

Nehru's "liberal democratic socialism" has been generally accepted as the guiding philosophy for India's social, economic, and political development. Its wide acceptance has lent stability to India and provided a fundamental requisite for development and growth. However, healthily perhaps, other political philosophies exist and have articulate proponents. As many as five other schools of political thought are significant in India today: Hindu nationalism, dictatorial national socialism, revolutionary international communism, evolutionary national communism, and Gandhian decentralism. Should any of these groups gain political control of India, the direction of change is certain to be altered; but for the time being India, in spite of its lengthy period of rule by a single party, resembles a welfare democracy.

## *The Administration of Education*

Although education in India since 1921 has been under state (provincial) control, independent India has developed important educational responsibility at both the national and the local levels. With the important exception of higher and advanced technical education which are under the central government, the Constitution of India now provides for a continuation of the decentralized pattern of educational control. The states are still the responsible units for educational administration. However, Indian commitment to national planning means that the central government must be more than a disinterested spectator. The image of the New India is being shaped at the national level, and the aims, direction, and dimensions of the educational endeavor are regarded as foundational to success. Lacking specific constitutional rights, the central government has been assisted by three important factors in extending its educational influence: (1) the large-scale educational expansion or improvement requires the states to seek financial grants from the central government; (2) the states are dependent for statistical and other educational information on the central government which acts both as a repository and a clearinghouse; (3) lastly, the fact that the same political party has dominated both state and national politics since independence has reduced political conflict between the two levels which otherwise might have frustrated educational cooperation.

The official national body charged with planning, guiding, and coordinating educational reconstruction is the National Ministry of Education (see Figure 1). In addition to carrying out general policies of development the Ministry is charged with such specific functions as:

1. Providing exclusive educational direction in the centrally administered areas (the new Indian Union formed in 1956 includes fourteen states and six centrally administered territories).

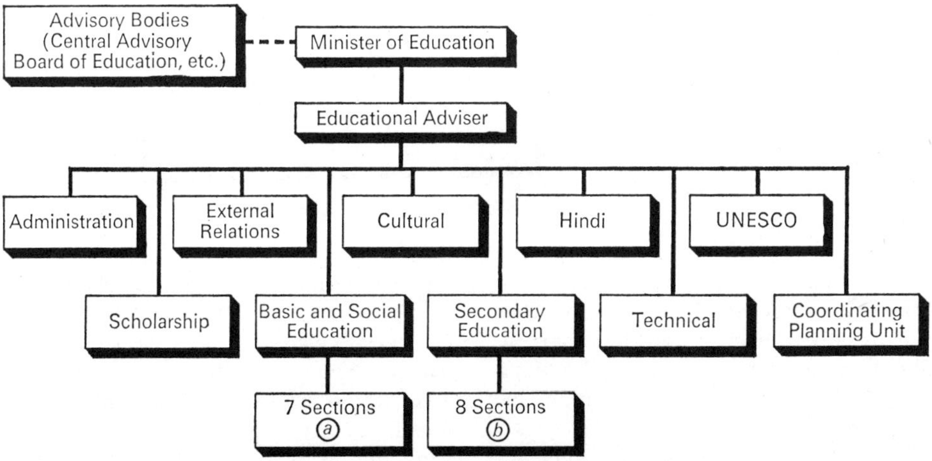


*Figure 1*

2. Directly administering to the eighteen *public schools*, four central universities and a variety of research and training centers.
3. Granting scholarships for scheduled castes, backward tribes.
4. Giving grants-in-aid to the states and, under certain conditions, directly to institutions of higher education.

The National Ministry is directly responsible to the Indian Parliament, and the Minister of Education is appointed by the Prime Minister (see Figure 2). The chief administrative officer of the Ministry is the Educational Adviser who advises the Minister on all matters of administration and policy (see Figure 1).

To promote a degree of uniformity and coordination among the states, various central advisory bodies have been created, the most important of which is the Central Advisory Board of Education. The members of this body include a number of specialists, all of the state ministers of education, and the national Minister of Education who acts as the chairman. By the very nature of its composition, recommendations of the Central Advisory Board carry considerable weight. In the fields of secondary and university education, the All-India Council for Secondary Education and the University Grant Commission provide similar advisory services. Uniformity of goals and standards gets additional impetus from India's commitment to central planning, and the National Planning Commission has included specific targets for educational progress in the first three Five-Year Plans.

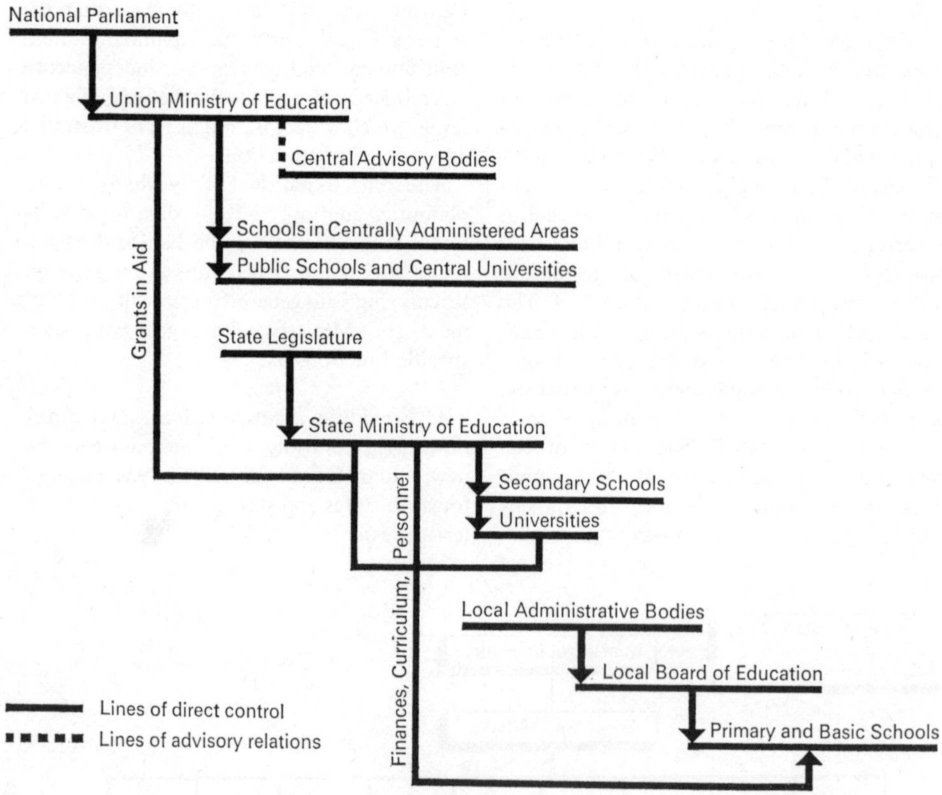


*Figure 2*

In addition to the Ministry of Education other central ministries, such as those of defense and railways, through various training programs are deeply involved in educational matters. Moreover, the relatively new Ministry of Scientific Research and Cultural Affairs whose functions until 1958 had been combined with those of the Ministry of Education is responsible for cultural activities, scientific research and survey, and technical and scientific education. The establishment of this separate body for scientific and technical matters demonstrates the government's expectations of the contributions by these fields to development.

State governments have full autonomy for the administration of their educational programs except those for which they receive grants-in-aid from the central government. The administrative hierarchy of the state is topped by an elected minister of education who is responsible to the state legislature of which he is a member. The director of public instruction, in some states called director of education, is the executive head of the department and is in charge of the inspecting and teaching staffs of government and recognized private schools. With respect to

### *Table 1—Number of Students by Stage of Education in India*

| *Stage of education* | *Boys* | *Girls* | *Total* |
|---|---|---|---|
| University stage: | | | |
| Ph.D./D.Sc./D.Phil./etc., arts and science only | 4,233 | 681 | 4,924 |
| M.A., arts and science only | 27,059 | 7,701 | 34,760 |
| M.Sc., arts and science only | 10,392 | 1,670 | 12,062 |
| M.Com., arts and science only | 5,333 | 48 | 5,381 |
| M.Ed., arts and science only | 972 | 424 | 1,396 |
| B.A., pass and hons. | 139,034 | 52,841 | 191,875 |
| B.Sc., pass and hons. | 111,638 | 19,027 | 130,665 |
| B.Com., pass and hons. | 51,181 | 697 | 51,878 |
| Teacher training, B.T/B.Ed. and equivalent diplomas: | | | |
| (1) Basic | 3,238 | 1,550 | 4,788 |
| (2) Nonbasic | 10,442 | 4,954 | 15,396 |
| B.P.E., bachelor of physical education and equivalent diplomas | 613 | 120 | 733 |
| Teacher training, undergraduate level: | | | |
| (1) Basic | 14,603 | 4,696 | 19,299 |
| (2) Nonbasic | 6,430 | 5,687 | 12,117 |
| Institutes of arts | 177,603 | 33,942 | 211,545 |
| Institutes of science | 23,818 | 3,071 | 26,889 |
| Preuniversity: | | | |
| (1) Arts | 105,504 | 36,023 | 141,527 |
| (2) Science | 82,671 | 8,965 | 91,636 |
| (3) Commerce | 23,034 | 561 | 23,595 |
| School stage: | | | |
| Classes IX and above | 2,469,165 | 581,773 | 3,050,938 |
| Classes VI–VIII | 5,680,711 | 1,878,681 | 7,559,392 |
| Classes I–V | 25,748,556 | 12,683,341 | 38,431,897 |
| Preprimary | 133,359 | 98,432 | 231,791 |
| Teacher training, primary: | | | |
| (1) Basic | 85,477 | 29,124 | 114,601 |
| (2) Nonbasic | 10,830 | 5,167 | 15,997 |
| Teacher training, preprimary | 178 | 1,661 | 1,839 |
| Commerce | 78,271 | 14,897 | 93,168 |
| Physical education | 2,885 | 438 | 3,323 |
| In schools for the handicapped | 6,723 | 1,885 | 8,608 |
| In schools for social workers, Janta colleges | 3,243 | 507 | 3,750 |
| In schools/centers for adults | 1,497,389 | 801,156 | 2,298,545 |

*Source:* India, Ministry of Education, *Provisional Educational Statistics:* (*As on 31st March 1962*), New Delhi, 1962, p.2.

higher education, the state governments share their power with the universities; with respect to primary education, they share power with local government bodies (panchayats). The trend in India has been for the local bodies or councils to assume more and more control over local affairs, including primary education. Typically the councils operate through the school boards to formulate policies for the financing, managing, and expanding of primary schooling. In some states the local boards even maintain their own supervisory and administrative staff.

#### EDUCATIONAL INSTITUTIONS

Article 45 of the Indian Constitution charged the states with responsibility for providing compulsory education up to fourteen years of age for all Indian children by the year 1960. Although this goal was far too ambitious, in the period between 1950 and 1962 the percentage of the six- to eleven-year age group in school grew from 42 to 66 and the percentage of the eleven- to fourteen-year age group climbed from 13.4 to 27.0. However, India still ranked well below the world mean with respect to primary enrollment ratio. (Table 1 shows the enrollment by school levels in 1962.) Most states, temporarily disregarding higher aspirations, were attempting to provide four to six years of education. Moreover, it should be emphasized that educational conditions vary widely throughout India. One Indian state, Kerala, as early as 1956–57 could boast that nearly all children of primary school age were attending school, while during the same year in the North East Frontier Agency, a centrally controlled territory, less than 7 per cent of the children were in school.

Although there is a propensity to describe elementary education as that which is provided children in the six- to fourteen-year age span, this structure is not uniform throughout the country. Most typically the initial stage of primary education, covering ages six to eleven years, approximately, takes place in what is called a primary school or junior basic school. For a simplified view of the school pyramid, see Figure 3. Three-year higher primary schools of vernacular middle schools have been established in a few states. This second stage usually is divided into two sections, the first of which covers ages eleven to fourteen, approximately, and is termed the senior basic or middle secondary school. In some cases a senior division extends from age fourteen for an additional three years. However, some of these have been made into four-year higher secondary schools by adding what has hitherto been the first year of the university preparatory stage. The first degree course at the university requires a minimum of three or four years, depending on whether or not the student has attended a regular or higher secondary school.

## *Educational Aspirations and Opportunities*

#### PRIMARY AND BASIC EDUCATION

Social reformers, particularly Mahatma Gandhi and his followers, have long been concerned with the character of primary education. In particular, the emphasis on memorization, the divorce of contents from the environment, the overwhelming costs, and the general impracticality of the curriculum of the primary school have come under criticism. As a cure for these ills, Gandhi, at a famous educational conference at Wardha in 1937, recommended a new concept of primary education, a concept he considered fundamental to his program of social reform. Gandhi, who believed that the teaching of handicrafts was essential to purposeful education, called his new approach "basic education" and described its objective and method as follows:

> The principal idea is to impart the whole education of the body and the mind and the soul through the handicraft that is taught to the children. You have to draw out all that is in the child through teaching all the processes of the handicraft, and all your lessons in history, geography, and arithmetic will be related to the craft.

In the basic schools the study of crafts, theoretically at least, consumes 20 to 25 per cent of the week's schedule. Typical subjects and the hours of instruction per week in each are as follows: mother tongue (regional vernacular), 8; mathematics, 5; social studies, 5; general science, 4; Hindi, 3; physical education, 5; arts and crafts, 12 (9 or 10 hours per craft); and extracurricular, 2. Crafts include: spinning and weaving; gardening leading to agriculture; book crafts, including paper and cardboard work, leading to wood and metal work; leatherwork; clay work and pottery; fisheries; housecraft. Since the reorientation of primary education involves this complex of changes, it might be expected to be a long-term process. Indian statistics bear this out, and by the end of the second Five-Year Plan (1961) only about 24 per cent of the elementary schools were of the basic pattern.

The terms used by Indian educators in condemning the traditional primary school and

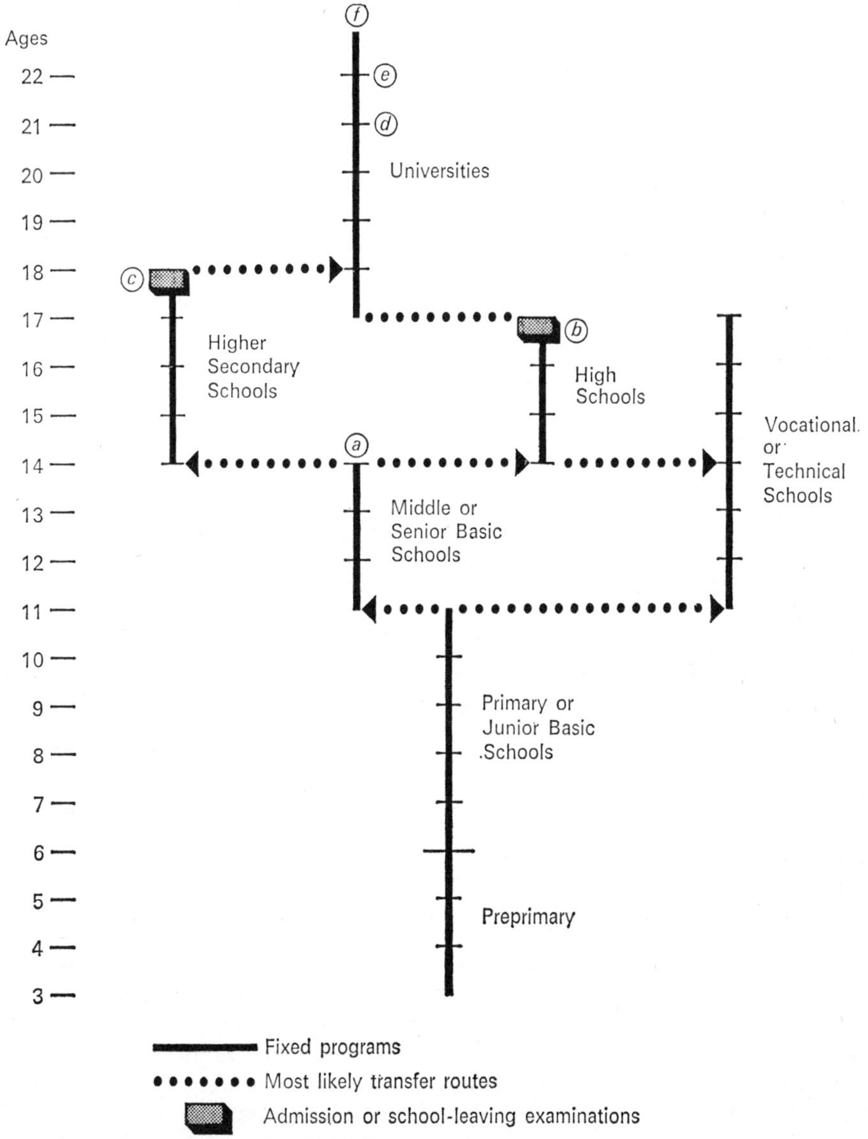


*Figure 3*

in justifying basic education are reminiscent of the arguments of the advocates of progressive education in the United States during the 1930s. Memorization and drill were to be replaced by purposeful and creative activity. Bookish, abstract content was to give way to content derived partly from the immediate community. Cooperation in socially useful endeavors was to replace harsh competition. Such changes, many Indian educators argued, were in keeping with the democratic goals of their nation, for education so conceived could help to break down class barriers and promote a respect for productive labor. A rural and vocational bias favoring primary education would slow the exodus to the already-overcrowded urban areas. Moreover, other advocates added, primary education built on functional experiences and the interest of the child was in keeping with the best learning theory.

In addition to the educational considerations, there was also an important economic reason for the expansion of basic education. Progress toward the goal of universal primary education placed a tremendous burden on the limited financial means of India, and any expensive system would be automatically ruled out. Under a system of basic education the items produced by the children had an economic value which could help meet schooling costs. Food, clothing, and the products of handwork could be utilized by the teachers and children within the school; and when the children became further skilled, the surpluses could be sold on the market.

As conceived by Gandhi and his followers the long-range goal of basic education was no less than a spiritual reconstruction of society. Gandhi, while concerned with the material poverty about him, was most disturbed by what he considered a prevailing spiritual poverty. Western culture and education inasmuch as they had divorced Indians from their own cultural heritage were, he felt, a major contributor to this latter problem. Indians had become strangers in their own land, a view often expressed by Nehru also, and political and social disunity were the result. Gandhi further deplored the lack of respect for manual labor in the imported English pattern of education.

Evaluations of the success of basic education in contributing to the new society envisioned by Gandhi have been mixed. While the basic education concept at the primary level has found general support, there appears to be more than a little lingering confusion about its precise purpose and content. Some Indians emphasize the contributions of basic education to rural reconstruction. Others claim the concept is equally valid in urban development. Primary schools which offer little or no handicraft classify their programs as basic education. Certainly a sizable group of social scientists and educators view basic education as hardly more than a romantic experiment with little relationship to social development, economic growth, or even sound education. Then, the increased centralization of Indian economy has not been conducive to a craft-centered education, nor, in fact, has the suspicion of material wealth, fostered by some of the advocates of basic education, supported the developmental goals of entrepreneurship and industrialization. It is probably fair to conclude that the contributions thus far of basic education toward producing the Gandhian ideal, a classless, nonviolent society, have been modest.

Although top priority is being given to creating basic schools through a reorientation of the primary curriculum, by 1960 three-fourths of the Indian primary schools were still of the nonbasic variety. These schools in general were faced with even greater shortages in financial and human resources than the basic schools. Merely keeping the children in school long enough to acquire a functional literacy was a major task. Obstacles to extension of the length of schooling included costs to pupils (noonday meal and clothing); ill health; and, most of all, parents unsympathetic to the values of education. A dearth of women teachers was particularly detrimental to any prolongation of the education of girls.

Indian leaders hope that increased financial support from national, state, and local levels will help make compulsory education a reality. Historically much of the expense for education has been borne by the community, and new laws enabling local authorities to levy a special tax for education should increase community responsibility and, hopefully, community initiative. Other steps taken by some communities under the five-year plans to extend opportunities in elementary education include initiation of a double-shift system to make maximum use of school facilities; extension of out-of-doors classes; experimentation with cheap building materials; and the establishment of short-term, streamlined teacher preparation programs. Finally, a continuing scheme of social education—programs in literacy, use of libraries, citizenship, group community development, etc.—is expected to assist adults in making more positive contributions to the education of their children.

The expansion and transformation of Indian primary schooling has brought new demands on the teacher training institutions. Teachers for the primary schools normally are prepared in middle schools and may or may not receive professional training. There is a strong movement to make high school graduation a requirement for primary teaching; yet by 1957, one-third of the primary school teachers were still without any professional preparation.

Since there are two types of primary school in India, basic and nonbasic, there are two kinds of institutions for the preparation of primary school teachers. By 1956 there were 520 schools specifically designed to prepare teachers for basic schools and 403 for nonbasic schools. These schools, over one-third of which were private, might admit either primary school graduates or secondary school graduates. The former group of students could expect to receive a junior teacher's certificate, while the matriculates could qualify for a senior teacher's certificate. The main difference in the curricula of the two kinds of training institutions is that those candidates preparing to teach in basic schools receive lengthy instruction in craft skills and intensive community observation and participation.

### SECONDARY EDUCATION

Under the British, secondary education in India served to introduce European culture and, less frequently, to teach certain vocational skills to a few selected Indian youths; in addition, it prepared young men for clerical positions in British administrative offices. English was the language of instruction, and the curriculum was dominated by university requirements. Although the Hunter Commission of 1882 and several later commissions recommended a dual-track system of secondary education, "one [track] leading to the Entrance Examination of the Universities, the other of a more practical character," no action in this latter direction was taken. Products of the secondary schools, together with the microscopic number of university graduates, formed an Indian elite whose cultural ties with the great proportion of the population were often very limited.

Independent India has attempted to Indianize and extend secondary schooling. Again, however, as with the primary schools, the exact role and structure of secondary education are still to emerge. Some Indians have been advocating a three- or four-year multipurpose secondary school, following eight years of primary (basic) education. This pattern appears to be gaining favor, but by 1961 few attempts had been made at actual implementation, and some differentiation of instruction before the age of fourteen is likely to persist for some time. Further, multiple institutions at the secondary level probably will continue, with certain curricular and administrative safeguards to ensure that no capable student in any stream is kept out of higher education.

A comparison of the analyses of the weaknesses of Indian secondary education shows considerable agreement. An examination of the publications of an Indian educator, a visiting American specialist, and the Indian Secondary Education Commission, revealed the following common recommendations:

1. The curriculum should be vitalized by supplementing verbal learning with practical and "lifelike" activities through utilization of community resources and by bringing

about a closer relation to community life.

2. More attention should be given to identifying and providing for individual differences through increased personal and vocational guidance.

3. Opportunities should be provided for the students to develop skills in group discussion and practice in planning, researching, and arriving at independent judgments.

The trends in Indian secondary education in the period since independence have been in the direction of meeting many of the needs recognized by these educators. As summarized by one Indian educator these trends are:

1. A strong movement for the diversification of the courses and introduction of vocational bias.

2. Enrichment of the curricula by introducing new subjects, such as civics, crafts, and agriculture.

3. Emergence of new types of post-primary schools, viz., the postbasic school and the higher secondary school.

4. Greater emphasis on the regional and the national languages.

5. Increasing recognition of the importance of physical education.

As suggested by this list the commitment to basic education at the primary level has had implications for the direction of secondary education. Indian leaders are reconciled to the fact that for many years secondary education, because of financial restrictions, must remain the prerogative of a few. Nevertheless, a secondary school whose curriculum is restricted to those subjects traditionally regarded as the best preparation for the university does not set well on an institution that stresses activities and socially useful labor. The role of crafts, the relationship between knowledge and work, and the importance of cooperative activity in Indian secondary schools are issues raised by the philosophy of basic education and are yet to be resolved.

The multiplicity of Indian languages (the Constitution has recognized fourteen) is a major problem for secondary education. The trend for several decades has been toward the use of the regional vernaculars as the languages of instruction in the secondary schools. In no region has the customary language of instruction been English, the language used in the universities.

The Indian solution to the language problem appears gradually to be taking shape, although dissenting opinions are still heard. The use of the mother tongue at the elementary and secondary levels now appears to be well accepted. Opinion continues to be split on the language of instruction at the university level, with the adoption of a regional language gaining support. These trends would place a heavy, but not impossible, language burden upon the secondary school students, since, at least for students for whom Hindi is not the mother tongue, two additional languages, Hindi and English, would need to be mastered. The former, because it is destined to be the national language, must be mastered by at least those students who extend their education beyond the elementary school, and the latter dare not be neglected because of its peculiar historical significance in India and its importance as a vehicle for modern scientific thought.

An even more fundamental problem facing Indian secondary education is related to its nonfunctional qualities in a developing democratic society. One Indian educator sees two conflicting philosophies operating in Indian secondary schools:

> One is represented by the traditional school which stands for authoritarianism, strict external discipline, a predetermined curriculum, and an attempt to discipline the mind for a remote future without paying due attention to the needs of the present. . . .
>
> The other is the democratic philosophy represented by the modernists who advocate cooperative planning and recognition of the present needs and problems of the learner. The modernists also assert that the teacher is not a dictator; he is merely a sympathetic guide. . . .

Attempts to broaden the scope of secondary education have led to the introduction of multipurpose high schools which provide instruction for several alternative courses.

The proponents of these schools argue that such institutions would reduce class distinctions, allow greater adaptation of the school to community needs, and perform an important guidance function by helping the student find a course to fit his aptitude. With the absence of an educational heritage friendly to the educational philosophy underlying multipurpose schools and the lack of teachers trained in the applied subjects, recognition of the potential value of these schools has been slow in coming. However, future years are likely to see increasing experimentation in this direction.

Although the first two Five-Year Plans proposed to emphasize expansion of primary education, the period covered by the two plans saw greatest expansion in secondary and higher education. Since many Indian educators have long considered the secondary schools the weakest educational link, this level received heavy emphasis throughout these two plans. Efforts were made to improve science instruction, extend facilities in vocational education, and as mentioned above, experiment with multipurpose schools. Before the first plan, only 5 per cent of the youth between the ages of fourteen and seventeen were in secondary schools. By 1961 this percentage had been raised to 12, and the 1965 target was set at 15 per cent. In the first two plans considerable attention was also given to developing higher secondary schools, increasing teachers' salaries, and improving their working conditions.

The expansion and redesign of Indian secondary education have made heavy demands on the teacher training institutions. Teachers in the high schools typically are prepared through one of two routes. They may attend a secondary teacher training institution whose course of study is two years for the holder of a high school or higher secondary school certificate. A second route for the prospective secondary teacher is to take a one-year course in a graduate teacher training institute after graduation from a university. Such a course leads to the degree of bachelor of teaching, bachelor of education, or licentiate in teaching. In spite of sizable expansion of both basic types of teacher training institutions, by 1962 nearly one-third of Indian secondary teachers still lacked minimum professional training.

A third and subtle problem encountered by Indian secondary schools as they attempt to orient themselves toward the demands of democracy, nationalism, and economic development is concerned with the selection of students. Admittedly in the past the most important single requisite for secondary schooling was wealth, not talent. The cost of attending secondary schools was prohibitive to lower-class families. Moreover, the cultural deprivation of the poorer Indian homes, as in other parts of the world, hindered the success of the poor children in the academic requirements. While the problem is well recognized, steps for its cure have only begun. New selection procedures have been developed that will ensure more objectivity in selecting students; and as a necessarily parallel step, scholarships are being provided for some able but poor students.

### HIGHER EDUCATION

The first modern universities in India were established in 1857 at Calcutta, Bombay, and Madras and were modeled after the University of London. The function of the universities, then, like that of the University of London, was to establish courses of study for the affiliated colleges, examine the candidates prepared by the colleges, and grant degrees to the successful candidates. This pattern has been modified in recent years, and most modern Indian universities are either classified as "teaching and affiliating" or "teaching and residential."

The course for most of India's forty-five universities traditionally has been four years beyond high school graduation. At the end of two years there is an intermediate examination. The successful candidate then proceeds for two more years and, if successful in his degree examination, is awarded the bachelor's degree. For some time there has been criticism of the two separate and essentially unrelated stages of university education, and there has been a long-standing argument for an integrated three-year university course leading to the bachelor's degree. By 1962 well over half of the universities had agreed to introduce a three-year course, and it is likely that the remainder will follow suit.

Beyond the bachelor's degree a master's degree is awarded after one or two years of additional study and completion of an examination. In some universities honor graduates—under one arrangement the honors' degree is awarded for three years' study after the intermediate examination—automatically receive their master's degree after the lapse of a prescribed period of time. A Ph.D. degree requires a thesis but no course work beyond the master's degree.

The changes recommended in a post-war report of the Central Advisory Board of Education, together with the report cited below, set the course for university education in independent India. Among the recommendations were: (1) the conditions for admission should be revised with the object of ensuring that students admitted to a university course would benefit by it; (2) the intermediate course should be abolished, one year being added to the high school and the other to the university, thereby making three years the length of the university degree course; (3) the tutorial system should be widely extended; (4) high standards and post-graduate courses and research should be maintained; and (5) an Indian university-grant committee should be constituted to exercise general supervision over the allocation of grants to universities from public funds.

A more definitive report on university education was presented in 1949 by the University Education Commission. This respected and influential report called upon the universities to prepare educated men and women for the leadership positions required by a modernizing nation. Higher education should be at once scientific, technical, and liberal. As stated in the report:

> Democracy depends for its very life on a high standard of general, vocational, and professional education. Dissemination of learning, incessant search for new knowledge, unceasing effort to plumb the meaning of life, provision for professional education to satisfy the occupational needs of our society are the vital tasks of higher education.

Committing itself to scientific progress, the report nevertheless warned against over-specialization and the dangers of

> . . . scientists without conscience, technicians without taste who find a void within themselves, a moral vacuum and desperate need to substitute something, anything, for their lost endeavor and purpose.

Indian universities, in their attempt to teach the myriad of cultural and vocational goals charged to them, have been beset with a host of problems, many of which are common to most underdeveloped countries but some of which are peculiar to India. Those university problems shared with other poor nations include the need for adjusting enrollments to fit manpower demands; the modernization of an outmoded curriculum, especially in the natural and social sciences; further development of native languages which have potential as effective vehicles for higher learning; provisions for increased opportunities for women's education; finding and keeping competent staffs; preventing urbanization of the country student; improvement of plant and equipment; and objectifying means by which students are selected. In India, as in most former colonial nations, higher education is often viewed as a route to secure and profitable government employment. Adjustments in the labor market are being considered to ease the pecuniary attraction of Indian higher education, for it is hoped that elimination of degree requirements for recruitment into public services will slow the rush of students to the arts colleges. Among the more or less peculiar problems facing Indian universities are those related to the process of synthesizing India's cultural traditions with the new knowledge from the West.

Indian leaders realize that the task of deliberately planning a nation's future without utilizing Draconian measures is fraught with obstacles. They further realize that the first requisite to the infusion of knowledge is a group of leaders who have a vision of India's future as an extension of the past. Indian universities thus far have not been able to integrate past modes of thought with modern European thought to form a new social philosophy that promotes development without forsaking cultural identity. In this regard Kabir points out:

> Even today European, Indian and Islamic philosophies are treated as isolated and self-contained subjects. What is worse, Indian philosophy is often treated as an alternative to Arab thought. A national system of education would require systematic and connected study of the three systems—Indian, Saracenic and European—which have influenced modern Indian consciousness.

The most concrete step taken to remedy this ill has been the introduction of experimental programs of general education at the university level.

## *Innovations and problems*

Many Indian educators would undoubtedly agree with Prof. S. N. Mukerji that "an educational apparatus which even after a hundred years has left 80 per cent of the people unable to read and write stands self-condemned." Yet since independence Indian educators have learned the hard fact that limitations of funds and trained personnel are at times as big an obstacle to progress as lack of vision.

In considering the priorities of development, Indian leaders have given much attention, too much in the view of some economists, to grass-roots change. A nationwide program of community development was instituted within the provisions of the first and second Five-Year Plans and received support not only from the Indian government but also from many foreign sources. To remold village life rural India is being divided into blocks of approximately one hundred villages and further subdivided for the sake of operational efficiency. Teams of specialists in such areas as agriculture, public health, cooperatives, small industries, village government, and social education, professionally supported by a national research center, are assigned to coordinate schemes of reconstruction. By 1961 impressive statistics had been compiled on the accomplishments. For example, under the technical assistance of the specialists and with the self-help of villages, millions of farming demonstrations were held, over 100,000 miles of roads constructed, and 3.7 million men and women taught to read through new adult literacy centers. The precise contributions of these activities for national development are yet to be measured.

Unfortunately, extension of educational opportunities in the villages and the establishment of governmental controls over the schools has brought about a reduction in the prestige of the teacher. In the past there were mostly single-teacher schools in the villages, and the schoolmaster was an important and respected figure. The contemporary system, which has eliminated student fees and holds the teacher responsible to the headmaster, inspectors, and local authorities, has made the teacher's economic position more precarious and reduced his independence. With his needs no longer met in a well-defined traditional procedure and with the ineffectiveness of teachers' associations in collective bargaining, the teacher can hardly be considered a leader in community development.

For a larger role in economic-development plans, education must be more attuned to manpower requirements. Secondary education, finding it difficult to free itself from a literary curriculum and white-collar vocational goals, has still been unable to fully adjust its program to the wide variety of needs of the terminal student; thus, large numbers of secondary school graduates are unemployed. The limited experiments in differentiating the curriculum at the upper secondary level hold promise, but first must win professional and public confidence. Also of possible far-reaching significance are experiments in newer methods of instruction, other techniques in student evaluation for the traditional year-end examination, establishment of guidance services, formation of academic clubs, and extension of the activities of the parent-teacher association. These attempts to increase the efficiency and broaden the concept of schooling may serve to modify the mechanical teaching procedures and reduce the preoccupation of Indian secondary schools with the meeting of diploma requirements. Empirical research is badly needed to judge the result of these and other innovations.

In higher education the number of graduates in arts, teaching, and commerce has been rising steeply, but the increase in medicine, science, and engineering has been disturbingly low, and in recent years no gain at all has been registered in forestry and agriculture. Moreover, universities remain predominantly urban; in 1957 only 4.4 per cent of the enrollment in universities came from rural areas, and university graduates show a strong preference for city life. Two types of experiments initiated under the first two five-year plans hold some promise for establishing closer ties between higher education and rural life. One experiment involves the development of people's colleges inspired by the famous Danish folk schools. A second experiment involves the creation of a number of rural higher institutes whose purpose will be to carry out rural extension programs and conduct research pertinent to rural problems. The people's colleges and rural higher institutes exist only in small number and their potential cannot be anticipated at this time.

Under the first two five-year plans investment in education lagged behind that in irrigation, power, agriculture, industry, and railways. Moreover the proportion spent on education was less for the second plan than for the first. Of further significance is the shift in emphasis in expenditures under the two plans, as shown in Table 2. The increased attention to secondary, vocational, and higher education under the second plan drew criticism from some Indian educators who pointed to the large number of unemployed graduates of secondary and higher educational institutions and argued that the most important immediate task was to promote mass education. The planners argued that, considering India's economic needs, the highest educational priority should be given to the development of technical and administrative skills which are attainable only through postprimary instruction.

The requirements for involving Indian educational institutions more deeply in social change are at least as subtle as gearing them more efficiently for economic growth.

### *Table 2—Proposed Expenditures for Education in India (Rs. in crores[a])*

| | *First plan* | *Second plan* |
|---|---|---|
| Elementary education | 93 | 89 |
| Secondary education | 22 | 51 |
| University education | 15 | 57 |
| Technical and vocational education | 23 | 48 |
| Social education | 5 | 5 |
| Administration and miscellaneous | 11 | 57 |
| Total | 169 | 307 |

[a] At the official exchange rate 1 rupee = U.S. $0.21. A crore = 10 million rupees.

*Source:* India, Government Planning Commission, *The Second Five-Year Plan*, Ministry of Publications, New Delhi, 1956, p. 500.

Indian leaders have shown admirable reticence in resisting what they have considered the dangers of dehumanization in the development process. Yet, protection of the human element need not mean reluctance to allow Indian institutions to give dynamic leadership to social change. One author has pointed out that the Indic-Hindu societal pattern has been "emotional, mystic, aesthetic, collectivistic, aristocratic, easygoing and conservative." These characteristics obviously conflict with the scientific, materialistic, aggressive pattern which is usually associated with rapid economic and social growth.

If, for example, India is to be a secular, democratic, industrial nation then the schools, as Indian educators have pointed out, need to assist the people in acquiring a new social philosophy. The implications of representative government, urbanism, and technological change must be made understandable at the popular level. To Gandhi this task meant preservation of the Indian spiritual strength through the perpetuation of the traditional crafts. Other Indians have argued that the Gandhian idealized society is not the image of future India and that his approach essentially negates development. Success in more clearly identifying the social pattern and value system consonant with the goals of New India and then communicating these through an advanced educational technology is fundamental to more dynamic educational planning.

27

# Communist China's Education: Policies, Problems, and Prospects

*Leo A. Orleans*

*From* An Economic Profile of Mainland China, Vol. II, *Studies Prepared for the Joint Economic Committee, Congress of the United States, February 1967, U.S. Government Printing Office pp. 501–18, with omissions. Reprinted by permission.*

## *Introduction*

THE VITAL ROLE of education in accelerating economic growth has become axiomatic. Every scheme for the development of a backward economy, whether by the indigenous government or by an inertnational organization, lays primary stress on education and on the qualitative improvement of the nation's human resources. Consequently, it would seem that given the necessary priorities and funds there should be no further problem in raising the people's educational level in an underdeveloped country. In practice, however, many problems arise that cannot be solved with money and good intentions. Among the most difficult problems in implementing educational policies is that of adjusting them to the economic conditions and specific requirements of the particular country. Furthermore, although the relationship of education to economy is rather direct, there is still inadequate exploration of the ways in which the contribution of education and training can best be made.

Communist China's efforts in the field of education over the past seventeen years have resulted in both striking successes and significant failures—illustrating clearly many of the problems faced by developing countries. The new regime was quick to realize that education must be given top priority if China's economy was to fulfill the Communist prophecy of internal growth and serve as an example of achievement under a "correct" political system. This priority was expressed through policy and through a rapidly increasing educational budget. It was not long, however, before the burgeoning enrollment resulted in predictable shortages in facilities and personnel, in a deterioration of the quality of instruction as well as in numerous problems stemming from poor planning and inadequate integration of educational and economic plans. Faced by these obstacles, and under constant and vacillating political pressures, the educational system in Communist China has had to "shift gears" with regard to both approach and content. Nevertheless, it has been able to show considerable achievement in providing elementary education and training for the masses while, at the same time, furnishing the best education available to a relatively small number of specialists in the priority fields.

It is the intent of this short paper to provide a bird's-eye view of the Chinese educational system, describe some of the policies, some of the achievements and problems, present some of the basic statistics, and finally to cover the most recent developments and to speculate a little on the future of China's education.

Before proceeding into any discussion on Communist China, a caveat with regard to data has become almost a rule—a rule which I am not able to break. In brief, statistical data on education in Communist China follow the pattern set by all other statistics. After reporting some of the basic figures on education for most of the 1950s, there has been a virtual statistical blackout during the current decade. Textual materials on education provide some idea of the general trends and activities, but they are not very helpful in any effort to estimate or project the size and quality of China's human resources. The problem is accentuated by the proliferation of different types of educational institutions and by a lack of adequate and stable definitions and standards. For example, it would be almost meaningless to estimate that there are 10 million persons in China's secondary schools because the qualitative differences between urban and rural schools, full-time and part-time schools, or any of a dozen other types of secondary level institutions, are too great. A distribution of students among these various types of institutions on the basis of currently available information is simply not possible.

## *Goals and Policies*

In assuming control over a largely illiterate and untrained population, it would seem that the primary goal of the Chinese Communist Party would be to establish a system that would raise the overall literacy and educational level of the masses and at the same time provide as many trained individuals as necessary to meet the demands of a growing economy. This pursuit of "expertness," however, is only part of the objective of China's education. Over the years, the pursuit of "redness," or political trustworthiness, has been given even more emphasis, and most of the vacillations in China's educational policies can be traced to the periodic shifts in emphasis between the "red" and the "expert." The ultimate goal of education is to "create conditions for the gradual elimination of differences between industry and agriculture, between town and countryside, and between manual and mental labor, and eventually to realize communism."

Briefly, the educational system has gone through several distinguishable periods. In education, as in all activities in China during the first few years under the new regime, the major emphasis was on reorganization, reorientation, and consolidation. A basic educational reform in 1951, which called for some changes in organization, established technical and specialized schools and colleges, stressed ideological "correctness," and guaranteed everyone in the country an opportunity to receive an education. The relative stability and development of the educational system that typified the first few years of the First Five-Year Plan (1953–57) was disrupted by developments resulting from Mao Tse-tung's invitation for a hundred flowers to bloom and for everyone to express opinions and criticisms of his personal lot under the new regime. The most vocal of the critics naturally were the country's students and teachers, who quickly experienced the retaliatory power of the regime. Many of the critics had to undergo reform through labor and self-criticism, political education was strengthened, and greater emphasis was placed on correct political thinking for entrants into the middle and higher educational institutions.

The ill-fated Great Leap Forward, which was launched in 1958 in order to transform China rapidly into an advanced industrial nation, brought about a number of significant changes in the country's educational policy so that it could better reflect the new mood and the new requirements of the economy. All education was combined with productive labor; by integrating manual work and intellectual pursuits the regime could further its objective of creating the "all-round man." At the same time, local communities, industrial units, and other institutions were made responsible for establishing and maintaining their own schools while the existing schools incorporated a variety of labor programs into their basic curriculums—some of them actually operated limited production facilities. This resulted in a proliferation of different types of schools and an immediate and drastic increase in enrollments—all at minimal cost to the government in Peking.

These developments associated with the Great Leap Forward had predictable results on the quality of the education received by the majority of the students. With shortages in teachers and facilities, with great emphasis on productive labor and political purity, only a relatively small segment of the student population was able to pursue their education seriously. The combination of mismanagement and natural calamities that forced a retreat from the Great Leap policies within the Chinese economy had parallel repercussions in the field of education. The overrapidly expanded educational system started to contract, substandard schools were closed, productive labor for students was relaxed, and by the 1961–62 school year most of the emphasis was again placed on diligent study, *i.e.*, "expertness."

Within the charged political atmosphere that exists in Communist China, this phase in education could not last long—and it did not. By 1963, ideological education and physical labor for students were again on the ascendancy, and the educational system was given the responsibility of supplying the state with revolutionary youth whose love of Mao and the motherland would transcend all personal considerations. Great emphasis was placed once again on the "work-study" and especially the "farm-study" schools. It was stated at a national educational conference that in the future these schools would "become the mainstay of our country's educational system." And yet the reversal was not complete, and the conditions did not revert to the period of the late 1950s. As recently as September 1965 the *People's Daily* was still saying that schools should implement "the policy of less quantity and high quality to enable the students to assume more initiative and to be more lively and free in their studies, with a view to creating conditions for the overall development of students—morally, mentally, and physically."

The reasons for the initiation of the "great cultural revolution" in Communist China in the summer of 1966 are complex and the subject of much speculation. The effect of this "cultural revolution" on the country's educational system, however, is clear in its consequences. When the schools were supposed to have opened in September 1966 they did not. The Red Guards, who are the activists of the "cultural revolution," consist, almost entirely, of students from China's middle schools and colleges. Since the major force of this revolution is to curb revisionist tendencies and rededicate China to world revolution, much of the attack is centered on the institutions of higher education which presumably are the focal point of revisionist activity.

On June 13, 1966, the Communist Party's Central Committee and the State Council decreed the abolition of the existing system of entrance examinations for higher educational institutions and the closing down of all institutes of higher learning for half a year because "the system of examinations and enrollment . . . has failed to free itself from the stereotype of the bourgeois system of examinations." According to this pronouncement, the old system "places school marks in command," encourages young people "to become bourgeois specialists," and makes them strive for "individual fame, wealth, and position." Also, "it is not only the system of enrollment that requires transforming; all the arrangements for schooling, for testing, for passing or not passing, and so on must be transformed, and so must the content of education."

Given their rein, the Chinese students took advantage of the existing turmoil—as would teenagers anywhere else in the world. Whether in or out of the Red Guards, everyone seemed to find major fault with the system, the school, or the individual teacher. Literally hundreds of articles appeared in the press proclaiming "enthusiastic support" for the pronouncement of the Central Committee and the State Council, with everyone "strongly demanding" drastic changes in the "vicious old educational system." The main points of these demands were (1) more emphasis on Chairman Mao's works and on class struggle; (2) more integration of study with "production and reality"; (3) remolding of all teaching staffs and abolition of all academic rank; and most important (4) abolition of college entrance examinations and deemphasis of academic competence in order to increase the proportion of outstanding workers and former poor and lower middle peasants and demobilized army men among the students.

The last point is worthy of special note, not only because of its drastic consequences (if actually implemented), but also because after seventeen years of encouragement and of special privileges, the students of worker and peasant background still constitute only two-thirds of the total enrollment in the institutions of higher education. This figure is generous; other sources have quoted figures that are as low as 50 to 55 per cent of the total student body above the secondary level. In other words, a large proportion of the students continue to come from families which, according to Peking's definition, have a bourgeois character—an affliction that apparently leaves lifelong scars. An example of the many exceptions made in order to provide "higher education" for workers is the Shanghai University of Science and Technology, which, since 1960, recruited 479 advanced workers for enrollment. The authorities felt that although very few veteran workers had a "higher cultural attainment," they should have an opportunity that was denied them under the old society. As a result, the following standards for admission were instituted in 1960: "good in politics, high awareness, 5 or more years of working experience, skilled in production techniques, a cultural standard equivalent to spare-time junior middle school, under the age of 30, in good health and capable of persisting in study."

The apparent enthusiasm of the young people of China for the closing of all schools is easy to understand. It is much more difficult to rationalize the actions of the leadership. One of the few consequences that is predictable in unpredictable China is the adverse effect of this "holiday" on the education system and consequently on China's economic goals.

## *Structure and Numbers*

Basically, there are three standard levels in the educational system of Communist China: primary, secondary, and higher. The variations within this system are anything but standard, often appear to be completely unchecked, and, as the Chinese would say, very difficult to grasp. The slogan, "walking on two legs," was introduced during the years of the Leap Forward and proclaims the need to approach all the goals through every available means, be they old or new, efficient or inefficient. The slogan is particularly applicable to the field of education where, over the years, China has been walking on the legs of a centipede.

Chinese education has a unified character in that all the basic goals and policies are established by the central government in Peking and communicated through the various administrative channels to the most distant rural schoolhouse. This is expected in a totalitarian state. What may seem surprising is the degree of discretion that is left to the individual school district, or even school, as to how these directives and policies are to be implemented. In this sense, the educational system is extremely diversified and decentralized, assuming many forms and utilizing many different methods and practices. When this multiple character of implementation is superimposed on the vacillating policies of the Peking regime, it is possible to appreciate the reason for the emerging confusion. Thus there are government-managed schools and schools that are run by factories, mines, people's communes, and other enterprises; general and technical schools; schools for adults and for children; full-time, part-time, and spare-time schools; free schools and those that require tuition; permanent and temporary schools. Within each category of schools, there are variations in terms of courses, their content, and length of the program so that there are both secondary and higher schools that may run anywhere from 2 to 6 years. A student who has completed, let us say, nine years of schooling in a commune-run school may be years behind a student who has completed the same number of years in a better urban school. The quality of education also varies depending on the particular period during which the individual was attending school.

Before discussing the more formal educational system, perhaps a few words should be said about adult education and preschool facilities. When the Chinese Communists took over the mainland and started to expand and reorganize the existing educational system, they knew that the greater part of the working force was beyond the school age and beyond the reach of formal education. In order to include this segment of the population in the educational system, the regime inaugurated a nationwide adult literacy program for the masses and a variety of technical and vocational training courses for persons already in the urban labor force.

Although the established criteria for literacy were extremely low, especially for the peasants, in 1956 the Minister of Education complained that almost four-fifths of the people were still illiterate. At the time of the Great Leap Forward, some 40 million people were presumably enrolled in "anti-illiteracy classes," but it was a slow battle. Not only were the illiterates continuing to enter adulthood at a rapid rate, but many of the peasants who apparently managed to get their "certificate of literacy" had no occasion to utilize their shaky knowledge and quickly forgot most of what they learned. At present, not too much is written about adult literacy programs. Obviously, China decided to concentrate on getting the children into school and not to spend too much effort in teaching adults to read.

In addition to the literacy programs, a great variety of other adult training programs were set up—some lasted only a few years while others survived over a longer period. Most of the training was designed to meet the needs of the urban worker. By attending spare-time schools, he could obtain the equivalent of a primary or secondary education, or he could participate in on-the-job and spare-time training courses operated by industries and other enterprises and institutions in order to improve his productive capabilities. At present the emphasis is on work improvement courses, and little is said about regular primary education for workers, which was emphasized in the 1950s.

More logically included under adult education rather than higher education are the spare-time and correspondence colleges. In 1965, there were over 1,000 of these institutions with a total enrollment of 430,000, of which 149,000 was in correspondence colleges. Many of these schools catered to rural areas and provided courses in agronomy, animal husbandry, water conservancy as well as "mechanical, electrical, and civil engineering."

At the other end of the spectrum are the country's nurseries and kindergartens which, in 1958, enrolled some 30 million children. Although no later figures have been published, preschool facilities undoubtedly continue to play an important role in the society in order to permit women to participate fully in the nation's economy. In addition to the more formal type of nurseries and kindergartens that would be found in the larger cities, most of the factories maintain child-care facilities for the working mothers while field nurseries are set up in the rural areas during the busy farming seasons.

## *Primary Schools*

Normally primary schools are started at the age of seven, continue for six years, and are divided into four-year junior and two-year senior primary schools. Actually, there are many schools, particularly in the rural areas, that do not go beyond the initial three or four years. and there are many children who do not get into school until they are well beyond the theoretical starting age. Primary school enrollment grew rapidly during the 1950s and reached some 90 million by 1960. Although there have been no figures published since then, it is unlikely that, despite a significant increase in the school-age population, the enrollment in primary schools ever reached 100 million, and it may have even declined since then. This conclusion is based on scattered data available for individual provinces. For example, in 1958 Kirin Province reportedly approached universal education, "but owing to the continued natural calamities . . . and all the shackles placed on us by capitalist educational thinking, this result has not been stabilized, so that universality of primary-school education has become an old and difficult problem in educational work." The same source states that "The lowest school attendance rate is usually found in rural areas, where it is only 50 to 60 per cent for communes and production brigades and where children not attending school are mostly from poor and lower middle peasant families." This low percentage may not be untypical for the country as a whole, especially because of the high rate of attrition between each grade. The Chinese themselves admit that "some children cannot enter school at the proper age or have to give up study in the middle of the school term and cannot finish their primary school education."

One of the ways in which the regime is trying to counteract this problem is by establishing farm-study primary schools in the rural areas. During the earlier years, schools that combined education with productive labor were primarily limited to secondary and higher education, but now similar schools have been established for the young children on the communes. It was reported that 17 million children were attending the farm-study schools in September 1965. It is interesting to note that, when possible, parents prefer to send their children to adjacent full-day schools, and the authorities have admitted considerable difficulties in "selling" farm-study primary schools even to the peasants. To transfer from a farm-study school into a state-operated full-day school, a student has to pass an entrance examination; few make the grade.

Another important reason for China's problems in achieving universal primary education is that not even these schools are entirely free of charge and, as a result, fewer children of poor families attend primary schools. Undoubtedly, this is also an important reason for the pressure to establish farm-study schools in China's villages; they make it possible for the children to compensate the local authorities for their education and thus avoid a monetary payment.

## *Secondary Schools*

There are many different types of courses that may be pursued by a boy or girl who has completed a six-year elementary school. Although statistics on this level of education are particularly confusing even for the period when data were reported, in 1959 somewhere between 8 and 9 million students were enrolled in China's secondary general schools. These schools are divided into two three-year levels, roughly comparable to our junior and senior high schools. Only approximately one out of six junior middle school students, however, has an opportunity to enter the senior middle schools which, of course, supply the great majority of entrants into the institutions of higher education.

Students who continue their education but do not enter the secondary general schools may choose from numerous specialized schools that are operated by the State or, more likely, by an individual enterprise which both instructs the students and utilizes their services. In addition to industrial vocational schools, there are secondary schools in the fields of agriculture and forestry, public health, finance and economics, as well as normal schools which train teachers for primary schools or even for junior middle schools. Despite the proliferation of specialized schools and other less formal educational arrangements, it would not be surprising if the enrollment in the general schools had remained fairly constant since the late fifties.

All the general (full-time) middle schools and the overwhelming proportion of the specialized middle schools are located in the urban areas of China. Until 1958, for all practical purposes, there were no middle schools in the Chinese countryside. With the Great Leap Forward, the regime introduced the part-work, part-study agricultural middle schools in the communes. Enrollment in these schools grew quickly and reportedly reached 3 million by 1959–60. Disrupted during the agricultural crisis of the early sixties, Peking started a new push on these schools in 1964 and 1965 when they directed the local authorities again to establish this type of education. Without any assistance from the Central Government, and to compensate for the limited local resources, the brigades (villages) had to place maximum emphasis on the "great red flag of Mao Tse-tung's thinking." "When they are devoid of school premises, teachers and students construct them with their own hands. When they are devoid of desks and chairs, teachers and students make them with their own hands."

These agricultural middle schools are ideally suited to meet the special problems and needs of rural China. They raise the general educational level of the rural population, without withdrawing any significant labor force from the rural economy since most of the study is done during the slack farming season. Like the primary level work-study schools, they are almost entirely locally subsidized and, therefore, do not present a financial burden to the government. Schools fees are low, and the students can meet part or even all of the study and livelihood expenses through their own labor. On the other hand, agricultural middle schools in no sense can be equated with the general middle schools located in the cities. Most of these schools provide only four courses: "political subjects, language, arithmetic, and agricultural knowledge," and follow these principles: "Teach whatever the people's communes want; teach whatever is needed locally; teach whatever the masses lack knowledge of; teach whatever is necessary for the current farming operations; teach first what is urgently needed for use and study in order to put the acquired knowledge into application." These courses make it possible for the students to "pass hard tests politically and pass muster technically." Although the agricultural middle schools are academically deficient, the students learn to read and become conversant with numbers, while in some more specialized schools they do acquire skills that are in very short supply in the countryside, such as learning to drive a tractor, repairing of machinery, and basic knowledge of electricity.

## *Higher Education*

Higher education, as education at the lower levels, is also "walking on many legs" in Communist China. It is, therefore, difficult to make meaningful evaluations of the number of institutions of higher education and of their enrollment.

At the apex of the higher education pyramid are about twenty comprehensive universities that have several academic departments and continue to offer courses to full-time students for a period of four or more years, as well as special universities such as the University of Science & Technology and the Tsinghua Polytechnic University, both in Peking. These universities provide China with her higher level personnel and leading scientists and engineers. In the middle of the pyramid are the hundreds of specialized colleges that have narrow fields of specialization, with courses lasting anywhere from two to four years. A rung below these colleges are the spare-time and part-time institutions of higher education that are usually run by individual enterprises, industrial ministries, or local governments. Most of the students in these institutions are workers, who are skilled in productive operations but do not have the formal education that would be required for entrance to the more legitimate institutions. At the bottom of the pyramid are the so-called worker and peasant colleges that first came into being during the 1958–59 Great Leap Forward and, in no stretch of the imagination, can be considered institutions of higher education.

Enrollment in the institutions of higher education grew rapidly during the 1950s, increasing by 50 per cent between 1957 and 1958 and 1958 and 1959 and reaching a peak of 810,000 by the 1960–61 school year. Although no enrollment figures have been published since then, there are indications that enrollment dropped off and may be in the vicinity of 700,000 at present. Until the closing of the schools by the "cultural revolution," admittance to a university depended, first of all, on the needs of the state. Quotas were set up for various specializations, whereupon selections were made on the basis of examination results, political conformity, and health of the individual student. The distribution of students by field of specialization reflected the regime's emphasis on those fields which had the most immediate practical application. Thus the greatest increase occurred in the fields of engineering and education, primarily at the expense of the social sciences, law, literature, and the arts. Although the growth in scientific education was impressive, it was not as rapid as the growth in engineering and technical education, because the contribution of a graduate in the physical sciences is not as immediate, in most cases, as that of an engineer. Furthermore, despite vigorous attacks on foreign science and technology, the Chinese Communists continue to rely heavily on borrowed scientific know-how.

It is estimated that at present (January 1967), there are slightly over 1.7 million persons on the Chinese Mainland who have completed some form of higher education. Of this total, roughly one-third are engineering graduates, one-quarter are graduates in education, while only about 6 per cent have majored in one of the natural sciences (see table). It is important to note that the two fields that account for over half of the personnel with completed higher education also have the largest number of graduates with less than a four-year education.

Universities did not award advanced degrees in pre-Communist China, and students seeking them went abroad, primarily to Japan, the United States, or Europe. A plan to award such degrees was finally formulated and announced in 1956, with most of the responsibility falling on research institutes of the Chinese Academy of Sciences, and specifically on qualified research personnel, who were to tutor small groups of students. Although figures on the number of entrants into the advanced degree program were published for a few years, none have been released on the number completing such a program. One of the reasons for the lack of such data is that the system was never adequately formalized and was not really successful. In all probability, any student who remained at the university for an additional period of time to participate in further study or research was considered to be a graduate student. Despite the ambiguity of the whole program, however, there must be an elite group of students, particularly in the fields of science and engineering, who continue to attain graduate level competence within their area of specialization.

Until 1960, the Soviet Union played an important role in training specialists for China. During the years of economic cooperation, hundreds of Soviet experts participated in China's economic planning and construction, in scientific research, and, to a more limited extent, in the field of education. At the same time, thousands of Chinese scientists, professors, and students were sent to the Soviet Union either on short professional tours or to receive training. It is estimated that of the 7,500 students who went to the Soviet Union between 1950 and 1960, 2,000 were graduate students. Since 1960, the number of Chinese students in the Soviet Union has decreased yearly, until in October 1966 the remaining 65 students were expelled by the Soviet Government.

It is estimated that the number of persons in China who have completed graduate studies, both in China and abroad, is in the vicinity of 10,000 to 12,000. At least three-quarters of them are believed to be scientists and engineers.

## *Quality of Education*

There are two possible approaches in evaluating Communist China's accomplishments in the field of education. One is to compare the training of an average Chinese youth with that of students in the West, a comparison which will be unfavorable to China since the majority of her schools cannot provide an education that will meet the standards of the world's advanced countries. It is much more realistic to consider China's accomplishments in the field of education in relation to her past and in the light of the problems she must face and the specific needs of her economy.

Determined to raise the overall educational level of the population but realizing the magnitude of the problem, the Communists decided to compromise by attempting to give the largest portion of the population a limited education (requiring minimum expenditure of capital and time away from production), and, at the same time, to train a smaller group more adequately, and to thoroughly educate a select handful of politically and scholastically qualified individuals.

The problems that the Chinese faced were

similar to those of all developing countries striving for modernization, but China's obstacles were on a much larger scale. With rapid growth in enrollment, there was, and continues to be, a severe shortage of qualified teaching personnel. The problem is serious at all educational levels, but most serious in China's countryside, where 80 to 85 per cent of the students are located. Typical is a complaint of one region with 161 agricultural middle schools that "85 per cent of the teachers today, judging by their cultural standards, are inadequately trained in their special fields and are in need of improvement." The standards referred to above are generally quite low. Thus, with the exception of some of the better urban schools, children in primary schools are, at best, taught by graduates of the junior middle schools; those in the junior middle schools are taught by graduates of the senior middle schools; the latter by graduates of the two-year normal schools. Quite often even these minimal standards are not achieved in rural China.

To a somewhat lesser degree, the problems of teaching personnel, facilities, and equipment also exist in institutions of higher education, particularly in those of the post-Leap Forward variety. Major universities that are on the standard itinerary of the touring scientists apparently are well provided for, however.

Few textbooks seem to find their way out of China, and a detailed evaluation of their content is difficult to make. With so many different types of schools, levels of education, and periodic shifts in emphasis, the writing and publication of textbooks could be—in a different economy—a lucrative business. Given the conditions in China, and the size of the student body, publication and distribution of appropriate texts could very well be a major problem. One solution that has been widely utilized by the school authorities is to translate, primarily Russian, textbooks into Chinese. It seems safe to assume that Russian texts are on the decline, but undoubtedly numerous college texts used in Europe and the United States continue to be translated. Of some 200 scientific books published by Science Press in Peking in 1965, about 50 per cent were translations of Soviet and Western publications.

A conclusion that need not be based on assumptions is that an inordinate amount of time is spent on political training, on the study of Marxism-Leninism, the history of the Communist movement, and the writings of Mao Tse-tung. The proportion of time spent on these subjects varies from one type of school to another and from one year to the next—depending on whether the "flowers are blooming," or the country is "contending and rectifying." In the legitimate institutions of higher education, the amount of time which the student must spend in political study usually averages between 10 and 20 per cent of the entire curriculum, while in the part-time schools for workers and peasants, one-third to one-half of the time may be spent on political topics. This excessive emphasis may well go beyond the prescribed requirements. In the first place, how better for a teacher to assure his personal security; in the second place, for a poorly trained individual it is much easier to read Mao's works to the class than to teach a regular course.

But this must be only part of the story, or else how could China have consolidated its controls over the economy? How could she have overcome the serious and prolonged economic crisis of the early 1960s? How could she have become one of only five world nuclear powers? Obviously Communist China's educational system has not been as ineffective as could be implied from the preceding paragraphs. The answer is in the "other leg" of China's education.

Urban areas of China maintain adequate numbers of schools that offer the students the best education China is able to provide. Numbers are not available, but over the years these urban primary and secondary schools have been able to supply the better institutions of higher education with more than enough candidates to fill the limited number of available openings. At the select universities, the student is provided with all the necessary facilities, as well as instruction by some of China's most competent professors, many of whom are Western-trained and must double as teachers and researchers at the Chinese Academy of Sciences.

It is difficult to criticize China for emphasizing physical sciences and technology at the expense of the social sciences and the arts. She is a country in a hurry and must pick and choose those areas of specialization that are likely to contribute more immediately and more directly to her economic growth. Many of the Chinese engineers, for example, are overly specialized, extremely weak on basic theory, and, in effect, little more than middle level technicians. But China needs this type of specialist. It would be a waste of time and money for China to produce nothing but highly trained engineers who have spent four, five, or more years at a university. While a nucleus of these people is available, the Chinese economy, in its present stage of development, would probably have difficulty in absorbing large numbers of these individuals.

Another good example of China's practical approach to education is in the field of medicine. There are many developing countries around the world which are desperately in need of medical personnel. But what is their solution? They train highly competent doctors who meet all the standards required by Western medicine, but who refuse to live in the countryside and to serve the needs of the peasant. The Chinese are much more realistic. They have neither the time nor the money to train only highly competent medical doctors; instead they are producing thousands of middle level medical personnel who return to serve in the village of their origin. They are not able to provide the professional care of the medical doctor, but they play a vital role in providing the masses with the basic medical needs, taking care of emergencies, and teaching the people the importance of sanitation and personal hygiene. Also, the thousands of medical practitioners (herb doctors) have been given equal status with the doctors trained in Western medicine and are fully utilized around the country. This does not mean that the Communists are blind to the differences between the native- and Western-trained doctors (although from their writings it is easy to come to that conclusion); it is again a case of "making do" with what is available until improvement can be brought about.

## *Education and the Economy*

More than forty years ago, the Soviet academician, Strumilin, estimated that primary education in the Soviet Union increased a worker's efficiency by over 40 per cent, secondary education by over 100 per cent, and completed higher education by over 300 per cent. The applicability of these specific figures either to China or to the present decade is not important; the message it conveys has not changed. The importance of investing capital in human resources through education has been expressed countless times and is universally accepted. In developing countries, the problem is how to integrate education with the economy rationally so that neither will suffer because of an inability of the other to provide for it.

Budgetary data on Communist China are scarce for the 1950s and almost nonexistent for the 1960s. Despite an admission that "the State is in no financial position at present to satisfy fully the needs of the people" in the field of education, Communist China spent an average of 7 per cent of its national budget on education between 1951 and 1956 and almost 10 per cent in 1957. Since 1957 China experienced many changes in its educational system, but because such a large share of the financial burden for education was relegated to the local communities which had to support schools with existing resources, it is unlikely that the proportion of the national budget allocated to education ever exceeded 10 per cent. As a matter of fact, it may have declined significantly since 1960. It is, of course, impossible to measure the cost of education at the local level.

As difficult as it is for Peking to allocate the necessary resources for education, it is just as difficult to achieve a happy medium between the quantity and quality of manpower produced by the educational system and the growing needs of an economy that relies equally on the simple plow and on the electronic computer.

China's population is growing by some 14 to 16 million persons per year. Over 10 million youths enter the labor force ages annually and must be absorbed into the economy. Even during the period of rapid industrial growth, the regime admitted that the cities could not effectively absorb much more than 1 million persons into the urban economy annually. As a result, China had to limit the so-called "blind infiltration" of rural population into the urban areas and periodically had to round up these peasant migrants and return them to their villages. The agricultural failures in the early sixties and the ensuing crisis in China's urban economy resulted in a major change in China's economic policies. Beginning in 1962, production priorities were shifted from industry to agriculture, thus further limiting the cities' requirements for additional skilled labor and contributing to the very basic and acute problem of having to absorb the bulk of the growing manpower into the rural economy.

To assist the rural areas in counteracting the increasing population pressure on arable land, Communist China has instituted a number of policies designed to help the economy to absorb this manpower. In recent years, in addition to continuing the mass labor projects in water conservancy, afforestation, flood control, land reclamation, road construction, and other miscellaneous activities, the Government has been emphasizing the so-called subsidiary occupations. These activities are primarily household oriented and are to occupy all those who can be spared from basic agricultural production. Members of the communes are encouraged to engage in handicraft activities, to plant additional fruit trees or bamboo plants, to raise domestic animals and fowl, to gather wild plants, and so forth. Material incentives are provided in order to secure some enthusiasm for these activities.

This thumbnail description of China's problems in utilizing rural manpower is directly pertinent to educational policies. Under these circumstances what should the role of education be? What type of education should be provided children and youth who have little, if any, possibility of leaving the farms for either white-collar or blue-collar employment? How can just enough education be provided to raise the overall cultural level of the rural youth, yet not enough to affect their morale adversely or make them rebel at the thought of a future of building up a Socialist countryside?

From what is known about China's educational trends and policies, it may be concluded that the questions raised above were not considered too seriously during most of the first decade under the new regime. The leadership was much more optimistic and idealistic: As much education as possible for as many people as possible. The limiting factor was cost to the economy, with little thought given to the economic and social consequences of this kind of philosophy. It was probably not until after the Great Leap Forward, and particularly during the critical years of 1961 and 1962, that the leadership has had to recognize some of the problems stemming from imbalances between education and the economy.

Although many of the urban students in the 1950s were required to participate in various forms of manual labor and, on occasion, to spend summers and holidays working in rural cooperatives and communes, it was not until 1961, when the deepening economic crisis decreed agriculture as the economic base and industry as the leading factor, that the regime implemented a policy of curtailing enrollment, closing substandard schools, and moving students to the countryside on a permanent basis. Hundreds of thousands of urban youths at various stages of completed schooling were prevented from pursuing their education. As of mid-1966 it was reported that "Well over a million educated young people from Chinese cities, determined to take the road of revolution and to become working people, have gone to live and work in the countryside since 1962." Although most of them were from middle schools, expendable college students were also included, that is, those who were studying subjects that ranged from the agricultural sciences to art, education, and law. *People's Daily* bluntly expressed China's dilemma: ". . . the desire of the young men and women for education cannot be fully satisfied."

The reaction of China's urban youth to these developments was predictably bitter, and the regime utilized all the facilities of China's vast propaganda machine to convince the students that whether they continue their studies or join in production they are part of the revolution. In 1965, an article in an educational journal, for example, discussed students who would complete their elementary and middle school studies during the summer: "Some of them will advance to higher levels and continue their studies, but the majority will enter into productive labor. . . . However, there are still quite a few students who are unable to correctly see the relationship between the desires of the individual and the needs of the state." In other words, you may want to go on with your education, but the state can't afford the luxury.

"Dear Abby" type columns have been extremely popular in China and are often more revealing than lengthy analyses in professional journals. A letter to "Comrade Editor" that appeared in *China Youth* states: "I am a third-year student in senior middle school. . . . Every day, I come to school early and leave late, studying hard. . . . But some fellow students say that I am wrong to think only of seeking admission into a university. . . . They even think that only going to the agricultural front is glorious and brave. . . ." The reply of the editor is typical: ". . . Provided we have a red heart and a wish to serve the people wholeheartedly and to labor, study, and struggle for the sake of the revolution, then we shall be able to make useful contributions to the motherland whether we continue our studies or take part in productive labor. . . . It is, of course, glorious for middle school students if they respond to the appeal of the motherland and go to the agricultural front, but it is equally glorious if, as required by the state, they go to schools of higher grade to continue their studies. . . ."

Propaganda notwithstanding, it would undoubtedly be difficult to find a youth so full of ideological fervor and revolutionary zeal that he would prefer to leave even the drab Chinese city for the healthy climatic and political atmosphere of the countryside. To some extent, the disappointment of the students must have had adverse reactions on their parents, and more important for the leadership, on the morale of students still in school. Many of them felt that ". . . since most of the graduates from the elementary and middle schools will have to go to work, they need not prepare for advanced studies and consequently neglected their studies."

Once among the peasants, the "young intellectuals" were to "temper themselves in hard manual work" and eventually to help raise the cultural level of the countryside by taking jobs as teachers and bookkeepers, for example. Unfortunately for the "urban intellectuals," most of the peasants were just as unhappy to see them arrive as the students were to come, thus creating difficult social problems of integration. An example of the difficulties is expressed in the following poem written by the "local masses":

> Behold the graduate of the ordinary
> middle school,
> He is capable of doing nothing correctly.
> Ask him to handle human manure,
> He complains it is not sanitary.
> Request him to make use of the abacus,
> He does not know how it is operated.
> Tell him to grow sweet potatoes,
> He raises a crop of onions instead.
> If you want an important job attended
> to,
> Better rely on one from an agricultural
> middle school.

## *Conclusions*

Without statistics, with only vague economic indexes, and during the height of the "great cultural revolution," projections or predictions of the future in Chinese education can be little more than a gesture of frivolity. Let us then be frivolous. If the cultural revolution will run its course and finally phase

## Graduates from Institutions of Higher Learning in Communist China by Field

| YEAR | TOTAL | | ENGINEERING | | NATURAL SCIENCES | | AGRICULTURE AND FORESTRY | | MEDICINE | | EDUCATION | | FINANCE AND ECONOMICS | | OTHER | |
|---|---|---|---|---|---|---|---|---|---|---|---|---|---|---|---|---|
| | Number | % | Number | % | Number | % | Number | % | Number | % | Number | % | Number | % | Number | % |
| *Total* | *1,716,000* | *100* | *577,840* | *34* | *98,387* | *6* | *140,149* | *8* | *184,868* | *11* | *468,417* | *27* | *87,140* | *5* | *159,199* | *9* |
| 1948–49 | 21,000 | 100 | 4,752 | 23 | 1,584 | 8 | 1,718 | 8 | 1,314 | 6 | 1,890 | 9 | 3,137 | 15 | 6,605 | 32 |
| 1949–50 | 18,000 | 100 | 4,711 | 26 | 1,468 | 8 | 1,477 | 8 | 1,391 | 8 | 624 | 4 | 3,305 | 18 | 5,024 | 28 |
| 1950–51 | 19,000 | 100 | 4,416 | 23 | 1,488 | 8 | 1,538 | 8 | 2,366 | 12 | 1,206 | 6 | 3,638 | 19 | 4,318 | 23 |
| 1951–52 | 32,000 | 100 | 10,213 | 32 | 2,215 | 7 | 2,361 | 7 | 2,636 | 8 | 3,077 | 10 | 7,263 | 23 | 4,235 | 13 |
| 1952–53 | 48,000 | 100 | 14,565 | 30 | 1,753 | 4 | 2,633 | 6 | 2,948 | 6 | 9,650 | 20 | 10,530 | 22 | 5,921 | 12 |
| 1953–54 | 47,000 | 100 | 15,596 | 33 | 802 | 2 | 3,532 | 8 | 4,527 | 10 | 10,551 | 22 | 6,033 | 13 | 5,959 | 13 |
| 1954–55 | 55,000 | 100 | 18,614 | 34 | 2,015 | 4 | 2,614 | 5 | 6,840 | 12 | 12,133 | 22 | 4,699 | 8 | 8,085 | 15 |
| 1955–56 | 63,000 | 100 | 22,047 | 35 | 3,978 | 6 | 3,541 | 6 | 5,403 | 9 | 17,243 | 27 | 4,460 | 7 | 6,328 | 10 |
| 1956–57 | 56,000 | 100 | 17,162 | 31 | 3,524 | 6 | 3,104 | 6 | 6,200 | 11 | 15,948 | 28 | 3,651 | 6 | 6,411 | 11 |
| 1957–58 | 72,000 | 100 | 17,499 | 24 | 4,645 | 6 | 3,513 | 5 | 5,393 | 8 | 31,595 | 44 | 2,349 | 3 | 7,006 | 10 |
| 1958–59 | 70,000 | 100 | (23,310) | (33) | (4.410) | (6) | 6,318 | 9 | 9,000 | 13 | (21,000) | (30) | (2,450) | (4) | (3,512) | (5) |
| 1959–60 | 135,000 | 100 | (44,955) | (33) | (8,505) | (6) | (10,800) | (8) | (14,850) | (11) | (40,500) | (30) | (4,725) | (4) | (10,665) | (8) |
| 1960–61 | 162,000 | 100 | 54,000 | 33 | 10,000 | 6 | 12,000 | 7 | 19,000 | 12 | 49,000 | 30 | (5,670) | (4) | (12,330) | (8) |
| 1961–62 | 178,000 | 100 | 59,000 | 33 | 11,000 | 6 | 20,000 | 11 | 17,000 | 10 | 56,000 | 32 | (6,230) | (4) | (8,770) | (5) |
| 1962–63 | 200,000 | 100 | 77,000 | 38 | 10,000 | 5 | 17,000 | 8 | 25,000 | 12 | 46,000 | 23 | 3,000 | 2 | 22,000 | 11 |
| 1963–64 | 200,000 | 100 | (70,000) | (35) | (11,000) | (6) | (18,000) | (9) | (23,000) | (11) | (56,000) | (28) | (6,000) | (3) | (16,000) | (8) |
| 1964–65 | 170,000 | 100 | (60,000) | (35) | (10,000) | (6) | (15,000) | (9) | (19,000) | (11) | (48,000) | (28) | (5,000) | (3) | (13,000) | (8) |
| 1965–66 | (170,000) | 100 | (60,000) | (35) | (10,000) | (6) | (15,000) | (9) | (19,000) | (11) | (48,000) | (28) | (5,000) | (3) | (13,000) | (8) |

*Note.*—Numbers in parentheses are estimates. Percentage detail may not add to totals because of rounding.

1948–49—1962–63: C. Y. Cheng, *Scientific and Engineering Manpower in Communist China, 1949–63,* National Science Foundation, Washington, 1965, p. 78.

1963–64: Total reported in *Chung-kuo Ching Nien Pao* (China Youth Daily), Aug. 13, 1964. Distribution based on the average for the previous 3 years (1960–61 to 1962–63).

1964–65: Total reported in *Jen-min Jih-pao* (People's Daily), Aug. 11, 1965. Distribution, same as for 1963–64.

1965–66: In a sense, these figures are completely fictitious. The Cultural Revolution interfered with the orderly completion of the 1965–66 school year, so that most probably the majority of the students received neither a certificate of completion nor a job assignment. Nevertheless, it would be inaccurate to exclude these individuals since they did pursue their studies during most of the school year. There is no reason to believe that there was a drastic change in the number and distribution of students scheduled for graduation and the 1964–65 figures are repeated.

out into a condition of relative stability, what can be expected of the next decade in the field of education? It is difficult to foresee any drastic changes.

The situation in the urban areas should stabilize so that in the future it will not be necessary to send urban students to the countryside. Even assuming that China's industrial development will accelerate over the rate of the past half dozen years, the urban areas of China should be able to supply most of the skilled manpower necessary for a growing urban economy. This, of course, means that the nature of education in the rural areas will have to be molded in a way that will provide hundreds of millions of children and youths with the three R's and a much more select group of students with training that will meet the limited requirements for semiprofessional personnel to fill administrative and technical positions in rural China. Six-year universal primary education will not be achieved in rural China within the next decade, but it is quite possible that a four-year primary education will become available to almost all the children in the country. Relatively few offspring of peasants will be able to leave the village and to improve their social and economic status within the urban economy. Probably most schools in rural areas will continue to be of a farm-study variety. If the economic situation improves, a larger proportion of the urban training will be on a full-time basis.

Thus, China will continue to "walk on many legs" and to support and encourage many different types of schools to meet a variety of conditions and needs that evolve from continued use of both labor-intensive and capital-intensive projects.

Assuming no economic crisis of the 1961 variety, enrollments in institutions of higher education should increase again, but they should not experience another Leap Forward. Emphasis on science and technology will persist indefinitely at all educational levels and so will concentration on the practical and the immediate. With the continued emphasis on teacher training and special schools for teacher improvement and advancement, the general quality of education should improve gradually; nevertheless, only select urban schools will continue to train the Chinese elite.

Communist China's accomplishments in education cannot be slighted. It can be said that, except for periodic disruptions, Communist China has managed to create and operate an educational system that is ideally suited to her conditions and goals. Unable to provide the hundreds of millions of people with first-rate education, she has encouraged an atmosphere of learning, has made literacy among the masses one of the primary goals, has managed to elevate the overall educational level of rural youth, has trained adequate numbers of middle-level specialists and technicians, and, at the same time, has not neglected the economy's requirements for higher level professional personnel, particularly engineers and scientists. China has done this with a minimum of disruption to individual productivity, in most instances, by combining education with work and at a minimum cost to the state, by making the local authorities responsible for the education of the people within their jurisdiction.

China's achievements in education would have been even more impressive had it not been for the constant emphasis on political orthodoxy and political training. By encouraging educational achievements and, at the same time, distrusting those who do achieve a high level of competence, Communist China has had one foot on the accelerator and one on the brake throughout most of her 17 years of existence. In the final analysis China's future thus depends on whether she persists in placing politics above all else or gradually deemphasizes political control. Although education in Communist China is "on the right track" in many ways, only when "expertness" will take precedence over "redness" will China truly be in a position to move forward toward her ambitious economic goals.

V

# International Economic Relations—Trade and Aid

# International Economic Relations—Trade and Aid

HISTORICALLY, FOREIGN TRADE and foreign capital have played an important role in the economic development of a number of countries. This may be clearly seen in the economic history of India and China during the past two decades. Furthermore, both these underdeveloped countries have themselves extended aid to other countries.

Datt's article analyzes the trends in India's foreign trade by dividing the period, 1948–49 to 1965–66, into four parts: (1) 1948–49 to 1950–51, (2) 1951–52 to 1955–56, (3) 1956–57 to 1960–61 and (4) 1961–62 to 1965–66. Because the value of imports—raw materials and capital goods required for industrial development and of foodgrain for consumption—was greater than the foreign exchange earnings from export, the trade balance was negative for every year during that period. The trade deficits were financed by foreign grants and loans.

The pattern of India's imports changed significantly during this period. The shares of capital goods and foodgrain in the total imports increased whereas the shares of raw materials and consumer goods declined. This reflects the increasing tempo of industrial investment in that period. No definite trend is noticeable in the pattern of exports, but consumer goods and raw materials accounted for the bulk of exports. Although exports of sewing machines, electric fans, bicycles, and other items have expanded in recent years, tea, jute, and cotton manufactures still make up more than half of India's total exports.

Before independence India's foreign trade was heavily oriented toward the Sterling Area. The Sterling Area still absorbs the largest share of India's exports, but imports now come chiefly from the Dollar Area. Indian trade with Eastern Europe has increased in recent years. The two countries that provide the main export market for Indian goods are the United States and Britain.

The article by Philip Phibbs describes in detail Indian foreign aid programs. The bulk of India's aid has been concentrated in Nepal, Sikkim, and Bhutan. Loans and technical assistance have also been extended to some Asian and African nations. Joint economic ventures between Indian industrialists and local groups in foreign countries have been encouraged by the Indian government. Although Phibbs does not provide the total value of aid extended by India, adding all the figures mentioned in the article gives a figure of 1,300 million rupees. This is the equivalent of about 270 million United States dollars (at the

1960–61 exchange value of 4.77 rupees to $1.00) during the period covered in Phibbs' article.

The article by Paul Streeten and Roger Hill analyzes foreign aid to India. During the period 1947–66 the total authorized external assistance to India is estimated to have been 58 billion rupees, of which 77 per cent has been utilized. Although India received large sums in total amount of aid, the aid on per capita basis is still small because of the size of population. A special feature of the composition of aid is the declining trend of grants. Around 60 per cent of the aid authorized up to the end of the First Plan was in loans, 36 per cent in grants, and only 4 per cent in PL 480 funds and the like. But during the Third Plan the share of loans increased to 81 per cent while the share of grants dropped to 3 per cent and that of PL 480, etc. rose to 16 per cent.

The problem of debt servicing obligations became difficult in the late 1960s. While such obligations rose by 84 per cent between 1962 and 1966, export earning—a source for debt servicing—increased by only 14 per cent. Between 1966–67 and 1980–81 India will need $18 billion in foreign aid to carry out her development plan, but her debt servicing liability will be as high as $14 billion. This is partly due to the hardness of the terms on which some of the loans are incurred and renewed. India has now learned that slow utilization of aid already authorized can be speeded up by more non-project aid and the softening of terms as well as the improvement in the administrative machinery.

The distribution of total aid utilized so far shows that the highest proportion—58 per cent—was allocated for industrial development. Railway, power, iron, and steel took up 34 per cent. About 1.0 per cent was utilized for agricultural development and about 4.0 for wheat imports. The remainder was allocated for port and transportation improvement.

The contribution of external finance to total public outlays under India's Five Year Plans is large. About 10 per cent of the total public outlay during the First Plan was financed through external aid. The proportion increased to 22 per cent and 28 per cent during the Second and Third Plans respectively. It is estimated that the corresponding figure would be somewhat lower during the Fourth Plan. Because considerable unused industrial capacity in India has been largely the result of inadequate import of raw materials, components, and spare parts, the role of external aid in filling the foreign exchange gap could also be crucial. Thus Streeten and Hill concluded that any additional foreign exchange shortage would have led to a severe cut in the size of the Second and Third Plans even if domestic savings had been available. In addition, the lag in agricultural output also created a serious hindrance for the foreign aid in speeding up development. United States food aid under PL 480 did help in easing a part of such difficulties.

Robert Price's article on China covers several aspects of Chinese international economic relations. Chinese foreign trade with communist countries shows a sharp upward trend between 1950 and 1959 and continues on a downward trend after 1959. Trade with the non-communist countries shows an upward trend after 1952. In 1955 75 per cent of her trade was oriented toward communist countries. This proportion dropped to 34 per cent in 1965 and again to 23 per cent in 1968.[1] Because of China's goal of economic independence, no single trade partner has shared more than 20 per cent of her total foreign trade in recent years.

Notes to this Part appear on page 396

The pattern of Chinese trade shows heavy orientation toward industrial development. The import of machinery and equipment made up about 48 per cent of China's total imports in the peak year, 1959; the proportion dropped to a low figure of 10 per cent in 1962 and has probably crossed the 20 per cent mark in recent years. Agricultural products continue to make up 40 per cent of China's exports while each of the three categories—industrial materials, textiles, and other manufactured goods—make up about 20 per cent. As the growth rate of foodgrain output continues to exceed the rate of population growth, the import of machinery and equipment is expected to make up a greater share of the total import in the future.

During the 1950s most of China's imports of industrial equipment came from the Communist Bloc. Since the early 1960s, China's imports of these items have depended heavily on the capitalist industrialized nations. A special feature of her foreign relations since 1963 has been the purchase of complete plants from these nations and the continuing large purchases of wheat from Canada and Australia. As a result China has had trade deficits with the Western industrial countries and Japan in recent years. These deficits, however, are covered largely by her trade surplus from Hong Kong and Singapore.

In the 1950s the USSR was the only supplier of foreign loans to China. Soviet economic loans amounted to between $475 million and $795 million, depending on the interpretation of the five-year loan of $320 million in 1961. This fairly moderate sum of credit did allow China to have a trade deficit with Soviet during the first half of the 1950s. After 1956 China had a trade surplus with the Soviet, and by 1965 she had virtually liquidated her indebtedness.

Thus the most valuable aspect of the Soviet aid to China was in the form of technical assistance and the supply of critical machine and equipment, especially the complete plants which China was not able to obtain from the West. In addition the trade policy of the Soviet Union had ensured a market for the products of China's textile and food industries.

Between 1953 and 1965 communist China extended credits and grants of slightly more than $2 billion to other nations. About 60 per cent of the aid went to the less developed communist nations, and the remainder to the less developed non-communist nations in Asia and Africa. It was estimated that the aid program never exceeded 0.2 to 0.3 per cent of the national income in any year.[2] In recent years the annual foreign economic aids of China amounted to about $250 million. Some of the aid projects are long-term in nature, including the one for the 1,100 mile railway line between Tanzania and Zambia. During the past twenty years China has extended more credit to other nations than she has received. Thus for that period as a whole she was a net capital exporter.

India and China undoubtedly have benefited from foreign aid during the past two decades. Both have been fairly successful in utilizing foreign aid and trade to stimulate economic development at home. Because the prospect of expanded external aid to these two countries in the 1970s is not so promising as in the past, the success of their future economic development efforts will depend in part on how skillfully they utilize the aid extended to them. (And China may receive no aid at all.) The lessons learned from their experience in the past two decades should provide them with insight into how to coordinate aid, trade, and domestic economic policy to their greatest economic advantage.

28

# Foreign Trade of India During the Post Independence Period

*Ruddar Datt*
*K. P. M. Sundharam*

*From Ruddar Datt and K. P. M. Sundharam,* Indian Economy *(New Delhi: Niraj Prakashan, 1969), pp. 638–48 with omissions. Reprinted with permission.*

## *Introduction*

For the study of trends of India's foreign trade during the post independence period, it is convenient to divide the entire period into four periods (a) 1948–49 to 1950–51—the period of planning (b) 1951–52 to 1955–56—the period of the First Plan, (c) 1956–57 to 1960—the period of the Second Plan and (d) 1961–62 to 1967–68.

### 1948–49 TO 1950–51—ON THE EVE OF PLANNING

On the eve of planning, the foreign trade of India showed an excess of imports over exports (refer Table 1). The rise in imports was largely due to (a) pent-up demand of the war and the post-war period as a consequence of various controls and restrictions, (b) the shortage of food and basic raw materials like jute and cotton as a result of partition, (c) the rise in the imports of machinery and equipment—or capital goods—to meet the needs of replacement of war-time worn-out machinery as also to meet the growing demand for hydro-electric and other projects started during the period.

### 1951–52 TO 1955–56—THE FIRST PLAN PERIOD

During this period, imports rose further in value (refer Table 2). The annual average value of imports during the period was Rs. 730 crores and that of exports Rs. 622 crores. In this way, the average annual trade deficit worked out to be Rs. 108 crores. Over

**Table 1—Trade Balance During 1948–49 to 1950–51[a]**

| Year (April–March) | Imports c.i.f. | Exports f.o.b. | Balance of Trade |
|---|---|---|---|
| 1948–49 | 766.3 | 482.5 | −238.8 |
| 1949–50 | 603.9 | 514.0 | −89.9 |
| 1950–51 | 650.3 | 646.8 | −3.5 |
| Total 1948–49 to 1950–51 | 2,020.5 | 1,643.3 | −332.2 |
| Annual average | 673.5 | 547.8 | −110.7 |

[a] In Rs. crores.
*Source: Reserve Bank of India Bulletins.*

**Table 2—Trade Balance During First Plan[a]**

| Year (April–March) | Imports c.i.f. | Exports f.o.b. | Balance of Trade |
|---|---|---|---|
| 1951–52 | 962.9 | 730.1 | −232.8 |
| 1952–53 | 633.0 | 601.9 | −31.1 |
| 1953–54 | 591.8 | 539.7 | −52.1 |
| 1954–55 | 689.7 | 596.6 | −93.1 |
| 1955–56 | 773.1 | 640.3 | −132.8 |
| Total 1951–52 to 1955–56 | 3,650.5 | 3,108.6 | −541.9 |
| Annual average | 730 | 622 | −108 |

[a] In Rs. crores.
*Source: Reserve Bank of India Bulletins.*



Notes to chapter 28 appear on page 396

the five-year period, the cumulative trade deficit was of the order of Rs. 540 crores. Trade deficit was largely due to programs of industrialization which gathered momentum and pushed up the imports of capital goods. Imports of raw materials showed a slight decline as a proportion of total imports. Foodgrains worth Rs. 595 crores were imported during the period. The import of consumer goods was of the order of Rs. 878 crores during the First Plan, but the bulk of consumer goods imports were accounted for by foodgrains. The pattern of exports did not change significantly and was restricted to jute manufactures, tea and cotton manufactures. They are counted for about half of the total exports. Raw material exports are counted for between one-fourth to one-fifth of total exports.

### 1956–57 TO 1960–61—THE SECOND PLAN PERIOD

During the Second Plan, a massive program of industrialization was initiated. This included the setting up of the steel plants, heavy expansion and renovation of railways and modernization of many industries and as a result, the quantum of imports reached a very high level. Besides this, the maintenance imports required for a developing economy further increased our imports. Foodgrain imports had also to be continued and during the Second Plan, foodgrain imports were of the order of Rs. 805 crores.

Exports under the Second Plan did record some change in their pattern. Export earnings averaged Rs. 603 crores per annum (refer Table 3). The figure of average export earning for the Second Plan was lower than that under the First Plan, which shows that the much needed diversification of exports and export promotion drive did not materialize. Consequently, the trade balance became heavily adverse. During the Second Plan, the annual average adverse balance of trade was of the order of Rs. 467 crores which is in sharp contrast to the adverse trade balance of the order of Rs. 108 crores per year during the First Plan.

### 1961–62 TO 1965–66—THE THIRD PLAN PERIOD

The Third Plan document targeted for exports worth Rs. 3,700 crores and imports worth Rs. 5,750 crores during the five-year period. The record of exports during the plan shows that although in the first two years—1961–62 and 1962–63—export earnings did not rise significantly, but in 1963–64 and 1964–65 export earnings shot up to Rs. 802 crores. But in 1965–66, there was a slight decline in exports to Rs. 782 crores (refer Table 4). In this way the average export earnings worked out to be Rs. 747 crores and, thus, the export target set for the Third Plan was achieved.

On the other hand, the target for imports was fixed at Rs. 5,750 crores—out of which Rs. 1,900 crores were to be for the import of machinery and equipment for plan projects, Rs. 200 crores for the import of components, intermediate goods, etc., for raising productivity and Rs. 3,650 crores for maintenance imports. For an expanding economy, imports of this order are a necessity. During the Third Plan, we imported goods worth Rs. 6,119 crores. In other words, the target of

***Table 3—Trade Balance During Second Plan***[a]

| *Year (April–March)* | *Imports c.i.f* | *Exports f.o.b.* | *Balance of Trade* |
|---|---|---|---|
| 1956–57 | 1,102.1 | 635.2 | −466.9 |
| 1957–58 | 1,233.2 | 594.2 | −639.0 |
| 1958–59 | 1,029.3 | 576.3 | −453.0 |
| 1959–60 | 932.3 | 627.4 | −304.9 |
| 1960–61 | 1,105.7 | 630.5 | −475.2 |
| Total 1956–57 to 1960–61 | 5,402.6 | 3,063.6 | −2,338.1 |
| Annual Average | 1,080 | 613 | −467 |

[a] In Rs. crores.
*Source: Reserve Bank of India Bulletins.*

imports had to be relaxed in order to permit a larger quantum of imports. This was largely necessitated by two factors: firstly, the defense needs had increased, and, secondly, larger quantity of foodgrains had to be imported.

Although after the devaluation of the rupee, exports touched a record level of Rs. 1,255 crores in 1967–68, but on account of relative inelasticity of imports, the import bill also reached an all-time record of Rs. 2,042 crores. As a consequence, the balance of trade situation worsened still further.

## *Composition of India's Foreign Trade*

In order to study the composition of India's foreign trade, it is necessary to analyze the changing pattern of imports and exports.

### PATTERN OF IMPORTS

Indian imports are broadly classified into three categories—capital goods, raw materials and consumer goods. The capital goods category includes machinery of all kinds, metals—iron and steel—other non-ferrous metals and transport equipment. The raw materials category includes mineral oils, raw cotton and waste, raw jute, dye-stuffs and chemicals. The consumer goods category consists of electric goods and apparatus, drugs and medicines, rayon textiles, paper and paper board, etc., and foodgrains.

Table 5 reveals the changing pattern of imports during the seventeen-year period—1950–51 to 1967–68. The share of capital goods imports which was 28.8 per cent during the First Plan period increased to 42.2 per cent during the Second Plan period. As against it, the import of raw materials as also of consumer goods is on the decline. Raw material imports which accounted for 27.5 per cent of total imports during the First Plan came down to 17.7 per cent during the Second Plan period. Similarly the import of consumer goods declined from 24.0 per cent during the First Plan to 19.8 per cent during the Second Plan period. The most important single item in our consumer goods imports is foodgrains which accounted for 16.3 per cent of total imports during the First Plan and which stood at about 15 per cent during the Second Plan period. In other words, the import pattern during the first decade of planned economic development changed rapidly in favor of capital goods imports and raw materials and consumer goods imports (other than foodgrains) declined slowly. This changing pattern is an index of the growing industrialization of our economy. The only disquieting feature of our import trade is the continuance of foodgrain imports which are the result of the failure of agricultural production to rise corresponding to our growing demand for foodgrains with a rapidly increasing population.

During the Third Plan, capital goods worth Rs. 2,912 crores were imported and

**Table 4—Trade Balance During 1961–62 to 1967–63[a]**

| Year (April–March) | Imports c.i.f. | Exports f.o.b. | Balance of Trade |
|---|---|---|---|
| Third Plan | | | |
| 1961–62 | 1,006.0 | 668.3 | −337.7 |
| 1962–63 | 1,096.8 | 680.9 | −415.9 |
| 1963–64 | 1,245.0 | 801.6 | −443.4 |
| 1964–65 | 1,420.8 | 800.9 | −619.9 |
| 1965–66 | 1,350.0 | 783.3 | −566.7 |
| Total 1961–62 to 1965–66 | 6,118.6 | 3,735.0 | −2,383.6 |
| Annual Average | 1,224 | 747 | −477 |
| 1966–67[b] | 1,885.6 | 1,079.3 | −806.3 |
| 1967–68[b] | 2,042.8 | 1,254.6 | −788.2 |

[a] In Rs. crores.
[b] Provisional.
*Source: Reserve Bank of India Bulletin,* March 1969.

this accounted for 47.8 per cent of the total imports. Similarly, raw materials and mineral oils accounted for 17.0 per cent of total imports. The import of consumer goods was of the order of Rs. 938 crores, *i.e.*, 15.4 per cent of total imports. Foodgrain imports were 19.8 per cent of total imports.

During 1966–67 and 1967–68, the composition of imports changed. On account of the drought that resulted in a sharp fall of agricultural production, the demand for foodgrain imports increased. Foodgrains worth Rs. 1,105 crores were imported during this period which accounts for 28.3 per cent of the total imports. Similarly, the demand for raw materials also went up. On account of the recessionary trend in the economy, the demand for capital goods imports declined. Capital goods imports declined from 47.8 per cent of total imports during the Third Plan to 37.0 per cent during 1966–68.

The trend of imports in selected commodities is given in Table 6.

*Foodgrains*—The principal item of import is foodgrains. The imports were necessitated by the partition of the country and the growing demand for food for the rising population. The average annual imports of foodgrains which were about Rs. 120 crores during the First Plan, rose to Rs. 160 crores during the Second Plan, and have further increased to an average rate of Rs. 241 crores during the Third Plan. Foodgrain imports can be curtailed only if there is a sharp improvement in

## *Table 5—Structure of Indian Imports*[a]

| | *1951–52 to 1955–56 (First Plan)* | *1956–57 to 1960–61 (Second Plan)* | *1961–62 to 1965–66 (Third Plan)* | *1966–67*[b] *to 1967–68* |
|---|---|---|---|---|
| Total Imports | 3,651 | 5,399 | 6,093 | 3,903 |
| | (100) | (100) | (100) | (100) |
| (a) Capital goods | 1,053.6 | 2,283.0 | 2,912 | 1,445 |
| | (28.8) | (42.2) | (47.8) | (37.0) |
| (b) Raw materials | 1,060.8 | 918.8 | 1,039 | 1,022 |
| | (27.5) | (17.7) | (17.0) | (26.0) |
| (c) Consumer goods | 877.8 | 1,074.2 | 938 | 331 |
| | (24.0) | (19.8) | (15.4) | (8.6) |
| (d) Foodgrains | 595.2 | 804.7 | 1,204 | 1,105 |
| | (16.3) | (14.9) | (19.8) | (28.3) |

[a] In Rs. crores.
[b] Provisional.
*Note.*—Figures in brackets indicate percentage of imports in the group to the total imports.
*Source:* RBI, *India's Balance of Payments 1948–49 to 1961–62. Reserve Bank of India Bulletins.*

## *Table 6—Average Annual Imports of Principal Commodities*[a]

| | *1951–52 to 1955–56* | *1956–57 to 1960–61* | *1961–62 to 1965–66* | *1966–67*[b] *to 1967–68* |
|---|---|---|---|---|
| 1. Foodgrains | 120 | 161 | 241 | 552 |
| 2. Machinery (including locomotives) | 116 | 265 | 472 | 514 |
| 3. Mineral oils | 73 | 80 | 85 | 68 |
| 4. Raw cotton | 77 | 45 | 54 | 70 |
| 5. Metals (ferrous and non-ferrous) | 54 | 131 | 172 | 184 |
| 6. Chemicals, drugs and medicines | 34 | 53 | 55 | 90 |
| 7. Fertilizers | — | — | 28 | 110 |

[a] In Rs. crores.
[b] Provisional.
*Source: Reserve Bank of India Bulletins.*

food production within the country. So far, the achievement in food production has been rather slow. As a result, imports of foodgrains on a significant scale have continued. The drought of 1965–66 further worsened the situation and consequently, foodgrains imports worth Rs. 1,105 crores were done during 1966–67 and 1967–68.

*Machinery*—In a country which is rapidly industrializing her economy imports of machinery are bound to increase. Compared to the average annual import of machinery which was about Rs. 116 crores during the First Plan period, the annual average during the Second Plan rose to Rs. 265 crores and during the Third Plan, the annual average jumped to Rs. 472 crores. Imports of machinery include electrical and non-electrical equipment as also locomotives. The average annual imports of machinery during the two-year period following the Third Plan were Rs. 514 crores.

*Mineral Oils*—Imports of mineral oils are also on the increase. India is short in the supply of mineral oils, especially petroleum. The average annual imports of mineral oils which were Rs. 73 crores during the First Plan period are about Rs. 85 crores during the Third Plan period. There was a decline in the import of mineral oils during 1966–68.

*Metals*—India imports iron and steel and also some non-ferrous metals. The annual average imports of ferrous and non-ferrous metals which were about Rs. 54 crores during the First Plan have gone up to Rs. 172 crores during the Third Plan. Import of metals on such a large scale is necessitated by the vast programs of industrial expansion, development of railways and hydro-electric projects. During 1966–67 and 1967–68 imports of ferrous and non-ferrous metals averaged Rs. 184 crores per annum.

*Chemicals, drugs and medicines*—There has been an increase in the import of chemicals, drugs and medicines. The imports of these items during the First Plan period were about Rs. 34 crores per annum; they increased to Rs. 53 crores per annum during the Second Plan period and the average annual imports during the Third Plan also work out to be Rs. 55 crores. Imports of chemicals, drugs and medicines have risen sharply to Rs. 90 crores per annum on the average during 1966–68.

*Raw Cotton*—Imports of raw cotton and waste are graduaully on the decline. During the First Plan, average annual imports on this item were of the order of Rs. 77 crores, but annual average imports came down in the Third Plan to Rs. 54 crores. Imports of raw cotton rose to Rs. 70 crores per annum during 1966–68. This was largely the result of a fall in agricultural production.

Besides these items, India also imports electrical goods and apparatus, paper, paperboard and stationery, raw jute and vehicles. The imports of raw jute which were about Rs. 40 crores year per during 1948–49 to 1950–51 came down to a bare Rs. 5 crores per annum during the Third Plan period. Following the adoption of the New Strategy in Indian agriculture, the imports of fertilizers were stepped up. The average annual imports of fertilizers which stood at Rs. 28 crores during the Third Plan rose to Rs. 110 crores during 1966–68.

## PATTERN OF EXPORTS

The Director General of Commercial Intelligence has classified Indian exports into three categories—(a) consumer goods, (b) raw materials or intermediate goods, (c) others. Among consumer goods exports are included tea, cotton cloth, black pepper, cashew kernels, tobacco and oil cakes. Among raw materials or intermediate goods are included jute manufactures, hides and skins (raw and tanned), metallic ores, raw and waste cotton, vegetable oils, oil seeds, etc. Among "others" are wool, lac, lubricants, art silk, machinery and transport equipment. The last category was relatively unimportant but with the diversification of items of exports, these commodities are also acquiring some significance in our exports. In Table 7 is given the percentage distribution of exports in these categories.

No definite trend is noticeable from the figures given in Table 7, but it obviously shows that bulk of Indian exports (74 to 79 per cent) consists of consumer goods and raw materials. Items of machinery or transport equipment such as sewing machines, electric fans, bicycles, etc., have entered recently in Indian exports but they are relatively unimportant. Tea, jute and cotton manufactures—these items account for more than half of our exports.

Annual average exports of a few principal commodities are given in Table 8.

*Tea*—Tea is one of the most important items of Indian exports. It held the first position in our export items in certain years, while jute held the first position in other years. The average annual export of tea was Rs. 106 crores during the First Plan period and it increased to Rs. 132 crores in the Second Plan period. A slight deterioration occurred in tea exports in the Third Plan. During 1966–67 and 1967–68 tea exports picked up to an average annual level of Rs. 167 crores. Tea ranks as the second most important export item. Our principal customers of tea are UK, USA, Canada, Australia, USSR, Egypt and West Germany.

*Jute Yarn and Manufactures*—Jute has been our principal item of export. At present, jute manufactures rank at the top in our export list. Our biggest rival in jute goods is Pakistan. Our exports have not gone up significantly in this commodity. From Rs. 129 crores per annum during 1948–49 to 1950–51, exports of jute goods went up to Rs. 149 crores during the First Plan, then declined to Rs. 120 crores during the Second Plan but again rose to Rs. 157 crores during the Third Plan. The value of jute yarn and manufactures exported during 1966–67 and 1967–68 rose to an annual average level of Rs. 225 crores. Since part of the rise in the value of exports is accounted for by a rise in prices of jute manufactures, increase in the volume is very little.

*Cotton Yarn and Manufactures*—During the First Plan period, the average annual exports of cotton yarn and manufactures touched Rs. 81 crores, but this declined to Rs. 76 crores during the Second Plan period and to a small figure of Rs. 55 crores during the Third Plan. On account of relatively high

### *Table 7—Percentage Distribution of Exports*

| | *1950–51* | *1955–56* | *1960–61* | *1965–66* |
|---|---|---|---|---|
| (*a*) Consumer goods | 41 | 33 | 37 | 40 |
| (b) Raw materials or intermediate goods | 36 | 41 | 36 | 39 |
| (c) Others | 23 | 26 | 27 | 21 |
| Total | 100 | 100 | 100 | 100 |

### *Table 8—Average Annual Exports of Principal Commodities*[a]

| | *1951–52 to 1955–56* | *1956–57 to 1960–61* | *1961–62 to 1965–66* | *1966–67 to 1967–68* |
|---|---|---|---|---|
| 1. Tea | 106 | 132 | 120 | 167 |
| 2. Jute, yarn and manufactures | 149 | 120 | 157 | 225 |
| 3. Cotton, yarn and manufactures | 81 | 76 | 55 | 75 |
| 4. Hides and skins (raw and tanned) | 32 | 35 | 35 | 67 |
| 5. Metallic ores (iron, mica and manganese) | 30 | 37 | 50 | 96 |
| 6. Cotton, raw and waste | 27 | 18 | 16 | 18 |
| 7. Tobacco | 15 | 16 | 20 | 26 |
| 8. Vegetable oils | 27 | 16 | 10 | 4 |

[a] In Rs. crores.
*Source:* (1) *India's Balance of Payments 1948–49 to 1961–62.*
(2) *Reserve Bank of India Bulletin.*

cost in Indian textile industry, India finds it difficult to capture the international market. In fact, high costs are due to rising labor costs and use of old and worn-out machinery. In the post-devaluation period, exports of cotton textiles have increased because their competitiveness in the international market improved. During 1966–67 and 1967–68, average annual exports of cotton textiles improved to Rs. 67 crores.

*Hides and Skins*—One of the traditional items of Indian export is raw hides and skins. But recently, in the exports of this item, the proportion of leather to raw hides and skins is on the increase. This is really a healthy development. India earned about Rs. 67 crores per annum from this item during 1966–68.

*Metallic Ores*—India exports mica, iron ore and manganese. The average annual exports of these metallic ores was Rs. 6 crores only in 1945–69 to 1950–51 but it has been gradually on the increase and India has started earning about Rs. 50 crores per year on this account. During 1966–67 and 1967–68, export of mineral ores rose further to Rs. 96 crores per annum. This is a significant gain.

Besides these items, India exports raw cotton and waste, tobacco and vegetable oils. These commodities also earn about Rs. 48 crores worth of foreign exchange per year. There is no doubt that the pattern of Indian exports shows dependence on a few items. Diversification of exports, finding new commodities and markets is one of the most urgent necessities to boost up our export trade.

## *Direction of India's Foreign Trade*

In order to study the regional direction of India's foreign trade, the countries of the world are grouped under four categories—(i) Sterling Area, (ii) Dollar Area, (iii) O.E.E.C. Countries and (iv) Rest of the Non-Sterling Area. In Table 9 the percentage share of these four broad groups of countries in India's foreign trade has been presented.

The Sterling Area due to its historical association with India was very important in our foreign trade. It was on account of this factor that 54 per cent of our exports were directed to the Sterling Area, and our imports from this area were of the order of 46 per cent during the First Plan period, but our trade with this area is on the decline. During the Second Plan period, exports to the Sterling Area were 50 per cent of the total exports and during the Third Plan, they further declined to 38.7 per cent. Exports to the Sterling Area declined further to about 31.8 per cent during 1966–68. Similarly, imports from the Sterling Area declined from 46 per cent during the First Plan to 38 per cent during the Second Plan, and they fell further to 22.2 per cent during the Third Plan. They have further declined to a low figure of 17.9 per cent during 1966–68.

### *Table 9—Percentage Share in India's Foreign Trade*

| | *1951–52 to 1955–56 (First Plan)* | *1956–57 to 1960–61 (Second Plan)* | *1961–62 to 1965–66 (Third Plan)* | *1966–67 to 1967–68* |
|---|---|---|---|---|
| EXPORTS | | | | |
| Sterling Area | 54 | 50 | 38.7 | 31.8 |
| Dollar Area | 21 | 19 | 21.2 | 20.6 |
| OEEC Countries | 10 | 9 | 9.1 | 8.8 |
| Rest of Non-Sterling Area | 15 | 22 | 30.9 | 38.8 |
| IMPORTS | | | | |
| Sterling Area | 46 | 38 | 22.2 | 17.9 |
| Dollar Area | 24 | 26 | 36.2 | 39.7 |
| OEEC Countries | 16 | 21 | 15.4 | 14.4 |
| Rest of Non-Sterling Area | 14 | 15 | 26.1 | 28.0 |

*Source: Reserve Bank of India Bulletin,* July 1967 and March 1969.

Our trade with the Dollar Area on the export front has remained virtually unchanged. Our exports during 1950–51 and 1967–68 (*i.e.*, seventeen-year period) were between 19 to 21 per cent of total exports. But imports from the Dollar Area have improved significantly during the recent years. Imports from the Dollar Area which represented 24 per cent of total imports during the First Plan improved to 26 per cent during the Second Plan and further rose sharply to 36.2 per cent during the Third Plan. During 1966–67 and 1967–68, imports from the Dollar Area were about 40 per cent of total imports.

The share of the O.E.E.C. countries[1] in Indian exports has remained between 9 to 10 per cent during the seventeen-year period (1950–51 and 1957–68), but share in imports from this area rose from 16 per cent during the First Plan to 21 per cent during the Second Plan and then came down again to 14.4 per cent during 1966–68. In this group, India had heavy trade deficits with the E.C.M. countries. During the Second Plan period (1956–57 to 1960–61) the trade deficit with E.C.M. countries[2] was of the order of Rs. 711 crores and during the Third Plan, the trade deficit amounted to Rs. 592 crores. It is, therefore, essential to secure proper safeguards for Indian exports to the European Common Market.

The regional group "rest of the non-Sterling Area" has significantly improved its position. Indian exports to this area have risen from 15 per cent during the First Plan to 22 per cent during the Second Plan and to 30.9 per cent during the Third Plan. Exports to this area have further increased to about 39 per cent of total exports. Similarly, imports from this area have also improved from 14 per cent during the First Plan period to 26.1 per cent during the Third Plan, and further to 28.0 per cent during 1966–68.

Among the non-Sterling Area countries, trade with USSR and other East European Socialist countries like Poland, Rumania, Bulgaria, Hungary, East Germany, Czechoslovakia and Yugoslavia has also developed during the recent years. The main items of imports from these countries are iron and steel, non-ferrous metals, chemicals, capital equipment, railway stores, etc. These countries in return exported tea, cashew kernels, spices, tobacco, oil seeds, hides and skins, metallic ores, jute manufactures, etc.,—the traditional items of Indian exports. The composition of imports from these countries suggests the significance of the trade with this area from the viewpoint of economic development.

It would be of interest to examine the direction of trade with reference to some important countries (refer Table 10).

Although UK was of prime importance in our foreign trade before independence, USA is now shaping as the premier country. Imports from USA were 39.1 per cent of total imports in 1967–68 whereas imports from UK accounted for only 8 per cent. On the export side Indian exports to UK were always higher than the exports to USA but during the Third Plan, the exports to USA have leveled off with exports to UK Our imports with West Germany are on the increase, although our exports to this country are not expanding.

***Table 10—India's Foreign Trade with Selected Countries[a]***

| COUNTRY | Imports | | | Exports | | |
|---|---|---|---|---|---|---|
| | *1950–51* | *1960–61* | *1967–68* | *1950–51* | *1960–61* | *1967–68* |
| USA | 18.5 | 29.2 | 39.1 | 18.5 | 16.0 | 17.3 |
| UK | 20.8 | 19.3 | 8.0 | 22.4 | 26.9 | 9.1 |
| West Germany | 2.0 | 10.9 | 7.3 | 1.7 | 3.1 | 1.9 |
| USSR | 0.0 | 1.4 | 4.9 | 0.2 | 4.5 | 10.1 |
| Japan | 1.6 | 5.4 | 5.4 | 1.6 | 5.5 | 11.3 |
| Australia | 5.2 | 1.6 | 3.4 | 4.8 | 3.5 | 2.3 |
| Pakistan | 6.7 | 1.3 | 0.4 | 4.9 | 1.6 | 0.6 |

[a] In percentages.
*Source: Planning Commission, Basic Statistics relating to the Indian Economy.*

This accounts for the heavy trade deficit with West Germany. Japan and USSR are both growing in importance in our foreign trade. We had trade relations with Japan in the pre-war period, but trade was cut off during the war. But now, it has been revived again. With USSR foreign trade is of a recent origin but the share of imports from this country ranges between 5 to 6 per cent, but our exports to USSR have risen very sharply to 10.1 per cent in 1967–68. With Australia and Pakistan, our foreign trade is on the decline. The deterioration of our political relations with Pakistan is responsible for this trend. Foreign trade with Pakistan accounts for just less than one per cent of our total foreign trade.

29

# India's Economic Aid Programs

*Philip M. Phibb*

*From* Current History *54, no. 320, (April 1968): 232–38, 242, with omissions. Reprinted with permission.*

INDIA IS AT ONCE the recipient of the largest quantity of foreign aid in the world and, among those who received aid, the donor of the most assistance to others. Her program is small when compared to those of the developed countries, but it represents a significant sacrifice in view of her own critical needs.

The bulk of India's aid has been concentrated in the three Himalayan kingdoms—Nepal, Sikkim and Bhutan. In these states, India is either a major or the sole contributor of foreign assistance.

## *Aid to Nepal*

India's largest aid program is in Nepal, where she first became involved on a limited scale in 1951 with the loan of an Indian administrative official and an offer to train two Nepalese. At the same time, India built a temporary landing strip at Kathmandu. During the following year she agreed to construct a highway from the Kathmandu valley to India and to convert the airstrip into a permanent airport. Both projects were to be financed by a loan to Nepal.[1]

From these modest beginnings the program has grown steadily. By mid-1966 India had actually expended 312 million rupees in aid to Nepal.[2] Future commitments for a number of major highway and power projects suggest that Indian aid will remain at an extremely high level in the years immediately ahead.

India's aid has played a major role in Nepal's development. Until 1956, India provided more assistance than any other country. The United States outstripped her effort for a time, but in 1965–66, the leadership passed back to India, and she has agreed to provide nearly three times as much aid as the United States in 1966–67. Of the total assistance provided for Nepal from 1952 through 1967, India's share has been 34.6 per cent, while the United States has contributed slightly more, 42.1 per cent. Russia with 10.1 per cent and China with 8.8 per cent have made much smaller efforts.

The bulk of India's aid has gone to the development of transportation and into power and irrigation projects. Highway construction alone accounts for 29 per cent of the Indian assistance, and power projects account for 25 per cent. But horticulture, education, forestry and many other fields have also received attention.[3] Virtually all of India's aid has been given in the form of grants. The original proposal for a loan to build the Tribhuvan Rajpath and Gaucher Airport was quietly forgotten in 1954 and these funds, like all subsequent aid (with one exception), were provided as a gift.[4]

## *Aid to Sikkim*

Indian aid to Sikkim began at about the same time that India first took an interest in Nepal's development. In 1950, a grant of Rs. 50 thousand was given to Sikkim for a land reform program and a forest survey.[5] In 1952, the Maharaja of Sikkim asked Prime Minister Jawaharlal Nehru for economic assistance, and the latter readily agreed. An Indian team drew up a Seven Year Plan which was approved by the Indian Planning Commission in June, 1954. The plan originally called for a grant of Rs. 20.2 million and a separate loan of Rs. 2.1 million for an aerial ropeway between Gangtok and the Tibetan border. This aid was to be added to the Rs. 5.5. million which India had spent on road construction in Sikkim prior to 1954.[6]

**Notes to chapter 29 appear on page 396**

Subsequent road construction funds were included in Sikkim's plan, and roughly half of the first plan was devoted to this item.

India apparently expected to complete her participation in Sikkim's development during that initial seven-year period. In addition to road construction, the plan emphasized revenue-producing projects like a fruit-preservation factory, the aerial ropeway, and a timber-floating project. It was hoped that these commercial enterprises would produce sufficient revenue by 1961 to maintain and continue other projects.

Internal and external events intervened, however. During the first year of the plan only about one-half the funds made available were actually used. Lack of trained personnel and an inadequate administrative machine were the main problems.

Developments across Sikkim's northern border and Sino-Indian difficulties also affected the original assumption that India's obligation could cease in 1961. Despite the slow beginning made in the first year of the plan period, India decided in 1957 to increase the size of the plan to Rs. 30 million. It ultimately grew to about Rs. 35 million and most of the added expenditures were for road construction and communications.[7]

In September 1960, there was an incident involving Chinese forces at Jelep La Pass in Sikkim. Shortly thereafter discussions began on the second plan. India eventually committed herself to provide more than twice as much in the second five years (Rs. 81.3 million) as she had given in the first seven. Once again, nearly half the funds were allocated to roads and transport. All the revenue for the plan was provided by India as a grant.[8]

## *Aid to Bhutan*

Indian assistance to Bhutan began much later than it did to Nepal and Sikkim. This was not due to any lack of interest in Bhutan or concern about developments there. R. K. Nehru, a high official in the Ministry of External Affairs, visited Bhutan in 1955 and reportedly offered aid to Bhutan, but it was declined.

In 1958 Prime Minister Nehru himself journeyed to the country. The main topic of conversation during the visit was economic development, and the Indian leader stressed the need for roads which would link the two countries directly. He was apparently impressed by the fact that his journey to this neighboring state, for whose foreign policy India was responsible, took six days and required the permission of the Chinese government, since the best access to central Bhutan from India was through Tibet's Chumbi Valley. The Bhutanese accepted a small sum for road-building material and equipment and a loan for an orange-crushing factory, but they remained cautious and reluctant.[9]

There was a significant change in their attitude as the Chinese presence in Tibet became more ominous in 1959. In the autumn of that year it was agreed that India would provide an annual grant from 1960 onward of Rs. 700 thousand. The funds would enable Bhutan to plan its expenditures on a sounder basis. India also announced a road-construction program for Bhutan which would eventually provide four north-south roads linking Bhutan and India and one east-west highway to unify the system internally. The cost of the entire program was estimated at Rs. 150 million.

In February of 1961, Bhutan invited a team from the Indian Planning Commission to devise a development plan for the country. India subsequently agreed to provide the entire expenditure for the plan, Rs. 174.7 million. About 70 per cent of the funds were allocated to road construction and transportation.

## *Role of the Programs*

The most obvious fact about the area in which India has concentrated most of her aid is that it is of immense strategic importance to her. The Himalayan states provide a major mountain barrier protecting India's northern border.

The British had established special relations between their government in India and these three states. Independent India inherited the British role and confirmed the special status of the area in a series of treaties in 1949 and 1950. Nepal continued as nominally independent state but with especially close relations with India.[10] Sikkim agreed to continue as an Indian protectorate, and Bhutan once again agreed to be guided in its external relations by the government in India. Each state also continued to receive the financial grants which the British had begun.[11] The transfer was so complete and the continuity so smooth that the Indians even moved into the British Residencies in Kathmandu and Gangtok.

The decision to extend technical and economic assistance to these three countries, then, did not represent a new policy departure, but was simply the addition of a basically post-war instrument of diplomacy to the methods already in use to maintain Indian influence in the Himalayas and protect her security.

The second noteworthy feature of India's aid program is that she decided to use this new diplomatic weapon because existing techniques were inadequate to meet the situation there. By 1950, India was seriously concerned about the stability and security of the three countries. The underlying cause of her apprehension was, of course, the advent of a Communist government in China and its increasing pressure on and eventual occupation of Tibet. The traditional cultural, economic and political ties between the three states and Tibet provided a basis for Chinese intervention; their internal instability and socioeconomic backwardness provided the opportunity.

If China's potential activity was the cause of concern, immediate events indicated the urgency of the situation and forced India to act. All three countries had autocratic governments and what might be described as semi-feudal economies. Indian aid began in Nepal and Sikkim under remarkably similar circumstances. In 1949 a demonstration in Gangtok which began as a demand for economic reforms quickly degenerated into an insurrection against the Maharaja. Order was restored only by the intervention of Indian troops. Shortly thereafter, the first Indian aid was provided to enable the Sikkimese government to undertake urgently needed economic reforms.

In Nepal, India had encouraged more democratic practices for some time but with little success. In 1950, revolt broke out and India helped the various factions reach a compromise solution in 1951. Aid began soon thereafter to assist the new, liberalized regime perform its responsibilities.

Bhutan's isolation and greater political stability provided no similar occasion for Indian involvement at this time. Increasing Sino-Indian tensions led the Indians to propose aid after 1955, but not until 1959 did the Bhutanese become sufficiently alarmed about Chinese intentions to accept Indian aid on a large scale.

There seem to have been three objectives in India's response to this situation: to increase the links between India and the Himalayan region, to promote economic progress, and to encourage political stability.

The first of these objectives was relatively simple. The major portion of Indian aid to the region went to the development of roads and transportation. A number of new north-south highways were built or are being built which link each of these three countries more closely with India. At the same time these projects have considerable strategic value, for they provide avenues by which Indian forces can reach the interior of the countries if and when they are needed.

Road construction was not, however, wholly self-interested, for without improved transportation little development would be possible. Roads were the prerequisite for economic advance. Moreover, India is building not only north-south roads but also east-west highways which will connect each of these countries internally for the first time. These lateral connections will reduce their dependence upon India and promote internal communications.

The new roads would tie the Himalayan states to India physically. Other aid projects should produce the desired economic and social change. The third problem was political stability, and this was intimately connected to the aid program. It was this concern that triggered the initial assistance to both Sikkim and Nepal; it would be a necessary condition to achieve the long-term objective and purpose of the aid program.

In Nepal, India repeatedly urged democratic reforms in 1949 and 1950. In the early 1950s, she intervened in Nepalese political life to this end, creating considerable resentment in the process. When King Mahendra assumed personal control of the Government in 1960, New Delhi openly indicated its disapproval. Subsequent outbreaks of violence encouraged by Nepalese politicians in exile in India increased the strain. Only the timely intervention of the Chinese by their attack on India in 1962 reversed the trend. India has since made strenuous efforts to improve relations and now accepts the Mahendra government.

In Sikkim where, ironically, India's influence and leverage are far greater, she has not promoted democratic government with comparable fervor. Her initial intervention in 1949 and her subsequent aid preserved the authority of the Maharaja. Political reforms have been initiated gradually, but Sikkim is still far from popular democratic government.

This is not to condemn the Indian government, for the political situation in Sikkim is extremely delicate. About 1890, the British began to encourage Nepalese to settle in sparsely populated Sikkim. By 1947, the Nepalese constituted the majority of the population. The indigenous Bhutia-Lepcha community was a minority in its own land. The basic political problem to this day is that while the Nepalese represent the majority, the Bhutia-Lepchas—through the person of the Maharaja (now styled, Chogyal)—dominate the government.

In this situation, India has been circumspect. She has not openly promoted the one-man, one-vote principle she advocates elsewhere, nor has she promoted the same measure of reform in Sikkim that she sought in Nepal.

In Bhutan, India has made no overt move to encourage democratic reform. She has respected the absolute internal autonomy assured to Bhutan by the treaty of 1949. By 1959, when India became involved in the country, the border situation was so tense that it probably seemed unwise to disturb Bhutan's apparently stable, but autocratic, regime.

India has become a major aid donor in an area where existing diplomatic methods were inadequate to meet a serious threat to her security. Her initial commitments were limited and considered temporary. Involvement has escalated, however, and the Indian aid program in the Himalayas now appears to be a semi-permanent feature of her diplomacy there.

Aid has enabled India to defend herself more effectively in the region. It has also improved economic conditions and has probably added to the internal stability of the three kingdoms. But aid has also aroused a desire for new, less dependent relations between India and the three countries. India has been forced to adjust herself to a new relationship. The process has been painful and the result is potentially hazardous because it reduces India's influence.

All three countries have traditionally been suspicious of India, as most small countries are of a large and powerful neighbor. The close connection between the commencement of Indian aid in Nepal and Sikkim and overt Indian intervention in domestic political struggles did little to assuage fears. The presence of large aid missions adds to the concern, and in Sikkim at least there is some apprehensions about "Indianization" of the local culture.

Aid has required Indian presence and involvement. The three countries have tried to counteract this potential danger by seeking new, less dependent, formal relations with India.

## *Other Indian Aid Programs*

Indian aid to other regions of the world has been smaller in quantity and more limited in its political and economic impact. Until 1963, it consisted of minor assistance provided on an *ad hoc* basis and three rather substantial, organized efforts.

The first gesture was made in 1947 when four students from East Africa came to India for study on Government of India Scholarships. In the next year, India extended her first foreign loan—to Indonesia—in the amount of Rs. 75 thousand. The forms of assistance multiplied. Technicians and skilled personnel were lent to other countries, sometimes at their expense, sometimes at India's; training was provided in a variety of fields; and India helped other governments to recruit skilled Indian manpower for service abroad. Ethiopia, for example, regularly hires several hundred Indian teachers. All assistance was provided in response to requests.

However, three programs, each operating independently, did provide more substantial assistance. In 1949, India initiated a scholarship program for Indian and indigenous students from Asian and African countries. At first, a large number of the grants went to Indians resident abroad, and until 1965 a number were specifically reserved for this group, but increasingly the emphasis was placed on selection of indigenous students and these are now preferred. The number of scholarships offered has grown steadily.[12] In addition, since 1960, India has offered 50 grants annually for post-graduate study in India under the new Commonwealth Scholarship/Fellowship Program. Altogether, from 1949 to 1966, India allocated over Rs. 24 million for these two schemes.

India has also extended technical assistance to Asian and African countries through two international programs—the Colombo Plan and the Special Commonwealth Africa Assistance Program (SCAAP). The two plans might be described as multilateral arrangements to provide bilateral assistance.

India has been both a major donor and a major recipient of assistance under the Colombo Plan. She has, on balance, received far more than she has given, but her contributions have been significant.[13]

Three types of assistance are provided under the plan—training, experts and equipment. India has provided more training to nationals of other plan countries than all but four other members—the United States, Great Britain, Australia and Canada. India's status as one of the technically more advanced developing countries is emphasized by the fact that she provides 80 per cent of the training offered in the Colombo Plan region, and her share has been growing. In 1965–66, she provided 93 per cent of the training places.

In the field of expert assistance, the record is even stronger. India has provided the services of nearly a thousand of her skilled technicians, an effort which is second only to that of the United States. In the provision of equipment, India's contribution is smaller, but it surpasses that of any other Asian member of the plan except Japan. Similarly, among the Asian states only Japan has exceeded India's total expenditure, nearly Rs. 35.5 million, on the three forms of technical assistance. Pakistan made the next largest total effort, but spent less than two million rupees.[14]

India has also played an ever-increasing role in SCAAP since its founding in 1960. The same three types of assistance were extended at a total cost to India of Rs. 1,269,700 by the end of 1966.

## *Aid Programs After 1962*

After the Sino-Indian conflict of 1962, India began a searching reexamination of her relations with other developing countries. The failure of many of these states to support her was a cause of concern and disappointment.

In 1963, Indian ambassadors to West Asian, African and South East Asian countries met in special conferences to consider ways to build wider support for Indian policies. One result of these meetings was a new emphasis upon technical assistance programs and economic collaboration with developing countries.

There are three major aspects to the new assistance programs. First of all, various existing technical assistance schemes have been continued and expanded. These include the deputation of experts and skilled personnel for service abroad, assistance in recruitment of trained Indians by foreign governments, the donation of equipment and the training of foreigners in Indian institutions.

This assistance has gone to a considerable

number of states and clearly is not used exclusively or primarily for political purposes. It can and apparently has been used for this reason, however. In early 1962, India and Yemen established diplomatic relations. It was noted simultaneously that there were over 500 Chinese technicians in the country. In September 1962, civil war erupted in Yemen and in October India recognized the new government.

In 1964–65 India allocated Rs. 1 million for assistance to Yemen, and Rs. 600 thousand was budgeted in 1965–66. The assistance included hospital equipment, medicine, water pumps, technicians and training for Yemeni students.

Indian aid to Somalia also appears to have some political motivation. Until 1964, most of India's technical assistance in the "Horn of Africa" went to Kenya and Ethiopia. There were also a number of joint economic ventures linking India with these two countries. In 1963, Chinese assistance was extended to Somalia, with whom both Kenya and Ethiopia have border disputes. In 1964–65, India set aside Rs. 260 thousand for assistance to Somalia and more than doubled that figure in 1965–66. The sums were small, but they demonstrated India's interest and impartiality.

Loans to other developing countries were the second form of assistance to receive new emphasis after 1962. Loans provide somewhat limited help because they obviously have to be repaid and have usually been extended only for the purchase of Indian goods. Yet they can provide temporary relief in moments of economic crisis, and they make it possible for recipients to begin industrial ventures with Indian capital goods obtained on deferred payment.

India had provided loans before 1962. The aid programs to Sikkim and Bhutan initially included loans, and funds had been advanced in this form to Burma and Indonesia to help them through temporary difficulties shortly after they became independent.[15]

In recent years, however, the number of loans offered by India has increased substantially. By 1966, seven Afro-Asian countries—Ceylon, Nepal, Sudan, Kenya, Uganda, Tanzania and Ghana—had received offers of loans totaling Rs. 235 million for the purchase of Indian goods and assistance in establishing industrial ventures.

The loan to Ceylon is of particular interest because it represents a significant shift in the pattern of Indian assistance to that country. Relations between the two are complicated by their proximity, relative size, and the large Indian community in Ceylon. India sought to avoid creating additional tensions and concern by channeling her assistance to Ceylon through the Colombo Plan.

By 1960, China had become a major trading partner for Ceylon and the source of considerable assistance. Ceylonese neutrality in the Sino-Indian conflict deeply disturbed India. The form of Indian assistance now changed. In December of 1962, India, for the first time, offered Ceylon direct bilateral assistance, a loan of Rs. 50 million. The offer could not be accepted at the time, but when Ceylon encountered serious economic difficulties in 1965, India again came forward.

India made a similar gesture to Indonesia at a critical moment in 1966. In the early years after they became independent, ties between the two countries were unusually close, but gradually differences developed. Indonesia became friendly with China and openly supported Pakistan in the Indo-Pakistan conflict of 1965. India, in turn, backed Malaysia in her "confrontation" with Indonesia. The trend was dramatically reversed by India in 1966. The change in government in Indonesia had created a new situation, and the country's desperate need for economic assistance provided the opportunity. While other nations waited to see how stable and effective the new government would be, India stepped in with an offer of a loan amounting to Rs. 100 million for the purchase of Indian goods.

### *Joint Ventures*

The last area on which the Indian government has put renewed emphasis since 1962 is economic collaboration with other developing countries. India is herself short of capital so her ability to assist in foreign economic development is limited. However, she does have a considerable pool of technically trained personnel and experienced managerial talent. She also has the industrial capacity to produce capital equipment in a number of areas. The government of India has, therefore, been actively encouraging the establishment of joint economic ventures between Indian industrialists and local groups in other Asian and African states. In these enterprises, India's share of the capital is provided in the form of trained personnel and Indian-built machinery.

The first joint venture was set up in 1958 in Ethiopia. Only six others were established in succeeding years, but in 1964 alone twelve new proposals were approved by the Indian government. In 1965, fifteen were sanctioned and in 1966, twelve.

Joint ventures provide a number of dividends to India. First of all they demonstrate India's capacity to produce capital goods. This may open new markets for the sale of similar equipment to other firms in the same country. The joint venture is, in a sense, a form of export promotion. Secondly, many Afro-Asian states are beginning to develop indigenous industry to reduce imports. The joint venture enables India to remain in the market as a local producer even though her exports to the country are beginning to decline. Finally, India hopes that economic collaboration will improve relations with Afro-Asian countries by promoting new ties and demonstrating India's concern for and contribution to local industrial development.

India has engaged in an extensive assistance program for a variety of reasons. She seems sincerely to feel that developing countries have a duty to help one another, a duty which becomes evermore urgent as assistance from the developed countries decreases.[16] India's considerable industrial experience and her extensive training facilities enable her to play a larger role in this respect than other Afro-Asian states. This, in turn, brings political dividends. It gives substance to the leading political role which India has played among the developing states since she became independent.

Aid also plays more precise and concrete roles in Indian diplomacy. In the countries where India has concentrated her assistance, it performs the vital political function of promoting national security. Aid is a new diplomatic instrument which India uses to cope with the changed nature of her traditional security problem in the Himalayas.

In areas where Indian aid has been small in quantity and necessarily limited in impact, its function has been different. Aid is expected to promote good will, a sense of solidarity and friendly relations. The objective is to obtain wider support for Indian foreign policy.

30

# Aid to India

*Paul Streeten*
*Roger Hill*

*From* Crisis of Indian Planning, Economic Policy in the 1960's, *edited by Paul Streeten and Michael Lipton and published by the Oxford University Press for the Royal Institute of International Affairs. Reprinted by permission.*

## *The Terminology of Aid*

AN IMPORTANT DISTINCTION is that between *project aid* and *non-project aid.* The former is a specific sum of money which is intended to cover the foreign exchange cost of an identifiable project within the total aid allocation. Such aid need not cover the whole foreign exchange component of the project, though it normally does. Donors provide aid to the Government of India, which makes the funds available, on its own terms, to the authority responsible for the project. Conditions may be attached by the donor to consultancy, supervision, bidding for contracts, shipping arrangements, etc. These "strings" are of a different nature from the more general "conditions" relating to performance in the economy at large, although they too can give rise to disagreements between donors and recipients.

Non-project aid refers to all other goods provided under the aid program: primary products, semi-finished products, spare parts, components, machine tools, equipment, etc., which are needed to keep existing firms going or to start new projects and generally to support the balance of payments. Most of U.K. non-project aid consists of general purpose loans, which the Indians are free to spend on a wide range of imports from the donor country. The rest is devoted to purposes agreed on with the Indians. For example, the so-called "Kipping aid"[1] is used to supply components and spares to metal-using industries which look to Britain as their source of supply. Similarly, a loan in 1963 was made for the procurement of steel plate in this country. Other donors, particularly the U.S., tie their non-project aid to specific commodities, though the range of these may be very wide.

In addition to being tied to projects, aid may be tied to purchases in the donor country. This is *procurement-tying*. At present nearly all bilateral U.S. aid and over half of bilateral U.K. aid is wholly or partially tied in this manner. Only a small proportion of German aid is formally tied, though in effect the proportion is much higher, for the Germans tend to avoid making commitments for projects in sectors in which German firms are not competitive. Donors tie their aid to protect their balances of payments. For the recipient country the main disadvantage is that it cannot buy its imports in the cheapest market, although a certain amount of "switching," *i.e.*, using aid to buy products on which "free" foreign exchange would otherwise have been spent, is usually possible. The opportunity to switch will be greater, the larger are the commercial imports from the donor country and the more diversified the tied aid, while the desire to switch will depend on competitiveness of the products of the supplier. Mahbub ul Haq has estimated for Pakistan that aid-tying has raised the average price of all commodities imported under aid arrangements by 15 per cent.[2] In addition, aid-tying complicates the administration of aid.

*Double-tying* occurs when aid is both project- and procurement-tied. Donors double-tie to make it more certain that aid will produce extra demand for their goods. With procurement-tied aid for programs, a recipient can select those commodities he would buy from the donor in any case. Double-tying makes such selection more difficult, since it is unlikely that a single donor will be the cheapest supplier of all the goods required for a project.

There are three stages in the process of


Notes to chapter 30 appear on page 397

aid-giving and aid-receiving: pledging, committing, and disbursing. First, each donor *pledges* a total amount at the annual meetings of the Aid India Consortium.[3] Pledges of one donor influence pledges of others, and Britain (giving about 10 per cent of Consortium aid to India) can therefore exercise some leverage on total aid contributions. Non-Consortium aid to India is largely Soviet aid. Not all aid provided by members of the Consortium has been pledged. Thus PL 480 aid was independent of the U.S. pledge until 1967. Pledges are considered binding, although the Americans did not in fact commit aid pledged in 1965 after the Kashmir hostilities.

At the next stage, the pledged aid is *committed, allocated*, or *authorized.* At this stage aid is divided between project and non-project aid. The initiative for suggesting projects lies with the Indians, though representations from industrial and commercial interests are made to the donor country's authorities. The result is a compromise between Indian wishes and British commercial and prestige interests. The process of committing can take some time. For the U.K., after the 1963 pledge it took nine months; after the 1964 pledge only three. Lags have also been reduced for other countries.

The final stage is that of *disbursements* or *utilization.* The rate of disbursement is clearly faster for non-project aid than for project aid, because the range of imports is wider, and for soft loans than for hard loans, because higher interest rates, payable when goods have been ordered, induce greater caution in giving orders. It is in the nature of a project that it takes time to negotiate, prepare, and execute, and disbursements are bound to be less than commitments. This shortfall rises as commitments increase. But slow disbursements can also be due to inadequate or inefficient administration by the Indians. Most of the U.K. non-project aid is normally spent within the financial year of the pledge, though delays in the disbursements of Kipping aid beyond that have been known. Delays are longer in the disbursement of non-project aid from other donors, including IDA. The lag of disbursements behind commitments creates the *pipeline* which consists of unspent claims arising from past authorized loans. The pipeline permits the continuation of expenditure for a time when new commitments are run down. It creates problems for British economic policy, for it can give rise to unplanned claims on British resources. The size of the pipeline can be reduced by spreading commitments over the period of construction of projects. The lag of disbursements behind commitments, which can also be reduced by raising the proportion of general purpose aid to the total, and by softening the terms of aid, has the added drawback for India that commitments are made in terms of money, and rising prices wipe out part of the real value of the aid.

*Gross aid* disbursed in a year exceeds net aid by payments of interest on past loans and repayment of capital, *Debt relief* is perhaps the most urgent need. To avoid default, debt can be *rescheduled* or *refinanced.* Rescheduling means lengthening the period of the loan. Refinancing means making new loans to meet obligations on outstanding loans. Loans may be advanced with *grace periods* before interest falls due. This is another way of easing the terms of loans.

The provision of a *bisque*, advocated by some, is modeled on the waiver clause in the American loan to Britain of 1946, which allows Britain to opt out of capital repayments (though not interest), in an agreed number of years.

In tackling the debt problem, one has to distinguish between *new* debt—the problem of the *terms of aid*—and *old* debt, which may be rescheduled or refinanced. The link between the two is that the attitude to accepting and servicing new debt will be influenced by the manner in which old debts are settled.

## *Review of Past Aid to India*

Up to the end of March 1966 aid authorizations from all sources amounted to Rs. 58,015 mn, of which 77 per cent (Rs. 44,818 mn) had been utilized. Only Rs. 290 mn, of the authorized aid and Rs. 220 mn of the utilized aid were received prior to the First Plan.

Table 1 shows external assistance by sources. The donors' list is dominated by the U.S., which provided over half the authorized aid, and a little under three-fifths of the utilized aid. Aid authorizations under PL 480 accounted for 51 per cent (Rs 13,860 mn) of U.S. aid. IBRD and IDA, the main multilateral donors, have been responsible for just over 12 per cent of the aid received by India. Table 2 provides a more detailed breakdown of the sources of aid.

Table 3 breaks down external assistance by form. The outstanding feature here is the decline in grants: from 36 per cent of authorizations in the First Plan to 3 per cent in the Third Plan. Loans amounted to Rs 22,690 mn during the First Plan, but the 1951 Wheat Loan accounted for Rs 9,030 mn (40 per cent) of this figure. Over two-thirds of the aid utilized in the Third Plan has been in loan form. Authorizations of PL 480 aid reached very high levels during the Second Plan and provided a large "carry-over" into the Third Plan. For this reason utilization of PL 480 aid between 1961–66 was nearly double the authorization during the same period.

## *External Debt*

External debt servicing charges rose from $250 mn in the Second Plan (just under 4 per cent of export earnings) to $1,150 mn during the Third Plan (about 14 per cent of merchandise export earnings) and to 22 per cent in 1966. During the period 1966–70 these charges are estimated as $3,050 mn—28 per cent of estimated export earnings and 36 per cent of aid requirements. The total outstanding external public debt has risen from $400 mn in 1955 to $6,900 mn in June 1966.[4] The problem of external debt was a major one in the late 1960s. While debt servicing obligations rose by 84 per cent between 1962 and 1966, exports increased by only 14 per cent. This is the legacy of past loans. However, a marked softening of aid terms has taken place recently. The average rate of interest on new external debt contracted during 1960 was 4.19 per cent, the average grace period 4.0 years and the average term to maturity 16.7 years.[5] In 1965 the corresponding figures were 3.18 per cent interest rate, 7.4 years grace period, and 31.3 years to maturity.[6] This reflects an even greater improvement if account is taken of the general rise in commercial interest rates. Nevertheless, further renegotiations, rescheduling, consolidations and waivers of loans must be expected during the Fourth Plan period, for servicing charges are likely to account for 28 per cent of a very optimistic export projection of Rs 80,330 mn (Rs 51,000 mn in pre-devaluation rupees).

The problem of debt service has several aspects:

1. In the 1970s the debt servicing problem will become even more serious. From 1966–67 to 1980–81 India will require some $18,000 mn of foreign aid but her debt servicing liability will come to $14,000 mn. After 1975 the planners expect repayments to outstrip inflows of capital.

2. Next, there are the terms on which loans are incurred and renewed. India herself has in the past declared that she does not wish to receive grants. Some donors believe that soft terms discourage economic use and encourage waste. There cannot be much in this argument because the Government of India can lend at appropriate interest rates and can require these rates of return for its own projects. Soft terms are intended to get over the foreign exchange difficulty, and do not reduce the need to calculate adequate domestic returns on expenditure. Whether local currency counterpart funds for interest receipts should be accumulated by the creditor country is another question.

3. Most bilateral aid is tied to procurement from the donor and often tied to projects as well. Repayment, on the other hand, is demanded in convertible currency, and the use of such funds is not tied to Indian exports. This asymmetry introduces an additional element of hardness. The exception is aid from Russia and certain European countries which is usually repaid in the recipient's traditional exports; thus, in effect, repayment is in the borrower's own currency.

4. It is not sufficient to give debt relief

## *Table 1—External Assistance by Sources*[a]

| *Sources of Aid* | *Aggregate External Assistance Since Independence* | | | |
|---|---|---|---|---|
| | *AUTHORIZED UP TO MARCH 1966* | | *UTILIZED UP TO MARCH 1966* | |
| | *Amount* | *% of Total* | *Amount* | *% of Total* |
| IBRD/IDA | 7,415 | 12.8 | 5,815 | 13.0 |
| US | 30,487 | 52.5 | 26,052 | 58.1 |
| USSR | 4,855 | 8.4 | 2,833 | 6.3 |
| W. Germany | 4,444 | 7.7 | 3,417 | 7.6 |
| UK | 3,660 | 6.3 | 2,931 | 6.6 |
| Others | 7,154 | 12.3 | 3,770 | 8.4 |
| Total | 58,015 | 100.0 | 44,818 | 100.0 |

[a] In Rs. mn.
*Source:* Reserve Bank of India, *Report on Currency and Finance 1965–66* (1966), p. 28, Table 28.

## *Table 2—Sources of External Assistance*[a]

| | *Aid authorized up to end of 1st Plan* | *Aid authorized during 2nd Plan* | *Aid authorized during 3rd Plan* |
|---|---|---|---|
| Loans | | | |
| Repayable in foreign currencies | | | |
| International institutions | 572 | 2,612 | 4,231 |
| US | 903 | 1,085 | 7,917 |
| Canada | — | 157 | 310 |
| UK | — | 1,226 | 2,420 |
| W. Germany | — | 1,342 | 3,081 |
| Japan | — | 268 | 1,381 |
| USSR | 648 | 3,190 | 1,005 |
| Switzerland | — | 65 | 180 |
| France | — | — | 571 |
| Italy | — | — | 813 |
| Poland | — | 143 | 270 |
| Yugoslavia | — | 190 | 24 |
| Czechoslovakia | — | 231 | 400 |
| Austria | — | — | 85 |
| Belgium | — | — | 114 |
| Netherlands | — | — | 219 |
| Sweden | — | — | 22 |
| Denmark | — | — | 14 |
| Total | 2,123 | 10,509 | 23,057 |
| Rapayable in Rupees | | | |
| Denmark | — | — | 10 |
| US | 146 | 2,304 | 486 |
| Total | 146 | 2,304 | 496 |
| Grants | | | |
| US | 918 | 546 | 200 |
| Canada | 323 | 571 | 551 |
| Australia | 111 | 22 | 22 |
| New Zealand | 17 | 17 | 7 |
| UK | 4 | 4 | 6 |
| W. Germany | — | 21 | — |
| Norway | 7 | 19 | 20 |
| USSR | — | 12 | — |
| Total | 1,380 | 1,212 | 806 |
| PL 480, 665, and Third Country Currency Assistance | 169 | 11,307 | 4,506 |
| Grand Total | 3,818 | 25,335 | 28,865 |

[a] In Rs. mn.
*Source:* Reserve Bank of India, *Report on Currency and Finance 1965–66* (1966), Statement 82.

when the time for debt repayment arrives. Foreign exchange has to be accumulated in the form of extra reserves, and hence diverted from development imports well in advance of the date when debt payments are due, and debt relief promised in advance is worth more than relief that comes later.

5. From the point of view of any one creditor, debt relief should be given by all creditors. Otherwise the relief given by one can be regarded as being used to pay the obligations to others. (The same applies to giving aid on soft terms.) The World Bank, because of its need to raise money in the capital markets of the West, is in a special position and may not be able to give relief without impairing its impeccable credit standing. But bilateral Consortium donors normally consider that they must act in consort.

Until recently, a characteristic of Indian aid was the large proportion authorized but not disbursed. To help remedy this slow disbursement of aid, the Rao Report recommended in 1964 that a larger proportion of aid should be non-project.[7] In the years 1963–64 India received considerable quantities of non-project assistance (apart from PL 480) for the first time. In the years 1965–66 about half the aid pledged was non-project, while for 1967 Consortium members have agreed to about $900 mn (Rs 6,800 mn) of non-project aid.

However, the causes of slow disbursements are to be found on both sides. In India, slow disbursements may occur because of (*a*) inadequate project planning, *i.e.*, faulty project preparation, programming, and scheduling, (*b*) faults in complementary actions, *e.g.*, failure of supplies of raw materials and com-

### *Table 3—External Assistance by Form*[a]

| Form | *Authorizations* | | | *Utilization* | | |
|---|---|---|---|---|---|---|
| | *UP TO END OF 1ST PLAN* | *DURING 2ND PLAN* | *DURING 3RD PLAN* | *UP TO END OF 1ST PLAN* | *DURING 2ND PLAN* | *DURING 3RD PLAN* |
| Loans | 2,269 | 12,813 | 23,553 | 1,264 | 7,247 | 19,094 |
| (i) Repayable in foreign currencies | 2,123 | 10,509 | 23,057 | 1,241 | 6,079 | 17,530 |
| (ii) Repayable in rupees | 146 | 2,304 | 496 | 23 | 1,168 | 1,564 |
| Grants | 1,380 | 1,212 | 806 | 702 | 1,603 | 877 |
| PL 480 and PL 665 aid and Third Country Assistance (gross), | 169 | 11,280 | 4,506 | 51 | 5,423 | 8,532 |
| Total | 3,818 | 25,305 | 28,865 | 2,017 | 14,273 | 28,503 |
| Debt Servicing Payments | n.a. | n.a. | n.a. | n.a. | 1,192 | 5,470 |
| Net Aid | | | | | 13,081 | 23,033 |
| Net Aid at 1965–66 import prices | | | | | 13,769 | 25,403 |
| IMF | 476 | 952 | | 476 | 952 | |
| Percentage Distribution | | | | | | |
| Loans | 59.5 | 50.7 | 81.6 | 62.7 | 50.7 | 67.0 |
| Grants | 36.2 | 4.8 | 2.8 | 34.8 | 11.2 | 3.0 |
| PL 480 and PL 664 aid and Third Country Assistance (gross) | 4.3 | 44.5 | 15.6 | 2.5 | 38.1 | 30.0 |
| Total | 100.0 | 100.0 | 100.0 | 100.0 | 100.0 | 100.0 |

[a] In Rs. mn.
n.a. = not available.
*Source:* Reserve Bank of India, *Report on Currency and Finance 1965–66* (1966), Statement 82.

ponents, and services like electricity and transport, and (*c*) failures in aggregate planning, *e.g.*, non-availability of rupee resources, inadequate aggregate demand, wrong choice of top personnel, and other wrong decisions. Even forms of aid which are avowedly the most useful, because they are not tied to projects, have been slowly disbursed. Thus "Kipping loans" have, astonishingly, suffered from slow disbursements.

But the main reason for slow disbursement is found, the Rao Committee suggested, in the fact of project aid. Aid geared to the creation of capacity, it is said, is of little use and can be an obstacle if the main bottleneck is imports of raw materials and components, especially fertilizers, and spare parts. The superiority of general-purpose aid over project, and even non-project but specific-purpose aid, has been increasingly recognized, and the change in the composition has contributed to speedier disbursements. The need for non-project aid grows as development progresses. A final reason for delays has been the terms of aid. The harder the terms, the more reluctant the borrower will be to draw quickly on a loan, because interest is charged from the date of drawing, not from the date of commitment. Thus the share of loans tends to be higher in the aid pipeline than in total aid commitments.

However, more non-project aid and softening of terms, together with changes in the administrative machinery, especially in the vetting of import requirements, have produced in 1964 and 1965 a marked improvement in the rate of aid utilization. This is borne out by Table 4.

***Table 4—Utilization of Loans[a]***

| | *Authorized and Undisbursed (1)* | *Used in Following Year (2)* | *2/1 per cent* |
|---|---|---|---|
| March 1961 | 6,571 | 2,296 | 34.9 |
| 1962 | 8,378 | 3,058 | 36.5 |
| 1963 | 11,292 | 3,918 | 34.7 |
| 1964 | 11,755 | 4,831 | 41.1 |
| 1965 | 11,886 | 4,991 | 42.0 |

[a] In Rs. mn.
*Source:* Reserve Bank of India, *Report on Currency and Finance 1965–66*, Part I, Table 2.

## *The Impact of Aid*

There is a widespread impression that India receives large sums of aid. This is, of course, true in the sense that India is a large country, containing 30 per cent of the population of the under-developed world. But it is not true if the relevant measure, viz. aid per head, is used. India received in 1961 \$1.5, in 1962 \$1.7, and in 1963 \$2.1 from OECD countries and multilateral agencies, compared with Pakistan's massive doses: \$2.8 excluding Indus Waters Scheme, \$4.0 including it (some of this should, however, be credited to India) in 1962; \$4.2 excluding, \$4.9 including it (1963), and a further rise to about \$6.0 in 1964. Stepping up gross aid to \$10,000 mn for the period 1966–70 would mean raising aid per head to \$4 a year, still considerably below the level of Pakistan and of many other aid recipients. Whatever aid criteria one wishes to choose. India should be given much higher priority than it receives now.[8] India is one of the poorest countries. Its development potential is high. It has an efficient administration, a high level of education and skills, and a reserve of potential entrepreneurship. Its plans are well conceived and it has applied stringent import controls and high levels of domestic taxation. There can be no doubt that it has a structural balance of payments problem and considerable absorptive capacity. It enjoys constitutional democracy and has been the victim of an attack by China. What India does will serve as an example to others. Whether one's criteria are cold war, the encouragement of democratic government, the promotion of self-help, good performance, the relief of the needy, or the activation of development potential, India should qualify for massive aid. In fact it is grossly under-aided.

Both the Right and the Left have attacked India's reliance on foreign aid, which both tend to exaggerate. The Right argues that aid, by encouraging central planning and public prestige projects, discourages the growth of private savings and private initiative, frightens away foreign enterprise, discourages economy in the use of capital, and generally destroys the basis of decentralized decision-taking which, on this view, is the prerequisite of development. Aid thus is thought to perpetuate the system which makes aid necessary; some go further and say that it pauperizes the country, making it increasingly dependent on external assistance.

The Left attacks aid on the ground that, by supporting reactionary groups in power, it retards the introduction of the institutional and political reforms, particularly effective land reform, which are necessary for development. Aid, on this view, props up reform-resisting oligarchies and conservative and feudal social systems, and again perpetuates the system which makes it necessary.

These arguments, which fit in well with the general disenchantment with aid among donors, are difficult to quantify and to assess. We shall discuss the argument in the context of food aid below. In order to bring out the costs and benefits of aid, and also in order to present clear political choices, it might be possible to draw up two simultaneous plans: one with a somewhat smaller reliance on aid, the other with somewhat more aid and with possible concessions to the donors. The cost of aid in the widest sense, including policies adopted or sacrificed, would thus be brought out clearly.

Table 5 shows the uses to which aid has been allocated. It adds to the total resources available to the community. It may be used to raise consumption, private investment, or government expenditure. In this general case, the value of aid to India is equal to the value of these additions. But if it helps to break a bottleneck—foreign exchange, particular items of equipment, or particular skills—the value of aid to India exceeds the nominal value of aid given. It makes fuller utilization of capacities in other sectors of the economy possible. Against this, it is possible that an aid-financed project imposes a burden of recurrent or other contributory expenditure on the domestic economy, and that these resources could have been used more productively in other lines. In such conditions the value of aid to India falls short of its nominal value. In so far as aid is available in freely-spendable foreign exchange, its value is likely to exceed its nominal value. The more it is tied to projects and donor procurement, the less likely this will be.

The conventional approach to analyzing the impact of aid is to regard it as filling either of two gaps, depending upon which is larger. If growth is seen as a function of the ratio of investment to national income, aid is seen as filling the gap between target investment and domestic savings. Alternatively, if growth is regarded as constrained by foreign exchange, aid fills the gap between the foreign exchange required to achieve a given growth target, and the foreign exchange earned by visible and invisible exports plus private capital flows.

The weakness of the double gap approach is that it makes assumptions, sometimes justified in advanced economies, which are unwarranted for India. The savings gap approach assumes that the relationship between investment and additional output is fairly stable, that consumption makes no contribution to output, and that home and foreign savings are interchangeable. But in the diagnosis of India it is normal to assume that the dominant bottleneck is not savings, but foreign exchange. And we have certainly witnessed situations in which potential domestic savings have run to waste for lack of foreign exchange. Aid requirements therefore tend to be approached through the trade gap. This analysis assumes that growth of domestic production could be accelerated with more foreign exchange.

We see from Table 6 that the contribution of external finance to public plan outlay is large. However, the apparently greater dependence on external assistance in the Draft Fourth Plan is due to the rise in the

## Table 5—Distribution of Foreign Loans / Credits by Purposes[a]

| LOANS/CREDITS | AUTHORIZED | | | | | | | | UTILIZED | | | | | | | |
|---|---|---|---|---|---|---|---|---|---|---|---|---|---|---|---|---|
| | (1) Up to end of 1st Plan | | (2) During 2nd Plan | | (3) During 3rd Plan | | Total 1 to 3 | | (1) Up to end of 1st Plan | | (2) During 2nd Plan | | (3) During 3rd Plan | | Total 1 to 3 | |
| 1. Railway development | 156 | (6.9) | 1,952 | (15.1) | 1,392 | (6.1) | 3,500 | (9.2) | 156 | (12.3) | 1,432 | (20.1) | 1,850 | (10.1) | 3,438 | (12.8) |
| 2. Power projects | 196 | (8.6) | 623 | (4.8) | 2,414 | (10.5) | 3,233 | (8.5) | 121 | (9.6) | 293 | (4.1) | 1,529 | (8.3) | 1,943 | (7.2) |
| 3. Iron and steel projects[b] | 786 | (34.7) | 2,242 | (17.4) | 2,078 | (9.1) | 5,106 | (13.4) | 27 | (2.1) | 2,541 | (35.6) | 1,049 | (5.7) | 3,617 | (13.5) |
| 4. Ports and development | — | — | 205 | (1.6) | 186 | (0.8) | 391 | (1.0) | — | — | 68 | (0.9) | 180 | (1.0) | 248 | (0.9) |
| 5. Transport and communication | — | — | 148 | (1.2) | 930 | (4.1) | 1,078 | (2.9) | — | — | 90 | (1.3) | 759 | (4.1) | 849 | (3.2) |
| 6. Industrial development | 193 | (8.5) | 7,555 | (58.7) | 15,266 | (66.7) | 23,014 | (60.5) | 23 | (1.8) | 2,554 | (35.8) | 12,836 | (69.6) | 15,413 | (57.5) |
| 7. Agricultural development | 34 | (1.5) | — | — | 621 | (2.7) | 655 | (1.7) | 34 | (2.7) | — | — | 225 | (1.2) | 259 | (1.0) |
| 8. Wheat loans | 903 | (39.8) | 157 | (1.2) | — | — | 1,060 | (2.8) | 903 | (71.5) | 157 | (2.2) | — | — | 1,060 | (3.9) |
| Total | 2,268 | (100.0) | 12,882 | (100.0) | 22,887 | (100.0) | 38,037 | (100.0) | 1,264 | (100.0) | 7,135 | (100.0) | 18,428 | (100.0) | 26,827 | (100.0) |

[a] In Rs. mn. Figures in brackets show percentage of distribution.

[b] Includes Orissa Iron Ore Project.

*Source:* Reserve Bank of India, *Report on Currency and Finance 1965–66* (1966), Statement 83.

rupee figure resulting from devaluation; in fact, if corrected for devaluation, the proportion of aid-financed public outlay is less in the Fourth than in the Third Plan. It may be that without aid India would have increased its already strong tax efforts even more, but it is impossible to dispute that the Second and Third Plans would have been smaller without aid.

Consider aid as a provider of foreign exchange, assuming that domestic savings are not the dominant constraint. The withdrawal of aid would then have necessitated a combination of four courses of action: non-development import retardation, development import substitution, export expansion, and a shift of plan outlay into areas with low foreign exchange requirements. Since the foreign exchange crisis of 1957–58 India has imposed the most stringent controls on imports of consumer goods. Table 7 shows that if foodgrains, 82 per cent of which consist of PL 480 imports, are excluded, the total value of consumer goods imports was lower in the Third Plan than in the First. Little foreign exchange can be gained by further restrictions of consumption imports. As for the second course, development-import substitution, raw materials, and equipment are closely scrutinized for possible indigenous replacement. In any case, import substitution of equipment requires, in the initial stages, larger, not smaller, imports. It is the strenuous attempt to set up domestic import-substituting capital goods industries which is responsible for the growth of raw material and capital imports.

There has been considerable unused capacity in Indian industry, largely as a result of inadequate imports of raw materials, components, and spare parts. A change in the composition of imports—a higher proportion of maintenance imports and a lower proportion of imports tied to new industrial capacity—would indeed lead to higher capacity utilization. But there is little scope for substituting domestic production for imports in such a way as to reduce import requirements substantially in the near future.

Export expansion, unaccompanied by an

### *Table 6—Financing of Public Outlay*[a]

| *Sources* | *1st Plan* | *2nd Plan* | *3rd Plan* | *4th Plan* |
|---|---|---|---|---|
| 1. Balance from Current Revenues | 3,820 | 110 | −4,730 | 33,450 |
| 2. Surpluses of Public Enterprises | 1,150 | 1,670 | 6,960 | 13,450 |
| 3. Capital Receipts | 6,860 | 14,390 | 21,390 | 38,800 |
| 4. Deficit Financing | 3,330 | 9,540 | 11,510 | — |
| 5. Additional Taxation | 2,550 | 10,520 | 26,600 | 27,300 |
| 6. Budgetary Receipts corresponding to External Assistance | 1,890 | 10,490 | 24,550 | 47,000[b] |
| 7. Total Resources | 19,600 | 46,720 | 86,280 | 160,000 |
| Row 6/Row 7 per cent | 9.6 | 22.5 | 28.5 | 29.4[c] |

[a] In Rs. mn.
[b] Post devaluation.
[c] This figure is not comparable with the previous figures because of devaluation (see text).
*Source: MFB*, pp. 117–18, Table FR 2.

### *Table 7—Imports of Consumer Goods*[a]

| | *1st Plan* | *2nd Plan* | *3rd Plan* |
|---|---|---|---|
| Consumer Goods | 8,878 | 10,742 | 12,786 |
| Foodgrains | 6,015 | 8,046 | 10,330 |
| Non-foodgrains | 2,863 | 2,696 | 2,456 |
| PL 480 | 51 | 5,448 | 8,800 |
| PL 480 as percentage of total foodgrains | 1.8 | 68.0 | 85.0 |

[a] In Rs. mn.
*Source: 4DO*, pp. 100–02.

equivalent fall in unit prices of exports, is the third way of reducing dependence on aid. Indian exports stagnated during the First and Second Plans. They rose between 1960 and 1964–65, but seem to have run out of steam since. Traditional exports (tea, jute, cotton) run into limitations of demand, and non-traditional exports, though they showed impressive increases, are still a small proportion of the total. Exports of engineering goods, iron ore and steel, and chemicals are still less than 10 per cent of total exports. No doubt it is in the expansion of these exports that future earnings prospects lie, but foreign exchange will be needed in order to build up this export potential.

The fourth method of saving foreign exchange is to change the composition of plan outlay in the direction of economizing in foreign exchange. This means more for agriculture, less for industry. In the Third Plan public outlay in agriculture and irrigation was Rs 14,600 mn, exclusive of industries producing agricultural inputs such as fertilizers, and in medium and large industries Rs 25,700 mn. If aid reductions had forced a substantial switch of investment from industry to agriculture, some foreign exchange could have been saved, though limitations of absorptive capacity may have retarded growth. An increase in agricultural inputs such as fertilizers does require foreign exchange, directly if these are imported, and indirectly if domestic fertilizer plants are to be put up.

We conclude that added foreign exchange shortages would have led to even more severe cuts in the Second and Third Plans, even if domestic savings had been available. In addition, it is most unlikely that the Government of India could have raised enough resources to maintain the size of the plans even if structural balance of payments problems had not constituted an obstacle. These considerations suggest that the Second and Third Plans would have been reduced by an amount greater than the aid provided, if aid had been reduced. Or, to put the same point the other way around, in spite of some waste in the preparation, execution, and management of some projects, additional aid enables India to mobilize a multiple of the resources provided by aid.

## *Aid and the Draft Fourth Plan*

In the Draft Fourth Plan aid plays a crucial role. Economic planning aims ultimately at a "steady and satisfactory rate of growth, without inflation and without dependence on foreign aid."[9] It is planned to bring about a sharp fall in imports in the Fifth Plan coupled with a continued increase in exports, so that by 1977 the balance of payments gap will be closed even after providing for debt repayments, and no more aid will be needed. To do this, the Indians estimate that they will require gross external assistance of between $8,500 and $9,000 mn exclusive of PL 480 aid during the 1966–71 period. About $2,000 mn was in the pipeline at the end of the Third Plan, so that disbursements of new aid will have to be about $7,000 mn. To provide this volume of disbursement, commitments of between $8,000 and $10,000 mn will have to be made for the plan period. Since debt servicing during the period 1966–70 is likely to absorb around $3,000 mn of gross aid, net aid should amount to about $6,000 mn or Rs 45,000 mn. This is over 20 per cent of total estimated investment. In addition, external finance is to be the main source of public outlay during the Fourth Plan, accounting for 30 per cent of total planned development expenditure.[10]

But aid needs may be even greater than indicated by these figures. The aid requirements calculations are based on very optimistic assumptions about domestic production, exports, and savings. Already, domestic production of fertilizers and steel shows shortfalls, and higher imports will be required to make up for them. The export earning projections seem over-optimistic, particularly the projected increase in jute and tea exports.

These are India's aid needs, but how much it will actually receive is another question. Germany has indicated that its aid to India will remain at its existing level during the period to 1970. American and Britain both have balance of payments problems, and until these are solved India cannot expect large increases of aid from these countries, unless there are major changes in the distribution of their aid. So far Aid India Consortium members have pledged sums of $900 mn of non-project financial aid each year for 1966–67 and 1967–68. To meet the aid requirements of the Draft Fourth Plan, India must receive in addition to the promised Russian aid ($1,000 mn for the Draft Plan, or more) about $1,600 mn of gross aid per year from the Consortium. The amount of aid India is receiving is therefore well below the aid requirements of the Plan. However, the virtual moratorium on Indian debt repayments during 1967–68 will save it some $400 mn of foreign exchange. How much the debt burden will be reduced in the later years of the Plan depends upon the outcome of the bilateral rescheduling negotiations.

In spite of errors and some faulty management, there is no doubt that India could absorb substantially more aid than it receives now. But the solution is more complex than simply changing the composition of aid in the direction of more maintenance imports. The contrast between project- and non-project aid over-simplifies the real issues. Not all capacity which has been created in India is equally valuable from a development point of view, and to underwrite maintenance imports for all existing capacity may lead to fuller utilization of capacity that should not be more fully used and may encourage the creation of undesirable capacity. On the other hand, economic progress, the unequal degree of capacity under-utilization, and the fact that fuller utilization of the capital goods industries is possible only if new projects are started, imply that *some* new projects will have to be started, say some new fertilizer plants, while there is still under-utilization in less important sectors. It is then essential that these projects should be well selected, well prepared, and well executed. Donors should offer assistance in sector and project selection, execution, and planning, as well as raising the proportion of non-project aid. These measures would not only raise the productivity of aid directly, but would also lead to fuller utilization of existing capacity, thereby raising output indirectly. They would reduce the need for detailed physical controls, economize in scarce administrative talent, and thus contribute to higher productivity and better morale.

But all this is relevant largely for the urban industrial sector. The most serious constraint on development, apart from population growth, is the relative stagnation until recently in many rural areas. Even a substantial speeding up of the already high industrial growth rate is bound to be halted unless food production is raised by much more than it has been in the past. Project the figures for 1961–65 into the future. Industrial output increased annually by 7.4 per cent, services by 6.7 per cent, and agricultural output by 2.7 per cent.[11] Weighting these growth rates by their respective shares in 1964–65 in net domestic product at factor cost, the total growth rate is 4.8 per cent, which is 0.8 per cent per annum less than the projected rate of growth 1964–65 to 1970–71 (see Table 8). Even if we assume that industrial output is raised by the planned 10 per cent per annum, the aggregate growth rate is raised, initially, to only 5.3 per cent. The lag of agricultural production constitutes a serious brake on the power of foreign aid to speed up development. Slow growth in agriculture limits essential supplies to industry, demand for mass-produced industrial products, and the savings ratio. And can, of course, also contribute to the growth of agricultural output and to rural development, particularly through higher fertilizer imports,

## *Table 8*

| | *% of net domestic product at factor cost 1964–65* | *Annual growth rates 1961–65* | *Weighted growth* |
|---|---|---|---|
| Agriculture | 51 | 2.7 | 1.4 |
| Industry | 18 | 7.4 (assume 10) | 1.3 (1.8) |
| Services | 31 | 6.7 | 2.1 |
| All sectors | 100 | 4.8 (5.3) | 4.8 (5.3) |

but its efficacy there is more limited than in urban manufacturing industry. It can do relatively little to promote land reform or effective agricultural extension services on the spot. But more recently there have been promising signs that farmers, encouraged by high prices and responding to new techniques, have in some areas substantially increased production.

### *Food Aid from America*

Over half the aid India has received from the U.S. and slightly less than a third of the total aid it has utilized has been in the form of commodities. (Part of the non-project aid also takes the form of commodities.) A small amount of this was received under the U.S. Mutual Security Act (PL 665), but by far the greater part has come under the U.S. Agricultural Trade Development and Assistance Act (PL 480), particularly under Title I which authorizes the sale of U.S. agricultural commodities for foreign currencies. Between India's first PL 480 agreement with the U.S. in 1956 and the end of the Third Plan, the total sales proceeds of PL 480 imports amounted to Rs 156,730 mn. Four-fifths of these counterpart funds were lent or granted to India; 7 per cent were loaned to U.S. private enterprises,[12] the remaining funds (13 per cent) have been retained by the U.S. Government for its own use.

Though self-sufficiency in foodgrains received top priority in the Third Plan, imports of PL 480 foodgrains have increased markedly since 1961–62. And this rise is not solely the result of large imports in 1965–66 following the disastrous harvest; year by year throughout the Plan, cereals imports have increased. Table 9 shows that nearly all the increase in imports during the Third Plan can be accounted for by larger quantities of PL 480 imports. Domestic production of foodgrains stagnated during the first three years of the Plan and fell severely in the fifth year, so that dependence on imported food has increased: in 1961 net imports of cereals were just over 5.2 per cent of net production; by 1963 this figure had risen to 7.8 per cent, and by 1964 to over 11 per cent.[13]

But the growing size of U.S. food shipments is entirely contrary to American aid philosophy. U.S. aid, perhaps more than that of other donors, is intended to promote self-reliance, not to undermine it. America has expressed its dissatisfaction with India. The most obvious expression of this dissatisfaction was President Johnson's four-month delay at the end of 1966 in sanctioning new PL 480 agreements with India, but another sign was the American stipulation in 1965 that India must pay in foreign currencies the whole cost of PL 480 freight, not just 50 per cent as previously. This has been followed by the U.S. Food for Freedom Act which is intended to move countries receiving American food aid from soft currency payments to a system of dollar payments on long terms, but the Act is unlikely to be applied in its full rigor to India for some time. The U.S. has in effect indicated to India its reluctance to continue food shipments at the present high levels. For one thing, the Americans feel that others should share the burden of feeding India. It is for this reason that the U.S. has been the major force in getting food and food-related aid coordinated through the World Bank Consortium. Also, U.S. Government wheat stocks have in recent years fallen dramatically, largely because of increased food aid, especially to India. This has led to the removal of area limits in order to stimulate U.S. grain production.

There is, however, a deeper reason for the American reluctance to continue large-scale commodity shipments to India. The Americans fear that dependence on PL 480 food will breed ever greater dependence. It is felt by some Indians as well as Americans that U.S. surplus food, available almost for the asking in years of good harvests as well as bad, had undermined India's determination to tackle its agricultural problem seriously. In particular, food management, and especially efforts to draw out the marketable surplus, may have suffered as a result of PL 480 aid. True, self-sufficiency in foodgrains received top priority in the Third Plan. But this was not achieved and has now been carried over to become a major target in the Fourth Plan. Though weather played its part in this failure, it is not yet clear that India has yet hit upon a combination of policies which will ensure a high and sustained rate of growth in agriculture. India has cut the share of investment in agriculture and has not a sufficiently strong policy to get trained personnel into rural areas. Such policies will involve difficult and unpopular choices and changes, and the Indians may prefer to postpone making them as long as possible. Certainly such postponement will be easier the more India can rely upon the U.S. to bail it out of its worst consequences.

But U.S. commodity aid may have had a more direct impact on agricultural production via its effect on cultivator incentives. PL 480 funds have been a major source of aid to the public sector. It is estimated that during the Third Plan funds arising from PL 480 aid financed over 10 per cent of public developmental outlay. PL 480 aid accounted for 56 per cent of the external assistance to public outlay. Because of the dangers of too much deficit financing and of the unpopularity of higher taxes, the Indian Government has had an interest in making PL 480 imports and sales as large as possible, to raise funds to finance its plans. Larger PL 480 sales exert a downward pressure on food prices, and thus may reduce incentives for cultivators. They also divert limited sources of

### Table 9[a]

| | *1961–62* | *1962–63* | *1963–64* | *1964–65* | *1965–66* |
|---|---|---|---|---|---|
| Total imports | 11,071 | 11,356 | 12,229 | 13,490 | 13,490 |
| PL 480 foodgrains | 710 | 1,120 | 1,730 | 2,250 | 2,680 |
| Net total imports | 10,361 | 10,236 | 10,499 | 11,240 | 10,810 |

[a] In Rs. mn.
*Source: 4DO,* p. 102.

### Table 10—Percentage Changes in Net Production and Net Availability

| | *1956–57* | *1957–58* | *1958–59* | *1959–60* | *1960–61* | *1961–62* | *1962–63* | *1963–64* | *1964–65* |
|---|---|---|---|---|---|---|---|---|---|
| Net production | +4.7 | −6.3 | +16.1 | −0.9 | +6.7 | +2.4 | −5.6 | +4.7 | +8.3 |
| Net availability | +4.0 | −4.7 | +14.8 | −0.3 | +6.3 | +2.8 | −4.7 | +9.1 | +5.7 |

*Source:* Ministry of Finance, *Economic Survey of India 1965–66* (1966).

### Table 11

| | *1* *Net Production of Cereals (a)* | *2* *Imports of Cereals* | *3* *Change in Govt. Stocks* | *4* *Imports Plus Stock Reductions* | *5* *Net Availability of Cereals* | *6* *Index No. of Cereals Prices (b)* | *7* *Cultivators' Terms of Trade* |
|---|---|---|---|---|---|---|---|
| 1956 | 50.34 | 1.04 | −0.60 | 1.64 | 52.34 | 96 | 91 |
| 1957 | 52.68 | 3.63 | +0.86 | 2.77 | 55.45 | 101 | 93 |
| 1958 | 49.36 | 3.22 | −0.27 | 3.49 | 52.85 | 107 | 95 |
| 1959 | 57.30 | 3.86 | +0.49 | 3.37 | 60.67 | 104 | 90 |
| 1960 | 56.77 | 5.13 | +1.40 | 3.73 | 60.50 | 104 | 83 |
| 1961 | 60.65 | 3.49 | −0.17 | 3.66 | 64.31 | 102 | 82 |
| 1962 | 62.08 | 3.64 | −0.36 | 4.00 | 66.08 | 106 | 83 |
| 1963 | 58.63* | 4.55* | −0.02 | 4.57 | 63.20 | 116 | 86 |
| 1964 | 61.41* | 6.26* | −1.26 | 7.52 | 68.93 | 139 | 91 |
| 1965 | 66.52* | 7.45* | +1.12 | 6.33 | 72.85 | 148 | — |

* Provisional.
Cols. 1, 2, 3, 4, and 5 units: mill. tons.
(*a*) Refers to agricultural year July–June: 1956 figure refers to net production in 1956–56. Net production is 8.75 per cent of total production, 12.5 per cent being provided for feed, seed requirements, and wastage.
(*b*) Refers to financial year March to February: 1956 figure for example refers to 1956–57. The base year of the Index is 1952–53 (= 100), as for col. 7.
*Sources: Economic Survey of India 1965–66.* Reserve Bank of India, *Report on Currency and Finance 1965–66* (1966), statements 12 and 13.

credit away from agriculture. A difficult choice has therefore faced the Indian Government: to acquire a non-inflationary source of finance for its plans, or to provide incentives for agriculture. The critics argue that the Government has favored the former too much.

There are two ways for the Government to control the net availability of cereals directly. It can vary PL 480 imports, or it can vary the level of its cereal stocks. Table 10 shows increases over the previous year of net production of cereals and of net availability, *i.e.*, net production plus imports less additions to stocks. It will be seen that Government imports and stocks policy has in most years had a stabilizing effect on the supply of cereals. However, this stabilizing effect has been very slight; in 1958–59, for example, the Government did very little to offset the large increase in the supply of cereals following the excellent harvest. In Table 11, column 4 shows the contribution to net availability of imports of cereals and changes in stocks. The trend of imports less additions to stocks has clearly been upward. Only in two years since 1956—when the first PL 480 agreement was made with the U.S.—has this trend been halted: 1958–59 and 1960–61, both years of bumper harvests. But the fall in imports less stock additions in these two years has been very small. The pattern is now clear: in years when agricultural production has fallen or risen only slightly, imports less stock additions have increased; in years of good harvests, they have remained stable. In years of bad harvests, therefore, the Government has used imports and stocks to put downward pressure on cereal prices, but in good years it has not lowered imports and added to stocks to offset the downward pressure on prices exerted by domestic production, but has simply kept cereal imports less stock additions at their former levels.

Turning now to the actual prices of cereals, it can be seen from Table 11 that cereal prices rose from 1956 to 1958. Also the cultivators' terms of trade, *i.e.*, the ratio of the wholesale price index of cereals to the general wholesale price index, improved. But in 1959 production was 8 mn tons higher, while imports and stock withdrawals were still at the same level as in 1958—the net result was a fall in cereal prices from 107 to 104, and in the cultivators' terms of trade from 95 to 90.

In 1960 net availability of cereals was just below that of 1959, since the small fall in net production was offset by a large increase in imports, most of which was used to build up Government stocks. The quantity of cereals available was not sufficient to push cereal prices down, but it was sufficient to prevent them from sharing in the general price rise; as a result the cultivators' terms of trade fell from 90 to 83. In 1961 net output increased by 6.7. per cent; imports and stock withdrawals fell only slightly; net availability increased by 6.3 per cent; cereal prices and cultivators' terms of trade again fell. There followed three years of stagnation in agriculture.

The evidence linking PL 480 imports and lower levels of cereal production is strong but circumstantial. There are a number of possible objections. Firstly, while PL 480 imports are mostly in the form of wheat, a high proportion of cereal consumption is in the form of rice. The two are not perfect substitutes. Secondly, the ratio of the wholesale price index of cereals to the general wholesale price index may be a poor indication of the actual terms of trade of agriculturalists.[14] Thirdly, though the agricultural stagnation of the early 1960s came after large imports of PL 480 cereals, the weather and shortages of agricultural inputs were probably more important contributing factors. Fourthly, change in area cultivated is possibly a more accurate indication of producers' decisions than output. The impact of PL 480 on crop areas is less clear—in 1964, for example, the area under cereals was slightly higher than in 1961, and the area under wheat, the commodity most affected by PL 480, was only slightly lower. However, a recent econometric study of PL 480 in India by J. S. Mann lends support to the view that PL 480 has had a depressing effect on cereal prices and production.[15] In this study Mann estimates that an increase in per capita imports of cereals under PL 480 of one pound (219,995 metric tons with the estimated 1962 population of 485 mn) has resulted in a 0.54 per cent drop in wholesale cereal prices in the same year and a decline in output in the second year of about 0.5 pounds of cereals per capita (about 109,997 tons with the same population). Output tends to rise in later years so that the depressing impact on output is trimmed to about 0.3 pounds per capita in the long run. This study measures only the direct impact of PL 480 imports; the indirect impact via the effect of readily available food aid on planners' attitudes to agriculture is not estimated.

The conclusion is not that ending PL 480 imports is an urgent matter deserving a higher priority. Indeed, Mann uses his analysis to argue the opposite: that since PL 480 cereal imports are only partially offset by the decline in domestic supply, they can make a positive contribution to filling the food gap. The inescapable fact is that for the time being India simply cannot do without food from abroad. In the two years 1965–66 India will have received about 19 million tons of food aid, which is equal to the Draft Outline estimate for the whole Plan period. As late as 1975–76, minimum likely average import requirements for foodgrains will still be as high as 7 million metric tons per year.[16] This continuing need for foreign food is reflected in the special Consortium arrangements for coordinating food aid to India; they amount in essence to a method which enables the U.S. to share with other donors the task—one it considers far from finished—of feeding India. Given a still sizeable flow of food aid to India over the next decade, the important lesson from past experience is the need to control the amount reaching the consumer, in particular to limit it when domestic harvests are good. In years of good harvests PL 480 cereals should be stockpiled.

## *New Initiatives*

### U.K. POLICY AND THE FOURTH INDIAN FIVE-YEAR PLAN

Apart from trying to clear away the obstacles to the traditional methods of raising aid to India, it is worth exploring new methods. There are a number of ways in which modernization in the U.K. could be geared to assist India. In these sketchy remarks no clear distinction will be drawn between aid and trade reforms.

### MATCHING MARKETS

The late John Strachey proposed a scheme by which Britain and India would agree to identify specific markets in each country to be supplied by the other. The intention was to treat such markets separately from aid arrangements through the Consortium. Britain would reduce barriers to specified Indian exports. Particular areas hit thereby, such as Lancashire or Dundee, would erect factories producing goods for which a ready, guaranteed market in India would be found. Thus the problem of raising Indian exports, of transferring workers from declining industries, and of finding new export markets would be solved simultaneously.

It may be asked whether the best location for these new factories would necessarily be the areas hit by the additional imports. Furthermore, there would be the question whether the new British export industries would supply the desired products at competitive prices to India. It is not, on the face of it, obvious that a bilateral arrangement is necessarily better than some more indirect way of substitution. But it is worth exploring methods of shifting resources in Britain so as to permit better access to Indian exports.

### AID FROM SURPLUS CAPACITY

The problem of aid from surplus capacity, additional to existing aid, is also worth exploring. There are three main objections: (*a*) delays in getting orders so that the surplus capacity has disappeared by the time the process is completed; (*b*) uncompetitively high prices and undesired products; (*c*) the difficulty of avoiding underwriting malinvestment in the U.K. The Indians are confident that they could give an answer to the question whether specific types of goods would be required within fifteen days. In any case, a glance at the list of Indian imports should make it fairly clear what types of goods are required. The problem of uncompetitive prices, which has been made a lot of in Britain, does not seem to worry the Indians. To the problem of preventing desirable adjustments in Britain, the answer is that aid from surplus capacity should be found for those sectors in which demand has *temporarily* receded, and resources are not intended to be redeployed. It is important that aid from surplus capacity would have to be additional to other aid.

#### SECONDHAND EQUIPMENT

Since modernization often involves the replacement of physically workable but technologically obsolete machinery, it would be worth looking into the question whether, subject to arrangements about transport costs, such secondhand machinery could be used by India. It may, however, be true that breakdowns may occur more frequently, that maintenance costs are higher and that for export industries only modern equipment can be used.

#### LONG-TERM PLANNING

Our own five-year and fifteen-year projections should accommodate not only increased trade with India, but also the flow and composition of aid. Debt servicing has to be reflected in admitting more Indian exports into the U.K.

The value of aid to India could be greatly increased if the quantum, pattern, and terms were pledged over five or ten years, and committed, not annually, but for several years ahead. Not only the Indian Perspective Planning Division, but also such commissions as the Energy Commission (with Prof. E. A. G. Robinson) aim at projections for 1975, and a longer-term view, which embraces at least two plans, would give a more rational and effective pattern of aid.

#### JOINT ENTERPRISES

Another idea worth exploring is that of joint U.K.-Indian enterprises, whose aim it would be to promote exports to Europe and other developed countries. They would join U.K. private firms to either Indian private or public enterprises. What appears to be lacking in India is know-how of export promotion, and in particular of styling, design, etc., suited for selling light labor-intensive goods. An increase in export earnings must have a very high priority in Indian development. To provide not only export know-how but also easier entry into European markets would make it possible for Indian industry to earn foreign exchange. In addition to consumer goods such as dresses, shoes, ties, etc., there should be emphasis on light engineering goods.

#### AID FOR POPULATION CONTROL

One area where the U.K. can take a major initiative is aid for population control. In the next five years India will add to its population a number of people roughly equal to the present population of this country. It is this rapid rate of population growth rather than the modest though not unsatisfactory increase in incomes which makes the outlook for India disturbing. However, India is one of the few countries which has taken up family planning as a national program—Rs 950 mn were to be spent in this field between 1960 and 1970, while Britain is the major donor with few religious and other objections to giving aid for population control. But British policy has been to wait until asked for assistance. The result is that British aid for population control has been very small—£11,000 in 1965–66 and possibly £40,000 in 1966–67. Since there is a willingness on both sides, Britain should prompt India to ask for more assistance for population control. This should be in addition to the aid India is already receiving.

But all the initiatives discussed in this section are of comparatively minor importance. It is important to recognize that India is grossly under-aided by whatever criteria one may wish to apply, and to break through the crust of pessimism, cynicism, and disenchantment which has weakened effective cooperation on both sides.

31

# International Trade of Communist China, 1950–65

*Robert L. Price*

*From* An Economic Profile of Mainland China, Vol. II, *Studies Prepared for the Joint Economic Committee, Congress of the United States, February 1967, U.S. Government Printing Office pp. 583–607, with omissions. Reprinted by permission.*

## *Foreign Trade and the Economy of Communist China*

### AN OVERVIEW

FOREIGN TRADE IN Communist China is a state monopoly that is used by the Party leaders as an important instrument of national policy for the pursuit of political objectives, both at home and abroad. The Chinese Communist regime seeks to create a strong, unified, and thoroughly communized China capable of achieving an independent great-power status and a position of leadership in Asia. This objective requires the transformation of China from a backward agrarian country into an industrialized state, with a powerful military establishment and broad international recognition. Specifically, foreign trade is directed toward assisting in obtaining these policy objectives by: (1) providing capital-goods imports embodying modern technology for the development of industry, (2) compensating for serious shortfalls and relieving bottlenecks in domestic production, and (3) developing trade as a wedge to promote Chinese influence abroad, both in other Communist countries and in less-developed Free World countries.

Up to 1960, Communist China's pattern of trade was dominated by the exchange of Chinese agricultural and mineral products and increasingly textiles, for machinery and raw materials contributing to the growth of the industrial base. Although the physical makeup of imports and exports reflected economic goals, the geographical direction of China's trade was strongly influenced by ideology. Mao established the "lean-to-one-side" policy for China at the beginning of the Communist regime. This policy resulted in China's economic orientation toward other Communist countries, particularly the U.S.S.R. This policy was reinforced by the Western trade embargo against China imposed in 1950 following China's intervention in the Korean war. Imports were obtained from the Free World chiefly when they were not available or were in short supply in the Communist world.

Since 1960, both the commodity and geographical patterns of Communist China's foreign trade has shifted dramatically. The collapse of the Great Leap Forward and the withdrawal of Soviet technicians from China in 1960, the persistent need for imports of Western grain, and the continuing deterioration of Sino-Soviet relations have combined to lower the volume of trade and to alter sharply its direction and composition. China's total trade rose from $1.2 billion in 1950 to a peak of $4.3 billion in 1959, and then declined to a level of $2.7 billion in 1962. This downturn was reversed in 1963, and by 1965 trade had increased to an estimated $3.7 billion. Since 1960 a major realinement in China's trading partners has taken place. Communist countries used to account for two-thirds of China's trade before 1960, but today the share is reversed, the Free World now accounting for 70 per cent of China's total trade. (Table 1.)

The Chinese acted with some deliberation in their liquidation of Mao's "lean-to-one-side" policy. After such Soviet actions as the cancellation of a "defense technology" agreement in 1959 and the abrupt withdrawal of Soviet specialists in 1960, the Chinese set about to lessen their dependence on the Soviet Bloc, and, if necessary, to be in a position to adjust to a break in relations. One of their earliest acts was to maintain the priority for the development of China's petroleum industry, even during the time when the overall investment program was being slashed. The earlier concentration on development of petroleum exploration and extraction was followed by a few orders for refining equipment and petrochemical plants for delivery by the Free World in 1964–65. Thus China was unable to reduce sharply its imports of petroleum from the U.S.S.R. Another of China's priority objectives was the rapid elimination of debt to the U.S.S.R. Simultaneously, the Chinese moved toward a phasing out of Soviet deliveries of equipment for complete plants and toward a careful cultivation of Free World contacts and detailed knowledge of Free World market conditions. The decision to purchase Free World equipment for high priority plants was apparently reached at the 10th Plenum of the Eighth Congress of the Chinese Communist Party in September 1962, but orders were not placed until August 1963.

The commodity composition of Communist China's foreign trade has continued to follow the trend set in 1961, despite the substantial recovery in both imports and exports since 1963. (Table 2.) Imports of agricultural products (largely wheat, raw cotton, sugar, and jute) and chemical fertilizers continued to dominate China's imports, and accounted for 47 per cent of China's total imports in 1965. In contrast, in 1959 imports of agricultural products and chemical fertilizer amounted to only 4 per cent of China's total imports. Imports of machinery and equipment, although showing a substantial rise in 1965, amounted to only \$330 million, still far short of the nearly \$1 billion in 1959. Part of this increase in imports of machinery and equipment in 1965 was accounted for by complete plants from the West contracted for in 1963, and just beginning to enter the country.

The major trend in Communist China's exports since 1963 has been the recovery in the export of agricultural products. For the first time in recent years food exports in 1965 drew roughly even with food imports in value. China exchanged high-value food products (rice, vegetables, processed foods, and meat products) for the cheaper wheat. After foodstuffs, textiles remained the single largest export earner, but exports declined slightly in 1965 as increased shipments to the West failed to offset the decline in exports to the Soviet Union. Exports of minerals and

***Table 1—Direction of Chinese Communist International Trade[a]***

| Year | *Total international trade* | | | *Trade with Communist Countries[b]* | | | *Trade with Free World[c]* | | |
|---|---|---|---|---|---|---|---|---|---|
| | *TOTAL* | *EXPORTS* | *IMPORTS* | *TOTAL* | *EXPORTS* | *IMPORTS* | *TOTAL* | *EXPORTS* | *IMPORT* |
| 1950 | 1,210 | 620 | 590 | 350 | 210 | 140 | 860 | 410 | 450 |
| 1951 | 1,895 | 780 | 1,115 | 975 | 465 | 510 | 920 | 315 | 605 |
| 1952 | 1,890 | 875 | 1,015 | 1,315 | 605 | 710 | 575 | 270 | 305 |
| 1953 | 2,295 | 1,040 | 1,255 | 1,555 | 670 | 885 | 740 | 370 | 370 |
| 1954 | 2,350 | 1,060 | 1,290 | 1,735 | 765 | 970 | 615 | 295 | 320 |
| 1955 | 3,035 | 1,375 | 1,660 | 2,250 | 950 | 1,300 | 785 | 425 | 360 |
| 1956 | 3,120 | 1,635 | 1,485 | 2,055 | 1,045 | 1,010 | 1,065 | 590 | 475 |
| 1957 | 3,025 | 1,595 | 1,430 | 1,935 | 1,065 | 870 | 1,090 | 530 | 560 |
| 1958 | 3,735 | 1,910 | 1,825 | 2,350 | 1,250 | 1,100 | 1,385 | 660 | 725 |
| 1959 | 4,265 | 2,205 | 2,060 | 2,960 | 1,595 | 1,365 | 1,310 | 615 | 695 |
| 1960 | 3,975 | 1,945 | 2,030 | 2,605 | 1,320 | 1,285 | 1,370 | 625 | 745 |
| 1961 | 3,015 | 1,525 | 1,495 | 1,680 | 965 | 715 | 1,335 | 560 | 775 |
| 1962 | 2,675 | 1,525 | 1,150 | 1,410 | 920 | 490 | 1,265 | 605 | 660 |
| 1963 | 2,755 | 1,560 | 1,200 | 1,245 | 820 | 425 | 1,510 | 740 | 770 |
| 1964 | 3,245 | 1,770 | 1,475 | 1,125 | 730 | 395 | 2,120 | 1,040 | 1,080 |
| 1965[d] | 3,695 | 1,955 | 1,740 | 1,125 | 645 | 480 | 2,570 | 1,310 | 1,260 |

[a] Because of rounding to the nearest \$5,000,000, components may not add to the total shown.
[b] Including trade with Yugoslavia.
[c] Trade reported by Free World countries has been adjusted for time leads and lags in shipping, shipping costs, double-counting, and unrecorded transactions.
[d] Preliminary estimates based on incomplete data.

metals, once a prime earner of foreign exchange, continued to lag.

CREDIT AND FOREIGN EXCHANGE LIMITATIONS

Communist China's exports have been by far the dominant source of foreign exchange, accounting for four-fifths of total receipts. The receipts of foreign credits, overseas remittances, and other earnings have played a less important role in financing China's imports. (See Figure 1.) During 1950–57 the rapid growth of the economy provided an upsurge in exports, which, supplemented by more than a billion dollars in long-term foreign aid from the U.S.S.R. and almost another billion in remittances from overseas Chinese, helped China meet its expanded requirements for foreign machinery and raw materials. In contrast, the excesses of the Great Leap Forward (1958–60) caused imports quickly to outpsace exports, resulting in a sharp rise in short-term foreign indebtedness and a decline in China's international reserves. The deterioration of China's international payments position was slowed in 1961–62 by deep cuts in imports from Communist countries and by new infusions of foreign credit.

By 1963, China's international financial position began to improve because of a revival of exports and continued restrictions on purchases of machinery and raw materials from both the U.S.S.R. and the West. By the end of 1964, China's clearing indebtedness with Communist countries (especially the U.S.S.R.) amounting to about $360 million had been almost eliminated. Moreover, by generating a large export surplus with the U.S.S.R. each year, the Chinese were able by 1965 to finish repaying their long-term debt to the U.S.S.R.

### *Table 2—Communist China: Commodity Composition of Trade*[a]

| | *1959* | | | *1962* | | | *1964* | | | *1965*[b] |
|---|---|---|---|---|---|---|---|---|---|---|
| | *Total* | *Free World* | *Communist countries* | *Total* | *Free World* | *Communist countries* | *Total* | *Free World* | *Communist countries* | *total* |
| Exports | 2,205 | 615 | 1,595 | 1,525 | 605 | 920 | 1,770 | 1,040 | 730 | 1,955 |
| Agricultural products | 1,100 | 390 | 720 | 425 | 285 | 140 | 650 | 515 | 135 | 775 |
| Foods | (820) | (300) | (520) | (250) | (175) | (80) | (375) | (275) | (100) | (520) |
| Industrial materials | 360 | 70 | 290 | 300 | 125 | 175 | 320 | 150 | 170 | 400 |
| Textiles | 620 | 120 | 500 | 535 | 155 | 375 | 440 | 200 | 240 | 425 |
| Other manufactured goods | 115 | 35 | 85 | 265 | 40 | 225 | 350 | 175 | 175 | 355 |
| Imports | 2,060 | 695 | 1,365 | 1,150 | 660 | 490 | 1,475 | 1,080 | 395 | 1,740 |
| Agricultural products | 10 | 10 | | 575 | 455 | 120 | 820 | 735 | 85 | 700 |
| Foods | | | | (460) | (345) | (110) | (600) | (525) | (75) | (530) |
| Fertilizers (chemical) | 70 | 70 | | 40 | 40 | ([c]) | 60 | 60 | ([c]) | 140 |
| Industrial materials | 740 | 500 | 240 | 305 | 125 | 180 | 325 | 195 | 130 | 485 |
| Machinery and equipment | 980 | 70 | 910 | 120 | 20 | 105 | 200 | 70 | 130 | 300 |
| Other | 260 | 45 | 215 | 110 | 25 | 85 | 70 | 20 | 50 | 115 |

[a] In millions of U.S. dollars. Data have been rounded to the nearest $5,000,000. Because of rounding, components may not add to the total shown.
[b] Preliminary estimates based on incomplete data.
[c] Not available.

Communist China for the first time turned to the West in 1961 for credits and by the end of 1964 had received credits of almost $1.2 billion. Unlike the credits from Communist countries, however, those from the West have provided only short- and medium-term financing, most of which have been 18-month credits to cover China's huge annual grain purchases. Other short-term credit from the West has covered China's large fertilizer purchases. Western credits have given little respite to China in meeting its hard currency obligations, however, because repayments each year now almost offset new drawings. If the Chinese leaders continue to rely on medium-term credits, repayments may even surpass new drawings in the next few years. China, therefore, may seek long-term credits from the West to finance imports of additional plants and equipment needed to accelerate their industrial development. China's failure to seek long-term credits from the West probably reflects the uncertainty of the leadership over future requirements for Western grain and the high cost of credit.

Chinese holdings of Western currency and gold reached a peak of about $650 million at the end of 1957. These holdings were heavily drawn on during and following the Great Leap Forward from 1958 to 1962. By 1964 they were probably only about $400 million, well below the peak level of 1957. Thus holdings of Western currency and gold now are much less than in 1957, but trade with the Free World now is more than double the 1957 level. (See Table 3.)

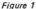

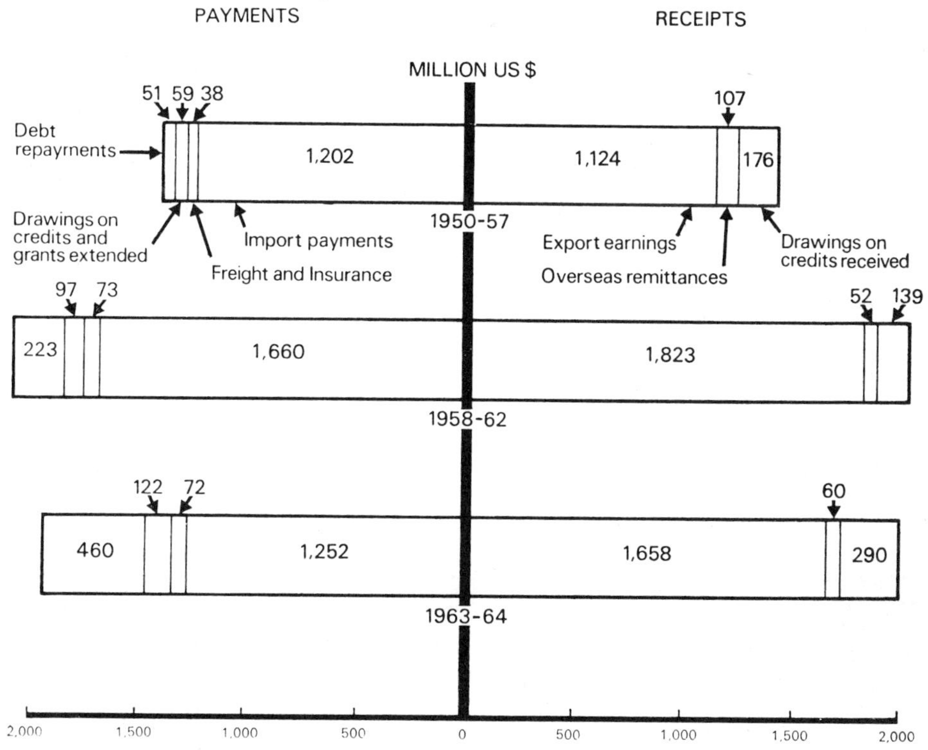


*Figure 1*

Communist China's foreign exchange holdings do not allow for any sustained trade expansion. China, when the Communists took it over in 1949, had almost no international financial resources. But China was able to build up its international reserves by imposing a strict and highly effective system of trade and foreign exchange controls, by borrowing from the U.S.S.R., and by obtaining foreign currencies from overseas remittances and from the "surrender" by private individuals of foreign exchange and gold.

During 1965 Communist China's holdings of gold and convertible currencies probably rose by $100 to $150 million as China increased the use of its export earnings to build up reserves. In 1965, China made its first purchases of gold on the world market, which amounted to $135 million and were paid for in sterling. This exchange of sterling for gold reflected not only the leadership's decision to diversify its international reserves, as a hedge against the possible devaluation of sterling, but also its more immediate concern over the deepening political and military crisis in southeast Asia. The Chinese nevertheless must have continued to hold some sterling balances overseas.

#### FOREIGN AID

Communist China has used its foreign aid program in an attempt to extend its political influence in both Communist and Free World countries. (See Tables 4 and 5.) Although the Chinese have directed their trade toward the West in recent years, China continues to channel its foreign economic assistance largely to Communist countries, especially those of Asia, as shown in the following tabulation:

### *Communist China: Extension of Credits and Grants to Communist and Free World Countries, 1953–65*

| | *U.S. dollars in millions* |
|---|---|
| Communist countries | 1,223.5 |
| North Vietnam | 457.0 |
| North Korea | 330.0 |
| Outer Mongolia | 115.0 |
| Albania | 164.0 |
| Cuba | 100.0 |
| Hungary | 57.5 |
| Free world countries | 815.0 |
| Asia | 410.0 |
| Africa | 264.0 |
| Middle East | 141.0 |
| Total | 2,038.5 |

The bulk of the actual drawings on these credits—at least $1 billion—has gone to Communist countries, chiefly North Vietnam and North Korea. Drawings by the less-developed Free World countries have lagged considerably behind credit extensions and through December 1965 were estimated at some $200 million, only about 25 per cent of total foreign-aid expenditures. China made record aid extensions in 1964 to the less-developed Free World countries of $338 million but, as in the past, drawings against these recent credits to the Free World probably will be extremely slow.

The predominant role of the Communist countries in China's foreign-aid program is likely to continue, inasmuch as these nations are the main areas in which China and the U.S.S.R. are competing for influence. The increasing political isolation of China in the international Communist movement, however, may narrow the scope of China's aid program. North Vietnam and Albania have been the only Communist nations recently receiving Chinese aid. The principal focus of Sino-Soviet aid competition is in North Vietnam. Both China and the U.S.S.R. have stepped up their economic and military aid to North Vietnam, partially as a result of U.S. air strikes, but also for the prosecution of the war in South Vietnam.

## *Trade with the Communist Countries*

#### THE SOVIET BLOC

*Mutual Cooperation During the 1950s*—Communist China based its industrial and technological growth of the 1950s on the rapid buildup of trade with the Soviet Union, in particular the flow of Soviet-produced machinery and equipment to China. Sino-Soviet trade grew more than fivefold from $320 million in 1950 to more than $2 billion in 1959. More than $12 billion in goods were exchanged between the two partners during this period. Of this amount, more than $1 billion worth of machinery and equipment for complete industrial installations was supplied China by the Soviet Union. Financial aid extended to China by the Soviet Union has been relatively small. The Soviet Union extended loans to China amounting to about $1.4 billion, of which $430 million was for economic development and the rest primarily for military purchases. The Soviet Union provided significant technical aid to China over the decade of the 1950s including (*a*) supplying vast quantities of blueprints and technical information, (*b*) sending 10,000 Soviet advisers and technicians to China to perform a wide variety of tasks, and (*c*) making available its own teaching facilities in the U.S.S.R. for training 8,000 Chinese technicians and researchers and 7,000 academic students.

*Industrial Projects in China*

The core of Communist China's program for rapid industrialization was the Soviet commitment to assist China in the building of 291 major industrial plants by 1967. The Soviet equipment for these plants was valued at $3.3 billion, or some $11 million on the average for each project. By the end of 1959, $1.35 billion worth of equipment for these projects had been delivered and about 130 projects had been completed. (See Table 6.) With Soviet and Eastern European support, Communist China expanded production of heavy industry from 1952 to 1959 at an annual average rate of about 25 per cent; without this aid the rate would have been far lower. This flow of equipment and technical assistance had a vital effect on the quality of China's industrialization, en-

### *Table 3—Communist China: International Financial Resources, Year-end Balances*[a]

| | 1957[b] | 1959 | 1960 | 1961 | 1962 | 1963 | 1964 |
|---|---|---|---|---|---|---|---|
| Foreign exchange reserves | 645 | 530 | 415 | 355 | 320 | 335 | 400 |
| Foreign currency balances[c] | 610 | 450 | 300 | 215 | 155 | 145 | 185 |
| Monetary gold holdings[d] | 35 | 80 | 115 | 140 | 165 | 190 | 215 |
| Clearing account balances (with Communist countries)[e] | −360 | −435 | −625 | [f]−260 | −205 | −120 | −55 |
| Net international financial resources | 285 | 95 | −210 | 95 | 115 | 215 | 345 |

[a] Table 3 is from CIA/RR ER 66–17, "Communist China's Balance of Payments, 1950–65," Washington, D.C., August 1966, p. 7. Data are rounded to the nearest $5,000,000. In millions of U.S. dollars.
[b] Because foreign exchange reserves were negligible at the beginning of 1950, reserves at the end of 1957 represent the net changes during 1950–57.
[c] Net balance of errors and omissions (from China's balance of payments with the Free World), which are almost entirely changes in foreign currency balances arising from transactions with the Free World.
[d] Net balance of changes in holdings of monetary gold.
[e] Net balance of errors and omissions (from China's balance of payments with the Communist countries), which are almost entirely clearing account balances arising from transactions with Communist countries.
[f] The reduction in the clearing debt in 1961 and the consequent improvement in China's clearing and foreign exchange position are due almost entirely to the U.S.S.R.'s funding of China's clearing debt of $320,000,000.

### *Table 4—Communist China: Economic Credits and Grants to Communist Countries*[a]

| | Total | Albania | Cuba[b] | Hungary | North Korea | North Vietnam | Outer Mongolia |
|---|---|---|---|---|---|---|---|
| 1953 | 200.0 | | | | 200 | | |
| 1954 | | | | | | | |
| 1955 | 204.0 | 4 | | | | 200 | |
| 1956 | 49.5 | 2 | | 7.5 | | | 40 |
| 1957 | 54.0 | 4 | | 50.0 | | | |
| 1958 | 55.0 | 5 | | | 25 | | 25 |
| 1959 | 119.0 | 19 | | | | 100 | |
| 1960 | 220.0 | 5 | 60 | | 105 | | 50 |
| 1961 | 282.0 | 125 | | | | 157 | |
| 1962 | ([c]) | ([c d]) | | | | | |
| 1963 | 40 | | 40 | | | | |
| 1964 | | | | | | | ([e]) |
| 1965 | ([c]) | ([c]) | | | | ([c]) | |
| Total | 1,223.5 | 164 | 100 | 57.5 | 330 | 457 | 115 |

[a] With the exceptions noted, source of table is Alexander Eckstein, *Communist China's Economic Growth and Foreign Trade,* (New York: McGraw Hill, 1966), app. E, p. 306. In millions of U.S. dollars.
[b] Figures revealed by Prime Minister Fidel Castro in speech on Jan. 2, 1966.
[c] Not available.
[d] Albanian press reported additional aid extended by Communist China, but amount not known.
[e] Negligible.

## *Table 5—Communist China: Economic Credits and Grants to Free World Countries*[a]

| | 1956–65[b] | 1964[c] | 1965[b] |
|---|---|---|---|
| Total | 815 | 337.8 | 59 |
| Africa | 264 | 115.1 | 15 |
| Algeria | 50 | 0 | 0 |
| Central African Republic | 4 | 4.0 | 0 |
| Congo (Brazzaville) | 25 | 25.2 | 0 |
| Ethiopia | 0 | 0 | 0 |
| Ghana | 40 | 22.4 | 0 |
| Guinea | 25 | 0 | 0 |
| Kenya | 18 | 18.0 | 0 |
| Mali | 20 | 0 | 0 |
| Somalia | 22 | 0 | 0 |
| Tanzania | 45 | 45.5 | 0 |
| Uganda | 15 | 0 | 15 |
| Asia | 410 | 114.2 | 44 |
| Afghanistan | 28 | 0 | 28 |
| Burma | 85 | 0 | 0 |
| Cambodia | 50 | 0 | 0 |
| Ceylon | 42 | 4.2 | 0 |
| Indonesia | 105 | 50.0 | 16 |
| Nepal | 40 | 0 | 0 |
| Pakistan | 60 | 60.0 | 0 |
| Middle East | 141 | 108.5 | 0 |
| Syrian Arab Republic | 16 | 0 | 0 |
| United Arab Republic | 85 | 80.0 | 0 |
| Yemen | 40 | 28.5 | 0 |

[a] In millions of U.S. dollars.
[b] U.S. Department of State, "Communist Governments and Developing Nations: Aid and Trade in 1965," research memorandum, RSB–50, June 17, 1966.
[c] Alexander Eckstein, *Communist China's Economic Growth and Foreign Trade* (New York: McGraw Hill, 1966), app. E, p. 307.

## *Table 6—Soviet Project Construction Agreements with Communist China*

| *Date of agreement* | *Economic credits (million U.S. dollars)*[a] | *Number of projects* | *Value of complete sets of equipment*[b] *(million U.S. dollars)*[a] |
|---|---|---|---|
| February 1950 | 300 | 50 | ([c]) |
| September 1953[d] | 0 | 91 | 1,300[e] |
| October 1954 | 130 | 15 | 100 |
| April 1956 | 0 | 55 | 625 |
| August 1958 | 0 | 47 | ([c]) |
| February 1959 | 0 | 78 | 1,250 |
| Total | 430 | [f] 291 | 3,275 |

[a] Converted from rubles at the official rate of exchange of 4 rubles to 1 U.S. dollar.
[b] Including technical assistance related to these projects.
[c] Not available.
[d] An agreement signed to deliver equipment for a total of 141 projects.
[e] This sum includes the value of equipment and technical assistance for all of the 141 projects.
[f] The Chinese announced in April 1959 that the 211 major Soviet-assisted projects agreed on through April 1956 were reduced in number to 166 as a result of merging of some projects during their construction. Thus, the total of 336 projects was reduced to 291.

abling China to produce such prestige items as jet aircraft, submarines, large electric-generating equipment, metal-cutting machine tools, tractors, trucks, and electronic equipment. Soviet aid to China also included extensive training of Chinese scientists and technicians in the nuclear sciences in both the U.S.S.R. and China, including the supply of experimental reactors and other nuclear related technology, designed to eventually provide a base which could support native Chinese production of Soviet-designed weapons.

The sudden withdrawal of Soviet support in mid-1960 was, in the words of Chinese economic planner Po I-po, like "taking away all the dishes when you have only eaten half a meal." About 20 per cent of the Soviet aid plants begun under agreements concluded prior to 1958 were incomplete. For example, much work remained to be done on the important steel complexes of Pao-t'ou and Wu-han, and on construction of the large hydroelectric station in San Men Gorge on the upper reaches of the Yellow River. Most of the 125 Soviet aid plants contracted for under agreements concluded in August 1958 and February 1959 and scheduled for completion by 1967 were still in the planning stage. These latter projects included facilities for the production of chemicals, the development of a more balanced steel industry, additional support to defense industries, and the provision of specialized machine tools and precision instruments. Thus, the Chinese were still highly dependent on the Soviet Union for new plants and product designs involving technology not already furnished or with which the Chinese had little experience. The degree of dependence varied, some industries requiring only capital equipment for further development, others needing only technical assistance, and still other more complex industries—depending on both imported knowledge and equipment.

Although none of the European satellites extended long-term financial assistance for Communist China's development efforts, they did negotiate assistance agreements calling for the construction in China of a number of large projects. Agreements for at least 100 projects were signed and construction of about two-thirds of these projects were completed and placed into operation by 1959, including electric power, chemical, and sugar-refining plants.

*Trade Flows*

The U.S.S.R.'s share in China's foreign trade increased from a mere 5 per cent before the Communist revolution to approximately 50 per cent in 1959. By 1959, Soviet exports to China were as large as those to all Free World underdeveloped countries combined. One-sixth of Soviet exports of machinery and nearly three of every four complete plants sent abroad went to China. (See Table 7.)

At the height of Sino-Soviet commercial relations in 1959, Communist China rivaled East Germany as the Soviet Union's principal trading partner. China supplied one-fifth of the Soviet Union's total imports, two-thirds of her food imports and three-quarters of her textile imports. Soviet willingness to accept Chinese agricultural raw materials and large amounts of industrial consumer goods, especially textiles, permitted China to pay for the large-scale imports of machinery and equipment needed for industrialization. (See Table 8.)

Communist China has acknowledged the receipt of long-term credits from the Soviet Union amount to $1,405 million. These included an economic loan of $300 million granted in 1950; a further economic credit of $130 million in 1954; a loan in 1955 covering the transfer to China of Soviet holdings in four joint-stock companies and other Soviet-owned assets in China believed to total $330 million; and other miscellaneous credits totaling $645 million, probably mainly used for military purposes. The Soviet Union provided some additional financial aid to China following the collapse of the Great Leap Forward by funding $320 million of outstanding short-term indebtedness in 1961 over a 5-year period, and by extending a loan of $46 million for the import of 500,000 tons of Cuban sugar.

Sino-East European trade started from a negligible base in 1950, but increased rapidly and by 1959 accounted for 15 per cent of

## Table 7—Soviet Exports to Communist China[a]

| | 1958 | | 1959 | 1960 | 1961 | 1962 | 1963 | 1964 | | 1965 | |
|---|---|---|---|---|---|---|---|---|---|---|---|
| | VALUE | % | value | value | value | value | value | VALUE | % | VALUE | % |
| Total exports | 634.0 | 100.0 | 954.5 | 817.1 | 367.3 | 233.4 | 187.2 | 135.2 | 100.0 | 191.7 | 100.0 |
| Machinery and equipment | 318.0 | 50.2 | 597.5 | 503.9 | 108.1 | 27.3 | 42.2 | 57.6 | 42.6 | 77.0 | 40.2 |
| Complete plants | (166.2) | (26.2) | (399.8) | (373.8) | (78.9) | (8.8) | (14.6) | (12.3) | (9.1) | (3.9) | (2.0) |
| Industrial raw materials | 173.4 | 27.4 | 176.3 | 188.7 | 166.9 | 127.0 | 107.4 | 56.7 | 42.0 | 71.9 | 37.5 |
| Petroleum and petroleum products | (92.4) | (14.6) | (117.7) | (113.1) | (120.7) | (80.5) | (60.7) | (21.6) | (16.0) | (2.2) | (1.1) |
| Ferrous metals | (60.8) | (9.6) | (48.0) | (59.3) | (34.7) | (28.2) | (27.4) | (20.8) | (15.4) | (34.7) | (18.1) |
| Nonferrous metals | (15.8) | (2.5) | (6.4) | (10.5) | (6.5) | (5.6) | (4.9) | (3.1) | (2.3) | (3.8) | (2.0) |
| Consumer goods | 9.2 | 1.5 | 6.6 | 4.4 | 67.2 | 30.6 | 14.2 | 7.2 | 5.3 | 1.4 | 7 |
| Foods | (1.1) | (.2) | (.5) | ([b]) | (63.8) | (20.8) | (.7) | (.1) | (.1) | ([b]) | ([b]) |
| Other merchandise | 17.0 | 2.7 | 12.3 | 13.1 | 6.1 | 3.4 | 2.3 | 5.6 | 4.1 | 16.9 | 8.8 |
| Unspecified | 116.4 | 18.4 | 161.4 | 107.0 | 19.1 | 45.1 | 21.2 | 8.2 | 6.1 | 24.5 | 12.8 |

[a] Figures based on *Vneshniaia Torgovlia S.S.S.R. za 1965 god,* Ministerstvo Vneshnei Torgovli S.S.S.R. (Moskva, 1965) and other volumes. Exports are f.o.b. Because of rounding components may not add to total shown. In millions of U.S. dollars.

[b] Negligible.

## Table 8—Soviet Imports from Communist China[a]

| | 1958 | | 1959 | 1960 | 1961 | 1962 | 1963 | 1964 | | 1965 | |
|---|---|---|---|---|---|---|---|---|---|---|---|
| | VALUE | % | value | value | value | value | value | VALUE | % | VALUE | % |
| Total imports | 881.2 | 100.0 | 1,100.0 | 848.1 | 551.4 | 516.3 | 413.0 | 314.2 | 100.0 | 225.6 | 100.0 |
| Industrial materials | 233.3 | 26.5 | 277.2 | 218.4 | 128.4 | 103.8 | 79.0 | 56.9 | 18.1 | 29.7 | 13.2 |
| Ores and concentrates | 74.0 | 8.4 | 73.3 | 61.2 | 48.3 | 35.3 | 25.9 | 13.2 | 4.2 | 11.6 | 5.1 |
| Ferrous metals | 19.2 | 2.2 | 7.6 | 12.8 | 8.7 | 6.6 | 10.9 | 10.6 | 3.4 | | |
| Nonferrous metals | 48.9 | 5.5 | 54.9 | 48.9 | 34.2 | 25.9 | 12.5 | 3.1 | 1.0 | 1.4 | .6 |
| Textiles | 37.5 | 4.3 | 91.6 | 65.3 | 22.7 | 13.9 | 8.6 | 6.7 | 2.1 | 3.6 | 1.6 |
| Consumer goods | 483.0 | 54.8 | 644.4 | 518.4 | 360.6 | 382.3 | 309.6 | 230.1 | 73.2 | 172.9 | 76.6 |
| Food | 230.1 | 26.1 | 219.1 | 127.9 | 17.4 | 38.1 | 21.9 | 51.9 | 16.5 | 78.2 | 34.7 |
| Fabrics and clothing | 158.4 | 18.0 | 306.3 | 293.2 | 277.1 | 299.4 | 256.6 | 165.2 | 52.0 | 81.3 | 36.0 |
| Other merchandise | 160.7 | 18.2 | 171.6 | 96.6 | 31.0 | 26.6 | 19.0 | 15.5 | 4.9 | 13.4 | 5.9 |
| Unspecified | 4.0 | .5 | 7.2 | 14.7 | 31.4 | 3.6 | 5.5 | 11.8 | 3.8 | 9.6 | 4.3 |

[a] Figures based on *Vneshniaia Torgovlia S.S.S.R. za 1965 god,* Ministerstvo Vneshnei Torgovli S.S.S.R. (Moskva, 1965) and other volumes. Imports are f.o.b. Because of rounding, components may not add to totals shown. In millions of U.S. dollars.

Communist China's total trade. (See Table 9.) Up to 1960 East Germany and Czechoslovakia have accounted for approximately two-thirds of Chinese trade with the European Communist countries, Poland and Hungary for less than 30 per cent, and Rumania, Bulgaria, and Albania the remainder. Although there are indications that imbalances have developed in Sino-East European trade, Chinese imports from these countries are not known to have been financed by long-term credits.

### *Table 9—Communist China: Trade with Eastern European Communist Countries*[a]

| | *Total* | *China's imports* | *China's exports* |
|---|---|---|---|
| 1950 | 20 | 5 | 15 |
| 1951 | 205 | 65 | 140 |
| 1952 | 320 | 155 | 165 |
| 1953 | 340 | 190 | 150 |
| 1954 | 370 | 240 | 130 |
| 1955 | 435 | 235 | 200 |
| 1956 | 465 | 265 | 200 |
| 1957 | 500 | 275 | 225 |
| 1958 | 670 | 410 | 260 |
| 1959 | 655 | 325 | 330 |
| 1960 | 640 | 340 | 300 |
| 1961 | 325 | 165 | 160 |
| 1962 | 230 | 80 | 150 |
| 1963 | 225 | 70 | 155 |
| 1964 | 245 | 85 | 160 |
| 1965[b] | 299 | 132 | 167 |

[a] Including Albania and excluding Yugoslavia. Totals have been rounded to the nearest $5,000,000. In millions of U.S. dollars.
[b] Preliminary trade estimates compiled primarily from official yearbooks and monthly statistical bulletins of the East European Communist countries.

Next to the U.S.S.R., Eastern Europe has been the largest supplier of machinery and equipment to China, including industrial, transport, agricultural, and communications equipment. East Germany and Czechoslovakia have been the chief exporters of machinery and equipment to China. During 1950–59, China received from Eastern Europe machinery and equipment valued at about $1.7 billion, approximately 40 per cent of Chinese imports of these items from all sources. The Chinese have paid for imports by exports of basic raw materials and foodstuffs required by Eastern Europe. In the past some Eastern European nations on occasion supplemented their own exports to the West by reexporting Chinese products.

*Mutual Discord During the 1960s*—Toward the end of the 1950s discord between the Soviet Union and Communist China grew over a widening range of political and economic matters. For example, the Soviets had second thoughts over the wisdom of supplying China with nuclear information and the Soviets had grave doubts about China's freewheeling Leap Forward economic policy. Matters came to a head with the abrupt withdrawal of the Soviet technicians from China in mid-1960. Their departure was a serious blow to the Chinese economy at an already critical time, and marked the end of the period of large-scale Sino-Soviet economic collaboration. Trade fell rapidly. (See Figure 2.)

*Union of Soviet Socialist Republics*

Sino-Soviet trade has declined each year since 1960, dropping to a level of $450 million in 1964, only one-quarter the level of 1959, and in 1965 amounted to only $417 million. Despite this reduction in trade, China maintained a large export surplus with the U.S.S.R. in order to pay off its indebtedness ahead of schedule. In 1963 and 1964 alone, China maintained an export surplus of over $400 million with the Soviet Union. In an attempt to bring trade into better balance in 1965, China increased its imports from the Soviet Union by over $50 million to $192 million, while decreasing exports by $90 million to, $225 million, reflecting the completion of Chinese debt payments.

After the withdrawal of Soviet assistance, Communist China's imports of machinery and equipment from the Soviet Union fell to a trickle, amounting to only $27 million in 1962. With the gradual upturn in China's industrial production since 1962, imports of machinery and equipment from the Soviet Union have revived slightly, reaching a level of $58 million in 1964 and $77 million in 1965. Though still not importing any complete plants, China has been purchasing more spare parts and replacements for existing stocks of Soviet equipment, particularly civil aircraft and transportation and construction equipment. As for exports, in 1964 China reduced shipments to the Soviet Union of almost all items. The sharpest drops were in fabrics (down $51 million), garments (down $40 million), ores and concentrates (down $13 million), metals (down $9 million), and construction materials, mainly cement (down $8 million). In 1965, China further reduced shipments to the U.S.S.R. of fabrics and clothing (down $84 million), and metals (down $12 million).

*Eastern Europe*

Following 1960, Sino-East European trade also dropped sharply, and in 1961 amounted to only one-half the level of 1960. This sudden drop in trade created difficulties for Eastern Europe both in marketing machinery produced to Chinese specifications and in finding alternate sources of supply and the means of financing of materials that were normally imported from China. Sino-European trade continued to fall sharply in 1962, trade with some nations falling more sharply than that with others. China's trade with East Germany, Czechoslovakia, and Hungary, the important Chinese trade partners in Eastern Europe and those countries most strongly supporting the Soviet position in the Sino-Soviet political dispute, declined by 40 to 50 per cent, while trade with Poland declined by some 20 per cent. Chinese trade with Albania—China's strongest ally in the Sino-Soviet dispute—increased in 1962 chiefly due to increased Chinese aid deliveries to Albania under long-term credit arrangements.

By 1964, total Sino-East European trade increased by 6 per cent over the 1962 level. Of this total increases in trade with Albania, Rumania, and to a lesser extent, Poland, offset a decline in trade with East Germany and Czechoslovakia. In 1965, China's trade with Eastern Europe jumped 22 per cent over 1964, the largest increases occurring with East Germany (up $16 million) and Rumania (up $15 million). (See Table 10.) The bulk of China's imports continue to be machinery and equipment.

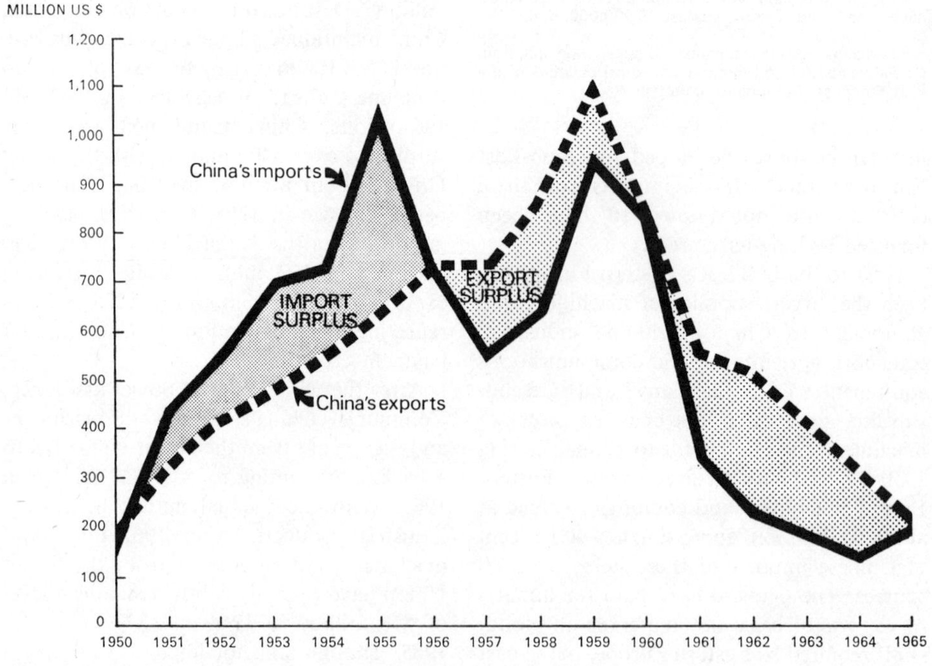


*Figure 2*

Communist China's total trade with North Vietnam, North Korea, and Mongolia has been small, amounting to less than 10 per cent of China's total trade and has been governed largely by its economic assistance programs to these countries. The rivalry between China and the U.S.S.R. in the extension of aid to these countries has been exacerbated since the flaring up of the Sino-Soviet dispute as each country has maneuvered to win adherents in the political struggle. As a result of this struggle, China's trade with North Korea and Mongolia has declined, while trade with North Vietnam has increased.

The extension of credits and grants by China has played an important role in the economic development of these nations. (See Tables 11 and 12.) Communist China has supplied economic and technical assistance for the development of both light and heavy industry in North Vietnam including the Thai Nguyen iron and steel plant, and the rehabilitation and development of North Vietnam's transportation and communications facilities as well as in the improvement of its irrigation system. North Korea has received equipment and technical assistance from China for light industrial projects and powerplants. China and North Korea are cooperating in the building of a large hydroelectric power station on the Yalu River. Chinese economic aid to Mongolia has been concerned primarily with the development of light industry and with housing

### *Table 10—Communist China: Trade with Eastern Europe*[a]

| | *China's exports* | | | | *China's imports* | | | |
|---|---|---|---|---|---|---|---|---|
| | *1962* | *1963* | *1964* | *1965*[b] | *1962* | *1963* | *1964* | *1965*[b] |
| Total | 147.1 | 156.6 | 160.8 | 167 | 78.0 | 72.7 | 85.5 | 132 |
| Albania | 42.1 | 41.7 | 61.7 | 70 | 11.7 | 23.4 | 23.9 | 25 |
| Bulgaria | 3.2 | 2.3 | 1.1 | 1 | 3.3 | 1.3 | 1.5 | 1 |
| Czechoslovakia | 25.6 | 29.0 | 20.6 | 13 | 11.9 | 9.3 | 9.3 | 19 |
| East Germany | 32.0 | 24.7 | 19.5 | 25 | 21.9 | 10.4 | 15.6 | 26 |
| Hungary | 11.0 | 20.0 | 14.9 | 11 | 11.9 | 3.3 | 4.3 | 15 |
| Poland | 22.7 | 24.8 | 25.0 | 25 | 15.1 | 11.2 | 15.0 | 19 |
| Rumania | 10.5 | 14.1 | 18.0 | 22 | 2.2 | 13.8 | 15.9 | 27 |

[a] Trade data for 1962–64 are from CIA/RR ER 65–37, "Foreign Trade of the European Satellites in 1964: A Statistical Summary," Washington, D.C., December 1965. In millions of U.S. dollars.
[b] Preliminary trade estimates compiled primarily from official yearbooks and monthly statistical bulletins of the East European Communist countries.

### *Table 11—Derivation of Chinese Communist Trade with the Far Eastern Communist Countries*[a]

| | *1950* | *1951* | *1952* | *1953* | *1954* | *1955* | *1956* | *1957* | *1958* |
|---|---|---|---|---|---|---|---|---|---|
| Total trade[b] | 5 | 20 | 30 | 50 | 95 | 115 | 120 | 130 | 160 |
| Exports on credit or grant basis | [c] 3 | [c] 14 | [c] 21 | [c] 35 | [d] 75 | [d] 97 | [d] 82 | [d] 48 | [d] 58 |
| Commercial trade (excluding credits and grants) | [c] 2 | [c] 6 | [c] 9 | [e] 15 | [e] 20 | [e] 18 | [e] 38 | [e] 82 | [e] 102 |
| Derived trade:[b] | | | | | | | | | |
| Imports[f] | 0 | 5 | 5 | 10 | 10 | 10 | 20 | 40 | 50 |
| Exports[g] | 5 | 15 | 25 | 40 | 85 | 105 | 100 | 90 | 110 |

[a] Table from CIA/RR ER 66–17, "Communist China's Balance of Payments, 1950–65," Washington, D.C., August 1966, p. 37. In millions of U.S. dollars.
[b] Includes North Korea, North Vietnam, and Mongolia. Data are rounded to the nearest $5,000,000.
[c] During 1950–54, as China restored and expanded its economy, commercial trade probably increased rapidly, although it amounted to a relatively small percentage of the aid goods which China provided to North Korea for its war with South Korea and to Viet Minh forces in Vietnam. Thus, commercial trade during 1950–53 is assumed to amount to about 30 per cent of total trade. Exports on credit or grant basis are the residual of total trade less commercial trade.
[d] Based on announced credit extensions and drawings and related data.
[e] Total trade less exports on credit or grant basis.
[f] Half of the value of commercial trade, on the assumption that commercial trade has been balanced each year.
[g] Total trade less imports.

construction. In addition, between 1956 and 1964 large numbers of Chinese laborers were sent to work on Mongolian construction projects.

Communist China's trade with Mongolia

### *Table 12—Communist China: Trade with Far Eastern Communist Countries*[a]

| Year | Total trade[b] | Imports | Exports |
|---|---|---|---|
| 1959 | 244 | 83 | 161 |
| 1960 | 255 | 96 | 159 |
| 1961 | 257 | 93 | 164 |
| 1962 | 262 | 88 | 174 |
| 1963 | 263 | 96 | 167 |
| 1964 | 227 | 92 | 135 |

[a] Table from CIA/RR ER 66–17, "Communist China's Balance of Payments, 1950–65," Washington D.C., August 1966, p. 40. In millions of U.S. dollars.

[b] Includes North Korea, North Vietnam, and Mongolia. Data based on miscellaneous and incomplete trade data of the Far Eastern Communist countries and information on the extension and implementation of Chinese credits and grants. In the absence of clearing account data, commercial trade is assumed to have been balanced between exports and imports. China's aid deliveries were largely estimated on the assumption of a straightline drawing of credits and grants.

has declined in importance since 1959 largely because of Mongolia's firm commitment to the U.S.S.R. in the Sino-Soviet dispute. A similar decline in China's exports to North Korea since 1962 probably reflects the completion of drawings on credits provided by China in 1960 as well as the more recent political leanings of North Korea toward the U.S.S.R. Counter to this declining trend has been an increase in China's trade with North Vietnam. China supplied large-scale assistance in support of North Vietnam's First Five-Year Plan (1961–65). But perhaps the large stimulus to increasing Sino-North Vietnamese trade has been China's increasing technical and material support to the bomb-damaged economy of North Vietnam and for the prosecution of the war with South Vietnam.

#### CUBA

Sino-Cuban trade first began to assume significant proportions in 1960 following the establishment of formal trade relations and the extension by Communist China of a $60 million interest free credit. This credit was to be drawn between 1961 and 1965 to finance exports of complete plants and for other technical aid to help Cuba develop its economy. Trade between the two countries developed rapidly, and between 1961 and 1965, the average annual turnover amounted to about $180 million.

The growth of Sino-Cuban trade between 1961 and 1965 was based chiefly on the exchange of Cuban sugar for Chinese foodstuffs, including rice, soybeans, textiles, machinery, and other industrial equipment, part of which was financed under the $60 million economic credit. (Table 13.) Appa-

### *Table 13—Communist China: Trade with Cuba*[a]

| Year | Total trade | Imports | Exports |
|---|---|---|---|
| 1960 | 42 | 32 | 10 |
| 1961 | 182 | 92 | 90 |
| 1962 | 171 | 89 | 82 |
| 1963 | 156 | 73 | 83 |
| 1964 | 180 | 81 | 99 |
| 1965 | 213 | 98 | 115 |

[a] Compiled from Chinese and Cuban sources but excluding shipping costs (which the Cuban sources apparently included), which are estimated at 10 per cent of the value of imports. In millions of U.S. dollars.

rently, Sino-Cuban trade will decline in 1966 because of a rapid deterioration in political relations. According to statements by Fidel Castro, China has decided to reduce its trade with Cuba in 1966 by importing less Cuban sugar and exporting less rice and other commodities than in 1965. China, moreover, has insisted that trade should be balanced and press announcements from Havana indicate that a total trade turnover of about $170 million is expected in 1966. This level of trade is slightly below the average annual turnover for 1961–65 and considerably below the record level reached in 1965.

## *Trade with the Free World*

#### THE 1950s—THE MARGINAL SUPPLIER

Communist China's trade with the Free World during the first half of the 1950s declined sharply in total value and in relative importance. China's total foreign trade doubled in the five years from 1950 to 1954, but trade with the Free World, which accounted for 70 per cent of total trade in 1950, dropped in absolute value by nearly 30 per cent and in relative terms to only 25 per cent of total trade in 1954.

During the second half of the decade trade with the Free World revived, rising from $785 million in 1955 to $1.4 billion in 1958 and to about $1.3 billion in 1959, when it accounted for about one-third of total Chinese trade. This upsurge was furthered by the rapid economic advance in Communist China, and, in part, it represented an effort to develop alternate sources for industrial materials in short supply or not readily available within the Bloc. Growth in trade with Western Europe was particularly rapid, reflecting the rising Chinese need for chemicals and metals. Thus, while China's trade with Western Europe more than tripled, China's trade with less-developed countries —southeast Asia—grew by only 50 per cent. Trade with the less-developed areas expanded in large measures to promote the political policy of developing closer relations with many of the uncommitted countries of this area, and, where possible, to acquire foreign exchange to cover purchases from Western Europe. However, China's preoccupation with its own industrialization limited its expansion of economic assistance to the less-developed areas.

### THE 1960S—THE MAJOR SUPPLIER

Communist China's trade with the Free World has grown rapidly since 1960, and by 1965 accounted for more than two-thirds of China's total trade. (See Table 14.) China's economic difficulties and the impact of the Sino-Soviet dispute have been the principal factors in the redirection of trade. Beginning in 1961, agricultural failures forced China to import 6 million tons of grain annually. At first, these purchases were financed by means of drastic cuts in imports of machinery and other investment goods, emergency sales of precious metals, and credits from Canada and Australia, the principal grain supplying countries. Later, China was able to shift exports to markets where urgently needed hard currency could be obtained.

Rapid shifts also occurred in the geographic distribution of trade with the Free World. Canada and Australia increased their exports (grain) to China manyfold in 1961 whereas Western Europe's exports (industrial products) declined by 75 per cent. Imports of capital goods from the industrial West, however, have revived since 1962, following the gradual recovery in China's industrial production. In 1963, for the first time since 1950, the Free World accounted for more than half (55 per cent) of China's trade. Moreover, since 1960 the greatly altered emphasis of China's investment program has meant a growing demand for chemical and petrochemical plants, mining equipment, and other capital goods that the Soviet Bloc economies are less able to supply.

Trade with Free World countries has been important to Communist China for certain raw materials (cotton, rubber, wool), producers' goods (some types of steel and nonferrous metal manufactures, chemical fertilizers, artificial fibers), and more recently grain and complete industrial installations. The Chinese also have benefited from small purchases of special purpose items embodying advanced designs such as instruments, machine tools, and electronic equipment. Particularly since the loss of Soviet technical assistance in 1960, China's entry into advanced fields of production will depend largely on the acquisition of Western equipment and technical knowledge. The Free World, on the other hand, has received useful but not critical imports from China; including an increasing range of textiles and light industrial products, agricultural commodities ranging from rice and tea through Chinese specialities such as tung oil, bristles, feathers, processed food, hog casings, oilseeds, and essential oils; and metals and minerals including tin, wolfram, mercury, pig iron, and coal. For individual Free World trade partners, except Hong Kong,

## *Table 14—Communist China: Trade with Countries of the Free World*[a]

| | 1961 | 1962 | 1963 | 1964 |
|---|---|---|---|---|
| Exports | 560 | 605 | 740 | 1,040 |
| Total, industrial West | 222 | 210 | 265 | 415 |
| Western Europe | 181 | 149 | 172 | 229 |
| Of which— | | | | |
| United Kingdom | 73 | 50 | 47 | 59 |
| West Germany | 35 | 32 | 34 | 49 |
| France | 13 | 15 | 19 | 28 |
| Italy | 10 | 12 | 19 | 21 |
| Japan | 29 | 44 | 71 | 150 |
| Australia, Canada, and New Zealand | 12 | 17 | 22 | 36 |
| Total, less developed countries | 223 | 259 | 304 | 371 |
| South and southeast Asia | 165 | 194 | 226 | 270 |
| Of which— | | | | |
| Burma | 21 | 27 | 25 | 34 |
| Ceylon | 21 | 20 | 32 | 39 |
| Indonesia | 40 | 46 | 34 | 38 |
| Malaya and Singapore | 54 | 64 | 90 | 95 |
| Pakistan | 3 | 4 | 6 | 17 |
| Middle East | 27 | 32 | 42 | 45 |
| Africa | 29 | 31 | 34 | 54 |
| Latin America | 2 | 2 | 1 | 2 |
| Of which Argentina | ([b]) | ([b]) | ([b]) | ([b]) |
| Hong Kong[c] | 115 | 138 | 170 | 253 |
| Imports | 775 | 660 | 770 | 1,080 |
| Total, industrial West | 692 | 473 | 582 | 684 |
| Western Europe | 234 | 170 | 184 | 196 |
| Of which— | | | | |
| United Kingdom | 52 | 28 | 35 | 56 |
| West Germany | 46 | 36 | 18 | 20 |
| France | 41 | 51 | 67 | 43 |
| Italy | 38 | 23 | 21 | 20 |
| Japan | 17 | 40 | 66 | 160 |
| Australia, Canada, and New Zealand | 350 | 263 | 332 | 328 |
| Total, less developed countries | 174 | 186 | 188 | 394 |
| South and southeast Asia | 109 | 100 | 94 | 131 |
| Of which— | | | | |
| Burma | 40 | 20 | 13 | 18 |
| Ceylon | 16 | 33 | 22 | 25 |
| Indonesia | 32 | 40 | 37 | 68 |
| Malaya and Singapore | 9 | ([b]) | 6 | 1 |
| Pakistan | 10 | 2 | 12 | 13 |
| Middle East | 27 | 30 | 34 | 54 |
| Africa | 28 | 22 | 54 | 54 |
| Latin America | 9 | 34 | 7 | 155 |
| Of which Argentina | 5 | 33 | 4 | 112 |
| Hong Kong | 1 | 2 | 2 | 2 |
| Total, Free World | 1,335 | 1,270 | 1,510 | 2,120 |

[a] Data are based on the official statistics of Free World countries, adjusted to approximate Chinese foreign trade on an export f.o.b. and an import c.i.f. basis. Adjustments also have been made for double counting and for undercounting such as Chinese grain purchases sent to other countries. Because of rounding, components may not add to the totals shown. In millions of U.S. dollars.

[b] Less than $500,000.

[c] Net of entrepôt trade with 3d countries.

trade with China has represented less than 10 per cent of their total trade. But Chinese purchases of individual commodities have been quite important at times, such as in the case of Ceylonese rubber and Australian and Canadian grain.

*Grain*—Chinese Communist purchases of grain have become an established fact of life in the Chinese economy and purchases since 1961 have averaged about 6 million tons a year at an average annual cost of $400 million, as shown in the following tabulation.

### *Communist China: Grain Purchases from the West*[a]

| *Year* | *Million metric tons* | *Value (c.i.f.)* |
|---|---|---|
| 1961 | 6.2 | 434 |
| 1962 | 5.3 | 371 |
| 1963 | 5.7 | 400 |
| 1964 | 6.8 | 475 |
| 1965 | 5.7 | 400 |
| Total | 29.7 | 2,080 |

[a] In millions of U.S. dollars.

China's retained imports, *i.e.*, grain imports less grain exports, are lower than this, since each year there are shipments on Chinese account to other countries, notably Albania. About 80 per cent of these imports of grain have come from the industrial West (Canada, Australia, and France), although other suppliers such as Argentina and Mexico have also been significant. (See Table 15.) China's continued need for large grain imports is demonstrated by a contract signed with Canada in October 1965, which calls for the purchase of 5 million to 12.5 million tons over the next three to five years.

The reasons for China's concern to insure future supplies are not difficult to find. Over the past few years, food production has barely kept up with the growth in population, and domestic production of food may now be as much as 10 per cent below the per capita level of 1957. Thus, China will have to continue importing grain for the foreseeable future, and probably at a gradually increasing rate to say 7 to 8 million tons a year. The Chinese claim they are buying wheat to facilitate the sale of more expensive rice. This trade makes economic sense as the caloric value of wheat per pound is almost equal to a similar amount of milled rice. However, this claim is only partly true as sales of rice in the past few years have averaged about 800,000 tons per year, or only about 14 per cent of average annual grain imports.

As a consequence, agriculture now contributes far less to industrialization than it did in the 1950s. This is shown quite dramatically by the shift in export earnings from food. In 1959, China earned $820 million net from the sale of food abroad; from 1961 to 1965, however, there was an average annual net deficit of about $125 million in food sales. As a result, China's capacity to import capital goods declined sharply; im-

### *Table 15—Communist China: Net Trade in Grain*[a]

| | *1957–58*[b] | *1961–62* | *1962–63* | *1963–64* | *1964–65* | *1965–66*[a] |
|---|---|---|---|---|---|---|
| Retained imports: | | | | | | |
| Canada | | 2.5 | 1.7 | 1.3 | 1.8 | 2.3 |
| Australia | | 2.1 | 2.0 | 2.7 | 2.2 | 1.8 |
| Argentina | | .2 | .3 | 1.2 | .7 | 2.2 |
| France | | .5 | .9 | .3 | .1 | |
| Other | | .7 | .5 | .4 | .5 | |
| Total | | 6.0 | 5.4 | 5.9 | 5.3 | 6.3 |
| Exports | 0.7 | 1.1 | .8 | .9 | .8 | .8 |
| Net trade | —0.7 | +4.9 | +4.6 | +5.0 | +4.5 | +5.5 |

[b] In millions of metric tons.
[c] July 1–June 30.
Tentative figures.

## Table 16—Communist China: Purchase of Whole Plants from Western Europe and Japan, August 1963–December 1965

| *Plant and equipment* | *Country of Origin* | *Value*[a] | *Capacity* | *Date of Contract* | *Remarks* |
|---|---|---|---|---|---|
| Whole Plants: | | | | | |
| Vinylon fiber plant | Japan | 20.0 | 11,000 metric tons per year | August 1963 | Trial production began in September 1965. |
| Urea plant | Netherlands | 6.0 | 175,000 metric tons per year | September 1963 | Scheduled to begin production of fertilizer by October 1966. |
| Synthetic ammonia plant | United Kingdom | 7.0 | 105,000 metric tons per year | October 1963 | This plant is to complement the Dutch urea plant. |
| Petroleum refinery | Italy | 5.0 | 150,000 to 200,000 metric tons per year | December 1963 | |
| Ammonium nitrate plant | Italy | 14.2 | 110,000 metric tons per year | December 1963 | This plant is being built in Albania. The contract includes facilities for the production of ammonia, nitric acid, and ammonium nitrate fertilizer. |
| Synthetic ammonia plant | Italy | 3.6 | Not available | December 1963 | |
| Industrial alcohols plant | France | 3.0 | Not available | January 1964 | |
| Palm oil processing plant | Netherlands | 2.0 | Not available | May 1964 | |
| Crude oil cracking and olefins separation plant. | West Germany | 12.5 | 50,000 metric tons per year | July 1964 | The scheduled startup is mid-1967. |
| Synthetic fiber plant (nylon) | West Germany | 1.5 | Not available | July 1964 | |
| Polyethylene plant | United Kingdom | 12.6 | 24,000 metric tons per year | September 1964 | This plant will use ethylene produced by the olefins separation plant purchased from West Germany. |
| Polypropylene plant | United Kingdom | 7.3 | Not available | November 1964 | Both resin and fiber products will be made from propylene produced by the olefins separation plant. |
| Complete plant for the manufacture of porous silica material. | Sweden | 1.8 | 150,000 cubic meters per year | December 1964 | |
| Acetylene generating plant | Japan | .3 | 1,100 cubic meters per year | May 1964 | This plant is in operation and complements the vinylon fiber plant. |
| Air liquefaction plant | Japan | 1.7 | Not available | September 1964 | This plant was delivered in August 1965. |
| Precision measuring instrument plant | Japan | .8 | Not available | November 1964 | To be delivered by the end of 1966. |
| Oil hydraulic equipment manufacturing plant | Japan | 1.8 | Not available | March 1965 | Construction to be completed in December 1966. |
| Acrylonitrile plant | West Germany | 4.6 | 10,000 metric tons per year | May 1965 | Equipment is to be delivered by mid-1967. |
| Glass plant | West Germany | 3.5 | Not available | Mid-1965 | |
| Polyester resin plant | United Kingdom | .1 | Not available | July 1965 | This plant is scheduled to begin production before the end of 1966. |
| Acrylic fiber plant | United Kingdom | 8.4 | Not available | August 1965 | |
| Condenser manufacturing plant | Japan | 2.0 | 200,000 condensers per year | September 1965 | |
| Air liquefaction plant | West Germany | 3.3 | Not available | August 1965 | |
| Wire drawing plant | Japan | 5.0 | Not available | 1965 | |
| Instrument plant | United Kingdom | 1.0 | Not available | 1965 | |
| Tube-expanding pipe plant | Italy | 3.0 | Not available | 1965 | |
| Straw cellulose plant | Finland | ([b]) | 62.5 metric tons of semichemical cellulose daily. | 1965 | |
| Bleaching plant | Finland | ([b]) | 80 metric tons of bleached sulfur cellulose daily. | 1965 | |
| L–D steel plant | Austria | 12.0 | 650,000 metric tons per year | 1965 | |
| Cold strip steel rolling mill | West Germany | 17.0 | Not available | 1965 | |

[a] In millions of U.S. dollars.
[b] Not available.

ports of machinery and equipment were only $300 million in 1965, compared with almost $1 billion in 1959. China's purchases of a few key plants from the West since mid-1963 have just begun to enter into China's trade returns in 1965, but these orders add up to a little less than one-tenth of the $2 billion spent for grain during 1961–65. The prospects that another $2 billion may have to be committed for grain purchases in 1966–70 must indeed be a sobering thought for the Chinese planners.

*Completed Industrial Installations*—A major feature of Communist China's foreign economic relations since mid-1963 has been the purchase of complete industrial installation from the Free World, financed in part by medium-term credits, and including, in some cases, the services of Western technicians. Contracts for 30 to 40 complete plants from Western Europe and Japan, valued at more than $170 million, have been negotiated since mid-1963. Over half the value of the contracts have been chemical plants, including plants for the production of chemical fibers, chemical fertilizers, plastic materials, and petrochemicals. (See Table 16.) These plants, most of which will not be in operation until 1967–68 or later, will either supply vital products for the Chinese economy or will advance Chinese technical competence in important branches of industry. China is currently negotiating with a West German consortium for a steel-mill complex valued at between $125 and $175 million. If this contract is successfully concluded, it will almost double the value of Free World plants known to have been purchased by China through December, 1965. China also has placed several large orders for other machinery in the past two years, particularly transportation equipment and heavy-duty equipment for construction purposes.

### INDUSTRIAL WEST AND JAPAN

*Industrial West*—Communist China's trade with Japan and the industrial West has grown from about $700 million in 1962 to $1.4 billion in 1965—an annual average growth of roughly 25 per cent. This growth can be accounted for chiefly by grain imports from Canada and Australia, the two main suppliers, and Peking's turn to Japan and Western Europe as its major source of foreign technology. The growth of trade with Japan has been particularly rapid, and in 1964–65 this trade greatly surpassed the earlier peak of $150 million reached in 1956. By 1965 trade with Japan had risen to $470 million, and Japan had replaced the U.S.S.R. as China's No. 1 trading partner. Although China's trade with Western Europe jumped by about 40 per cent in 1965—to $600 million—this level of trade was still slightly less than the 1959 peak of $670 million. The bulk of China's imports from Japan and Western Europe have been machinery and equipment, steel products, and chemical fertilizer.

With the exception of Japan, the countries from which Communist China mainly wishes to import do not offer comparable markets for China's exports. This is particularly true of Canada and Australia with whom China has had an annual average import surplus of close to $300 million during 1961–64. Although China has managed to triple her exports to these two countries over this period, reaching some $35 million in 1964, the scope for additional increases does not appear to be large. China has managed to maintain a small export surplus with Western Europe in 1964 but it remains to be seen whether China can keep pace with a strong upward trend in imports once this is resumed in earnest. Western Europe probably would buy more Chinese agricultural products and industrial raw materials, but does not offer a ready market for low-quality Chinese manufactured products. The Chinese export drive must therefore be concentrated in the growing markets of the less-developed countries, particularly in the large overseas Chinese communities in southeast Asia.

*Japan*—The ability of industrial Japan to complement underdeveloped China is reflected in the rapid increase in recent years of Sino-Japanese trade, which has grown as follows:

### *Communist China: Trade with Japan*[a]

| | *Exports* | *Imports* | *Total* |
|---|---|---|---|
| 1956–58 average | 72.8 | 59.4 | 132.2 |
| 1960 | 20.4 | 2.8 | 23.2 |
| 1961 | 29.0 | 17.0 | 46.0 |
| 1962 | 45.9 | 38.6 | 84.5 |
| 1963 | 74.8 | 62.4 | 137.2 |
| 1964 | 157.9 | 152.9 | 310.8 |
| 1965 | 225.0 | 245.0 | 470.0 |

[a] In millions of U.S. dollars.

Japan is the most important customer for Chinese bulk products such as coal, pig iron, iron ore, salt, coke, soybeans, some perishable foodstuffs, and minerals. In turn, China has been purchasing from Japan an increasing quantity of steel products, chemical fertilizer, chemicals, machinery, synthetic fibers, motor vehicles, earthmoving equipment, and various other manufacturers.

#### THE LESS-DEVELOPED COUNTRIES

Communist China has met only with partial success in fashioning trade as a political weapon to capture the countryside of the world; that is, the less-developed countries of Africa, Asia, and Latin America. Basically, each side has an underdeveloped agricultural economy often producing the same type goods, or suffering from similar scarcities best supplied by more technically advanced and industrialized countries. China's trade with the less-developed countries almost doubled between 1959 and year-end 1965—reaching an estimated level of $825 million, or about 22 per cent of China's total foreign trade in 1965. Over half of that trade was conducted with only five countries: Argentina, Indonesia, Malaysia, the United Arab Republic, and Ceylon. Trade with these countries was of special importance to China's own economy; either for earnings of scarce hard currency as in the case of its lopsided trade with Malaysia (about $100 million in net exports), or for essential commodities as grain from Argentina, rubber from Indonesia and Ceylon, and cotton from the United Arab Republic. With the exception of grain purchases, China has run a trade surplus with the less-developed nations.

#### UNIQUE ROLE OF HONG KONG

The tiny British Crown Colony of Hong Kong inhabited by approximately 4 million Chinese and a small Western community provide Communist China with its most important source of hard currency. Hong Kong serves as China's largest customer while selling only a minimal amount to China as the following figures show:

### *Communist China: Trade with Hong Kong*[a]

| | *1963* | *1964* | *1965* |
|---|---|---|---|
| Exports by China | 259 | 345 | 407 |
| Imports from Hong Kong | 12 | 10 | 13 |
| Export surplus of China | 247 | 335 | 394 |

[a] In millions of U.S. dollars.

With the present level of her trade surplus running about $400 million, China can buy almost all her annual grain imports from the West with earnings from Hong Kong. China faces a leveling off of these earnings, however, as the colony can use only so much food, which is China's primary export to Hong Kong.

Hong Kong depends on Communist China for meat, fruit, and vegetables, dairy products and oil seeds, rice, wheat, and sugar. It also provides a growing market for Chinese textiles, simple machinery, and other manufactured goods.

Hong Kong also serves as an important trading outpost for Communist China. Hong Kong reexports a portion of the foodstuffs, textiles, and other products obtained from China to other southeast Asian countries, Japan, and Europe. This entrepôt trade is believed to have been running close to $90 million annually in the past few years.

The many economic benefits that Peking derives from Hong Kong would be lost or greatly diminished if it were a part of Communist China. Foreign exchange earnings would be sharply reduced because deliveries to Hong Kong for local consumption would be paid for in domestic currency. The ready exchange of non-Bloc currencies would disappear with the loss of British backing, and the loss as a British-sponsored port would bring a sharp reduction in the use of the commercial and financial facilities in Hong Kong by businessmen of non-Bloc countries.

## *Outlook*

The Chinese have claimed that the abrupt ending of Soviet economic assistance, although extremely damaging in the short run, would be to China's ultimate advantage, since it would force China to redouble its efforts to widen its own manufacturing capability and to reduce dependence on imports. This widely proclaimed policy of national self-reliance has not been so restrictive as to have kept China from contracting for complete plants, machinery, and equipment and in some cases even for technicians, from Japan and Western Europe.

There are few sectors of Communist China's industrial economy that would not gain considerably from imports of plant and equipment and production technology; in fact, for the future development of many branches of the chemical, metallurgical, transportation, and machine-building industries such imports appear essential. There are, moreover, various raw materials which China must buy, perhaps in increasing quantities including rubber, cotton, copper, chrome, nickel, cobalt, and special alloy steels. Imports of chemical fertilizers, pesticides, and farm machinery also remain vital and may well maintain their upward trend. Even in the case of petroleum, where the advance toward self-sufficiency has been unusually rapid, some imports of high quality lubricants almost certainly will be needed for some time to come. Last but not least, Chinese imports of grain may well rise gradually over the next few years.

Communist China then has fundamental economic needs for large-scale trade with the outside world during the Third Five-Year Plan (1966–70). The prediction of the future rate of growth of foreign trade, its commodity composition, and its geographical distribution is made doubly hazardous by the current political turmoil in China. The so-called Proletarian Cultural Revolution is in part directed against "foreign" elements that have sneaked into the society. Conceivably the strong xenophobic elements in the political situation could hamper trade; already, foreign businessmen find that trade officials in China are reluctant to make decisions or enter into new agreements. No general policy decision, however, has been made to curtail trade. In any case, the strong unpredicted switches in the volume, composition, and distribution of China's foreign trade in the last six years should serve as an object lesson to those seers who attempt to foretell the future of trade in 1966–70.

Over the next five years—to lay aside these disturbing political elements—the extent to which foreign trade can expand will depend on how successfully the leadership deals with the problems of expanding agricultural and industrial production. Although China has managed over the past five years to make progress in narrow sectors of the economy—including its nuclear weapons program—the country has not regained the economic momentum that marked the 1950s. The economy has never recovered from the dual setback of Leap Forward economic policies and the withdrawal of Soviet economic assistance.

Communist China's foreign trade over the next five years will continue to grow, but will be tied more closely to production capabilities—particularly in agriculture—and thus a slower rate of growth subject to considerable fluctuations can be expected than in 1964–65. The trend toward increased trade with the West is likely to continue. The major growth in exports will still be in agricultural products and textiles although there should be some increase in mineral and metal exports. Imports of Western grain have become a continuing necessity and will require the expenditure of a large share of China's annual hard currency earnings. Thus, grain purchases will continue to restrict the import of capital equipment needed for the expansion of modern industry. Barring the receipt of long-term credits which would help trade expand greatly, or a sustained increase in the export of agricultural products, there is little likelihood that imports of capital equipment will increase sufficiently during the Third Five-Year Plan (1966–70) to make the contribution to industrial development that they made in the 1950s.

VI

# Looking Forward

# Looking Forward

During the past two decades both China and India have made substantial gains in their economic development. The planning mechanism of India has gradually attained a high degree of sophistication and is in a much better position than before to implement the new plans. Economic planning in China has become more and more decentralized and has adjusted to the newly emerged patterns of her economic organization. The industrial bases in both countries are now more diversified and balanced. In both countries agriculture is now offering greater promise than one or two decades ago of providing a better diet for the people. What, then, are the prospects for these two economies in achieving a sustained growth in the decade ahead? The following two papers provide us with some insight into this question.

The article on India, "Looking Ahead," projects the future progress of the economy through a series of Five Year Plans under a number of assumptions. It predicts that the growth rate for national income will accelerate from the annual 5.64 per cent during the Fourth Plan (1966–71) to 6.34 per cent during the Fifth Plan (1971–76) and to the high rate of 9.1 per cent rate for 1976–81. The achievement of the 9.1 per cent rate for 1976–81 truly will represent a breakthrough and must depend a great deal on the attainment of food self-sufficiency and favorable trade balance, the latter through the maturing of machine industries and expansion in new lines of imports. Even with a population growth rate of slightly over 2 per cent until 1971 and a little under 2 per cent in the following decade, the growth rate of per capita income should increase from 3.4 per cent annually during 1966–71 to 7 per cent during 1976–81. Thus in 1981 the national income would be 3.6 times and the per capita income 2.4 times as large as in 1961. In terms of the United States dollar (converted at the foreign exchange rate of 7.50 rupees per dollar), the national income would be around $69.9 billion and the per capita income around $105.5 in 1981. (The 1981 national income in rupees is measured in 1960–61 prices. In terms of the 1960–61 United States dollar, converted at the 1960–61 foreign exchange rate of 4.77 rupees per dollar, the national income will be around $110 billion and the per capita income around $166 in 1981).

To achieve these goals the saving rate is envisaged to increase from 14 per cent of the national income during 1966–71 to 21 per cent during 1976–81. Any gap between the savings funds and the investment outlay will be filled by foreign capital.

Modern factory production in India should attain an annual growth rate of 13 per cent whereas the output in small-scale industry should grow at about 6 per cent between 1961 and 1981. The agriculture sector is expected to improve at a more moderate rate, and foodgrain production is expected to reach a level of 166 million tons by 1981. This will enable India to build up an impressive stock of foodgrains. Growth in agriculture will come mainly from the extensive adoption of double cropping practices, improved irrigation, and greater use of chemical fertilizers and new seeds.

The foreign trade sector is anticipated to have a surplus in trade balance. Because of the great expansion in the output of consumer goods, the absolute level of India's import will decline between 1961 and 1981 while import of intermediate and capital goods will be stepped up considerably.

The achievement of these plans will provide a much higher living standard for the average Indian citizen in 1981 than in 1961. Of course the success of these plans depends on a number of factors. For example, the anticipated increase in production of steel ingots from 3.5 million tons in 1961 to 50 million tons in 1981 will require a very large amount of investment funds. The output for 1968 was estimated at 6.4 million tons.[1] Thus there must be an *average* increase of 3.3 million tons in output per year (as much as one-half of the estimated output in 1968) between 1968 and 1981. In order to reach the 1981 goal of steel output, the steel industry will have to make greater effort in the near future. At the time of writing this article (1962), the promise of the "Green Revolution" did not look as bright as at present. Judging from the developments during the past few years, the goal of 166 million tons of foodgrains in 1981 may materialize. Even though the actual performance of the economy on the whole may fall short of the goal by a considerable margin, India in 1981 will be in a much better position to generate sufficient investment funds for a self-sustained growth in the future.

The article on China first analyzes the newly emerged pattern of economic institutions and policies since the Cultural Revolution. Within the framework of these new economic organizations and policies, Chen assesses the prospects of attaining a growth rate of about 6 per cent for the 1970s. This rate of growth represents the average rate for the period 1950–66 and is close to the rate of growth achieved in 1966—a year prior to the Cultural Revolution. The current saving and investment ratio seems adequate to support such a growth rate provided the incremental-capital-output ratio does not greatly exceed 3.3 during the 1970s. To achieve an annual GNP growth rate of 6 per cent, the foodgrain sector must grow at an annual rate of 2.5 per cent to provide sufficient food, raw materials, and foreign exchange. Judging the performance of agriculture in the past few years and the current expanded efforts the prospect of achieving a growth rate of 2.5 per cent in the foodgrain sector is fairly promising. Chen also assesses the prospects of attaining an annual growth rate of 9 per cent in GNP (which was achieved during the heyday of Chinese economic development, 1950–57). For this growth rate a saving and investment rate at 27 per cent of GNP and a growth rate of 3.5 per cent in foodgrain output would be required. Chen feels this will be difficult to achieve.

**Note to this Part appears on page 397**

Chen's final conclusion is that the Chinese economy may be able to achieve an annual GNP growth rate of 6 per cent or slightly higher during the 1970s. Thus by 1980 the GNP may reach $180 to $190 billion and the per capita GNP around $200. The output of foodgrain may reach 290 to 300 million tons in 1980. The output of modern manufacturing industry may grow at an annual rate of 10 per cent, and the volume of foreign trade may reach $7 to $8 billion in 1980. Despite a substantial improvement in the per capita GNP, the average citizen in China would still be living at a subsistence level in 1980.

It is interesting to note that political stability, agriculture growth, population control, and improvement in technology will all be crucial for the economic development of both India and China. Although these two countries will rank among the ten largest economies in the world, their per capita income will still be among the lowest in the world around 1980–81. With the achievement of their respective economic goals by 1980–81 the two countries will begin to enter the stage of self-sustained economic growth. Only after a few more decades beyond 1980–81 can they hope to approach the living standard already attained by the more affluent countries today.

32

# Looking Ahead

*National Council of Applied Economic Research, New Delhi*

*From* Looking Ahead *(New Delhi: National Council of Applied Economic Research, 1962), pp. 3–25, with omission. Reprinted with permission.*

## *Introduction*

THIS IS AN essay on the shape of the Indian economy as it might be in 1981. It gives certain broad economic and social objectives and indicates possible means to achieve them. It is thus an outline plan of what is desirable and what appears to be feasible under certain assumptions.

The broad purposes of our planning have been often stated both in plan reports and elsewhere. Eradication of mass poverty, substantial improvement in the standard of living of the growing millions, liquidation of illiteracy, provision of fuller employment to all, reduction of inequalities in income and wealth, reduction of regional disparities and similar economic and social purposes are our accepted goals. But these goals cannot be achieved if we restrict our vision only to narrow horizons. Problems which in the short period baffle solution may become easier to manage if our time perspective is sufficiently long. Hence, the need to look ahead and gaze at the somewhat distant horizon and see what effort is involved in the attainment of our national goals.

The object of this paper is primarily to focus attention on planning efforts in terms of mobilization of human and material resources in the most productive way so as to achieve these national goals in the shortest possible time. There are, of course, all sorts of difficulties which the nation will encounter in its march—difficulties from within and those which may emanate from abroad. But these difficulties are not insurmountable and if we are prepared to take the rough with the smooth, in course of time, we should be able to overcome them.

The projections that have been made in this paper are based on fairly reasonable assumptions and highlight the issues involved in transforming the present low-gear economy into a self-sustaining one. No one can claim that these projections, because they have been set forth in specific values and quantities, are certain to be realized. But they would help to bring to our attention the many-sided nature of our goals and the need for simultaneous effort on a number of fronts. They would serve to bring out the need for integration in planned efforts and the necessity to ensure that the demand for and supply of a large variety of materials and equipment match each other at the right time.

While recognizing the limitations necessarily involved in Looking Ahead, it seemed worthwhile to present a paper of this nature to the members of the NCAER and the general public. In taking this decision the object was not so much to set up firm targets, as to lay emphasis on the necessity for having a long term perspective, and to stimulate discussion on vital issues.

## *Progress in the Last Decade*

India is now on the threshold of the Third Five Year Plan. A decade of effort in planned economic development has yielded substantial results; the output of a wide variety of commodities has increased; structure of the economy has become diversified and broad-based; people have more opportunities for productive employment and on an average they have a higher standard of living today than in 1951.

Between 1951–61 India's national income increased by 42 per cent, reaching a level of Rs. 14,500 crores in 1961.[1] Though population increased at the rate of about 2 per cent



Notes to chapter 32 apppear on page 397

per annum, the per capita real income was Rs. 331 in 1961—16.5 per cent higher than in 1951. Net agricultural output as a whole rose by 36 per cent during this period. The output of foodgrains increased by 27 million tons from a level of 52 million tons in 1951.[2] The output of oilseeds, cotton and sugarcane also increased substantially.

More striking has been the progress in industry. Output from industry increased by 60 per cent over the decade.[3] The production of cotton textiles and engineering industries registered substantial increases. At the same time new lines of manufacture have been taken up. In the Second Plan foundations of industrial development were greatly strengthened by the establishment of new basic industries and a rapid expansion of existing key industries such as steel and heavy chemicals. India's capacity for manufacturing machine tools, industrial machinery, boilers, locomotives and wagons, heavy electrical equipment, motor cycles, scooters, bicycles and basic metals like aluminium was also considerably augmented. With these developments, Indian industry was greatly diversified.

Economic overheads, namely, transport and power were extended and strengthened. Railway freight traffic increased from 91.5 million tons to 154 million tons, motorable road mileage from 98,000 miles to 144,000 miles and the number of commercial vehicles rose from 116,000 to 210,000. The installed capacity for power increased two and a half times reaching a level of 5.7 million kW in 1961. However, the supply of transport facilities and power was not wholly adequate to meet the growing demands of the economy. Serious bottlenecks occurred particularly in and around the large industrial and mining areas, hindering the achievement of targets in several industries.

On the whole, progress made over the decade brought about several welcome changes in the structure of the economy. The proportion of agricultural output in the total national income declined from 55 per cent in 1951 to 53 per cent in 1961 and that of mining and manufacturing, increased from 13 per cent to 15 per cent. Productivity per worker (net output per worker) in agriculture increased from Rs. 545 in 1951 to Rs. 645 in 1961, that is, by 18 per cent, and in industry from Rs. 1,016 to Rs. 1,414 or by 41 per cent.

Owing to improved medical facilities the death rate fell sharply from about 27 to 19 per 1,000 and the population multiplied at a compound annual rate of about 2 per cent. This rather high rate of population growth resulted in a large increase in the labor force, from 147 million to 181 million. Larger production in agricultural and non-agricultural sectors resulted in substantial increases in employment opportunities though not on a scale sufficient to reduce the severity of unemployment. Actually, the volume of unemployment at the beginning of the Third Plan, estimated at 9 million, was higher than at the beginning of the decade.

However, during the last decade the structure of employment changed for the better. Agriculture, which engaged 72.5 per cent of the working force in 1951, absorbed 70 per cent in 1961. Though the proportion of industrial working force declined slightly from 9.2 per cent to 8.9 per cent, the services sector compensated by absorbing 21 per cent, as against a little over 18 per cent in 1951. These changes resulted in a higher overall productivity for the Indian economy—Rs. 850 per worker in 1961 compared with Rs. 716 in 1951.

The consumption pattern of the people also showed signs of change for the better. The proportion of expenditure on foodgrains declined and that on cloth and other items increased. In the villages, people looked better fed and clothed, and throughout the decade there was absence of widespread famines or scarcity. There was a general increase in activity; people everywhere were on the move by rail, road and air, more than ever before.

Nevertheless, the growth and structural changes in the economy that came about over the decade 1951–61, were by no means dramatic or radical. The First Five Year Plan did not involve much purposeful, well directed or integrated planning. The Second Five Year Plan on the other hand was conceived of within a more rigid framework of physical planning. But, the foreign exchange crisis of 1957–58, inadequate development of power and coal resources, bottlenecks in railway and road transport and shortages in skilled and technical manpower combined to thwart the achievement of output and income targets.

## *Looking Ahead*

The Third Five Year Plan would however seem to justify the belief that with time, planning in India will deepen and become well-stratified and integrated and the implementation more rigorous. If this happens, then on certain reasonable assumptions, it would be interesting to look ahead, say, over a twenty-year period and consider the structure of the Indian economy, the levels of sectoral development and the growth rates as they would then be. It would also be fruitful to do so, as we could then have a long term perspective of the economy and plan for the achievement of self-sustained growth in the shortest possible time.

The main assumptions and conditions for development on which this Looking Ahead is based are:

1. Land reforms will be implemented during the early years of the Third Plan.
2. Agricultural prices will be stabilized and inflationary pressures held in check.
3. Livestock and forest policies will become development oriented.
4. Fisheries will receive far greater attention than at present.
5. Minerals development policy particularly with regard to iron ore, coal, limestone and manganese will be geared to the short- and long-term requirements of industrial development and export trade, without undue insistence on reserving coal and iron ore mining for the public sector on non-economic considerations.
6. Industrial development policy will be made far more dynamic, and redesigned specifically to foster rapid and well-integrated growth of metallurgical, heavy chemical industries, industrial intermediates, machine-building and engineering industries.
7. The private sector will also have the fullest scope to develop different types of industries to the extent of its capacity, without being restricted as now on mere ideological considerations.
8. Existing transport and power deficiencies will be removed in the next two or three years.
9. Transport and power facilities will be developed ahead of their actual requirements.
10. Educational system will be re-oriented in the shortest possible time so as to create, sufficiently ahead of demand, the requisite supply of technically trained manpower and managerial personnel of different categories.
11. India will continue to have a stable Government and there will be no major world crisis.

On present indications these assumptions seem reasonable. Still, a horizon which extends over twenty years necessarily involves changes which cannot be easily foreseen. Consequently, the targets indicated here are essentially dimensional in character.

## *National and Per Capita Incomes*

If the above conditions obtain, India's national income in real terms could be expected to increase from its 1961 level of Rs. 14,500 crores to Rs. 52,540 crores in 1981, that is, by more than 250 per cent. The compounded annual growth rate of the economy over the span of twenty years will thus be 6.6 per cent. At the end of the Third Plan, national income will reach a level of Rs. 19,000 crores with an annual growth rate of 5.55 per cent. There will be no significant acceleration in the growth rate during the Fourth and Fifth Plans; the national income will rise to Rs. 25,000 crores in 1971 and Rs. 34,000 crores in 1976, at a rate of 5.64 per cent and 6.34 per cent respectively.[4]

By the end of the Fifth Plan, large capacities in basic and heavy industries—steel, heavy forge and foundry, machine-building, sulphuric acid, fertilizers and other heavy chemicals—will have been firmly established. Transport facilities will have been closely integrated to serve as a stimulus to all-round economic growth. The infra-structure will have reached a high level of development and become closely geared to the needs of rapidly growing industry and agriculture.

As a result, by 1976, the Indian economy will have acquired the vigor to go foward at an accelerated rate. The growth rate of national income during the Sixth Plan period (1976–81) will reach a level of about 9 per cent—nearly one and a half times as high as the rate for the Fourth and Fifth Plan periods taken together.

Such a jump in the rate of growth is not impossible. Two vital long term targets will have been achieved by the Sixth Plan: food self-sufficiency and a favorable trade balance, the latter through maturing of machinery industries and expansion in new lines of export. With the marginal propensity to save rising by one per cent every year as before, there will be enough internal resources to make India independent of foreign aid and to achieve a much higher rate of growth. Similar jumps have also occurred in the growth rates of other planned economies when crucial developments have fructified. In Poland, for example, the rate of growth jumped from 12 per cent a year between 1950–56 to 16 per cent between 1956–60. In Russia, the rate of growth which for the past five years has been a little below 7 per cent is expected to go up to over 9 per cent over the next 10 years. Japan provides another example of a country whose rates of growth have been, in the last few years, of the order of 8 to 10 per cent per annum.

The population of India will grow from 438 million in 1961 to 663 million in 1981, at an annual rate of slightly more than 2 per cent until 1971 and a little less than 2 per cent in the subsequent decades. This rapid growth of population will dampen the increase in per capital income. Yet the real per capita income will rise at an annual rate of over 4.4 per cent from its 1961 level of Rs. 331 to Rs. 792 in 1981. Like the national income, per capita income will also increase without much acceleration till 1976. In the Third, Fourth and Fifth Plans it will increase at a rate of 3.23 per cent, 3.37 per cent and 4.25 per cent respectively. During the Sixth Plan, there will be a break through and the per capita income will increase at a rate of 7 per cent—about one and a half times as rapidly as in the preceding years. By 1981 it will be 2.4 times as large as in 1961.

## *Savings*

On reasonable expectations of domestic saving and foreign aid, these growth rates and levels of national and per capita incomes are well within our reach. Considering the growth of national income envisaged by the Planning Commission during the Third, Fourth and Fifth Plans, and on reasonable assumptions about average saving rate and the marginal propensity to save, it would appear that between 1961 and 1981 Indian economy can save about Rs. 99,000 crores and attract some Rs. 6,200 crores of foreign capital aid. The saving-income ratio for the whole period will be 17 per cent. Realization of foreign aid to the tune of Rs. 6,200 crores will, of course, rest on the assumption that there will be no major international crisis, and our relations with the U.S.A., the U.K., the European Economic Community, the U.S.S.R. and the Eastern European countries will become increasingly closer. Aggregate investible resources amounting to Rs. 105,000 crores would be sufficient to raise the per capital income from Rs. 331 in 1961 to Rs. 792 in 1981. This will be the overall position over the entire twenty-year period and will be the outcome of progressively improving economic condition of the country.

Total investment outlay in the Third Plan is estimated at Rs. 11,600 crores, implying a capital-output ratio of 2.3. Considering the nature of developments visualized, this appears to be an underestimate. To achieve the income target set for 1966 it would, therefore, be necessary to provide for a larger quantum of investment. In our view this can be done from domestic resources. According to NCAER estimates, net domestic saving for the Third Plan period would be of the order of Rs. 9,965 crores. With the external aid of Rs. 2,600 crores now planned, the total resources for the Third Plan would come to about Rs. 12,600 crores. This level of investment outlay has been accepted in this paper.

The saving estimate for the Third Plan implies an average saving-income ratio of 11.6 per cent and a marginal propensity to save of the order of 20 per cent. These ratios appear quite realistic against the NCAER estimates of 10 per cent and 20 per cent respectively for the last few years of the Second Plan. Even otherwise, in a planned economy an average saving rate of 11 to 12 per cent, and a marginal rate which implies setting aside some 80 per cent of the incremental income for improving consumption standards, cannot be regarded as unreasonable or overoptimistic.

In the Fourth Plan (1966–71) the financial resources position will be somewhat better. As against the investment requirement of Rs. 18,000 crores, the economy will save some Rs. 15,700 crores, leaving a deficit of Rs. 2,300 crores to be met by foreign capital aid. This will happen despite the fact that in the Fourth Plan the marginal saving rate will have increased to 25 per cent and the average rate to 14 per cent. However, given world peace and amicable relations with the capital supplying countries, foreign aid to the tune of Rs. 2,300 crores can be expected to be forthcoming and the economy will continue to grow according to plan.

Toward the end of the Fifth Plan (1971–76), there will be some relief from these difficulties, and the economy will become more self-reliant. As against the investment requirement of Rs. 27,000 crores, the economy will generate saving of the order of Rs. 25,700 crores, thus reducing the need for foreign aid to a level of Rs. 1,300 crores, compared with Rs. 2,300 crores for the Fourth Plan. This welcome change will be the real turning point in the economic development of the country. The marginal propensity of the economy to save will have then risen to 30 per cent, and the average saving rate to 17 per cent.

It is a fundamental condition for the higher rate of growth in the Sixth Plan that substantial additions to capacity in heavy industries, transport and power are made during the Fourth and Fifth Plans. As these developments, particularly the latter two, are capital-intensive, the capital-output ratio for these plans will be relatively high. It has been assumed that it will be 3 for the ten-year period 1966–76. This assumption, however, does not preclude the possibility that it may be lower in the Fourth and higher in the Fifth.

Somewhere by the middle of the Sixth Plan the Indian economy will have reached the "take-off" point. The entire investment of Rs. 47,800 crores will be financed from domestic savings. It is also anticipated that in 1981 there might be a trade surplus of about Rs. 250 crores and the balance of payments position favorable.

## *Structural Changes*

By 1981, there will be radical changes in the structure of the Indian economy. The share of industrial output[5] in the national income will go up from a meager 15 per cent in 1961 to 33 per cent in 1981, giving industry a status in the country's economy comparable to that obtaining in some of the advanced nations like the U.S.A., the U.K., Canada and Japan. Simultaneously the share of agriculture will decline from a level of 53 per cent in 1961 to a little over 33 per cent in 1981. The tertiary sector, comprising transport, trade, services and construction, will also register a small increase from its current level of 32 per cent to 34 per cent. Employment structure will also change for the better. The proportion of the working force engaged in agricultural activities will decline from 70 per cent at present to nearly 62 per cent, and that in industry increase from 9 per cent to 12 per cent. Transport, trade, services and construction will also account for a higher proportion of employment by 1981—26 per cent as against 21 per cent in 1961.

## *Productivity Changes*

These changes in the structure of output and employment will be accompanied by rising overall as well as sectoral productivity. Per worker productivity of the whole economic system will go up at a compounded rate of 4.3 per cent from a level of Rs. 850 in 1961 to about Rs. 2,000 in 1981. The most marked increase in productivity will be witnessed in industry, where it will rise at a rate of 7 per cent per year, from a level of of Rs. 1,400 in 1961 to Rs. 5,340 in 1981. Structural changes in industry and adoption of modern technology on an increasing scale will be the major factors in raising industrial productivity to a high level. Manpower development on scientific lines will also play an important part in this sector.

In spite of a large movement of agricultural labor to industry and services the working force in agriculture is expected to increase from 120 million in 1961 to 163 million in 1931. But the output from the agricultural sector in the same period would rise to a greater extent, from Rs. 7,680 crores to Rs. 17,310 croes, resulting in a 66 per cent increase in labor productivity over the 1961 level of Rs. 645 or at an annual compounded rate of 2.57 per cent. Because of the existence of underemployment in agriculture, transfer of labor from land to industry and services would no doubt contribute to the rise in labor productivity. But the major share would come from the rise in the productivity of land. Increased use of fertilizers, irrigation, improved cultural practices and extensive adoption of double cropping will raise the productivity of land by about 100 per cent over the 1961 level of Rs. 200 per acre. Labor productivity in the services and construction sector will go up at a higher rate. It will increase at an annual compounded rate of 3.6 per cent, from Rs. 1,300 to Rs. 2,600, or by about 100 per cent.

These rates are not unrealizable in a planned economy, but they presuppose technological improvements at a fairly rapid pace, early establishment of a dynamic infra-structure and substantial advances in social and economic organization through education and institutional developments.

## *Industrial Growth*

A rapid growth of modern industries will bring about major structural changes. In 1981, the net output of industrial sector including mining will be about eight times the level of 1961. This will imply an annual growth rate of 11 per cent. In the initial stages, however, say, till the end of the Fourth Plan, owing to organizational difficulties and long gestation periods for basic and heavy industries, the rate of growth would be much less. But thereafter, industrial development will gather great momentum; the Fifth and Sixth Plans will witness a veritable explosion in industrial growth. The main drive for this development will come from the rapid expansion of modern factory industry. By 1981, net output of this sector will be nearly Rs. 13,000 crores, compared to Rs. 1,100 crores in 1961 or about 12 times. The annual growth rate will be about 13 per cent.

The growth rate of small scale industry will however be more modest—about 6 per cent per annum. But in 1981 this sector will provide employment to about 14 million workers —a little more than the modern large scale industry. Throughout the twenty-year period it will also continue to function as one of the major instruments for ensuring a wider dispersal of industry and as a nursery for cultivating new entrepreneurship.

This dramatic rise in industrial output will be made possible through the achievement of high production goals in a number of key industries. Production of basic metals such as steel and basic chemicals like sulphuric acid will be the kingpin of this growth. Also the development of petro-chemical industries and of substitute materials of all kinds, foreseeable and unforeseeable, will affect the structure of the economy. Steel output will increase by 13 times from its 1961 level of 3.5 million ingot tons to nearly 50 million tons by 1981. This will provide about 33 million tons of finished steel for domestic consumption and about 5 million tons for export. This large increase envisaged for the steel output will require the establishment of several additional steel plants each of 2.5 to 3.5 million tons annual capacity as well as the expansion of existing plants. If the heavy forge and foundry plant, now planned to manufacture equipment for making 5 million tons of steel in a five-year period gets into full production by the end of the Third Plan and another similar unit is established during the Fourth Plan to go into full production in the later stages of the Fourth Plan, it will not be difficult to achieve the steel targets.

The expansion in the steel industry will make possible considerable increase in the output of machinery and tool making industry. It is expected that by 1981 this industry will be nearly 100 times its present size, its net value of output increasing from Rs. 22 crores in 1961 to Rs. 2,200 crores in 1981. Transport equipment industry would be nearly twenty-four times its size in 1961, with its net output going up from Rs. 16 crores to Rs. 385 crores. The volume of electrical equipment produced will also increase by nearly 80 times, the net output increasing from Rs. 120 crores to Rs. 1,000 crores.

Nitrogenous and phosphatic fertilizers will register large increases—27 times and 23 times the present levels of output, the former rising from a level of 125,000 tons (N) to 3.5 million tons (N) by 1981 and the latter from 67,000 tons to 1.6 million tons ($P_2O_5$). Other important industrial chemicals will likewise register high levels of production. Sulphuric acid production will expand by some sixteen times, from a level of 360,000 tons in 1961 to 6 million tons in 1981. Output of caustic soda will be 0.7 million tons—nearly 8 times its 1961 level, and that of soda ash nearly nine times the 1961 output of 140,000 tons. Output of cement, so important for the expansion of construction activity, will increase to a level of 48 million tons—six times the 1961 level, providing an exportable surplus of 8 million tons. These basic developments will foster similar large scale growth in ancillary and related industries with the result that by 1981 the net output of organized manufacturing sector will be some 12 times its size in 1961.

Expansion of major consumer goods industries will be relatively modest, but still enough to bring about a marked improvement in the standard of living of the people. Output of cotton textiles, for instance, will increase by 240 per cent reaching a level of 17,000 million yards. Together with about 2,000 million yards of handloom cloth and other fabrics the total production will be 19,000 million yards. After exporting about 2,000 million yards, this will provide 26 yards of cloth per capita, against the present figure of 16 yards. The output of hydrogenated oil industry will increase 10 times reaching a level of 3.5 million tons in 1981. Sugar industry will expand three-fold reaching a level of 10.5 million tons by 1981. At this level of output and an export of about 1.5 million tons, per capita consumption of sugar will go up by about 85 per cent.

Mining will also develop at a rapid pace to cater both to the raw material requirements of manufacturing industry and an expanding export trade. By 1981 its net output will reach a level of Rs. 1,200 crores, 8 times the 1961 level. Major expansion in this sector will be in iron ore and coal mining, output of the iron ore rising from 10 million tons in 1961 to over 100 million tons by 1981 and that of coal from nearly 53 million tons to over 350 million tons. Production of lignite, bauxite, manganese, copper ore, lead and zinc ores, gypsum, limestone as well as chromite, magnesite, etc., would also register large increases. Iron ore will be the major mineral for export with a target of 40 million tons.

## *Agricultural Development*

Compared to industrial growth agricultural development by 1981 will be modest, but this will not mean any neglect of agriculture. The net output will have increased by about 125 per cent over the 1961 level of Rs. 7,680 crores. Even by 1966, India will be free from dependence on imported foodgrains to meet domestic demand. In fact, by 1981, the anticipated supply would be sufficient to enable the country to build up adequate stocks of about 9 million tons. By then, foodgrains production will have reached a level of 166 million tons. The per capital consumption will have attained the level of about 18 ozs. per day, the accepted nutritional standard, even earlier than 1981. In addition, the supply of agricultural raw materials will be adequate not only to meet the needs of the domestic industry but also to provide reasonable surpluses which can be exported to augment foreign exchange earnings of the country.

The output of oilseeds will increase by more than 200 per cent by 1981 over the 1961 level estimated at 6 million tons; this will result in a 100 per cent increase in oil crushing capacity. The supply projections of edible oils suggest that per capita consumption will increase from 5 lbs. to more than 10 lbs. per annum between the period 1961 and 1981. The supply of oilseeds will leave a surplus of about 1.5 million tons, which can be reckoned as equivalent to about 0.5 million tons of hydrogenated oil for export purposes.

Sugarcane output will go up four-fold increasing sugar and gur production to the same extent. Allowing for an export of about 1.5 million tons of sugar, per capita sugar consumption will increase by about 85 per cent.

Cotton production will go up by 180 per cent, from 4.7 million bales to 13.2 million bales, between 1961 and 1981 and will permit a large expansion of cotton textile industry. Further, about 300,000 to 350,000 bales of cotton will be available for export, although some long staple and superior varieties of cotton will have to be imported to meet the special needs of the industry.

There will be 140 per cent increase in the output of tobacco, reaching by 1981 a level of 720,000 tons. This will enable the country to export about 100,000 tons of tobacco per year. However, the country may still depend on foreign sources for superior varieties which cannot be locally grown, to meet the needs of the domestic cigarette industry.

The output of manufactured tea will stand at 1,000 million lbs, in 1981—54 per cent higher than the current production of about 650 million lbs. After meeting the internal consumption there will be an exportable surplus of about 500 million lbs.

Jute output will increase but the extent of increase will depend more on the internal demand for jute goods rather than export markets. The output of natural rubber will substantially increase, rising from about 24,000 tons in 1961 to about 60,000 tons by 1981. The production of synthetic rubber will also have to be expanded substantially to meet the growing demand. The output of coffee will be doubled and bring about 100 per cent increase in the current level of exports estimated at 20,000 tons reaching roughly a level of 40,000 tons by 1981.

These major goals in agriculture will be reached though a series of developments leading to substantial increase in gross area sown as well as higher yield per acre. The net area sown will increase only by 5 per cent, *i.e.*, from 322 million acres in 1961 to 338 million acres by 1981. However, the gross area sown which stood at 380 million acres in 1961, will increase by about 36 per cent by 1981 on account of extensive adoption of double cropping practices. Of much greater importance will be the large increase in gross irrigated area which will be up by 240 per cent from about 79 million acres in 1961 to 235 million acres by 1981, bringing the proportion of irrigated areas to total cropped area to about 45 per cent as compared with 21 per cent in 1961.

The area under cash crops will increase from 94 million acres to 125 million acres by 1981. Its proportion to the gross sown area will, however, remain more or less unchanged at about 25 per cent.

Despite these developments a major part of the increase in crop yields as well as output will come through increased application of fertilizers and manures. By 1981, 3.5 million tons (N) of nitrogenous, 1.6 million tons ($P_2O_5$) of phosphatic, and about 900,000 tons ($K_2O$) of potassic fertilizers will be used as compared to the existing levels of 230,000 tons, 48,000 tons and 26,000 tons respectively. In addition, there will be a substantial increase in the use of green and other organic manures.

New developments envisaged for the creation of irrigation potential, substantial increase in the supply of chemical fertilizers and increased production of organic manures will be accompanied by commensurate improvements in other directions. These measures constitute increased transport facilities especially in rural areas, extension of regulated markets to all areas, stabilization of agricultural prices, adequate expansion of sources for rural credit and some measures of mechanization of agriculture especially in regions such as eastern Madhya Pradesh and Rajasthan where labor is likely to be in short supply.

It is expected that by 1981 breeding programs currently in operation will have upgraded the quality of Indian cattle significantly. The problem of excessive pressure of livestock population may, however, continue to be a serious hindrance in the way of proper planning for livestock development.

On the basis of past trends it can be expected that production of milk and its products, poultry products, hides and skins and other animal by-products, will be roughly doubled by 1981. While this increase is not substantial, considering the present level of production and the potential, the principal achievement of the period will be the introduction of schemes on an organized basis for the development of livestock industry on scientific and commercial lines.

The present trend in gearing silviculture to the requirements of industry will have spread to most of the areas in the country by 1981. Introduction of fast maturing species, planned afforestation programs and improvements in felling and logging techniques, which would be the core of this change, would have begun to yield substantial results. It is expected that these developments would bring about a 100 per cent increase in forest produce by 1981.

In the coming two decades the vast fishery resources of the country will receive progressively greater attention. Modern pisciculture practices, including mechanization of coastal fishing already introduced, will spread on a much wider scale. Commensurate cold storage and refrigerated transport facilities necessary for marketing fish on a large scale will also be developed. As a result it is expected that fish output by 1981 will be twice as large as in 1961.

## *Energy Development*

Rapid developments contemplated in the different sectors of the economy will depend upon a sharp increase in the supply of all forms of energy and especially electricity.

The non-commercial sources[6] of energy cannot be expected to increase their share in meeting the rising demand for energy. In fact their use should be restricted as far as possible, for, already they impose a heavy strain on the country's natural resources. A rapid switch over to commercial forms of energy[7] is, therefore, desirable and necessary. Further, energy-intensive industries like iron and steel, aluminum, cement, fertilizers and chemicals are expected to register a rapid growth. All these factors enhance the need for large scale, comprehensive and co-ordinated development of commercial sources of energy.

The overall requirement of commercial energy in 1981 is estimated at about 465 to 470 million tons of coal equivalent or about 3,300 billion kWh of electricity equivalent[8] Of this, the known resources of hydro-electricity when fully harnessed, can contribute energy equal only to 25 million tons of coal equivalent, that is, 180 billion kWh. The remainder will have to be shared by coal, petroleum products and nuclear power as shown below:

| | *Electricity equivalent (million kWh)* | *Coal equivalent (million tons)* |
|---|---|---|
| Hydro power | 180 | 25.0 |
| Coal | 2,450 | 350.0 |
| Petroleum products | 630 | 90.0 |
| Nuclear power | 20 | 3.0 |
| Total | 3,280 | 468.0 |

Nearly three-fourths of the energy consumed in 1981 will be derived from coal. This will necessarily put a heavy pressure on the country's coal resources. Fortunately, recent technological advances enable the use of low grade coal for power generation by having pithead stations with large generating sets operating at high thermal efficiencies. As there are very large resources of low grade coal in the country the achievement of energy target based on coal should be feasible.

An all-India super grid may be expected to materialize well before 1981. This will facilitate transfer of electric power over large distances and make it possible to increase utilization of the installed capacity to about 5,500 kWh per kW from the current level of 4,000 kWh. Based on this factor, the installed capacity for power in 1981 will have to be nearly 75 million kW against 5.7 million kW in 1961. Of this, 32 million kW will be hydro (43 per cent), 40 million kW thermal (53 per cent) and about 3 million kW nuclear (4 per cent).

Increase of this order in installed capacity for electric power and other energy requirements would call for considerable efforts in other fields. Roughly, 110 million tons of coal would have to be mined and a large refining capacity for crude petroleum has to be established for other forms of energy for power generation. In addition, coordinated developments of transport facilities and machinery manufacture will also have to take place.

Experience of the first decade of planned development in our country has shown clearly that serious bottlenecks can arise in case energy supplies are not kept ahead of the demand. Efforts must therefore be made from the start to ensure that energy supplies always outpace the maturing of demand.

## *Transport Development*

Like power, the development of transport facilities should not only match industrial and agricultural growth but keep well ahead of all the emerging requirements. By 1981, the output of industrial and agricultural commodities will have increased by over 250 per cent of their 1961 level. On top of this, increasing monetization in agriculture and the relatively rapid growth of distributive trade will require additional transport. From the transportation point of view a substantially greater freight carrying capacity will need to be created. In concrete terms, the capacity of the transportation system will have to be expanded by about 500 per cent over the twenty-year period. An increase of this magnitude will call for proper planning, development and coordination of all forms of transport—rail, road, river, coastal shipping, air and pipeline.

The importance of coordinated and integrated planning of the transport system is being recognized more than ever before and the expectations are that appropriate action will be taken to implement such planning as early as possible so as to make for the development of adequate and efficient transport capacity. Between 1961 and 1981 the net freight ton mileage will increase from about 70,000 million to 420,000 million, that is, by about 500 per cent. Over the same period medium and long distance road traffic register an increase of 1,900 per cent and coastal shipping of some 1,000 per cent. The volume of traffic that railways and road transport (feeder and local) may be handling by 1981 would be 400 to 500 per cent higher than in 1961. These increases will have the effect of reducing the share of rail traffic from about 79 per cent in 1961 to about 70 per cent in 1981. The balance of 30 per cent will be moved by other forms of transport.

The share of local traffic on road will remain about the same in 1981 as in 1961.[9] However, the proportion of the tonnage moved by road feeder services linked with the railways is expected to come down. The share of medium and long distance traffic may increase from 1.5 per cent to 3.1 per cent. Slight variations in shares of coastal shipping and inland waterways would also occur. One new factor which will have entered the scene by 1981 is the network of pipelines which are expected to handle the bulk of long distance distribution of oil.

The passenger traffic by rail and bus services, amounting to 2.62 billion in 1961 may be expected to go up to 9.9 billion by 1981, a little less than four times. The demand for urban transport will require special consideration and calls for extension of suburban electrified services to the existing network as well as to a number of additional towns. Passenger mileage on rail transportation may be expected to increase from 49 billion at present to about 125 billion by 1981, an increase of about two and a quarter times. As against this, the number of passengers travelling by rail is likely to be about twice the present figure.

As a result of the extension of the network of roads to all the rural areas, quick, efficient and cheap modern transport will bring about an increase from about 1 billion bus passengers in 1961 to about 7 billion by 1981.

In view of the rapid strides made by domestic air transport in recent years, it is expected that the number of passengers travelling by air will increase from 800,000 in 1961 to somewhere between 8 to 10 million by 1981.

In order to cope with these large increases in traffic, the railway route and track mileage will have extended from 35,000 and 50,000 in 1961 to 50,000 and 80,000 respectively by 1981.[10] The mileage of National Highways likewise will go up from 15,000 to 32,000 by 1981. The mileage of other roads will increase from 380,000 to 630,000 by 1981. These developments are already visualized in the Chief Engineers' Plan and the expectation is that a properly phased and well integrated program of transport development will be undertaken in each of the Plans from the Third Plan onward. Port development and coastal shipping programs will also keep in step with expanding coastal traffic.

Moreover, there would be certain important changes having the effect of substantially enhancing the general efficiency of the national transportation system. Electric and diesel traction will replace steam traction on main lines. The entire railway system will be geared to operate at much higher speeds. The average speed of all passenger trains will have been considerably accelerated and of goods trains doubled. The necessary technological improvements, such as, improved signalling, centralized traffic control, automated classification in yards, adoption of larger capacity stock, use of light-weight material for construction of rolling stock, and progressive reduction in the tare ratio, will have been introduced.

Trailer's on flat cars, called piggy-backs, are expected to come into general use and thus achieve effective operational coordination between rail and road services.

It is expected that the present obstacles to efficient operation of road transport, such as inadequate bridging, lack of by-passes, etc., would all have been eliminated. Similarly it is also expected that between 1961 and 1981, improvements of ports and port facilities, canals and inland waterways, and the air ports commensurate with the traffic increases indicated will all have been carried out.

By 1981, one of the major changes brought about in rural economy, through transport development, will be that no village will be more than one and a half miles away from a feeder road and four to five miles from a metalled road.

## *Manpower Development*

Concentration on material capital formation without commensurate investment in manpower cannot bring about the acceleration in economic growth aimed at by most developing countries. From the very outset, therefore, human resource development in India will demand far greater attention than hitherto accorded to it. To this end, several strategically planned lines of advance are necessary.

First of these is the creation of sufficient job opportunities to employ all those who offer their services in the labor market. No manpower development can be conceived of without a simultaneous increase in the scope of employment. By 1981, this objective will be adequately met and unemployment will cease to exist as a problem; some frictional unemployment of the order of one to two per cent or so of the labor force may, of course, persist due to seasonal and other factors. While in the country as a whole, the number of jobs created will be sufficient for the labor force, it is possible that workers from rural areas may not move to the non-agricultural sector on the scale visualized. To start with, distribution of the increase in non-agricultural activity may not match region-wise the distribution of increase in labor force. This discrepancy will be accentuated by the fact that industrial development is likely to take place in a relatively few concentrations. Such factors as cost of migration, social attitudes, and lack of training may also inhibit the movement of people on the requisite scale. Further, if agricultural output increases at the rate anticipated, the output per worker and hence average real income in rural areas will increase. This may dampen an important force which leads people to migrate from rural areas. On balance, it is possible that while in areas such as Kerala, Uttar Pradesh, Madras and West Bengal, there may be a regional surplus of labor toward the end of 1981, in other areas such as Madhya Pradesh and Rajasthan there may be a shortage of labor.

The structure of employment will improve significantly. About 62 per cent of the working population will be engaged in agriculture as against 70 per cent in 1961. Both industry and services (including construction) will register gains in their shares: industry from 9 per cent to 12 per cent and services from 21 per cent to 26 per cent.

Some degree of underemployment may, however, still persist. While it is difficult to quantify it, there is no doubt that it will be considerably lower by 1981. In all sectors labor will be markedly more productive in 1981 than in 1961. In agriculture where underemployment primarily exists, productivity will rise by 66 per cent. As this increase will come about mainly through intensive cultivation techniques without any marked increase in the application of labor saving devices, the intensity of employment will rise.

New employment opportunities will be increasingly more for persons having skills of different categories. Growth of industries, transport, power, agriculture, education and medical and public health services will require a large number of engineers, managerial personnel, supervisors, teachers, extension workers, skilled and semi-skilled workers, doctors, compounders, nurses, etc.

Though it is difficult at present to make a projection of all the categories of trained personnel for the next 20 years, the order of magnitude for the more important categories are indicated below:

| *Category* | *Availability (1961)* | *Requirement (1981)* |
|---|---|---|
| Graduate engineers | 58,000 | 600,000 |
| Diploma holders | 90,000 | 1,000,000 |
| Craftsmen | 1,500,000 | 16,000,000 |
| Doctors | 80,000 | 220,000 |
| Teachers | 1,260,000 | 4,200,000 |
| Agriculture and veterinary, etc. | 24,000 | 190,000 |

In each of these categories there will be an enormous increase. The requirement of engineers and craftsmen will be ten times more than the availability in 1961, diploma holders ten times, doctors three times, teachers three times and trained workers in agriculture, veterinary, etc., eight times. Comparable increases would also occur for other trained personnel such as nurses, compounders, etc.

For the level of industrial activity anticipated here for the next twenty years research effort will have to grow manifold. On a rough estimate about 260,000 scientists in various fields would be required in 1981 for this purpose. Similarly, a very much larger pool of managerial personnel, well trained both at the university level and in apprenticeship programs, will be needed. Even allowing for the fact that on the whole there will be consolidation of units of production as well as an increase in general efficiency, the requirement of managerial personnel may well be of the order of 500,000.

To make sure that these requirements are met by 1981, requisite training facilities tailored to the needs of planned economic growth will have to be provided before the end of the Fifth Plan. This will be an enormous undertaking. The intake capacity for engineers, for example, will have to expand eight to ten-fold over a period of fifteen years. Even on the average, this will involve about 3,000 additional admissions every year. In fact, the annual increase in admissions in the Fifth Plan will be considerably higher as the increase in requirements in absolute terms will be much larger as we move from Plan to Plan.

Projections for the requirements of skilled

manpower are generally made by assuming certain changes in the structure of industry and the levels of techniques employed. As development proceeds, variations from these assumptions often occur. If the system of training is rigid, short term adjustments to suit the needs of industry cannot be made. It will, therefore, be necessary to design training programs in such a way that alterations in the supply of different categories of trainees can be made over a relatively short period. This might involve shorter periods of training with broad-based course and partial specialization, leaving the final stages of specialization to be provided through apprenticeship programs.

For lower levels of skill a large network of craftsmen training centers will need to be created. In addition, compulsory apprenticeship programs and expansion of in-plant training schemes would also be necessary. These training facilities would have to be widely spread in the country, for, it is through them that a large section of the rural manpower will shift into non-agricultural occupations. Unless these facilities are available in time, regional as well as rural urban mobility may be impeded, giving rise to regional shortages in this category of skilled workers.

In addition to the increase in the number of exclusively technical training institutions extension as well as improvement in general education will also have to take place. Free primary education will become universal by the end of the Fourth Plan. By the end of the Fifth Plan nearly all children between the ages of eleven to fourteen will also receive free education. Even at this stage curricula will have acquired a much greater vocational bias than at present.

At the secondary stage, however, the object of education will be more specifically directed toward preparation of students for professional careers. At this stage educational programs at every level will be guided by the needs of the economy. Broadly speaking, this will mean that about half the students would receive instruction in technical and scientific subjects as well as commerce and business administration, a quarter towards the teaching profession and the remaining quarter in liberal arts.

Not all students passing the secondary stage need enter the higher secondary or university stage. On a rough estimate about half or a little less would go into trade schools in various fields such as crafts, nursing, agriculture, public health, veterinary, etc. The rest would go into higher secondary schools. Again about half of those who get through this stage would enter productive careers and only the remaining qualify for university education. The university selection as well as immediate requirements of the economy would determine how many should take courses leading up to supervisory careers and how many prepare for higher levels of technological training. Similar procedures would also determine the numbers to enter the fields of science, commerce or liberal arts. For the former a further division will have to be made between those who will devote themselves exclusively for research and those preparing for the teaching professions. In each case the nature of courses provided by universities would be different. On the whole research orientation of universities will have become much more marked.

Besides education, development of manpower also involves improvement in the physical capacity of the population to work. At present the general health of the working class is palpably impaired by poor diet, insanitary living conditions and inadequate precautionary and curative medical service. Improvements in health in these circumstances would undoubtedly contribute to the productivity of the workers as they become more capable of standing sustained work at higher levels of efficiency. It is expected that by 1981 significant improvements in the diet of the people would take place both in the way of increased quantity and more balanced intake of nutrients. However, this by itself is not sufficient; substantial development of medical, public health and sanitation facilities is also necessary. It is expected that significant improvements in these fields would take place by 1981.

## *Foreign Trade and Balance of Payments*

With growing output, India's total foreign trade will expand by 1981 and there will be a surplus trade balance. The direction as well as the pattern of imports and exports will have materially altered. It is, however, expected that the volume of trade as proportion of the national income may be smaller.

In 1961, India's imports totalled Rs. 1,070 crores, of which about 30 per cent represented capital goods, 47 per cent intermediates and 23 per cent consumer goods. By 1981, India will be producing a large variety of capital goods now being imported. However, it is likely that equipment for some of the new steel plants, components for the machinery already installed, certain industrial materials and petroleum and its products may still have to be imported. Till the end of the Fourth Plan imports would increase and may well reach a level of Rs. 1,500 crores a year.[11] It is only in the Fifth Plan that indigenous production of capital goods and intermediates will begin to replace some of the imports of traditional items. But this will be more than offset by the greater need for imports of new items, such as equipment for atomic power stations, petro-chemical industries, etc., inevitable in a growing economy. On balance, it is likely that the aggregate imports by 1981 may well stabilize at a level of Rs. 1,500 to Rs. 1,600 crores a year—about 3 per cent of the national income, compared to 7 per cent in 1961.

The pattern of imports by 1981 compared with 1961 may be as given below:

| | *1960–61* | | *1980–81* | |
|---|---|---|---|---|
| *Category of goods* | *Rs. crores* | *Percentages* | *Rs. crores* | *Percentages* |
| Capital goods | 327 | 30 | 600 | 37.5 |
| Intermediates | 503 | 47 | 800 | 50 |
| Consumer goods | 240[a] | 23 | 200 | 12.5 |
| Total | 1,070 | 100 | 1,600 | 100 |

[a] Of this at present more than Rs. 140 crores are food imports which will cease. Rs. 200 crores which is the figure for 1980–81 will therefore provide a reasonable margin for other imports.

On the other hand, by 1981, India's exports might well be about three times the 1961 level of Rs. 643 crores. The main items in the future export trade of India will be 5 million tons of finished steel (Rs. 400 crores), 1 million tons of jute goods (Rs. 170 crores), 1,500 million yards of cloth (Rs. 150 crores), 0.5 million tons of hydrogenated vegetable oil (Rs. 75 crores), 1.5 million tons of sugar (Rs. 60 crores), 250,000 tons of tea (Rs. 150 crores), 8 million tons of cement (Rs. 80 crores), 2 million bicycles (Rs. 24 crores), 85,000 tons of tobacco (Rs. 25 crores), 40 million tons of iron ore (Rs. 200 crores), and other items like electric fans, bulbs, household electrical equipment, sewing machines, etc. In addition it may also be possible to export aluminum, heavy chemicals and paper. All told a level of exports of Rs. 1,800 crores will be well within the reach, by 1981.[12]

On this basis, by then, there would be an export surplus to the tune of Rs. 200 to 300 crores, and the total volume of trade would be Rs. 3,300 to 3,400 crores, *i.e.*, nearly 6 per cent of the national income in 1981 estimated at Rs. 52,500 crores, as against about 12 per cent in 1961. The pattern of export trade will have significantly altered in the sense that by 1981, India will be exporting large quantities of commodities like steel, machinery, cement, bicycles, electrical goods, etc., which were so far imported. Some of these items might continue to be imported till the end of the Fifth Plan, though with a declining trend.

In 1961, nearly 65 per cent of India's imports came from four countries, 27 per cent from the U.S.A., 20 per cent from the U.K., about 12 per cent from West Germany and 6 per cent from Japan. By 1981, there will, however, be some change in the direction of import trade. India's imports from the U.S.A. will probably be Rs. 400 crores, about 50 per cent more than the 1961 level of Rs. 270 crores, but the share of the U.S.A. in India's import trade will be somewhat smaller. The pattern will be rather weighted towards new types of capital goods, and consumer durables and superior quality consumer goods. This will come about through relaxation of import controls on these goods, as the economy reaches the self-sustaining stage. Imports from the U.K. amounting to Rs. 200 crores in 1961 will probably increase by 50 per cent to Rs. 300 crores, but their share in the total will remain at the 1961 level—20 per cent. Imports from other European Common Market countries may also increase by 50 per cent and reach a level of Rs. 250 crores by 1981. The quantum as well as the share of imports from the U.S.S.R. and the Eastern European countries will increase from Rs. 33 crores or 3.8 per cent in 1961 to nearly Rs. 150 crores or 10 per cent. Imports from Japan may more than double and reach a level of Rs. 150 crores. Despite development of oil resources and agricultural production in India, traditional imports from the Middle East and other Asian and African countries will increase. In addition, there will be sizable imports of copper, lead, zinc, tin, etc. from African and Asian countries. Imports from these areas will, therefore, go up to about Rs. 300 crores, but their share may go down to 20 per cent.

During the Third and Fourth Plans there will be some difficulties in the way of expanding the export trade, and the increases in volume of exports will be gradual. But thereafter it will go up at a rapid rate and by 1981 the volume of exports will be nearly three times that in 1961.

As the volume of exports increases from a level of Rs. 640 crores to Rs. 1,800 crores by 1981, the direction of export trade will undergo a change. The U.K., which now takes about 27 per cent of India's exports, may account for about 20 per cent of exports in 1981. However, this will mean nearly doubling the volume of exports to the U.K. With the reduction of tariffs, the U.S.A. also may be expected to absorb about twice the present volume of exports estimated at Rs. 100 crores. However, even with this increase the share of the U.S.A. in India's export trade may decline from 16 per cent at present to 10 per cent by 1981. The share of Japan may increase to a level of 10 per cent. The share of African countries and Asian countries excluding Japan, and the Middle Eastern nations may also go up to 15 per cent each from the existing levels of 4 to 5 per cent. The share of the U.S.S.R. may also double itself and reach a level of 8 per cent, and that of the Eastern European countries increase to a level of 5 per cent from the negligible proportion obtaining in 1961. ECM countries (excluding the U.K.) will probably maintain their present share of 10 per cent, but this would mean doubling the volume of export to these countries by 1981. Australia and New Zealand will also be in a similar position, maintaining their current shares of about 4 per cent in India's exports.

The balance of payments which now shows a deficit may be expected to turn into a surplus by 1981. This will, however, occur only by about the middle of the Sixth Plan. Till the Fourth Plan the volume of imports will be rising, as India will still be dependent on foreign countries for certain capital goods, intermediates and petroleum. Exports during this period may show some increase, but the rate of increase will be quite small. Consequently the adverse balance of payments which stood at Rs. 365 crores in 1961 may worsen. This trend will be reversed during the Fifth Plan and a period in which exports will expand while imports remain stable, will follow. By 1981 exports will be 180 per cent higher and imports only 50 per cent resulting in a trade surplus of the order of Rs. 250 crores. In the invisibles while the receipts and payments on such items as insurance, travel, freight, etc., are likely to be of the same order the net outflow on account of investment income (interest payment on loans and returns on foreign private investment) will be sizable and may well wipe off the trade surplus. On the capital side foreign private capital will continue to flow into the country and together with the reinvestment of part of the returns on existing foreign private investment is likely to set off the normal loan repayment obligations of the country. In such a situation there will be no balance of payments problem.

## *Standard of Living*

By 1981, substantial gains will be made in the living standards of the people. The per capita income will go up from Rs. 331 to Rs. 792, by 140 per cent—resulting in an increase in both savings and consumption. The average rate of saving will rise progressively from 10 per cent in 1961 to 21 per cent in the Sixth Plan and marginal rate from 20 per cent to 35 per cent. Per capital consumption expenditure will go up from about Rs. 300 to over Rs. 600 between 1961 and 1981[13] and the altered distribution of income will be reflected in the pattern of consumer expenditure.

Consumption of essential articles will increase as shown below:

### *Per Capita Consumption*

| *Articles* | *1961* | *1981* | *Percentage Increase* |
|---|---|---|---|
| 1. Foodgrains | 15.60 ozs. per day | 18.00 ozs. per day | 15 |
| 2. Edible oils | 0.22 | 0.44 | 100 |
| 3. Milk and milk products (in milk equivalent) | 4.70 | 10.00 | 112 |
| 4. Sugar | 0.590 | 1.10 | 85 |
| 5. Tobacco | 0.0630 | 0.085 | 35 |
| 6. Cotton cloth[a] | 16.20 yds. per annum | 26.00 yds. per annum | 62 |

[a] Includes handloom cloth and other fabrics. Comparable figures for other countries are: U.S.A. 50 yds., Japan 35 yds., U.S.S.R. 31 yds.

These increases will represent not only an absolute gain in each item but also an improvement in the pattern of consumption. Protective and energy giving foods will constitute a much more important part of the daily diet of the average Indian than at present. Improvement in the health of the worker brought about by this change will strongly influence the increase in his productivity.

Availability of durable consumer goods in India is still extremely low as compared with some of the advanced countries. At present perhaps one out of 300 persons in India has a radio set, one in 20,000 a car, or a jeep, one in 500 has a sewing machine, one in 100 a bicycle, and one in 200 an electric fan. By 1981, the per capita availability of these and other durables will increase several-fold. For radio sets and cars, it will be several times more than at present level. On an average by 1981 there will be a bicycle for every second family and an electric fan for every family. A reasonably large supply of refrigerators, air conditioners, washing machines, electric cooking ranges, etc., will also be on the market, at prices which the urban middle class can afford.

Despite these improvements in the standard of living, the consumption level of an average Indian will be far below that of an average American, Englishman, Russian, Japanese, and for that matter an average European or Latin American. For instance, when one Indian in forty will have a radio set by 1981, in America, there are 4 sets for every 5 persons, even now. In England this ratio would be about half. When we in India may have a car for every 700 of population, there may be more than one car for every family in the U.S.A. and the U.K.

However, apart from the higher level of average consumption, by 1981 there will be a more equitable distribution of incomes and a definite uplifting of the consumption levels and improvement in the consumption pattern of the people in the lower income brackets in urban and rural areas. They will be better fed, clothed and housed. Their children will be having the benefit of education at all levels. Modern medical care would be available to all. A national social insurance scheme will be in operation. Most of the villages will be electrified; and industries will have spread to larger rural areas; and while extent of urbanization will be much more than at present, dispersal of industries will have prevented undue concentration in metropolitan areas and carried the benefits of modern science and technology to much wider areas in the countryside.

## *Rationale of the Approach*

An attempt has been made in this paper to project the growth of the economy over a period of next twenty years on the basis of assumptions indicated in the beginning. These assumptions are by no means unrealistic. Nevertheless, the projections are open to criticism that they are at best speculative exercises, and there may occur many changes which might alter the entire picture. The longer the time span over which targets are projected and forecasts made, the greater the chances of uncertainty and the possibility of events turning out differently. To look very far ahead might involve the risk of ignoring the possibility of a very radical change in the pattern of the economy due to unforeseen technical and social innovations. There are many factors which might upset one's calculations.

Admitting, however, all limitations of Looking Ahead for several years, one should also recognize not only the usefulness of such projections, but perhaps the inevitability of some of the targets which have to be achieved. Given the fact that our population will increase from its present level to as much as 663 million in 1981 and given also the assumption that our objective should be to raise the level of living by at least 4 to 5 per cent per annum per capita, certain implications inevitably follow. The additional population has to be fed, clothed, housed, educated and provided with medical, sanitary and other amenities. The additional labor force has to be found useful opportunities of employment. These inevitably mean increased production of food, increased manufacture of textile and other consumer goods, increased supply of building materials, all of which in turn mean corresponding inputs of various kinds of seed, fertilizer, water and technology for increased agricultural production; inputs of bricks, cement and steel for building, increased supply of trained manpower and of scientists and technologists. A number of consequences in terms of increased production of material goods and expansion of skills will follow. It is not, therefore, correct to think that the projections which have been presented in the previous pages are just a play of mind. On the contrary most of the targets that have been indicated in the previous pages more or less fix themselves. The degree of maneuverability is not even as much as one might think. Many things are a "must" and failure to achieve production of the order of magnitude indicated in the previous pages would result in seriously undermining the economy. The targets set, therefore, are necessary. But are they feasible and consistent? In our view, they are. India's resources in material and human terms are by no means insignificant. It is more a question of organization and administration of investment in man and the upgrading of the skills of the people, of a proper manpower planning and, above all, of a determination and will to achieve. Given Government's determination to develop and given the right kind of attitudes and values among the people, the rate of growth envisaged in this paper is not beyond our capacity. Even if the goals are achieved, India would remain a relatively poor nation whose per capital income would be only about 150 U.S. dollars and far below that of most of the countries of the world, including some Asian countries.

Very much will depend upon the patterns of investment and adjustments to accelerated growth of Indian economy. It is investment in education and training, in other words, investment in man which is crucial. It has been pointed out that for the U.K. capital and labor inputs accounted for only one-fourth of the increased output per head in manufacturing industry between 1948 and 1954. The residual factors accounted for as much as three-fourths and among those education and basic science appeared to play the predominant role. A country's human capital is not only its physical labor force but also knowledge and skills which should grow at a faster rate than the rate of growth of national product.

It is, therefore, clear that the growth rate of a country has at least as much bearing upon the development of human resources and the building up of people and institutions, as upon the accumulation of material capital. Our investment program should, therefore, be well balanced and adequate to meet the requirements of accelerated growth.

33

# Prospects for the Chinese Economy

*Kuan-I Chen*

TO EVALUATE THE prospects for future growth in the Chinese economy, we must first analyze the basic changes which have occurred in the economy and in economic policy during the past twenty years. We can then deduce from the substances of these changes the more probable direction of Chinese economic policy for the coming decade and the prospects for the economy under such direction.

## *Changes in Economic Organization and Policy*

Looking back at the past two decades one can discern several phases of changes. During the first phase, 1949–57, the development of industry followed the Soviet model of emphasizing heavy industries. The sources of growth in agricultural output mainly came from the more intensive use of traditional methods of production such as flood control, minor irrigation of traditional type, fuller use of double cropping, farm manure, and the like. Nationalization of industries and collectivation of agriculture (converting small private farms into collective farms prior to the introduction of the commune in 1958–59) were virtually completed. Despite some disruptive effects resulting from such rapid changes in economic organization the GNP manage to increase at an annual rate of about 9.0 per cent for the period, 1950–57.[1]

The second phase, 1958–66, started with the experiment of "big push" strategy, the Great Leap Forward. When the new communes rapidly came into existence during the Great Leap, 1958–59, garden plots and livestock were confiscated and rural free markets largely abolished; the household was no more considered as the basic unit of society. The excesses of the commune system brought significantly greater disruptive effects to the economy than the reorganization of institutions during 1949–57. In addition to such disruptive effects, expedients such as the backyard furnace, deep plowing, and so on combined with overemphasis on heavy industry, the withdrawal of Russian experts in 1960, and successive years of poor weather caused the Great Leap to end in deep economic crisis. This fiasco, however, did pave the way for a number of important changes in economic policy and rural organization. These changes have long-range significance to economic and technical development in China.

The new policy in 1961–62 gave priority to agriculture and consumer goods industries, particularly those turning out goods for peasant consumption. Heavy industries were geared to support these two sectors. The sources of recovery and new growth in agriculture after 1962 came increasingly from greater use of modern technology such as electrification, extension of irrigation and improvement of its effectiveness, chemical fertilizers, mechanization, and improved seeds. The commune system was greatly modified to provide more incentives for the peasants. Economic planning was further decentralized.

In response to the withdrawal of Russian technical experts in 1960 a policy of self-reliance in technology was seriously pursued; applied industrial and agricultural research was greatly encouraged. Thus the result was a rising level of diversification and self-sufficiency in industrial products, especially machinery and equipment, in recent years.

Prior to 1950 China's technical level was as a whole several decades behind that of Japan. According to a study made by the Japanese Ministry of Foreign Affairs, the Chinese technical level in 1965 was fifteen years behind Japan in machine tools and irons and steel, ten years in hydraulic machines and chemical industry, and twenty



Notes to chapter 33 appear on pages 397-398

years in automation (Takahashi, p. 59). Thus China has succeeded in reducing her technical gap relative to Japan during the past decade or so.

The last phase, 1967–present, covers the Cultural Revolution and the return to normalcy. There are indications that China's economic policy since the end of the Cultural Revolution has been concerned with building up a new economic structure (MacDougall, October 2, 1969, p. 43). It was apparent, by the beginning of 1970 that the new program of industrialization of the countryside had already been carried out on a fairly wide scale. The means for development of industry, both heavy and light, was the further decentralization of industries and the increase in the number of small- and medium-sized industries in the countryside. The emphasis of industry is, as it has been since 1962, on the production of chemical fertilizers, agricultural machinery, and other food production aids.[2]

The chief aim of the new policy is to make the countryside self-supporting. Every commune not only grows its own food but also produces its own fertilizers and tools (or purchases them from a nearby town). In addition it also generates its own electricity, runs its own small factories, health schemes, and primary schools. Intensified efforts were also made to expand roads, waterways, telecommunication, and health services and to construct more irrigation and water-control projects.[3]

To finance these programs peasants were asked to mobilize their savings. The amalgamation of communes was to make the production unit larger and economically more capable of financing these investments. The workpoints of commune members were awarded increasingly on a political basis. The needed skills for such programs are to be supplied by the expansion of rural part-work, part-time vocational schooling and by the 15 to 20 million of better educated or trained urban dwellers sent to the countryside during the past few years. One by-product of the movement from town to countryside and the expansion of rural health services is the improvement in human and physical resources for implementing the birth control scheme in rural areas.

## *The Probable Direction of Economic Policy for the 1970s*

Although the economic policy pursued in 1969 has incorporated some elements of the Great Leap program it continues to embrace the basic programs of "agriculture first" policy adopted since 1961–62. The recent changes in the commune structure have been far less drastic than they were in 1958, and more consideration is given to local attitudes and traditions. Some lessons have been learned from the fiasco of the Great Leap. New small-scale plants are more sophisticated than the disastrous backyard iron smelters of 1958, and a market guarantee for their products is offered. Also more thought has been given to the selection of the best location for the plants.[5]

In so far as the current (new) social and economic policies are concerned, do they represent the trend for this decade or do they merely represent a step forward toward other drastic changes which may be envisaged? In order to provide the answer we must analyze the relevance of these current policies in terms of the long-range social-economic policies for economic development expressed so often by the Chinese leadership during the past fifteen years or so. These long-range policies include: (1) building up the countryside, reducing the town population, and narrowing the gap in standard of living as well as the difference in mental attitudes between the country and town population, (2) the use of the "mass line," the system of calling upon workers and peasants to take responsibility and initiative with less emphasis on material incentives, (3) "the walking on two legs," the policy of simultaneous use of modern and traditional methods of production, and (4) "taking agriculture as the foundation and industry as the leading factor."[6]

The first policy was based on Mao's May 7, 1966 directive and obviously was pursued with increasing vigor during the past year (MacDougall, October 2, 1969, p. 43). The second policy represents the philosophy of the Great Leap period and has been incorporated into the current policies. The "walking on two legs" is an old slogan. This policy was further emphasized after the withdrawal of Russian experts in 1960. It responded to the need to industrialize in a way that China could afford without outside help. The current policy of further decentralization and of building small industries in rural areas actually continues to pursue the goal of self-reliance and economic independence. The fourth policy was said to have been originated by Mao in 1957. He stated then that the most logical way for China to develop heavy industry was to use the rural areas both as a market and as a source of investment funds. Thus the way of expanding industry was to invest in industry the profits derived from the sale of agricultural and light industrial products.[7] This policy was adopted four years later by the "agriculture first" policy and continues to be a part of the current economic policy. It is apparent, then, that the current social and economic policies do not actually deviate in any basic way from the long-range policies envisioned by the leaders in the past. Actually they are not simply measures designed to boost the economy for the immediate future but are part of a long-term scheme. In view of these facts it is most likely that the current policies will represent the trend for the coming decade. In the event that Mao passes from the scene sometime during the 1970s, a new coalition form of leadership may adopt the present policy with some modifications. It is expected that ideological extremism will be tempered somewhat and that monetary incentive will be used to a greater extent.

## *Prospect of Growth During the 1970s*

If the present policies and economic organization should prevail, what then are the prospects for China's economic growth in the 1970s? Clearly the growth rate to be attained will vary with the economic and political environments. It is, therefore, appropriate to assess the range of growth rates that could possibly be realized under different environments. Before we go into the assessment, we shall give the two following general assumptions for the coming decade:

1. No large scale war with a superpower.
2. No major civil turmoil.

*Prospects of an Annual GNP Growth Rate of about 6 per cent for the 1970s.*—Why should an annual GNP growth rate of about 6 per cent be chosen as the yardstick for the 1970s? A growth rate of 6 per cent is very close to the middle of the estimated range of annual growth rate of 5.5 to 7.2 per cent for the period 1950–66 (Richman, p. 598) or of 5.2–7.0 per cent for the period 1951–66, and is also close to the 6 per cent rate (at least) estimated for the period 1949–66 (Gurley, p. 188). These rates reflect the actual economic performance for a fairly long period of sixteen or eighteen years.

A growth rate of about 6 per cent is also very close to the rate probably attained in 1966.[8] Why should the annual growth rate for 1966 be taken into consideration here? During most of the period 1962–65, China was in a state of recovery from the economic crisis of 1960–61. Thus the growth rate attained in 1962–65 does not truly represent new growth. The year 1966 represented a year of new growth after the recovery from the 1960–61 crisis and the last relatively normal year before the main thrust of the Cultural Revolution. The new growth in 1966 also reflected the result of the new economic policy introduced after 1961 and was achieved on a more self-dependency basis than ever before. If it had not been for the Cultural Revolution, this rate of growth would more likely have been sustained into the following few years.

The rising foodgrains output between 1962 and 1965 or 1966 did contribute to the overall economic recovery during 1962–65 and to the new economic growth in 1966.[9] The foodgrain output increased at an annual rate of 4.2 per cent during 1962–65 and 3.0 per cent during 1962–66.[10] By 1965 foodgrain output had largely recovered to the record level prior to the crisis years, 1960–61. The agriculture performance for 1967 and 1968[11] was reported as rather good despite the interruption of the Cultural

Revolution, and the 1969 harvest could be an unprecedentedly good one due to the wider use of Los Banos rice seeds, new wheat and corn strains of higher yield, increased use of fertilizer, new irrigation projects, and favorable weather.[12] If we compare the conservative estimates of foodgrain output in 1966 to the preliminary estimate of 1969 output, the rate of increase in output should be between 2.3 per cent and 5.6 per cent for the period 1966–69.[13]

Thus the rather good performance in agriculture during the past three years would reflect the result of a continued basic improvement of the productive capacity for agricultural growth rather than the result of a temporary improvement in weather conditions. It would appear that the expanded effort on agriculture since 1962 has begun to show results. As of today China is in a much better position than ever before to ward off natural disasters. The past two decades saw drastic policy shifts, constant experimentation, and reorganization of rural institutions on an unprecedented scale; but now relatively stable rural institutions have finally emerged. The coming decade should be a period of relative stability for rural organization in China. In view of the relative stability in rural institutions and the expanded effort on supporting agriculture under the current economic policy, the foodgrains output (or total agricultural output) may be able to increase approximately 2.5 per cent annually during the 1970s.[14] This moderate prospective rate of increase will be sufficient to provide food for an annual population increase of 1.5 per cent to 2.0 per cent, agricultural products for export, and raw materials for light industry. Output of light industry could be expected to increase about 5 to 6 per cent, and part of the increase would be available for export (Dernberger, p. 22).

The beginning of an upturn in the economy occurred in 1962, following the 1960–61 crisis. In that year as much as 50 per cent of of imports was in agricultural products (40 per cent in food), 4 per cent in chemical fertilizer, and only 37 per cent in industrial materials, machinery, and equipment (27 per cent and 10 per cent respectively for these two categories). By 1965 about 40 per cent of imports was in agricultural products (30 per cent in food), 8 per cent in chemical fertilizers, and 45 per cent in industrial materials, machinery, and equipment (28 per cent and 17 per cent respectively).[15] It is probable that a similar composition prevailed in 1966 with the proportion in agricultural products probably somewhat lower and that in the last two categories somewhat higher. This trend of a declining proportion of agricultural products and a rising proportion of the two latter categories may continue into the 1970s if agricultural production keeps ahead of population growth by a small margin.

Because foodgrains make up a considerable fraction of total imports, an increase in their production and the consequent reduction of food imports will mean a substantial saving in the foreign exchange position. In 1962 the total value of food imports ($460 million) exceeded the value of food export ($250 million) by a wide margin (Price, p. 586). By 1965 the value of food exports ($520 million) began to match the value of food imports ($530 million) owing to the expanded domestic output as well as the policy of exporting high-priced food products (rice, eggs, and so on) and importing low-priced grains (wheat). The net food import deficit declined from $210 million in 1962 to $10 million in 1965, resulting in a saving of $200 million in foreign exchange between 1962 and 1965. If foodgrain output were to increase at a rate of 2.5 per cent during the period 1967–80, the annual net food export surplus would be somewhere between $600 million and $900 million. The stipulated range assumes no allowance for diet improvement, and the actual achievement within the range depends on the rate of population growth. (For details of estimates, see Part A of Appendix.)

The anticipated increase of net export earning from agricultural products ($600 million to $900 million) and light industrial products ($50 million to $100 million) resulting from a 2.5 per cent annual increase in agricultural output would go a long way toward meeting the need of additional foreign exchange for imports of machinery, equipment, and industrial raw materials.

It would contribute greatly to the necessary annual expansion of heavy industry of 10 to 12 per cent (Robert Dernberger, p. 23) required to provide producers' goods and defense hardware commensurate with an investment rate of some 20 per cent of GNP. This rate is close to the rate estimated for 1965.[16] Apparently an annual GNP growth rate of 6 per cent can be accomplished with more or less the same investment rate as that realized in 1965–66 even if the gross (total) incremental-capital-output ratio for the coming decade turns out to be as high as 3.2.[17] In that case no greater saving rate than the current one is required to accomplish an annual GNP growth rate of approximately 6 per cent.

As stated previously the current (new) social and economic policies include the sending of city dwellers to the countryside and the amalgamation of communes in order to make the production units larger and economically more capable of assuming the costs of rural health schemes and rural education, as well as administrative and welfare expenses. When the communes and other local governments finally assume the full cost of these functions, the central government will be able to make substantial savings on these functions. It has been estimated that the central government, with its new education and health policies, might be able to reduce its total expenditure in a few years by as much as 15 to 20 per cent (MacDougall, June 26, 1969, p. 706). If we use the ratio of government expenditure to GNP for 1957 (26 per cent) as the yardstick, the savings in expenditure may amount to 3.9 to 5.2 per cent of GNP. These savings could then be channeled to the investment sector, especially investment in heavy industry.

Even if this new policy were to increase the government saving fund by an amount equivalent to only 4 per cent of GNP during the second half of the 1970s, this would still be a boon to the national capital formation. It would either accelerate the GNP growth rate beyond the 6 per cent level or at least keep the growth rate from falling below that level, provided such new policy does not have a net disincentive effect on the peasants

Judging from the various assessments made so far, it seems that attaining an annual GNP growth rate of 6 per cent for the coming decade is well within the realm of possibility for the Chinese economy; the ingredients for this achievement are present, provided there is no sustained ideological extremism which would create disincentive effects on the peasants and workers. Compared to the Chinese economic performance since 1949 this is not an unreasonably high rate to expect from its economy.[19] With relative institutional and organizational stability the GNP might grow less erratically in the coming decade than in the past. Assuming the Chinese GNP to be in the neighborhood of $94 billion[20] (in 1966 U.S. dollars) in 1969, a 6 per cent growth rate will yield a GNP of about $178 billion (in 1966 U.S. dollars) by 1980, which is only about one-fifth of the 1968 American GNP.

*Prospects of an Annual GNP Growth Rate for The 1970s Close to That Attained During the Period 1950–57.*—During the period 1950–57, the Chinese GNP increased at an annual rate of 9 per cent despite the disruptive effects resulting from the rather rapid change in economic organization.[21] This period represents the heyday of China's economic development. What are then the prospects of achieving such a relatively high rate of growth during the 1970s? Let us first look into the would-be burden on the saving and investment sector.

Hollister calculated the gross (fixed) incremental-capital-output ratio (ICOR) at 1.8 for 1950–57 and at a higher ratio, 2.3, for 1952–57. Liu and Yeh derived a gross (fixed) ICOR of 2.8 for 1952–57. The gross (total) ICOR was estimated to be 3.1 for the period 1963–66. (For details, see footnote 17). It seems that the ICOR may have increased gradually during the past two decades. The past record of ICOR, of course, does not necessarily provide us with a reliable clue to the prospective ratio for the coming decade. In addition there is no simple and direct relationship between the rate of investment, ICOR, and growth rate. Other factors such as the morale of the workers, the efficiency of utilizing existing productive capacity, the pattern of allocation of available investment funds, and the like would influence the growth rate which in turn would affect the ICOR. The substantial increase in output over the present level, as required by a GNP growth rate of 9 per cent, would need large-scale capital investment to build new plants and to replace worn-out equipment. In view of the rather long gestation period of many capital-intensive projects, we should be prudent not to take the optimistic view that ICOR in the coming decade will be lower than that of 1963–66.

Even if the ratio turns out to be no greater than 3.0 during the coming decade, the required saving and investment would have to be stepped up greatly to the level of about 27 per cent of the GNP, as compared with 20 per cent level in recent years. Even the latter percentage is already quite high for a low-income country like China.

In what ways could the government increase the national saving or its investment revenue by an amount equal to 7 per cent of the GNP or about $6.6 billion (in terms of 1969 GNP)? Judging from the past record of its tax policy as well as its sensitivity to the potential repercussions of this policy, the central government is not prone to raise agricultural and other tax rates beyond the present levels. The expedient scheme would, then, be the gradual reduction of its expenditures on a number of functions.

As mentioned previously, the central government with its new education and health policies hopes to cut the subsidies to local units and communes and thus ultimately create a saving in government expenditures amounting to 3.9 to 5.2 per cent of GNP (or $3.7 to $4.9 billion) for capital construction purposes. However, it may take several years to accomplish this feat. Ironically, in some local areas the central government must initially absorb a greater burden for the health program; this represents a retrogression from the policy of transferring costs downward.[22] Even if the government enthusiastically pursues a policy of expenditure cutback during the 1970s, the first two years would not yield a saving of any significant amount. Thus the saving rate gap, in relation to the required 27 per cent investment rate, could be as much as 6 to 7 per cent for the first two years; and in terms of the absolute amount, the gap would be about $6.0 billion. As the government succeeds in creating a saving in expenditure amounting to 3.9 to 5.2 per cent of GNP during the second half of the 1970s, the annual saving rate gap, relative to the 27 per cent rate, would then still be 1.8 to 3.1 per cent. Taking the 1970s as a whole, the budgetary savings may amount to 3.1 to 4.0 per cent of the GNP and the annual saving rate gap would average 3.0 to 3.9 per cent. This fiscal scheme probably opens the largest possible domestic source for tapping investment funds; but even the successful execution of this scheme could hope to raise the annual saving and investment rate only from 20 per cent to 23.1 to 24.0 per cent during the coming decade.

The success of this fiscal scheme depends upon the cooperation of the communes and other local units in assuming the full costs of health and education, as well as administrative and welfare expenditures. In order to finance these services the communes and local units must now charge a higher price, or charge a price if none was charged previously, for these services; otherwise an additional local tax will have to be levied. If peasants and non-agricultural workers are not willing to forego these services, they must reduce their consumption of other goods and services. These practices may have a net disincentive effect on the peasants and workers because their present level of consumption is still close to subsistence.

The other major source of financing required investment depends mainly on the performance of the agricultural sector during the coming decade because the exports of agricultural products (mainly food products) and of industrial products based on agricultural raw materials make up the lion's share of total export earnings. In order to sustain a GNP growth rate of 9 per cent, average annual imports of machinery, equipment, and industrial raw materials during the 1970s should be $850 million to $1,500 million over those of 1965–66. To have a net export surplus of that magnitude the food grain output per capita during this period must be as high as 310 to 320 kilograms as compared with 295 kilograms for the period 1952–58. Table 1 shows the possible foodgrain output per capita in 1980 at various growth rates of population and grain output, projected from the per capita output of 283 kilograms in 1967. With an output growth rate of 3.5 per cent the output per capita in 1980 would be 365 kilograms and 342 kilograms at a population growth rate of 1.5 per cent and 2.0 per cent respectively. The *average* (annual) output per capita for the total period 1967–80 would then be about 324 kilograms and 312 kilograms at the respective population growth rates. With such a high rate of growth it is reasonable to expect that per capita consumption would also rise somewhat for diet improvement. Allowing 10 kilograms per capita for diet improvement in the form of poultry and livestock products, the net increase in per capita output over that of 1967–31 kilograms and 19 kilograms for the respective population growth rates—would be available as raw materials for light industry and for export.

Depending on the population growth rate, the margin over population growth and diet improvement would yield $700 million to $1,500 million from food export surplus annually after the allowance for the increase of chemical fertilizer import, provided the 3.5 per cent in foodgrain output could be achieved. (For details of estimates see Part B of Appendix). The output of light industry could then be expected to increase about 8 to 9 per cent; part of the increase would be available for export providing additional export earnings of $90 to $180 million. The total increase of export earnings would contribute heavily to the required expansion of heavy industry in the neighborhood of 15 per cent per year. Thus a 3.5 per cent growth rate in foodgrain output would more or less cover the increased foreign exchange need. If the total net increase in foreign exchange were to be devoted to capital formation in the form of imported plants and equipment, the annual investment rate as a percentage of GNP could be increased by 0.5 to 1.1 per cent during the 1970s. Adding this investment percentage to the projected 23.1 to 24.0 per cent associated with the fiscal scheme mentioned above, the annual gross investment rate for the economy would reach the level of 23.6 to 25.1 per cent during the 1970s. Even these rates, if ever attained, still fall short of the required investment and saving rate of 27 per cent by 1.9 to 3.4 per cent.

But could a growth rate as high as 3.5 per cent in the agricultural sector be attained in the 1970s? The present expanded rate of increase in agricultural inputs would most likely ensure a growth rate of 2.5 per cent. However, the current base of heavy industry is simply not large enough to provide all the modern inputs required for a growth rate of 3.5 per cent in agriculture without greatly affecting its supply of inputs to other sectors.

***Table 1—Possible Foodgrain Output Per Capita in 1980 at Various Growth Rates of Population and Foodgrain Output Between 1967[a] and 1980[b]***

| *Annual Increase in population (%)* | *Annual Increase in Foodgrain Output (%)* | | | | | | |
|---|---|---|---|---|---|---|---|
| | *1.0* | *1.5* | *2.0* | *2.5* | *3.0* | *3.5* | *4.0* |
| 1.00 | 283 | 310 | 331 | 353 | 376 | 401 | 426 |
| 1.50 | 257 | 283 | 302 | 321 | 342 | 365 | 388 |
| 1.75 | 249 | 274 | 292 | 311 | 332 | 353 | 376 |
| 2.00 | 242 | 265 | 283 | 302 | 321 | 342 | 364 |
| 2.50 | 224 | 249 | 266 | 283 | 301 | 321 | 342 |

[a] Per capita foodgrain output was estimated to be 283 kilograms for 1967.
[b] In kilograms.
*Source:* Foodgrain output for 1967 was put in the range of 190 to 210 million metric ton. The middle figure, 205 million metric tons, in that range is used here. See *Far Eastern Economic Review, 1969 Yearbook*, p. 150. Population in 1967 was estimated at 724.9 million. See Leo Orleans "Propheteering: The Population of Communist China," *Current Scene*, December 15 ,1969, p. 15.

(For explanation, see Part C of Appendix.) Thus for any growth rate beyond the 2.5 per cent, much depends upon a host of unknown factors such as the morale of the peasants, the improvement in the incentive system in rural areas, the rate of extension of improved seeds which offer a sure way to attain significantly higher yields, and weather conditions.

One other way to close the savings gap is to obtain long-term loans from other countries to finance imports. Foreign loans serve the dual purpose of filling both saving and foreign exchange gaps. Since 1962 China has sought loans and regular trade credit only in connection with individual transactions such as the eighteen-month short-term credit for grain imports from Canada and Australia and the medium-term loan for the import of a steel mill from West Germany. Owing to her policy of economic independence, China thus far has not made any serious attempt to obtain large-scale long-term loans for imports from the West. In general China's reputation for honoring its trade agreements and commitments, including payment, has been rather good (Eckstein, p. 272). It was estimated that China may be able to obtain loans from Western and Japanese enterprises of five to seven years term in amounts of $1 billion to $2 billion with export credit guarantees from their governments. The exact magnitude of such loans for imports of industrial plants on an individual basis would of course depend on the ability of Western and Japanese enterprises to ignore United States pressure attempting to prevent the extension of long-term credit to China. Because the United States further relaxed its embargo on non-strategic trade with China toward the end of 1969, it should not be long before the relaxation of such restriction on long-term credit follows suit.

Should the Chinese government make a serious attempt to seek loans from the West and Japan, it may succeed in the coming decade in obtaining loans of up to $2 billion with a grace period of ten years. Even loans of such magnitude would amount only to $200 million a year and would enlarge China's imports of needed machinery and equipment by 10 per cent annually during the decade of 1970s. Although the contribution of such loans to the foreign exchange sector is substantial, their contribution to the total saving and investment picture is rather insignificant. Any large-scale foreign long-term credit could come only from intergovernmental loans; but any large-scale extension of such loans is ruled out for the foreseeable future unless some dramatic change in China's political relations with capitalist industrialized countries occurs in the early part of the 1970s.

One aspect of the foreign trade policy which should be pursued by China during this decade is to develop the labor-intensive industries and handicrafts for export to the affluent Western nations. The labor-intensive modern industries such as sporting goods, musical instruments, gourmet foods, clothing articles, electronics, and optical goods offer China a favorable competitive position in the world market. The expansion of handicraft goods such as arts and crafts, unique clothing articles, jewelry, rugs, and the like also have good prospects for the export market. These are the industries in which China has a comparative advantage. However, before large-scale commercialization of such products can be realized, great effort in the areas of quality control, style, and marketing organization must first be made. Ultimately these industries would provide China with export earnings of a few hundred million dollars to import machinery and equipment for capital formation. If the recent partial relaxation by the United States on the embargo of non-strategic trade with China were to be followed by a full-scale resumption of non-strategic trade, an additional export market for such labor-intensive products, though minor at first, would be available to China. Even if China were to pursue this aspect of foreign trade seriously in the immediate future, the earnings from the export of these items would not make a significant contribution to the total export earnings until the latter part of the 1970s.

The assessments made so far lead to the following conclusions:

1. Even the full realization of both the

fiscal scheme and the 3.5 per cent growth rate in the agricultural sector would provide altogether a gross investment and saving rate of 23.6 to 25.1 per cent of GNP and thus fall short of the required rate of 27 per cent by 1.9 to 3.4 per cent.

2. The full realization of a growth rate of 3.5 per cent in the agricultural sector would generate sufficient extra foreign exchange earnings for expanded imports of machinery, equipment, and industrial raw materials if the annual population growth rate is less than 2 per cent during the 1970s. Any shortage of foreign exchange resulting from a population growth rate of 2 per cent or more may be taken care of by the partial realization of the acquisition of foreign loans as well as an export drive on labor-intensive products, including handicrafts.

3. However, the ambitious fiscal scheme would most likely not be realized because of the current low per capita personal income and the possible disincentive effect on the peasants and workers.

4. The full realization of the 3.5 per cent growth rate in agriculture demands not only good weather conditions, which are beyond the control of the planners, but also the presence of a social climate geared to high productivity (good morale, an effective incentive system, and so forth). As of this date, the latter is as much an unknown quantity as the former. Given the considerable degree of ideological extremism still prevalent on the Mainland, it is doubtful if the desired and necessary increase in agricultural productivity could ever be realized.

If the conditions of the intangible factors—the morale of the peasants and workers, the incentive system, and the efficiency of utilizing existing productive capacity—are unusually favorable toward economic growth, the economy could achieve a rate of growth higher than it could under less favorable conditions even with the same saving and investment rate. This may partly explain the reason why countries with similar rates of capital formation achieve substantially different growth rates. Because these intangible factors are not unusually favorable in China today and are not expected to be so in the near future, the prospects of China's attaining an annual growth rate of 9 per cent in the 1970s may not be very promising.

## Conclusion

Judging from the assessments made so far, during the 1970s the Chinese economy may be able to achieve an annual GNP growth rate of somewhere between 6 per cent and 9 per cent with the likelihood of a rate not much higher than 6 per cent. The GNP may have a fairly good chance of reaching $180 billion (1966 United States dollars) or may be even as high as $190 billion in 1980, as compared with $94 billion in 1969 (1966 U.S. dollars) (see Table 2). But even these levels of GNP would amount to only about 20 per cent of the United States GNP in 1968 and 1969.

**Table 2—Projected Estimates of GNP in 1980 at Various Growth Rate and Projected Estimates of Per Capita GNP in 1980 at Various GNP and Population Growth Rates Between 1969 and 1980**

| Annual Growth Rate of GNP | Projected Estimates of GNP in 1980[a] | Projected Estimates of Per Capita GNP in 1980 at The Following Annual Growth Rates of Population[a] | | | | |
|---|---|---|---|---|---|---|
| | | 1.00% | 1.50% | 1.75% | 2.00% | 2.50% |
| 4% | 145 | 166 | 157 | 153 | 149 | 141 |
| 5% | 161 | 184 | 174 | 170 | 165 | 156 |
| 6% | 178 | 204 | 193 | 188 | 183 | 174 |
| 7% | 198 | 226 | 214 | 209 | 203 | 193 |
| 8% | 219 | 251 | 238 | 231 | 225 | 213 |
| 9% | 243 | 278 | 263 | 256 | 249 | 236 |

In billions of 1966 U.S. dollars.

*Source:* See Footnote No. 13 for the estimate of GNP and Per Capita GNP in 1969. The GNP was estimated at $94 billion (in international purchasing power rate in 1966) and the Per Capita GNP at $120 in 1969.

The total value of China's foreign trade has amounted to 4 per cent of her GNP in recent years. The policy of economic independence, which set the priority on the production of import substitutes, may reduce the import need for a growing number of products. However, the expanding capital investment necessary for an investment rate of 20 to 27 per cent (of GNP) would require a large increase in the import of advanced machinery and plants. Thus, it is anticipated that the volume of trade would grow as fast as the GNP, and the proportion of the value of foreign trade in the GNP in 1980 would be close to the current rate of about 4 per cent. The total volume of Chinese foreign trade would, therefore, reach a level of $7 to $8 billion in 1980.

The agricultural sector is expected to improve at a moderate rate. The foodgrain output would increase at an annual rate of 2.5 per cent, or may even be somewhat higher, and reach a level of 290 to 300 million metric tons in 1980. Modern heavy industrial output is expected to grow at a rate of about 10 per cent whereas the growth rate of modern light industrial output is projected at about 6 per cent. The aggregate output of modern (manufacturing) industry would, therefore, increase at a rate of 10 per cent. (See Part D, Appendix.) With such a growth rate the output of modern industry would reach a level of $48 billion by 1980. Because the agricultural sector will grow at only a moderate rate, it is expected that by 1980 this sector will make up about 30 per cent of the GNP, as compared with over 40 per cent of the GNP in recent years. The value of the modern industrial output would account for 24 to 27 per cent of the GNP in 1980, as compared with 17 to 18 per cent of GNP in recent years. (See Part D, Appendix.)

Because the new economic policy favors decentralization of industry and planning, it is expected that small-scale industries in communes will be developed at a rapid rate. By 1980 communes will be more self-sufficient as economic units than at the present time. A new agro-industrial production unit will then begin to take shape, and this unit will play an increasing role in the process of economic planning.

If the population grows at an annual rate of 1.5 per cent, the per capita GNP in 1980 would be within the range of $190 to $210; this would represent a gain of 60 to 75 per cent over the $120 level in 1969. However, with a population growth rate of 2.0 per cent the per capita GNP would be $180 to $200, thus reducing the gain to 50 to 66 per cent.

Thus even with a respectable growth rate of 6 to 7 per cent in the 1970s the average Chinese citizen on the Mainland would find himself still living close to the subsistence level in 1980. However, a per capita GNP of about $200 in 1980, low though it may be, will be able to generate a higher investment rate than the $120 per capital GNP did in 1969, thus providing a stronger base for further growth in the future.

According to Table 2, a GNP growth rate of 6 per cent would attain a per capita GNP of $183 in 1980 if the population growth rate is 2.0 per cent, whereas a GNP growth rate of only 5 per cent would also attain the same level of per capita GNP if the population growth rate is at the low level of 1.0 per cent. In view of the unfavorable impact of a high birth rate on economic growth, the prospects of the Chinese economy developing on a sustained and respectable scale would improve, especially in the decades to come, if the birth rate is substantially reduced in the near future.

The other crucial factor which greatly affects the future performance of the economy is the question of ideological extremism versus managerial, technical, and economic rationality. The prevailing ideology in China continues to deny self-interest and material gain as major motivating forces for managers, technicians or workers, and it still aims to eliminate the distinctions between experts and non-experts, mental and physical work, managers and workers, etc.[23] If carried too far, this ideology would greatly hinder managerial effectiveness and thus the efficient performance of the economy. If ideological extremism could be tempered permanently, the Chinese economy would have much brighter prospects of achieving an impressive, self-sustained growth rate, similar to that achieved during 1950–57.

# Appendix
# Notes
# References

# Appendix

# Appendix

1. *Orleans' population figures are used here (Orleans, p. 15).*
2. *Foodgrain output for 1967 is assumed to be 205 million metric tons which represents the middle of the estimated range of 190 to 220 million tons* (Far Eastern Economic Review, *1969 Yearbook, p. 150).*
3. *Foodgrain output for 1952–57 are the estimates of O. L. Dawson (Jones, p. 93).*
4. *Import and export values are compiled from Eckstein's data (Eckstein pp. 106–7; 114–5).*

*Construction cost of fertilizer plant (Walker, p. 45). Total net fixed investment in 1965 yuan (Eckstein p. 164). Conversion factor to 1957 yuan (Liu & Yeh, p. 235). The share of fixed investment in heavy industry for 1965 was assumed to be the same as in 1957. For 1957 ratio, see Hollister, p. 128.*

## *Part A: Foodgrain Output at 2.5 per cent Growth Rate*

The per capita foodgrain output was estimated to be about 283 kilograms in 1967. In that year probably the value of food exports was close to the value of food imports, and the net food exports, if any, were minimal. If we assume an annual growth rate of 2.5 per cent for foodgrains during 1967–80, by 1980 per capita output would be 302 kilograms, 311 kilograms, or 321 kilograms at a population growth rate of 2.00 per cent, 1.75 per cent or 1.50 per cent respectively, Table 1. In order to save calculation, we may take the *average* of the 1967 and the 1980 per capita outputs to represent the *average* of output per capita for the period 1967–80. The *average* for this period would be 293 kilograms, 297 kilograms, and 302 kilograms at the respective population growth rates. The average per capita output was 291 kilograms for 1952–57 and 318 kilograms for the exceptionally good crop year, 1958. The average per capita output for the period 1952–58 was 295 kilograms. The import of foodstuffs averaged about $23 million for 1955–57, and the export of foodstuffs (excluding $79 million of inedible livestock products and tobaccos) about $505 million, given an average yearly foodstuffs export surplus of $482 million. For 1958 the import of foodstuffs was $34 million, and the export was $592 million (excluding $81 million of inedible livestock products and tobaccos), leaving a surplus of $558 million. The surplus was $566 million in 1959 (excluding $80 million of inedible livestock products and tobaccos). According to another source, the surplus in 1959 was $820 million (Price, p. 586).

The estimates of foodgrain export earning for the period 1967–80 are based on the relationship between foodgrain output per capita and food export earnings that existed during 1952–59 and in 1967. It also gives due allowance to the fact that even if per capita output remained unchanged, the greater total population in 1967–80 would provide greater export capacity in this period than in the period 1952–59. At an annual growth rate of 2.5 per cent no allowance is made for the improvement of diet. Therefore, depending on the population growth rate, the annual food export surplus could be somewhere between $600 million and $900 million for the period 1967–80.

## *Part B: Foodgrain Output at 3.5 per cent Growth Rate*

If we assume an annual growth rate of 3.5 per cent for foodgrains during 1967–80, by 1980 per capita output would be 342 kilograms, 353 kilograms, and 365 kilograms at a population growth rate of 2.00 per cent, 1.75 per cent and 1.50 per cent respectively, Table 1. Again we take the *average* of the 1967 and the 1980 per capita outputs to represent the *average* of output per capita for the whole period 1967–80. The *average* for this period would come to 312 kilograms, 318 kilograms, and 324 kilograms at the respective population growth rates.

A growth rate of 3.5 per cent in foodgrain is considered a rather successful one, and some improvement of diet is bound to happen. If 10 kilograms is given for such purpose, the *average* of output per capita for 1967–80 would be reduced to the net level of 302 kilograms, 308 kilograms, and 314 kilograms respectively. Based on the same method as used in Part A of the Appendix, the annual food export surplus would be estimated at somewhere between $1,000 million and $1,800 million, depending on the population growth rate.

At a growth rate of 3.5 per cent, total foodgrain output would increase from 205 million metric tons (M.M.T.) in 1967 to 320 M.M.T. in 1980, an increase of 115 M.M.T. To achieve this output in 1980, the use of fertilizer must also be greatly increased. Assuming one half of this 115 M.M.T. would come from improved seeds, irrigation, expanded acreage, and so on, the remaining 58 M.M.T. must depend on chemical fertilizers. Given a ratio of 1 M.M.T. of fertilizer to 2 M.M.T. of foodgrain, the supply of fertilizer should be 29 M.M.T. in 1980. In 1967 the fertilizer imports amounted to 3.5 M.M.T. while domestic production was 6.0 M.M.T. Projection of the past rate of increase in domestic production would put the output at 16 M.M.T. by 1980.

Fertilizer imports must therefore be stepped up to 13 M.M.T. by 1980. During the period 1968–80 the annual import level would exceed the 1967 import level (of 3.5 M.M.T.) by about 5.0 M.M.T. on the average. With a price of $60 per ton including freight, insurance, and the like, the average annual *extra* cost of importing fertilizers (over the cost of 1967) would amount to $300 million. Deducting from the annual net food export earnings cited above, net annual earnings of $700 million to $1,500 million would be obtained.

## *Part C: Estimates of Fertilizer Requirement and the Capacity of Heavy Industry*

According to the estimates presented in Part B of the Appendix, by 1980 the total required supply of chemical fertilizers would be 29 M.M.T. higher than that in 1967. Thus between 1967 and 1980 the annual increase of fertilizer production capacity would average about 2.2 million tons. The annual cost of constructing such additional capacity would be about 1.93 billion (1957) yuan, which would amount to 46 per cent of the estimated net fixed investment, 4.2 billion (1957) yuan, allocated to heavy industry in 1965. In the meantime the heavy industry sector is also expected to step up its support to industries producing insecticides, irrigation pumps, and the like, which normally go together with chemical fertilizers. It is obvious, then, that the heavy industry sector will be overburdened by the large order of machinery and equipment for fertilizer production if this plan is to be implemented. Consequently either the heavy industry sector will be compelled to reduce its supplies to a number of other industries, or the expansion of fertilizer production capacity must be curtailed.

An increase in the imports of fertilizer would, of course, reduce the burden on the heavy industry sector, but the ability to import additional large amounts of fertilizers depends on the realization of the increase in foodgrain output per capita. Thus there is no assurance that additional foreign exchange will be available for such increased imports prior to the actual increase in foodgrain output.

So far our estimates are based on the rather optimistic assumption that one-half of the additional 115 M.M.T. of foodgrains would come from improved seeds, irrigation, and so on. If we accept the (less optimistic) assumption that only four-tenths of the additional foodgrain would come from improved seeds, irrigation, and so on, the required supply of fertilizers in 1980 would be 34.5 M.M.T. higher than that in 1967. Thus between 1967 and 1980 the annual increase in fertilizer production capacity would *average* about 2.65 M.M.T. The annual cost of constructing these new facilities would amount to 55 per cent of the net fixed investment funds allocated to heavy industry in 1965. The adverse effects on the other industries, which also need support from the heavy industry sector, would be so great that modification on the fertilizer production goal would have to be made.

## *Part D: Estimates of Foreign Trade, Foodgrain Output and Modern (manufacturing) Industrial Output*

The value of China's foreign trade has amounted to 4.0 per cent of GNP in recent years. Because of the policy of economic independence, this rate may remain the same in 1980. Thus with a GNP of $180 to $200 billion in 1980, the foreign trade would be in the neighborhood of $7.2 billion to $8.0 billion by 1980.

Foodgrain output was estimated to be $205 M.M.T. in 1969 (see Table 1). With a growth rate of 2.5 to 3.0 per cent, it may reach the level of 290 M.M.T. to 300 M.M.T. in 1980.

Heavy industrial output is expected to grow at a rate of 12 per cent, and the growth rate of light industrial output is projected at 6 per cent. Heavy industrial output made up about 70 per cent of the total modern manufacturing output, and light industry constituted 30 per cent (Richman, Table 7–6, p. 620, for 1965). The aggregate manufacturing output should, therefore, increase at a rate of 10 per cent. If modern (manufacturing) industrial output made up about 18 per cent of GNP in 1969, the value of modern industrial output would amount to $17 billion in that year. At a growth rate of 10 per cent it may reach the level of $48 billion in 1980 and would thus account for 24 to 27 per cent of the projected GNP of $180 to $200 billion. The 18 per cent figure mentioned above approximates the 1957 figure as reported in Richman, p. 617 and the 1967 figure as reported in Richman, p. 658.

Agricultural production in recent years probably still made up 40 to 45 per cent of the GNP (Richman, pp. 617–18). If agricultural output grows at an annual rate of 2.5 to 3.0 per cent and the GNP grew at a rate of 6 to 7 per cent during 1969–80, agriculture would account for only 27 to 33 per cent of the GNP in 1980.

# Notes

# Notes

## 1. INDIAN AGRICULTURE: AN ANALYSIS OF RECENT PERFORMANCE

*Pranab Bardhan*

[1] *The New York Times*, "Hong Kong Report," October 26, 1969.

[1] All the data in this paper are from publications of the Ministry of Food and Agriculture, Government of India, unless otherwise mentioned.

[2] See P. V. Sukhatme, "Food and Nutrition Situation in India," *Indian Journal of Agricultural Economics*, April–June and July–September, 1962. One might also note here that about 75 per cent of calorie intake in the average Indian's diet is from foodgrains.

[3] See the estimate by Yamada, as reported in B. F. Johnston, "Agriculture and Economic Development: The Relevance of the Japanese Experience," *Food Research Institute Studies*, No. 3, 1966.

[4] See P. Bardhan, "Chinese and Indian Agriculture: A Broad Comparison of Recent Policy and Performance," MIT Department of Economics Working Paper No. 13, January, 1968.

[5] National Council of Applied Economic Research, *Long Term Projections of Demand for and Supply of Selected Agricultural Commodities*, 1962, p. 123.

[6] See, for example, E. Mason, *Economic Development in India and Pakistan* (Cambridge: Center for International Affairs, Harvard University, 1966).

[7] It should be noted, however, that the 1952–53 level of this ratio was much higher than that in the prewar period.

[8] See U. Datta Choudhury, "Technological Change in the Indian Economy, 1950–60," *Economic and Political Weekly* (Bombay), August 20, 1966.

[9] According to U.N. publications, in 1949–58, agriculture accounted for 13 per cent of gross fixed investment in Italy, 8.8 per cent in Yugoslavia, 11.2 per cent in France, 6.6 per cent in the U.S.; in Japan, agriculture accounted for 19 per cent of total investment in the period between 1956–57 and 1960–61.

[10] Let us cite not a very uncommon example of water distribution from the Thorners' observations on the operation of Sarda Canal in Uttar Pradesh: "Throughout the Sarda system it is the general rule that the strong, the powerful, the well-connected, the local bullies dominate the use of irrigation water. They get water first and they tend to take as much of it as they please. Only after they are satisfied do they permit the mass of ordinary, unimportant, petty cultivators to have access to it. The mass of ordinary cultivators have to conduct their affairs as though the supply of canal water was problematical, an intermittent blessing to be welcome when it comes, but not to be counted on. . . . This was our finding in more than half of the 68 villages we visited." See Daniel and Alice Thorner, *Land and Labour in India* (New York: Taplinger, 1962).

[11] See P. S. Sharma, "A Study of the Structural and Tenurial Aspects of the Rural Economy in the Light of 1961 Census," *Indian Journal of Agricultural Economics*, October–December, 1965.

[12] It has been estimated that for the areas with assured rainfall (of 1,150 mm. a year or more) the area covered by holdings under pure and mixed tenancy is 27.6 per cent, and for areas with extensive irrigation (with 50 per cent or more of gross sown area under irrigation), it is as high as 35.3 per cent.

[13] Holdings get progressively smaller through the operation of the law of inheritance. Legislation has been adopted in the several states to prevent subdivision below a prescribed minimum size. But on account of excessive pressure on land, such laws have not been effective at all.

[14] It has been calculated on the basis of Farm Management Studies data that the minimum size of holding for employing a pair of bullocks fully is about 7.5 acres, and that for yielding a minimum net farm business income of Rs. 1,200 per family is about 15 acres under average Indian conditions.

[15] According to the All-India Rural Credit Survey of the Reserve Bank, cooperatives provided only 3.1 per cent of the total annual borrowings of cultivating households in 1951–52; according to the recent All-India Rural Debt and Investment Survey of the Reserve Bank, it has gone up to 15.5 per cent in 1961–62. The total value of agricultural produce handled by cooperative marketing societies has gone up from Rs. 530 million in 1955–56 to Rs. 3,010 million in 1964–65. The total value of agricultural supplies like fertilizers, seeds, pesticides and implements handled by cooperatives was about Rs. 30 million in 1955–56 and Rs. 1,040 million in 1964–65.

[16] For example, in 1961–62 the proportion of annual borrowings from cooperatives to aggregate annual borrowings by all rural households increased uniformly from 4 per cent for the lowest asset group to 20.5 per cent for the highest asset group, according to All-India Rural Debt and Investment Survey data.

## 2. THE GREEN REVOLUTION

*Ruddar Datt and K. P. M. Sundharam*

[1] M. S. Swaminathan, Scientific Implications of HYV Programme, Economic and Political Weekly, Annual Number, January, 1969, p. 67.

[2] Ibid., p. 69.

[3] Ibid.

[4] Ibid., p. 75.

[5] P. N. Radhakrishnan, Management of HYVP, Economic and Political Weekly, January 25, 1969, p. 251.

## 4. RECENT DEVELOPMENT IN CHINESE AND INDIAN AGRICULTURE

*Pranab Bardhan*

[1] Raj [28] has a brief but illuminating general discussion of comparative agricultural performance. Ishikawa's recent book [16] also provides a very useful framework for a comparative study of agricultural development "in Asian perspective."

[2] Even the Chinese officials now do not seem to believe in them, otherwise it is hard to reconcile their claim in 1966 that 1966 foodgrains output was a record in Chinese history with their figure for 1958.

[3] To some observers our Chinese output figures for 1966 and 1967 may seem too high. In calculating the rate of growth we have *also* tried an alternative, more conservative, set of data for these two years. For 1966 we have taken in this alternative set the estimate of 210 million tons (indicated by Jones) of unhusked (170.1 million tons of husked) grains and 221 million tons (179 million tons husked) for 1967. These two figures are consistent with Hsieh Fu-chih's statement above and Chou En-lai's statement of April 28, 1968 that the 1967 grains production was about 5 per cent higher than that of 1966.

[4] The estimates of per capita foodgrains production for China should be taken as very crude approximations; among other things, the population figures underlying them are subject to doubts by some observers. The population figures for 1960 and 1965 are those used by Edwin Jones [21] p. 93. For 1965, Jones takes the official estimate after the mid-1964 "census" and projects it to the end of 1965. Population estimates and projections on the basis of several alternative hypotheses made by John Aird [1] seem to suggest that 728 millions for 1965 is an underestimate. (For a contrary view, however, see W. Klatt's comment in *China Quarterly*, July-September 1967.) Aird arrived at an estimate of 1965 total population of somewhere between the extremes of 714.6 million and 874.6 million. As Eckstein, Galenson and Liu [11] p. 13 comment, "judged by what is known about the food supply and employment, the true magnitude is probably nearer the lower limit."

[5] With the alternative, more conservative, estimates for 1966 and 1967 mentioned above, the rate of growth $b = 1.7$ per cent for China (with standard error $= .005$).

[6] This is as reported in Johnston [20]. Recently some of the past estimates of growth in agricultural production in Meiji Japan have been seriously questioned by Nakamura [24] who shows that agricultural production was grossly underreported in the earlier part of the Meiji era as a tax evasion device, and that this underreporting tended to decline over time. Yamada has now undertaken a careful revision of official estimates, and arrives at a rate of growth smaller than that of, say, Ohkawa but much higher than that of Nakamura.

[7] See State Statistical Bureau [30] and Jones [21].

[8] See Ishikawa [18], and N.C.A.E.R. [25], p. 123. The N.C.A.E.R. estimate for India does not include rural compost and is, therefore, an underestimate.

[9] Official reports claim that between 1949 and 1960 an estimated 50 billion man-days were spent on water-conservancy projects and a total of 70 billion cubic meters of earthworks and masonry —equivalent to excavating 960 Suez Canals—were completed.

[10] "Statistical Data of China's Irrigated Area in Recent Years," *Hydroelectricity* No. 7, April 11, 1957.

[11] Throughout the period, however, the proportion of minor to major irrigation projects has been much higher in China than in India. See Ishikawa [16], p. 152.

[12] This was to some extent due to mistakes of policy measures regarding ownership, use and raising of existing livestock in the period of agricultural cooperativization. For the same reason some of the increased use of chemical fertilizer in China in the 1960s was to make up for the loss of animal manure.

[13] For a detailed discussion of price policy in China, see Perkins [26] and Swamy [31]. For a good summary of the different aspects of price policy in India see Dantwala [7].

[14] These data are from Perkins [26], p. 30, except for the 1963 figures which are from Swamy [31].

[15] See Datta Roy Choudhury [8]. It should be pointed out here that the estimate for China is at current prices and excludes change in inventories, whereas the Indian estimate is at 1960–61 prices and includes change in inventories.

[16] As, to cite only two examples, in cases of sugar and rayon and staple fiber.

[17] In the Third Five Year Plan period less than 30 per cent of the target was achieved in production of both nitrogenous and phosphatic fertilizers. In the Second Plan period also, actual production at the end year was 34 per cent of target in nitrogenous fertilizers and 45 per cent of target in phosphatic fertilizers.

[18] Chinese performance in the production of agricultural machinery and implements has also been substantially better than that of India, particularly in recent years, although in neither country for obvious reasons of factor proportions agricultural mechanization is an immediate

objective. Chinese production of powered machinery for irrigation and drainage went up from 0.56 million HP in 1957 to 7.28 million HP in 1964, that of tractors from 2,720 in 1953 to 124,000 in 1964 and that of medium and small-scale agricultural machinery and implements quadrupled between 1957 and 1965; see Kojima [22], Table 3. In India the production of tractors was negligible in 1955–56 and was 5,600 in number in 1965–66; that of power-driven pumps went up from 37,000 in 1955–56 to 200,000 in 1965–66, and that of diesel engines (stationary) from 10,000 to 500,000 in the same period.

19 It is to be remembered that water conservation absorbed a major portion of agricultural investment. Investment in water conservation constituted an estimated 62 per cent of total state investment for capital construction in agriculture during the First Five Year Plan. See Ishikawa [16], pp. 161–63.

20 See, for example, Yang [36], p. 26.

21 This has been noted by, among others, Perkins [26] and E.C.A.F.E. [12].

22 See, e.g., Thorner [34] on the water distribution from Sarda Canala in U.P.

23 The actual importance of tenancy in rural India may, however, be more important than suggested by this figure on account of two major reasons. Since the prevalence of tenancy is significantly higher in the wet, and therefore generally more productive, areas (including irrigated land) than in dry areas, the loss from tenant cultivation is more than what may be suggested from the all-India average figure.

Secondly, what may not have come out in official data is that land legislation in some areas has in fact driven underground some forms of tenancy, numerous cases of eviction of tenants have taken place under the guise of "voluntary surrender" and that informal arrangements have been made with share-croppers disguised as agricultural laborers. The high pressure of population on land as well as the balance of social and political forces in the countryside has made it possible for land owners to impose such arrangements on the landless and defenceless agricultural population. This has tended to defeat the major aim of protective tenancy reforms.

24 The share is, however, relatively small; the agricultural tax rate was about 15.5 per cent of output in the 1950s.

Besides, the tax is fixed according to the so-called "normal" yield of land, *i.e.*, the amount the land *should* produce in an ordinary year. This considerably reduces the disincentive effects.

25 It has been calculated by Jung-Chao Liu [23] from data on relative price and yield response functions of rice to Ammonium Sulphate that with the 15.5 per cent proportional agricultural tax rate the Chinese farm gains only 41.2 per cent of the increase in revenue when 15 kg. of N is applied per hectare of rice production, 33.1 per cent of increase in revenue when 30 kg. of N is applied per hectare and only 9.8 per cent of increase in revenue when 60 kg. of N is applied per hectare.

26 Holdings get progressively smaller through the operation of the law of inheritance, Legislation has been adopted in several States to prevent subdivision below a prescribed minimum size. But on account of excessive pressure on land such laws have not been effective at all.

27 It has been calculated on the basis of Farm Management Studies data that the minimum size of holding for employing a pair of bullocks fully is about 7.5 acres, and that for yielding a minimum net farm business income of Rs.1,200 per family is about 15 acres under average Indian conditions.

28 For example, in 1961–62 the proportion of annual borrowings from cooperatives to aggregate annual borrowings by all rural households increased uniformly from 4 per cent for the lowest asset group to 20.5 per cent for the highest asset group, according to All-India Rural Debt and Investment Survey data (see *Reserve Bank of India Bulletin*, September 1965).

29 There is some evidence in Indian Farm Management Studies data that land productivity is invariant with respect to the size of farm when holdings are corrected for fertility differences.

30 An official survey in 1957 covering 228 agricultural cooperatives in twenty-four provinces showed that saving in these cooperatives came to about 15 per cent of net income, and this marked a significant increase over earlier years.

31 According to one estimate based on reports of agricultural producers' cooperatives, the share of labor in total cost of irrigation projects was as high as 95 per cent.

32 See Ishikawa [19] for a similar opinion.

## 5. INDUSTRIAL PROGRESS IN INDIA UNDER PLANNING

*Wilfred Malenbaum*

1 *Far Eastern Economic Review, 1970 Yearbook*, December 1, 1969, p. 146.

2 *Far Eastern Economic Review, 1970 Yearbook*, December 1, 1969, p. 113.

1 India's Third Five Year Plan indicates that, within a 70 per cent increase projected in the total index of industrial production, there would be the following increases: cotton textiles, 18 per cent; machinery (all types), 143 per cent; chemicals, 150 per cent; iron and steel, 160 per cent.

2 India's sales abroad, some Rs. 575 crores in early plan years, were dominated (about 60 per cent) by jute and cotton yarn and textiles, and by tea. Manufactured goods other than textiles contributed less than 10 per cent of the total.

3 Government demand also declined because of reduced flows of foreign assistance.

4 *Fourth Plan* (draft).

5 *Ibid.*

6 *Fourth Plan* (draft).

### 6. PATTERN OF INDUSTRIAL DEVELOPMENT IN INDIA
*Ruddar Datt and K. P. M. Sundharam*

[1] Myrdal, *Asian Drama*, Vol. II, p. 1173.

[2] George Rosen, *Industrial Change in India*, (1958), pp. 182–83.

[3] Datta, B., "Growth of Business Houses, Tatas, Birlas and Mafatlal," *Mainstream*, March 22, 1968, p. 26.

### 10. ADMINISTRATIVE PROBLEMS OF ECONOMIC DEVELOPMENT
*M. Abel*

[1] Jawaharlal Nehru, "Annual Address to the Indian Institute of Public Administration," 1963.

[2] Planning Commission, *Third Five-Year Plan: Summary*, New Delhi, 1962, p. 8.

[3] *Ibid.*, p. 59.

[4] *The Constitution of India*, Seventh Schedule.

[5] Planning Commission, *Second Five-Year Plan*, p. 353.

[6] Planning Commission, *Review of the First Five-Year Plan*, p. 165.

[7] *The Hindu*, May 1, 1962.

[8] Planning Commission, *Second Five-Year Plan*, p. 349.

[9] Paul H. Appleby, *Public Administration in India, Report of a Survey*, p. 17.

[10] For more information see: *Second Five-Year Plan*, pp. 602–03.

[11] *The Constitution of India*, Article 162.

[12] Paul H. Appleby, *Public Administration in India, Report of a Survey*, p. 10.

[13] *The First Five-Year Plan*, p. 532.

[14] Paul H. Appleby, *op. cit.*, p. 17.

[15] Paul H. Appleby, *ibid.*, p. 18.

[16] Paul H. Appleby, *Re-Examination of India's Administrative System with Special Reference to Administration of Government's Industrial and Commercial Enterprises*, New Delhi, 1956, p. 17.

[17] *The Hindu*, November 14, 1961.

[18] Paul H. Appleby, *op. cit.*, p. 17.

[19] *Idem.*

[20] Paul H. Appleby, *op. cit.*, p. 31.

[21] *Third Five-Year Plan: Summary*, p. 59.

[22] *Report of the Foodgrains Enquiry Committee*, 1957, pp. 112–18.

[23] *The Second Five-Year Plan*, p. 131.

[24] *Evaluation Report on Second Year's Working of Communiy Projects*, Vol. 1, p. 7.

[25] *The Fifth Evaluation Report*, 1958, p. 37.

[26] *Report of the Foodgrains Enquiry Committee*, p. 107.

[27] Planning Commission, *Programme Administration Adviser's Report*, 1959, p. 130.

[28] John Dewey, *Logic, the Theory of Inquiry* (New York), 1938, p. 508.

[29] *The Second Five-Year Plan*, p. 251.

[30] The Program Evaluation Organization has conducted studies of "input requirements" to determine "a budget of resources required for the current input per acre." It has also conducted sociological surveys of several Indian villages to study "faction and leadership, and the impact of the development program on village social life." See *Evaluation Report on Second Year's Working of Community Projects*, New Delhi, 1955, Vol. I, pp. 68–69.

### 13. INCENTIVES AND PROFITS IN CHINESE INDUSTRY
*Dwight H. Perkins*

[1] "On Khrushchev's Phoney Communism and Its Historical Lessons for the World," Comment on the Open Letter of the Central Committee of the CPSU (IX), Foreign Languages Press, Peking, 1964.

[2] Robert W. Campbell, "Economics: Roads and Inroads," *Problems of Communism*, November-December 1965.

[3] See, for example, Joseph S. Berliner, "Marxism and the Soviet Economy," *Problems of Communism*, September-October 1964.

[4] See, "China in World Trade," *Current Scene*, Vol. IV, Nos. 3 and 4, February 1 and 15, 1966.

[5] For a more complete discussion, see D. H. Perkins, *Market Control and Planning in Communist China*, Harvard University Press, Cambridge, 1966.

[6] See speech by Ch'en Yün.

[7] Ma Wen-kuei, "China's State-Owned Industrial Enterprises—Their Nature and Tasks," *Peking Review*, Peking No. 26, June 26, 1964.

[8] Ministry of Finance, "Methods of Dividing and Using Profits of State Enterprises in Excess of the Plan in 1954," *A Compilation of the Laws and Regulations of the People's Republic of China*, II.

[9] Ministry of Finance, "Regulation on 1956 State Enterprise Profits," and State Council, "Regulation Putting into Effect the Enterprise Retained Profits System," *A Compilation of the Laws and Regulations of the People's Republic of China*, IV and VII.

[10] For a more complete discussion see D. H. Perkins, *op. cit.*, Chapters V-VI.

[11] Sung Hsin-chung, "The System of Retaining a Percentage of Profits by Our Enterprises," *Ta-kung Pao*, Peking, May 12, 1961.

[12] *E.g.*, Ch'en Kung, "Questions Concerning the Meaning and Jurisdiction of Socialist Finance," *Economic Research*, No. 8, August 20, 1965, and Wang Chen-chih and Tuan Chien-k'e, "Several Questions About the Prices of Heavy Industrial Products," *Economic Research*, No. 12, December 20, 1964.

[13] Joseph S. Berliner, *Factory and Manager in the USSR*, Harvard University Press, Cambridge, 1957.

[14] On the latter point see Ch'ai Yen-hsieh, "Several Questions Concerning the Correct Disposal of Financial Relations between the State and State-run Enterprises," *Economic Research*, No. 10, October 20, 1965.

[15] See, for example, Peter Schran, "The Structure of Income in Communist China," unpublished dissertation, University of California, 1961, pp. 300–32.

[16] Yang Po, "Several Opinions on the Problem of Accumulation and Consumption," *Red Flag*, Peking, No. 21, November 1, 1962.

## 15. IMPLEMENTATION OF LAND REFORM LEGISLATION IN INDIA—A STUDY OF TWO VILLAGES IN PUNJAB

*J. S. Uppal*

[1] United Nations, *Land Reforms, Defects in Agrarian Structure as Obstacles to Economic Development*, 1951, p. 18.

[2] Planning Commission, India, *The Fourth Five Year Plan—A Draft Outline* (New Delhi: Manager of Publications, 1967), p. 125.

[3] V. M. Dandekar and G. J. Khudanpur, "Working of the Bombay Tenancy Act 1948–1962," Bombay, 1966. (Mimeographed.)

[4] Planning Commission, India, *Progress of Land Reforms* (New Delhi: Manager of Publications, 1963).

[5] *The Fourth Five Year Plan—A Draft Outline*, *op. cit.*, p. 221.

[6] M. B. Desai, *Report on an Enquiry into the Working of Bombay Tenancy and Agricultural Act 1948* (Bombay: Indian Society of Agricultural Economies, 1958); A. M. Khusro, *An Analysis of Agricultural Land in India by Size of Holdings and Tenure* (Delhi: Institute of Economic Growth, 1962); L. Krishnamurty, "Land Legislation in Andhra Pradesh," *Indian Journal of Agricultural Economics*, Vol. XVII (1962), pp. 161–74; M. B. Navanati and J. J. Anjaria, *A Pilot Survey of Fourteen Villages in U.P. and Punjab* (Bombay: Asia Publishing House, 1959); Walter Neale, *Economic Change in Rural India* (New Haven: Yale University Press, 1962).

[7] Nanavati and Anjaria, *The Indian Rural Problem* (Bombay: The Indian Society of Agricultural Economics, 1954).

[8] C. B. Mamoria, *Agricultural Problems of India* (Allahbad: Kitab Mahal, 1966), p. 452.

[9] A standard acre means an acre of land yielding between 10 and 11 maunds of wheat per acre matured. One maund is 82 pounds.

[10] Well-run farms have been defined under specially framed rules. For purposes of exemption, each farm will be inspected and allotted marks. The aggregate marks would be 1,000. Half of them would be allotted on the basis of yields, and the other half on the basis of other criteria such as layout, cultivation and sowing practices, use of manures, soil conservation, plant protection, development of irrigation facilities, etc.

[11] *Batai* rent is the rent paid in kind as a proportion of the total gross produce from the land, while cash rent is fixed for a year.

[12] Planning Commission, India, *The Third Five Year Plan* (New Delhi: Manager of Publications, 1961), pp. 130–31.

## 18. THE POPULATION OF INDIA

*Thomas E. Dow, Jr.*

[1] *Current Scene*, December 15, 1969, pp. 13–19.

[1] Kingsley Davis, *The Population of India and Pakistan* (Princeton: Princeton University Press, 1951).

[2] *The Times of India: Directory and Yearbook* (Bombay: The Times of India Press, 1967), p. 241.

[3] Ansley J. Coale, "Population and Economic Development," in Philip M. Hauser (ed.), *The Population Dilemma* (Englewood Cliffs: Prentice-Hall, Inc., 1963), p. 63.

[4] In the case of Gandhi it must be noted that although he supported the idea of family planning he considered abstinence the only acceptable means to this end.

[5] The First Five-Year Plan, as quoted by Dr. Sripati Chandrasekhar in *The New York Times* (April 4, 1965), p. 33.

[6] In the last few months Dr. Chandrasekhar's activities have been somewhat curtailed, and it is now clear that the more radical legal and economic incentives he suggested in connection with sterilization will not be acted upon in the near future.

[7] By making extensive use of legal abortion, Japan was able to reduce its birth rate by 50 per cent in a 10 year period.

[8] W. Parker Mauldin, "Fertility Studies: Knowledge, attitude, and practice," *Studies in Family Planning*, The Population Council, Number 7 (June 1965), pp. 1–10.

[9] Kingsley Davis, "Population Policy: Will Current Programs Succeed?," *Science*, 158 (November 10, 1967), p. 733.

[10] Davis, *op. cit.*, "Population Policy," pp. 733–34.

[11] Frank W. Notestein, "The Population Crisis: Reasons for Hope," *Foreign Affairs*, (October 1967), p. 170. See also Donald J. Bogue, "The End of the Population Explosion," *The Public Interest*, 7 (Spring 1967), pp. 11–20.

[12] T. J. Samuel, "The Development of India's Policy of Population Control," *The Milbank Memorial Fund Quarterly*, XLIV (January 1966), pp. 63–64.

[13] The Population Council, "India: Report of the U.N. Advisory Mission," *Studies in Family Planning*, Number 12 (June 1966), p. 6.

[14] The situation with regard to personnel suggests the scale of the problem. The government is trying to recruit and train an army of 125,000 family planning workers, only one-third of whom are available so far. This must be measured against the need to place such workers in each of India's more than 550,000 villages.

### 26. INDIAN EDUCATION: SEARCH FOR ECONOMIC AND POLITICAL INDEPENDENCE
*I. N. Thut and Don Adams*

[1] *Far Eastern Economic Review, 1970 Yearbook*, pp. 102–4.

### 28. FOREIGN TRADE OF INDIA DURING THE POST INDEPENDENCE PERIOD
*Ruddar Datt and K. P. M. Sundharam*

[1] *Current Scene*, July 1, 1969, p. 4.

[2] Alexander Eckstein, *Communist China's Economic Growth and Foreign Trade* (New York: McGraw-Hill Book Company, 1966), p. 166.

[1] Organization of European Economic Cooperation (OEEC) Countries: Austria, Belgium, Denmark, West Germany, France, Italy, Luxemburg, the Netherlands, Norway, Portugal, Sweden, Switzerland, Turkey and Spain.

[2] European Common Market countries are France, West Germany, Italy, Belgium, Luxemburg and the Netherlands.

### 29. INDIA'S ECONOMIC AID PROGRAMS
*Philip M. Phibbs*

[1] Eugene Mihaly's *Foreign Aid and Politics in Nepal* (London: Oxford University Press, 1965) provides an excellent, if somewhat overly critical, study of Indian aid to Nepal through 1962. It should be remembered, however, that Indian aid has increased substantially since then, and the administration of the program has changed significantly. See *Cooperation for Progress in Nepal* (New Delhi: Ministry of Information and Broadcasting, Government of India, 1966) for details on the total program. The aid figures for Nepal used in this paper do not include various special grants and programs like technical assistance provided through the Colombo Plan, a special annual diplomatic expenditure, and other small items.

[2] Figure provided by the Indian Cooperation Mission, Kathmandu. The rate of exchange for figures used in this text is U.S. \$1.00 = Rs. 4.76.

[3] Statistics provided by the Indian Cooperation Mission, Kathmandu. For details see *Cooperation for Progress in Nepal.*

[4] The exception is a loan of Rs. 10,000,000 negotiated in September of 1964 for the purchase of Indian equipment and machinery for industrial enterprises in Nepal.

[5] India, *Parliamentary Debates*, III (1950), 1661–62.

[6] India, *Lok Sabha Debates*, VII (1954), 1638; Ministry of External Affairs, *Annual Report, 1955–56*, p. 8; and Ministry of External Affairs, *Foreign Affairs Record*, I (1955), 64. All aid figures for Sikkim do not include the annual treaty subsidy which India provides or the special scholarship program for Sikkimese students.

[7] *Statesman*, June 3, 1960 and December 4, 1960, and *Hindustan Times*, January 31, 1960.

[8] Total plan outlay was Rs. 81,300,000 of which Rs. 35,000,000 was devoted to transportation. India, *Lok Sabha Debates*, Appendix III (1961), Annexure, No. 24. In addition, India and Sikkim agreed to establish the Sikkim Mining Corporation with a capital of Rs. 10,000,000 to exploit Sikkim's copper deposits. India provided 49 per cent of the capital and Sikkim the remaining 51 per cent, but India loaned Sikkim the funds to meet the cost of its share! *Annual Report, 1960–61*, p. 13.

[9] *Annual Report, 1958–59*, p. 12. Rs. 150,000 for roads plus free material and a loan of Rs. 220,000 for the factory were offered. Details of the aid actually provided are found in *Lok Sabha Debates*, XXVII (1959), 6351–52.

[10] For the text of the new treaty see *Foreign Policy of India, Text of Documents, 1947–64* (New Delhi: Lok Sabha Secretariat, 1966), pp. 56–58.

[11] Nepal receives Rs. 1,000,000 each year. This is described in the Government of India's budget as a "special diplomatic expenditure." See India, Ministry of External Affairs, *Demands for Grants*. Under the treaties negotiated in 1949 and 1950, Bhutan receives annually a subsidy of Rs. 500,000 and Sikkim Rs. 300,000 as long as the terms of the treaties are duly observed by the states. The Indian Government has been far more generous than the British. Bhutan's subsidy was initially set at Rs. 50,000 in 1865; in 1910 it was raised to Rs. 100,000, and in 1942 to Rs. 200,000. Sikkim's grant rose even more dramatically. British India provided only Rs. 12,000; Independent India contributes Rs. 300,000.

[12] For details of the scholarship program see the *Annual Reports* of the Ministry of Education.

[13] The details provided in the text of India's participation in the Colombo Plan come from *Technical Co-operation under the Colombo Plan* (Colombo: Colombo Plan Bureau, 1966).

[14] Technically Ceylon has made a somewhat larger expenditure than Pakistan and has contributed more equipment than India, if Ceylon's donation of the Colombo Plan Bureau headquarters is included.

[15] India offered Burma a loan of one million pound sterling in 1950 as part of a six million pound Commonwealth loan to help Burma put down an insurrection. In 1955 another loan of Rs. 200,000,000 was offered to help Burma through a difficult economic situation. Neither loan was used at the time although the second offer was renewed and accepted in 1957. Ministry of External Affairs, *Annual Report, 1949–59*, pp. 5–6 and *1956–57*, p. 11.

[16] This feeling is expressed repeatedly by Indian officials both publicly and in private conversation. It is given substance by India's practice of providing assistance to any country which requests her help.

## 30. AID TO INDIA
*Paul Streeten and Roger Hill*

[1] Named after Sir Norman Kipping who led a mission which recommended it.

[2] Mahbub ul Haq, "Tied Credits—A Quantitative Analysis," in *Capital Movements and Economic Development*, ed. J. Adler for the International Economic Association (London, 1967).

[3] It was set up by the World Bank in 1958 and consists of the U.S., Britain, Canada, Japan, West Germany, France, Italy, Netherlands, Belgium, Austria, the World Bank and, since 1959, IDA.

[4] IBRD, *Ann. Rep., 1965–66* (1967), p. 33, Table 5, and *1966–67*, p. 31, Table 6.

[5] *Ibid.*, p. 36, Tables 7 and 8.

[6] *Ibid.*, p. 35, Table 9.

[7] Cte on the Utilization of External Assistance, *Report* (Min. of Finance, 1964.)

[8] This is powerfully argued in I. M. D. Little and J. M. Clifford, *International Aid* (London, 1965), pp. 226, 231, 234.

[9] It is envisaged that in the course of the Sixth Plan the stage will be reached when "further economic growth will no longer require any net increase in our foreign indebtedness" (*4DO*, p. 28).

[10] These ratios are based on post-devaluation figures and cannot be compared with the same ratios for previous plans.

[11] Calculated from *4DO*, pp. 62–63.

[12] Under the Cooley Amendment, Cooley rupees have, according to AID, attracted over fifty American investors to India.

[13] Min. of Finance, *Economic Survey of India 1965–66* (1966), Table 1:4.

[14] See in this connection V. G. Mutalik-Desai, "Terms of Trade and Food Surplus," *Indian J. Agric. Econ.*, January-March 1966 (Bombay).

[15] J. S. Mann, "The Impact of P.L. 480 Imports," *J. of Farm Economics*, February 1967, vol. 49, 1, pt. 1.

[16] U.S. Dept. of Agriculture, *Supply of and Demand for Selected Agricultural Products in India, Projections to 1975–76*, ERS For. 100.

## 32. LOOKING AHEAD
*National Council of Applied Economic Research, New Delhi*

[1] *Far Eastern Economic Review*, 1970 Yearbook, p. 146.

[1] All income and other estimates are in terms of 1960–61 prices.

[2] *Third Five Year Plan.*

[3] Includes Mining and Small Scale Industries.

[4] At 1960–61 prices.

[5] Includes mining.

[6] Dung, firewood, bagasse and agricultural wastes.

[7] Petroleum, coal, hydroelectricity and natural gas.

[8] Hydro or thermal energy in kWh = 1/7000 ton of coal. One ton of petroleum = 1.5 tons of coal.

[9] Expressed in tonnage.

[10] These figures include the new construction of lines in areas not previously served by railways.

[11] At 1960–61 prices.

[12] At 1960–61 prices.

[13] At 1960–61 prices.

## 33. PROSPECTS FOR THE CHINESE ECONOMY
*Kuan-I Chen*

[1] Hollister's estimate put the GNP growth rate at 8.9 per cent for this period. GNP was measured in constant market price (Hollister, p. 126).

[2] *The New York Times*, November 2, 1969, p. 5; January 11, 1970, p. 3.

[3] *Far Eastern Economic Review, 1970 Yearbook*, p. 105.

[4] *Ibid.*, pp. 104, 106.

[5] *Ibid.*, p. 106.

[6] *Ibid.*, pp. 103, 105.

[7] *Ibid.*, p. 105.

[8] A GNP growth rate of at least 6 per cent for 1966 was estimated by Barry Richman. He put the upper limit at 8 per cent (Richman, p. 616). Also see his estimates for aggregate GNP in various years (Richman, pp. 600–601).

[9] No data of total agricultural production are available and foodgrain output is used in lieu of total production. Foodgrains include rice, wheat, corn, sorghum, millets, other miscellaneous grains, and tubers. The conversion ratio of tuber to grain is 4-to-1 grain equivalent.

[10] Estimated from the output data of FAO. (See FAO, p. 85.)

[11] *Far Eastern Economic Review, 1970 Yearbook*, p. 110 reported a bumper crop for 1967 and an average harvest in 1968 owing partly to the weather condition and partly to the unfavorable impact of the Cultural Revolution.

[12] *The New York Times*, October 26, 1969, p. 21; January 19, 1970, p. 49c.

[13] The conservative estimate made by *Current Scene* (March 31, 1969, p. 8) in Hong Kong put the 1966 output at 178 million metric tons. The report of Hong Kong on 1969 output ranged from 190 to 210 million metric tons (*The New York Times*, January 19, 1970, p. 49c). If we use 190 million metric tons for 1969, the annual growth rate would be 2.3 per cent between 1966 and 1969. If the middle of the range, 200 million metric tons is used for 1969, the annual growth rate would be 4.0 per cent. If the upper limit, 210 million metric tons is used for 1969 the annual growth rate would be 5.6 per cent.

[14] The annual growth rate for Chinese foodgrain output was estimated by Pranab Bardhan to be 1.9 per cent for the period 1952–67. If the

unusually disastrous years of 1960 and 1961 were excluded, the growth rate would be 2.5 per cent. These rates were accomplished during a period of fundamental rural transformation and interruptions on an almost unparallelled scale. (See Bardhan, p. 55.)

[15] Compiled from data presented in (Price, p. 586) for these years.

[16] Jones' data (Jones, p. 96) would yield a 19 per cent figure for 1965. Most likely a rate of 19–20 per cent was maintained in 1966 and in 1969.

[17] Liu and Yeh estimated the net (total) incremental-capital-output ratio (ICOR) to be 3.3 for the period 1952–57 and gross (fixed) ICOR to be 2.8 (Liu, p. 62). Hollister's estimate gave a gross (fixed) ratio of 1.8 for 1950–57 and 2.3 for 1952–57. (Hollister p. 126,). The ratio of 3.3 is rather high for a developing nation such as China which has carried out numerous labor-intensive projects in both the agricultural and industrial sectors. Even the gross (fixed) ratios of Japan and Taiwan were only 2.4 and 1.7 respectively for the period 1950–59. Jones' 1965 data (Jones, p. 96) would yield a 19 per cent figure for the proportion of GNP in gross (total) investment. This figure may well represent the proportion for the period 1963–66. If we use Richman's lower estimate of GNP growth rate, 6.0 per cent, for the period 1963–66 (Richman, p. 598) the gross (total) ICOR would be 3.1 for this period. If Richman's higher estimate of growth rate, 8.3 per cent, is used, the ICOR would be 2.3.

[18] The ratio was derived from an estimated state budget expenditure of 29 billion yuan (Godaire, p. 157) and an estimated GNP of 112 billion yuan (Hollister, 1967, p. 125). No data for state budget were published after 1960; 1958, 1959 and 1960 were not considered normal years. Therefore, the figures for 1957 were used here.

[19] This 6 per cent rate would be considered a fairly high rate to achieve if we use Liu's estimated figures for the period 1952–65. His exploratory estimate approximated a net domestic product of 71.4 billion yuan for 1952 and 108.1 billion yuan (1952 yuan) for 1957. A rate of 3.3 per cent is derived for this period. He reconstructed the estimate made by the Communists and his reconstructed communist estimate yielded a rate of approximately 4.9 per cent for this period (Liu, p. 50).

[20] The GNP and per capita GNP for 1966 were estimated to be $90 billion and $120 respectively. These figures were obtained by converting yuans into U.S. dollars at an international purchasing power rate (see Richman, p. 607). It was estimated that by 1969 the industrial production might exceed the level of 1966 by a narrow margin (Cheng, p. 4) and that foodgrain output was significantly higher than in 1966 (*The New York Times*, January 19, 1970, p. 49c). (Also see footnote 13.) A conservative educated guess would suggest that the GNP made some gain between 1966 and 1969 and probably increased at least as much as the population growth. The growth of population was estimated to be about 4.5 per cent between 1966 and 1969 (Orleans, p. 15). If the "conservative educated guess" is correct, then 1969 GNP might be estimated at $94 billion, with per capita GNP stationary at $120.

[21] It was estimated that the pre-1949 peak output was surpassed in 1951 (Richman, p. 600) but not in 1950. Some readers may like to point out that this 9 per cent rate might not have been achieved during 1950–57 if 1950 were a year of normal conditions with the economy operating close to capacity. But one should not ignore the fact that the U.S.S.R. had removed $1 to $2 billion worth of industrial equipment from Northeastern China to the U.S.S.R. during 1945–46. In order to regain the pre-1949 peak output, therefore, it would require not only resumption of production to the former level from the existing plants but also rehabilitation and reconstruction of plants which required substantial investment expenditures.

[22] *Current Scene*, December 15, 1969, p. 2.

[23] According to Hoffman, the Chinese structure of material incentives in industry and agriculture is much the same as the Russian, but the Chinese have not, however, pushed material incentives to the same extent as the Russians (Hoffman, p. 117). During past periods of ideological extremism, when the non-material incentive schemes were emphasized and material incentive schemes de-emphasized, the performance of the economy was generally poor. It is expected that the effectiveness of non-material incentives in raising output would be even poorer in the future than in the past. Thus greater emphasis on material incentives is a requisite for the rapid future growth of the economy.

# References

# References


**References to Chapter 2**

1. Swaminathan, M. S., "Scientific Implications of HYV Programme," *Economic and Political Weekly*, January, 1969.
2. Minhas, B. S. and Srinivasan, T. N., "New Agricultural Strategy Analysed," *Yojana*, January 26, 1966.
3. Laxminarayan, H., "The small farmers should be the strategy base," *Yojana*, December 8, 1968.
4. Vyas, V. S., "The New Strategy—Lessons of first three years," *Economic and Political Weekly*, October 26, 1968.
5. Sengupta, S. and Ghosh, M. G., "HYVP for Rice—Performance in Bengal District," *Economic and Political Weekly*, October, 26, 1968.
6. *Indian Journal of Agricultural Economics*, Conference Number, October–December, 1966 and October–December, 1968.
7. *Eastern Economist*, Annual Number, 1969, "The Green Revolution," pp. 1147–66.

**References to Chapter 4**

1. Aird, J. S. "Population Growth and Distribution in Mainland China," in [35].
2. Bardhan, P. K. "Agricultural Output, Input and Prices in China and India," *Economic and Political Weekly*, Annual Number, February 1969.
3. Bardhan, P. K. and Bardhan, K. "The Problem of Marketed Surplus of Cereals in India," *Economic and Political Weekly*, June 28, 1969.
4. Bardhan, P. K. "Chinese and Indian Agriculture: A Broad Comparison of Recent Policy and Performance," *Journal of Asian Studies*, February 1969.
5. Buck, J. L. *Land Utilization in China*, 1937.
6. Buck, J. L., Dawson, O. L. & Wu, Y. L. *Food and Agriculture in Communist China*, 1966.
7. Dantwala, M. L. "Incentives and Disincentives in Indian Agriculture," *Indian Journal of Agricultural Economics*, April-June 1967.
8. Choudhury, U. Datta Roy "Technological Change in the Indian Economy, 1950–60," *Economic and Political Weekly*, August 20, 1966.
9. Dawson, O. L. "Irrigation Developments under the Communist Regime," in [6].
10. Eckstein, A. *Communist China's Economic Growth and Foreign Trade*, 1966.
11. Eckstein, A., Galenson, W. and Liu, T. C. (ed.), *Economic Trends in Communist China*, 1968.
12. E.C.A.F.E. *Community Development and Economic Development*, Part 1, 1962.
13. Hoffman, C. "Work Incentives in Chinese Industry and Agriculture," in [35].
14. Hollister, W. W. "Trends in Capital Formation in Communist China," in [35].
15. Hou, Chi-Ming "Agriculture in Mainland China," *Journal of Asian Studies*, August 1968.
16. Ishikawa, S. *Economic Development in Asian Perspective*, 1967.
17. Ishikawa, S. "Resource Flow, Between Agriculture and Industry: The Chinese Experience," *The Developing Economies*, March 1967.
18. Ishikawa, S. "Factors Affecting China's Agriculture in the Coming Decade," Institute of Asian Economic Affairs, November 1967, unpublished.
19. Ishikawa, S. "Agrarian Reform and its Productivity Effect—Implication of the Chinese Pattern," 1968, unpublished.
20. Johnston, B. F. "Agriculture and Economic Development: The Relevance of the Japanese Experience," *Food Research Institute Studies*, No. 3, 1966.
21. Jones, E. F. "The Emerging Pattern of China's Economic Revolution," in [35].
22. Kojima, R. "Self-sustained National Economy in Mainland China," *The Developing Economies*, March 1967.
23. Liu, J. C. "Fertilizer Application in Communist China," *China Quarterly*, October-December 1965.
24. Nakamura, J. I. *Agricultural Production and Economic Development of Japan, 1873–1922*, 1966.
25. National Council of Applied Economic Research, *Long Term Projections of Demand for and Supply of Selected Agricultural Commodities*, 1962.
26. Perkins, D. H. *Market Control and Planning in Communist China*, 1966.
27. Perkins, D. H. "Comments on Professor T. C. Liu's Paper," in Ho and Tsou (ed.), *China's Heritage and Communist Political System*, 1968.
28. Raj, K. N. *India, Pakistan and China: Economic Growth and Outlook*, 1967.
29. Shen, T. H. *Agricultural Resources of China*, 1951.
30. State Statistical Bureau, *Ten Great Years*, 1960.
31 Swamy, S. "Price Policy in the People's Republic of China," Harvard Institute of Economic Research Discussion Paper No. 4, November 1967.
32. Tang, A. "Policy and Performance in Agriculture," in [11].
33. Thamarajakshi, R "Inter-Sectoral Terms of

Trade and Marketed Surplus of Agricultural Produce, 1951–52 to 1965–66," *Economic and Political Weekly*, June 18, 1969.
34. Thorner, D. and A. *Land and Labor in India*, 1962.
35. United States Congress, Joint Economic Committee, *An Economic Profile of Mainland China*, VII, 1, 1967.
36. Yang, C. K. *A Chinese Village in Early Communist Transition*, 1959.

### References to Chapter 6

1. United Nations, *World Economic Survey*, 1961.
2. United Nations, *Processes and Problems of Industrialization in Underdeveloped Countries* (1955).
3. Planning Commission, *Five Year Plans*.
4. Government of India, *Economic Survey* (1968–69).
5. Myrdal, G. *Asian Drama*, Vol. II.
6. Rosen, G. *Industrial Change in India*.

### References to Chapter 16

1. Dey, S. K. *Community Development, a Bird's-eye view*.
2. Krishnamachari, V. Y. *Community Development in India*.
3. United Nations, *Community Development and Economic Development*.
4. Chaudhuri, P. K. "Panchayati Raj in Action," *Economic Weekly, Annual*, February, 1964.
5. Planning Commission, *Annual Evaluation Reports* (Summary) I–VII, P.E.O.
6. Dayal, Rajeshwar *Community Development*, Panchayati Raj and Sahakari Samaj.
7. Myrdal, G. *Asian Drama*, Vol. II, Ch. 26.

### References to Chapter 26

*Books*

1. Chaube, S. P. *Secondary Education for India*, Atma Ram & Sons, New Delhi, 1956.
2. Datta, Dhirendra Mohan *The Philosophy of Mahatma Gandhi*, The University of Wisconsin Press, Madison, Wis., 1953.
3. Dean, Vera Micheles *New Patterns of Democracy in India*, Harvard, Cambridge, Mass., 1959.
4. de Bary, Wm. Theodore (ed.) *Sources of Indian Tradition*, Columbia, New York, 1958.
5. Despai, A. R. *Recent Trends in Indian Nationalism*, Popular Book Depot, Bombay, 1960.
6. Dube, S. C. *Indian Village*, Routledge, London, 1955.
7. Dube, S. C. *India's Changing Village*, Routledge, London, 1958.
8. Gandhi, Mahatma *All Men are Brothers*, UNESCO and Columbia, New York, 1958.
9. Ghush, O. K. *Problems of Economic Planning in India*, Kitabistan Allahabad, 1957.
10. Ginsburg, Norton *Atlas of Economic Development*, The University of Chicago Press, Chicago, 1961.
11. Harap, Henry *Improvement of Curriculum in Indian Schools*, Government of India Press, New Delhi, 1959.
12. Hartog, Sir Philip *Some Aspects of Indian Education Past and Present*, Oxford, Fair Lawn, N.J., 1939.
13. Hutton, J. H. *Caste in India: Its Nature, Function, and Origins*, Cambridge, New York, 1946.
14. India: *Review of the Third Five-Year Plan*, Ministry of Publications, New Delhi, n.d.
15. India, Estimates Committee *Seventeenth Report, 1957–58*, Ministry of Education and Scientific Research, Lok Sabha Secretariat, New Delhi, 1958.
16. India, Government Planning Commission *The Second Five-Year Plan*, Ministry of Publications, New Delhi, 1956.
17. India, Government Planning Commission *The Third Five-Year Plan: Draft Outline*, Ministry of Publications, New Delhi, 1960.
18. India, Ministry of Education *Education in India: A Graphic Presentation*, New Delhi, 1959.
19. India, Ministry of Education *Provisional Educational Statistics: (As on 31st March 1962)*, New Delhi, 1962.
20. India, Ministry of Education *Report of the Secondary Education Commission*, October 1952–June 1953, Hindu Union Press, New Delhi, 1953.
21. Kabir, Hamayan *Education in New India*, G. Allen, London, 1956.
22. McCully, Bruce T. *English Education and the Origins of Indian Nationalism*, Columbia, New York, 1940.
23. Mayhew, A. *The Education of India*, Faber and Gwyer, London, 1928.
24. Mudaliar, A. L. *Education in India*, Asia Publishing House, Bombay, 1960.
25. Mukerji, Shridhar Nath *Education in India: Today and Tomorrow*, 4th ed., Acharya Book Depot, Baroda, 1960.
26. Mukerji, Shridhar Nath *History of Education in India*, Acharya Book Depot, Baroda, 1951.
27. Myers, Edward F. *Education in the Perspective of History*, Harper & Row, New York, 1960.
28. Nehru, Jawaharlal *The Discovery of India*, John Day, New York, 1946.
29. Nurallah, Syed, and Naik, J. P. *A History of Education in India*, Macmillan, New York, 1951.
30. Panikar, K. M. *A Survey of Indian History*, Meridian Books, Ltd., London, 1948.
31. Philips, C. H. *India*, Hutchison's University Library, London, 1948.

32. Rawlinson, H. G. *India: A Short Cultural History*, Frederick A. Praeger, Inc., New York, 1937.
33. Riencourt, Amaury de *The Soul of India*, Harper & Row, New York, 1960.
34. Saiyidain, K. G. *Education, Culture and the Social Order*, Asia Publishing House, Bombay and Calcutta, 1952.
35. UNESCO *World Survey of Education II: Primary Education*, UNESCO and Evans Brothers, London, 1958.
36. UNESCO *World Survey of Education III: Secondary Education*, UNESCO and Evans Brothers, London, 1961.
37. Wallbank, T. Walter *India in the New Era*, Scott, Foresman, Chicago, 1951.
38. Wallbank, T. Walter *A Short History of India and Pakistan*, New American Library, New York, 1958.

*Pamphlets and periodicals*

39. Basu, Sobharani "Forest Universities in Ancient India," *The Year Book of Education*, World, Tarrytown-on-Hudson, N.Y., 1957.
40. Deshpande, A. R. "Education for Social Change," *Journal of Education*, vol. 89, pp. 378–81, London, September 1957.
41. Fowlkes, J. G. "Where India Is Going," *Phi Delta Kappan*, vol. 38, no. 2, p. 64, November 1956.
42. Hingorani, D. K. "Education in India before and after Independence," *Educational Forum*, vol. 19, pp. 217–25, January 1955.
43. Hingorani, D. K. "Higher Education in India: Recent Developments," *Higher Education*, vol. 11, pp. 77–86, February 1955.
44. *Journal of Educational Sociology*, vol. 28, January 1955.
45. Kabir, Hamayan "Basic Education: Indian Experiment," *Journal of General Education*, vol. 8, pp. 93–99, January 1955.
46. Kabir, Hamayan "Indian Education since Independence," *Phi Delta Kappan*, vol. 39, no. 3, pp. 107–17, December 1957.
47. Maw, E. W. "Impressions of Education in India," *Educational Outlook*, vol. 30, pp. 55–62, January 1956.
48. Rice, T. C., and Roy, B. "Some Aspects for Youth in India," *Journal of Educational Sociology*, vol. 28, pp. 194–236, January 1955.
49. Ward, F. F. "Some Polarities in Indian Educational Thought," *Phi Delta Kappan*, vol. 39, pp. 108–11, December 1957.

## References to Chapter 28

1. Planning Commission *Third Five Year Plan*, Ch. VIII.
2. Singh, Manmohan *India's Export Trends*.
3. Reserve Bank of India "India's Balance of Payments, 1948–49 to 1961–62," *RBI Bulletin*, March 1969

## References to Chapter 33

1. Bardhan, Pranab, *Economic and Political Weekly*, Bombay, India, January 1969, pp. 53–65.
2. Cheng, Chu-Yuan, "The Effects of The Cultural Revolution On China's Machine-Building Industry," *Current Scene*, January 1, 1970.
3. Dernberger, Robert F., "China's Foreign Trade: The See-Saw Pattern," *Columbia Journal of World Business*, November-December 1968, pp. 17–26.
4. Eckstein, Alexander, *Communist China's Economic Growth and Foreign Trade*, McGraw-Hill, 1966, pp. 106–7; 114–15.
5. *Far Eastern Economic Review*, 1970 Yearbook, December 1, 1969, pp. 102–15.
6. FAO, *Production Yearbook, 1967*, p. 85.
7. Gurley, John G., Statement of John G. Gurley in *Mainland China In The World Economy*, Hearings Before The Joint Economic Committee, Congress of the United States, April 5, 10, 11 and 12, 1967, pp. 184–88.
8. Hoffman, Charles, *Work Incentive Practices and Policies in the People's Republic of China, 1953–1965*, State University of New York Press, 1967.
9. Hollister, William W., "Trends In Capital Formation in Communist China," *An Economic Profile of Mainland China*, vol. I, U.S. Joint Economic Committee, February 1967, pp. 121–53.
10. Jones, Edwin, "The Emerging Pattern of China's Economic Revolution," *An Economic Profile of Mainland China*, vol. I, U.S. Joint Economic Committee, February 1967, pp. 77–96.
11. Liu, Ta-Chung, "The Tempo of Economic Development of The Chinese Mainland, 1949–65," *An Economic Profile of Mainland China*, U.S. Joint Economic Committee, vol. I, February 1967, pp. 45–75.
12. Liu, Ta-Chung and Yeh, Kung-Chia, *The Economy of the Chinese Mainland: National Income and Economic Development, 1933–1959*, Princeton University Press, 1965.
13. MacDougall, Colina, "The Chinese Economy," *Far Eastern Economic Review*, June 26, 1969, pp. 706–08.
14. MacDougall, Colina, "Economy: Forward and Back," *Far Eastern Economic Review*, October 2, 1969, pp. 43–44.
15. Orleans, Leo, "Propheteering: The Population of Communist China," *Current Scene*, vol. 7, no. 24, December 15, 1969.
16. Price, Robert, "International Trade of Communist China, 1950–1965," *An Economic Profile of Mainland China*, U.S. Joint Economic Committee, vol. 2, February 1967, pp. 579–608.